The Lockheed Martin C-130 Hercules

By the same author

Destroyer Leader (The Story of HMS Faulknor 1934-46)
Task Force 57: The British Pacific Fleet 1944-45
Pedestal: The Malta Convoy of August 1942
Stuka At War
Hard Lying: The Birth of the Destroyer 1893-1914
British Battle Cruisers
War in the Aegean
The Story of the Torpedo Bomber
Heritage of the Sea
Royal Navy Ships' Badges
RAF Squadron Badges
Battles of the Malta Striking Forces
Per Mare, Per Terram
Fighting Flotilla
Arctic Victory
Battle of Midway
The Great Ships Pass
Hit First, Hit Hard: HMS Renown 1916-48
Destroyer Action
Impact! The Dive Bomber Pilots Speak
Action Imminent
Cruisers in Action
Dive Bomber!
Hold the Narrow Sea: Naval Warfare in the English Channel 1939-45
HMS Wild Swan
Into the Assault: Famous Dive-Bomber Aces of the Second World War
Vengeance! The Vultee Vengeance Dive Bomber
Jungle Dive Bombers at War

Victoria's Victories: Seven Classic Battles of the British Army 1849-1884
The Royal Marines – A Pictorial History
Massacre At Tobruk
Dive Bombers in Action
Battleship Royal Sovereign
Stuka Squadron: StG77: The Luftwaffe's Fire Brigade
T-6: The Harvard, Texan & Wirraway
Eagle's War: The War Diary of an Aircraft-Carrier
Close Air Support
Douglas SBD Dauntless
Stuka Spearhead
Stukas over the Steppe
Ship Strike! The History of Air-to-Sea Weapons Systems
Curtiss SB2C Helldiver
Junkers Ju 87 Stuka
Aichi D3a1/A2 Val
Douglas AD Skyraider
Stukas over the Mediterranean
Fairchild-Republic A-10 Thunderbolt-II
Straight Down! The North American A-36 Dive Bomber
Petlyakov Pe-2 Peshka
The Sea Eagles: Luftwaffe's Maritime Operations 1939-45
Luftwaffe Colours – Stuka (2 Vols)
Into the Minefields
Skua!
Fist from the Sky
Midway Dauntless Victory
Cruise Ships

The Lockheed Martin C-130 Hercules
A Complete History

Peter C Smith

Crécy Publishing

First published by Airlife, Shrewsbury, 2001
This expanded and updated second edition published in 2010 by Crécy Publishing Ltd

Copyright © Peter C. Smith 2001 and 2010

A CIP record for this book is available from the British Library

ISBN 9 780859 791533

Printed and bound in Great Britain
by MPG Books

See all Peter C Smith books at www.dive-bombers.co.uk

Crécy Publishing Limited
1a Ringway Trading Estate, Shadowmoss Road, Manchester M22 5LH
www.crecy.co.uk

Frontispiece: The strength of the C-130 is her versatility, which has attracted world-wide customers for over half-a-century. She is a truly International aircraft. *Hayakawa, JASDF*

Contents

Preface 8

Acknowledgements 9

Chapter 1   The family of Hercules...11

Chapter 2   The versatile Hercules...74

Chapter 3   The multiple roles of the American Hercules variants 181

Chapter 4   The worldwide operators of Hercules: military 249

Chapter 5   The worldwide operators of Hercules: civilian 324

Appendices

      1   Model summary...373

      2   Model list..374

      3   C-130: major sub-contractors 383

      4   Verifiable losses of C-130s 385

      5   Museum Hercules 400

      6   Chase the Herk: strange happenings! 402

      7   Latest USAF C-130 Serial Numbers 403

Select bibliography...404

Index...406

Preface: an explanation of the book's layout

There have been an enormous number of books on the C-130 Hercules, and I have consulted most of them. For those who also wish to do so a Bibliography is included at the rear of the book. So complex has the Hercules family tree become, however, that I found most of these books rather confusing to find one's way around, and not a single one of them contained information about every single variant or proposed design that might not have come to fruition. As I intended my book to be not a repeat of all these, but more a warm tribute to the C-130 in all its many facets, with both facts and photographs, I decided to abandon traditional chapters and divide the book into headed sub-sections under five main divisions, supported by a comprehensive Index. This, I hope, will allow easier access to the multitude of Hercules varieties, and although some duplication results, it is *deliberate*. Despite some petty criticisms I consider that this is well worthwhile for clarity, as it enables the reader to quickly reach the information required from whatever designation he currently has to hand. Likewise I consider the construction number (c/n) number of each aircraft as the anchor on which to base the equally diverse changes and shifts of these long-lived aircraft, and these are therefore always included in any references. Individual aircraft histories are *not* included here, and the reader is strongly recommended to consult the current edition of Lars Olausson's definitive *Lockheed Hercules Production List* for these.

The result will be, I hope, a rather different look at the Herk in all her many faces, and any errors or omissions I would hope to rectify in future editions.

Peter C. Smith
Riseley
Bedfordshire
March 2010

Acknowledgements

To list in full the kind and helpful persons who have contributed their knowledge and expertise to the compilation of this book would require about as much space as the cargo hold of a 'stretched' Hercules! Few aircraft generate such a warmth of affection and eagerness of response than the Herk and this has been reflected in the enormous help I have been freely given. The majority of these contributors, mainly serving personnel, aircrew and groundcrew, engineers and constructors alike, have requested anonymity, but I know who they are and to them all I extend my gratitude and indebtedness, especially all those who were so helpful during my visits to various locations in Washington DC; in Maryland and Virginia; in Atlanta, Georgia; in Seattle and Redmond, Washington State; in San Diego, Long Beach, and San Francisco, California; in Pensacola and Fort Myers, Florida; in Portland, Oregon and at Hill AFB, Utah; and around Nagoya, Japan, especially Norio Aoki at Kakamigahara Air & Space Museum; the Directorate of Public Information at the Department of Defence, Canberra ACT, Australia; National Oceanic and Atmospheric Administration, at Rockville, Maryland; Smithsonian Museum, Washington DC; the United States Marine Corps Museum, USMCB Quantico, Virginia; and the United Nations Office, New York. I hasten to add that any mistakes I accept entirely as my own.

I would like to thank by name a few of these people who went out of their way to assist me, and these include Mollie Angel, RAAF Historical Records, Canberra ACT; Norio Aoki and *401st Hikotai*, JASDF, Komaki Air Base, Japan; Captain Dave Becker, South African Air Force Museum, Pretoria, Republic of South Africa; Major Donald L. Black, Director, Media Division, United States Air Force, Headquarters Tactical Air Command, Langley Air Force Base, Virginia; Martin W. Bowman, Norwich; Mark Farrar, *Flightpath*; Colonel A. C. J. Collocott, South African Defence Force, Pretoria, Republic of South Africa; Eric F. Deylius, 731st Tactical Airlift Squadron (AFRES), Peterson Air Force Base, Colorado; J. C. David, United States Department of Commerce, National Oceanic and Atmospheric Administration, Rockville, Maryland; D. L. Dick, Headquarters Third Air Force (USAFE), RAF Mildenhall, Suffolk, UK; Russell D. Egnor, News Photo Branch, Office of Information, Department of the Navy, Washington DC; Giancarlo Garello, Venice, Italy; Jeffrey S. Halik, Chief Media Relations, Office of Public Affairs, Headquarters 5135th Tactical Airlift Wing (USAFE), RAF Mildenhall, Suffolk, UK; Mario Isack, Hellenhahn, Germany; Lieutenant Alena Kotas, Air Force Headquarters, Pretoria, Republic of South Africa; Stephanie Mitchell, Pima Air & Space Museum, Tucson, Arizona; Audrey Pearcy, Sharnbrook, for the free use of the late Arthur Pearcy's photographs, letters, and documents; Lars Olausson, Satenas, Sweden; Sharon Peterson, Department of the Air Force, Headquarters United States Air Forces in Europe, Flugplatz Ramstein, Germany; First Lieutenant Jay W. Pyles, Department of the Air Force, 67th Aerospace Rescue and Recovery Squadron (MAC), New York; Gene Queson, Johnson Controls Incorporated, March ARC, California; R. K. Salmon, Air Staff Headquarters, Royal New Zealand Air Force, Wellington, New Zealand; Seán O'Brien, Shannon Airport, Eire; K. O'Donoghue, Safair Freighters, Kempton Park, Republic of South Africa; Rosemary Roth, Australian Defence Headquarters, Canberra, ACT; Simon Watson of the Aviation Bookshop, Holloway Road, London, for yet again coming up trumps with all my unusual book needs; Captain Lindajean H. Western, USMC, Headquarters United States Marine Corps, Washington, DC; Peter Williams, Dowty Aerospace, Staverton; and especially Nick Williams, AAHS, Waverly, Iowa.

Thanks also to good friends Ken and Roma Smith, for their hospitality at their home in Fredericksburg, Virginia, and enormous enthusiasm in visiting important research sites; Barry Petty, Barry Ketley; Kurt A. Viegelmann and Jonathan Falconer for absorbing details of the C-130 hijacking mystery; and Ali Reza; TomCarter, Juan K. Benitez, Martin W. Bowman, Diego Ruiz de Vargas, Alastair T. Gardiner, Michael Gothic, Kian Hong, Mathias Henig, W. T. Liew, Michal Nowicki, Rafael Nunes, Pablo Andres Ortega, Cornelius Saayman, Mark Smith, Konstantin von Wedelstaedt, Tim McLelland, Ben Jones, Craig Dow, James Newton, Alan Sim and Richard Vandervord, all of whom either supplied photos or contributed welcome help in securing good photos for the new edition.

Special thanks to Philip Rood (EXP), Head of Media Relations, Lockheed-Martin UK and Peter C. Simmons, Lockheed-Martin Aeronautics Company, Marietta, Georgia, for detailed information updates on C-130 production and for permission to reproduce official LM photographs.

In this connection, one of most stupid comments I have ever seen concerning reference books on historical aircraft is that it is unnecessary for them to contain photographs, and that only an ample text is necessary – in fact, the exact reverse is the case if the book is to be of any value at all and, despite such myopic viewpoints, it is to be hoped that the more than 450 photographs included here illustrate most aspects of the Herk's story and its varied career. That being said, this book also comprises more than 125,000 words, which is probably more than the above critic has ever written in his entire life, and therefore cannot be said to be cursory coverage.

Finally, this book does *not* claim, as do some, to be the final word on the Hercules, or the final history – how can it possibly be when the Herk herself continues to be built and to take part in missions worldwide. Every day this remarkable aircraft is making fresh history and is likely to continue doing so far into the future.

Chapter 1

The family of Hercules

Origins of the Herky Bird

Aerial transportation came into its own during the Second World War and has played an ever-increasing role in international warfare ever since. The ability to move troops, military equipment and supplies quickly to trouble-spots around the globe is now a basic requirement for the world's major air forces, rather than a desirable luxury. With the aggressive expansion of communism from its centralised position in the Asian land-mass (the then Soviet Union and China), the free world found itself on the peripherals of an amoeba that was probing and growing out into South East Asia (South Korea, Vietnam, Cambodia, Tibet) and Eastern Europe (Rumania, Czechoslovakia, Bulgaria, Yugoslavia and Poland being swallowed up, Greece being threatened), while yet further afield the newly independent colonial states of Africa and even the Caribbean were being subverted. In order to deal with many 'brush fire' situations, and supporting the statement by an American Civil War General that the winner would usually be 'the firstest with the mostest', speed of response was a growing military requisite. Sea power, of which the Western alliance had total dominance for the first 15 years of the Cold War only, would always be necessary for heavy equipment, but it was in nipping situations in the bud, or in trying to restore deteriorating war situations, that the bulk air lift came into its own.

The situation in the Korean War in the early 1950s brought these facts into sharp focus, and in the United States – which by then had taken over the former duty of the rapidly fading British Empire as the world's policeman – the matter was the subject of hard study. The Korean War had almost been lost before it had begun, when the North suddenly invaded and there were almost no United Nations troops in the area to stem its rapid advance. Only a last-ditch stand in the Pusan perimeter and a subsequent seaborne landing at Inchon in the rear of the communist lines had saved the day. It took six weeks to get two US Army divisions into line to begin the counter-attack. It had been, as Wellington said of Waterloo, 'a damn close-run thing'. Existing air transport in the United States Air Force was based on the C-124 'Globemaster' and the C-54 'Skymaster', both strategic air transports, but with limited capacity and range, while in Korea aircraft like the old piston-engined C-48, C-47 and the newer C-110 'Flying Boxcar' did their best, but the whole effort was too small, too limited in capacity and scope and too obsolete to do the job well. A solution therefore had to be found, and right speedily, before the next nasty surprise being brewed up in the Kremlin or Beijing. Rapid mobility was the keynote of all subsequent thinking on the issue.

On the last day of July 1950, barely a week after the communist invasion armies had poured over the 38th parallel, Lieutenant General Gordon Saville called a meeting at USAF HQ in Washington DC to discuss how best to implement the speedy introduction into service of new types of military combat aircraft for which a supplemental research and development (R&D) budget of $105,000,000 had just been assigned. Eventually they got around to discussing transport aircraft needs. Already awed by such a sum, the parties to the discussion on that hot summer Sunday got bogged down in rambling discussion and seemed to be getting no-place until a Air Force Colonel voiced his exasperation by wryly stating that what they needed was, '...a medium transport than can land on unimproved ground, be extremely rugged, be primarily for freight transport, with troop-carrying capability, and carry about 30,000 pounds to a range of 1,500 miles!'[1]

The accountant was no flying expert, and did not realise that what was being asked for was far more than anyone had hitherto deemed possible in a transport aircraft, so he did not smile. Instead, as accountants always do, he asked, 'How much would that cost?' The deadlock was broken and a

---

[1] Quoted by Mr H. H. Test, Military Officer assigned to USAF HQ, and present at that meeting.

provisional figure of a few million dollars per airplane was tossed into the discussion and duly gravely recorded. When the entire supplementary budget was finally approved, the funding allocated for the transport was retained and preparations for a General Operational Requirement (GOR) put in train. The transport GOR was not finally issued until some months later, on 2 February 1951, but the need had not lessened in the intervening period. The aircraft was still urgently required by the Tactical Air Command (TAC), Military Air Transport Service (MATS) and the US Army. As was normal practice, what followed was the initiation of a Request for Proposal (RFP), which would be sent to all major aircraft manufacturers, inviting them to respond with their own ideas.

The Air Force's RFP took the original throw-away line and turned it into hard figures, and these proved hardly less daunting to the manufacturers who received it – Boeing, Douglas, Fairchild and Lockheed – all of whom had high expertise in this particular field of aeronautical design. The basic requirements for the new aircraft were that she be a medium transport (this applying to both payload and range), and capable of performing both the tactical and logistic mission as required. The devil was in the detail. As a troop transport they wanted ninety men hauled to any point in the globe in 2,000-mile (3,220km) hops. The same aircraft should be capable of carrying up to 30,000lb (13,600kg) of military hardware (of any type) into unpaved battle-zone air strips. Oh, and she should also have the ability to get off a mud, sand or clay airstrip on three engines and be able to make paratroop drops at low speeds as well, and be reliable and fully controllable in such a scenario. There was the need for an 8,000-foot (2,438m) pressure altitude, not just for the aircrew but for the cargo hold as well, for the carriage of seventy-two stretcher cases, as well as an integral ramp and rear door, both capable of in-flight operations. To ensure versatility of loading capability, an obstruction-free cargo compartment should have the dimensions 41 feet 5 feet by 10.3 feet by 9 feet (12m 62cm by 3.14m x 2.74m), and a deck that was able to accommodate existing truck heights from ground level had to be built in.

The Lockheed team had already ensured that they knew what the practicalities were by dispatching Al Lechner, a design engineer, and Chuck Burns, from the sales team, on an exploratory visit to the Pentagon in Washington DC, Andrews Air Force Base in Maryland and the Strategic Air Command (SAC) HQ in Nebraska, and to watch a field paratroop drop exercise at Fort Bragg, North Carolina, the US Army Airborne HQ. They learned a lot, including an estimate from SAC that at least 2,000 such aircraft would be required. These were dizzy numbers to the starved, post-Second World War aircraft manufacturers and well worth putting themselves out for, even if the RFP seemed ambitious, or even, to some, almost unattainable with the then current state of the art. To reinforce the full picture Lockheed also consulted with the Air Force's Air Research & Development Command, the Joint Airborne Troop Board, the Joint Air Transport Board and No 1 Field Forces Board of the Army.

All this input, and much more, was taken on board by the Lockheed Advanced Design Team, which was brought together at Burbank, California, under Willis Hawkins, to initiate the Model 82, following the signing of the contract for detail design work on 11 July 1951. The team he headed up included his deputy, Eugene Frost, with Robert W. Middlewood, later to become chief engineer, Art Flock as Project Leader, Preliminary Design, E. C. Frank and E. A. Peterman, with Dick Pulver joining in as the programme got rolling. Others heavily involved with their specialist areas were Willard Thossen and Merrill Kelly for the engines – early on Lockheed decided that they would have to be (then) revolutionary turbo-props, which gave excellent range at high altitude – and Jack Lebold, who concentrated on the new-design tandem-wheel and landing-gear to get this new bird in and out of all the precarious situations envisaged for her by the USAF and Army, while the general arrangements fell to the province of Al Lechner. Thus came about the Lockheed Model L-206 concept. The watchwords became 'Keep it simple' and 'Keep it light but strong'.

Gradually the design came together, with a high-aspect-ratio wing (a 10 aspect ratio, with a 132-foot (40m) wingspan giving a 1,745sq ft/162.1158m² wing area) adopted to accommodate a low (45-inch/114.3cm) cargo flooring requirement. Four engines were considered essential to meet the Air Force specification, despite the extra cost that this would involve. The 3,750 equivalent shaft horsepower (eshp) Allison YT56-A-1A axial-flow propeller turbine engines had a weight of 1,600lb (725.74kg) and were contained in slim, titanium-built nacelles to lessen drag. Not only did they combine the best features of both propeller and jet propulsion, but they were also to prove highly efficient in fuel consumption, another important factor. The four engines each drove a three-bladed

Curtiss turbo, variable-pitch, constant-speed propeller. The pitch of the propeller was reversible, enabling the wondrously fast stopping distances in which the Hercules was to revel down the years. In an age of sleek jet engines, this radical adoption of the turboprop, the first for an American aircraft, seemed a retrospective step, yet it proved the making of the design.

The landing arrangement ditched the usual wing-mounted layout for side blister accommodation outside the fuselage itself, so it did not restrict capacity, and featured soft, low-pressure, 'doughnut', semi-recessed tyres, and smoothed-in fairings for good flotation effect and low structural weight. Anti-skid brakes were also fitted.

New thinking on airframe design flattened out the usual fuselage cross-form from the traditional oval shape. The wings were mounted across the top of the fuselage, well out of the way, and had a 2.5-inch (6.35cm) dihedral. The in-built ramp gave unrestricted access for both wheeled and tracked heavy vehicles to drive straight in, and when shut it smoothed right into the after ventral fuselage, while the huge cargo door had an inward-opening top section so that similar heavy and wide loads could be dispatched straight out in air-drops without difficulty.

To give this 'flying boxcar', with its ungainly loads, the maximum stability in all the various mission profiles she was expected to undertake, similar new thinking was applied to the empennage. The after ventral hull swept up at a high angle to give clearance for loading, and culminated in a huge 'sail' 38 feet (11.6m) high, the vertical stabiliser, yet another truly distinctive Hercules feature, along with a beaver tail and large, low-mounted horizontal stabilisers to ensure maximum lift and excellent handling at low speeds for such a large airplane.

Finally, in order to maximise visibility for the pilot and aircrew, who had to manoeuvre this bulky flying machine fully laden with freight in and out of tiny and unprepared airstrips anyplace from a tropical jungle clearing to a cleared stretch of Antarctic ice, the whole aircraft terminated forward in a blunt, chopped-off nose, almost a straight cliff-like frontage that did little to redeem the overall appearance of the Hercules, which was unique in so many ways. The so-called 'Roman nose', ugly as it might be, gave the aircrew an unprecedented 20 degrees of down vision, which was to prove invaluable. Further enhancement to the ground steering of this big machine on primitive airstrips was the provision of an abnormally large number of windshield windows, some twenty-three in all, with some ventrally mounted for maximum visibility in difficult situations.

One of the first! 'Roman-nosed' C-130A 53-3131 (c/n 3003) carries the national flag on her tail on the apron at Palmdale, California, in October 1965. *Nick Williams, AAHS*

Air National Guard C-130A Hercules 1639 (c/n 3026), also with the 'Roman nose', is seen in July 1981 with all ramps down. *Nick Williams, AAHS*

Internally the required pressurisation was achieved, despite the huge rear door, the ramp, the multi-faceted windows of the cockpit, the crew door and two troop doors that pierced the mighty hull in so many places. Bleed air from the engines fed both air-conditioning and pressurisation systems. The hydraulics featured a 3,000psi high-pressure system. Apart from the pumps, every other feature of the system was located inside the fuselage and could be readily accessed by the flight engineer. The electrics were of the high-voltage Alternating Current (AC) type. Another smart new innovation was the fitting of servo controls to ease the work on the flight deck in operating all this complex equipment.

All this was achieved with around 75,000 component parts, which made for ease of construction of the 54-ton (48,987.97kg) aircraft, in an age when complexity was increasing with each new aircraft design. The designated five-man aircrew consisted of two pilots, a navigator, a systems manager and a loadmaster

Despite the many different or unusual features, the preliminary design and estimated performance figures that Lockheed came up with impressed the people who mattered and, on 2 July 1951, the company were announced the winner of the RFP. Awarding Lockheed the contract, the Air Force required two prototypes YC-130s, as the new aircraft was designated. Work on these commenced in Lockheed's C-1 Plant at Burbank, but already Building No 1 at the new Marietta plant in Georgia, located immediately to the north of the sprawling city of Atlanta, had been earmarked for the full production run. On 19 September 1952 Lockheed was awarded a contract for an initial production run of seven C-130 (Model 182) aircraft, confirmed on 10 February for an initial production run of seven aircraft.

The company followed earlier precedent by naming the new aircraft after one of the constellations, and 'Hercules' was certainly the most apt! The name was a legendary one, being bestowed on the son of Zeus and Alcmene, who was renowned for his physical strength and for his many incredible feats, which included the famous twelve labours he had to perform to appease the Gods. Lockheed's product took the legendary name and also became an aeronautical legend, while the number of labours the latter-day Hercules has performed are almost without number.

Top: A view of the packed C-130 production line at Marietta. The Hercules proved herself to be one of the most versatile and popular transport aircraft of all time. *Lockheed-Georgia, Marietta, via Audrey Pearcy*

Bottom: The Lockheed-Georgia Marietta plant in full swing in the 1950s, with the B-47 line on the left at the rear, and C-130A 53-3132 (c/n 3004) prominent in the foreground. *Lockheed*

The impressive C-130 Hercules line-up at Marietta *Lockheed*

Flanked by the Lockheed C-130 production line at the Georgia plant, the then President of the company, Larry Kitchen, makes a Christmas 1970 address to the employees. *Lockheed*

Workers on the Hercules production line at Lockheed's Georgia plant give blood to the Red Cross during a working day in 1970. *Lockheed*

The designated production team for Marietta was headed up by Al Brown, with Project Engineer E. A. Peterman, and they were brought across to California to familiarise themselves with the project in readiness. They returned to Marietta and were joined by a 100,000lb (45,359.237kg) mock-up built of wood, which was shipped from the West Coast via the Panama Canal to Savannah, then via a convoy of low-loader trucks before being placed in Building B-4.

The C-130 programme

The two YC-130-LOs (Model 082-44-01) prototypes received the USAF serials 53-3396 (c/n 1001) and 53-3397 (c/n 1002) respectively. They were completed without radar and navigator's station and with the minimum of internal and radio fittings at Burbank in August and September 1955. This partly accounts for the fact that the gross weight of the first aircraft was 108,000lb (48,987.97kg) instead of the 113,000lb (51,255.9kg) proposed, with an empty weight of 57,500lb, while the designed payload was 25,000lb (11,339.809kg). This lead aircraft, completed on 26 August, was used for static tests at the Air Research & Development Centre at Edwards Air Force Base with the 6515 MAIGP. On 23 March 1956 she joined USAF Logistics Command at Marietta and was transferred to the engine manufacturer's plant at Indianapolis that same December so that Allison's engineers could conduct further testing.

The second aircraft made her maiden flight from the Lockheed Air Terminal on 23 August 1954, piloted by Stanley Beltz, the Lockheed Engineering Flight Test Pilot, with Roy Wimmer as co-pilot and flight engineers Jack Real and Dick Stanton as the Flight Test Group engineers. At 14.45 she became airborne at 855 feet (260.6m), making a steep 30° ascent, setting many mouths agape and proving her STOL qualities right from the outset. With two chase aircraft, a P-2V with Chief Designer Kelly Johnson aboard (still unhappy and far from impressed with the design as it was) and a B-25 conducting in-flight photographs, she flew the 61 minutes to Edwards AFB, in the Mojave Desert, at 10,000 feet (3,048m) to join her sister. Beltz landed the aircraft within an equally impressive short distance, and later boasted to the base commandant, Brigadier-General Albert Boyd, that had he wanted to, he could '…land it cross-ways of the runway…'

Here vigorous trials were conducted, which resulted in the Herk passing most of the tests with flying colours. The resultant aircraft improved on the USAF's own minimum flying requirements in several vital areas, with 20% better average cruising speed; 35% higher normal power, three-engine power ceiling, normal ceiling and rate of climb; and 55% faster than predicted, with the required take-off distance at maximum power decreased by 25% and landing without reverse thrust at 40% less. These figures were very impressive. The two prototypes continued to be used as engine installation test-frames at the Allison plant for the rest of their lives. In 1959 they were both redesignated as NC-130s and were consigned to Warner Robins AFB, where they were both finally broken up in October 1960 and April 1962 respectively. They were the only Hercules to be built at Burbank.

The original profile of the basic C-130

The Air Force was impressed enough to order an additional twenty aircraft for Tactical Air Command in April 1954. All twenty-seven Hercules from the initial orders bore close resemblance to the prototypes in appearance, with the 'Roman nose'. They featured the improved T56-A-9 engines and had 15-foot (4.572m), three-bladed Curtiss-Wright hollow propellers, and also had provision for a pair of optional, externally slung fuel tanks with a capacity of 450 US gallons (1,703 litres), each carried outboard of the engine nacelles, to materially increase range. They had a 3g load factor, which enabled the airplane to be pushed hard in the air. The initial order was followed in the September by another firm Air Force order for no fewer than four dozen more.

All these eighty-five aircraft became the C-130A (Model 182-1A). The first of them, serial 53-3129 (c/n 3001), was completed at Marietta on 10 March 1955. As she emerged the Governor of the State of Georgia, one Marvin Griffin, repeatedly tried to break a bottle of Chattahoochee River water on her nose during a christening ceremony. After this debut, she made her maiden flight on 7 April, lifting off after an 800-foot (243.84 m) run at 11.39 with Bud Martin at the controls, Leo Sullivan as co-pilot and Anthony 'Bob' Brennan, Jack Gilley and Chuck Littlejohn as flight engineers. After undercarriage tests at 5,000 feet (1,524m) she was taken to twice that height and put through her paces. Everything went well and Bud Martin, the Lockheed Chief Pilot, was quoted as saying that in all his twenty years of flying, he had '…never flown an airplane as easy to handle'.

A USAF TAC Herk comes in to land. *Author's collection*

The first flight of the first production Hercules, 53-3129 (c/n 3001), on 7 April 1955. A crowd greets the returning aircraft and congratulates the pilots. This batch featured the original 'Roman nose', as is clearly seen in this photograph. Later they were converted to the more usual Herk profile, as can be seen in the following photograph, which shows the same aircraft at Dukes AFB, Florida, many years later. *Lockheed-Georgia, Marietta, via Audrey Pearcy*

The grandmamma of them all! *The First Lady*, 53-3129 (c/n 3001), at Marietta on 7 April 1955 and with 415 SOTS in 1975. *Lockheed-Georgia, Marietta, via Audrey Pearcy*

Maiden flight: the take-off of 53-3129 (c/n 3001) from Marietta on 7 April 1955. *Lockheed-Georgia, Marietta*

The First Lady taking off. *Lockheed-Georgia, Marietta, via Audrey Pearcy*

The C-130A-LM

The basic layout of the C-130A formed the general outline for all early Herk development. The fuselage was of a semi-monocoque design, divided into a flight station and a cargo compartment, with seating for each flight station. Full pressurisation maintained a cabin pressure-altitude of 5,000 feet (1,524m) at an aircraft altitude of 28,000 feet (8,534.4m). The full cantilever wing contained four integral main fuel tanks and two bladder-type auxiliary tanks; the weight of the fuel gave the Hercules a marked 'wing-droop' when sitting on the ground. The empennage comprised horizontal stabiliser, vertical stabiliser, elevator, rudder, trim tabs and a tail cone, and was also an all-metal full cantilever semi-monocoque structure, bolted to the after fuselage section.

The four Allison turboprop engines were attached to the wings, with nacelles that had cowl panels and access doors forward of the vertical fire wall. Clam-shell doors were situated aft of the vertical fire wall and air entered the engine through a scoop assembly at the front of the nacelle. Four independent oil systems provided an oil capacity of 12 US gallons (45.4249 litres) for each engine, with oil serviced through a filler neck located on the upper right engine cowling. The fuel system comprised a modified manifold-flow type, which incorporated fuel crossfeed, single point refuelling (SPR) and defuelling. Later models incorporated fuel dumping and blue fire suppression foam.

The landing gear was of the modified tricycle type, and consisted of dual nose gear wheels and tandem main wheels. The main gear retraction was vertical, into fuselage fairings, while the nose gear folded forward into the fuselage, and had power steering. The brakes were of the hydraulically operated, multiple-disc type, and the system incorporated differential braking and parking brake control with a modulating anti-skid system.

The hydraulic system comprised four engine-driven pumps supplying 3,000psi pressure to the utility and booster systems, and maintained a constant pressure during zero or negative 'g' conditions. The 25-litre (6.6043 US gallons) liquid oxygen (LOX)-type system provided for 96 man-hours of oxygen at an altitude of 25,000 feet (7,620m). It used diluter-demand automatic pressure-breathing regulators, and the system pressure was maintained at 300psi.

The primary flight control system of conventional aileron, elevator and rudder systems had hydraulic power boost. The wing flaps were also conventional, being of the high-lift Lockheed-Fowler type, hydraulically operated but with an emergency hand crank. De-icing was effected by engine bleed air on the wing and empennage leading edges, the radome and the engine inlet air ducts. The propellers had electrical heating, as did the windshield and pitot tubes.

The basic figures came out as follows:

Overall length	97ft 9in (29.3m) (with retro-fitted radome)
Span	132ft 7in (40.41m)
Overall height	38ft 3in (11.4m)
Horizontal tailplane overall length	52.7 inches (133.858cm)
Main landing gear overall width	14.3 inches (36.322cm)
Cabin to ramp cargo length	40.4 feet (12.31392m)
Cabin to ramp cargo width	123.2 inches (3.12928m) tapering to 120 inches (3.12928m) at rear entrance
Maximum ramp weight	124,200lb (56,336.17kg)
Maximum landing weight (5 fps)	124,200lb (56,336.17kg)
Maximum landing weight (9 fps)	96,000lb (43,544.86kg)
Operating weight	61,842lb (2,8010.5kg)
Empty weight without external tanks	72,231lb (32,763.43kg)
Maximum payload	35,000lb (15,875.73kg)
Fuel capacity @ 6.5lb/gal	39,975lb (18,132.35kg)
internal tanks	5,250 US gallons (19,873.41 litres)
external tanks	900 US gallons (3,406.87 litres)
total fuel volume	6,150 US gallons (23,280.28 litres)
Engines	four Allison turboprop constant-speed T56-A-9s; provision for eight 1,000lb (453.5923kg) thrust-assisted take-off (ATO)
Engine take-off power	3,750eshp
Auxiliary power	one auxiliary power unit (APU) to provide air during ground engine starting, for air-conditioning and electrical power, and emergency electrical power during flight up to 20,000 feet (6,096m)
Propellers	four Aeroproducts electro-hydromatic, constant-speed, full-feathering, reversible-pitch
Number of propeller blades	three
Diameter of propellers	15 feet (4.572m)
Outboard propeller ground clearance	68 inches (0.4064m)
Inboard propeller ground clearance	60.6 inches (1.53924m)
Inboard propeller/fuselage clearance	28.8 inches (0.73152m)
Performance: maximum speed	383mph (616km/h)
cruise speed	356mph (573km/h)
rate of climb	1,700ft/min (518m/min)
Service ceiling at 100,000lbs	34,000ft (10,360m)
Range with maximum payload	1,830 miles (2,945km)
Range with external tanks	3,359 miles (5,390km)
Wing area	1,745sq ft (162.1158048m²)
Wing loading	71.2lb (32.749kg)/sq ft
Wing aspect ratio	10.09
Cargo compartment floor length	41.0 feet (12.4968m)
width	120 inches (3.048m)
height	108 inches (2.7432m)
floor area	533sq ft (162.458m²) including ramp space
useable volume	4,500cu ft (127.4258m³)
Wing tip turning radius	85.0 feet (25.908m)
Nose gear turning radius	37.0 feet (11.2776m)
Wheelbase	32.1 feet (9.784m)
Main gear tyre size	20:00-20
Nose gear tyre size	12:50-16

The 'Thunderbirds' crew plane, Hercules C130-A 55-0026 (c/n 3053), serving with 317 Tactical Control Wing, is pictured at Cedar Rapids, Iowa, in October 1964. *Nick Williams, AAHS*

Oil capacity	8 US gallons (30.283 litres); independent system per engine
Fuel	modified manifold-flow type incorporating fuel cross-feed, single-point refuelling (SPR) and defuelling
Electrics	four 40kva engine-drive DC generators for 28-volt system; one 20kva APU-driven generator; one 24-volt, 36-ampere-hour battery
Hydraulics	four engine-driven pumps supplying 3,000psi pressure to utility and booster systems; one compressed-air pump supplying pressure to auxiliary system, backed up by hand-pump
Air-conditioning and pressurisation	two independent systems for flight deck and cargo compartment, bleed-operated from engine compressors in flight, or APU on ground; each systems provides 15,000 feet (4,572m) cabin at 35,000 feet (10,668m) altitude; maximum pressure differential of 7.5psi maintains an 8,000-foot (24,384m) cabin at the same altitude
Oxygen	gaseous-type system providing 36 man-hours of oxygen at 25,000 feet (7,620m) with diluter-demand automatic pressure-breathing regulators; also portable units
Cargo fittings and fixtures	10,000lb (4,535.925kg) D-ring tie-down floor fittings on 20-inch (0.508m) centre-on-centre grid pattern; six 25,000lb (11,339.8092kg) tie-down rings each side of floor; additional 5,000lb (2,267.96185kg) tie-down rings along fuselage walls and on ramp; interchangeable troop seats/litter racks with special overhead, sidewall and floor fittings, normally stowed
Mechanised loading system	USAF 463L MLS, with dual-rails, comprising roller conveyors attached to floor with tie-down fittings, locking devices for cargo restraint and remote-operation release capable of handling both 88-by-54-inch (2.2352-by-1.3716m) or 88-by-108-inch (2.2352-by-2.7432m) pallets.

A laden C-130A Herk from Naha AB, Okinawa, climbs from Hickam, AFB, Hawaii, in July 1967. *Nick Williams, AAHS*

The euphoria that followed the maiden flight debut of the Herk was followed by a near-disastrous in-flight fire that broke out in the No 2 engine of 53-3129 (c/n 3001) on 14 April 1955 as she was landing at Dobbins AFB. The Lockheed test pilots Leo Sullivan and Art Hansen had been conducting routine aerial engine tests on the aircraft's third flight under the supervision of Chief Development Test Engineer Lloyd Frisbee and his team. Each engine was feathered in turn, then air-started again. The trials went well but, while landing, the Royln coupling, which had not been properly locked, came apart and the quick-disconnect fuel line came loose at the fuel tank boost pump. Within seconds JP-4 oil started pumping out from the No 2 nacelle, and subsequently ignited. Although the aircraft survived, the fire spread and the port wing broke in half on the runway as the crew abandoned the aircraft.

Subsequently repaired, she was later converted into a JC-130A and served a long life in various capacities, including gunship combat duty in Vietnam, surviving a direct hit by a 37mm (1.456-inch) round. Named *The First Lady*, she ended up in the USAF Armament Museum at Eglin AFB. All that could be was salvaged from her and transferred to serial 54-1624 (c/n 3011), which became the new flight test programme aircraft in her stead.

Retro fittings on forty-nine production aircraft included the substitution of the original Curtiss-Wright variable-pitch, electric, three-bladed, hollow-steel propellers for the four-bladed Hamilton Standard type. This followed continuing problems with the former due to the reduction gear system being unable to cope with pitch control changes resulting in propeller oscillation and numerous defective units. This threatened the whole programme, and aircraft serial 53-3134 (c/n 3006) was used to experiment with a different design, the Aeroproducts hydraulically operated propeller, built by General Motors Detroit Diesel Allison Division from 26 November 1955 to July 1956. This led to it being adopted for the C-130A for a time. However, this proved but a temporary expedient and a second change was made to the Hamilton Standard product, which became the standard Hercules power plant until the C-130J arrived on the scene decades later.

The 3245th Test Group (Bombardment) based at Eglin AFB conducted a series of trials in mid-1956 in conjunction with Continental Army Command Board Five at Fort Bragg and the 3rd Aerial Port Squadron. One C-130A flew from El Centro, California, and made a para-drop of what was then a world record single load of 27,000lb (12,246.99kg) of iron. This was followed by another Hercules, serial 54-1623 (c/n 3010), which conducted a series of eighty-six sorties from Pope AFB, North Carolina, in which a total of 160 tons (145,149.5584kg) of supplies, 485 paratroops and 315 dummies were dropped successfully. The conversion versatility figures were equally impressive, with just 20 minutes being taken to change the configuration of thirty troop seats to the heavy freight hold, and 40 minutes to change from a forty-seater to the heavy freight platform dropper. During a trial a 22,235lb (10,085.626kg) Marine Corps weapons-carrier was dropped, followed

THE LOCKHEED MARTIN C-130 HERCULES

immediately by paratroops. During a six-day test period a freight platform was dropped from the ramp, again closely followed by five parachutists.

The USAF in Europe conducted an early loading demonstration during which a 13,000lb Matador missile was engorged by a Hercules in less than 15 minutes. At the US Army Engineer Research & Development Laboratories at McGuire AFB, New Jersey, the Army's Corps of Engineers offloaded trucks carrying Bailey Bridge sections from a Hercules at the rate of one every 15 seconds, and the airplane proved capable of airlifting an 18-ton (16,329.32kg) D7 bulldozer, a wheeled asphalt plant, road graders and scrapers, heavy highway rollers and similar road- and runway-building heavy equipment with ease. It also shifted a Bell XH-40 helicopter from Fort Worth, Texas, to Edwards AFB, California, together with a test crew of eight in just a few hours.

The 463rd Troop Carrier Wing (TCW) of Tactical Air Command was present at these trials and assessments were made of spare parts availability, maintenance requirements and crew-training needs. This unit subsequently took delivery of the first four C-130As at Ardmore AFB, California, on 9 December 1956. The first aircraft to arrive, the fiftieth to come off the production line, was 55-0023 (c/n 3050), which was named *City of Ardmore*. She also gave good service, surviving combat damage in Vietnam and being preserved at the Texas Museum of Military History (now Linear Air Park at Dyess AFB).

City of Ardmore, 55-0023 (c/n 3050), was the first C-130A to go on operational duty with the USAF and was still flying regular airlift missions a decade or more later with the Air Force Reserve after a worldwide career that included Purple Heart action in Vietnam. This aircraft was assigned to the 928th Tactical Airlift Group based at O'Hare Airport, Chicago, and is pictured over that city. She was later transferred to the Air National Guard at Nashville, Tennessee. *Lockheed-Georgia Newsbureau*

The most significant retro-fit of all (from the public perception of the Hercules, if nothing else) was the introduction of the AN/APS-42 and AN/APS-59 search radar sets, which were fitted to the lower half of the blunt front of the fuselage. This transferred the stern 'Roman nose' appearance of the Hercules into a softer 'Baby seal'-type profile, and the Herk took on a whole new image, which, if not beautiful, was more enduring!

Between 1958 and 1969 all C-130As were progressively given make-overs; re-skinning of 30% of the fuselage with thicker panels made them capable of carrying a 20-ton (18,143.694kg) payload to 35,000ft (10,668m). In addition a tandem rudder boost system was installed and electrical systems redesigned. Provision was also made to carry two under-wing pinion fuel tanks with a capacity of 450 US gallons (1,703.4435 litres) outboard of the engines. The propeller speed was reduced, both to lower the internal noise level and decrease vibration, but without any reduction in performance.

The C-130B-LM

The C-130B-*LM* (Model 282), which first flew on 20 November 1958, had an improved engine, the four-bladed propeller, stronger landing gear and additional in-built centre-wing-section fuel tanks, thus doing away with the optional pylon-mounted tanks of the C-130A. The forward cargo door on the port side remained but was sealed, bunks for the aircrew were provided in a deepened cockpit space, and the centre wing section was strengthened. Some had the AN/URT-26 Crash Position Indicator (CPI) in the extended tail cone, and a Tactical Precision Approach System (TPAS). The new dimensions were as follows:

Overall length	97ft 8in (29.79m)
Span	132ft 7in (40.41m)
Overall height	38ft 3in (11.66m)
Horizontal tailplane overall length	52.7 inches (1.33858m)
Main landing gear overall width	14.3 inches (0.36322m)
Cabin to ramp cargo length	40.4ft (12.3139m)
Cabin to ramp cargo width	123.2 inches (3.12928m) tapering to 120 inches (3.048m) at rear entrance
Maximum ramp weight	135,000lb (61,234.969kg)
Maximum landing weight (5 fps)	135,000lb (61,234.969kg)
Maximum landing weight (9 fps)	118,000lb (53,523.8996kg)
Operating weight	69,376lb (31,468.424kg)
Maximum payload	35,000lb (15,875.73295kg)
Fuel capacity @ 6.5lb/gal	45,240lb (20,520.5188kg)
internal tanks	6,960 US gallons (26,346.46 litres)
external tanks	nil
total fuel volume	6,960 US gallons (26,346.46 litres)
Engines	Four Allison turboprop, constant-speed T56-A-7s; provision for eight 1,000lb (453,592kg) thrust-assisted take-off (ATO)
Engine take-off power	4,050eshp
Auxiliary power	one auxiliary power unit (APU) to provide air during ground engine starting, for air-conditioning and electrical power, and emergency electrical power during flight up to 20,000 feet (6,096m)
Propellers	four Hamilton Standard electro-hydromatic, constant-speed, full-feathering, reversible-pitch
Number of propeller blades	four
Diameter of propellers	13.5 feet (4.1148m)
Outboard propeller ground clearance	79 inches (2.0066m)
Inboard propeller ground clearance	69.6 inches (1.7678m)
Inboard propeller fuselage clearance	37.8 inches (0.960m)
Performance: maximum speed	383mph (616km/h)
cruise speed	356mph (573km/h)

rate of climb	1,700ft/min (518m/min)
Service ceiling at 100,000lb	34,000 feet (10,360m)
Range with maximum payload	1,830 miles (2,945km)
Range with external tanks	3,359 miles (5,390km)
Wing area	1,745sq ft (531.876m²)
Wing loading	77.4lb (35.108kg)/sq ft
Wing aspect ratio	10.09
Cargo compartment floor length	41 feet (12.496m)
width	120 inches (3.048m)
height	108 inches (2.743m)
floor area	533sq ft (162.458m) including ramp space
useable volume	4,500cu ft (1371.6m³)
Wing tip turning radius	85.0 feet (25.908m)
Nose gear turning radius	37.0 feet (11.2776m)
Wheelbase	32.1 feet (9.78408m)
Main gear tyre size	20:00-20
Nose gear tyre size	12:50-16
Oil capacity	12 US gallons (45.4249 litres); independent system per engine
Fuel	modified manifold-flow type incorporating fuel cross-feed, single-point refuelling (SPR) and defuelling; provision for fuel dumping
Electrics	four 40kva engine-driven AC generators for 28-volt system; one 20kva APU-driven generator; one 24-volt, 36-ampere-hour battery
Hydraulics	four engine-driven pumps supplying 3,000psi pressure to utility and booster systems; one electrical motor-driven pump supplying pressure to auxiliary system, backed up by hand-pump
Air-conditioning and pressurisation	two independent systems for flight deck and cargo compartment, bleed-operated from engine compressors in flight, or APU on ground; each system provides 15,000 feet (4,572m) cabin at 35,000 feet (10,668m) altitude; maximum pressure differential of 7.5psi maintains an 8,000-foot (2,438m) cabin at the same altitude
Oxygen	gaseous-type system providing 40 man-hours of oxygen at 25,000 feet (7,620m) with diluter-demand automatic pressure-breathing regulators; also portable units
Cargo fittings and fixtures	10,000lb (4,535.923kg) D-ring tie-down floor fittings on a 20-inch (0.508m) centre-on-centre grid pattern; six 25,000lb (11,339.809kg) tie-down rings on each side of floor; additional 5,000lb (2,267.9618kg) tie-down rings along fuselage walls and on ramp; interchangeable troop seats/litter racks with special overhead, sidewall and floor fittings, normally stowed
Mechanised loading system	USAF 463L MLS, with dual-rails, comprising roller conveyors attached to floor with tie-down fittings, locking devices for cargo restraint and remote-operation release capable of handling both 88-by-54-inch (2.2352-by-1.3716m) or 88-by-108-inch (2.2352-by-2.7432m) pallets.

This is Hercules C-130B-15-*LM*, 58-0728 (c/n 3523), on 7 May 1964. *Nick Williams, AAHS*

While the engines were rated at 300hp above those of the -A, they still revolved at 13,820rpm, with a 10,000rpm ground operation selection available. One engine had to be operated at full rpm for AC generator operation or the ATM switched on. The -B had no provision for any under-wing pinion-mounted tanks.

As just one example of the C-130B's longevity, as late as June 1988 the 731st Tactical Airlift Squadron (AFRES) at Peterson AFB, Colorado, was running seventeen -Bs: serials 58-0713 (c/n 3508), 58-0723 (c/n 3518), 58-0738 (c/n 3535), 58-0757 (c/n 3558), 59-1526 (c/n 3563), 59-1527 (c/n 3568), 59-1530 (c/n 3576), 59-1531 (c/n 3579), 59-1537 (c/n 3589), 60-0294 (c/n 3593), 60-0295 (c/n 3596), 60-0296 (c/n 3597), 60-0299 (c/n 3603), 60-0300 (c/n 3604), 60-0303 (c/n 3613), 60-0310 (c/n 3622) and 61-0948 (c/n 3624). The airframe with the highest time at that date was 59-1527, which had 18,194.2 hours on her clock on 24 June 1988.[2]

Seen over Hickam Air Force Base in June 1969 is a C-130B of 11 JDS/355. *Nick Williams, AAHS*

[2] Letter from Flight Engineer Eric P. Deylius, 731st TAS, AFRES, Peterson Air Force Base, Colorado, dated 24 June 1988.

Hunched up against a dusk sky, Hercules C-130B 58-0728 (c/n 3523) of the 145th Tactical Air Group is seen at Lambert AFB on 7 May 1977. *Fred Harl via Nick Williams, AAHS*

It has been placed on record that at least one C-130B – 60-0308 (c/n 3620) – was fitted as a so-called 'Talking Bird' by the installation of Mobile Radio Communications equipment, MRC-108, developed by the Air Force Communications Service (AFCS) to maintain reliable contact with the Defense Communications Agency (DCA) [3] when operating in areas with no reliable or secure landline connections.

The suite included radio on a narrow band, Morse, fax, voice and a 12/16-channel multi-channel telex (known as teletype to the Americans) output at a speed of 75 baud. This particular aircraft, and no doubt others, worked on secondment from the 313th Tactical Airlift Wing with the Mobile Communications Group based at Warner-Robbins AFB in Georgia.

A Lockheed Georgia company engineer tests a ground-based mobile communications unit developed by the firm. The aircraft in the background is C-130H 78-0807 (c/n 4817). *Lockheed-Georgia, Marietta, via Audrey Pearcy*

[3] The DCA had been established at Arlington, Virginia, in 1960.

A Hercules of Military Airlift Command in the 1960s. *USAF*

The C-130E-LM

On 15 August 1961 the C-130E made her debut, being specifically designed for the Military Airlift Command (MAC) with its longer-range Logistic Supply role. Fuel bunkerage was accordingly increased, and larger, optional under-wing tanks could be carried, necessarily this time further inboard, being positioned between the two engine nacelles. The large cargo-loading door on the port side of the forward fuselage had been found to be virtually redundant in earlier models and was seldom used, and with the C-130E it was done away with completely.

The -E's dimensions were as follows:

Overall length	97ft 8in (29.79m)
Span	132ft 7in (40.41 m)
Overall height	38ft 3in (11.66m)
Horizontal tailplane overall length	52.7 inches (1.33858m)
Main landing gear overall width	14.3 inches (0.36322m)
Cabin to ramp cargo length	40.4 feet (12.31392m)
Cabin to ramp cargo width	123.2 inches (3.129m) tapering to 120 inches (3.048m) at rear entrance
Maximum ramp weight	155,000lb (70,306.817kg)
Maximum landing weight (5 fps)	155,000lb (70306.817kg)
Maximum landing weight (9 fps)	130,000lb (58,967kg)
Operating weight	73,563lbs (34,274.8kg)
Maximum payload	45,579lbs (20674.286kg)
Fuel capacity @ 6.5lb/gal	62,920lb (31,715.178kg)
internal tanks	6,960 US gallons (26,346.46 litres)
external tanks	2,720 US gallons (10,296.32 litres)
total fuel volume	9,680 US gallons (36,642.78 litres)
Engines	four Allison turboprop, constant-speed T56-A-7s; provision for eight 1,000lb (453.59kg) thrust-assisted take-off (ATO)
Engine take-off power	4,050eshp
Auxiliary power	one auxiliary power unit (APU) to provide air during ground engine starting, for air-conditioning and electrical power, and emergency electrical power during flight up to 20,000 feet (6096m)
Propellers	four Hamilton Standard electro-hydromatic, constant-speed, full-feathering, reversible-pitch
Number of propeller blades	four
Diameter of propellers	13.5 feet (4.1148m)
Outboard propeller ground clearance	79 inches (2.0066m)
Inboard propeller ground clearance	60.6 inches (1.5392m)
Inboard propeller fuselage clearance	37.8 inches (0.960m)
Performance: maximum speed	384mph (618km/h)

cruise speed	368mph (558km/h)
rate of climb	1,830ft/min (518m/min)
Service ceiling at 100,000lb	23,000 feet (7,010m)
Range with maximum payload	2,420 miles (3,895km)
Range with external tanks	4,700 miles (7.560km)
Wing area	1,745sq ft (531.876m)
Wing loading	88.8lb (40.279kg)/sq ft
Wing aspect ratio	10.09
Cargo compartment floor length	41.0 feet (12.4968m)
width	120 inches (3.048m)
height	108 inches (2.743m)
floor area	533sq ft (162.584m^2) including ramp space
useable volume	4,500cu ft (1371.6m^3)
Wing tip turning radius	85.0 feet (25.908m)
Nose gear turning radius	37.0 feet (11.2776m)
Wheelbase	32.1 feet (9.784m)
Main gear tyre size	20:00-20
Nose gear tyre size	12:50-16
Oil capacity	12 US gallons (45.4249 litres); independent system per engine
Fuel	modified manifold-flow type incorporating fuel cross-feed, single-point refuelling (SPR) and defuelling; fuel dumping provision
Electrics	four 40kva engine-driven AC generators for 28-volt system; one 20kva APU-driven generator; one 24-volt, 36-ampere-hour battery
Hydraulics	four engine-driven pumps supplying 3,000psi pressure to utility and booster systems; one electric motor-driven pump supplying pressure to auxiliary system, backed up by hand-pump
Air-conditioning and pressurisation	two independent systems for flight deck and cargo compartment, bleed-operated from engine compressors in flight, or APU on ground; each system provides 15,000 feet (4,572m) cabin at 35,000 feet (10,668m) altitude; maximum pressure differential of 7.5psi maintains 8,000-foot (2,438m) cabin at the same altitude
Oxygen	300psi liquid-type system providing 96 man-hours of oxygen at 25,000 feet (7,620m) with diluter-demand automatic pressure breathing regulators; also portable units
Cargo fittings and fixtures	10,000lb (4,535.92kg) D-ring tie-down floor fittings on a 20-inch (0.508m) centre-on-centre grid pattern; six 25,000lb (11,339.809kg) tie-down rings each side of floor; additional 5,000lb (2,267.96kg) tie-down rings along fuselage walls and on ramp; interchangeable troop seats/litter racks with special overhead, sidewall and floor fittings, normally stowed.
Mechanised loading system	The USAF 463L MLS, with dual-rails, comprising roller conveyors attached to floor with tie-down fittings, locking devices for cargo restraint and remote-operation release capable of handling both 88-by-54-inch (2.2352-by-1.3716m) or 88-by-108-inch (2.2352-by-2.7432m) pallets.

The extra fuel bunkerage enabled the -E to haul a 35,000lb (15,875.73kg) payload 900 nautical miles (1,666.84km) further than the -B and about 1,200 miles (1,931.21km) further than the -A, greatly increasing its value.

In June 1980 Lockheed announced that a USAF C-130E from Pope AFB had been equipped with the experimental two 7-foot-long 'tail fins', which they termed 'afterbody strakes', together with strain gauges and flight test instrumentation equipment. The strakes consisted of lightweight aluminium/fibreglass fins, 7 feet (2.15m) long, 4 inches (10.16 cm) thick and 20 inches (50.8cm) high, installed ventrally on the after fuselage. They were designed to smooth the air flow over the rear of the fuselage, reducing the Herk's aerodynamic drag. Although not a new concept at that time, those carried by the C-130 were the first to be fitted solely with the aim of improving fuel conservation. Mr L. R. Woodward of Lockheed's aerodynamic section went on record as claiming that, as a result of tests at the Warner Robins Air Logistic Center, a 3 to 3.5% fuel consumption saving could result, which would save the USAF $9 million annual on J-4 aviation fuel. Each strake fitted to the USAF's 550 Herks would therefore pay for itself within three months. Further air-drop trials at Pope confirmed that these strakes did not interfere with routine cargo handling operations.

A C-130E from Hickam AFB, Hawaii, in 1968. *Nick Williams, AAHS*

Military Airlift Command C-130E 63-7829 (c/n 3897) of 438 MAW, MAC, in June 1968. *Nick Williams, AAHS*

THE LOCKHEED MARTIN C-130 HERCULES

Cutting a clean line as she cruises from Hickam AFB in Hawaii in June 1969 is this C-130E of the 776 TAS, 314 TAW, out from Ching Chang Kang AB, Taiwan, and coded DL. *Nick Williams, AAHS*

A study in power: C-130E Herk 72-1288 (c/n 4499) revs up to full power as her sister climbs into the sky astern of her during exercises held in 1970. *USAF*

A Lockheed C-130E from Pope AFB displays her unique camouflage markings in April 1989. *Nick Williams, AAHS*

In May 1964 a specially-prepared C-130E, registration N11390E (c/n 3946), painted red, white and blue, carried out a round-the-world, record-breaking flight covering 50,000 miles (80,462.2km) of zig-zag flight, touching down in sixteen different countries, starting with the 11th Annual Italian International Air Show at Turin. The crew was headed by pilot Joe Garrett, with Ira Giles as navigator, Al Barrett as chief flight engineer, Bob Hill as flight engineer and Ralph Evans as co-pilot. Also in 1964 the same C-130E, the *One-World* machine, broke the First Production Flight Record with an endurance flight of 25hr 1min 8sec on April 20/21, with Joe O. Garrett at the helm.[4] This broke the record formerly held by an HC-130 of the USAF Aerospace Rescue & Recovery Service (ARRS), which had flown 8,790 miles (14,146.13km) from Taiwan to Scott AFB, Illinois, in 21hr 12min on 20 February 1972. The -E never looked back from then on.

A USAF MAC Hercules undergoing electrical checks. *Author's collection*

[4] See *Southern Star*, the newspaper of the Lockheed Corporation, April/May 1964 issues.

Air Force Reserve C-130E 63-7848 (c/n 3918) of the 756 TAS, nearest the camera, proudly displays the unit crest while lined up at Willow Grove Air Base in July 1978. *Bruce Stewart via Nick Williams, AAHS*

On 20 April 1964 a World First Flight Endurance Record was established by Lockheed with factory-fresh Hercules N 1130E (c/n 3946), which remained aloft for more than 25 hours. *via Audrey Pearcy*

Air Force Reserve Hercules, with 63-7848 (c/n 3918) of the 756 TAS nearest camera, lined up at Willow Grove Air Base July, 1978. *Bruce Stewart via Nick Williams, AAHS*

The C-130H-LM

By far the most prolific of all the Hercules variants to date, the C-130H (Model 382C) first appeared in March 1965 when the Royal New Zealand Air Force (RNZAF) took delivery of the first, serial NZ 7001 (c/n 4052), having made her first flight on 19 November 1964. Again the engines were improved with the adoption of the 4,910eshp T56-A-15 (de-rated to 4,508eshp in service). The opportunity was taken to make strength improvements to the centre-wing box assembly, and the aircraft were fitted with a beefed-up brake system.

This 'long-life' improved-design wing box included fatigue-resistant fasteners. The new wing structure was fatigue-tested to 40,000 simulated flight hours and all the US services had their fleets (except the -As) retro-fitted with the new centre wing section, and Australian, Brazilian, Colombian, Indonesian, Iranian, New Zealand, Pakistani and Saudi Arabian Herks all followed suit.

A C-130H of the USAF Military Airlift Command comes in to land. *USAF*

THE LOCKHEED MARTIN C-130 HERCULES

In 1972 the C-130's outer wings were given the same fatigue standards, with the wing structural aluminium alloy upgraded to stress-corrosion-resistant 7057-T73 material and using the latest sulphuric-acid-anodised surfaces as a base for a polyurethane protective coating, and these were all incorporated in the later production-line aircraft of later marks. The wing boxes were flay-surface sealed on assembly with corrosion-inhibitive polysulphide sealant, and structural fasteners were wet-installed with the same material, while external joins and seams were further protected with environmental 'aerodynamic smoother' sealant. The integral fuel tanks thus formed by the sealed structure were further sealed by fillet-sealing and fastener over-coating techniques. For extra corrosion protection within the integral tanks, and to eliminate the bacteria-promoting 'water bottoms', the new wings were equipped with a water-removal suction system actuated by the fuel boost pumps, which was pioneered on the C-5A.

The -H's dimensions were as follows:

Overall length	97ft 9in (29.79m)
Span	132ft 7in (40.41m)
Overall height	38ft 3in (11.66m)
Horizontal tailplane overall length	52.7 inches (1.338m)
Main landing gear overall width	14.3 inches (0.3632m)
Cabin to ramp cargo length	40.4 feet (12.3139m)
Cabin to ramp cargo width	123.2 inches (3.129m) tapering to 120 inches (3.048m) at rear entrance
Maximum ramp weight	155,000lbs (6,803.885kg)
Maximum landing weight (5 fps)	155,000lb (6,803.885kg)
Maximum landing weight (9 fps)	130,000lb (5,896.6kg)
Operating weight	75,381lb (34,192.246kg)
Empty weight	73,618lb (33,392.567kg)
Empty weight without external tanks	72,231lb (32763.43kg)
Maximum payload	43,761lb (19,849.655kg)
Fuel capacity @ 6.5lb/gal	62,920lb (28,540kg)
internal tanks	6,960 US gallons (26,346.46 litres)
external tanks	2,720 US gallons (10,296.32 litres)
total fuel volume	9,680 US gallons (36,642.78 litres)
Engines	four Allison turboprop, constant-speed T56-A-9s; provision for eight 1,000lb (453.59kg) thrust-assisted take-off (ATO)
Engine take-off power	4,508eshp
Auxiliary power	one auxiliary power unit (APU) to provide air during ground engine starting, for air-conditioning and electrical power, and emergency electrical power during flight up to 20,000 feet (6,096m)
Propellers	four Hamilton Standard electro-hydromatic, constant-speed, full-feathering, reversible-pitch
Number of propeller blades	four
Diameter of propellers	13.5 feet (4.1148m)
Outboard propeller ground clearance	79 inches (2.0066m)
Inboard propeller ground clearance	69.6 inches (1.7678m)
Inboard propeller fuselage clearance	37.8 inches (0.96m)
Performance: maximum speed	385mph (620km/h)
cruise speed	332mph (535km/h)
rate of climb	1,900ft/min (579m/min)
Service ceiling at 100,000lb	33,000 feet (10,060m)
Range with maximum payload	2,356 miles (3,791km)
Range with external tanks	4,894 miles (7,867km)
Wing area	1,745sq ft (531.876m²)

Wing loading	88.8lb (40.279kg)/sq ft
Wing aspect ratio	10.09
Cargo compartment floor length	41.0 feet (12.49m)
width	120 inches (3.048m)
height	108 inches (2.74m)
floor area	533sq ft (including ramp space)
useable volume	4,500cu ft (1,371.6m³)
Wing tip turning radius	85.0 feet (25.908m)
Nose gear turning radius	37.0 feet (11.27m)
Wheelbase	32.1 feet (9.78m)
Main gear tyre size	20:00-20
Nose gear tyre size	39 x 13
Oil capacity	12 US gallons (45.4249 litres); independent system per engine
Fuel	modified manifold-flow type incorporating fuel cross-feed, single-point refuelling (SPR) and defuelling; fuel dumping provision
Electrics	four 40kva engine-driven AC generators for 28-volt system; one 20kva (40kva on some) APU-driven generator; one 24-volt, 36-ampere-hour battery
Hydraulics	four engine-driven pumps supplying 3,000psi pressure to utility and booster systems; one electric motor-driven pump supplying pressure to auxiliary system, backed up by hand-pump
Air-conditioning and pressurisation	two independent systems for flight deck and cargo compartment, bleed-operated from engine compressors in flight, or APU on ground; each system provides 15,000 feet (4,572m) cabin at 35,000 feet (10,668m) altitude; maximum pressure differential of 7.5psi maintains an 8,000-foot (2,438m) cabin at the same altitude
Oxygen	300psi liquid-type system providing 96 man-hours of oxygen at 25,000 feet (7,620m) with diluter-demand automatic pressure-breathing regulators; also portable units
Cargo fittings and fixtures	10,000lb (4,535.9237kg) D-ring tie-down floor fittings on a 20-inch (0.508m) centre-on-centre grid pattern; six 25,000lb (11,339.80kg) tie-down rings each side of floor; additional 5,000lb (2,267.86kg) tie-down rings along fuselage walls and on ramp; interchangeable troop seats/litter racks with special overhead, sidewall and floor fittings, normally stowed
Mechanised loading system	USAF 463L MLS, with dual-rails, comprising roller conveyors attached to floor with tie-down fittings, locking devices for cargo restraint and remote-operation release capable of handling both 88-by-54-inch (2.2352-by-1.3716m) or 88-by-108-inch (2.2352-by-2.7432m) pallets.

The upgrading of the engines gave standard day operators an increase of about 150eshp per engine, making for greatly improved aircraft performance. This increased potential was particularly noticeable in hot weather conditions (103°F+) when the A-15 engine delivered 24% greater shaft horsepower. This in turn translated itself into as much as 500 feet (152.4m) less take-off ground run and 1,000 feet (304.8m) less total distance in order to clear a 50-foot (15.24m) obstacle, as well as lessening the landing distance – no mean attributes in the type of environment that the Herk regularly operates in! Also the -H could cruise some 3,000 feet (914.4m) higher and 5 knots faster, and had 2% greater range than the -E.

The C-130J-LM

Enduringly durable as the Hercules was (by 1999 she had accumulated more than 20 million flight hours and was in use by sixty nations), with airframes that went on for decades while their internal equipment was revamped and revamped again to keep up to date with half a century of fast technological advances, there eventually came a time when the building of a brand-new aircraft became a more viable and, in some cases, cheaper option, in the long term, than continual upgrading. At that point, in 1991, the C-130J concept was born.[5] A projected production run of 600 machines was envisaged at that time.

The RAF was particularly anxious to replace its ageing, twenty-seven-year-old Hercules fleet, but, as always, any decision was preceded by a whole raft of speculation in the British media, ranging form the sublime to the ridiculous, and a hostile attitude from the Treasury, traditionally opposed to any form of spending on the defence of the realm. Contenders (real or imaginary) were touted almost daily, and ranged from the European consortium Future Large Aircraft (FLA)[6], an updated, upgraded version of the British HS.681 (which had been killed off by the 1964 defence cuts), to the Russian-designed Antonov An-70T built in Kiev, Ukraine[7]. It seemed that nothing was too bizarre for the experts to tout as a Hercules replacement. The scowling Treasury had yet another option – don't buy any, just refurbish the existing aircraft and keep them going somehow

A dramatic artist's impression of the proposed C-130J powering off a desert track strip.
Robert F. Dorr via Nick Williams

[5] The 'J' suffix had been briefly assigned to the projected design that became the C-130SS, but was not officially adopted – see the appropriate section.

[6] See 'Tailskid', article in *Full Circle*, in *Air Pictorial* magazine, October 1993.

[7] See Harvey Elliott, 'RAF could replace its trusted Hercules with Russian aircraft', article in *The Times*, 29 December 1992.

A C-130J banks toward camera. *Lockheed-Martin*

until the proposed British Aerospace FLA might eventually arrive (a date of 2003 was given for this)[8]. Air Chief Marshal Sir Patrick Hine, BAe's military advisor, stated that for the FLA to be selected, 'There has got to be a will within government to support this programme, but that will in the MoD is not there.' For the other side, Micky Blackwell, President of Lockheed's Aeronautical Systems Company, put it clearly: 'Even the current-model Hercules can't go on for ever. Most of the aircraft have been in service between twenty and thirty years.'[9]

---

[8] As early as May 1961, the then British Aircraft Corporation had proposed building the BLC-130 Tactical Transport, which would be known as the BAC 222, and which was to have been powered by Rolls-Royce R Ty 20-15 engines to meet UK Specification OR 351.

[9] See John Davison and Andrew Lorenz, 'Funding row hits Hercules', article in *The Times*, 1993.

The first C-130J completes her acceptance trails. *Lockheed-Martin*

An on-board C-130 maintenance team at work. (Lockheed Martin)

The first C-130J Super Hercules to be assigned to fleet at the Ramstein Air Base, Germany, taxies under pressured water from two base fire trucks during an arrival ceremony. The aircraft's owning unit, the 86th Airlift Wing, celebrated not only the arrival of the J-model during the ceremony, but also a new era of operations for the Wing. This aircraft was the first of fourteen J-models scheduled to arrive over a 120-month period to replace the old E-models. *Airman 1st Class Kenny Holston, USAF official*

C-130J cockpit detail. *Lockheed-Martin*

An RAF C-130J in flight. *All Martin Bowman*

In the end the British Government accepted the view (highly predictable for most outside observers, if not the press) that 'Only a Hercules can replace a Hercules'. However, in 2000 the RAF was also looking at the European Airbus A400M as a possible replacement for the rest of the C-130Ks.[10] With the direct British involvement and technological input of major companies like Rolls-Royce, Dowty Aerospace, Lucas Aerospace and GKN Westland, with more than forty others, and spurred by the urgent need to upgrade the obsolescent RAF transport fleet, work pressed ahead. The stated aim of Lockheed-Martin was to produce a state-of-the-art Hercules for the new millennium, a low-cost, low-risk aircraft, one that retained and capitalised on the Herk's name and fame, and even looked superficially the same, but was a brand-new aircraft. The RAF placed an order for twenty-five of these 'second generation' Herks in 1995 at a total cost of £1.1 billion, and the C-130J and C-130J-30 were designated the Hercules C4 and C5 respectively.

Even the Test Team was international in its composition, with Test Pilots including Lockheed-Martin's Chief Pilot Bob Price working with Major Dave Alvin USAF, Flight Lieutenant Muz Colquhoun RAF, and Squadron Leader Robyn Williams RAAF, all involved in the programme.

The C-130J has essentially much the same dimensions as the C-130E/H, while the stretched J-130J-30 has 15 extra feet built into her in the form of two extension plugs. The forward extension plug is 100 inches (2.54m) long and the rear one 80 inches (2.032m) to give a total of 180 inches (4.572m).

Internally things are very different. The 'glass cockpit' concept prevails, with multi-function displays. Each system component has its own computer and everything can be controlled: mission planning, digital mapping, monitoring and advisory systems, integrated systems diagnostic testing and maintenance data recording and advisory systems. Each of the dual Flight Dynamics (Collins-Kaiser) holographic Head-Up Displays (HUD) has a wide-angle field of view (FOV) of 240 vertical by 300 horizontal, and is the primary flight display for the first time ever on a transport aircraft. The HUD gives the pilot the whole control scenario, including altitude, attitude, roll scale, flight path, airspeed, vertical velocity and heading, as well as projecting flight director cues, time displays, reference settings and the like. This system minimises 'head-down' display transitions and maintains full situational awareness during air-drop and in-flight refuelling profiles when maximum up-to-the-second data is essential, as well as simplifying approach and landing operations. The HUD is not only a boon, but also has reliability with a mean time between failure (MTBF) of 5,400 hours. Straight away its introduction reduced the aircrew to just two, together with a loadmaster, eliminating the flight engineer and navigator, an enormous saving in personnel and costs.

The four Head-Down Displays' (HDD) colour, multifunctional, liquid crystal displays (LCDs) are equally impressive and feature the Avionic Display Corporation's high-resolution, active matrix, flat-panel LCDs that are able to present twelve alternative formats or pages of data. This LCD also permits overlaying the formats with route of flight (ROF) and colour weather information. This system alone obviates the need for in excess of 90 electromechanical flight deck displays, an enormous simplification. It also has durability, with an MTBF of 8,900 hours. Each internal display is also fully compatible with the Night Vision Imaging System (NVIS), with night vision goggles with Type 1, Class A or Type II Class B systems. Both interior and exterior lighting is controlled through the Avionics Management Unit (AMU) of the -J and is compatible with this, including the internal light in the cargo compartment with the use of Class B, Types I and II systems. This lighting system supports night formation flying, air-to-air refuelling (both as tanker and receiving aircraft), night take-off and landing operations, and night covert ground work. Exterior lights, formation lights and navigation lights all have a normal and a covert option.

The Automatic Thrust Control System (ATCS) was introduced, which automatically reduces asymmetric engine thrust should there be unexpected outboard engine failure. Power is automatically restored on the good engine as the airspeed increased, the system's computer-fed software working with the outboard engines' own computers.

Features include All-Weather Airdrop Capability (AWADS), one every aircraft, to replace the fifty or so C-130E/Hs that had that capability. High-resolution ground-mapping capability with the APN-

[10] See Paul Jackson, 'In the Pipeline?', article in *The Royal Air Force Yearbook 2000*, PRM Aviation, Bristol, UK.

An RAF C-130J. This page shows the flight deck detail and overleaf the loading and unloading. *All Martin Bowman*

241 Low Power Colour Radar, coupled with the Honeywell dual embedded INS/GPS and digital mapping systems, makes this possible. The weather/navigation radar is the Westinghouse AN/APN-241 Colour/Navigation Radar, specially developed for the C-130 with high-resolution ground-mapping, predictive windshear detection, and an Enhanced Traffic Avoidance System (E-TCAS) and a Ground Avoidance System (GCAAS) are provided. The Advisory Caution & Warning System (ACAWA) has been installed as well as the SKE-2000 Station Keeping Equipment and Instrument Landing System (ILS). The Alliant Defense AN/AAR-47 missile-warning system uses electro-optic sensors to detect missile exhaust, and advanced signal processing algorithms and spectral selection to analyse and prioritise threats through sensors nose-mounted below the second cockpit window and in the tail cone. The Tracor AN/ALE-47 countermeasures system dispenses chaff and infrared flares in addition to the Primed Oscillator Expendable Transponder (POET) and Generic Expendable (GEN-X) active expendable decoys. The Lockheed-Martin AN/ALQ-157 infrared countermeasures system, mounted at the aft end of the main undercarriage bay fairing, generates a varying IR jamming signal and gives all-round protection. The Northrop Grumman MODAR 4000 colour weather and navigation radar, installed in the upward hinged dielectric radome in the nose, has a range of 250 nautical miles (463km) and completes the sophisticated electronics suite.

The power plant for the aircraft is the Rolls-Royce Allison AE2100D3 turboprop, rated at 4,591eshp (3,424kW).[11] There is automatic thrust control to the fly-by-wire propulsion system with the Lucas Aerospace Full-Authority, Digital Engine-Control (FADEC) system. The propeller driven by each engine is of the R391 composite, scimitar-shaped, six-bladed type of Dowty Aerospace, Staverton, Gloucestershire. They have a diameter of 13ft 6in (411.48cm) and the whole system, including control modules, weighs about 750lb (340.194kg) as against the C-130H's propellers, which Dowty also service, which weigh about 500kg (110,231.3lb). These distinctively shaped Series D600 propellers, so called because they can generate 6,000shp, act as one of the -J's few external identifying points against earlier models, the other being that the refuelling probe is now mounted on the port side of the aircraft, above the cockpit, housed in a Westland-modified nacelle. Ground feathering of the propeller blades (HOTEL mode) is another built-in option, and does away with troublesome prop blast while loading or offloading troops and other personnel. Ease of replacement is another feature; a change of propeller takes 45 minutes to complete compared to 8-10 hours on the C-130E/H.

[11] On 17 April 2006 it was reported that these Rolls-Royce AE21000D3 engines had notched up one million flight hours.

A close-up view of the unique scimitar-bladed D600-series propellers on a C-130J. *Courtesy of Dowty Aerospace Propellers, Gloucester*

There is a new and much-improved auxiliary power unit with double the life of the old one, the AiResearch APU. The fuel supply shows an equally impressive simplification, with just a solitary cross-ship manifold with foam installation in dry bays for extra fire safety. The landing gear shares the general upgrading with a newly designed nose gear strut and a modular wheel fitting with self-jacking struts incorporated for faster wheel changing. A new automated braking system is installed, married to an anti-skid mechanism as well as the Mk IV carbon brakes themselves.

During trials unexpected stall characteristics were experienced and Lockheed developed an enhanced stall warning system with a stick pusher to help in this. The initial audible stall warning indication is given through the headset while speed is still in excess of 40 knots above stalling speed. When this drops to 7% above stall speed there is also a pilot visual indicator on both sides of the HUD and HD in addition to an audible one. Should these warnings not be acted upon and the aircraft continues to decelerate, the stick pusher activates and automatically puts the aircraft in a nose-down attitude.

The -J tankers are equipped with a new boom refuelling option developed by Lockheed-Martin in order to provide them with the capability of refuelling aircraft like the F-15 and F-16, which do not have the drogue-and-probe system in their build. A pump rate for this boom is 800 US gallons (3,028.329 litres) per minute.

All these modifications gave impressive results, with General Walt Kross, Commander of USAF Air Mobility Command, lifting off a -J from Lockheed-Martin's Aeronautical Systems runway on 4 April 1997 in less than 800 feet of rolling length at a speed of 76 knots and a nose-up angle of 200. Range was also increased to an impressive 3,000 nautical miles (5,556km). As a KC tanker aircraft, the offloading rate for each refuelling pod is up to 300 gallons/2,040lb (1,135 litres/925kg) per minute simultaneously, with a load of 45,000lb.

As cost-saving was a prime selling point, Lockheed was at pains to point out the estimated advantages of the new C-130J over a revamped C-130E. The company gave the following figures: a 50% reduction in maintenance man-hours; 50% improved reliability; a 46% reduction in total manpower requirements; and 47% savings in operating and support cost.

How some of these savings were achieved becomes clearer when one looks at the enhanced servicing and maintenance facilities of the C-130J over earlier models. For a start the old maintenance plan based strictly on flying-hour totals has been completely done away with. The new concept is for calendar-based servicing. Regardless of major usage, the new aircraft will receive servicing to the following schedule:

Every 30 weeks: Primary Servicing (two days instead of up to a week)
Every 120 weeks: Intermediate Minor Servicing
Every 480 weeks – Major Servicing

Making all this possible is the new Hercules's Integrated Diagnostic System (IDS), which communicates to all the on-board computers via the MIL-STD-1553[12] data bus. Into the onboard reader is inserted a PCMCIA[13] card that is written to by the MCs after they have interrogated the onboard systems records. The fully downloaded card is removed and reinserted into the Ground Maintenance System (GMS) computer, which analyses all the card's data and makes diagnostic fault evaluations. This system will eventually do away with the time-consuming Form 700 Aircraft Maintenance Record.

Of course the PCMCIA card will also have stored on it the whole sum of each flight's data, including duration, engine hours, fuel usage, system malfunction and so on, and this data will also be downloaded to the GMS to build up a permanent record for each aircraft. As most of the onboard systems are modular in design, replacement is relatively simple and straightforward, with Lockheed-Martin establishing warehouses containing most of them at strategic points both in the USA and overseas.[14]

The development of the new technology was difficult, resulting in delivery delays. The US Federal Aviation Administrations did not grant approval until September 1998, some four weeks after the first C-130J had been delivered to the RAF, a delay of twenty-one months. The first in-flight refuelling demonstrations by an RAF C-130J-30 utilising the HUD, with Lockheed-Martin Chief Test Pilot Bob Price and Flight Lieutenant Mark Robinson at the controls, took place from a VC- tanker aircraft on 17 and 20 February 2000 at an 18,000-foot (5,486.4m) rendezvous 100 miles east of Charleston, South Carolina. Some 30,000lb (13,607.77kg) of fuel was transferred.

At Edwards AFB, Dave Shaw of Lockheed took an RAF C-130J-30 successfully through a fortnight of air and ground propeller blade strain tests to comply with FAA regulations.

The maiden flight of the first of the twelve RAAF C-130J-30s took place on 16 February 2000 with Robyn Williams RAAF and Lyle Schaefer, Lockheed Test Pilot, and James Bragg RAAF and Steve Bloodworth, Lockheed-Martin, as flight test engineers, together with Lockheed's Jerry Edwards and Paul Budge. This aircraft is flying a dedicated avionics testing programme in service.

Meanwhile the USAF, having ordered twenty-eight aircraft, anticipates buying at least 150 at twelve per year commencing in 2006. The first trio of J-30s underwent a comprehensive test plan to test the take-off and landing performance and their paratroop-drop capabilities, before joining their assigned unit, 143 Airlift Wing, Air National Guard, at Quonset State Airport, Rhode Island.

[12] MIL-STD-1553 is the military standard bus originally developed to define a communications bus to interconnect different sub-systems that needed to share and exchange information. It evolved to become the predominant, internationally accepted data bus standard for military platforms and was adopted by the air forces, navies, armies and space agencies of nations worldwide. In addition to military aircraft this standard is used on tanks, warships, missiles, satellites and the International Space Station, as well as ground-based support in test equipment, simulators and trainers.

[13] PCMCIA (Personal Computer Memory Card International Association) is the international standards body and trade association founded in 1989 to establish standards for integrated circuit (IC) cards and to promote interchangeability among mobile computers. It currently has more than 300 members and its mission in the twenty-first century is to develop standards for modular peripherals and promote their worldwide adoption.

[14] For example, the Lockheed Martin storage facility for the RAF in the UK is at Cheney Manor Industrial Estate, Swindon, which was at the time convenient for the aircraft's main operational base of RAF Lyneham. With the closing of Lyneham this no longer applies.

Order from Italy for eighteen and from the Marine Corps for five more followed. Marine Corps Brigadier General Randall L. West, the Legislative Assistant to the Commandant, flew a C-130J on 16 May 1997 in a demonstration that moved sixty fully equipped Marines more than 1,200 miles (1,931.21km) to their forward operating base. Take-off was achieved in less than 700 feet (213.36m). Additional Italian orders increased that country's total take of twelve C-130Js and ten C-130J-30s. Their instrumentation included UHF/VHF combined multi-band radios and a laser warning receiver system. They are operated by the 46° Air Brigade, based at Pisa.

Perhaps one of the greatest boosts to the -J's fledgling career came with the award of the National Aeronautic Association's (NAA) 'Most Memorable Record Flights of 1999'. In the spring of that year, with Lockheed Test Pilots Lyle Schaefer and Arlen Rens at the helm, an unmodified C-130 took off from Dobbins ARB, Georgia, with a 22,500lb (10,205.8kg) payload in a distance of 915 feet (278.89m), then flew to an altitude of 40,386 feet (12,309.65m), breaking both the US and World 10,000kg (22,046lb) payload records. She landed in a distance of 1,224 feet (373m). The same flight also saw the breaking or setting of no fewer than fifty other world records in both the C-1.N and STOL categories. These records included speed over both 1.000km (621.37 miles) and 2,000km (1,242.74 miles); closed courses with payload; altitude; greatest altitude in horizontal flight; and time-to-climb to 3,000m (9,842.5 feet), 6,000m (19,685 feet) and 9,000m (29,527ft) respectively with a payload. By the end of that year the C-130J held a total of fifty-four world records, with an average of one a week being set, itself a unique record! By May 2000 orders had built up to ninety-six aircraft, thirty-seven for the US Government including one Air National Guard EC-130J Psychological Warfare aircraft for 2001 delivery, and fifty-nine internationally.

The dimensions are as follows:

Overall length	97ft 9in (29.3m)
Span	132ft 7in (39.7m)
Overall height	38ft 3in (11.4m)
Horizontal tailplane overall length	52.7 inches (1.3385m)
Main landing gear overall width	14.3 inches (0.363m)
Cabin to ramp cargo length	40.4 feet (12.3m)
Cabin to ramp cargo width	123.2 inches (3.12928m) tapering to 120 inches (3.048m) at rear entrance
Maximum ramp weight	155,000lbs (70,306.8kg)
Maximum landing weight (5 fps)	155,000lbs (70306.8kg)
Maximum landing weight (9 fps)	96,000lbs (43,544.867kg)
Operating weight	79,090lb (35,875kg)
Empty weight	73,618lb (33,392kg)
Empty weight without external tanks	72,231lb (32,763kg)
Maximum payload	41,043lb (18,617kg)
Fuel capacity @ 6.5lb/gal	39, 975lb (18,132kg)
internal tanks	45,900lb (20,820kg); 43,900lb (20,723kg) with foam
external tanks	18,700lb (8,482.17kg)
total fuel volume	64,100lb (29,075.27kg)
Engines	four Allison AE2100D3 two-spool turboprops; oil-bath starter and modular gearbox; provision for eight 1,000lb thrust-assisted take-off (ATO)
Engine take-off power	4,591eshp (3,424kW)
Auxiliary power	one auxiliary power unit (APU) to provide air during ground engine starting, for air-conditioning and electrical power, and emergency electrical power during flight up to 20,000 feet (6096m)
Propellers	four Dowty Aerospace composite R391 scimitar-shaped units
Number of propeller blades	six
Diameter of propellers	13ft 6in (411.48cm)

Outboard propeller ground clearance	5ft 10in (1.778m)
Inboard propeller ground clearance	5ft 7in (1.7018m)
Inboard propeller fuselage clearance	38 inches (96cm)
Performance: maximum cruise speed	400mph (645km/h)
rate of climb	1,700ft/min (518m/min)
Service ceiling at 100,000lb	34,000 feet (10,360m)
Range with maximum payload	1,830 miles (2,945km)
Range with external tanks	3,359 miles (5,390km)
Wing area	1,745sq ft (161.12m²)
Wing loading	71.2lb (32,295kg)/sq ft
Wing aspect ratio	10.09
Cargo compartment floor length	56.0 feet (17.068m)
width	120 inches (3.048m)
height	108 inches (2.743m)
floor area	533sq ft (162,485m²) including ramp space
useable volume	4,500cu ft (1,371.6m³)
Cargo loading	37,216lb (16,880.89kg)
Wing tip turning radius	85 feet (25.90m)
Nose gear turning radius	37 feet (11.27m)
Wheelbase	32.1 feet (9.784m)
Main gear tyre size	20:00-20
Nose gear tyre size	12:50-16
Oil capacity	12 US gallons (45.4249 litres); independent system per engine
Fuel	modified manifold-flow type incorporating fuel cross-feed, single-point refuelling (SPR) and defuelling.
Electrics	four 40kva engine-driven DC generators for 28-volt system; one 20kva APU-driven generator; one 24-volt, 36-ampere-hour battery
Hydraulics	four engine-driven pumps supplying 3,000psi pressure to utility and booster systems; one compressed-air pump supplying pressure to auxiliary system, backed up by hand-pump
Air-conditioning and pressurisation	two independent systems for flight deck and cargo compartment, bleed-operated from engine compressors in flight, or APU on ground; each system provides 15,000 feet (4,572m) cabin at 40,000 feet (12,192m) altitude; maximum pressure differential of 7.5psi maintains an 8,000-foot (2,438m) cabin at the same altitude
Oxygen	gaseous-type system providing 36 man-hours of oxygen at 25,000 feet (7,620m), with diluter-demand automatic pressure-breathing regulators; also portable units
Cargo fittings and fixtures	10,000lb (4,535.92kg) D-ring tie-down floor fittings on a 20-inch (0.508m) centre-on-centre grid pattern; six 25,000lb (11,539.809kg) tie-down rings each side of floor; additional 5,000lb (2267.96kg) tie-down rings along fuselage walls and on ramp; interchangeable troop seats/litter racks with special overhead, sidewall and floor fittings, normally stowed

Mechanised loading system	integral flip-over roller conveyors and dual-row, right/left centreline container delivery system (CDS), centre vertical restraint (CVR) rails; variable-speed electric winch flush-mounted in front cargo compartment floor; loadmaster console controls electric load-sensing locks on low-profile rails; electric towplate flush-mounted in ramp for accurate air-drop load extraction; aerial delivery system (ADS) ramp support arms remain connected for all operations; also new cargo ramp and door-opening capability for high-speed target ingress/egress.

Comparison loadings for the C-130J and the C-130J-30 are:

Aircraft	C-130J	C-130J-30	Increase (%)
Cargo floor	40 feet (12.192m)	55 feet (16.764m)	37
463L cargo pallets	6	8	34
Litters	74	97	31
Container bundles	16	24	50
Combat troops	92	128	39
Paratroops	64	92	44

Currently 168 C-130Js of both types are built or building for US users.

America

C-130J: Serials 94-3026 (c/n 5413), later civilian N130JC, then 94-8151 used for various flight testings; 94-3027 (c/n 5415), later civilian N130JG, then 94-8152 flight test machine; 96-8153 (c/n 5454), former civilian N4099R scheduled for 'Commando Solo III' palleting 2005, named *Spirit of Biloxi*; 96-8154 (c/n 5455), 'Commando Solo II' pallet 2006, *Spirit of Biloxi* 2007; 97-1351 (c/n 5469) Air National Guard; 97-1352 (c/n 5470) Air National Guard; 97-1353 (c/n 5471) Air National Guard; 98-1355 (c/n 5491) Air National Guard; 98-1356 (c/n 5492) Air National Guard; 98-1357 (c/n 5493) Air National Guard; 98-1358 (c/n 5494) Air National Guard.

EC-130J: All Air National Guard (ANG): 97-1931 (c/n 5477), 'Commando Solo II' palleted; 98-1932 (c/n 5490), 'Commando Solo III' 2008; 99-1933 (c/n 5502), 'Commando Solo III' 2008; 00-1934 (c/n 5522); 01-1935 (c/n 5532).

HC-130J: All US Coast Guard (USCG):

Customer	Registration	c/n	Type
USCG	CG2001	5524	383U-35J
USCG	CG2002	5533	383U-35J
USCG	CG2003	5534	383U-35J
USCG	CG2004	5535	383U-35J
USCG	CG2005	5541	383U-35J
USCG	CG2006	5542	383U-35J

HC/MC-130J: All Air Force Special Operations Command (AFSOC):

Customer	Serial	c/n
AFSOC	09-	5633
AFSOC	09-	5634
AFSOC	09-	5656
AFSOC	09-	5657
AFSOC	09-	5658
AFSOC	09-	5659

KC-130J: All US Marine Corps (USMC):

Customer	BuOrd No	c/n	Type
USMC	165735	5488	382U-11J
USMC	165736	5489	382U-11J
USMC	165737	5499	383U-11J
USMC	165738	5506	383U-11J
USMC	165739	5507	382U-11J
USMC	165809	5508	383U-11J
USMC	165810	5509	382U-11J
USMC	165957	5515	382U-33J
USMC	166380	5516	382U-33J
USMC	166381	5527	382U-38J
USMC	166382	5528	382U-38J
USMC	166472	5543	382U-38J
USMC	166473	5544	382U-38J
USMC	166511	5553	382U-38J
USMC	166512	5554	382U-38J
USMC	166513	5555	382U-72J
USMC	166514	5556	382U-72J
USMC	166762	5562	382U-72J
USMC	166763	5563	382U-72J
USMC	166764	5564	382U-72J
USMC	166765	5565	382U-72J
USMC	167108	5577	382U-72J
USMC	167109	5578	382U-72J
USMC	167110	5579	382U-72J
USMC	167111	5580	382U-72J
USMC	167112	5602	382U-72J
USMC	167923	5590	382U-72J
USMC	167924	5591	382U-72J
USMC	167925	5592	382U-72J
USMC	167926	5593	382U-72J
USMC	167927	5618	382U-72J
USMC	167981	5617	382U-72J
USMC	167982	5603	382U-72J
USMC	167983	5604	382U-72J
USMC	167984	5605	382U-72J
USMC	167985	5606	382U-72J
USMC	168074	5631	382U-72J
USMC	168075	5632	382U-72J
USMC	168065	5644	382U-72J
USMC	168066	5645	382U-72J
USMC	168067	5646	382U-72J
USMC	168068	5647	382U-72J
USMC	168069	5660	382U-72J
USMC	168070	5661	382U-72J
USMC	168071	5676	382U-72J
USMC	168072	5677	382U-72J

MC-130J: All Air Force Special Operations Command (AFSOC):

Customer	c/n	Type
AFSOC	5680	382U-73J
AFSOC	5681	382U-73J
AFSOC	5682	382U-73J
AFSOC	5695	382U-73J
AFSOC	5696	382U-73J
AFSOC	5697	382U-73J

WC-130J: All USAF Reserve (AFRES):

Customer	Serial	c/n	Type
AFRES	96-5300	5451	382U-04J
AFRES	96-5301	5452	382U-04J
AFRES	96-5302	5453	382U-04J
USAF	97-5303	5473	382U-07J
USAF	97-5304	5474	382U-07J
USAF	97-5305	5475	382U-07J
USAF	97-5306	5476	382U-07J
USAF	98-5307	5486	382U-12J
USAF	98-5308	5487	382U-12J
USAF	99-5309	5501	382U-12J

C-130J-30: All USAF except where indicated:
99-1431 (c/n 5517) ANG; 99-1432 (c/n 5518) ANG; 99-1433 (c/n 5519) ANG; 01-1461 (c/n 5525) ANG; 01-1462 (c/n 5526) ANG; 02-0314 (c/n 5545); 02-8155 (c/n 5546) AFRES; 02-1434 (c/n 5547) ANG; 02-1463 (c/n 5551) ANG; 02-1464 (c/n 5552) ANG; 03-8154 (c/n 5557) AFRES; 04-3142 (c/n 5558); 04-3143 (c/n 5559); 04-3144 (c/n 5560); 04-8153 (c/n 5561) AFRES: 05-8152 (c/n 5566); 05-3146 (c/n 5567); 05-3147 (c/n 5568): 05-3145 (c/n 5569); 05-8157 (c/n 5570); 05-8156 (c/n 5571); 05-1435 (c/n 5572) ANG; 05-8158 (c/n 5573); 05-1465 (c/n 5574) ANG; 05-1436 (c/n 5575) ANG; 05-1466 (c/n 5576) ANG; 06-8159 (c/n 5581); 06-4631 (c/n 5582); 06-1438 (c/n 5584); 06-1467 (c/n 5585); 06-1437 (c/n 5586); 06-4632 (c/n 5587); 06-4633 (c/n 5588); 06-4634 (c/n 5589); 07-1468 (c/n 5594); 07-4635 (c/n 5595); 07-4636 (c/n 5596); 07-4637 (c/n 5597); 07-4638 (c/n 5598); 07-4639 (c/n 5599); 07-46310 (c/n 5600); 07-46311 (c/n 5608); 08-8601 (c/n 5609); 07-46312 (c/n 5610); 08-8602 (c/n 5611); 08-8604 (c/n 5612); 08-8603 (c/n 5613); 08-8606 (c/n 5614); 08-8605 (c/n 5615); 08-8607(c/n 5616); 08-8611(c/n 5619); 08-8612 (c/n 5620); 08-8610 (c/n 5621); 07-8608 (c/n 5622); 07-8609 (c/n 5623); 08-8613 (c/n 5624); 08-8614 (c/n 5625) ;07-31701(c/n 5628); 06-03171 (c/n 5641); 09-0108 (c/n 5633); 08-31704 (c/n 5643); 08-3174; (c/n 5648) 08-3172 (c/n 5642); 08-3173 (c/n 5643) and 09-0109 (c/n 5634).

The following were on order for the USAF at time of writing:
c/ns 5670, 5671, 5672, 5673, 5674, 5675, 5678, 5679, 5683, 5684, 5685, 5686, 5691, 5692, 5693, 5694

Great Britain
Serials ZH880 (c/n 5478), former civilian registration N73238; ZH881 (c/n 5479), former civilian N4249Y; ZH882 (c/n 5480), former civilian N4081M; ZH883 (c/n 5481), former civilian N4242N; ZH884 (c/n 5482), former civilian N4249Y; ZH885 (c/n 5483), former civilian N41030; ZH886 (c/n 5484), former civilian N73235; ZH887 (c/n 5485), former civilian N4187W; ZH888 (c/n 5496), former civilian N4187; ZH889 (c/n 5500).

Italy
Serials 46-21 (c/n 5497) MM 62176; 46-22 (c/n 5498) MM 62177; 46-46 (c/n 5510) MM 62181; 46-47 (c/n 5511) MM 62182; 46-48 (c/n 5512) MM 62183; 46-49 (c/n 5513) MM 62184; 46-50 (c/n 5514) MM 62185; 46-51 (c/n 5520) MM 62186; 46-53 (c/n 5521) MM 62187; 46-54 (c/n 5523) MM 62188; 46-55 (c/n 5529) MM 62189; 46-56 (c/n 5530) MM 62190; 46-57 (c/n 5531) MM 62191; 46-58 (c/n 5539) MM 62192; 46-59 (c/n 5540) MM 62192; 46-60 (c/n 5548) MM 62194; 46-61 (c/n 5549) MM 62195; 46-62 (c/n 5550) MM 62196

All the main types, C-130A, C-130B, C-130E, C-130H and C-130J, have spawned a huge number of sub-types and variants with specialised spin-offs from the 'norm', and these are all described in their appropriate sections.

The C-130K

First flown on 19 October 1966, the C-130K (Model 382-19B) was stated officially to be the British equivalent of the C-130H for RAF Support Command[15] but with much locally supplied components supplied by Scottish Aviation, and with UK electronics and instrumentation fitting the responsibility of the Cambridge-based company, Marshall Engineering.

Some sixty-six of this Variant C.1 were delivered, and were known in the RAF as the Hercules C Mk I. Six C.1s were modified to tankers as the C.1K, serials XV192 (c/n 4212); XV201 (c/n 4224); XV203 (c/n 4227); XV204 (c/n 4228); XV213 (c/n 4240) and XV296 (c/n 4262), while twenty-six had in-flight refuelling added to become C.1Ps – serials XV178 (c/n 4188); XV179 (c/n 4195); XV181 (c/n 4198); XV182 (c/n 4199); XV185 (c/n 4203); XV186 (c/n 4204); XV187 (c/n 4205); XV191 (c/n 4211); XV192 (c/n 4212); XV195 (c/n 4216); XV196 (c/n 4217); XV200 (c/n 4223); XV205 (c/n 4230); XV206 (c/n 4231); XV210 (c/n 4236); XV211 (c/n 4237); XV215 (c/n 4242); XV218 (c/n 4245); XV291 (c/n 4256); XV292 (c/n 4257); XV293 (c/n 4258); XV295 (c/n 4261); XV297 (c/n 4263); XV298 (c/n 4264); XV300(c/n 4267) and XV306 (c/n 4274).

[15] However, in 2005 it was stated that '…the RAF C-130K is nothing more than a 1968-70E model but with Dash 15 engines (as fitted to the later H model)' and again 'The K model only designated UK specified avionics, ie – it wasn't a *bona fide* Lockheed model designation.' Also that 'Most of the older RAF C130s were given newer centre-sections in the mid-'70s to mid-'80s at Marshalls of Cambridge, and the outer wings were rebuilt with new planks top and bottom. This was done specifically to address the fatigue problems with the older type wing.' The RAAF had also had to fit wing patches on its older models prior to selling them to Pakistan.

The C-130K being refurbished at Marshalls of Cambridge. *Marshall of Cambridge (Engineering) Ltd, via Audrey Pearcy*

RAF C-130K XV181 (c/n 4198) starting engines at Lyneham. *RAF official*

Dawn operations, with one aircraft taking off over another at a gloomy British base. *Author's collection*

Subsequently thirty C.1 aircraft were modified with 'stretched' fuselages like the civilian L-100-30s, with a 15-foot (4.57m) extension, and these became the Hercules C.3P. These then had in-flight refuelling added to become the C.3P. They were serials XV176 (c/n 4169); XV177 (c/n 4182); XV183 (c/n 4200); XV184 (c/n 4201); XV188 (c/n 4206); XV189 (c/n 4207); XV190 (c/n 4210); XV193 (c/n 4213); XV197 (c/n 4218); XV199 (c/n 4220); XV202 (c/n 4226); XV207 (c/n 4232); XV209 (c/n 4235); XV212 (c/n 4238); XV214 (c/n 4241); XV217 (c/n 4244); XV219(c/n 4246); XV220 (c/n 4247); XV221 (c/n 4251); XV222 (c/n 4252); XV223 (c/n 4253); XV290 (c/n 4254); XV294 (c/n 4259); XV299 (c/n 4266); XV301 (c/n 4268); XN302 (c/n 4270); XV303 (c/n 4271); XV304 (c/n 4272); XV305 (c/n 4273) and XV307 (c/n 4275).

XV208 (c/n 4233) was modified by Marshalls of Cambridge in 1975 to become the unique Hercules W.2 for use as a Meteorological Research platform, operating with the A&AEE and operated by the RAE, Farnborough. Christened 'Snoopy', she made her final weather flight in July 2002 after clocking up 11,900 flight hours. In 2005 she was reacquired by Marshalls from QinetiQ, and modified for Risk Reduction flight trials for the Europrop International TP400-D6 turboprop

THE LOCKHEED MARTIN C-130 HERCULES

engine, which are destined for the Airbus A400M Military Transporter programme. The aircraft's distinctive nose boom, radar and wing pods were removed, and the systems, fuselage, pylons and wings were adapted to mount the test engine. The TP400-D6 itself is mounted on the inner port wing location and is fitted with an eight-bladed Ratier-Figeac propeller of 5.33m (17.5-foot) diameter. Ground tests commenced in 2008 and she made her first flight in her new configuration that same December, with full power flights commencing a year later.

The unique Hercules W.2 XV208 (c/n 4233), a modified aircraft that first flew on 31 March 1973. Some twenty-two scientists could be embarked, together with their laser projector, cameras and other sophisticated equipment. *Lockheed-Georgia, Marietta*

One RAF Hercules W.2, XV 208 (c/n 4233), was converted by Marshalls of Cambridge into a flying test bed for the Meteorological Flight of the Royal Aircraft Establishment at Farnborough. She presented a truly unique profile, as this photograph shows. *AP Publications*

Civilian use – the basic L-100

Enormously useful and efficient in proven military service the world over, Lockheed was obviously not overlooking the huge potential civilian market for such a versatile aircraft. Since she first obtained her FAA type certificate on 16 February 1965, the basic civilian variant, the L-100 series (Models 382 and 382B), which was derived from the C-130E model, has proved to be just about the most popular bulk-hauler there is and has been operated by the full range of users, scheduled airlines, contract carriers, leasing companies and quasi-governmental agencies in the Third World, where they double as military transports whenever the need arises. Like their air force counterparts, these civilian operators have found that the Hercules can get into, and get out of, practically any airstrip, from jungle clearing, mountain-hemmed patch to compacted desert sand.

In the same manner as the C-130 variants, the first L-100, registration N1130E (c/n 3946), which made her maiden 25hr 1min flight on 20/21 April, 1964, most of it on just two engines, had fully air-conditioned and fully pressurised cockpit and cargo compartments, both on the ground and in the air. Many of the military fittings were extraneous to commercial operation and were done away with, including the aerial delivery system, troop seating and litter racking; even the navigator's station was redundant, while the under-wing fuel tanks were also omitted. Aircrew accommodation was for three men plus one observer, while the cargo compartment, 10 feet (3.048m) wide and 9 feet (2.7432m) high, gave easy access and wide, straight-in loading, as useful for moving freight as for moving tanks. The truck-level integral ramp, 42 inches (1.0668m) high and adjustable to ground level, was just as useful for loading from a freight dock and gave a further 10 feet.

The cargo compartment itself was fitted out with the same 20-inch (0.508m) centre-on-centre grid patter of 10,000lb (4535.92kg) D-ring tie-down floor fittings and 25,000lb (11,339.8kg) tie-down rings along the sides of the fuselage and on the ramp. The flooring, strengthened with military vehicles and equipment in mind, was therefore quite capable of carrying the heaviest machinery, such as oil rig parts and heavy trucks as well as anything else that could be palletised. The loading system employed on the L-100 was a dual rail-roller with removable side restraint rails and rollers on the cargo floor, plus a 9g barrier net at the forward end. The guide rails along the outboard rollers were movable, accommodating pallets 88, 109 or 118 inches (2.2352, 2.7686 or 2.9922 metres) wide, or containers 8 feet (2.4384m) wide. The L-100 could therefore swallow with ease either the standard 8 by 8 feet (2,4384 by 2,4384m) container straight from the haulage vehicle, or a selection of palletised loads, including, with length-wise loading, the 88-by-125-inch (2.2352m) pallet, or, conventionally, half-sized pallets of 88 by 118 inches (2,2352 by 2.9972m), 88 by 108 inches (2.2352 by 2.7432m), or 88 by 54 inches (2,2352 by 1,3716m), all of which could be secured by hand-operated 9g restraining locks. The first airline to operate the L-100 was Alaskan on 8 March 1965, when it leased the lead demonstrator aircraft from Lockheed. Twenty-one Model 382B production aircraft followed. Initial cargoes ranged from supplies for Alaskan bases to copper bar transportation in Africa. Most were subsequently 'stretched' to L-100-20, and some were stretched again to L-100-30 standard.

The figures for the basic original L-100 were as follows:

Overall length	97ft 8in (29.79m)
Span	132ft 6in (40.386m)
Overall height	38ft 3in (11.66m)
Horizontal tailplane overall length	52.7 inches (1.3385m)
Main landing gear overall width	14.3 inches (0.36322m)
Cabin to ramp cargo length	40.4 feet (12.31392m)
Cabin to ramp cargo width	123.2 inches (3.12928m) tapering to 120 inches (3.048m) at rear entrance
Maximum ramp weight	155,800lb (70,669.691kg)
Maximum landing weight (10 fps)	130,000lb (58,967.0081kg)
Operating weight	69,926lb (31,717.90kg)
Maximum payload	47,990lb (21,767.89kg)
Fuel capacity @ 6.7lb (3.039kg)/gal	64,668lb (29,332.9kg)
internal tanks	6,942 US gallons (26,278 litres)
external tanks	2,712 US gallons (10,266.0367 litres)

total fuel volume	9,654 US gallons (36,544,365 litres)
Engines	four Allison turboprop, constant-speed 501-D22s
Engine take-off power	4,050eshp flat-rated (sea level)
Auxiliary power	one auxiliary power unit (APU) to provide air during ground engine starting, for air-conditioning and electrical power, and emergency electrical power during flight up to 20,000 feet (6,096m)
Propellers	four Hamilton Standard electro-hydromatic, constant-speed, full-feathering, reversible-pitch
Number of propeller blades	four
Diameter of propellers	13.5 feet (4.1148m)
Outboard propeller ground clearance	79.0 inches (2.066m)
Inboard propeller ground clearance	69.6 inches (1.76784m)
Inboard propeller fuselage clearance	37.8 inches (0.96012m)
Performance: maximum speed	343mph (552 km/h)
rate of climb	1,700ft/min (518m/min)
Service ceiling at 100,000lb	34,000 feet (10,360m)
Range with maximum payload	1,569 miles (2,526km)
Range with external tanks	5,733 miles (9,227km) with zero payload
Wing area	1,745sq ft (531.876m²)
Wing loading	86.2lb (39.099kg)/sq ft
Wing aspect ratio	10.09
Cargo compartment floor length	49.0 feet (14.9352m)
width	120 inches (3.048m)
height	108 inches (2.7432m)
floor area	533sq ft (162.458m²) including ramp space
useable volume	4,500 cu ft (1,371.6m³)
Wing tip turning radius	85.0 feet (25.908m)
Nose gear turning radius	37 feet (11.2776m)
Wheelbase	32.1 feet (9.784m)
Main gear tyre size	20:00-20
Nose gear tyre size	12:50-16
Oil capacity	12 US gallons (45.4249 litres); independent system per engine
Fuel	modified manifold-flow type incorporating fuel cross-feed, single-point refuelling (SPR) and defuelling and fuel dumping
Electrics	four 40kva engine-driven AC generators for 28-volt system; one 20kva APU-driven generator; one 24-volt, 36-ampere-hour battery; four 200-ampere transformer-rectifier units converting AC to DC power, both of which can also be supplied by external power sourcing
Hydraulics	four engine-driven pumps supplying 3,000psi pressure to utility and booster systems; one electric motor-driven pump supplying pressure to auxiliary system, backed up by hand-pump
Air-conditioning and pressurisation	two independent systems for flight deck and cargo compartment, bleed-operated from engine compressors in flight, or APU on ground; each system provides 15,000 feet (4,572m) cabin at 35,000 feet (10,668m) altitude; maximum pressure differential of 7.0psi maintains an 8,000-foot (2,438m) cabin at 32,000 feet (9,753m) altitude

Oxygen	gaseous-type system providing 10 man-hours of oxygen at 25,000 feet (7,620m), with diluter-demand automatic pressure-breathing regulators; also portable units
Bulk loading: clear cube volume	3,670cu ft (11,18.616m³)
cheek volume	200cu ft (60.97m³)
ramp volume	630cu ft (192.024m³)
Total volume	4,500cu ft (1,371.6m³)
Palletised loading: no of pallets	six*
Main compartment loading	2,825cu ft (861.06m³)
Ramp volume	490cu ft (149.352m³)
Total volume	3,315cu ft (1,010.412m³)
Containerised loading: no of containers	six** (five in hold and one on ramp)
Main compartment volume	2,725cu ft (830.58m³)
Ramp volume	490cu ft (149.352m³)
Total volume	3,215cu ft (979.932m³)

* Based on standard pallet 118 by 88 inches (2.922 by 2.2352m), loaded 102 inches (2,5908m) high, with a weight of 361lb (163.7468kg). With a cargo setback of 2 inches (0.0508m) from each pallet edge, volume was 565cu ft (172.212m³).

** Based on fibreglass containers in main compartment, 114 inches (2.8956m) wide by 84 inches (2.1336m) long by 101 inches (2.564m) high, with a weight of 680lbs (308.44kg) each. Volume was 545cu ft (166.166m³). Plus ramp-mounted, contoured fibreglass container with a weight of 650lb (294.835kg); volume 490cu ft (149.352m³)

The L-100s produced, with the first civilian/military registrations, were as follows:

Model 382: N1130E (c/n 3946), Lockheed demonstration aircraft, leased to Alaskan Airlines in March 1965

Model 382: N9260R (c/n 4101); N9261R (c/n 4109); 9J-RBW (c/n 4129); N9263R (c/n 4134); 9J-RBX (c/n 4137); AP-AUT (c/n 4144); AP-AUU (c/n 4145); N9267R (c/n 4146); N9268R (c/n 4147); N9258R (c/n 4170); N9259R (c/n 4176); N9269R (c/n 4197); N9227R (c/n 4208); 9J-REZ (c/n 4209); N9248R (c/n 4221); N9254R (c/n 4222); N759AL (c/n 4225); N7999S (c/n 4234); N9262R (c/n 4248); N9266R (c/n 4250)

The L-100-20

Useful and versatile as the standard L-100 proved to be in civilian usage, there soon came calls for a 'stretched' version to cope with the ever-increasing demands of heavy airlifting the world over. Lockheed responded with two such extended variants. The first of these was the L-100-20, which gave an extra 9 feet of cargo compartment length, now 48.7 feet (14.84376m). Six containers could be accommodated plus one, contoured, on the ramp. But this was at the cost of external fuel tanks and a shortening of range. Nine L-100s were converted and sixteen built from new to this specification, the first of the type being FAA certified on 4 October 1968 and joining Interior Airways. Most utilised the alternate 4,508eshp 501-D22A engines, the commercial equivalent of the T56-A-15. Subsequently eight were extended even further to L-100-30 standard.

The following figures applied to the L-100-20:

Overall length	106ft 7in (32.4866m)
Span	132ft 6in (40.3860m)
Overall height	38ft 3in (11.66m)
Horizontal tailplane overall length	52.7 inches (1.33858m)
Main landing gear overall width	14.3 inches (0.36322m)
Cabin to ramp cargo length	40.4 feet (12.31392m)

Cabin to ramp cargo width	123.2 inches (3.12928m) tapering to 120 inches (3.048m) at rear entrance
Maximum ramp weight	155,800lb (70,669.691kg)
Maximum landing weight (10 fps)	130,000lb (58,967.0081kg)
Operating weight	73,236lb (33,219.29kg)
Maximum payload	46,764lb (21,211.79kg)
Fuel capacity @ 6.7lb/gal	46,498lb (21,211.79kg)
internal tanks	6,942 US gallons (26,278.328 litres)
external tanks	nil
total fuel volume	6,942 US gallons (26,278.328 litres)
Engines	four Allison turboprop, constant-speed 501-D22As
Engine take-off power	4,508eshp flat-rated (capable of 4,910eshp)
Auxiliary power	one auxiliary power unit (APU) to provide air during ground engine starting, for air-conditioning and electrical power, and emergency electrical power during flight up to 20,000 feet (6,096m)
Propellers	four Hamilton Standard electro-hydromatic, constant-speed, full-feathering, reversible-pitch
Number of propeller blades	four
Diameter of propellers	13.5 feet (4.1148m)
Outboard propeller ground clearance	79 inches (2.066m)
Inboard propeller ground clearance	69.6 inches (1.76784m)
Inboard propeller fuselage clearance	37.8 inches (0.96012m)
Performance: maximum speed	363mph (584.19km/h)
rate of climb	1,700ft/min (518m/min)
Service ceiling at 100,000lb	34,000 feet (10,360m)
Range with maximum payload	1,569 miles (2,526 km)
Range with external tanks	5,733 miles (9,227 km), with zero payload.
Wing area	1,745sq ft (531,87m²)
Wing loading	88.8lb (40.279kg)/sq ft
Wing aspect ratio	10.09
Cargo compartment floor length	49.3 feet (15.02664m)
width	120 inches (3.048m)
height	108 inches (2.7431m)
floor area	602sq ft (including ramp space)
useable volume	5,307cu ft (1,617.268m)
Wing tip turning radius	88.0 feet (26.8224m)
Nose gear turning radius	43.0 feet (13.1064m)
Wheelbase	37.1 feet (11,308m)
Main gear tyre size	56 x 20:00-20
Nose gear tyre size	39 x 13
Oil capacity	12 US gallons (45.4249 litres); independent system per engine
Fuel	modified manifold-flow type incorporating fuel cross-feed, single-point refuelling (SPR) and defuelling and fuel dumping
Electrics	four 40kva engine-driven AC generators for 28-volt system; one 20kva (40kva on some) APU-driven generator; one 24-volt, 36-ampere-hour battery; four 200-ampere transformer-rectifier units converting AC to DC power, both also able to be supplied by external power sourcing

A view of the interior of the hold of an L-100-20 loading a Rolls Royce RB.211 jet engine in 1979. *Lockheed-Georgia, Marietta, via Audrey Pearcy*

THE LOCKHEED MARTIN C-130 HERCULES

Hydraulics	four engine-driven pumps supplying 3,000psi pressure to utility and booster systems; one electric motor-driven pump supplying pressure to auxiliary system, backed up by hand-pump
Air-conditioning and pressurisation	two independent systems for flight deck and cargo compartment, bleed-operated from engine compressors in flight, or APU on ground; each system provides 15,000 feet (4,572m) cabin at 35,000 feet (10,668m) altitude; maximum pressure differential of 7.0psi maintains an 8,000-foot (2,438.4m) cabin at 32,000 feet (9,846m) altitude
Oxygen	gaseous-type system providing 10 man-hours of oxygen at 25,000 feet (7,620m), with diluter-demand automatic pressure-breathing regulators; also portable units
Bulk loading: clear cube volume	5,101cu ft (1,554.78m³)
cheek volume	326cu ft (99.3648m³)
ramp volume	630cu ft (192.024m³)
Total volume	6,057cu ft (1,846.1736m³)
Palletised loading: no of pallets	eight
Main compartment loading	3,955cu ft. (1205.484m³)
Ramp volume	490cu ft (149.352m³)
Total volume	4,445cu ft (1,354.836m³)
Containerised loading: no of containers	eight (seven in hold and one on ramp)
Main compartment volume	3,815cu ft (1162.812m³)
Ramp volume	490cu ft (149.352m³)
Total volume	4,305cu ft (1,312.164m³)

The L-100-20s (Model 382E), with their first civilian/military registrations, were N9232R (c/n 4299); N9265R (c/n 4300); N7951S (c/n 4301); N7952S (c/n 4302); N9237R (c/n 4303); N7957S (c/n 4333); N7954S (c/n 4350); N7960S (c/n 4355); N7985S (c/n 4358); N7982S (c/n 4361); N7984S (c/n 4362); N7986S (c/n 4364); N10ST (c/n 4383); N11ST (c/n 4384); ZS-GSK (c/n 4385); 318 (c/n 4412); OB-R-956 (c/n 4450); N7967S (c/n 4512); RP-C101 (c/n 4593); OB-R-1183 (c/n 4706); 383 (c/n 4708); TR-KKB (c/n 4710); 384 (c/n 4715); N4080M (c/n 4830); N4081M (c/n 4832); N4115M (c/n 4850) and N4119M (c/n 4853).

The solitary Model 382 L-100, registration N1130E (c/n 3946), was extended to an L-100-20 (Model 382E). Similarly modified were six former Model 382Bs, registrations N9268R (c/n 4147); N9258R (c/n 4170); N9259R (c/n 4176); N9248R (c/n 4221); N9254R (c/n 42222) and N759AL (c/n 4225).

Two other Model 382Bs were stretched to L-100-20s (Model 382F), N109AK (c/n 4129) and N9266R (c/n 4250).

The L-100-30

Even the L-100-20 proved insufficient for some operators and Lockheed took the basic L-100 Hercules and extended her even further, a full 15 feet over the L-100, giving an overall cargo compartment length of 55 feet. As such she became the L-100-30 Super Hercules. Yet another container could now be embarked, seven in the hold and one, contoured, on the ramp. It also enabled wide-bodied jet engines to be engorged for transatlantic flights from Rolls-Royce in the UK, and this engine hauling was done by Saturn Airways for Lockheed, among others. Space vehicles were among the new range of cargos that this enhancement opened up for the Herk, and civilian L-100-30s were also in demand by the US Air Force and Navy, which contracted several for such duties on regular-schedule LOGAIR and QUICKTRANS route systems. This further extension was done to several L-100s and also retro-fitted to some L-100-20s, in addition to the fifty-three new-build aircraft of the type.

As part of the flight test demonstration programme for the C-130H-30 Super Hercules to show off the increased volume capacity, at Fort Bragg, North Carolina, on 1 September 1987, an Army 'Gamma Goat' is one of three pallets dropped on a single pass together with an eight-man crew. *Lockheed*

Details for the L-100-30 were:

Overall length	132ft 7in (40.41m)
Span	132ft 6in (40.386m)
Overall height	38ft 3in (11.66m)
Horizontal tailplane overall length	52.7 inches (1.338m)
Main landing gear overall width	14.3 inches (0.3632m)
Cabin to ramp cargo length	40.4 feet (12.3139m)
Cabin to ramp cargo width	123.2 inches (3.129m) tapering to 120 inches (3.048m) at rear entrance
Maximum ramp weight	155,800lb (70,669.69kg)
Maximum landing weight (10 fps)	135,000lb (58,967kg)
Operating weight	73,889lb (33,219.29kg)
Maximum payload	51,111lb (23,183.559kg)
Fuel capacity @ 6.7lb/gal	46,498lb (21,091.138kg)
internal tanks	6,942 US gallons (26,278.32 litres)
external tanks	nil
total fuel volume	6,942 US gallons (26,278.32 litres)
Engines	four Allison turboprop, constant-speed 501-D22As
Engine take-off power	4,058eshp flat-rated (capable of 4,910eshp)
Auxiliary power	one auxiliary power unit (APU) to provide air during ground engine starting, for air-conditioning and electrical power, and for emergency electrical power during flight up to 20,000 feet (6,096m)
Propellers	four Hamilton Standard electro-hydromatic, constant-speed, full-feathering, reversible-pitch
Number of propeller blades	four
Diameter of propellers	13.5 feet (4.1148m)
Outboard propeller ground clearance	79 inches (2.0066m)
Inboard propeller ground clearance	69.6 inches (1.76784m)
Inboard propeller fuselage clearance	37.8 inches (0.955m)
Performance: maximum speed	363mph (583km/h)
rate of climb	1,700ft/min (518m/min)
Service ceiling at 100,000lb	34,000 feet (10,360m)
Range with maximum payload	1,569 miles (2,526km)

Range with external tanks	5,733 miles (9,227 km) with zero payload
Wing area	1,745sq ft (531,87m²)
Wing loading	88.8lb (40.279kg)/sq ft
Wing aspect ratio	10.09
Cargo compartment floor length	56 feet (17.0688m)
width	120 inches (3.048m)
height	108 inches (2.7432m)
floor area	666sq ft (202.996m²) including ramp space
useable volume	6,057cu ft (1846.176m³)
Wing tip turning radius	90.0 feet (27.432m)
Nose gear turning radius	46.8 feet (14.264m)
Wheelbase	40.4 feet (12.3139m)
Main gear tyre size	56 x 20:00-20
Nose gear tyre size	39 x 13
Oil capacity	12 US gallons (45.4249 litres); independent system per engine
Fuel	modified manifold-flow type incorporating fuel cross-feed, single-point refuelling (SPR) and defuelling, and fuel dumping
Electrics	four 40kva engine-drive AC generators for 28-volt system; one 20kva (40kva on some) APU-driven generator; one 24-volt, 36-ampere-hour battery; four 200-ampere transformer-rectifier units converting AC to DC power; both can also be supplied by external power sourcing
Hydraulics	four engine-driven pumps supplying 3,000psi pressure to utility and booster systems; one electric motor-driven pump supplying pressure to auxiliary system, backed up by hand-pump
Air-conditioning and pressurisation	two independent systems for flight deck and cargo compartment, bleed-operated from engine compressors in flight, or APU on ground; each system provides 15,000 feet (4,573m) cabin at 35,000 feet (10,668m) altitude; maximum pressure differential of 7.0psi maintains an 8,000-foot (2,438.4m) cabin at 32,000 feet (9,846m) altitude
Oxygen	gaseous-type system providing 10 man-hours of oxygen at 25,000 feet (7,620m), with diluter-demand automatic pressure-breathing regulators; also portable units
Bulk loading: clear cube volume	3,670cu ft (1,118.6m³)
cheek volume	200cu ft (60.96m³)
ramp volume	630cu ft (192.024m³)
Total volume	4,500cu ft (1,371.6m³)
Palletised loading: no of pallets	six
Main compartment loading	2,825cu ft (861.06m³)
Ramp volume	490cu ft (149.352m³)
Total volume	3,315cu ft (955.548m³)
Containerised loading: no of containers	six (five in hold and one on ramp)
Main compartment volume	2,725cu ft (830.58m³)
Ramp volume	490cu ft (149.352m³)
Total volume	3,215cu ft (979.932m³)

The L-100-30s (Model 382G), with the first civilian/military registrations, were N7988S (c/n 4388); N15ST (c/n 4391); ZS-RSB (c/n 4472); ZS-RSC (c/n 4475); ZS-RSD (c/n 4477); ZS-RSE (c/n 4558); N20ST (c/n 4561); ZS-RSF (c/n 4562); ZS-RSG (c/n 4565); TR-KKA (c/n 4582); N21T (c/n 4586); ZS-RSH (c/n 4590); ZS-RSI (c/n 4600); ZS-RSJ (c/n 4606); N108AK (c/n 4610); ZS-JIV (c/n 4673); ZS-JVL (c/n 4676); ZS-JIW (c/n 4679); ZS-JIX (c/n 4684); ZS-JIY (c/n 4691); ZS-JIZ (c/n 4695); ZS-JJA (c/n 4698); ZS-JVM (c/n 4701); N108AK (c/n 4763); 9Q-CBJ (c/n 4796); N4301M (c/n 4798); C-GHPW (c/n 4799); N4304M (c/n 4800); PK-PLU (c/n 4824); PK-PLV (c/n 4826); PK-PLW (c/n 4828); N4083M (c/n 4833); N4085M (c/n 4834); N4110M (c/n 4839); N4116M (c/n 4851); N4148M (c/n 4880); N4152M (c/n 4883); N4160M (c/n 4886); PK-PLR (c/n 4889); N4170M (c/n 4891); N4175M (c/n 4893); TR-KKD (c/n 4895); N4185M (c/n 4915); PK-PLT (c/n 4923); N4107F (c/n 4949); N4253M (c/n 4950); N4249Y (c/n 4951); N4254M (c/n 4952); N4242N (c/n 4953); HZ-117 (c/n 4954); N4232B (c/n 4955); N4255M (c/n 4956); N4261M (c/n 4957); N4266M (c/n 4960); N4248M (c/n 4992); N4269M (c/n 5000); N4272M (c/n 5022); N4274M (c/n 5024); N4276M (c/n 5025); N4278M (c/n 5027); N4232B (c/n 5029); N4281M (c/n 5032); N82178 (c/n 5048); N8213G (c/n 5055); N8218J (c/n 5056); N4161T (c/n 5225); ET-AKG (c/n 5306); N41030 (c/n 5307) and N4080M (c/n 5320).

Four L-100s were extended to L-100-30s, these being N24ST (c/n 4101), N16ST (c/n 4134), N18ST (c/n 4208) and N101AK (c/n 4248).

Eight L-100-20s were also extend to L-100-30s: N19ST (c/n 4147); N14ST (c/n 4225); N9232R (c/n 4299); N104AK (c/n 4300); N7951S (c/n 4301); N17ST (c/n 4333); N10ST (c/n 4383) and N11ST (c/n 4384).

The L-100-50 (GL-207)

This was a proposed further extended commercial Hercules, with the addition of yet another 20-foot (6.10m) section, but nothing came of it. The passenger deck floor was to be raised by 23 inches (58.4cm) to give the passenger cabin the full width of the Hercules widened girth. The proposal for the GL-207 Super Hercules had some interesting details in its data, among which were the following:

The original artist's concept of the stretched 'high-capacity' Herk, the proposed L-100-50, which would have featured an additional 20-foot stretch over the existing L-100-30 Super Hercules, or a total stretch of 35 feet over the standard C-130 or L-100. *Lockheed-Georgia, Marietta, via Audrey Pearcy*

Engines	four Allison T-61B7s rated at 5,500ps
Wing span	44.00m (144.35 feet)
Length	36.8m (120.75 feet)
Height	11.60m (38 feet)
Wing area	190sq m (2,045sq ft)
Track	4.75m (15.58 feet)
Wheelbase	13.6m (44.6 feet)
Capacity	19.8m (64.96 feet) long by 2.77m (9.08 feet) high by 3.12m (10.23 feet) wide
Empty weight	41,800cu m (137,139.10cu ft)
Loaded weight	92,000cu m (301,837.27cu ft)
Fuel capacity	39,000 litres (10,302.71 US gallons)
Maximum speed	680km/h (422.53mph)
Maximum cruising speed	640km/h (397.677mph)
Rate of climb	595m/min (1,931ft/min)
Service ceiling	13,000m (42,650.9 feet)
Range, maximum	7,200km (4473.87 miles)
Useful payload	20,500kg (45,194.76lb)[16]

To meet the Air Forces Advanced Civil/Military Aircraft (ACMA) specification, the proposed Super Hercules had a cabin girth 3 feet wider than the DC-9, with two-abreast, dual-aisle seating, recessed overhead lighting and luggage compartments, and a fully pressurised air-conditioned ambiance. Operating costs were estimated as 25% less than the four-engined C-130/L-100. In May 1980 Lockheed announced that it had awarded a contract to Rohr Industries Incorporated, of Chula Vista, California, for eighteen sets of powerplant nacelles for the L-400. Despite this, the aircraft never materialised.

The L-100-PX

As a cheap airline alternative for Third World nations with limited spending power, Lockheed drew up a proposal for a passenger-carrying variant of the L-100 series. This was a 100-seater aircraft with palleted units, but, again, she never appeared.

The L-100-30QC

Yet another proposal that has so far come to naught was for convertible airliner/freighter versions of the extended L-100-30, which could be readily adapted to either market as the world situation fluctuated. Again, it was a good concept in theory but one that aroused little or no interest and never happened.

The L-400 Twin Hercules

Lockheed continue to scout new variations of the Herk on the world markets and this idea, first made public in January 1989, was for a lightweight and more affordable version of the standard commercial aircraft. Lockheed proposed a twin-engine design, using two of the new Allison 501-D22D engines, rated at 4,910eshp.

The same airframe and fuselage structure as the standard Hercules was to be used and the same cargo bay, 10 feet wide, 9 feet high and 40 feet long (3 by 2.7 by 12.5 metres), with a loading floor height of 3.4 feet (1 metre) above the ground. The concept was for a lightweight, in-country airlifter for short-haul work. The L-400 was seen as the natural successor to older types then in the process of being phased out of service, such as the DC-3, C-119, C-123 and C-54. The L-400 would carry a 22,500lb (10,205.82kg) payload over 550 miles (885.13km) and operate from 3,600-foot (1,098m) runways, being able to land and take off from dirt, gravel, sand or snow.

---

[16] See 'Von de Hercules zur Super-Hercules', article in *Der Flieger* magazine, issue 10, 1959.

The President of the Lockheed-Georgia company, Robert B. Ormsby (left), goes over details of the proposed Lockheed Hercules airline with Charles Cannon, Lockheed's engineering programme manager, advance programmes, on 6 April 1978. The wide-girth Hercules was designed to accommodate three lanes of seats and two aisles. The aircraft design utilised the in-service L-100-30 Hercules version, which was 15 feet longer than the standard C-130. It was designed to be either an all-passenger airliner or a cargo/passenger convertible. *Lockheed-Georgia, Marietta, via Audrey Pearcy*

The major changes were in the wing, landing gear and power plant. The L-400 was to have a new centre wing, 22.5 feet (6.858m) shorter than the existing L-100, while the span of the outer wings was to be extended by adding 4.5 feet (1.3716m) wing tips. The Allison 501-D22A engine was to be emplaced in a strengthened nacelle capable of accommodating the engine's full 4,910shp. A water-alcohol system was added to retain this power for hot-day take-offs. In order to increase the efficiency of the propellers at the high shp, a new Hamilton Standard propeller of 14 feet (4,267m) diameter was to be shipped, 6 inches larger than that on existing C-130s.

The main landing gear for a predicted take-off weight of 84,000lb (38,101.759kg) was reduced from four to two wheels. The crew was also reduced to two, with simplified systems and instrumentation together with a raft of easy-maintenance features to enable small operators to keep the machine in the air for maximum usage and turn-round; however, many of the parts were to be fully compatible with the larger C-130 as an attraction for larger companies who might wish to operate both types.

Lockheed's marketing organisation canvassed thirty-nine countries and identified a sizeable potential market of more than 250 aircraft of the Twin Hercules specification. Robert B. Ormsby, Lockheed-Georgia's President at that time, went on record as saying that they expected to go into full-scale production, with first deliveries in 1981.[17] In the event, however, no actual orders were forthcoming, and the concept was finally abandoned for good.

Some Hercules projections that have never got off the ground (in any sense!) reappear as 'new' concepts from time to time on web forums. Among such speculations are Lockheed-Georgia's 1973 concept of an L-100 Amphibian to operate short-haul commuter traffic. The design featured a fibreglass hull, the mounting of the engines on top of the wings and the fitting of a retractable hydro-ski. It joined in the reject tray of aviation history such equally visionary ideas as the C-130VLS (Volume-Loadability-Speed), the 1972 VSTOL vision with the Pegasus engine, and the C-130SS (STOL/stretch), which had horsal and dorsal extensions, spoilers, and double-slotted flaps. More recently, in 2008, Lockheed-Martin's Jim Grant touted the idea of a short-fuselage variation,

---

[17] See Robert B. Ormsby, 'Lockheed launches world-wide sales drive for its L-400 "Twin-Hercules" transport', Newsbureau, 30 November 1977.

The twin-engine L-400 design in a contemporary artist's impression, 30 November 1977. At this time Lockheed-Martin launched a worldwide marketing drive to sell the new aircraft, offering potential customers firm prices and delivery positions. The L-100 derivative was a medium-size cargo and personnel transport aircraft that featured the same structure and versatility of its progenitor, the four-engined C-130. *Lockheed-Georgia, Marietta, via Audrey Pearcy.*

a wide-bodied C-130XL, with alternate 62,000lb, 72,000lb and 85,000lb payloads, in order to cope with predicted Army requirements beyond 2020 for the FCS (Future Combat Systems) hardware for Joint Future Theatre Lift mobility, and both VTOL and STOL requirements reappeared. Who knows in what direct future C-130 developments might take her?

Military/civilian use – the L-130H-30

Finally the governments of many countries found that the versatility of the Hercules, in both military and civilian usage, gave her to a wide range of interchangeability possibilities, which proved irresistible to nations strapped for cash. By extending the fuselage of the military C-130H by 15 feet (4.6m) in the same way as the L-100-30, the result was an all-round aircraft that, if sales are any indication, proved the ideal solution. These became the L-130H-30, and their ambiguity of use is reflected in the many changes of military serial/civilian registration they have undergone. At the time of writing the following nations have taken delivery of this most successful version of the Herk, the first being A-1317 (c/n 4864) to Indonesia in September 1980.

Algeria
Eight aircraft: serials 7T-VHN (c/n 4894); 7T-VHO (c/n 4897); 7T-VHM (c/n 4919); 7T-VHP (c/n 4921); 7T-WHD (c/n 4987); 7T-WHL (c/n 4989), formerly civilian 4989; 7T-WHA (c/n 4997); 7T-WHB (c/n 5224)

Cameroon
One aircraft: registration TJX-AE (c/n 4933), former civilian N4206M

Canada
Two aircraft: serials 6801 (c/n 4749) and 6802 (c/n 4753)

Chad
One aircraft: registration TT-AAH (c/n 5184)

Dubai
One aircraft: serial 312 (c/n 4961)

Egypt
Three aircraft: serials 1293 (c/n 5187), later civilian SU-BKS; 1294 (c/n 5191), later civilian SU-BKT; 1295 (c/n 5206), later civilian SU-BKU

France
Nine aircraft: serials 61-PD (c/n 5140), formerly civilian F-RAPD; 61-PE (c/n 5142), formerly civilian F-RAPE; 61-PF (c/n 5144), formerly civilian F-RAPF; 61-PG (c/n 5150), formerly civilian N4242N and F-RAPG; 61-PH (c/n 5151), formerly civilian F-RAPH; 61-PI (c/n 5152), formerly civilian F-RAPI; 61-PJ (c/n 5153), formerly civilian N73235 and F-RAPJ; 61-PK (c/n 5226), formerly civilian F-RAPK; 61-PL (c/n 5227) formerly civilian F-RAPL

Indonesia
Seven aircraft: serials A-1317 (c/n 4864); A-1318 (c/n 4865); A-1319 (c/n 4868); A-1320 (c/n 4869); A-1321 (c/n 4870); A-1321 (c/n 4925); A-1324 (c/n 4927)

A group of Indonesian technicians receive a briefing in Marietta. *Lockheed-Georgia, Marietta, via Audrey Pearcy*

Malaysia

Six aircraft: serials M30-10 (c/n 5268); M30-12 (c/n 5277); M30-11 (c/n 5309); M30-14 (c/n 5311); M30-15 (c/n 5316); M30-16 (c/n 5319)

Netherlands

Two aircraft: serials G273 (c/n 5273), formerly civilian N4080M, and G275 (c/n 5275), formerly civilian N4080M

Nigeria

Three aircraft: serials NAF916 (c/n 4962), formerly civilian N4081M; NAF917 (c/n 4963), formerly civilian N4099R, and NAF918 (c/n 5001)

Portugal

Two aircraft: serials 130343 (c/n 5307), formerly civilian N41030, 130344 (c/n 5320), formerly civilian N4080M, and 6806 (c/n 5264)

Saudi Arabia

Two aircraft: registrations HZ-MS8 (c/n 4986), formerly civilian N4243M, and 1622 (c/n 5212)

South Korea

Four aircraft: serials 5006 (c/n 5006), formerly civilian N4080M; 5019 (c/n 5019), formerly civilian N73232; 5030 (c/n 5030), formerly civilian N4249Y; 5036 (c/n 5036), formerly civilian N4161T

Spain

One aircraft: serial TL10-01(c/n 5003), formerly civilian N7323D

Thailand

Six aircraft: serials 60104 (c/n 4959); 60105 (c/n 5146): 60106 (c/n 5148); 60107 (c/n 5208); 471 (c/n 5211); 60111 (c/n 5280); 60112 (c/n 5281)

Chapter 2

The versatile Hercules

Aerial delivery

The transportation of personnel and all manner of goods, stores and equipment from one base to another is the basic function of the Hercules, but equally important is her ability to precisely deliver the same payloads without touching down, due to inaccessibility, lack of or totally unsuitable landing sites, combat danger, or required speed of turn-around. Lockheed therefore developed the Aerial Delivery System (ADS), taking advantage of the Herk's wide, obstruction-free belly, and utilising standardised palleting capable of carrying just about anything and offloading it accurately and safely to the customers below. The inherent stability of the aircraft ensures safe control at all heights and during the sudden transference of weights off the cargo ramp.

For air-drop missions, the basic personnel exit procedure applies to the military aspects of the aircraft, with paratroop-dropping as a prime function. With the capacity to embark sixty-four fully equipped paratroopers, the early marks of Hercules could offload these in only 30 seconds via the two paratroop doors located on either side at the after end of the cargo compartment. Alternately, the troops could go out via the lowered ramp. This ensures that the unit stays relatively close together when they hit the ground and can reform into fighting formation quickly.

A fisheye camera catches a volunteer stepping off the ramp during trials of the Human Retrieval System. *Lockheed-Georgia Newsbureau*

THE LOCKHEED MARTIN C-130 HERCULES

A C-130 air-drop. *US Defense Department official*

Their associated military equipment – light vehicles and small tracked vehicles, even 105mm (4.13-inch) howitzers – could be equally accommodated, the C-130A and C-130B being able to cope with single loads of up to 25,000lb (11,339.80kg), which was increased to 35,000lb (15,875.73kg) in the C-130H and offloaded via the ramp. In one test conducted by the USAF, a record air-drop for a single palleted discharge was 41,740lb (18,937.48kg)! Air-drop speeds range between 115 and 150 knots (59.16 and 77.16 m/sec), and the normal altitude of the drop (if 'normal' actually exists for the Hercules!) is around 1,200 feet (365.76m).

A more precise method of aerial placement was devised, this being the Ground Proximity Extraction System (GPES), which is based on a low-level approach guided from the ground. This sub-system comprises an extraction line, hook and pole assembly in the aircraft, and a pair of rotary hydraulic energy absorbers (known as 'water twisters', as the retardant vaned rotors turn in a housing filled with water) with their associated ground anchoring equipment and a steel pendant cable, which have to be pre-set on the landing site. The aircraft has to steer a straight and level course no more than 5 feet (1.524m) from the ground, with the ramp open and the hook fully extended, similar to a carrier-based aircraft's tail-hook approach. When the hook touches the ground an audible warning is sounded to the pilot so he knows he has the right height to hold. The hook catches the stretched-out pendant cable held between the two energy absorbers on either side of the airstrip. As the cargo comes clear, its forward momentum is slowed by the action of the 'water twisters', and in 5 seconds the palleted load is dumped safely and the Herk can climb free. Such deliveries require a steady pilot and a high degree of nerve and skill, but it enables loads of up to 25,000lb (11,339.80kg) to be delivered into delivery areas only 1,200 feet (365.76m) in length. Naturally this form of low, slow approach is considered near suicidal in combat conditions (but, needless to say, it *has* been done!).

Dependant as it is upon the ground equipment being set up, which is not always a practical option given the range of missions the Hercules has to cope with worldwide, an alternative aerial delivery system was perfected, the Low-Altitude Parachute Extraction System (LAPES). This method employs a ring-slot extraction parachute to pull the palleted cargo via the hatch and bring it quickly to a standstill with minimum impact. Loads to be thus delivered are stacked in either single or multiple platforms and retained in the cargo hold of the C-130, utilising restraining gear on the 463L dual-rail cargo handling system. According to load size and weight, either a single 28-foot (8.53m) extraction parachute is deployed, or multiple chutes. The approach is similar to the GPES drop and, once over the predesignated drop point, which is about 600 feet (182.88m) from the target zone, or about 3 seconds' flight time, the basic Aerial Delivery System (ADS) is activated, whereupon the extraction chute or chutes are released into the aircraft's slipstream. The extraction force required to move the cargo is 2g, and a single chute can extract a load maximum of 12,000lb (544.31kg). A pair of chutes is required for loads of double that weight, and the maximum load thus delivered by LAPES with multiple chutes deployed is 50,000lbs (22,679.61kg). The cargo slides about 100-200 feet (30.48-60.96m) on hitting the ground.

A similar method, or refinement of the LAPES method, is the Parachute Low-Altitude Delivery System (PLADS). This enables special loads (electronics, medical equipment and the like) to be parachute-dropped from low levels while ensuring that delicate or sensitive cargo reaches the ground safely because the impact shock is minimised. These loads are securely packaged in supply containers of 2,000lb (907.184kg) capacity, which have plywood bases to absorb the impact. Up to sixteen such containers could be embarked in the Herk, and could be dropped singly or in pairs to within 25 feet (7.62m) of the aiming point by this method. While the approach speed at 130 knots (66.87m/sec) indicated air speed (IAS) is similar to LAPES, the height is greater, at 250 feet (76.2m). The reefed extraction parachute, when deployed, is towed against the container until it reaches the required extraction deployment. When this happens an electrically actuated pyrotechnic cutter slices the reefs, the parachute inflates and the load is pulled clear. Impact speeds are between 70 and 90 feet (21.366 and 27.432 metres) per second down a projected trajectory, and the horizontal velocity is a predicted zero at point of touch down of the load.

Very low-level supply drops with the Air Supply Platform. *Author's collection*

Another parachute-assisted air-drop system adopted specifically for the accurate delivery of multiple small resupply loads is the Container Delivery System (CDS). It lacks the accuracy of a LAPES delivery, but can be made from great heights, up to 400 feet, and this form of stick release ensures better ground distribution than conventional methods. Each load is securely packed in A-22 containers, 52 by 65 inches (1.32 by 1.65m), which have a maximum capacity of 2,200lbs (997.9kg). Eighteen such containers are loaded nine to a side, and can be simultaneously delivered by the Herk in two sticks, totalling 39,600lb (17,962.25kg). Again the ADS system kicks in at the desired position during the approach and releases the extraction chute, one of which is attached to the first-out container of either stick. As this occurs the Herk's nose is pulled up at an angle of 6° and gravity does the rest. Once clear of the ramp, the parachute of each individual container is activated in the normal way by static lines.

During famine-relief operations in Ethiopia in 1985, the Belgian Air Force Hercules pilots developed their own unique method of delivery, the Very Low Altitude Gravity Extraction System (VLAGES), or Green Light-Gate System. Due to appalling Ethiopian Government restrictions, which prevented them from making parachute drops in case supplies reached the rebels by mistake, many areas full of starving citizens were unable to be supplied. Determined to overcome this awe-inspiring bureaucratic idiocy, the Belgians adopted this method for supply areas such as Mehoney.

Under the VLAGES system, eight 1.5-tonne pallets of sacked supplies were prepared by Belgian paratroopers and loaded in a single line down the Herk's cargo hold. The whole process of installing the roller conveyors and pallets took almost an hour per load. A forward restraining buffer was emplaced at the cockpit end in case of shifting through turbulence. During the approach the team of three paratroopers took off the main lashings as the seconds were counted off by the navigator, leaving just one restraining strap in place. The main restraining band behind the ramp was fitted with a large knife. A static line followed after each pallet, which had a small amount of slack in it. As the loadmaster activated a handle, located just below the cockpit, it tightened this slack and activated the knife, which severed each pallet's last restraint. Any pallets that jammed, or sacks that fell off the pallets, were dealt with by this team to ensure free flow over the drop zone.

Again, the sudden trim-change called for expert flying. Drop heights were initially trialled at about 30 feet, but this resulted in too many split sacks and lost food. Height was gradually increased to 50 feet, with a 130-knot (66.87m/sec) approach speed, and this worked well; increasing the vertical speed and decreasing the horizontal speed made for less spoilage and a failure rate that came down to three or four sacks out of 240 per drop, especially when British polypropylene sacks were superseded by Belgian jute and plastic dual ones, which proved far tougher in practice.

Aerial photography and mapping

The RC-130 was developed specifically as a long-range, steady aerial photography platform in order to conduct accurate worldwide photogrammetric mapping and electronic geodetic surveying by the USAF.

A prototype RC-130A (R for Reconnaissance), serial 54-1632 (c/n 3019), was modified from a TC-130A and first flew in this configuration on 8 November 1957. She served with the 1375 Mapping & Charting Squadron for several years, but was subsequently converted back to a standard C-130A.

Fifteen RC-130As were specifically built for the Hiran Electronic Surveying, Hiran Controlled Photography and Mapping Photography missions. Both high-altitude photography and electronic measuring could be operated simultaneously, which made for far more accurate charting and mapping. These aircraft were delivered to the USAF between March and November 1959 for use by the Military Air Transport Service. They were serials 57-0510 (c/n 3217); 57-0511 (c/n 3218); 57-0512 (c/n 3219); 57-0513 (c/n 3220); 57-0514 (c/n 3221); 57-0515 (c/n 3222); 57-0516 (c/n 3223); 57-0517 (c/n 3224); 57-0518 (c/n 3225); 57-0519 (c/n 3226); 57-0520 (c/n 3227); 57-0521 (c/n 3228); 57-0522 (c/n 3229); 57-0523 (c/n 3230) and 57-0524 (c/n 3231).

These aircraft showed little exterior differences from their conventional sisters; about the only give-aways as to their role were the addition of a Television Viewfinder bubble under the nose radome, the large camera windows for the Prime Vertical Cameras (forward) and Fixed Convergent Cameras (aft), and the Viewfinders for the Precision Automatic Photogrammetric Intervalometer (PAPI) cut into the underside of the main fuselage. The hand-held Oblique camera was sited just forward of the rear hatch. Internally removable provision was made in the cargo hold to house a Chief Photographer, two Hiran operators and an Airborne Profile Recorder (APR) operator, together with their huge cameras, electronic, photographic and surveying instruments and installations, photographers' racking, stowage for dropsondes (instruments containing high-frequency radio and sensing devices), and a darkroom for developing film. By removing the operators' stations, extra cargo capacity was available almost instantly, while, with the palleted Hiran apparatus also taken out, four extra standard recliner passenger seats could be fitted abaft the main leading gear wheel well. Alternatively, TAC-type jump seats could accommodate twenty passengers in considerably less comfort! A temperature and humidity probe was mounted on the port side forward of the cabin, and a driftmeter in a ventral position below the cabin.

The Hiran Electronic Surveying devices could ensure precise scientific measurements with an accuracy of 1/50,000 (or less than 1 foot in an 8-mile length). The method used was trilateration, whereby the exact distance between two fixed ground points was acquired after the Hercules had flown a 'racetrack crossing path' several times between them, the instruments electronically measuring and recording the data for comparison until the optimum was achieved. The Hiran Photographic equipment worked from this precise data, feeding signals to a A-1 Straight Line Indicator. The Hiran instruments ensured that a series of parallel runs could be made with a high degree of guaranteed accuracy, with timed photographs of the terrain being taken to give an overlapping and total picture. In conditions where the Hiran control method could not be operated, the RC-130As used standard Mapping Photography, using visually referenced flight lines, less accurate and requiring greater overlap.

All served in 1375 Mapping & Charting Squadron, 1370 Photomapping Group, which was based at Turner AFB, Georgia. This outfit later became the 1370 Photomapping Wing in 1960, and was subsequently based at Forbes AFB, Kansas, until it was deactivated in June 1972. Some RC-130As also served with 1 Aerospace Cartographic & Geodetic Squadron and 1866 Facility Checking Squadron, with serial 57-0515 taking part in the US-Ethiopian Aerial Mapping Survey in 1963/64.

All were subsequently converted to C-130As in the 1970s, except 57-0523, which became a DC-130A.

A further refinement of the type was the RC-130S. Two JC-130As, serials 56-0493 (c/n 3101) and 56-0497 (c/n 3105), were fitted with searchlight pods for experiments from 1965 onward, but these were both later reconverted back to standard C-130As.

RC-130A 57-0516 (c/n 3223) of 1370 Photo Mapping Wing, seen at Forbes AFB in October 1967. *Nick Williams, AAHS*

RC-130A 57-0515 (c/n 3222) of 1375 Photo Mapping Wing undertaking the US-Ethiopian Mapping Survey in 1964. *Nick Williams, AAHS*

Aerial search and rescue

There was no doubting that the Hercules was the optimum aircraft for any number of jobs that required long range, high endurance and fuel economy coupled with the ability to conduct broad-altitude search patterns and carry a wide variety of customised and palletised packages. Search & Rescue (SAR) potential was automatic, and both the USAF and the USN were quick to exploit the C-130s potential in this area. These aircraft were originally designated as the SC-130B (USAF) or R8V-1G (USN).

In total twelve such Search & Rescue conversions were made for both services, and they were allocated those services' respective serials. In September 1962 these designations were combined as the HC-130G, but this was quickly replaced by the designation HC-130B-LM, and all twelve aircraft were instead allocated to the US Coast Guard, thus: CG 1339, ex-58-5396 (c/n 3529); CG 1340, ex-58-5397 (c/n 3533); CG 1341, ex-58-6973 (c/n 3542); CG 1342, ex-58-6974 (c/n 3548); CG 1344, ex-60-0311 (c/n 3594); CG 1345, ex-60-0312 (c/n 3595); CG 1346, ex-61-0958 (c/n 3638); CG 1347, ex-61-2082 (c/n3641); CG 1348, ex-61-2083 (c/n 3650); CG 1349, ex-62-3753 (c/n 3745); CG 1350, ex-62-3754 (c/n 3763); and CG 1351, ex-62-3755 (c/n 3773).

US Coastguard HC-130B Herk CG-1351 (c/n 3773), coded 'San Francisco', on the apron. *Thompson Productions via Nick Williams, AAHS*

The colourful display of US Coast Guard Herk CG 1342 (c/n 1341) operating from Elizabeth City, New Jersey, on 26 April 1968. *Nick Williams, AAHS*

These aircraft differed from the standard C-130B in the flight deck and aft observation window layouts. The former was redesigned to accommodate a radio operator and an On-Scene-Commander (OSC) situated where the normal crew rest bunks had been located, in addition to the pilot, co-pilot, flight engineer and navigator. Two clear-vision observer stations were built into the aft cargo compartment to give a wide field of vision via the paratroop door apertures. A manually controlled observation door was placed to shield this embrasure during any wave-top-type visual searches, as the aircraft were not pressurised at such low altitudes. Of course, when in pressurised flight configuration this door was stowed and the paratroop door closed.

Two alternative mission scenarios were catered for, dependant on whether the aircraft was employed as a search platform or as a support aircraft deploying men and equipment to reinforce a search area. Dependant on the requirement, a removable command/passenger interior module could be shipped, which had fourteen airliner-type seats for use by the OSC and his staff for the coordination of large rescue operations, or for the transportation of personnel to the scene of the mission.

In the case of the former requirement, the cargo hold could stow droppable rescue kits on ramps. As a support aircraft, disassembled helicopters could be transported to the search area, disembarked, assembled and used in the work. For the latter, the cargo compartment behind the control module could accommodate either a further twenty-four airliner-type seating module or a forty-four standard troop-seater module in addition to the normal C-130B ambulance configuration of seventy-four patients and two attendants. The shipping of these modules required just simple modifications to the electrical power and air-conditioning equipment.

Far more common in their twenty years of sterling USCG service was patrol duty, in both the Atlantic and the Pacific. The most high-profile missions were the Ice Patrols: the northern ice pack and western Greenland area was patrolled daily during the spring and summer months when the glaciers were 'calving' to give continuously updated records on the number, size and direction of the bigger bergs deemed hazardous to shipping.

The 67th Aerospace Rescue & Recovery Squadron (ARRS), equipped with five HC-130s and five HH-53 'Super Jolly Green Giant' helicopters, moved to RAF Woodbridge, Suffolk, from Moran, Spain, in March 1970 in order to provide greater rescue coverage in the North Atlantic. The 67th was then providing rescue coverage from the North Pole to the South Pole and from mid-Atlantic in the west to the Indo-Burmese border in the east, approximately 68,000,000 square miles

(176,119,191.5km²). The unit had as its primary mission Combat Rescue and Support of Special Operations NATO in Europe, with the secondary role of peacetime Search & Rescue. The Herks carried a team of para-rescue specialists, called 'PJs', who could parachute, scuba or mountain climb their way to a survivor and provide him with medical attention as necessary.

Aerial search, rescue and recovery ('Combat Talon I')

The USAF had for many years utilised the Douglas HC-54 in its Air Rescue Service units, and they had perfected the techniques and equipment suitable for their era. With the increased need for offshore out-of-the-water pick-ups with the Vietnam operations, and the burgeoning aerospace programme also calling for high numbers of water retrievals, the arrival of the Hercules enabled these units to be updated and upgraded and for improved equipment and techniques to be employed.

With the primary mission of searching for, locating and retrieving both personnel and/or material in support of global air and space operations, including those associated with research and development activities, the Aerospace Rescue & Recovery Service (ARRS) was established, and a programme was initiated that originally included forty-five specially equipped Hercules. Known as the 'Crown Birds', eventually only forty-three were so completed: 64-14852 (c/n 4036); 64-14853 (c/n 4037); 64-14854 (c/n 4038); 64-14855 (c/n 4055); 64-14856 (c/n 4072); 64-14857 (c/n 4073); 64-14858 (c/n 4081); 64-14859 (c/n 4082); 64-14860 (c/n 4084); 64-14861 (c/n 4088); 64-14862 (c/n 4089); 64-14863 (c/n 4094); 64-14864 (c/n 4097); 64-14865 (c/n 4098); 64-14866 (c/n 4099); 65-0962 (c/n 4102); 65-0963 (c/n 4103); 65-0964 (c/n 4104); 65-0965 (c/n 4106); 65-0966 (c/n 4107); 65-0967 (c/n 4108); 65-0968 (c/n 4110); 65-0969 (c/n 4111); 65-0970 (c/n 4112); 65-0971 (c/n 4116); 65-0972 (c/n 4120); 65-0973 (c/n 4121); 65-0974 (c/n 4123); 65-0975 (c/n 4125); 65-0976 (c/n 4126); 65-0977 (c/n 4127); 65-0978 (c/n 4130); 65-0979 (c/n 4131); 65-0980 (c/n 4132); 65-0981 (c/n 4133); 65-0982 (c/n 4135); 65-0983 (c/n 4138); 165-0984 (c/n 4139); 65-0985 (c/n 4140); 65-0986 (c/n 4141); 65-0987 (c/n 4142); 65-0989 (c/n 4150); and 65-0990 (c/n 4151). These were designated as the HC-130H.

A magnificent view of Rescue Hercules HC-130H 65-0985 (c/n 4140), of 79 ARRS, Military Air Command, climbing from Hickam Air Force Base, Hawaii, in June 1964. *Nick Williams, AAHS*

The radome-fitted HC-130H Hercules 64-14859 (c/n 4082) of 76 ARRS is seen over Hickam AFB on 12 January 1968. *Nick Williams, AAHS*

Human Retrieval experiments underway with a volunteer seen leaving the after bay of 64-14859 (c/n 4082), equipped with the Surface-to-Air recovery system. *USAF*

A good rear-view aerial shot of the same aircraft, Military Airlift Command's 64-14859 (c/n 4082), of 76 ARRS, taken on 19 January 1968. *Nick Williams, AAHS*

HC-130H Hercules 64-14852 (c/n 4036) was equipped with the Surface-to-Air recovery system and was flown by Atlantic Aerospace Rescue & Recovery Center units based at Moran Air Base, Spain, and Lajes Filed, in the Azores. *USAF*

The flight crew board HC-130H Hercules 64-14855 (c/n 4055) of 76 ARRS, converted to carry the Surface-to-Air recovery system and flown by Atlantic Aerospace Rescue & Recovery Center air teams. *USAF*

The two faces of rescues: USAF HC-130H 65-0975 (c/n 4125) is over-flown by a ski-fitted Helo during a demonstration. *Lockheed-Georgia Newsbureau*

THE LOCKHEED MARTIN C-130 HERCULES

A trio of USAF Rescue HC-130Hs, with 65-0970 (c/n 4112) in the centre, are seen at Moran Air Base, Spain. This and Lajes Field, Azores, were used by the Hercules for the delivery of rescue teams. All in all, the Atlantic Rescue Teams were credited with saving 120 lives in just one year of operations, in conditions ranging from the tropics, the frozen north, deserts, oceans and the crowded air space of Europe. *USAF*

An awards ceremony at 5 ARRS, with 65-0972 (c/n 4120) in the background *Author's collection*

Their specialised equipment included the Fulton Surface-to-Air Recovery System (STAR), which enabled repeated pick-ups, from both land and water, of personnel or material with weight loading up to 500lb (226.79kg), including recoverable gear. The STAR kit comprised a nose-mounted, vee-shaped yoke, which folded back on either side of the nose radome when not in use, with fending lines stretching from the nose to both wing tips. The 137-metre (450-foot) lift-line was actuated by the rescuee and elevated via a helium balloon. With the yoke extended, the Hercules made its approach at about 240km/h (150mph) and snagged the line, lifting the personnel clear. A crew member then winched in the rescued man via the rear cargo door aperture. This was not carried on every mission but could easily be fitted.

Seen in June 1967, USAF Rescue HC-130H adaptation 64-14864 (c/n 4097) of 67 ARRS, Military Airlift Command, features the cable snagger on her nose. *Nick Williams, AAHS*

Also carried in a fairing built atop the aircraft's nose was the Cook AN/ARD-17 Electrical Aerial Tracking System (EATS). It was anticipated at the time that NASA space capsule re-entry would be a large part of the Hercules remit, but in the event none of this type of operation ever took place. Scanner windows were built into either side of the fuselage aft of the flight deck, while ten parachute flare/illumination markers/smoke markers, sonar buoys and beacon-launching tubes were installed in the rear cargo door.

Increased accommodation totalled five flight deck personnel (with a special radio operator station replacing the crew bunks, which were relocated in the main cargo hold), two loadmasters and two para-rescue technicians carried in the cargo compartment. The latter had two observer window positions with fully swivelling seats, mounted aft of the forward bulkhead. To increase range, either one or two cradle-mounted fuel tanks with a capacity of 1,800 US gallons (6,814 litres) could be carried. They were also fitted with overhead delivery system tracking recovery winches. A range of three palleted MA-1/2 rescue/recovery packages was carried, each of which contained cylindrical bundles, two of which held inflatable and three waterproof store containers. All these bundles were linked together by four buoyant 210-foot (46m) polyethylene linking straps.

The normal recovery technique was for an initial pass to be made over the target zone during which a personnel rescue kit was dropped to the group awaiting rescue. The harnessed suits were donned and the inflatable helium-filled balloon was released on its 500-foot (152.4m) nylon line. Meantime the Hercules had gone round again, and made a second pass at less than 140 knots (72.62 m/sec) airspeed to facilitate the deployment of the recovery yoke to its full extension. The yoke then snared and trapped the nylon line suspended below the balloon. The hoisted personnel or package was then reeled into the cargo hold from the trail position astern of the aircraft, with the subject experiencing no more impact than that felt during a normal parachute descent. Two people could be snatched from the ground or the sea at one pass by this method.

THE LOCKHEED MARTIN C-130 HERCULES

The system was first used effectively by the HC-130H on 3 May 1966, when two personnel were plucked from the runway at Edwards AFB, California. This first test was followed by a second on 5 May when, in a simulation of an Apollo splash-down and pick-up, three volunteers were lifted from the sea by the same method. In a continuation of this aspect of the programme, a special team was attached to the 6593rd Test Squadron, based at Hickam Field, Hawaii. It comprised six aircraft specially converted to snatch the Apollo capsule crews from above the Pacific, and redesignated: 64-14858 (c/n 4081) became the solitary JC-130H-LM and 64-14854 (c/n 4038) and 64-14857 (c/n 4073) became JHC-130Hs, as did 65-0979 (c/n 4131) for a while before being redesignated as a DC-130H-LM.

Tail down, wheels down, a Herk up from Hickam AFB, Hawaii, in classic pose. *Nick Williams, AAHS*.

The majority of the HC-130Hs, as 'Combat Talons', found more than adequate employment in the rescue of downed US pilots off the coast of Vietnam during the American involvement in that war. Combat pilots hit over North Vietnam quickly found that they stood a far better chance of survival if they ditched at sea ('Feet Wet') instead of ashore ('Feet Dry') in hostile territory (and large parts of South Vietnam were also hostile territory for most of the time). A considerable number of aircrew owe their lives to the Herky Bird in this configuration.

A further twenty-four Hercules for the US Coast Guard received similar HC-130H modifications, but did not feature the ARD-17 Cook aerial tracker, the HRU pods or the Fulton STAR recovery yoke. These aircraft were produced in two batches of twelve aircraft, the first being CG 1452, ex-67-7183 (c/n 4255); CG 1453, ex-67-7184 (c/n 4260); CG 1454, ex-67-7185 (c/n 4265); CG 1500, ex-72-1300 (c/n 4501); CG 1501, ex-72-1301 (c/n 4507); CG 1502, ex-72-1302 (c/n 4513); CG 1503, ex-73-0844 (c/n 4528); CG 1504, ex-73-0845 (c/n 4529); CG 1603, ex-77-0320 (c/n 4764); CG 1602, ex-77-0319 (c/n 4762); CG 1601, ex-77-0318 (c/n 4760); and CG 1603, ex-77-0317 (c/n 4757), the second being serials CG 1710 (c/n 5028); CG 1711 (c/n 5031); CG 1712 (c/n 5033); CG 1713 (c/n 5034); CH 1714 (c/n 5035) and CG 1715 (c/n 5037).

A further eleven US Coast Guard Hercules were produced – serials CG 1700 (c/n 4947); CG 1701 (c/n 4958); CG 1702 (c/n 4966); CG 1703 (c/n 4967); CG 1704 (c/n 4969); CG 1705 (c/n 4993); CG 1706 (c/n 4996); CG 1707 (c/n 4999); CG 1708 (c/n 5002); CG 1709 (c/n 5005); and CG 1790 (c/n 4931) – and they were fitted with the Side-Looking Airborne Radar (SLAR) and Forward-Looking Infra-Red (FLIR). This latter system, intended for use in tracking drug-smuggling vessels at sea, also utilised the Lockheed Special Avionics Mission Strap-On Now system (SAMSON), which coupled the FLIR with an optical data link and a display and recording console to record and register evidence as it came in. They were designated as HC-130H-7s.

Later many of these latter aircraft were given the additional duty of in-flight helicopter refuelling like the HC-130Ps, and were fitted with wing pods carrying hose-and-drogue gear for this mission. They were also equipped with Night Vision Goggles (NVG), while both cockpit lighting and navigation capability was also upgraded. All these aircraft have served with the USCG from their seven bases in North America, and while some have been reduced to care at the AMARC in Arizona, many others are still working today.

Seventeen C-130Es and one NC-130E were similarly converted to the STAR system by the USAF to rescue downed combat flyers in Vietnam, but were mainly used for clandestine operations behind enemy lines as 'Combat Talon Is'. These were serials 62-1843 (c/n 3806); 63-7785 (c/n 3852); 64-0508 (c/n 3992); 64-0523 (c/n 4007); 64-0547 (c/n 4040); 64-0551 (c/n 4046); 64-0555 (c/n 4056); 64-0558 (c/n 4059); 64-0559 (c/n 4062); 64-0561 (c/n 4065); 64-0562 (c/n 4068); 64-0563 (c/n 4071); 64-0564 (c/n 4074); 64-0565 (c/n 4077); 64-0566 (c/n 4080); 64-0567 (c/n 4083); 64-0568 (c/n 4086); and 64-0572 (c/n 4090).

Human Retrieval System testing being conducted by C-130E 64-0572 (c/n 4090). *Lockheed-Georgia, Marietta*

Aerial search, rescue and helicopter in-flight refuelling

The usefulness of the HC-130H type was indisputable and a further twenty aircraft were allocated for that role, the first being completed in 1966: 65-0988 (c/n 4143); 65-0991 (c/n 4152); 65-0992 (c/n 4155); 65-0993 (c/n 4156); 65-0994 (c/n 4157); 66-0211 (c/n 4161); 66-0212 (c/n 4162); 66-0213 (c/n 4163); 66-0214 (c/n 4164); 66-0215 (c/n 4165); 66-0216 (c/n 4166); 66-0217 (c/n 4173); 66-0218 (c/n 4174); 66-0219 (c/n 4175); 66-0220 (c/n 4179); 66-0221 (c/n 4183); 66-0222 (c/n 4184); 66-0223 (c/n 4185); 66-0224 (c/n 4186); and 66-0225 (c/n 4187). They still featured the Cook AN/ARD 17 aerial tracking antenna and carried the Fulton STAR recovery equipment as before, but now an additional role was incorporated for this group, that of Helicopter In-Flight Refuelling. These aircraft were designated as the HC-130P and were initially all assigned to the Aerospace Rescue & Recovery Service (ARRS).

Below: USAF Military Air Command's HC-130P 66-0222 (c/n 4184) of 76 ARRS is seen on 19 January 1968. *Nick Williams, AAHS*
Bettom: Wheels down, Hercules HC-130P 66-0223 (c/n 4185) of 79 ARRS, Military Air Command, prepares to land at Hickam Air Force Base, Hawaii, in June 1964. *Nick Williams, AAHS*

Naturally the versatile Herk found the air-to-air refuelling mission added to her enormous repertoire. This sequence shows 65-0988 (c/n 4143) refuelling a Sikorsky helicopter during trials. *Sikorsky Aircraft, United Aircraft Corporation*

THE LOCKHEED MARTIN C-130 HERCULES

During the air war in Vietnam HC-130P Hercules 66-0220 (c/n 4179) refuels an HH-3C 'Jolly Green Giant' 'copter over the Mekong River. *USAF*

The HC-130Ps were fitted with two under-wing refuelling probe-and-drogue pods some 90 feet apart beneath the outer wing sections, with the associated plumbing reels containing 85 feet (25.9m) of hose. This Helicopter Refuelling Unit (HRU) equipment enabled them to replenish two turbine-powered helicopters simultaneously.

Two cradle-mounted fuel tanks with a capacity of 1,800 US gallons (6,813.74 litres) were installed in the cargo compartment and a pair of reel observer seats were fitted. The fuel carried in the aircraft's wing tanks could be transferred in addition to these fuselage-carried tanks at a maximum pumping rate of 200 US gallons (757.08 litres) per minute if just one receiving aircraft was being replenished, or 165 US gallons (624.59 litres) per minute if two helicopters were simultaneously receiving fuel from the 'mother ship'.

The technique normally employed was for the HC-130P to fly at an altitude of between 4,000 and 5,000 feet (1,219.2 and 1,524m), with 70% flaps applied and at an indicated airspeed of between 105 and 120 knots (54 and 61.7m/sec). The helicopter herself maintained a set course, allowing the Hercules to approach the rendezvous from astern and some 200 feet (60.96m) below. Once the tanker pulled ahead and stabilised her speed, the helo would descend, the probe would engage the drogue and fuelling would commence.

Again, the war in Vietnam showed just how important this mission was, with both the big HH-3E 'Jolly Green Giant' and HH-53B 'Super Jolly Green Giant' rescue helos having their range and endurance considerably enhanced by this method. These aircraft saw considerable combat service and two, 66-0214 and 66-0218, were lost on the same night, 29 July 1968, to Viet-Cong ground attacks at Tuy Hoa airbase, South Vietnam. A third loss was recorded on 2 April 1986, when 66-0211 lost her starboard wing and crashed in a bad weather incident in the Magdalena area of New Mexico. Subsequently thirteen surviving aircraft were redesignated as MC-130Ps and assigned to special service units.

A simplified version was produced, designated as the HC-130N, which dropped the nose yoke, fending lines and associated recovery equipment carried by the HC-130P, and also did not carry the fuselage tanks, but was otherwise was almost identical. Fifteen of these aircraft were produced for the ARRS in the 1970s: serials 69-5819 (c/n 4363); 69-5820 (c/n 4367); 69-5821 (c/n 4368); 69-5822 (c/n 4370); 69-5823 (c/n 4371); 69-5824 (c/n 4372); 69-5825 (c/n 4374); 69-5826 (c/n 4375); 69-5827 (c/n 4376); 69-5828 (c/n 4377); 69-5829 (c/n 4378); 69-5830 (c/n 4379); 69-5831 (c/n 4380); 69-5832 (c/n 4381); and 69-5833 (c/n 4382).

Wheels are coming down as HC-130N rescue aircraft 69-5833 (c/n 4382) of the 1550th Aircrew Training & Test Wing (ATTW) comes in to land at Hill AFB, near Salt Lake City, Utah, in 1975. *USAF*

    The success of the HC-130P and HC-130N variants led to a further pair of aircraft being delivered in 1990 – serials 88-2101 (c/n 5202) and 88-2102 (c/n 5210) – with a third, 90-2103 (c/n 5294), in 1992, and three more – 93-2104 (c/n 5381), 93-2106 (c/n 5387) and 93-2105 (c/n 5388) – in 1995. They were basically similar to the HC-130P with the HRU units beneath the wings as before, but with updated and upgraded electronics, and auxiliary fuel tanks carried within the fuselage. They received the designation HC-130-(N). All were allocated to the Air National Guard (ANG) in Alaska were they perform both Rescue & Recover Missions and Helicopter In-Flight Refuelling duties.

    Some twenty-nine former HC-130N/Ps were redesignated as MC-130P-*LM* ('Combat Shadows') in February 1996. They were modified with Forward-Looking Infra-Red scanners, Night Vision Goggles (NVG) and lighting, a self-contained Integrated Navigation System (INS) of the ring-laser gyro type, a Secure Communications Suite, Global Positioning System (GPS), Digital Scan Dual-Navigation radar systems, and enhanced ECM capability and incoming missile detection scanners.

Wheels and flaps down, Air National Guard 20061 makes a steady approach. *Courtesy of Mark Smith*

These aircraft were serials 64-14854 (c/n 4038); 64-14858 (c/n 4081); 65-0971 (c/n 4116); 65-0975 (c/n 4125); 65-0991 (c/n 4152); 65-0992 (c/n 4155); 65-0993 (c/n 4156); 65-0994 (c/n 4157); 66-0212 (c/n 4162); 66-0213 (c/n 4163); 66-0215 (c/n 4165); 66-0216 (c/n 4166); 66-0217 (c/n 4173); 66-0218 (c/n 4174); 66-0219 (c/n 4175); 66-0220 (c/n 4179); 66-0223 (c/n 4185); 66-0225 (c/n 4187); 69-5819 (c/n 4363); 69-5820 (c/n 4367); 69-5821 (c/n 4368); 69-5822 (c/n 4370); 69-5823 (c/n 4371); 69-5825 (c/n 4374); 69-5826 (c/n 4375); 69-5827 (c/n 4376); 69-5828 (c/n 4377); 69-5831 (c/n 4380); and 69-5832 (c/n 4381).

In their new role the MC-130P-*LM*s act as refuelling hosts for deep-penetration Special Operations helicopter missions into hostile territory with minimum-risk environments. They are distributed among various Special Operations Squadron (SOS) units including 5 Special Operations Wing, and 9, 17, 58 and 67 Special Operations Squadrons at bases in Florida, New Mexico, England and Japan.

Airborne drone launch and control

Seventeen examples of the C-130A, C-130E and C-130H were modified into Airborne Drone Launch & Control platforms for Air Research Development Command. Modifications for this duty were not very extensive, the chief physical changes being the adoption of two (outboard) or four (under-wing) pylons for carrying the drones and an extended (30 inches/76.2cm) 'Pinocchio' nose radome, which in some was later modified to a small 'thimble' nose radome that carried the AN/APN-45. Many also carried a small ventral chin-mounted Microwave Command Guidance System (MCGS) with a blade antenna on the tip of the tail-fin. Modular internal changes, mounted on portable consoles in the cargo compartment, were two launch officer stations, with square observation windows, *a la* the KC-130A, cut in the paratroop doors; outward-facing lights added to the external fuel tank pylons; and a three-man tracking and control station together with avionics command and control equipment. The four-bladed Hamilton Standard propellers replaced the original three-bladed Curtiss Electric ones on many. As the drones increased in size and weight, additional stronger three-strut sway-braces were added.

The ability of the Hercules to loiter for long periods awaiting the most suitable launch times according to the dictates of weather or other operational parameters, coupled with her ability to cruise at a wide range of speeds to altitudes of 35,000 feet (10,668m), made her an particularly appropriate vehicle for these duties.

Four drones (officially designated Remotely Piloted Vehicles, or RPVs) could be carried, or, as an alternative longer-range loading, two on the outer pylons and two external fuel tanks on the internal, of both subsonic and supersonic varieties, such as the Teledyne Ryan BQM-34 'Firebee'. They could be launched and remotely controlled from the Hercules 'mother ship' to provide more realistic training in detection, interception and defensive action postures against hostile missiles. The extra crew members were two launch control officers and two remote controllers. As such the modified Hercules was used by both the US Air Force (DC-130A and DC-130E) and the US Navy (DC-130A).

USAF Herk 56-0514 (c/n 3122) with extended nose and carrying two BQM-34 'Firebee' target drones during trials for the US Navy. *McDonnell Douglas*

The first pair of USAF C-130As to be so adapted were 57-0496 (c/n 3203) and 57-0497 (c/n 3204), which were converted in 1957. They were sent to the Air Force Missile Development Center, working from Holloman AFB, New Mexico. Their initial flights were concerned with the Northrop Radioplane Q-4B programme. Originating in 1955, this supersonic target drone was designated XQ-4, and saw its first launching in January 1956. It had an overall length of 10.7 metres (35 feet), and a wingspan of 3.7 metres (12 feet), with a ceiling of 18,300 metres (60,000 feet). It had a Westinghouse XJ81-WE-3 turbojet propulsion plant giving it a speed of around Mach 2; the DC-130As air-launched it and it was radar-guided, with an inbuilt three-stage parachute final recovery. A later model, the XQ-4B, had a more powerful General Electric J85-GE-5 engine. By 1961 the USAF redesignated these as the Q-4A and Q-4B, and in June 1963 redesignated them again as the AQM-35A and AQM-35B before abandoning further development.

An aerial under-view of DC-130A 57-0497 (c/n 3204) carrying an XQ-4B remote-controlled piloted vehicle in 1976. *Author's collection*

The DC-130As were also used for the Ryan Model 147B High-Altitude Reconnaissance 'Lightning Bug' flight testing programme. These were a development of the 'Firebee' and development extended over several types, both recce and decoy variants being employed. They had a 4-metre (13-foot) wingspan and an operating ceiling of 19,000m (67,500 feet). Still later in their careers, the two DC-130As acted as the launch vehicles for the first Model 147B reconnaissance sorties flown over China, flying from Kadena AFB in Okinawa from 20 August 1964 for a month, making five combat sorties. After being handed over to the US Navy, both DC-130As transferred to Point Magu, California; they clocked up 147 test flights with this drone.

A close up of the XQ-4B on the special under-wing pylon of 570497 (c/n 3204). *Author's collection*

They had originally received the official designation GC-130A, as did the succeeding conversions that followed during the 1960s, when combat mission requirements over Vietnam clearly called for more launch vehicles to cope with the increased usage. Thus three further former C-130As – 57-046 (c/n 3168), 56-0514 (c/n 3122) and 56-0527 (c/n 3135) – and a former RL-130A, 57-0523 (c/n 3230), were selected. In 1962 they were all redesignated as the DC-130A-*LM*.

In 1969 the US Navy converted C-130A 55-0021/158228 (c/n 3048) and a JC-130A, 56-0491/158829 (c/n 3099), but they remained without the standard 'Pinocchio' radomes. They briefly replaced the old Lockheed DP-2E Neptunes it had previously employed for target launch.

Next for conversion in 1967/68 were seven of the early-production C-130Es, the first pair being 61-2361 (c/n 3662) and 61-2362 (c/n 3663). These were assigned to Holloman AFB, Tularosa, New Mexico, for the AFMDC test programme of the Teledyne-Ryan 'Firefly' Model 154 'Compass Arrow'. This was also based on the 'Firebee' concept but was far more sophisticated, and was the first of the second-generation Unmanned Aerial Vehicles (UAVs); it even incorporated early attempts at 'stealth' technology in its design, with Radar Absorbent Materials (RAM) and inwardly canted wings to reduce its radar footprint. With a length of 10.36m (34 feet) and a wingspan of 14.63m (48 feet), it was developed from 1966 onward. It was launched from the DC-130, then became self-propelled via its General Electric J-97-GE-100 engine, and self-navigated itself 2,000 miles at a height of 23,744.4m (78,000 feet) to photograph such potential vital targets as the Red Chinese nuclear facility at Lop Nor near Xinjiang, using an inbuilt panoramic IT-K-80A camera. In the end political manoeuvring led to the abandonment of this programme, after which the aircraft were transferred to 432 Tactical Drone Group (TDG) at Davis-Monthan AFB, near Tucson, Arizona, until the cancellation of the entire drone programme in 1979, when they reverted to their former status.

Additionally the following were part of the programme at the Missile Development Center in 1968: USAF 61-2363 (c/n 3681); 61-2364 (c/n 3687); 61-2368 (c/n 3713); 61-2369 (c/n 3714) and 61-2371 (c/n 3716). The usual conversions followed the usual pattern, with these aircraft having the 'chin' (microwave guidance) and the 'thimble' (tracking radar) radomes to become DC-130E-*LM*s. They served with the 408th/100th Strategic Reconnaissance Wing, mainly in the SW Pacific area, before reverting to their former configuration and service in the 314th TAW.

Two former Rescue HC-130Hs, 65-0971 (c/n 4116) and 65-0979 (c/n 4131), were planned to be modified to DC-130Hs in 1977, with four under-wing pylons to carry the Ryan BGM-34C multi-mission drones. With the ending of the Vietnam War and cutbacks, only one aircraft, 65-979, was actually converted, becoming the solitary DC-130H-*LM*. After she was converted the pair joined the 6514th Test Squadron, based at Hill AFB, Utah. 65-979 was claimed by Lockheed to have achieved the turboprop external weight record on 26 July 1976 when, piloted by Carl Hughes, she lifted off from Edwards AFB, California, with four 'Mass Simulators'[1] weighing a total of 20,189.39kg (44,510lb) in place.

After some eighteen months of trials, the whole RPV programme was summarily abandoned as Electronic Countermeasures (ECM) advances rendered them increasingly vulnerable. The APVs were scrapped and the bulk of the Hercules 'mother ships' allocated to the MASDC. The two -Hs were subsequently reconverted to an MC-130P and an NC-130H respectively.

The US Navy took delivery of its first two DC-130As on transfer, as its BuNos 158228 (c/n 3048), with a normal radome, and BuNo 158229 (c/n 3099) in 1969. These were followed by a further three conversion transfers, BuNo 56-0514 (c/n 3122), BuNo 57-0496 (c/n 3203) and BuNo 57-0497 (c/n 3204), which joined the Navy's Composite Squadron Three (VC-3) in the early 1970s.

[1] These are especially constructed 'mock-ups' constructed by Lockheed to duplicate actual or intended underwing loadings and their effects , in this case, of larger drones than normally carried.

A US Navy Herk flying along the coast. *Author's collection*

Subsequent to their naval service life, the latter three were contract-operated in the same task by civilian companies, initially Lockheed Aircraft Service Company (LASC) and subsequently by Avtel Services Inc working out of Mojave Airport, California.

Aircraft carrier operation – COD

Experimental trials were conducted by the US Marine Corps and US Navy in 1963 to see whether so large an aircraft as the C-130 Hercules could operate from an aircraft carriers. Contrary to what has been written elsewhere, there was no question of making the Herky Bird a permanent carrier-borne operator, but it was thought that it would be useful during Combined Operations of the kind in which the USMC specialised, with its ability to use offshore carriers as safe bases from time to time during combat and supply operations in hostile territory. The vast wingspan of the Hercules would preclude any other of the ship's aircraft complement being able to operate on deck while she was landing or taking off, which would have been too big a price to pay for regular usage, even had there been an overriding need.

Accordingly sea trials were held using the aircraft carrier USS *Forrestal* (CVA 59) and a Marine Corps KC-130F tanker aircraft (BuNo 149798, c/n 3680), which was adapted for the job by the removal of the in-flight wing pylon-mounted refuelling pods and the 3,600-US gallon (13,627.48-litre) fuselage tank. This programme was designated Carrier Onboard Delivery (COD) and was organised from the US Navy's Air Testing Centre at Patuxent River. An improved Hytrol anti-skid brake system was fitted, together with a more sensitive speed-sensing system and strengthened nose-wheel doors. For these sea trials the USMC markings were temporary replaced by US Navy markings. The modified aircraft was at Patuxent on 8 October 1963 and initially the trials were conducted on a land simulation of the carrier deck, where some ninety-five take-offs and 141 landings were carried out.

Opposite page, top: On the mat, United States Navy DC-130A 158228 (c/n 3048) displays her stunning paint scheme with US Navy Fleet Composite Squadron Three (VC-3) at Davis-Monthan AFB in July 1979. *Bruce Stewart via Nick Williams, AAHS*
Bottom: The same aircraft is seen off Point Magu, California, carrying three BOM-345 'Firebee' target drones. *Navy Photograph Center, Washington DC*

Deck landing trials aboard the USS *Forrestal* (CVA 59) in October 1963 by KC-130F 149798 (c/n 3680), named *Look Ma, No Hook*. *Lockheed-Georgia, Marietta*

THE LOCKHEED MARTIN C-130 HERCULES

The trials then moved out to sea off the Massachusetts coast for the real thing. Piloted by Lieutenant James H. Flatley USN (later a Rear-Admiral), a series of fifty-four experimental approaches were made, which included sixteen touch-and-go 'bolters'. This phase was followed by twenty-one unarrested full-stop landings, during which the Herk was brought to a halt in distances that ranged from 270 feet (82m) to 495 feet (151m). Shipborne take-offs were carried out, with the test aircraft configured with various loading weights up to a maximum of 121,000lb (54,340kg). The maximum length of deck required was 745 feet (227m). Only normal braking and full-reverse throttle procedures were followed in these trials, all of which were accomplished with no problems whatsoever. In theory these trials showed that the KC-130F could deck-land a load of 25,000lb (11,340kg) with perfect safety. The Hercules remains the largest aircraft to have ever operated from any aircraft carrier.

Had the planned rescue of the American Embassy personnel, illegally held captive by Revolutionary Guards in Iran, been brought to fruition (Operation 'Eagle Claw'), Hercules fitted with tail-hooks were readied to take them to safety aboard a US aircraft carrier offshore, but unfortunately this part of the daring plan was never to be put into effect.

Air emergency hospitals

Taking the Relief & Rescue concept to its final extreme, the Saudi Government had Lockheed Aircraft Service Company (LASC) at Ontario, California, make a very special conversion of a C-130H, civilian registration N4098M (c/n 4837), to serve as the King's own special flying hospital and surgery aircraft. She was outfitted internally with the full range of medical equipment and necessities for any conceivable emergency, including an operating theatre and an intensive care unit, and staffed with a standby medical team of doctors and nurses. Special APUs were installed, contained in under-wing pods, and these could provide on-ground power to run all these facilities for up to 72 hours. She was delivered in September 1981, and became HZ-MS019, operated by Saudia.

She became the first Airborne Emergency Hospital (AEH). The Saudis then considered the prospect of bringing such fast aerial surgical aid to disaster areas in its remote desert hinterland. They extended the programme and the first AEH was followed by more of the same type, similarly converted by LASC, carrying the special registration letter MS (for Medical Services). These AEH aircraft were three more conversions from C-130Hs – registrations HZ-116 (c/n 4915), HZ-MS021 (c/n 4918) and HZ-MS7 (c/n 4922) – and six aircraft converted from L-100-30s – registrations HZ-117 (c/n 4954); HZ-MS05 (c/n 4950); HZ-MS06 (c/n 4952); HZ-MS09 (c/n 4956); HZ-MS10 (c/n 4957); and HZ-MS 14 (c/n 4960). One of these, HZ-MS06 (c/n 4952), was specially equipped as a dental hospital.

No other nation followed the Saudi lead, probably due to the enormous cost and the limited usage to which the aircraft were subsequently put.

Silhouetted against a dawn sky, this Hercules of Lockheed Air Services is seen outside the company hangars in May 1968. *Nick Williams, AAHS*

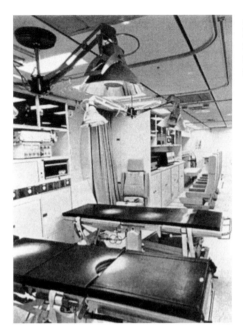

An interior view of one of the seven Saudi Arabian Hospital Ships, specially fitted-out L-100-30s. In front is the operating theatre, which could support two simultaneous operations, while in the centre section beyond can be seen a row of removable seats for medical personnel together with medical equipment and supply storage. *via Sven-Ake Karlson*

Aircraft in-flight refuelling

A natural assignment for so versatile and adaptable aircraft as the Hercules was that of an in-flight refuelling aircraft, and adaptations were made to the C-130A, C-130E, C-130H and C-130J variants accordingly, becoming the KC-130F, KC-130R, KC-130H and KC-130J respectively.

The US Marine Corps had an obvious interest in the Hercules's potential for in-flight refuelling (which it dubbed 'Bird Feeding'). The Corps was traditionally land-based and had for long been tasked for long overwater deployments, especially in the Pacific. To test the feasibility of such a conversion, two C-130As – 55-0046 (c/n 3073) and 55-0048 (c/n 3075) – were loaned from the USAF and initially designated as the GV-1.

They were fitted with two 934lb (424kg) pylon-mounted probe-and-drogue refuelling pods, which were positioned some 90 feet apart under the wings, outboard of the outboard engines. Thus they could refuel two Marine Corps aircraft simultaneously. To facilitate visual contact, large observer windows were cut in the aft personnel doors. Each HRU refuelling pod contained a hydraulically operated drogue-and-hose reel, with 91 feet (27.74m) of hose and the refuelling basket.

Internal modifications included increased flight-deck accommodation for five crew members together with the two refuelling observers positioned at the aft personnel doors. Two fuel tanks with a capacity of 1,800 US gallon (6,814 litres) were cradle-mounted and located in the cargo compartment. All the refuelling appendages were designed for quick removal so that the aircraft could be reconfigured to the pure transport role when required.

Commencing in 1957, the two trial aircraft were evaluated at the Naval Air Test Centre (NATC) at Patuxent River, Maryland, and these trials were declared successful. An ongoing programme of C-130B conversion to produce further such tankers (the US Navy's seven aircraft designated as GV-1Us) was therefore initiated, which finally produced no fewer than forty-six Tanker/Transport aircraft (see the table in the KC-130F-*LM* section in Chapter 3).

The original power plant for these aircraft was the T56-A-7 engine, which developed 4,050eshp, but later they were all converted to the improved T56-A-16, which was the US Navy's designation of the 4,910eshp T56-A-15 used on the standard C-130H at the time. (Interestingly, these were flat-rated to 4,508eshp for take-off in order not to exceed the nacelle/wing structural capability of the aircraft.) They were also redesignated as the KC-130F-*LM*. As would be expected in aircraft subjected to a salt water environment, extensive galvanising was undertaken throughout to protect against corrosion.

The aircraft proved most successful in this role. The technique employed was that the in-flight fuel transfer to the receiver aircraft could be made directly from the tanker's six wing tanks, even when the fuselage tank was installed. Fuel could be transferred from the internal fuselage tank to the tanker's own engines to extend her range if necessary. Once the Marine Corps fighters/attack aircraft had positioned themselves and locked onto the basket, fuel was transferred from the fuselage tank by two internally mounted electrically driven pumps, whose maximum pumping rate was 300 US gallons (1,135.62 litres) per minute to each host aircraft. Alternatively, the wing tanks could pump at half that rate to each host aircraft. A battery of three coloured lamps indicated: RED – Pressure OFF, YELLOW – Ready for Transfer, GREEN – Fuelling in Progress. In an emergency all the fuel could be jettisoned at a rate of 750 gallons per minute.

With the production of the C-130H Lockheed built on this experience to produce its KC-130H-*LM* tanker aircraft, aimed specifically at foreign air forces, and orders quickly followed. The aircraft utilised the same single or twin 1,800-US gallon (6,813.74-litre) fuel tanks initially, but these were later discontinued and replaced by a single 3,600-US gallon (13,627.48-litre) fuselage tank. A total of twenty such tankers were built from scratch, while a further six were conversions from C-130Hs (see the table in the appropriate section).

With the arrival of the KC-130H as a tanker version of the C-130H, the US Marine Corps placed orders that resulted in fourteen aircraft of this type being delivered between 1975 and 1978 (see the table in the appropriate section). As expected, the adaptations were basically similar to the KC-130F-LM but with increased capacity, and the USMC version was designated the KC-130R-LM. Fuel bunkerage went up to 13,320 US gallons (50,420 litres) carried in a single fuselage-mounted tank, which replaced the two smaller tanks of the earlier aircraft, whose capacity had totalled 10,623 US gallons (40,212.42 litres).

The latest tanker version for the US Marine Corps is based on the C-130J and is designated at the KC-130J. At the time of writing orders have been placed for seven such aircraft: serials 165735 (c/n 5488); 165736 (c/n 5489); 165737 (c/n 5499); 165738 (c/n 5506); 165739 (c/n 5507), 165809 (c/n 5508); and 169810 (c/n 5509).

Boundary Layer Control research

The testing of a new system (Boundary Layer Control, or BLC) to enhance the short take-off (STOL) performance characteristics of the C-130B from short air strips resulted in a one-off temporary conversion. A single C-130B, serial 58-0712 (c/n 3507), was flight-tested by Lockheed and several US Government agencies and was redesignated as the NC-130B-*LM*.

C-130B 58-0712 (c/n 3507) conducts the Boundary Layer Control (BLC) experiment. She was redesignated NC-130B for an intended C-130C STOL version. She first flew on 8 February 1969 and is depicted here during flight trials on unprepared ground at Eglin AFB, Florida. The angle of descent sharpens as the BLC noses down across the cameras. *Lockheed-Georgia, Marietta, via Audrey Pearcy*

　　　　　THE LOCKHEED MARTIN C-130 HERCULES

The intention was that, if the experiment proved successful, a new variant would result, the C-130-C, specifically for work with the US Army. The augmented air flow would increase STOL ability from close to the battle front airstrips and allow the supply situation of troops in forward positions to be vastly enhanced.

The BLC system as fitted comprised of two T56-A-6 engine load compressors, Allison YT56-A-6 turbojets operating as gas generators, which were pod-mounted (in 'clam shell' fairings) below the aircraft's outer wings, and had the associated ducting for the distribution of blown air in the wings, fuselage and empennage. Modifications also included the fitting of single-hinged flaps in place of the Fowler flaps, and increased rudder chord. The compressors forced the air out over the whole span of the upper sides of the flaps and ailerons and over each side of both the rudder and the elevator. In order to enhance the total flap area to maximise the effect during the tests, at low speeds the flaps were hinged so that they deflected the flow to a maximum of 90°, while the ailerons were depressed 30°.

The equipment and modifications resulted in a slightly increased operational weight of the test aircraft, and also a small reduction in the aircraft's payload and range. The first flight of the NC-130B took place on 8 February 1960. The US Army had already abandoned its requirement, but the USAF continued the programme for a while, and the aircraft even flew to England, where it was inspected at the Vickers Aircraft Company's airfield at Wisley, Surrey, in the spring of 1961. No British interest resulted, however, and the project was terminated. Having logged some 23 flight hours, the aircraft was placed in storage for a while.

Cargo transport

The basic duty for which the Hercules was built is often so routine and accepted as part of worldwide aerial activity as to be almost forgotten, or taken for granted amid the plethora of 'Special Mission' activities that have grown up around this legendary aircraft. Yet in this simple, basic role, the Hercules is unsurpassed and has a record that is as versatile as it is unassailable. Her basic built-in attributes assured this success from the onset of her long career. With design features that included a wide, encumbrance-free cargo hold, the straight-in, low-level, rear-loading cargo deck easily accessible with the minimum of outside specialised equipment, the large cargo doors for maximum capacity, and a fully adjustable ramp able to cope with everything from a low-loader downwards, the Hercules gulps down all manner of cargo, military and civilian, without effort. She thus proved able to cope with the diversity of air cargo across the whole spectrum, and even invented a few of her own as the decades rolled by.

'The Hercules gulps down all manner of cargo': loading drums into a Herk at a USAF base. *Lockheed-Georgia, Marietta*

Anything that required air-shipping from one part of the globe to another with the minimum of fuss and effort and with economy, range and reliability vanished into the Herk's maw and was duly disgorged, safely, at its point of destination, be it military vehicles (from full-size tanks and artillery, through tracked armoured personnel carriers and fuel trucks down to jeeps), military hardware (disassembled aircraft, helicopters, missiles, aircraft engines, lorries, ammunition and stores), civilian heavy equipment (road-building machinery, oil-rig assemblies, pipeline sections, mobile workshops and associated equipment and fittings), dangerous bulk fuels, sensitive electronics, emergency medical supplies, equipment and fully fitted laboratories, all manner of bulk livestock in internal pens (fish and animal containers, not forgetting displaced humans), fresh produce (fruit, grain, general foodstuff and relief supplies of every conceivable type and size), pail, parcels and packages, timber, metals and other raw materials, palletised or containerised – the list is endless.

In war situations from Vietnam to the Gulf, the Herk has truly proven herself indispensable. So reliant on the Hercules was the US war effort in Vietnam for supply and a myriad other duties that one high-ranking officer stated that without her the Allied attempts to stem the Communist invasion would have come to a complete stop. From 1972 they flew also with the Vietnamese Air Force (VNAF), the RAAF and the RNZAF. On 22 February 1967 they flew in the largest parachute drop of the war, Operation 'Junction City' at Tay Ninh. They ensured the survival of the Marine garrison at Khe Sanh between 21 January and 8 April 1968, logging 74% of the 1,128 transport missions flown. In many other dangerous supply runs the cost to the 'Trash and Ass Haulers', as the Hercules aircrew wryly dubbed themselves, was enormous, with heavy losses being incurred from ground fire, missiles and anti-aircraft batteries (see the accompanying table).

USAF/USMC Hercules losses in the South East Asia theatre

Serial	C/n	Serial	C/n	Serial	C/n
54-1625	3012	57-0467	3174	62-1815	3777
54-1629	3016	57-0475	3182	62-1840	3803
55-0002	3029	58-0718	3513	62-1843	3806
55-0009	3036	58-0722	3517	62-1853	3817
55-0038	3065	58-0737	3534	62-1854	3818
55-0039	3066	58-0743	3540	62-1861	3825
55-0042	3069	60-0298	3602	62-1865	3829
55-0043	3070	60-0307	3618	63-7772	3838
55-0044	3071	61-0953	3630	63-7780	3846
56-0472	3080	61-0965	3652	63-7798	3864
56-0477	3085	61-0967	3654	63-7827	3904
56-0480	3088	61-0970	3667	64-0508	3992
56-0490	3098	61-0972	3669	64-0511	3995
56-0499	3107	61-2637	3673	64-0522	4006
56-0502	3110	61-2644	3682	64-0547	4040
56-0506	3114	61-2649	3692	64-0563	4071
56-0510	3118	149809	3709	66-0214	4164
56-0521	3129	149813	3719	66-0218	4174
56-0533	3141	62-1785	3730	69-6571	4345
56-0548	3156	62-1797	3748		
56-0549	3157	62-1814	3776		

Having '…trash-hauled, air-dropped, flare-dropped, bombed, machine-gunned, fire-suppressed, drone-launched, photo-mapped, missile-tracked, air-evacuated, Fulton-rescued, capsule-recovered, air-refuelled, carrier-landed, ski-lifted everything from food, guns, toilet paper, jeeps, tanks, paratroops, bridges for the Dominican Republic and water for Peruvian earthquake victims, hay bales for starving cattle in North Dakota, wheat to starving Africans in Mali, and beer to fighter pilots at Phu Cat…'[2] with the TAC, the Herk was eventually phased out of that command. The TAC finally turned over the last of its Herks to the Military Airlift Command in December 1974, ending a unique era for the 'Trash and Ass Haulers'. But it was not the end of their military record by a long chalk.

In the Gulf several decades later the Herk logged 11,799 sorties during the defence 'Desert Shield' period, acting both as the prime tactical airlift facilitator and as one of the main struts of the air supply bridge between Europe and CONUS and the war zone. Some 130 C-130E/Hs were directly assigned to Operation 'Desert Storm'. Among their many heavy strategic and tactical airlift operations were the moving of the 82nd Airborne Division from Safwa, Saudi Arabia, to the Forward Operating Location (FOL) as part of Operation 'Desert Sabre'. There was just one war casualty, AC-130H 69-6567 (c/n 4341), which, on 28 January 1991, courageously remained over the battle zone south of Kuwait City after dawn in order to assist a US Marine Corps unit threatened by a Frog-7 missile site. She took a hit from a hand-held missile and crashed into the sea, killing all fourteen crew members.

A rocket-assisted take-off for a Herk during the Kuwaiti operation. *Courtesy of Simon Watson*

[2] From Major Joe Tillman, 'Farewell to the Herk', *TAC ATTACK* magazine, January 1975.

Earth survey programme

A standard C-130B, 58-0712 (c/n 3507), was modified prior to delivery, with blown flaps and control surfaces for Boundary Layer Control work, and given the civilian registration N707NA. Subsequent to this the test machine was reconverted back to normal C-130B configuration, with the modified wings and rudder being replaced by a conventional set from a damaged L-100 aircraft (c/n 4109); as N929NA, it arrived at the Johnson Space Center in July 1968. Purchased by NASA in September 1969, it resumed active duties on earth survey work with the NASA Earth Resources Programme, being initially based at Ellington AFB, Texas.

In 1979, as part of the Airborne Instrumentation Research Programme (AIRP) (Earth Survey 2), this aircraft was fitted out with a new nose section from a Lockheed P-3 Orion, which held a C-band microwave antenna together with a four-channel radiometer for remote sensing in addition to the normal C-130 sensors. A special camera bay was built into the aircraft's hold, which also contained a unique thermometer, eleven-channel and eight-channel scanners, and an active microwave scanner. At the rear a further microwave scanner was mounted on an extension to the tail, with three more on the upper rear ramp area, and two more were fitted on extensions that could be flown from the open ramp aperture.

During 1979 this aircraft surveyed the Arctic, covering a total of some 25,000 miles (40,225km). It was redesignated yet again in February 1982 as N707NA, and is currently still in service with NASA Dryden, flying from Edwards AFB, California.

Electronic reconnaissance and surveillance

There have been numerous special adaptations, modifications and conversions of standard USAF Hercules and other nations' variants to perform highly specialised ECM, ER and ES Electronic Intelligence-gathering (ELINT) and Communications Intelligence (COMINT) missions down the decades. The Herk had the bulk to accommodate the specialist equipment in all its complexity, and the room to house the operators, as well as having the range and endurance to put it to good use along the sensitive perimeters of the expanding communist world and to act as an airborne trip-wire for each new aggression, as well as in over-sensitive 'hot spots' like the Middle East cauldron and South East Asia.

The first such were twelve USAF C-130As, all Type 182-1As, modified from 1957 onward into C-130A-IIs specifically as Communications Intelligence and Signals Intelligence Gathering (COMINT/SIGINT) aircraft: serials 54-1637 (c/n 3024); 56-0534 (c/n 3142); 56-0484 (c/n 3092); 56-0535 (c/n 3143); 56-0524 (c/n 3132); 56-0537 (c/n 3145); 56-0525 (c/n 3133); 56-0538 (c/n 3146); 56-0528 (c/n 3136); 56-0540 (c/n 3148); 56-0530 (c/n 3138); and 56-0541 (c/n 3149).

The modification comprised the fitting of Direction Finding (D/F) equipment, Pulse and Signal receivers, recorders and analysers, and accommodation for up to fifteen operatives to work in shifts, with limited sleeping accommodation. They were flown by 7406 Operations Squadron, 7407 Combat Support Wing, along the Iron Curtain in Europe, and were based at Rhein-Mains airbase in what was then West Germany; for southern area and Middle Eastern missions they worked out of Athens Airport. It was during one of these flights along the Soviet border that serial 56-0528 was destroyed by Soviet fighter aircraft near Yerevan, Armenia, on 2 September 1958. All the surviving aircraft were reconverted to standard C-130As in 1971 on being replaced by the newer C-130B-II.

In May 1961 the patrols along the Demilitarised Zone (DMZ) that separated North and South Korea, which had to be constantly monitored against northern excursions, military build-up and spy penetrations, had their ageing Boeing RB-50Es replaced by thirteen newly built but modified RC-130Bs, which were redesignated as C-130B-IIs ('Sun Valley IIs'). These aircraft were serials 58-0711 (c/n 3506); 58-0723 (c/n 3518); 59-1524 (c/n 3560); 59-1525 (c/n 3561); 59-1526 (c/n 3563); 59-1527 (c/n 3568); 59-1528 (c/n 3571); 59-1530 (c/n 3576); 59-1531 (c/n 3579); 59-1532 (c/n 3581); 59-1533 (c/n 3586); 59-1535 (c/n 3585); and 59-1537 (c/n 3589).

They were equipped with Long Focal Length (LFL) oblique cameras and other electronic reconnaissance equipment and were flown by 6091 Reconnaissance Squadron, which was based at Yakota Airbase in Japan. From 1 July 1968 they were taken over by 556 Reconnaissance Squadron, performing the same role, and later joined 7406 Combat Support Squadron. They were all converted back to standard C-130Bs by the simple expedient of removing their specialised equipment and fittings in the early 1970s.

The white dome of USAF Hercules C-130B-II 58-0711 (c/n 3506) is seen flying over Hawaii. *Nick Williams, AAHS*

In October 1980 C-130B-II AFRES Herk 59-1524 (c/n 3560) stands ready to go. *Nick Williams, AAHS*

A single Coast Guard C130-E, serial 1414 (c/n 4158), was built in 1966 as a Long Range Navigation (Loran) A&C calibration aircraft and was initially designated as EC-130S (for Search); this was later changed to E on delivery. She operated from Elizabeth City, St Petersburg and Clearwater between August 1966 and July 1983, being again redesignated as HC-130E. After this she went to the Military Storage & Disposition Centre (MASDC) in Arizona, and received the USAF designation CF049 before being sold to Certified Aircraft Parts, which sold her cockpit to Reflectone, later Asia-Pacific Training & Simulation PTE Ltd; she was finally scrapped in November 1995.

In April 1967 this same designation, EC-130E, was applied to ten C-130E-IIs that had been modified for the Airborne Battlefield Command & Control Centre (ABCCC) role over Vietnam. These aircraft carried extra external antennae, which contained the USC-48 ABCCC-III, a $9 million self-contained palleted package or capsule 12 metres (40 feet) long and weighing 9,072kg (20,000lb); this platform comprised twenty-three securable radios, secure telex outputs and fifteen fully computerised consoles visually outletting the data to colour displays via rapid data retrieval. This enabled almost continuous monitoring of the battlefield conditions on the ground and enabled the current situation to be monitored back at Headquarters.

Aircraft thus configured were serials 62-1791 (c/n 3738); 62-1809 (c/n 3770); 62-1815 (c/n 3777); 62-1818 (c/n 3780); 62-1820 (c/n 3783); 62-1825 (c/n 3788); 62-1832 (c/n 3795); 62-1836 (c/n 3799); 62-1857 (c/n 3821); and 62-1863 (c/n 3827).

Two high-angle aerial views of USAF C-130E 62-1857 (c/n 3821). *USAF/Author's collection*

They were flown in combat by seven Airborne Command & Control Squadrons (ACCS) and one of them, serial 62-1815 (c/n 3777), was destroyed by enemy action at Da Nang airbase on 15 July 1967. The survivors soldiered on after the war and another example, serial 62-1809 (c/n 3770), became one of the casualties of the ill-fated and botched rescue mission into Tabas, Iran, when she collided with an RH53D at Posht-I-Badam on 24 April 1980. Many of these aircraft were modernised with 4,910eshp T56-A-15 engines (derated to 4,058eshp) and carried an in-flight refuelling receptacle forward, but retained their ABCCC status.

The ABCCCII capsules carried in Vietnam, which had manual plotting boards and grease pencils, were upgraded in two aircraft to the ABCCCIII system, which used secure communications equipment with computer-generated text and graphic displays, satellite communications equipment and a digital switching system (JTIDS) that could detect hostile ground forces and transfer the data and coordinates to aircraft such as the A-10A Thunderbolt-II ('Warthog') anti-tank aircraft for destruction. They were equipped with twenty-three fully secure radios, secure teletype and fifteen automatic fully computerised consoles, which allowed a quick analysis of any battlefield scenario for swift and accurate counter-action to be initiated. Two of the aircraft, 62-1791 (c/n 3738), named 'Grey Ghost', and 1825 (c/n 3788), named 'War Wizard', with the 7th ACC Squadron of 28 Air Division, headquartered at Kessler AFB, Mississippi, went out to Saudi Arabia during the Gulf War of 1990/91 and played a leading role in Operation 'Desert Storm'. In the actual aerial assault of the battle, they flew forty combat sorties totalling 400 hours flying time. They were credited with controlling almost 50% of all aerial attacks and also coordinated many of the SAR operations to get Allied pilots out from behind enemy lines.

Five C-130Es – serials 63-7783 (c/n 3850); 63-7815 (c/n 3889); 63-7816 (c/n 3894); 63-7828 (c/n 3896); and 63-9816 (c/n 3977) – were modified to EC-130E-(CL) between March and April 1979. These 'Comfy Levis'/'Senior Hunter' were configured by Lockheed Aircraft Service Company for both the Electronic Intelligence Acquisition and Electronic Jamming roles utilising palletised systems.

Three C-130Es – serials 63-7773 (c/n 3839), 63-7869 (c/n 3939) and 63-9817 (c/n 3978) – were similarly modified to EC-130E-(RR) between April and December 1979. This trio of 'Rivet Rider'/'Volant Scout' electronic surveillance aircraft, together with the EC-130E-(CL), were flown by 193 Tactical Early Warning Systems (TEWS) Squadron (Pennsylvania Air National Guard), and later by 193rd Electronic Countermeasures (ECS) Squadron, but with their missions directed by Electronic Security Command and their specialist equipment operated by National Security Agency personnel. From June 1987 all eight aircraft were upgraded with T56-A-15 engines, in-flight refuelling and Infra-Red Counter Measures (IRCM) jammers. In April 1980 one of the CLs, serial 63-7773 (c/n 3839), was modified to an RR.

An aerial view of EC-130(CL) 63-7869 (c/n 3939) in flight with 193rd TEWS from Olmstead-Harrisburg International Airport, Harrisburg, Pennsylvania. *Author's collection*

THE LOCKHEED MARTIN C-130 HERCULES

Four of the Harrisburg-based aircraft – 63-7773 (c/n 3839), 63-7783 (c/n 3850), 63-7869 (c/n 3939) and 63-9817 (c/n 3978) – were modified to 'Volant Solo' standard for Psychological Operations (PSYOP) duties. Large blade aerials were fitted on the upper rear fuselage and ventrally on the wings outboard of the engines. They later changed from 'Volant Solo II' to 'Coronet Solo' aircraft with the movement of the ANG unit from Tactical Air Command to Military Airlift Command. During Operation 'Just Cause' in Panama they flew as substitute radio and television stations when local facilities were poor, inadequate or simply non-existant, a mission they had also performed in similar circumstances over Grenada, West Indies, in 1989.

Their primary mission was to conduct psychological operations by use of electromagnetic transmissions that covered commercial AM and FM radio bands, VHF and UHF television bands and VHF, HF and FM military frequencies. The equipment includes prerecorded audio and video material, live broadcasts from eight aircrew broadcast microphones, using Army-supplied linguists if required, and cassette tape, reel-to-reel tape and video playback modulations. They also act as a link to re-transmit ground station signals. They have a five-man crew – two pilots, navigator, flight engineer and loadmaster – together with extra personnel, a third pilot, navigator and flight engineer, on special long-endurance missions, achieved by dropping some of the five communications systems operators, which are under the command of an electronic warfare officer.

The 193rd Special Operations Squadron, 193 Special Operations Group, deployed four CL and four RR 'Volant Solo IIs' during the Gulf War with spectacular results. Being stand-off platforms, they did not overfly enemy-held territory, but their sorties flew 8-to-10-hour missions along the existing front line with fighter cover at high altitudes. Arabic-speaking linguists were provided by the Army and the Kuwait Government in exile. Their broadcasts are credited with inducing thousands of Iraqi soldiers to lay down their arms and surrender without firing a shot. These Herks also flew other, very secret, 'Senior Scout'-type missions on behalf of Electronic Security Command.

These four aircraft were further modified to 'Commando Solo' status in 1992/93, in the light of the Gulf War experience. A pair of upgraded UHF/VHF antennae for the global capability TV broadcast system was fitted under each wing in pods measuring 23 by 6 feet (7 by 1.8 metres); the leading-edge blade aerial on the dorsal fin was removed, and in its place four forward-facing antenna pods are now carried for Low-Frequency (L/F) TV broadcasts. High-Frequency (H/F) broadcasts are by way of a trailing wire antenna, and AM broadcasts are also by a trailing wire antenna fitted with a 500lb (226.79kg) weight. In addition to their psychological broadcasting capability, this quartet also has huge civilian usage potential as airborne TV relay coordinators in times of natural emergencies or disasters.

A 'Commando Solo II' of the USAF with her tail-mounted arrays prominent. *US Department of Defense*

A C-130 makes a low pass over Haiti in 2009. *Courtesy of Ben Jones*

This system was first put to use during the Haitian crisis when paratroop and ground support units were placed on standby. The fact that the USA had heavy forces imminently poised to invade was broadcast, convincing the ring-leaders that resistance was futile; the President resigned and the whole of Operation 'Uphold Democracy' was made a bloodless episode.

The last of the EC-130E models was replaced by EC-130Js by 2006. Operating still with the 193rd under the auspices of the Special Operations Command's (SOC) Special Operations Wing (SOW) at Middletown, Pennsylvania, and working out of Harrisburg AFB, they issue psychological warfare broadcasts at specific audiences in AM, FM, HF, TV and military communication bands, most recently in the Gulf under Operation 'Iraqi Freedom' and in the ongoing 'war on terror' operations. One of the new aircraft was also utilised in the Haitian earthquake rescue missions in a humanitarian role by broadcasting warnings and advice to affected citizens. Previously the C-130 had performed excellent relief work in the aftermath of Hurricanes 'Katrina' and 'Rita'.

The EC-130E squadron based at Harrisburg IAP, Pennsylvania, is the 193rd SOS. These photos, taken on 20 December 1999, show the special antenna on the vertical tail surfaces and elsewhere on these aircraft – not bad for a 'logistics' squadron. *Kevin R. Smith*

THE LOCKHEED MARTIN C-130 HERCULES

The current fleet includes 97-1931 (c/n 5477), 98-1932 (c/n 5490), 99-1933 (c/n 5502), 00-1934 (c/n 5522) and 01-1935(c/n 5532).

In addition, six 'Combat Talons Is' were combat-operational during the Gulf War, these being serials 64-0523 (c/n 4007) and 64-0561 (c/n 4065) with 7 Special Operations Squadron, from Rhein-Main, Germany, and serials 64-0551 (c/n 4046), 64-0559 (c/n 4062), 64-0562 (c/n 4068) and 64-0568 (4086) from 8 SOS, Hurlburt Field, Florida. Their main role was inserting and retrieving Special Forces troops inside Iraq itself as well as behind enemy lines in occupied territory. They also cooperated with such units as the US Navy SEALS, the Army's Green Berets and the Joint-Service DELTA Force, as well as acting as refuelling tankers for the 20 SOS MH-53J 'Pave Low' helicopters working from behind enemy lines.

One unusual duty that came the way of the four 8 SOS birds was a mission to blast a path through Iraqi minefields by dropping 15,000lb (6,803.88kg) BLU-82/B 'Big Blue', 'Daisy-Cutter', fuel-air blasting bombs. Christened 'The Mother of All Bombs' in sarcastic reference to Saddam Hussein's boasts about the 'The Mother of All Battles' avidly lapped up by the western media, these were placed on pallets in the Herk's cargo hold and, at 17,000 feet (5,181.6m) over the target, simply rolled out down the rear ramp in a similar scenario to that used by the Vietnamese Herks twenty years earlier. With the spectacular results of 5 tonnes of their content counter-mining their target zones very obvious, the four Herks were duly dubbed by some wit as 8 Bomb Squadron!

The fifteen MC-130Es included, in addition to the above, serials 64-0547 (c/n 4040); 64-0555 (c/n 4056); 64-0558 (c/n 4059); 64-0564 (c/n 4074); 64-0565 (c/n 4077); 64-0566 (c/n 4080); 64-0567 (c/n 4083); and 64-0572 (c/n 4090), operated by 1 Special Operations Wing for the clandestine 'Combat Talon I' missions; these were replaced between June 1990 and November 1991 by twenty-four MC-130H 'Combat Talon IIs'.

A three-quarter port front view of an MC-130E 'Talon' flying a low-level mission during manoeuvres over the Arizona desert in December 1980. This aircraft was assigned to the 8th Special Operations Squadron (SOS) and based at Hulbert AFB, Florida. *USAF*

Developed from the experimental YMC-130H between 1981 and 1982, the introduction of the 'Combat Talon II' was subjected to a frustrating variety of political funding setbacks, internal cost-control feuding and internal squabbling, together with other unrelated factors that all delayed the entry into service of the first MC-130H – 83-1212 (c/n 5004) – until June 1984, and even then she lacked an appropriate navigational radar suite, which significantly reduced her effectiveness. The MC-130H featured a strengthened fuselage and modified cargo doors, together with GPI, bad-weather radars and NVG equipments. This gave the new aircraft the ability to operate at an Above Ground Level (AGL) height of 76 metres (250 feet) in poor visibility. Two fewer aircrew were required to operate the new aircraft due to automatic operational functions.

Although a further five of the new aircraft arrived the following year, the problems continued. The replacement for the now discontinued APQ-122 TF/TA system, contracted to IBM but sub-contracted to Emerson Electrics, failed to come up to scratch and the whole programme was seriously jeopardised as a result. Finally the AN/APQ-170(V)8 set arrived and performed satisfactorily, but overspend dried the supply of aircraft, being completed to a mere eighteen examples between 1987 and 1989, although none were combat-ready.

Therefore it was not until 20 June 1991 that 87-0024 (c/n 5092), the first fully operational 'Combat Talon II' MC-130H, joined 8 SOS at Hurlburt, followed by three others soon after and two more by the end of that year. By the new millennium four SOS Squadrons – 1, based at Kadena AB, Okinawa, 7 at RAF Mildenhall, UK, 15 at Hurlburt, Florida, and 550 at Kirtland AFB, New Mexico – were operational.

These aircraft were serials 83-1212 (c/n 5004); 86-1699 (c/n 5026), named *Merlin's Magic*; 84-0475 (c/n 5041); 86-0476 (c/n 5042), named *Hacker*; 85-0011 (c/n 5053); 85-0012 (c/n 5054); 87-0023 (c/n 5091); 87-0024 (c/n 5092); 87-0125 (c/n 5115); 87-0126 (c/n 5117); 87-0127 (c/n 5118); 88-0191 (c/n 5130); 88-0192 (c/n 5131); 88-0193 (c/n 5132); 88-0194 (c/n 5133); 88-0195 (c/n 5134); 88-0264 (c/n 5135); 88-1803 (c/n 5173), named *Dead Man's Party*; 89-0280 (c/n 5236); 89-0281 (c/n 5237); 89-0282 (c/n 5243); 89-0283 (c/n 5244); 90-0161 (c/n 5265); and 90-0162 (c/n 5266).

These aircraft were all former C-130Hs modified for the new role with all the tricks of the trade such as ground-mapping, Terrain-Following/Terrain Avoidance and navigation via the AN/APQ-170, AN/AAQ-15 detector, AN/AAR-44 missile launch warning, ANALQ-172 detector/jammer, AN/ALQ-69 warning and AN/ALQ-8 Electronic Countermeasure radar packages, as well as Internal Navigation System (INS) and infra-red jammers with associated flare/chaff dispensers. A system for high-speed, low-level (HSLL) delivery and container release, and an automatic computed air-release packaged was also shipped.

Three further C-130Hs – 74-2139 (c/n 4711), 74-2134 (c/n 4735) and 89-1185 (c/n 5194) – were converted to EC-130H-(CL) for use by the Air National Guard on the highly secretive 'Senior Scout' clandestine electronic intelligence-gathering and jamming missions between January 1993 and March 1994.

Sixteen Herks, comprising four EC-130Hs – 64-14859 (c/n 4082), 64-14862 (c/n 4089), 65-0962 (c/n 4102) and 65-0989 (c/n 4150) – and twelve C-130Hs – 73-1580 (c/n 4542); 73-1581 (c/n 4543); 73-1583 (c/n 4545); 73-1584 (c/n 4546); 73-1585 (c/n 4547); 73-1586 (c/n 4548); 73-1587 (c/n 4549); 73-1588 (c/n 4550); 73-1590 (c/n 4554); 73-1592 (c/n 4557); 73-1594 (c/n 4563); and 73-1595 (c/n 4564) – were modified to the Command, Control and Communications Counter-Measures (CCCCM) mission between 1981 and 1983. These 'Compass Call' aircraft are operated by 41, 42 and 43 Electronic Combat Squadrons of the 355 Wing based at Davis-Monthan AFB near Phoenix, with 43 working out of Sembach airfield in Germany.

Easily identifiable by their U-shaped antenna array mounted ventrally below the empennage, with streamlined blister fairings midway up the tapering section of the rear fuselage, they were also equipped with additional ram air inlets in the undercarriage bays on either side to improve air cooling for the increased electronic cabinets and displays carried internally. The Rivet Fire Operating System (RFOS) is a powerful ECM suite that is operated by a crew of thirteen, four of whom are flight operatives while the remaining nine comprise an electronic warfare officer acting as Mission Crew Commander (MCC); a cryptologic linguist; an Acquisition Operator, a High Band Operator, four analysis operators, and an Airborne Maintenance Technician (AMT). This team analyses the enemy signals capacity, then selects the most effective targeting, effectively jamming the most crucial enemy communications channels by high-energy radio frequency output that is microwave-generated, targeting intensive noise transmission over a wide range. In combat conditions this system was used to good effect in both Iraq and Panama. Lockheed's upgraded Block 30 System uses airborne fibre optics to the nth degree with the latest computer technology automatically reconfigurating the EC-130H's capabilities and constantly monitoring the system in a segmented and reintegrated approach to enhance the Offensive Counterinformation (OCI) reach over enemy Command and Control (C2) systems. Unfortunately the introduction of the further enhanced Block 40 System is liable to fall prey to financial restrictions.

These aircraft also came into their own during the Gulf War when 43 ECS Squadron was deployed to Riyadh King Khalid International Airport in Saudi Arabia, then moved forward to follow the flow of the battle during 'Desert Storm'. They successfully interrupted Iraq's tactical and strategic military communications and their jamming caused great inertia among enemy units. A detachment of EC-130Hs from 43 ECS also operated clandestinely over Iraq during Operation 'Proven Force', working out of Incirlik, Turkey.

Three EC-130Hs – serials 64-14862 (c/n 4089), 65-0962 (c/n 4102) and 65-0989 (c/n 4150) – still operate with 41 ECS, although fears have been expressed about the continued viability of these ageing airframes. Among the many operations to which these aircraft have contributed in recent years are 'Southern Watch', 'Just Cause', 'Desert Shield', 'Desert Storm', 'Uphold Democracy', 'Deny Flight', 'Vigilant Warrior', 'Provide Comfort', 'Decisive Edge', 'Deliberate Force', 'Enduring Freedom' and 'Iraqi Freedom'.

Two C-130Es were used as lead aircraft for the Electronic Special Operations Support (SOS) aircraft during trials and evaluations at Edwards AFB, California, and Wright-Patterson AFB, Ohio, these being 64-0571 (c/n 4087), used for Electronic Intelligence-gathering (ELINT) and named *Night Prowler*, and 64-0572 (4090) respectively. They were designated as NC-130E-*LM*s, but in 1979 their designations changed to MC-130E-S and MC-130E respectively (see below).

NC-130E 64-0571 (c/n 4087) of 4950 TWASD seen on 8 December 1977. *Nick Williams, AAHS*

These trials led to the conversion of fifteen Herks to 'Combat Talon Is'; they were re-engined with the T56-A-15 and an in-flight refuelling receptacle was mounted atop the forward fuselage to extend range. The electronics fitted included terrain-following AN/APQ-122(V)8 dual-frequency I/K band radar; an Internal Navigation System (INS); a special hush-hush communications pinpoint system enabling pinpoint air-drops of special forces units behind enemy lines; and Infra-Red Countermeasure (IRCM) carried in pods, with associated chaff dispensers and flare dispensers. In addition, the ten 'Rivet Clamp' aircraft were fitted with the Fulton Surface-to-Air Recovery (STAR) system (see the appropriate section).

These aircraft were in three groups, the first being designated as MC-130E 'Rivet Clamp', of which twelve aircraft were converted: serials 64-0523 (c/n 4007), named *Midnight Creeper*; 64-0547 (c/n 4040); 64-0551 (c/n 4046); 64-0555 (c/n 4056), named *Triple Nickel Ethel*; 64-0558 (c/n 4059);

64-0559 (c/n 4062); 64-0561 (c/n 4065); 64-0562 (c/n 4068); 64-0566 (c/n 4080); 64-0567 (c/n 4083); 64-0571 (c/n 4087); and 64-0572 (c/n 4090).

Four of these aircraft subsequently had ECM Update packages, and were re-rated as MC-130E (E), these being 64-0523 (c/n 4007), 64-0555 (c/n 4056), 64-0561 (c/n 4065) and 64-0566 (c/n 4080).

As mentioned, two of the trials aircraft became MC-130E-S 'Rivet Swap' aircraft, serials 64-0571 (c/n 4087) and 64-0572 (c/n 4090).

Finally there were four MC-130E-Y 'Rivet Yank' aircraft, two of which adopted the serials of crashed Herks and were used in clandestine operations; these were serials 62-1843 (c/n 3990), ex-64-0506; 63-7785 (c/n 3991), ex-64-0507; 64-0564 (c/n 4074), which crashed off Tabone Island, Philippines, on 26 February 1981; and 64-0565 (c/n 4077).

In 1981 the Lockheed Corporation put forward its idea of an Airborne Early-Warning aircraft, which it classified as the EC-130. The US State Department's Office of Munitions Control (OMC) authorised the company to release technical details to any potential overseas customer, and an artist's impression was printed by various magazines.[3] The concept was to incorporate a tail-mounted, updated version of the General Electric APS-125 surveillance radar to provide early detection of approaching airborne threats for both overland and overwater surveillance. Lockheed predicted a demand for such an aircraft, and the Hercules provided the most supportable platform of all the aircraft considered.[4]

The radar antenna would be housed inside a Rotodome 24 feet (7.315m) in diameter mounted atop the vertical stabiliser, which would be cut down in height by 65 inches (162.56cm) compared to a standard C-130. It was predicted that the interaction of the Rotodome and the stabiliser would continue to provide sufficient directional control despite the shorter tail. An antenna located thus was thought to be capable of providing an almost free-space field of view (FSFV) of 360° in azimuth and 21° in elevation to nominal ranges of 200 nautical miles. In addition to the radar the proposed design would also carry Identification Friend or Foe (IFF) equipment and passive electronic monitoring systems. The overall package would have the capacity to track 300 separate targets simultaneously and would be able to monitor up to 256 electronic threats. It would also be equipped with secure voice and data link communications for airborne early warning coordination.

One early-warning aircraft with Rotodome and AN/APAS-14S EC-130V, serial CG1721 (c/n 5121), was operated by the US Coast Guard for illegal anti-drug importation surveillance duties. She was modified by General Dynamics, Fort Worth, from an HC-130H in 1968 and designated as an EC-130V. She had the AN/APS-125 radar mounted above the after fuselage in a similar manner to the smaller Grumman E-2C Hawkeye early-warning aircraft already in use for the same mission. Additionally, various antennae sprouted from fairings around the nose. Three operatives had their associated cabinets, consoles and displays pallet-mounted in the cargo hold, and extra cooling vents were cut in order to give airflow around these additional electronic cabinets and equipment.

The Coast Guard briefly operated this aircraft from USCGS Clearwater, Florida, between 31 July 1991 and April 1992, then the USAF took an interest in her and her Coast Guard livery was replaced by camouflage. She was placed on the strength of 514 Test Squadron, being assigned the serial 87-0157, and in October 1993 was redesignated as NC-130H, flying with the 418 Test Squadron, before being assigned to the Naval Air Test Centre at Patuxent River in November 1998.

Forest-fire control

The United States has been plagued for decades with large-scale wildfires started accidentally or deliberately in areas of thick woodland or shrubland adjacent to its ever-sprawling city suburbs, which cause enormous damage running into billions of dollars. Airborne fire-fighting has long been a major weapon in the effort to contain these outbreaks, especially in inaccessible areas, and it was perhaps inevitable that the multi-talented Hercules should have quickly found herself a major contender in this specialised field.

[3] See for example, 'Lockheed Surveillance Concept Gains Favor', article in *Aviation Week & Space Technology*, 25 May 1981 issue.

[4] Other contenders were the Lockheed P-3 Orion and Boeing 737.

Lockheed worked with the existing services and the USAF in a series of tests in 1971. They developed the Modular Airborne Fire Fighting System (MAFFS), which could be quickly fitted to any standard C-130 with only the minimum of modification. The MAFFS was a modular system that was built around a core of six 500-US gallon (1,892.70-litre) pressurised air tanks, each tank having a pressure of 50lb (22.679kg) per square inch, with their associated plumbing and hardware consisting of dual nozzles and spraying gear located on the main ramp. The total spray cargo that a C-130 could dump was therefore 3,000 US gallons (11,356.23 litres).

Firefighting from the Herk: the twin foam release dispensers are seen in action at low level. *USAF*

The method adopted after trials was for the C-130 to fly straight and steady down to an altitude of only 200 feet (60.96m), and at a speed of 130 knots (66.87m/sec). The fire-retardant content of the tanks is forced out down the nozzles at a rate of 400 US gallons (1,514.16 litres) per second to lay a comprehensive field over the target zone. The tanks can be fired off as individual units or all six can be fired simultaneously to give a blanket cover. A C-130 spray pattern covers a rectangle some 2,000 feet (609.6m) long by 150 feet (45.72m) wide in about 6 seconds.

The retardant used is not only designed to be safe for humans or plants accidentally caught in the spray, but also acts as a fertiliser to regenerate vegetation in the burn area. C-130 FireShips did not have to wait long to prove their value, and a series of major wildfires in 1973 and 1974 saw them in action in states as far apart as California, Idaho, Montana and New Mexico. By 1975 the USAF Reserve and the Air National Guard units flying the Hercules had established no fewer than eight MAFFS units around the USA available when called upon, and in the ensuing decades the C-130 has performed frequently in this role. The USAF took over the job from the ANG and Reserves, but repeated cutbacks have today reduced their capability to just one unit, the 910th Airlift Wing (ALW), 773rd Airlift Squadron (ALS), which is a section of 22 Air Force (Air Mobility Command) based at Youngstown Warren Regional Airport in Ohio, flying C-130Hs.

However, the United States Forestry Service itself operated no fewer than twenty-two Hercules Fire aircraft via both the USAF and private companies, namely N1171TG (c/n 3018); 54-1639 (c/n 3026); N473TM (c/n 3081); N116TG (c/n 3086); N137FF (c/n 3092); N6585H (c/n 3095); N9724V (c/n 3099); N134FF (c/n 3104); N8055R (c/n 3115); N132FF (c/n 3119); N131FF (c/n 3138); N531BA (c/n 3139); N132FF (c/n 3142); N133FF (c/n 3143); N130RR (c/n 3145); N134FF (c/n 3146); N135FF (c/n 3148); N136FF (c/n 3149); N135HP(c/n 3166); N466TM (c/n 3173); 57-0479 (c/n 3186); and N8026J (c/n 1389).

The added strains of such duties showed up centre wing section metal fatigue faults earlier than on others, and some spectacular wing-folds resulted, which were caught on video. In September 2000 N116TG crashed at Burzet, France, during fire-fighting duties; in August 1998 N135FF crashed on Pallette Mountain, Palmdale, California, with metal fatigue in the underside of the centre wing section; and in June 2002 N130HP's wing broke during fire-fighting near Walker, California, due to metal fatigue.

The private company Aero Firefighting Services operated a further five machines, N134FF (c/n 3104); N132FF (c/n 3119); N131FF (c/n 3138); N135FF (c/n 3148); and N138FF (c/n 3227) (see the appropriate section).

With the unchecked sprawl of American cities into the countryside, and the increased temperatures and lack of rainfall due to global warming and increased pollution, the growth of the wildfire risk rises with each succeeding year, and never has the demand been higher for airtanker services. The August 2000 airtanker register of Fire & Aviation Management listed the following Hercules as still in service as part of the aerial combat teams desperately trying to contain such infernos.

No	Owner/operator	Type	Registration	Load (lb)	Volume (US gallons)
30	International Air Response	C-130A	116TG	27,000	3,000
31	International Air Response	C-130A	117TG	27,000	3,000
32	International Air Response	C-130A	118TG	27,000	3,000
63	TBM Inc	C-130A	473TM	27,000	3,000
64	TBM Inc	C-130A	466TM	27,000	3,000
67	TBM Inc	C-130A	531BA	27,000	3,000
81	Hemet Valley	C-130A	131FF	27,000	3,000
83	Hemet Valley	C-130A	132FF	27,000	3,000
88	Hemet Valley	C-130A	138FF	27,000	3,000
130	H&P Aviation	C-130A	130HP	27,000	3,000
131	H&P Aviation	C-130A	131HP	27,000	3,000
133	H&P Aviation	C-130A	133HP	27,000	3,000

The 115th Airlift Squadron, based at Port Hueneme, California, was the USAF fire-fighting unit at the forefront of the battle. Forward-deployed to Fresno from 24 July 2000, this outfit flew round-the-clock sorties under the direction of United States Forest Service and California Department of Forestry experts, who supplied the retardant and led the aircraft to the fires, and they were a key part of the Modular Airlift Fire Fighting System from the Air National Guard Channel Island Station.

Gunships

The aerial gunship concept was already well established in the USAF from the early 1960s with the converted C-47 Skytrain, which became the AC-47D, and which was used in combat from December 1964, but the arrival of the Hercules gave added scope and firepower to the type and it has been steadily developed ever since.

On 6 June 1967, under Operation 'Gunboat', the Aeronautical Systems Division, Air Force Systems Command, based at Wright Field, Ohio, produced the prototype of the AC-130A-*LM*-1 'Pave Pronto' and 'Pave Pronto Plus' aircraft; it was a conversion from a standard C-130A, serial 54-1626 (c/n 3013), named *Plain Jane*. She was equipped with the 'Stella Scope' Night Vision Device (NVD), Side-Looking

Radar (SLR), a Beacon Tracking device, Direction Finding Homer, FM band radio transceiver and Semi-Automatic Flare Dispenser, and on the after ramp was emplaced an AN/AVQ-8 steerable searchlight with an Infra-Red (IR) and an Ultra-Violet (UV) Xenon arc light. She was thus well equipped to find ground targets, but she was equally well armed in order to deal with the same targets once located and pinpointed. She had no fewer than four 20mm (0.787-inch) General Electric M061 cannon emplaced, firing obliquely downward from special gunports along her port fuselage; these had a fully computerised fire-control system. She also had an inert tank system.

Plain Jane was given two periods of combat experience in Vietnam, the first between October and December 1967 and the second between February and November of the following year. From her experience in the field the USAF decided that the experiment was highly successful and further Herk Gunships were an obvious requirement. The systems fit was modified in the light of these missions with the fitting of an AN/AWG-13 analogue computer to upgrade information faster, an AN/APQ-136 Moving Target Indicator (MTI) sensor and an AN/AAD-4 Side-Looking Infra-Red (SLIR) sensor.

Seven more conversions from JC-130As were carried out to this specification by LTV Electrosystems, at Greenville, Texas, and these were completed between August and December 1968. These seven all saw intense action at night against the infiltrating North Vietnamese and guerrilla armies invading South Vietnam, attacking their supply columns and vehicular traffic. They were later brought up to 'Pave Pronto' standard. The aircraft concerned were serials 53-3128 (c/n 3001), named *First Lady*, which survived battle damage to end her days in the USAF Armament Museum at Elgin AFB, Florida; 54-1623 (c/n 3010), named *Ghost Rider*; 54-1625 (c/n 3012), named *War Lord* and destroyed by enemy action over the Ho Chi Minh trail on 21 April 1970; 54-1627 (c/n 3014), named *Gomer Grinder*; 54-1628 (c/n 3015), named *The Exterminator*, which ended her days in Celebrity Row at the AC in Arizona; 54-1629 (c/n 3016), which was lost through enemy action and burnt out at Ubon Royal Thai Air Force Base on 25 May 1969; and 54-1630 (c/n 3017), named *Azrael*, which ended up at the USAF Museum, Wright-Patterson AFB, Ohio.

A further experimental aircraft was modified in November 1970 for all-weather capability, 'Pave Pronto', and with yet greater firepower. Produced under the 'Super Chicken'/'Surprise Package' programmes, this aircraft was a conversion from C-130A 55-0011 (c/n 3038), later named *Night Stalker*. Her box of tricks included an AN/ASQ-24A Stabilised Tracker, which incorporated ASQ-145 Low Light-Level Television (LLLTV) and Motorola AN/APQ-133 Beacon Tracking Radar (BTR). Added punch was provided by a pair of 7.62mm (0.3-inch) Miniguns, two clip-fed 40mm (1.57-inch) Bofors, mounted aft, and two 20mm (0.787-inch) Vulcan cannon emplaced forward.

She led to nine further 'Pave Pronto' aircraft conversions from C-130As, which carried yet further embellishments, the AN/ASQ-24A Stabilised Tracker and an AN/AVQ-18 Laser Designator/Rangefinder package with a bomb damage assessment camera built in. The conversions also featured for the first time the 'Black Crow' Truck Ignition sensor, and had dual AN/ALQ-87 Electronic Countermeasures (ECM) pods under each wing as well as SUU-42 flare ejectors. These nine aircraft suffered heavy casualties in the Vietnam War, so much so that they were nicknamed 'Mortar Magnets' by their long-suffering aircrews. They were intensively employed, not only in their own right but as target-markers for short-range aircraft such as the McDonnell F-4 Phantom.

The nine were serials 55-014 (c/n 3041), named *Jaws of Death*, which ended up in the Robins AFB Museum; 55-029 (c/n 3056), named *Midnight Express*; 55-040 (c/n 3067); 55-043 (c/n 3070), destroyed by an enemy SA-7 missile south-west of Hue on 18 June 1972; 55-044 (3071), named *Prometheus*, destroyed by an SA-2 missile south-east of Sepone, Laos, on 28 March 1972; 55-046 (c/n 3073), named *Proud Warrior*; 56-469 (c/n 3077), named *Grim Reaper*; 56-490 (c/n 3098), named *Thor* and lost to enemy action north-east of Pakse, Laos, on 21 December 1972; and 56-509 (c/n 3117), named *Raids Kill Um Dead*, which ended up at Hurlburt Field Memorial Air Park.

The next development followed in April 1970 and resulted in the AC-130E-LM ('Pave Spectre I'). These two aircraft were prototype conversions from C-130Es, and offered a greater payload, endurance and stability to the Gunship role. Both aircraft, serials 69-6576 (c/n 4351) and 69-6577 (c/n 4352), were therefore taken in hand by Warner-Robbins Air Material Area (WRAMA) and their initial armament was a pair of 7.62mm (0.3-inch) MXU-470 Miniguns, two 40mm (1.57-inch) Bofors and a pair of 20mm (0.787-inch) M-61 cannon.

Subsequently they were rearmed with the 'Pave Aegis' with one fewer 40mm (1.57-inch) but instead a huge 105mm (4.13-inch) howitzer firing obliquely downward from the port side for maximum impact on the target. This weapon, impressive though it was, was the downfall of 69-6576 for, when operating from Mombasa during the Somalia confrontation on 14 March 1994, a practice firing saw a premature detonation and the resultant explosion set fire to the port engines, the aircraft crashing into the sea south of Malindi on the Kenyan coast.

Six AC-130As took part in Operation 'Proven Force', working out of Turkey from February 1991 with 711 Special Operations Squadron, 919 Special Operations Group (headquartered at Duke Field, Florida). They were serials 54-1623, 54-1630, 55-0011, 55-0014 (which flew twenty combat missions), 55-0029 and 56-0509.

Nine further aircraft, conversions from C-130Es, were ordered in February 1971 and incorporated the latest state-of-the-art electronics; they became 'Pave Spectre Is'. An impressive array of equipment followed generally that of the earlier Gunships, but was much improved, with cockpit Head-Up Display (HUD); nose-mounted AN/APN-59B Navigation radar and MTI; AN/ASQ-150 Beacon Tracking radar; a stabilised AN/ASQ-24A Tracking radar with laser illuminator and range-finder; AN/ASQ-5 'Black Crow' TID; the AN/AAD-7 Forward-Looking Infra-Red (FLIR); AN/ALQ-87 ECM pods; an AN-AVQ-1720 kilowatt searchlight; and SUU-42A/A chaff and flare dispensers.

These aircraft went into action in South East Asia (Vietnam, Laos and Cambodia) from the spring of 1972 onward, by which time their targets were no longer just supply and ammunition trucks, but fully fledged North Vietnamese armoured regiments with Soviet-supplied heavy tanks. They were serials 69-6567 (c/n 4341); 69-6568 (c/n 4342); 69-6569 (c/n 4343); 69-6570 (c/n 4344); 69-6571 (c/n 4345); 69-6572 (c/n 4346); 69-6573 (c/n 4347); 69-6574 (c/n 4348); and 69-6575 (c/n 4349). One, 69-6571 (c/n 4345) was lost to enemy action in March 1972 at An Loc, Vietnam. The remainder were progressively upgraded from 1973 to the AC-130H configuration.

The AC-130H-*LM* upgrade was carried out on ten aircraft from June 1973 onward. They were converted from surviving AC-130E-*LM*s by replacing their engines with the 4,508eshp T56-A-15s; these were 69-6567 (c/n 4341); 69-6568 (c/n 4342); 69-6569 (c/n 4343); 69-6570 (c/n 4344); 69-6572 (c/n 4346); 69-6573 (c/n 4347); 69-6574 (c/n 4348); 69-6575 (c/n 4349); 69-6576 (c/n 4351); and 69-6577 (c/n 4352).

Subsequently all were given in-flight refuelling ability with a boom receptacle mounted atop the mid-section, and progressively upgrades have been made with the adoption of a Digital Fire Control Computer (DFCC) system, FLIR, LLLTV, ECM and navigation replacements, and, by the time of the 'Desert Shield'/'Desert Storm' contretemps with Iraq, they were fully upgraded. Five AC-130Hs were deployed for the war by 16 Special Operations Squadron, these being 69-6567, 69-6569, 69-6570, 69-6572 and 65-6576. Considered vulnerable to modern air defence systems, they operated by night over enemy lines, considered to be low-threat zones, but despite this caution 69-6567 fell victim to enemy defences on 31 January 1991 while attacking an enemy Free Rocket Over Ground (FROG-7) site that was threatening a US Marine force. The aircraft crashed into the sea off Kuwait, killing all fourteen crew members.

An AC-130H on display at an air show. This Close Air Support/Armed Reconnaissance variant was a gunship derived from the Vietnam War. *Author's collection*

Since then these aircraft have seen action in the world's trouble-spots such as Liberia, Bosnia and Somalia, and eight are still in service with 16 SOS. Under the designation Special Operations Force Improvement (SOFI), one aircraft, 69-6568 (c/n 4342), became the prototype MC-130P aircraft in October 1990 (see the appropriate section).

In July 1988 the first of thirteen AC-130Us ('Spectre)', serial 87-0128 (c/n 5139), based on the C-130H, was delivered to North America Aircraft Operations Division at Palmdale, California, part of the Rockwell International Corporation, for conversion. Not until January 1991 did the finished Gunship arrive at the Air Force Flight Test Centre at Edwards AFB for evaluation by 6510 Test Wing. She became known as 'The U-Boat' by her crews, and this nicknamed was also applied to her successors.

She featured a still further advance of the concept, incorporating a Battle Management Centre (BMC) whereby all her updated sensors fed into an IBM IP-102 computer system for input evaluation and decision-making data subjection. This has made both the Beacon Tracking radar and 'Black Crow' indicator sensor irrelevant. Firepower also saw the replacement of the 20mm (0.787-inch) Vulcan guns by a fully trainable 25mm (0.98-inch) General Electric GAU-12/U Gatling, a single 105mm (4.13-inch) howitzer and a single 40mm (1.57-inch) Bofors. Adverse weather conditions pose no problems with the choice of electronically slaved gunnery from these weapons linked to the Hughes AN/APQ-180 digital fire-control radar, the Forward-Looking Infra-Red AN/AAQ-117, emplaced on the port side of the aircraft's nose, or the Bell Aerospace All Light-Level Television (ALLTV) system. There are also special observer stations inbuilt on the starboard forward fuselage and at the rear ramp area. Target location is guaranteed by the Navstar Global Position System (GPS), and she carries combined INS and cockpit HUD.

Nor has the increasing risk posed to such aircraft by modern defence systems been overlooked. Following combat experience and losses, every attempt has been made to decrease the aircraft's vulnerability to ground fire. The AC-130U incorporates an ITT Avionics AN/ALQ-172 jamming system; the Texas Instruments AN/ALQ-117 Forward-Looking Infra-Red countermeasures system; and decoy equipment with MJU-7 or M296 IR flares and chaff bundles being released by three dispensers located ventrally on the main fuselage. The ability to absorb punishment is provided by a casing of 'Spectre' ceramic armour over areas most at risk.

The first 'Spectre' Gunship was followed by twelve more, which have joined 4 Special Operations Squadron, 16 Special Operations Wing, at Hurlburt Field, Florida. These are serials 89-0509 (c/n 5228); 89-0510 (c/n 5229); 89-0511 (c/n 5230); 89-0512 (c/n 5231); 89-0513 (c/n 5232); and 89-0514 (c/n 5233), which arrived between December 1990 and February 1991, and 90-0163 (c/n 5256); 90-0164 (c/n 5257); 90-0165 (c/n 5259); 90-0166 (c/n 5261); 90-0167 (c/n 5262); and 92-0253 (c/n 5279), which were received between August 1991 and March 1992.

The 'Spectre' force served in Operation 'Urgent Fury' in Grenada, Operation 'Just Cause' in Panama and Operation 'United Shield' in Somalia.

High Technology Test Bed (HTTB)

An L-100-20, N4174M (c/n 4412), originally sold to Kuwait in April 1971, was repurchased in May 1982 and re-registered as N130X in June 1984; she became the famous High Technology Test Bed (HTTB) aircraft, serial 23491 (c/n 3701), for the accumulation of STOL information for use on the C-130J project. The tests were in three phases from June 1984 onward. She had extensions forward from horizontal and vertical stabilisers ('horsals'), an extension to the dorsal fin, and was painted overall high-gloss black. In the second phase the leading edges of the wings were 'drooped' to change the airflow, and double-slotted flaps were fitted, together with spoilers. Extended chord ailerons and rudder were fitted and she had a special high-sink-rate undercarriage. The final phase saw her fitted with an FLIR (Forward-Looking Infra-Red) outfit in a turret and laser range-finder equipment. She later utilised the new T56A-1-1 Series IV 5,250shp prop-turbine engines, and established several climbing records. In February 1992 she was also tested with electro-hydrostatic aileron servo. During a high-speed ground test on 3 February 1993 she crashed on take-off and was a total write-off.

She had been practising touch-and-go landings all morning and was taking off on her eighth run from west to east along the main runway when she suddenly veered off course in a steep 60° to 70° bank. She reached an altitude of about 300 feet[5] then 'nosed-down steeply', according to one eyewitness. The aircraft crashed with yards of the Navy Dispensary building, then exploded, killing

Originally built for Kuwait, this 382E-16C L-100-20 became Lockheed's High Technology Test Bed (HTTB) aircraft in 1984. With the serial N130X and a stunning all-black gloss paint job, she is seen here on display at Le Bourget Airport on 30 May 1985. She created several climb records but was involved in a terminal accident in 1993, killing all seven crew members. *Both Paul Zethos*

all seven crew members.[6] Julius Alexander for Lockheed explained that the L-100-20 had been '…extensively modified to be a test vehicle for avionics and flight control systems. It was not an ordinary Hercules by any stretch of the imagination. It was an extraordinary airplane.'[7]

'Hurricane Hunters'

Perhaps not surprisingly it is the WC-130's most spectacular missions that have gained the most publicity down the decades, as with the famous 53rd Weather Reconnaissance Squadron, known as the 'Hurricane Hunters'. The 53rd became the first squadron to deliberately fly its aircraft into a hurricane when a B-17 made such a penetration in September 1945. Since that date this has become their prime mission, melded into the US Weather Bureau's around-the-clock hurricane warning service, first established on 16 June 1947. Reactivated at Bermuda on 21 February 1951, the first WC-130 Hercules came on strength in 1963. As an airborne early-warning system the Hercules had few equals and their timely information saved millions of dollars worth of property and prevented incalculable loss of life.

When not thus engaged, the WC-130s performed a wide variety of useful functions, including cloud-seeding, using silver iodide crystals to induce rainfall over drought areas, cold-fog-dispersal

[5] See Bill Torpy, 'Doomed plane's takeoff unplanned', article in *The Atlanta Constitution*, 5 February 1993.

[6] The aircrew that fatal day were Olin L. 'Oakie' Bankhead Jr, pilot; Troy Cleveland Castona, flight engineer; Malcolm Jesse Davis, flight engineer; Alan J. McLeroy, engineer; George Dennis Mitchell, engineering test pilot; Veda Ruiz, flight engineer, and William Boyd Southerland, specialist engineer.

[7] See Ron Martz, 'Plane "extensively modified" by Lockheed for test flights', article in *The Atlanta Journal*, 4 February 1993.

operations adjacent to US military airfields in Alaska, Europe and Asia, and patrol work locating and tracking normal winter storms of exceptional violence.

The 53rd was joined by the 815th WRS, AFRES, the 'Storm Trackers', in 1975, and the two units shared the role until the heavy defence cuts of 1991 obliterated the original Air Force 53rd for ever! The 815th then became the sole unit doing the job, and had to divide itself between this duty and its traditional tactical airlift (cargo) role. This rapidly proved impractical, however, and just two years later the unit split into two squadrons, the 815th reverting fully as the 815th TAS 'Flying Jennies', while the weather squadron was resurrected as the 53rd Weather Reconnaissance Squadron, AFRES, still based at Keesler, Biloxi, Mississippi, with currently ten WC-130s as part of the 403rd Wing, and with its proud nickname reinstated.

The first WC-130J was delivered to the USAF at Wright-Patterson AFB on 12 October 1999, and was assigned to the 53rd. She was followed by six more of the same type, with a further three in 2000. The $62.9 million upgrade – the installation and integration of the special avionics and weather sensors, in addition to the structural modifications required – was built in by the Defense Sciences Offices (DSO) original order in September 1998. The sensors mounted on the outside of the WC-130Js provide real-time temperature, humidity, barometric pressure, radar-measured altitude, wind speed and direction. This data is used to calculate a complete weather observation every 30 seconds during the flight. The WC-130J also deploys dropsondes, which are instruments containing high-frequency radio and sensing devices. Each cylindrical dropsonde is small, being approximately 40.6cm (6 inches) in length overall, with a maximum diameter of 8.3cm (3.25 inches). They are ejected from the stern of the aircraft at approximately 644km (400-mile) intervals and are deployed with a small stabilising parachute through the eye of storm areas down to sea level. As they descend they gather a real-time vertical atmosphere profile of weather data, including barometric pressures, humidity, temperature and wind speed, which is relayed back to the aircraft's computers. Once processed by the Dropsonde System Operator (DSO) aboard the parent aircraft, the analysed information is encoded before being relayed by satellite directly to the National Hurricane Centre (NHC) at the Tropical Prediction Centre (TPC) in Miami, Florida, for input into the national weather data networks.

Another modified C-130B served with the Research Flight of the US National Oceanic & Atmospheric Administration (NOAA). As an aerial laboratory for performing atmospheric and oceanic research missions, the Hercules proved invaluable, and she also doubled in her more usual logistic support role in supply and maintenance of far-flung weather research stations.

Maritime patrol

The Hercules had long seemed a natural candidate for the role of a maritime patrol aircraft, combining as she did a long-range, long-endurance, broad-altitude range of operations, superb low-speed handling ability and ample room in a converted cargo compartment for the stowage of specialist equipment. With the US Coast Guard having most successfully featured the HC-130H since 1977, a more specialised variant was expected to be in high demand.

In the 1970s it became common for nations to extend their exclusive economic zones (EEZs), over which they claimed jurisdiction, out to 200 miles (321.86km) from their shoreline, in order to protect their fishing rights, seabed mining, oil-drilling, smuggling prevention, unauthorised shipping entry and pollution monitoring. However, claiming these waters was one thing – protecting them against incursion or intrusion was quite another. What was required was an economical aircraft with long range and endurance able to sweep large areas both frequently and quickly. Strangely enough, the concept never really took off as it was expected to, but Lockheed did introduce a specialised variant designed specifically for this mission, the PC-130H.

Included in the Offshore Zone Patrol and Sea-search package, four observer stations were built into the fuselage forward and aft on a ramp pallet, with scanner seats and observer doors, those forward having large pressurised windows for high-altitude surveillance. Special USCG-type three-window observation doors were located at each side of the rear of the cargo compartment. Also included were high-intensity searchlights, with a 1,000-watt bulb providing 800,000 candlepower, carried on the leading edge of the wing, an Infra-Red (IR) scanner, a passive microwave imager, both search and Doppler navigation radar, a low-light-level (LLL) television, ten flare launch tubes installed on the aft ramp, and five para-drop rescue Medic kits, which were pallet-mounted and featured inflatable rafts in the package.

To photograph the targets by day or night the aircraft were equipped with a Hasselblad camera installed in the floor of the forward cargo compartment, which worked automatically with the Hercules's navigation equipment. Information was relayed and analysed by the aircraft's onboard computer and a resulting matrix, giving a perfect positional fix and time, was superimposed on each frame of film exposed. This provided essential evidence when perusing oil spillage or other pollution issues, disputed fishing ground infringement and the like.

Optional extras included an improved Sea-Search radar (APS-128) carried in the nose, which had dual search/weather radar. The aircraft could ship a rest module for relief crews, a ramp pallet with a rescue kit, flare launchers and loudspeakers, and a rear-looking observation station. They were also extensively galvanised throughout against salt corrosion.

A full crew for the PC-130H was eight men: pilot, co-pilot, flight engineer, navigator and four observers. The flight station and cargo hold were completely pressurised and air-conditioned both in flight and on the ground. To give adequate R&R facilities to crews on long-endurance patrols, there was a seating area and a rest area built into the hull with slide-in modules for crew rest and a two-lavatory/five-bunk/galley. A loudspeaker system was inbuilt.

To increase the range and endurance that maritime patrols entail, the aircraft were powered by four 4,509eshp Allison propjet T56-A-15 lean-burn engines, while the fuel bunkerage was increased with an 1,800-US gallon (6812.74-litre) tank in the fuselage. This gave the PC-130H a maximum range of 5,640 nautical miles (10,445.29km), based on 5% of initial fuel plus 30 minutes reserve. The scenario was that the PC-130H could use all four engines to get out into the patrol area fast, then idle around on just two engines. Thus on a mission of 1,000 miles (1,609.34km) radius with the same reserves, the maritime Hercules could loiter on just two engines at 5,000 feet (1,524m) for a maximum of 15 hours on station; the maximum mission range was 2,517 nautical miles (4,661km) with a search time of 21//2 hours at a mission radius of 1,800 nautical miles (3,334km). Of course, the search time was increased as the mission radius reduced, thus 16 hours of search time could be obtained at a range of 200 nautical miles (371km). Redesignated as the C-130H-MP (Maritime Patrol), such an aircraft seemed ideal also for submarine-hunting, ships and fleet surveillance, or SAR missions.

The first customer of what was expected to be many was the Malaysian Republic, with its myriad of islands and the whole of the South China Sea and parts of the Indian Ocean as part of its defence responsibility. Three C-130H-MPs were ordered in 1980, serials FM2451 (c/n 4847), FM2452 (c/n 4849), the former civilian N4123M, and FM2453 (c/n 4866). The next customer was Malaysia's 'confrontation' rival to the south-east; the *Angkatan Udara Republik* Indonesia, with 13,000 islands to patrol, ordered one aircraft, serial AI-1322 (c/n 4898), which was delivered in late 1981.

However, no further orders resulted.

Minelaying

In the summer of 1981 Lockheed, in conjunction with the US Navy, began a series of experiments to test the practicability of aerial minelaying being conducted from the Hercules. The concept was designated as the Cargo Aircraft Minelayer System (CAML). The Navy contracted Lockheed to built a ground test stand 180 feet (54.86m) long by 25 feet (7.62m) high, and the object of the ten-week test programme, initiated on 1 June, was to functionally evaluate hydraulically powered rapid sequence deployment of mines. The CAML Programme Manager, Joe D. Stites, explained that the test stand would simulate the system's drive and restraint conditions, and would enable engineers to develop the optimum sequence for firing.

The Navy's existing minelaying aircraft at that time included the P-3 patrol bomber and the A-6 and A-7 fighter bombers (the latter with very limited capacity), while the Air Force's B-52 bombers could also be adapted for this role. All had limited payload and range, however, and furthermore had greater priorities for their usage.

The Lockheed system had three major components – the mine-bearing pallets, the control/power pallet, and the ejector module. Each was designed to fit easily into the C-130's cargo

A dummy mine is loaded into USAF C-130H 74-1661 (c/n 4596) during early tests to utilise the Herk as a minelayer under the CAML system. Initial gravity drop tests were conducted by Lockheed and the US Navy at Eglin AFB, Florida, and full-powered tests were carried out in 1981. *Lockheed via Audrey Pearcy*

compartment. The actual mines were loaded in stacks three deep, then rolled into the hold of the Hercules, whereupon the pallets were locked into place using the conventional cargo restraints. At the rear of the loaded mine pallets, the ejector module was inserted on the C-130's cargo ramp, linked to the same hydraulic drive system as the pallets. Ahead of the foremost mine pallet was located the control/power pallet, which also housed the launch operator's control station.

A year prior to this the Hercules had been used at Eglin AFB, Florida, in a series of experimental mine gravity drop tests to examine just how feasible it was to utilise rear-loading aircraft for aerial minelaying operations. This was part of a 22-month development programme conducted for the Naval Surface Weapons Center, located at Silver Spring, Maryland. Some twenty-nine dummy mines were dropped in four sorties, from altitudes that varied from 1,000 to 2,000ft (304.8 to 609.6 metres), with the Hercules flying at a slightly nose-up attitude to simulate the hydraulic-powered thrust. The trials were considered effective and the mines dropped remained stable when thus seeded.

In the event, although the trials were relatively successful, the concept was abandoned as far as Hercules participation was concerned.

Missile and satellite tracking and recovery

In order to track and monitor the behaviour and flight patterns of guided missiles during testing over the Atlantic range, a total of sixteen aircraft were modified between 1958 and 1963. They were USAF serials 53-3129 (c/n 3001); 53-3130 (c/n 3002); 53-3131 (c/n 3003); 53-3132 (c/n 3004); 53-3133 (c/n 3005); 53-3134 (c/n 3006); 53-3135 (c/n 3007); 54-1625 (c/n 3012); 54-1627 (c/n 3014); 54-1628 (c/n 3015); 54-1629 (c/n 3016); 54-1630 (c/n 3017); 54-1639 (c/n 3026); 56-0490 (c/n 3098); 56-0493 (c/n 3101); and 56-0497 (c/n 3105). They were modified from C-130As for Missile Tracking Atlantic with removable test equipment. They carried extra sensor gear and a large radome atop the fuselage. Many were employed by the US Navy during the Polaris submarine-launched IBM launch firing programme to collect telemetry data, and these aircraft were designated as the JC-130A-*LM*. They were mainly based at Patrick AFB, Florida, for these duties, and later most were reconverted back to other duties.

Similar conversions were carried out to fourteen C-130Bs in connection with the location and aerial recovery of satellite capsules on their parachute descent to the oceans. These aircraft were designated as JC-130B-*LM*s and their USAF serials were 57-0525 (c/n 3501); 57-0526 (c/n 3502); 57-0527 (c/n 3503); 57-0528 (c/n 3504); 57-0529 (c/n 3505); 58-0713 (c/n 3508); 58-0714 (c/n 3509); 58-0715 (c/n 3510); 58-0716 (c/n 3511); 58-0717 (c/n 3512); 58-0750 (c/n 3549); 58-0756 (c/n 3557); 61-0962 (c/n 3647); and 61-0963 (c/n 3648).

They were utilised by the USAF Space Systems Division in both the Pacific (by 6593rd Test Squadron at Hickam AFB, Hawaii, for the recovery of Discovery military satellite ejected capsules) and in the Atlantic on the missile ranges. They carried a package of instruments in a radome atop the fuselage for electronic direction finding and tracking, telemetry reception and recording equipment.

In June 1968 USAF JC-130B 57-0526 (c/n 3502) provides a good view of the unique wingtip configuration and radome mounted atop the forward fuselage. *Nick Williams, AAHS*

Another view of the same aircraft in May 1969. *Nick Williams, AAHS*

USAF JC-130B 58-0713 (c/n 3508), of 6593 TS, displays her distinctive flap markings as she touches down at Hickam AFB, Hawaii. *Nick Williams, AAHS*

Fine study of this USAF Hercules JC-130B, 58-0756 (c/n 3557), climbing from Hickam AFB, Hawaii. *Nick Williams, AAHS*

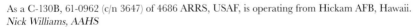

As a C-130B, 61-0962 (c/n 3647) of 4686 ARRS, USAF, is operating from Hickam AFB, Hawaii.
Nick Williams, AAHS

The white radar 'hump' is matched by the leading edges of fin and horizontal tail surfaces on 61-0962. *Nick Williams, AAHS*

Further aerial views of C-130B 61-0962 (c/n 3647) of 4686 ARRS on 21 January 1968. *Both Nick Williams, AAHS*

　　　　THE LOCKHEED MARTIN C-130 HERCULES

Seen taxiing down the pad at Hickam AFB, Hawaii, is JC-130B 58-0717 (c/n 3512). *Nick Williams, AAHS*

Converted JC-130Bs were utilised as aerial recovery vehicles for satellite capsules. *Author's collection*

For recovery of the capsules the Hercules were fitted with the All-American Engineering Company's Aerial Recovery System (ARS), which enabled them to snare their prey in mid-air. This retrieval system comprised a winch with a capacity of 3,000lb (1,360.77kg), an outer dolly and transfer boom, an energy-absorber, an inner dolly, a vehicle carriage, recovery poles and loop and tacks for guiding the dollies' and recovery poles' movements from within the cargo compartment. A control panel was provided at the winch operator's station.

The technique employed for aerial capsule retrieval was that, once positive lock-on of the target had been made, the Hercules positioned itself at not more than 15,000 feet (4,572m) altitude, and adopted a recovery speed of about 125 knots (64.305m/sec). Then the two recovery poles that held the loop in position were extended behind and below the open rear cargo ramp in order to snare the descending parachutes. Once the parachute was snagged, the winch furnished the braking and lifting forces required to arrest the whole package so it could be reeled into the after cargo hold like a fisherman landing his catch.

A further seven HC-130Hs were modified in 1965-66, serials 64-14852 (c/n 4036); 64-14853 (c/n 4037); 64-14854 (c/n 4038); 64-14855 (c/n 4055); 64-14856 (c/n 4072); 64-14857 (c/n 4073); and 64-14858 (c/n 4081). Later most were redesignated as HC-130H in 1986-87.

Personnel transport

Troop movements by air are an essential part of any modern combat scenario, and right from the beginning the Hercules was designed to maximise her potential in this field. With the main cargo compartment both fully pressurised (a first) and air-conditioned, the Herk could be fitted out to accommodate passenger variations that ranged between sixty-four paratroops, ninety-two combat-laden infantrymen or, in a casualty evacuation mode, seventy-four litter cases, stacked five high, together with two medics. Fold-down seating arrangements, which can be stowed between such missions, gave the Herk great versatility, and these also enabled various combinations of the three basic loadings to be made to accommodate all eventualities.

As cargo, heavy weapons and equipment were fully palletised according to type and need, and likewise various passenger-carrying modules were brought into service to fit the ever-changing mission profile of the Hercules. A Seat Conversion Kit capable of seating seventy-five civilians or hospital staff in standard airline-type seats was one refinement. The seats, being mounted on a standard 9g integral seat track, could be mounted on standard cargo pallets, with an all-steel base and fitted with casters to ease loading and unloading during turn-rounds. Separate Toilet and Galley modules could also be accommodated in the same manner, with three seats on either side of a centre aisle. Again, these standard pallets were designed to be interchangeable and flexible, and different loadings could be adopted with the minimum of delay or work involved. Even more luxurious accommodation modules were designed, suitable for the conveyance in some comfort of high-ranking VIPs or military top brass and staff, and these featured recliner seats, with separate modules for conference rooms, and also sleeping and rest rooms. Known as the Staff-Pak, each of these modular containers measured 44 by 88 by 88 inches (111.76 by 223.52 by 223.52cm) and there was also the Lounge-Pak, another totally self-contained unit that houses twenty personnel with seats, tables, bunks and a galley, measuring 10 by 30 by 9 feet (3.048 by 9.144 by 2.74m). These modules could be mounted in any combination straight from the truck and quickly connected up for use.

The record for the number of personnel transported in a Hercules was set up in tragic circumstances during the fall of South Vietnam, abandoned by its democratic allies to the communist northern armies, in 1975. In the final days of the collapse, on 29 April, one South Vietnamese C-130A somehow managed to cram 452 desperate refugees aboard for the last flight from Tan Son Nhut AB to the safety of Utapao, Thailand. The pilot who achieved this incredible feat commented that, 'I counted the people again as we disembarked. It is true – 452 people.'[8]

[8] See Newsbureau press release, 'The Versatile Hercules' – Lockheed-Georgia, Marietta, 1 January 1976.

An impressive line-up of Herks at Tan Son Nhut RVN base on 19 February 1968. In the foreground, with a QW code from Clark AB in the Philippines, is C-130B 60-0309 (c/n 3621) of 463 TAW. *Nick Williams, AAHS*

Pollution control

Although the only specialised Hercules that featured pollution control as one of their main functions were the PC-130Hs (see the appropriate section), which never really took off as a concept, the US Coast Guard has this as one of its mission capabilities.

Early experiments into the feasibility of the Hercules in this role were carried out in the 1970s. One of the Coast Guard's C-130Bs, CG 1350, the former 62-3754 (c/n 3763), was loaded with a pair of modules that held anti-pollution equipment and a fuel container bladder made from rubberised nylon. A simulated wrecked tanker with a large simulated oil slick were provided as the 'target' and the modules were dropped from an altitude of 800 feet. Nine US Marine Corps paratroops set the world free-fall record of 44,100 feet jumping from a Hercules.

Standby Coast Guard ships enabled the equipment to be retrieved and assembled, then connected to the derelict's fuel tanks and the simulated oil was then pumped out before it could leak into the sea. At a pumping rate of 1,300 US gallons (4,921.03 litres) per minute, the bladder siphoned off some 95,000 US gallons (4,354,486.782kg) of the simulated oil in an hour and a half. This, it was estimated, would enable about 4,800 tons of oil to be safely leached from any damaged or stranded tanker within a 24-hour period.

Rescue and relief operations

In the wake of both man-made and natural disasters all around the globe, from flood and famine to earthquake, war refugees and displaced populations, it has become an axiom that among the relief and rescue operations the Hercules is bound to appear. Indeed, if it could be calculated in terms of aid to ease humanitarian suffering around this troubled planet, the ubiquitous Herky Bird would easily prove more enduring than that older, equally welcome feathered friend, the Dove of Peace, the latter being sadly lacking in most places over the last six decades, but the former widespread.

Another trouble-spot erupts: the Congo, July 1960. Following the Security Council resolution of 14 July, authorising UN military assistance to the Republic of the Congo, soldiers from a number of nations were sent in to help restore law and order and impose calm on the rioting country. Here a contingent of Moroccan troops disembarks at Accra Airport, Ghana, en route to the Congo as part of the United Nations force sent to help maintain law and calm in that troubled nation. The Herk in the background is USAF C-130A 55-0006 (c/n 3032) of 314 TCW. *United Nations*

A comprehensive list of every operation in which the Hercules brought succour and some comfort in dire situations worldwide would require more pages than this book can encompass, but here are just a few representative cases down the decades. Others will be found among the illustrations.

Congo

1960	Agadir Earthquake Relief, Morocco
1965	Mendoza, Peru – road-building equipment supplies
1966	Kampuchea
1970s	South-West Africa drought, animal rescue
1973	Nepal
1976	Operation 'Thunderball' – Israeli rescue of hijacked hostages from Entebbe Airport, Uganda, with four C-130s and 245 commando troops
1980	Disastrous American attempt to rescue hostages held at Tabas, Iran, during which one Hercules, serial 62-1809 (c/n 3770), was lost.
1982	Search for Mark Thatcher, lost in the Algerian desert
1983	Operation 'Urgent Fury', Grenada
1984-85	Ethiopia famine relief
1988	Comic Relief aid, Africa
1989-90	Operation 'Just Cause', Panama
1990-92	Operation 'Provide Comfort', northern Iraq
1991	Operation 'Desert Shield'
	Operation 'Desert Storm'
	Operation 'Provide Hope',

Sudan

1992-93	Operation 'Provide Relief', Somalia
	Operation 'Restore Relief', Somalia
1992-94	Operation 'Provide Promise', Bosnia
1992-95	Operation 'Provide Comfort II', southern Iraq
1992	Sierra Leone I

Angola
1993	Operation 'Provide Hope II' –

Somalia

1995-97	Operation 'Joint Endeavour', Balkans
1997	Operation 'Bevel Edge', Cambodia
1999	Operation 'Stabilise', East Timor
2010	Operation 'Ice', Haiti

Many others are recorded elsewhere in these pages, and in other places[9]. Areas of rescue and relief operations range from Jordan and Turkey, through earthquake succour in Iran, Italy, Morocco, Nicaragua, Peru and Venezuela, famine relief from the Bay of Bengal to Chile, typhoon aftermath flights in Guam and Japan, hurricane relief flights to Harrisburg and Wilkes-Barre, Pennsylvania, Richmond, Virginia, Terre Haute, Indiana and Moline, Illinois, in the wake of Hurricane 'Agnes', and to Biloxi and Gulfport, Mississippi, after Hurricane 'Camile' the same year, together with cholera epidemics and food famine relief flights all over Africa (Congo and Chad) and in Nepal. They even helped save the roan antelope from extinction in southern Africa, airlifting tranquillised animals from the desert sands to protected areas. The odds are high that, even as you read these words, somewhere in the world a Herky Bird is bring hope and help to a despairing people. It is her finest legacy.

[9] See, for typical examples, 'Lockheed's Hercules – The goodwill aircraft', article in *Interavia* magazine, June 1972, and Earl and Miriam Selby, 'Hercules – Workhorse of the Air', article in *Readers Digest*, 1983.

At Accra Airport on 17 July 1960 the Moroccan contingent of United Nations soldiers lines up to embark aboard USAF C-130A 60-0529 (c/n 3137) for their transportation to the Congo. *United Nations*

How many evacuees can you cram into a Hercules? In many places and at many times the answer has been given, even if it varies. The official design accommodation for the C-130 is ninety-two persons, but here no fewer than 180 evacuees are jammed into the capacious hold of a USAF C-130. They are Indian refugees for a flight, under United Nations sponsorship, to move them from the overcrowded Tripura state to the less crowded Assam state in 1982. *Lockheed-Georgia Newsbureau*

Typical of the many mercy missions conducted by the Hercules down the decades, Indian families are transported to safe areas after floods devastated their homes. In the background stands a Pope AFB C-130E, 63-7803 (c/n 3869), of 779 TAS. *Lockheed*

Equipped with Tracor ALE-40 flare and chaff defences as part of the 'Snowstorm' system developed by Lockheed for UN flights over Bosnia, a C-130 gives a full defensive display. *Swedish Air Force official*

Australian troops of the international peacekeeping force embark on an RAAF C-130E Hercules transport at Darwin RAAF base to take part in Operation 'Stabilise' in East Timor, following the Indonesian military atrocities there after the independence referendum in September 1999. *Australian Defence Headquarters, Canberra*

Supplier Flight Sergeant Ray Loxley, from 1ATS DET Williamstown Air Movements, marshals a 36 Squadron, RAAF, Hercules on East Timor on 30 September 1999. *Australian Defence Headquarters, Canberra*

An RAAF C-130 departs from Dili Airfield on 30 September 1999 during the troubles in East Timor. *Australian Defence Headquarters, Canberra*

C-130E A97-172 (c/n 41720) of No 37 Squadron, RAAF, unloads medical equipment at Dili Airfield. *Australian Defence Headquarters, Canberra*

Short Take-off and Landing (STOL) and Jet Assisted Take-off (JATO)

Coupled with the unpaved runway capability (see the appropriate section), the ease with which the Hercules could get airborne from primitive landing fields with heavy burdens was another factor in making this aircraft legendary. The Short Take-off and Landing (STOL) requirement was built into the original design and was continually refined in subsequent models.

Lockheed had a multi-level approach to the subject of STOL, and many different configurations, which changed the aerodynamics of the wing and tail surfaces in order to facilitate lower take-off and landing speeds, coupled with better control. Double-slotted wing flaps with roll-control spoilers were fitted, a longer chord rudder and a larger dorsal fin were trialled together with new 'horsal' fins, and anti-skid brake gear was fitted.

An STOL take-off by 64-14863 (c/n 4094). *Lockheed-Georgia, Marietta, via Audrey Pearcy*

Both the High Technology Test Bed (HTTB) and the Boundary Layer Control experiments were offshoots of this facet of the Hercules's operational profile (see the appropriate sections). The C-130SS, the stretch/STOL and the C-130 'Option II-A' proposals were all Lockheed ideas to tackle and improve on the same area and meet the USAF AMST requirement to operate in and out of 2,000-foot (609.6m) unimproved strips with 27,000lb (12,246.99kg) of payload.

The fitting of Aerojet 15KS-1000 Jet Assisted Take-off (JATO) bottles (in two sets of four strapped either side of the rear fuselage), which developed 1,000lb (454kg) of thrust for additional boost during take-offs, was trialled with a modified C-130E-I, serial 64-0558 (c/n 4059), by 2 Detachment, 1 Special Operations Squadron, between 1967 and 1969, and later by the 318 Special Operations Squadron between 1971 and 1972, before that particular aircraft was lost in a collision with an F-102A over Myrtle Beach, South Carolina, on 5 December 1972. Each unit burns for just 15 seconds before abruptly cutting off. Use of this method reduced the length of the take-off from 1,000 feet (305m) to 790 feet (240m) at the designed weight of 108,000lb (48,988kg). This fitment became standard provision for all C-130As.

US Marines 'Blue Angels' support aircraft 149806 (c/n 3703) is boosted off by JATO bottles. *Jeffrey Wood, via Audrey Pearcy*

USMC C-130B 149804 (c/n 3695) of VMGR-352, Miramar MCAS, completes a JATO-assisted take-off from the McDonnell test field at Lakeside, California, in 1973. *Both McDonnell Douglas*

JATO equipment in place on a ski-equipped New York National Guard C-130. *Courtesy of Ben Jones*

The US Marines VMGR-352 also employed this method with a KC-130F, serial 149805 (c/n 3695), and the 'Blue Angels' TC-130-G support aircraft, serial 151891 (c/n 3878), also employed the system to add to the spectacle. This method was used extensively, especially in Antarctica, but was inherently dangerous, as witnessed in the loss of an LC-130F – serial 148321, ex-59-5925 (c/n 3567) – on 4 December 1971 when one JATO bottle separated from its mounting and struck the aircraft, causing the take-off from Carrefour D59 landing ground to be aborted and resulting in a crash-landing. The aircraft then lay ice-bound for fifteen years before being recovered.

A KC-130F of VMGR-352 fuelling two McDonnell F-4 Phantoms. *McDonnell Douglas, via Audrey Pearcy*

On 18 March 1987, covered by a fifteen-year accumulation of Antarctic ice and snow, US Navy LC-130F ski-equipped Hercules 148321 (c/n 3567) was pulled out of its icy grave in a remote region. The aircraft was uncovered in stages, first by hand and then by bulldozers. She was part of the Ski-Bird airlift fleet operated by the US Navy for the National Science Foundation (NSF), and suffered an aborted ski take-off from an open snowfield some 700 miles from McMurdo Sound, on 4 December 1971, while airlifting out a contingent of scientists. The pilot aborted the take-off and made a hard landing on the East Antarctic Ice Sheet. All the crew and passengers walked away safely. *Lockheed-Georgia, Marietta, via Audrey Pearcy*

Over a decade and a half after its aborted landing, the abandoned LC-130F was covered by ice and snow apart for the top 3 feet of the plane's 38-foot-high vertical stabiliser. Lockheed and Navy engineers who examined the aircraft found her structurally sound and fit, requiring just six weeks of preliminary repair before she could be flown out. The NSF was hopeful that this could be done and that the aircraft could be placed back in service. Dr Peter Wilkniss, director of the NSF Polar Programs Division, called the recovery 'a major feat'. The aircraft herself, with just 14,000 flight hours, he described as '...slightly used and rested for 15 years'. The LC-130 ski-equipped Hercules revolutionised the scientific exploration of Antarctica. The US Navy operated seven or eight such aircraft, which, during the 'off season', were based at Point Magu, California. *Lockheed*

Numerous examples of incredible landings and take-offs by the Hercules have been recorded down the decades. On 31 December 1966 a US Coast Guard HC-130B, piloted by Lieutenant Commander Clyde Robbins and Lieutenant Chester Wawrzynski, was brought down safely on the 2,500-foot gravel strip at Baja, Mexico, on a mission to pick up an injured seaman. Their recorded stopping time was 1,300 feet (396.24m) – lots of reverse thrust helped – and they also got safely off again with their patient. The same pilot also got down on the 2,380-foot (725.42m) strip at Bridgewater, California, which, located at an altitude of 7,000 feet (2133.6m), was hemmed in by the Sweetwater Mountains. Using JATO he got her safely up and out again.

Ski operations

In order to extend the useful area of operations of the versatile and indispensable Hercules to cover the snow- and ice-bound regions of the globe, a proposal was made as early as 1956 for the fitting of skis on this large aircraft. In particular, the supply and support of the Distant Early Warning (DEW) line of radar stations, constructed across Alaska and Greenland to give maximum warning of an incoming Soviet missile strike across the North Pole, was considered essential. A feasibility study was undertaken and one C-130A, serial 55-021 (c/n 3048), was modified accordingly, emerging in her new configuration of 29 January 1957. She retained her normal wheeled undercarriage and had a special nose ski and two main skis fitted over them.

A Herk over a snowy landscape. *Author's collection*

The nose ski was 3 metres (10 feet) in length and 1.8 metres (6 feet) wide, while the main skis measured 6 metres (20 feet) in length and had a width of 1.8 metres (6 feet), and weighed about 907kg (2,000lb). Each ski under-surface was Teflon-coated, which both lessened surface friction and ice and snow cling. While putting ski-fitted Hercules down on the deck proved similar to a conventional landing, getting the big bird airborne proved more problematical. A longer take-off run proved necessary, and a quartet of JATO bottles strapped on to each aircraft's flank for Rocket-Assisted Take-offs (RATO), each capable of an additional 1,000lb of thrust per 12-second burn, helped matters considerably.

These skis could only be raised or lowered with the undercarriage in the down position. Before the normal landing gear retracted, the skis automatically moved to the lowered position, and as the gear retracted they were drawn up against a fairing on the fuselage. The landing gear doors were therefore omitted. Two 'skegs' were fitted to the after ends of the nose skis, which made the normal nose-wheel steering system effective for directional control. Under normal conditions a utility hydraulic pressure system operated the skis, but should this fail, an emergency hydraulic system supplied pressure directly to the actuators via shuttle valves, which brought the skis from their lowered position to the raised position only. Ski unlocks and downlocks were achieved by blocking hydraulic fluid in the actuators. The aircraft pneumatic system was altered to allow for a hot bleed air flow to melt snow and ice from the external ports, while an air hose could be plugged into the regular external air supply coupling, positioned above the Gas Turbine Compressor (GTC) exhaust, and a check valve override control (with control located inside a small door aft the GTC exhaust above the main wheel wells) permitted the overboard flow of bleed air from the engine bleed air manifold.

In order to deal with the enormous distances involved between suitable landing sites, extra reserve and emergency fuel capacity was another essential built in, and these aircraft had a pair of 450-gallon under-wing pylon fuel tanks with the provision to embark a further two 500-gallon tanks in the cargo compartment. In 1966 a more permanent provision was made with the installation of a pair of 450-gallon fuel tanks in the inboard wing dry-bay area. This gave the original C-130D a return range of 2,296km (1,240 nautical miles) against the comparable Fairchild C-123J Provider's 1,430km (772 nautical miles) with the same 4,454kg (9,820lb) payload, and the Herk could do it at a higher cruising speed.

Thus equipped, and with JATO bottles to help with lift-off, this aircraft undertook a series of practical trials in Minnesota and Greenland. The outcome proved quite satisfactory and she was reconfigured back to a normal C-130A at the conclusion of the programme.

A series run of twelve ski-equipped Hercules was initiated, with late-production-line C-130As (airframes and engines) being completed as C-130Ds: serials 57-0484 (c/n 3191); 57-0485 (c/n 3192); 57-0486 (c/n 3193); 57-0487 (c/n 3194); 57-0488 (c/n 3195); 57-0489 (c/n 3196); 57-0490 (c/n 3197); 57-0491 (c/n 3198); 57-0492 (c/n 3199); 57-0493 (c/n 3200); 57-0494 (c/n 3201); and 57-0495 (c/n 3202). All these aircraft were allocated to the USAF Troop Carrier Squadrons (TCS) from January 1959 onward.

Ski-equipped C-130 57-0491 (c/n 3198). *Courtesy of Ben Jones*

In 1962-63 six of these aircraft had their skis removed once more and were redesignated C-130D-6s: they were serials 57-0484 (c/n 3191); 57-0485 (c/n 3192); 57-0486 (c/n 3193); 57-0487 (c/n 3194); 57-0488 (c/n 3195); and 57-0489 (c/n 3196). One aircraft, 57-0495 (c/n 3202), which carried the name *Frozen Assets* in the 1960s, and later *The Harker* in the 1970s, stalled and overshot at the Dye III landing strip east of Söndeström on 5 June 1972 and was written off. In 1975 the surviving aircraft were allocated to the 139th TAS, New York Air National Guard (ANG), and continued in operation until they were replaced by the LC-130Hs, the last retiring in April 1985.

Under lowering skies at Schlechty Airfield, New York, is C-130D 57-0487 (c/n 3194) *Hustling Husky*, of 109 TSAG, 139 TAS. *Nick Williams, AAHS*

Further examples of the type were requested and two standard C-130As, 57-0473 (c/n 3180) and 57-0474 (c/n 3181), were duly modified and served for a brief period under the designation C-130D, before converting back to C-130As once more.

The US Navy also had a use for ski-equipped Hercules aircraft, and in a similar manner four such aircraft – serials 148318, ex-59-5922 (c/n 3562); 148319, ex-59-5923 (c/n 3564); 148320, ex-59-5924 (c/n 3565); and 148321, ex-59-5925 (c/n 3567) – were ordered by the USAF as the C-130BL on behalf of the Navy. On delivery the Navy redesignated them as the UV-1L and they served as such until September 1962, when they received a new designation, becoming the LC-130F-*LM*.

Officials from the National Science Foundation and US Navy examine the special Antarctic ski fitting on an LC-130F, fresh off the line at Marietta. *Lockheed-Georgia, Marietta, via Audrey Pearcy*

THE LOCKHEED MARTIN C-130 HERCULES

A US Navy pilot straddles the front ends of the special Hercules LC1-30F 'Icebird' skis to give some indication of their size. *Lockheed-Georgia, Marietta, via Audrey Pearcy*

At Byrd Station, Antarctica, two LC-130F ski-fitted Herks of the US Navy's Development Squadron Six, VXE-6, 148319 (c/n 3564) and 148320 (c/n 3565), are ready to return to McMurdo Station. They have brought in supplies and equipment during Operation 'Deep Freeze' on 18 October 1968. *Navy Photograph Center, Washington DC*

On 26 October 1968 a propeller change is under way for an LC-130F at Williams AFB, Antarctica. The bleak, featureless icescape stretches away on all sides. *Navy Photograph Center, Washington DC*

Close-up detail of the front of the ski fixture on US Navy LC-130F 148321 (c/n 3567). This aircraft belonged to VXE-6 and is seen at NAS Barbers Point in June 1969. *Nick Williams, AAHS*

A starboard close-up of the equipment on the same aircraft. *Nick Williams, AAHS*

A long, long way from Georgia! Ski-equipped LC-130F 155917 (c/n 4305) of the US Navy is pictured on 22 December 1969 on the runway at the Soviet Vostok Station in Antarctica after bringing supplies to the Russian scientists there. *Navy Photograph Center, Washington DC*

A dramatic view of LC-130F Hercules 148318 (c/n 3562) blasting off from the ice strip at Beardmore Station, Antarctica, on 31 January 1970. *Navy Photograph Center, Washington DC*

LC-130F 148319 (c/n 3564) of XVE-6 on the ice runway at Beardmore in January 1970. *Navy Photograph Center, Washington DC*

An excellent close-up view of the forward ski arrangement on US Navy LC-130F 155917 (c/n 4305) as she takes off from the Annual Ice Runway at Williams AFB on 21 October 1970. *Navy Photograph Center, Washington DC*

THE LOCKHEED MARTIN C-130 HERCULES

A close-up of a US Navy LC-130F of VXE-6 having a bent propeller replaced in December 1970. The prop was damaged when the aircraft was blown off the runway as she touched down. *Navy Photograph Center, Washington DC*

An LC-130F of VXE-6 lifts off from the Annual Ice Runway for a resupply flight to the Ross Ice Shelf Scientific Drilling site on 23 October 1978. *Navy Photograph Center, Washington DC*

A ski-fitted New York National Guard Herk with rockets attached. *Courtesy of Ben Jones*

THE LOCKHEED MARTIN C-130 HERCULES

Warming up a USAF ski-fitted LC-130F. This and the previous photograph were taken on 13 June 2009 at ANC International during a brief visit, probably for a crew change. *Courtesy of Ben Jones*

They were operated by the US Navy's VX-6 unit (later redesignated as VXE-6 and christened 'Penguin Airline') as a key part of the 1960 Operation 'Deep Freeze', the supply and logistical support of the US Antarctic Survey programme, in conjunction with the National Science Foundation (NSF); the ski-fitted Hercules replaced the Douglas R4D hitherto used in that role. The four aircraft were all given names – 148313 became *City of Christchurch*, 148319 *Penguin Express*, 148320 *The Emperor* and 148321 *The Crown* – and all suffered accidents during their careers, but only the first-named was totally destroyed. In order to conduct a radar strip chart recording of the earth's surface beneath the Greenland icecap as part of the NSF Greenland Ice Sheet Project, one Navy LC-130, 148319 (c/n 3564), carrying the unique tail-marking letters JD, was modified with the installation of antenna arrays that operated on 60 and 300mc. The dipole antennae were horizontally polarised and were built with a balsa core, fibreglass outer skin and aluminium covering. The four 300mc antennae were carried under the port wing and were easily replaceable. The VHF radars were developed by the Technical University of Denmark for this work. In addition to the surface recordings, the installations simultaneously recorded icecap surface contours and variations in sub-surface strata layers in the ice. The aircraft flew from Söndeström Air Base in Greenland. The surviving three aircraft were retired when VXE-6 was disbanded in 1999.

The upper forward cabin area of ski-equipped LC-130F 148318 (c/n 3562) *City of Christchurch*, coded JD, of the US Navy's VXE-6 seen at NAS Barbers Point in June 1969. *Nick Williams, AAHS*

Ski-equipped LC-130F 145917 (c/n 4305) was also photographed on the same day. *Nick Williams, AAHS*

Ski-equipped LC-130F 148318 (c/n 3562) *City of Christchurch*, coded JD, of the US Navy's VXE-6 seen at NAS Barbers Point in June 1969. *Nick Williams, AAHS*

Seen on the same occasion is ski-equipped LC-130F 148320 (c/n 3565) *The Emperor. Nick Williams, AAHS*

Also present was 148321 (c/n 3567) *The Crown. Nick Williams, AAHS*

To replace the USAF's ageing ski-equipped C-130Ds, in 1985 four C-130Hs – 83-0490 (c/n 5007) *Pride of Clifton Park*, 83-0491 (c/n 5010) *Pride of Albany*, 83-0492 (c/n 5013) *City of Amsterdam* and 83-0493 (c/n 5016) *Pride of Scotia* – suitably equipped, were delivered to the 139th TAS, New York ANG. Ten years later another three ski-equipped aircraft were due to be delivered to the 139th TAS late in 1995, serials 92-1094 (c/n 5402), 92-1095 (c/n 5405) and 93-1096 (c/n 5410). Two of this trio also received names; 92-1094 became *Pride of Grenville* while 92-1096 took the now traditional name of *City of Christchurch NZ*. All these aircraft carry the designation LC-130H.

In a similar manner the NSF replaced its ski-equipped fleet with six special aircraft: serials 155917 (c/n 4305); 159129, ex-73-0839 (c/n 4508); 159130, ex-73-0840 (c/n 4516); 159131, ex-73-0841 (c/n 4522); 160740, ex-76-0491 (c/n 4725); and 160741, ex-76-0492 (c/n 4731). These received the designation LC-130R-*LM* and were, as before, operated for the NSF by US Navy squadron VC-6/VXE-6. As expected in such a hostile element, there were accidents, serial 155917 being involved in no fewer than three in 1975 and 1987 before being finally terminally damaged and written off charge. Serial 160740 crashed at Starshot Glacier, Antarctica, in December 1984 and lay in the snow for fourteen years until it was repaired in 1998. Dr Peter Wilkniss, of the NSF's Polar Programs Division, jested that she was, after all, 'only slight used' and that she had merely 'rested for fifteen years'! She was returned to service with the 139th AS, 109th AW, ANG, based at Schenectady County Airport, New York State, together with BuNo 160741.

All these aircraft received similar modifications to the standard models to enable them to operate within the Arctic, Antarctic, Alaska and Greenland. The ski installations were the largest ever to be incorporated on an aircraft and were designed to allow either wheeled or ski operation without further modification. By attaching the ski adaptations to the conventional landing equipment and arranging it so that they could be raised or lowered when the landing gear was in the lowered position, the resultant mechanism was extremely versatile.

The main ski 'shoes' fitted around the landing gear of the LC-130R are made of aluminium, with the bottom surfaces coated with Teflon plastic, which ensures completely free sliding in both snow and slush. The Teflon has the added advantage of minimising the freeze-down rate when the aircraft is parked. They are approximately 20.5 feet (6.25m) long and 5.5 feet (1.68m) wide and weight about 2,100lb (952.54kg). The solitary nose ski is 10.3 feet (3.14m) long and the same width as the main gear. Both the main skis and the nose ski have 8° nose-up and 15° nose-down pitch to enable them to coast over uneven terrain. The combined total weight of the ski gear and associated plumbing is 5,600lb (2,540.11kg). The equivalent reduction in the maximum payload of both the C-130D and the LC-130F was the penalty on ski or wheels, while for the LC-130R it was for wheels only. However, the LC-130R could not utilise its higher payload capability due to the fact that skis were not uprated to cope with the increased structural design weight of the C-130H.

The power plants on all were the same as for the standard C-130 equivalents. However, although the LC-130F original used the T56-A-7 engines, these were subsequently changed for T56-A-16s, which were flat-rated to 4,508eshp for take-off, for higher performance. The turning radii for skis came out at 122 feet (37.185m) for the wing tip turning radius and 64.5 feet (19.464m) for the nose gear.

The *Fuerza Aérea Argentina* also used about half a dozen Hercules to supply its bases in Antarctica, and some were fitted with RATOG and flew on skis. Other tasks have included the airlifting of machinery, vehicles, fruit, meat and other products all over South America and to African destinations, while the importation of 35 tons of soya beans from the USA was conducted by its C-130Bs. In 1974 an Argentine C-130 made a record first flight from Buenos Aires, across Antarctica to Australia and New Zealand.

Special concepts and conversions

Diverse and numerous as the speciality Herk designations became, some aircraft merit special attention as 'one-offs', which either acted as pioneers for variants to come, or were the answer to a specific mission profile and were never repeated. Among them were the following.

C-130BLC (serial 58-0712, c/n 3507)

This became the STOL test aircraft involved in the Boundary Layer Control experiments.

C-130J

This designation was originally briefly assigned to an Advance Assault Hercules concept, a modified version of the C-130E that incorporated the Assault Landing Gear. A new main gear oleo strut allowed 25 inches of wheel travel in order to dissipate the heavy shock and jarring received in rough field operations. Nose gear was redesigned and strengthened for the same reason and enabled operations to take place on airstrips with protruding obstacles and depressions up to 10 inches high or deep. A new and larger main gear fairing was deemed essential to house the main gear and the lower forward fuselage and radome were adapted for the new landing gear.

The rudder chord was to have been increased by 40%, giving increased directional control and lower engine minimum control speed. The aileron chord was increased by 30% to increase the low-speed rolling capability, while the flaps were modified to increase the maximum deflection to 50° and the elevator re-indexed to provide 5° additional down elevator deflection. Both rudder and aileron controls systems were actuated by fully powered servo systems. The A-15 engine replaced the A-7 and the propeller gearbox ratio was changed to 12.49:1, and this, combined with the additional rudder control, permitted the A-15 to be operated at the maximum rating of 4,591shp. The fuel tanks were given small arms fire protection, and there was an improved rate-of-sink indicator as well as an integrated instrument system.

This designation was soon abandoned and became the C-130SS (see below).

C-130SS

Another concept featuring stretch and enhanced STOL performance, this aircraft would have featured double-slotted flaps and roll-control spoilers and was Lockheed's reply to the Boeing YC-14 and McDonnell Douglas YC-15 projects. At a projected cost of $7.4 million per aircraft, including the development and production costs, this would be a fraction of the unit cost envisaged for these two fanjet models being prototyped for the AMST programme in 1976.

Based on the basic C-130 airframe, the C-130SS would feature a 100-inch fuselage stretch, a strengthened wing, a longer-chord rudder, a larger dorsal fin, new 'horsal' fins, a higher-strength landing gear and a new anti-skid braking system. Low-speed control would also be enhanced.

The strengthened wing would allow the aircraft to carry a 30,000lb (13,607.77kg) payload in a 3g flight manoeuvre on tactical or assault missions, and the designed landing gear structural strength would be increased to permit the same payload at a design sink rate of 15 feet per second (4.572m/sec). The penalty would be an increase in the aircraft's empty weight by 8,300lb (3,764.816kg), although Lockheed was to claim that '... this additional weight would increase structural strength, permitting significant increases in gross weight on strategic or routine airlift missions.'[10] The stretch was achieved by a 60-inch (1.52m) plug section forward of the wing and a 40-inch (1.016m) plug aft of the wing, which increased the cargo compartment length from 40.4 feet to 48.7 feet (12.313 to 14.84m), giving room for one additional 463L pallet. This was an increase of 85sq ft (7.896m^2) of floor area, to a total of 501.6sq ft (46.6m^2). Clear cube volume was to be increased by 769cu ft (21.664m^3) to a total of 4,514cu ft (127.878m^3). The new Hercules's palletised payload would increase from five to six pallets, or from 25,000 to 30,000lb (11,339.80 to 13,607.77kg) of cargo at an average of 5,000lb (2,267.96kg) per pallet.

The C-130SS would, it was claimed, carry a high percentage of US Army vehicles of the five type of divisions, 99.4% of airborne vehicles, 93.5% of infantry vehicles, 88% of mechanised vehicles and 87% of armoured division vehicles. Even those vehicles that would not fit into the Hercules, such as tanks and helicopters, would not fit the proposed replacements either, it was stated.

Two thousand hours of wind tunnel testing on the C-130SS was supplemented by STOL experience from the Boundary Layer Control aircraft tests. Lockheed further claimed that the new design could meet a mid-point, 2,000-foot (609.5m) assault runway requirement with a 3g payload of 30,000lb (13,607.77kg) for a 400-nautical mile (740.8 km) tactical mission.

Lockheed also pointed out the turboprop versus fanjet advantages, in that it considered the propeller more efficient for generation of take-off thrust and lift, since it acted upon a greater mass of air than the fan, but also that the slipstream affected the entire flap span, giving maximum lift effectiveness. By contrast, it was claimed, '…the propulsive lift of the fanjet engines in which the fan exhaust is concentrated over a smaller part of the flap span, and lift had to be attained by the addition of heavy, expensive and complicated equipment, such as ducting, valves or variable geometry nozzles.'[11] It was also stated that a modern high-bypass-ratio fan engine burned about half again as much fuel per pound of take-off thrust as did the C-130 turboprop, and that this was particularly significant on STOL aircraft. Lockheed claimed at that time that a fanjet-powered aircraft of similar size to the Hercules would require, on average, almost twice as much fuel to perform a typical mission of 400 nautical miles (740.8km) radius than the C-130 with an identical payload. Thus a fanjet would be twice as expensive to buy and operate, yet, while faster, the mission time required was only a few minutes less than that of the C-130 on short-range tactical assault missions.

It was conceded by Lockheed that the fanjet design was superior on two counts: the fuselage size could be made wider using C-5 philosophy, and the fan engines could provide some minutes of speed advantage. Lockheed proposed to the Air Force that two current production C-130Hs be modified to the C-130SS configuration for comparison trials, but the offer was not taken up.

EC-130E (serial CG 1414, c/n 4158)
This was a US Coast Guard aircraft that became the Loran A&C calibration test bed.

EC-130V (serial CG1721, c/n 5121)
This was a US Coast Guard HC-130H modified and fitted in 1992 by General Dynamics as a 'proof of concept' machine, combining an AN/APS-125 radar in a large rotodome and a ready-to-load 'palleted' US Navy 'Hawkeye' Mission System (MS) for early warning and detection usage. Cuts in the Coast Guard budget forced the early aborting of this experiment, and the aircraft was subsequently transferred to the USAF as the NC-130H 87-0157, working with 514 Test Squadron then 418 Test Squadron. She was again transferred to the US Navy at Patuxent River in 2000, becoming its 0157 870157, and conducted E-2C trials with the non-rotating radome. She continues to be employed by PEMCO as a test bed for the AN/APS-145 with the E-2C 'Hawkeye 2000' radar system.

AEWAC
Lockheed and the USAF are looking at AEWAC variants of a stretched C-130J with a new engine and propeller combination and a digital flight station for two pilots. A AN/APS-145 would be carried on pylons above the rear fuselage, like the EC-130V. A tactical command centre (TCC) and crew modules would be located in the hold with 7 operator consoles with the Northrop Grumman (ESID) Group II+ missile system emplaced.

---

[10] See 'The C-130SS – Lockheed Offers new Stretch/STOL Hercules at a fraction of the unit cost of the AMST', Lockheed Newsbureau, G-52176-1303N, 1976.

[11] Ibid

HOW

This acronym ('Hercules on Water') described the test bed flying-boat version of the Hercules with an elongated nose, reshaped ventral hull, wing-mounted floats and a hydro-ski, with US Navy requirements in mind. With regard to combat freight loading, HOW indeed!

HTTB (registration N130X, c/n 4412)

This became a Lockheed High Technology Test Bed aircraft that conducted vital research in the development of the C-130J programme.

JHC-130P (serial 65-0988, c/n 4143)

This was modified from an HC-130P for the ARRS for tests.

RC-130A (serial 54-1632, c/n 3019)

This was a proposed Hercules training aircraft variant prototype, modified from a standard C-130A. She was later rebuilt for the ATS as a Photo-Reconnaissance (PR) prototype, before again reverting to C-130A status.

TC-130A (serial 54-1632, c/n 3019)

This was both a prototype for the proposed TC-130A Training aircraft and for the RC-130A.

VC-130B (serial 58-0715, c/n 3510)

This was a JC-130B especially modified as a VIP transport. She later once more reverted to C-130B status.

W.2 (serial XV208, c/n 4233)

One of the most extraordinary (and ugly) aircraft ever to fly, this was a Marshalls of Cambridge modification of an RAF standard C.1 with an elongated nose probe and scientific instrument suites (internally displacing the radar scanner to an under-wing pod) for meteorological research duties. The 26-foot-long proboscis, painted with red-and-white stripes, had a laser projector and camera to take three-dimensional pictures of cloud samples.

The W.2 was operated from 31 March 1973 by the A&AEE at RAE Farnborough, then by DERA from Boscombe Down. She was nicknamed 'Snoopy'.

Most of these aircraft are more fully described in their own sections.

Training

Currently the bulk of USAF C-130 aircrew training is conducted by the 314th Airlift Wing, based at Little Rock AFB, Arkansas. This Wing is part of Air Education & Training Command, and has at its disposal the largest C-130 training fleet in the world. Its multiple squadrons and forty-four C-130s train not only USAF pilots but all the aircrew for the Department of Defense, US Coast Guard and twenty-seven foreign operators as well. The Wing also hosts the 463rd Air Mobility Command (AMC) group and the 189th Airlift Wing (Arkansas Air National Guard), which provides global tactical airlift capability. The 314th Wing has four groups – operations, logistics, support and medical – plus the HQ element. The 'Schoolhouse' is made up of two airlift squadrons, 53rd AS and 62nd AS, and the 314th Operations Support Squadron, together with the flight simulator contractor. The 189th Airlift Wing assists in the C-130 training programme in times of peace. The 463rd Airlift Group, with two Airlift Squadrons, 50th and 61st, carries out operational airlift missions worldwide, while the AMWC Combat Aerial Delivery School provides aircrews with graduate-level instruction in C-130 tactical employment.

Lockheed at Marietta is in itself a major training facility, with conversion training to the C-130 of thousands of foreign pilots, flight engineers, navigators and loadmasters from more than fifty nations over the decades. Courses vary from customer to customer, but a typical scenario for the Royal Thai Air Force was an eight-week ground school instruction that included a study of aircraft systems performance standards, weight and balance information, and emergency and normal operational procedure theory. Next came four weeks of flight training, with the emphasis on landing and taking off, instrument approach, stalls, day and night flying, emergency procedures, including engine-out landings, engine failure on take-off, and short field landings and take-offs,

A C-130 of the 50th Airlift Squadron lands at Little Rock AFB during Operation 'Millennium Challenge' in 2002. *Tom Bradbury, US Department of Defense official*

Royal Air Force and US Air Force C-130s each drop flares over central Arkansas during an Inter-Fly exercise. The low-level exercise was part of a week-long joint training mission between British and American airmen. *Staff Sergeant Norris Chandler, US official*

with flights conducted over northern Georgia, and instrument and visual landings at Dobbins AFB and municipal airports at Chattanooga, Tennessee, Huntsville, Alabama and Augusta, Georgia. The final phase was in-country operational training, which included long-range navigation operations on high-density traffic routes and short field take-off and landing from unpaved airstrips.

Unpaved airfield operation

From the earliest conception of the Hercules, the ability to work out of primitive airstrips in areas far distant from civilisation has always been a priority. The subsequent history of the Herk over five decades of peace and war has enshrined this versatility into its design and ensured that, whatever the situation on the ground, if any large transport could get in and out of dirt, mud, gravel, grass, asphalt or ice, the C-130 was usually the one to do so!

In a demonstration of the large aircraft's outstanding STOL ability, HC-130H 64-4863 (c/n 4094) lifts off from a 2,000-foot dirt strip at Elgin Air Force Base, Florida. Rough field tests conducted early in the Herk's career proved the rugged airlifter's ability to operate from unimproved airstrips. The tests included landing rollouts in which the aircraft sank deeper than 20 inches into the ground. As a result of its proven capability on such missions, the Hercules was used extensively during the Vietnam War as an assault tactical transport, landing and taking off from hundreds of rough, short strips in South East Asia. Subsequently her worldwide role found her able to operate with ease from sandy strips in the Sahara, unimproved dirt runways in Asia, Africa and South America, and frozen lake runways in Alaska. *Lockheed*

A great deal of study into the surface hardness and bearing strengths of differing types of unpaved landing sites the world over had already been made. The standard measuring methods to estimate these factors were the Modulus of Soil Reaction, known simply as the K-factor, or the California Bearing Ration (CBR), which grades surfaces on a scale of 1 to 10 CBR according to materials and the amount of moisture contained at a given time. With this measure the hardness and resistance to various types of aircraft and load displacements can be worked out and performance measured against it. The degree with which an aircraft can operate from such surfaces depends not only on the total weight of the aircraft and its loading, but on the spread of the load across the main undercarriage and the manoeuvrability and steerability of the aircraft to enable it to both touch down safely and 'unstick' from semi-boggy morasses or shifting sand-strips.

With her dual-wheel nose layout, combined with the reverse thrust of her engines, its wide distribution of load across the tricycle landing gear, and its single tandem wheels fitted with large-diameter, wide, low-pressure tyres, the Hercules came out well in the tests on the latter. These factors give the C-130 excellent flotation ability, and any doubts on the soundness of the many tests and experiments have been dispelled in hard practice time and time again down the years; the luxury of hard concrete or asphalt airfields has been a distinct rarity in Herk relief and combat operations.

The accompanying table shows the flotation characteristics of early model C-130s with the 'D' distance representing the gap between the rear of the lead tyre and the front of the after tyre on the main gear.

	C-130A	C-130B	C-130-E	C130-H
Gross weight (lb/kg)	124,200/ 56,336.17	135,000/ 61,234,96	155,000/ 70,306.817	155,000/ 70,306.817
Main gear load (lb/kg)	117,800/ 53,433.18	128,300/ 58,195.90	147,400/ 66,859.51	147,400/ 66,859.51
Single wheel load (lb/kg)	29,450/ 13,358.29	32,075/ 14,548.97	36,800/ 16,692.19	36,800/ 16,692.19
Normal tyre deflection (%)	35	35	35	35
Inflation pressure (psi)	72	80	95	05
Contact area (sq in/m²)	409/0.26387	400/0.2580	386/0.2490	386/0.2490
Maximum tyre deflection (%)	45	45	45	45
Inflation pressure (psi)	50	55	67	67
Contact area (sq in/m²)	589/0.379	582/0.375	459/0.296	549/0.354
'D' distance	-	-	-	-
Normal tyre deflection (in/cm)	29/73.6	29/73.6	29/73.6	29/73.6
Maximum tyre deflection (in/cm)	24/60.96	24/60.96	24/60.96	24/60.96

Weather tracking and research

Commencing on 7 August 1944 with the 3rd Weather Reconnaissance Squadron, Air Route, Medium, the weather tracking tradition is firmly established in the USAF.

In 1962 the USAF placed an order with Lockheed for five specially modified C-130Bs –serials 62-3492 (c/n 3702), 62-3493 (c/n 3707), 62-3494 (3408), 62-3495 (c/n 3721) and 62-3496 (c/n 3722) – to replace existing Boeing WB-50D aircraft in conducting detailed weather reconnaissance, monitoring and research missions under the auspices of the MATS Weather Reconnaissance Squadron, then based at Ramey AFB, Puerto Rico, with 55th Weather Reconnaissance Squadron. These modified machines were redesignated as WC-130B-*LM* 'Weatherbirds'. The first WC-130B (62-3492) was utilised as a flying test aircraft for the Kaman Airborne Weather Reconnaissance System, and following successful trials this became standard fitting to 'Weatherbird' machines.

A contrast in styles and size at Marietta: in the foreground is the XV4A Hummingbird I prototype, with, behind her, the 282-1B WC-130B 62-3492 (c/n 3702), flanked by early JetStar models. The small projections on the front fuselage were for atmospheric sampling, and she was later modified as a weather reconnaissance machine. *Lockheed*

An aerial view of USAF weather tracking WC-130B 62-33496 (c/n 3722). *Author's collection*

When Ramey AFB was shut down, the 55th relocated to Kessler AFB, near Biloxi, Mississippi. A further twelve aircraft were subsequently also converted to WC-130Bs and joined their sisters; these were serials 58-0725 (c/n 3520); 58-0726 (c/n 3521); 58-0729 (c/n 3524); 58-0731 (c/n 3526), which carried the name *NOAA's Ark*; 58-0733 (c/n 3528); 58-0734 (c/n 3530); 58-0740 (c/n 3537); 58-0741 (c/n 3538); 58-0742 (c/n 3539); 58-0747 (c/n 3545); 57-0752 (c/n 3551); and 58-0758 (c/n 3559); nine of them were surplus when 463rd Tactical Airlift Wing at Clark AB in the Philippines disbanded in 1970. Their numbers were gradually reduced as they were replaced by later conversions. Surplus aircraft were reconfigured as C-130Bs and subsequently served in Air Force Reserve (AFRES) or Air National Guard (ANG) units. One of the 53rd's WC-130Bs, 58-0731 was transferred out to the National Oceanic & Atmosphere Administration (NOAA) of the US Government's Department of Commerce, based at Miami, Florida, receiving the civilian registration N8037, which was later changed to N6541C.

A C-130B up from Hickam AFB gives a lot of flap as she climbs. She is tail-coded QB and is from 29 TAS, 463 TAW, based at Clark AB in the Philippines. *Nick Williams, AAHS*

Three modified C-130Es – 64-0552 (c/n 4047), 64-0553 (c/n 4048) and 64-554 (c/n 4049) – were ordered by MATS Air Weather Services in 1964, while a further three serving C-130Es – 61-2360 (c/n 3659), 61-2365 (c/n 3688) and 61-2366 (c/n 3706) – were similarly modified and fitted with the Kaman AWR. These aircraft served throughout the 1960s with the 53rd and also with the 54th WRS, based at Andersen AFB on Guam in the Pacific, and the 55th WRS based at McClellan AFB, California. In due course these were phased out and, although not reconverted, were utilised by the 815th TAS between 1989 and 1991 as Logistic Transports, before being retired to the Aerospace Maintenance & Regeneration Centre (AMARC) at Davis-Monthan AFB, Arizona.

The 53rd and 54th WRS of 9 WRW also operated in Europe, working from Bitburg, Hahn, Mildenhall, Ramstein, Rhein-Main, Spandahlem, Wiesbaden and Zweibrucken airfields. They called themselves Fog Floggers Ltd, as they had earlier carried out Operation 'Cold Cowl' from Elmendorf AFB in Alaska in the winters of 1967-68 and 1968-69, before they came to gloomy European skies to conduct similar flights under Operation 'Cold Crystal'.

The biggest increase came with the conversion of no fewer than fifteen HC-130Hs and C-130Hs in 1957; these were serials 64-14861 (c/n 4088); 64-14866 (c/n 4099); 65-0963 (c/n 4103); 65-0964 (c/n 4104); 65-0965 (c/n 4106); 65-0966 (c/n 4107); 65-0967 (c/n 4108); 65-0968 (c/n 4110); 65-0969 (c/n 4111); 65-0972 (c/n 4120); 65-0976 (c/n 4126); 65-0977 (c/n 4127); 65-0980 (c/n 4132); 65-0984 (c/n 4139); and 65-0985 (c/n 4140). The Fulton STAR recovery equipment was removed, except for the radome, and replaced by the Kaman system and a range of weather-monitoring systems. As well as the three WRS units, these machines also served with the 920th WRG (AFRES) based at Kessler AFB.

Four other aircraft completed as HC-130Hs were modified by the Lockheed Aircraft Service Company, at Ontario, California, to EC-130Hs in about 1985, these being serials 64-14859 (c/n 4082), 64-14862 (c/n 4089), 65-0962 (c/n 4102) and 65-0989 (c/n 4150), and served with 41 ECS. In 1996 the first-named reverted to C-130H standard with 16 Special Operations Wing working out of Hurlburt, while the remaining trio continue to operate as before.

Climbing steadily is HC-130H Herk 64-14859 (c/n 4082) of 76 ARRS, seen over Hawaii on 19 January 1968. *Nick Williams, AAHS*

Just how hazardous these missions could be was shown by the loss of 65-965 over the Taiwan Straits on 13 October 1974. The remainder have enjoyed a long service life, being utilised after 'retirement' by AFRES units, and a few are still currently active with the 53rd WRS and the 403rd AW at Kessler AFB, but are due to be replaced by the WC-130J. The remainder were steadily transferred to the AMARC from December 1997 onward.

The new generation WC-130Js first appeared with the introduction of three – serials 96-5300 (c/n 5451), 96-5301 (c/n 5452) and 96-5302 (c/n 5453) – that joined AFRES units. These have since been joined by a further seven aircraft - serials - 97-5303 (c/n 5473), 97-5304 (c/n 5474), 97-5305 (c/n 5475), 97-5306 (c/n 5476), 98-5307 (c/n 5486), 98-5308 (c/n 5487), 99-5309 (c/n 5501).

US Navy communications platform

The US Navy's airborne fleet broadcast system gave the Commander-in-Chief, Pacific, a mobile communications system in support of the Pacific Fleet's strategic forces. This obviated the need for fixed, land-based stations, which needed to be located in friendly or protected territory, an increasingly rare option for America as formerly friendly nations such as the Philippines and Okinawa turned against it. In 1962 the Defense Department charged the Director of Naval Communications with investigating and developing a highly reliable, mobile, very-low-frequency communications system, and studies showed that an airborne VLF communications platform would best fulfil that requirement. The order was given 'Take Charge and Move Out' and the acronym TACAMO followed and stuck. The new communications system necessitated the formation of a new squadron especially designed for it, Fleet Air Reconnaissance Squadron 3 (VQ-3).

Originally trials of the new system were held with two EC-130G aircraft assigned to VR-21 at Hawaii, both machines moving to Airborne Early Warning Squadron 1 (VW-1) in 1966 and working out of Naval Air Station Agana, Guam. They continued the test and evaluation of the system and at the end of two and a half years of research VQ-3 was commissioned at Agana on 1 July 1968. By June 1969 the unit had accepted the fourth EC-130Q aircraft.

The four EC-130Gs were received between December 1963 and January 1964, and were modified from C-130Gs for TACAMO III nuclear submarine communications work. The upgraded system gave increased communications flexibility, much improved in-flight maintenance, and a crew rest area. The aircraft were serials 151888 (c/n 3849), later modified to a TC-130G, receiving the civilian registration N93849 with Airplane Sales International; 151889 (c/n 3858), redesignated as TC-130G and scrapped in 1994; 151890 (c/n 3871), scrapped after in-flight fire damage in January 1971; and 151891 (c/n 3878), which was later used as a test bed for EC-130Q installations in May 1990 before being redesignated as a TC-130G and working with the 'Blue Angels' aerial demonstration team as their supply aircraft, based at Naval Air Station Pensacola, Florida, later carrying the name *Fat Albert Airlines*.

For the Take Charge and Move Out III (TACAMO III) system of nuclear submarine fleet VLF aerial communications relay aircraft, the US Navy replaced the EC-130Gs with some eighteen EC-130Q-*LM*s, these being serials 156170 (c/n 4239); 156171 (c/n 4249); 156172 (c/n 4269); 156173 (c/n 4277); 156174 (c/n 4278); 156175 (c/n 4279); 165176 (c/n 4280), which subsequently crashed into the sea off Wake Island on 21 June 1977; 156177 (c/n 4281); 159469 (c/n 4595); 159348 (c/n 4601); 160608 (c/n 4781); 161223 (c/n 4867); 161494 (4896); 161495 (c/n 4901); 161496 (c/n 4904); 161531 (c/n 4932); 162312 (c/n 4984); and 162313 (c/n 4988).

On the mat at Naval Air Station Atsugi, Japan, in September 1968 is EC-130G 151890 (c/n 3871) of VQ-32, flying with the US Navy. *Nick Williams, AAHS*

This US Navy is EC-130G is 151888 (c/n 3849), pictured in November 1975. *R. C. Stewart, via Nick Williams, AAHS*

A rocket-assisted take off for the 'Blue Angels' team's parent Herk. *Martin Bowman*

United States Navy EC-130Q 156177 (c/n 4281) displays the crest of the Naval Air Systems Command (and the Playboy 'bunny') at Naval Air Station BP. *Nick Williams, AAHS*

USN EC-130Q tanker 156171 (c/n 4249), with her drogue protruding from the rear fuselage doors and the special under-wing tank. *Nick Williams, AAHS*

These were basically standard C-130Hs powered by the T56-A-16 engine, rated at 4,910eshp. The ESM pods carrying the electronic and communications systems had dual trailing antennae, one, 26,000 feet (7.9km) long, dropped vertically from the tail cone, and the second, 5,000 feet (1.5km) long and also paid out ventrally, from the rear ramp. Each of these was fitted with a stabilising cone for deployment and this gear was steadily improved as time went on. To shield against Electro-Magnetic Pulse (EMP) interference, such as would be encountered in the aftermath of a nuclear missile exchange, equipment hardening was improved. By October 1976 VQ-3 had converted all aircraft to the TACAMO IV upgrading.

These aircraft served with the US Navy's VQ-3 based at Naval Air Station Agana on Guam Island, and, from 1 August 1981, back at Barber's Point, Hawaii, in the Pacific, serving the Pacific Fleet's nuclear submarines. The Atlantic Fleet was catered for by those serving with VQ-4, based at Naval Air Station Patuxent River, Maryland, until the surviving aircraft were replaced by Boeing E-6As and had their TACAMO removed, following which most were taken off charge.

A trio of these veterans, serials 156170 (c/n 4239), 159348 (c/n 4601) and 159469 (c/n 4595), saw renewed service usage as TC-13Q training aircraft and transports. One aircraft, 159348 (c/n 4601), after service in VXE-6, ended her days at the static park of Tinker AFB, while 156170 (c/n 4239) and 159469 (c/n 4595) were bought by Airplane Sales International from the AMARC in June 1996, becoming civilian registrations N15674 and N54595 respectively (see the appropriate section).

US Navy ski aircraft

There were four ski-equipped LC-130Fs. These were serials 148318 (c/n 3562), named *City of Christchurch*, which crashed at McMurdo on 15 February 1975; 148319 (c/n 3564), July 1960, named *Penguin Express*, then *Pride of McMurdo* and later *Betty*, which was struck off charge in 1999; 148320 (c/n 3565), July 1960, named *The Emperor* and later *Pete*, struck off charge in 1999; and 148321 (c/n 3567), August 1960, named *The Crown*, which crashed in ice on 1 December 1971, and was finally reclaimed and put back into service fifteen years later, aptly named *Phoenix*, and struck off charge 1999.

Salvage work on US Navy 148319 (c/n 3564) in 1977. *Lockheed-Georgia, Marietta, via Audrey Pearcy*

On the deck at Naval Air Station North Island in 1969 is C-130F 149795 (c/n 3661) of VRC-50. *Robert L. Lawson, via Nick Williams*

Seen at NAS Atsugi is US Navy C-130F 149793 (c/n 3660), tail-coded RZ, from NAS Barbers Point, Hawaii. *Nick Williams, AAHS*

Another view of 149793 (c/n 3660), this time at Barbers Point NAS, Hawaii. *Nick Williams, AAHS*

The same aircraft seen again at Barbers Point in 1972. *Nick Williams, AAHS*

US Navy transports/tankers

These were four C-130Fs: serials 149787 (c/n 3636), December 1961, which was sold to South Africa in 1996; 149790 (c/n 3645), March 1962, named *GoGo Airlines Naples*, and struck off in 1992; 149793 (c/n 3660), March 1962, sold to South Africa in 1996; and 149794 (c/n 3661), named *Sky Pig* and written off after hurricane damage at Guam in 1992.

Twenty C-130Ts, which were C-130H transports fitted with T56-A-16 engines and carrying refuelling packages, were received between August 1991 and October 1996. These were serials 164762 (c/n 5255), named *Dixie Belle*; 164763 (c/n 5258); 164993 (c/n 5298); 164994 (c/n 5299); 164995 (c/n 5300); 164996 (c/n 5301); 164997 (c/n 5304); 164998 (c/n 5305); 165158 (c/n 5341); 165159 (c/n 5342); 165160 (c/n 5344); 165161 (c/n 5345); 165313 (c/n 5383), named *Town of Townsham*; 165314 (c/n 5384), named *City of Abington*; 165348 (c/n 5404); 165349 (c/n 5406); 165350 (c/n 5407); 165351 (c/n 5409); 165378 (c/n 5429); and 165379 (c/n 5430). They are operated by United States Naval Reserve squadrons: VR-53, from Andrews AFB, Naval Airfield Washington DC; VR-54, from Naval Air Station New Orleans, Louisiana; VR-55, from Naval Air Station Santa Clara, California; and VR-62 from Naval Air Station New Brunswick, Minnesota.

The cockpit of US Navy C-130T L-382 164763 (c/n 5258) at Virginia Beach – Oceana Naval Air Station, Apollo Soucek Field. *Courtesy of Michal Nowicki*

Unloading JATOs from 'Fat Albert' 164763 at Virginia Beach. *Courtesy of Michal Nowicki*

Affixing JATOs to 'Fat Albert'.
Courtesy of Michal Nowicki

A close up of the JATOs affixed to 'Fat Albert'.
Courtesy of Michal Nowicki

US Marine Corps tankers

The US Marine Corps experimented with in-flight refuelling with two C-130As loaned from the USAF, serials 55-0046 (c/n 3073) and 55-0048 (c/n 3075). They were initially designated as the GV-1. Next C-130B conversions, designated as GV-1Us, followed, resulting in forty-six KC-130F tanker/transport aircraft in three batches.

Many of these saw extremely hard combat service. VMGR-152, Marine Air Group 36, Marine Air Wing 1, working from Marine Corps Air Station Futenma, on Okinawa, supported the Marines on the ground in Vietnam, supplying and air-dropping deep over enemy-held territory to surrounded garrisons like Khe San; not surprisingly, they suffered some casualties. They later moved out to Iwakuni Airfield, on Honshu, Japan. Several more of the type was lost in accidents, as recorded. Other units to employ this variant were VMGR-252 and VMGR-253, MAG-14, MAW-2, based at MCAS Cherry Point, North Carolina, and VMGR-352, MAG-11 and MAW-3, based at MCAS Miramar, California.

The first seven arrived between March 1960 and February 1961, being serials 147572 (c/n 3554); 147573 (c/n 3555); 148246 (c/n 3566); 148247 (c/n 3573); 148248 (c/n 3574); 148249 (c/n 3577); and 148890 (c/n 3592).

The second batch of twenty-one were purchased between April 1961 and June 1962. They were serials 148891 (c/n 3605); 148892 (c/n 3606); 148893 (c/n 3607), which served for a spell as the 'Blue Angels' support aircraft; 148894 (c/n 3608); 148895 (c/n 3619); 148896 (c/n 3623); 148897 (c/n 3627); 148898 (c/n 3631); 148899 (c/n 3632); 149788 (c/n 3640); 149789 (c/n 3644); 149791 (c/n 3657); 149792 (c/n 3658); 149795 (c/n 3664); 149796 (c/n 3665); 149798 (c/n 3680), which carried the name *Look Ma, No Hook* during her deck trials aboard the USS *Forrestal* in 1963 (see the appropriate section); 149799 (c/n 3684); 149800 (c/n 3685); 149802 (c/n 3693), which crashed at Hong Kong on 24 August 1965; 149803 (c/n 3694); and 149804 (c/n 3695).

Finally, another eighteen arrived on USMC strength between July and November 1962; these were serials 149806 (c/n 3703), which became the 'Blue Angels' support aircraft, before going to Naval Air Station Adak, Alaska, in the logistic support mission, then to the Naval Air Warfare Center, Patuxent River, from June 1994; 149807 (c/n 3704), written off after engine problems in 1997; 149808 (c/n 3705); 149809 (c/n 3709), destroyed by enemy action of Dong Hoi, Vietnam, on 1 February 1966; 149810 (c/n 3710), destroyed by fire at Lake City, Florida, on 15 January 1972; 149811 (c/n 3711); 149812 (c/n 3718); 149813 (c/n 3719), destroyed by enemy action at Khe Sanh, Vietnam, on 10 February 1968; 149814 (c/n 3723), destroyed in a mid-air collision with an F-4B over Vietnam on 18 May 1969; 149815 (c/n 3725); 149816 (c/n 3726); 150684 (c/n 3727), which was finally struck off charge in 1994; 150685 (c/n 3728), which crashed at El Toro, California, in July 1970; 150686 (c/n 3733); 150687 (c/n 3734); 150688 (c/n 3740); 150689 (c/n 3741); and 150690 (c/n 3742), also utilised as the 'Blue Angels' support aircraft in the 1970s.

With tail-code QB, KC-130F 149788 (c/n 3640) of the US Marine Corps VMGR-352, is seen at NAS Barbers Point in June 1969. *Nick Williams, AAHS*

Seen at Naval Air Station Atsugi is USMC KC-130F Herk 148895 (c/n 3619), also of VMGR-352. *Nick Williams, AAHS*

Another USMC VMGR-152 KC-130F, 148993 (c/n 3607), tail-code QD, out of MCAS Futenma, Okinawa, drops in at Da Nang RVN air base, South Vietnam. *Both Nick Williams, AAHS*

KC-130F 148892 (c/n 3606), coded QH, of VMGR-234, 4th Military Airlift Wing based at NAS Forth Worth, Texas, is seen at NAS Glenview, Illinois, on 11 February 1978. *M. J. Kasibuba, via Nick Williams, AAHS*

With the arrival of the KC-130R as a tanker version of the C-130H, the US Marine Corps placed orders that resulted in fourteen aircraft of this type, powered by the T56-A-16 engine rated at 4.910eshp. They had a fuel capacity of 13,320 US gallons (50,420 litres). These aircraft were delivered between 1975 and 1978. The first batch of eight aircraft arrived between September 1975 and October 1976, and were serials 160013 (c/n 4615); 160014 (c/n 4626); 160015 (c/n 4629); 160016 (c/n 4635); 160017 (c/n 4677); 160018 (c/n 4683); 160019 (c/n 4689); and 160020 (c/n 4696).

A nice view of the lowered after ramp and other detail of C-130F 149805 (c/n 3703), tail-coded RZ, of the VR-21, at NAS Barbers Point. *Nick Williams, AAHS*

Later KC-130F 149806 became part of the USMC 'Blue Angels' team, seen here with her brood of A-4F Skyhawk fighter-bombers over the Florida Keys. *McDonnell Douglas via Audrey Pearcy*

An aerial underside view of 149806, of the USMC 'Blue Angels' team. *McDonnell Douglas via Audrey Pearcy*

THE LOCKHEED MARTIN C-130 HERCULES

Coded BH, this is a KC-130F Herk 1492807 (c/n 3704) of the USMC VMGR-252 based at MCAS Cherry Point, North Carolina. *Nick Williams, AAHSv*

This is KC-130F 149811 (c/n 3711), of VMGR-234 from NAS Fort Worth, Texas, tail-coded QH, and seen in July 1977 at Tucson, Arizona. *Bruce Stewart, via Nick Williams, AAHS*

An underside view of the USMC's KC-130F 150684 (c/n 3727) of VMG-152, out of MCAS Futenma, Okinawa, with tail-code QD, turning low over Hickam AFB, Hawaii. *Nick Williams, AAHS*

USMC KC-130F 150689 (c/n 3741), of VNGR-352 out of MCAS Miramar, California, with tail-code QB, fires up her two inboard engines. *Nick Williams, AAHS*

This is USMC 'Blue Angels' support aircraft 150690 (c/n 3742), painted white on a California airfield. *McDonnell Douglas via Audrey Pearcy*

These were followed by six more of the same type between November 1976 and May 1978, these being serials 160021 (c/n 4702); 160240 (c/n 4712); 160625 (c/n 4768); 160626 (c/n 4770); 160627 (c/n 4773); and 160628 (c/n 47776).

This variant served with three units, VMGR-152, VMGR-252 and VMGR-352.

A further refinement, as tankers able to refuel both aircraft and helicopters, followed, this being the KC-130T. A total of twenty-six such aircraft were allocated to the US Marine Corps in five allotments, the first four between October and November 1983 being serials 162308 (c/n 4972), 162309 (c/n 4974), 162310 (c/n 4978) and 162311 (c/n 4981).

The initial quartet were followed by six more between September 1984 and November 1986, these being serials 162785 (c/n 5009); 162786 (c/n 5011); 163022 (c/n 5040); 163023 (c/n 5045); 163310 (c/n 5085), which worked as a 'Blue Angels' support aircraft; and 163311 (c/n 5087), whose completion marked the 1,800th Hercules built.

KC-130R of US Marines' VMGR-352, serial 160020 (c/n 4696) and tail-coded QB, is pictured at NAS Atlanta, Georgia, in October 1978. *Nick Williams, AAHS*

Between September 1988 and October 1989 a third batch of another six of the same type was received, these being serials 163591 (c/n 5143); 163592 (c/n 5145); 164105 (c/n 5147); 164106 (c/n 5149); 164180 (c/n 5174); and 164181 (c/n 5176).

Another pair were purchased from Lockheed's stock in October and November 1990, serials 164441 (c/n 5219) and 164442 (c/n 5222).

Next another batch of six arrived between November 1992 and February 1992; these were serials 164999 (c/n 5302); 165000 (c/n 5303); 165162 (c/n 5339), 165163 (c/n 5340); 165315 (c/n 5385); and 165316 (c/n 5386).

Finally a last duo was received in October 1995 and February 1996 respectively, these being serials 165352 (c/n 5411) and 165353 (c/n 5412).

A further pair of 'stretched' KC-130Ts were added, these being designated as the KC-KC-130T-30; they were serials 164597 (c/n 5260) and 164598 (c/n 5263).

The KC-130T saw service with VMGR-234, MAG-41 and MAW-4, flying from Naval Air Station Fort Worth, Texas, and VMGR-452, MAG-49 and MAW-4, based at Stewart International Airport, New York State.

The latest tanker version for the US Marine Corps is based on the C-130J and is designated the KC-130J. At the time of writing orders have been placed for nine such aircraft, serials 165735 (c/n 5488); 165736 (c/n 5489); 165737 (c/n 5499), 165738 (c/n 5506); 165739 (c/n 5507), 165809 (c/n 5508), 165810 (c/n 5509), 165957 (c/n 5515); and 165380 (c/n 5516). Early deliveries have joined the VMGR-252 at NAS Cherry Point.

US Coast Guard navigation/electronics platform

Twenty-four US Coast Guard HC-130Hs, which did not feature the ARD-17 Cook aerial tracker, the HRU pods or the Fulton STAR recovery yoke, were obtained between 1966 and 1985. A single EC-130E was obtained in August 1966, this being serial CG 1414 (c/n 4158). Her designation was later changed to HC-130E and she was struck off charge in 1983, going to the MASDC via the USAF and being sold to Certified Air Parts for breaking up; the cockpit ended up at Reflectone and later Asia-Pacific Training & Simulation PTE Ltd until finally scrapped in November 1995.

Further HC-130H aircraft were obtained in two batches. Twelve arrived between March 1968 and October 1977; they were serials CG 1452, ex-67-7183 (c/n 4255); CG 1453, ex-67-7184 (c/n 4260); CG 1454, ex-67-7185 (c/n 4265); CG 1500, ex-72-1300 (c/n 4501); CG 1501, ex-72-1301 (c/n 4507); CG 1502, ex-72-1302 (c/n 4513); CG 1503, ex-73-0844 (c/n 4528); CG 1504, ex-73-0845 (c/n 4529); CG 1603, ex-77-0320 (c/n 4764); CG 1602, ex-77-0319 (c/n 4762); CG 1601, ex-77-0318 (c/n 4760); and

CG 1600, ex-77-0317 (c/n 4757), which crashed near Attu, Aleutian Islands, on 30 July 1982. Six aircraft were then obtained between August and November 1985, serials CG 1710 (c/n 5028); CG 1711 (c/n 5031); CG 1712 (c/n 5033); CG 1713 (c/n 5034); CH 1714 (c/n 5035); and CG 1715 (c/n 5037).

A further eleven US Coast Guard Hercules were produced as HC-130H-7s between May 1983 and December 1984, these being serials CG 1700 (c/n 4947); CG 1701 (c/n 4958); CG 1702 (c/n 4966); CG 1703 (c/n 4967); CG 1704 (c/n 4969); CG 1707 (c/n 4993); CG 1706 (c/n 4996); CG 1707 (c/n 4999); CG 1708 (c/n 5002); CG 1709 (c/n 5005); and CG 1790 (c/n 4931). These were fitted with the Side-Looking Airborne Radar (SLAR) and Forward-Looking Infra-Red (FLIR). This latter system, intended for use in tracking drug-smuggling vessels at sea, also utilised the Lockheed Special Avionics Mission Strap-On Now system (SAMSON), which coupled the FLIR with an optical data link and a display and recording console to record and register evidence as it came in.

Some of these latter aircraft were given the additional duty of in-flight helicopter refuelling like the HC-130Ps, and were fitted with wing pods carrying hose-and-drogue gear for this mission. They were also equipped with Night Vision Goggles (NVG), while both cockpit lighting and navigation capability has also been upgraded. All these aircraft have served with the USCG from its seven bases in North America and, while some have been reduced to care at the AMARC in Arizona, many others are still working today.

Further HC-130Hs were taken on strength between August 1985 and May 1988, and served at Coast Guard Stations Clearwater, Barbers Point, Borinquen, Kodiak and Pemco; these were serials CG 1710 (c/n 5028); CG 1711 (c/n 5031); CG 1712 (c/n 5033); CG 1713 (c/n 5034); CG 1714 (c/n 5035); CG 1715 (c/n 5037); CG 1716, the former Lockheed N4272M (c/n 5023), built in January 1985 and sold to the Coast Guard in April 1986; CG 1717 (c/n 5104); CG 1718 (c/n 5106); CG 1719 (c/n 5107); CG 1720 (c/n 5120); and CG 1721 (c/n 5121), which was modified to an EC-130V with an AN/APS-125 rotodome installation and passed to the USAF's 514 Test Squadron, taking its serial 87-0157. In October 1993 she was again redesignated, this time as an NC-130H, before ending up at the US Navy test centre at Patuxent River in November 1998.

US Coast Guard Search & Rescue

Twelve Hercules HC-130B-L aircraft (which were originally designated as the R8V-1G, and later as the SC-130B, then the HC-130F, before finally becoming HC-130B-L) were fitted for the SAR role and featured two additional crew posts, two scanner stations with unrestricted fields of view, and internal adjustments to enable them to embark seventy-four litter patients. After the initial flight on 8 December 1964, they were allocated to the US Coast Guard. Built between December 1959 and February 1963, before conversion the fleet comprised serials CG 1339, ex-58-5396 (c/n 3529); CG 1340, ex-58-5397 (c/n 3533); CG 1341, ex-58-6973 (c/n 3542); CG 1342, ex-58-6974 (c/n 3548); CG 1344, ex-60-0311 (c/n 3594); CG 1345, ex-60-0312 (c/n 3595); CG 1346, ex-61-2081 (c/n 3638); CG 1347, ex-61-2082 (c/n 3641); CG 1348, ex-61-2083 (c/n 3650); CG 1349, ex-62-3753 (c/n 3745); CG 1350, ex-62-3754 (c/n 3763); and CG 1351, ex-62-3755 (c/n 3773).

They were fitted with Aerial Retrieval & Transport (ART) systems. For use with NASA's Space Program as recovery aircraft, extra equipment was installed including a brace of fuel bladders with an 1,800-gallon capacity, and could also be distinguished by a prominent blister atop the fuselage in front of the centre wing section, which contained the Cook Electric Re-Entry Tracking System, used in conjunction with the Gemini space vehicles. After good service, all were struck off charge between October 1983 and January 1987, and broken up for parts and scrap.

In general the US Coast Guard air forces are part of the armed forces set-up and work with the US Navy in times of war under the Maritime Defense Zone (MARDEZ) arrangement, which includes the search and rescue, anti-submarine and aerial harbour defence missions, together with major port security and limited surveillance interdiction, and the aircraft are funded via the Navy. In peacetime they are mainly responsible for the bulk of the North Atlantic ice patrol work, anti-drug-running operations in the Caribbean (Operation 'Opbat'), offshore oil installation pollution monitoring, and illegal immigration patrols. Bases include Barbers Point, Hawaii; Borinquen, Puerto Rico; Clearwater, Florida; Elizabeth City, North Carolina; Kodiak, Alaska; McClellan AFB, Sacramento, California; and St John's, Newfoundland.

Chapter 3

The multiple roles of the American Hercules variants

AC-130A-LM

One aircraft: prototype conversion from C-130A 54-1626.

Then in batches thus:

Seven aircraft, conversions from C-130As, serials 53-3128; 54-1623; 54-1625; 54-1627; 54-1628; 54-1629; 54-1630. Armament: four Miniguns and four cannon.

One aircraft, conversion from C-130A serial 55-0011.

Nine aircraft, conversions from C-130A, serials 55-0014; 55-0029; 55-0040; 55-0043; 55-0044; 55-0046; 56-0469; 56-0490; 56-0509. Armament: two Miniguns, two cannon, two 40mm Bofors.

The AC-130A gunship *Author's collection*

AC-130A 55-0046 (c/n 3073), of the Air Force Reserve, sits on the runway at Duke AFB on 29 September 1978. *Nick Williams, AAHS*

Customer	Serial	c/n	Type
USAF	54-1626	3013	182-1A
USAF	53-3129	3001	182-1A
USAF	54-1623	3010	182-1A
USAF	54-1625	3012	182-1A
USAF	54-1627	3014	182-1A
USAF	54-1628	3015	182-1A
USAF	54-1629	3016	182-1A
USAF	54-1630	3017	182-1A
USAF	55-0011	3038	182-1A
USAF	55-0014	3041	182-1A
USAF	55-0029	3056	182-1A
USAF	55-0040	3067	182-1A
USAF	55-0043	3070	182-1A
USAF	55-0044	3071	182-1A
USAF	55-0046	3073	182-1A
USAF	56-0469	3077	182-1A
USAF	56-0487	3095	182-1A
USAF	56-0509	3117	182-1A

AC-130E-LM 'Pave Spectre I'

Two aircraft, prototype conversions from C-130Es, serials 69-6576 and 69-65777.

Nine aircraft, conversions from C-130Es, serials 69-6567; 69-6568; 69-6569; 69-6570; 69-6571; 69-6572; 69-6573; 69-6574; 69-6575. One, serial 69-6571 (c/n 4345), was lost to enemy action in March 1972 at An Loc, Vietnam, while the rest were subsequently modified to AC-130H.

Customer	Serial	c/n	Type
USAF	69-6576	4351	382C-15D
USAF	69-6577	4352	382C-15D
USAF	69-6567	4341	382C-15D
USAF	69-6568	4342	382C-15D
USAF	69-6569	4343	382C-15D
USAF	69-6570	4344	382C-15D
USAF	69-6571	4345	382C-15D
USAF	69-6572	4346	382C-15D
USAF	69-6573	4347	382C-15D
USAF	69-6574	4348	382C-15D
USAF	69-6575	4349	382C-15D

AC-130H-LM

Ten aircraft, converted from surviving AC-130E-*LM*s, serials 69-6567 (c/n 4341); 69-6568 (c/n 4342); 69-6569 (c/n 4343); 69-6570 (c/n 4344); 69-6572 (c/n 4346); 69-6573 (c/n 4347); 69-6574 (c/n 4348); 69-6575 (c/n 4349), 69-6576 (c/n 4351); 69-6577 (c/n 4352).

AC-130U ('Spectre')

Thirteen aircraft, based on the C-130H, a gunship with three cannon and improved Rockwell electronics suite.

An AC-130U at sunset. *Author's collection*

Customer	Serial	c/n	Type
USAF	87-0128	5139	382C-86E
USAF	89-0509	5228	382C-97E
USAF	89-0510	5229	382C-97E
USAF	89-0511	5230	382C-97E
USAF	89-0512	5231	382C-97E
USAF	89-0513	5232	382C-97E
USAF	89-0514	5233	382C-97E
USAF	90-0163	5256	382C-19F
USAF	90-0164	5257	382C-19F
USAF	90-0165	5259	382C-19F
USAF	90-0166	5261	382C-19F
USAF	90-0167	5262	382C-19F
USAF	92-0253	5279	382C-40F

C-130A-LM

192 aircraft, for USAF Tactical Air Command:

Serial	c/n	Type	Serial	c/n	Type	Serial	c/n	Type
53-3129	3001	182-1A	55-0005	3032	182-1A	55-0036	3063	182-1A
53-3130	3002	182-1A	55-0006	3033	182-1A	55-0037	3064	182-1A
53-3131	3003	182-1A	55-0007	3034	182-1A	55-0038	3065	182-1A
53-3132	3004	182-1A	55-0008	3035	182-1A	55-0039	3066	182-1A
53-3133	3005	182-1A	55-0009	3036	182-1A	55-0040	3067	182-1A
53-3134	3006	182-1A	55-0010	3037	182-1A	55-0041	3068	182-1A
53-3135	3007	182-1A	55-0011	3038	182-1A	55-0042	3069	182-1A
54-1621	3008	182-1A	55-0012	3039	182-1A	55-0043	3070	182-1A
54-1622	3009	182-1A	55-0013	3040	182-1A	55-0044	3071	182-1A
54-1623	3010	182-1A	55-0014	3041	182-1A	55-0045	3072	182-1A
54-1624	3011	182-1A	55-0015	3042	182-1A	55-0046	3073	182-1A
54-1625	3012	182-1A	55-0016	3043	182-1A	55-0047	3074	182-1A
54-1626	3013	182-1A	55-0017	3044	182-1A	55-0048	3075	182-1A
54-1627	3014	182-1A	55-0018	3045	182-1A	56-0468	3076	182-1A
54-1628	3015	182-1A	55-0019	3046	182-1A	56-0469	3077	182-1A
54-1629	3016	182-1A	55-0020	3047	182-1A	56-0470	3078	182-1A
54-1630	3017	182-1A	55-0021	3048	182-1A	56-0471	3079	182-1A
54-1631	3018	182-1A	55-0022	3049	182-1A	56-0472	3080	182-1A
54-1632	3019	182-1A	55-0023	3050	182-1A	56-0473	3081	182-1A
54-1633	3020	182-1A	55-0024	3051	182-1A	56-0474	3082	182-1A
54-1634	3021	182-1A	55-0025	3052	182-1A	56-0475	3083	182-1A
54-1635	3022	182-1A	55-0026	3053	182-1A	56-0476	3084	182-1A
54-1636	3023	182-1A	55-0027	3054	182-1A	56-0477	3085	182-1A
54-1637	3024	182-1A	55-0028	3055	182-1A	56-0478	3086	182-1A
54-1638	3025	182-1A	55-0029	3056	182-1A	56-0479	3087	182-1A
54-1639	3026	182-1A	55-0030	3057	182-1A	56-0480	3088	182-1A
54-1640	3027	182-1A	55-0031	3058	182-1A	56-0481	3089	182-1A
55-0001	3028	182-1A	55-0032	3059	182-1A	56-0482	3090	182-1A
55-0002	3029	182-1A	55-0033	3060	182-1A	56-0483	3091	182-1A
55-0003	3030	182-1A	55-0034	3061	182-1A	56-0484	3092	182-1A
55-0004	3031	182-1A	55-0035	3062	182-1A	56-0485	3093	182-1A

Serial	c/n	Type	Serial	c/n	Type	Serial	c/n	Type
56-0486	3094	182-1A	56-0519	3127	182-1A	57-0453	3160	182-1A
56-0487	3095	182-1A	56-0520	3128	182-1A	57-0454	3161	182-1A
56-0488	3096	182-1A	56-0521	3129	182-1A	57-0455	3162	182-1A
56-0489	3097	182-1A	56-0522	3130	182-1A	57-0456	3163	182-1A
56-0490	3098	182-1A	56-0523	3131	182-1A	57-0457	3164	182-1A
56-0491	3099	182-1A	56-0524	3132	182-1A	57-0458	3165	182-1A
56-0492	3100	182-1A	56-0525	3133	182-1A	57-0459	3166	182-1A
56-0493	3101	182-1A	56-0526	3134	182-1A	57-0460	3167	182-1A
56-0494	3102	182-1A	56-0527	3135	182-1A	57-0461	3168	182-1A
56-0495	3103	182-1A	56-0528	3136	182-1A	57-0462	3169	182-1A
56-0496	3104	182-1A	56-0529	3137	182-1A	57-0463	3170	182-1A
56-0497	3105	182-1A	56-0530	3138	182-1A	57-0464	3171	182-1A
56-0498	3106	182-1A	56-0531	3139	182-1A	57-0465	3172	182-1A
56-0499	3107	182-1A	56-0532	3140	182-1A	57-0466	3173	182-1A
56-0500	3108	182-1A	56-0533	3141	182-1A	57-0467	3174	182-1A
56-0501	3109	182-1A	56-0534	3142	182-1A	57-0468	3175	182-1A
56-0502	3110	182-1A	56-0535	3143	182-1A	57-0469	3176	182-1A
56-0503	3111	182-1A	56-0536	3144	182-1A	57-0470	3177	182-1A
56-0504	3112	182-1A	56-0537	3145	182-1A	57-0471	3178	182-1A
56-0505	3113	182-1A	56-0538	3146	182-1A	57-0472	3179	182-1A
56-0506	3114	182-1A	56-0539	3147	182-1A	57-0473	3180	182-1A
56-0507	3115	182-1A	56-0540	3148	182-1A	57-0474	3181	182-1A
56-0508	3116	182-1A	56-0541	3149	182-1A	57-0475	3182	182-1A
56-0509	3117	182-1A	56-0542	3150	182-1A	57-0476	3183	182-1A
56-0510	3118	182-1A	56-0543	3151	182-1A	57-0477	3184	182-1A
56-0511	3119	182-1A	56-0544	3152	182-1A	57-0478	3185	182-1A
56-0512	3120	182-1A	56-0545	3153	182-1A	57-0479	3186	182-1A
56-0513	3121	182-1A	56-0546	3154	182-1A	57-0480	3187	182-1A
56-0514	3122	182-1A	56-0547	3155	182-1A	57-0481	3188	182-1A
56-0515	3123	182-1A	56-0548	3156	182-1A	57-0482	3189	182-1A
56-0516	3124	182-1A	56-0549	3157	182-1A	57-0483	3190	182-1A
56-0517	3125	182-1A	56-0550	3158	182-1A	57-0496	3203	182-1A
56-0518	3126	182-1A	56-0551	3159	182-1A	57-0497	3204	182-1A

At Da Nang RVN, Vietnam, in August 1968, C-130A 56-0543 (c/n 3151), tail-coded YD, of 21 TAS based at Naha, Okinawa, unloads in the simmering heat. *Nick Williams, AAHS*

C-130A 182-1A AF57-0479 (c/n 3186), coded MA, from Tachikawa AB, Japan with 315AD, is seen at an air display at Johnson Air Base, Japan. *Nick Williams, AAHS*

An underside aerial view of USAF C-130A 55-0026 (c/n 3053) landing. *Lockheed-Georgia, Marietta, via Audrey Pearcy*

THE LOCKHEED MARTIN C-130 HERCULES

Twelve aircraft for RAAF:

Serial	c/n	Type
A97-205	3205	182B-1A
A97-206	3206	182B-1A
A97-207	3207	182B-1A
A97-208	3208	182B-1A
A97-209	3209	182B-1A
A97-210	3210	182B-1A
A97-211	3211	182B-1A
A97-212	3212	182B-1A
A97-213	3213	182B-1A
A97-214	3214	182B-1A
A97-215	3215	182B-1A
A97-216	3216	182B-1A

Fourteen aircraft, former RC-130As:

Serial	c/n	Type
57-0510	3217	182-2A
57-0511	3218	182-2A
57-0512	3219	182-2A
57-0513	3220	182-2A
57-0514	3221	182-2A
57-0515	3222	182-2A
57-0516	3223	182-2A
57-0517	3224	182-2A
57-0518	3225	182-2A
57-0514	3221	182-2A
57-0520	3227	182-2A
57-0521	3228	182-2A
57-0522	3229	182-2A
57-0524	3231	182-2A

An early view of USAF C-130A 55-0005 (c/n 3032) over a European landscape early in her career. She was later to be transferred to the South Vietnam Air Force in November in 1972. (USAF Photo)

C-130A 56-0475 (c/n 3083), of the Air Force Reserve, is seen in September 1980. *Nick Williams, AAHS*

C-130A-II-LM

Twelve aircraft, C-130As modified for COMINT/SIGINT work from 1957:

Serial	c/n	Type
54-1637	3024	182-1A
56-0484	3092	182-1A
56-0524	3132	182-1A
56-0525	3133	182-1A
56-0528	3136	182-1A
56-0530	3138	182-1A
56-0534	3142	182-1A
56-0535	3143	182-1A
56-0537	3145	182-1A
56-0538	3146	182-1A
56-0540	3148	182-1A
56-0541	3149	182-1A

C-130B-LM

132 aircraft, for USAF Tactical Air Command:

On 12 January 1968 TC-130B 58-0717 (c/n 34512) of 6593 TS, USAF, lifts off from Hawaii. *Nick Williams, AAHS*

Serial	c/n	Type	Serial	c/n	Type	Serial	c/n	Type
57-0525	3501	282-1B	58-0751	3550	282-1B	61-0950	3626	282-1B
57-0526	3502	282-1B	58-0752	3551	282-1B	61-0951	3628	282-1B
57-0527	3503	282-1B	58-0753	3552	282-1B	61-0952	3629	282-1B
57-0528	3504	282-1B	58-0754	3553	282-1B	61-0953	3630	282-1B
57-0529	3505	282-1B	58-0755	3556	282-1B	61-0954	3633	282-1B
58-0711	3506	282-1B	58-0756	3557	282-1B	61-0955	3634	282-1B
58-0712	3507	282-1B	58-0757	3558	282-1B	61-0956	3635	282-1B
58-0713	3508	282-1B	58-0758	3559	282-1B	61-0957	3637	282-1B
58-0714	3509	282-1B	59-1524	3560	282-1B	61-0958	3639	282-1B
58-0715	3510	282-1B	59-1525	3561	282-1B	61-0959	3642	282-1B
58-0716	3511	282-1B	59-1526	3563	282-1B	61-0960	3643	282-1B
58-0717	3512	282-1B	59-1527	3568	282-1B	61-0961	3646	282-1B
58-0718	3513	282-1B	59-1529	3569	282-1B	61-0962	3647	282-1B
58-0719	3514	282-1B	59-1534	3570	282-1B	61-0963	3648	282-1B
58-0720	3515	282-1B	59-1528	3571	282-1B	61-0964	3649	282-1B
58-0721	3516	282-1B	59-1530	3576	282-1B	61-0965	3652	282-1B
58-0722	3517	282-1B	59-1531	3579	282-1B	61-0966	3653	282-1B
58-0723	3518	282-1B	59-1532	3581	282-1B	61-0967	3654	282-1B
58-0724	3519	282-1B	59-5857	3584	282-1B	61-0968	3655	282-1B
58-0725	3520	282-1B	59-1535	3585	282-1B	61-0969	3656	282-1B
58-0726	3521	282-1B	59-1533	3586	282-1B	61-0970	3667	282-1B
58-0727	3522	282-1B	59-1536	3588	282-1B	61-0971	3668	282-1B
58-0728	3523	282-1B	59-1537	3589	282-1B	61-0972	3669	282-1B
58-0729	3524	282-1B	60-0293	3591	282-1B	61-2634	3670	282-1B
58-0730	3525	282-1B	60-0294	3593	282-1B	61-2635	3671	282-1B
58-0731	3526	282-1B	60-0295	3596	282-1B	61-2636	3672	282-1B
58-0732	3527	282-1B	60-0296	3597	282-1B	61-2337	3673	282-1B
58-0733	3528	282-1B	60-0297	3600	282-1B	61-2638	3674	282-1B
58-0734	3530	282-1B	60-0298	3602	282-1B	61-2639	3675	282-1B
58-0735	3531	282-1B	60-0299	3603	282-1B	61-2640	3676	282-1B
58-0736	3532	282-1B	60-0300	3604	282-1B	61-2641	3677	282-1B
58-0737	3534	282-1B	61-2358	3609	282-1B	61-2642	3678	282-1B
58-0738	3535	282-1B	60-0301	3610	282-1B	61-2643	3679	282-1B
58-0739	3536	282-1B	60-0302	3611	282-1B	61-2644	3682	282-1B
58-0740	3537	282-1B	60-0304	3612	282-1B	61-2645	3683	282-1B
58-0741	3538	282-1B	60-0303	3613	282-1B	61-2646	3689	282-1B
58-0742	3539	282-1B	60-0305	3614	282-1B	61-2647	3690	282-1B
58-0743	3540	282-1B	60-0306	3617	282-1B	61-2648	3691	282-1B
58-0744	3541	282-1B	60-0307	3618	282-1B	61-2649	3692	282-1B
58-0745	3543	282-1B	60-0308	3620	282-1B	62-3487	3697	282-1B
58-0746	3544	282-1B	60-0309	3621	282-1B	62-3488	3698	282-1B
58-0747	3545	282-1B	60-0310	3622	282-1B	62-3489	3699	282-1B
58-0749	3547	282-1B	61-0948	3624	282-1B	62-3490	3700	282-1B
58-0750	3549	282-1B	61-0949	3625	282-1B	62-3491	3701	282-1B

In February 1968 at Da Nang, Vietnam, C-130B-II 59-1533 (c/n 3586) makes ready to run the gauntlet yet again. *Nick Williams, AAHS*

Coming in to land at Yokota Air Base, Japan, is C-130B 59-1532 (c/n 3581). *Nick Williams, AAHS*

In addition, five former WC-130Bs were modified to C-130Bs between 1976 and 1979:

Serial	c/n	Type
62-3492	3702	282-1B
62-3493	3707	282-1B
62-3494	3708	282-1B
62-3495	3721	282-1B
62-3496	3722	282-1B

Many others were produced for the Canadian, South African, Indonesian, Jordanian, Pakistani and Iranian air forces (see the appropriate sections).

C-130B-II

Thirteen aircraft, C-130Bs modified as 'Sun Valley II' electronics reconnaissance aircraft but later converted back:

Serial	c/n	Type
58-0711	3506	282-1B
58-0723	3518	282-1B
59-1524	3560	282-1B
59-1525	3561	282-1B
59-1526	3563	282-1B
59-1527	3568	282-1B
59-1528	3571	282-1B
59-1530	3576	282-1B
59-1531	3579	282-1B
59-1532	3581	282-1B
59-1533	3586	282-1B
59-1535	3585	282-1B
59-1537	3589	282-1B

C-130BL

Four aircraft, ski-equipped for the US Navy, were ordered by the USAF as the C-130BL on behalf of the Navy.

BuOrd No	Ex-USAF	c/n	Type
148318	59-5922	3562	282C-6B
148319	59-5923	3564	282C-6B
148320	59-5924	3565	282C-6B
148321	59-5925	3567	282C-6B

On delivery the Navy redesignated them as the UV-1L. In September 1962 they became LC-130F-*LM*s.

US Navy ski-equipped C-130BL 148318 (c/n 3652) gets ready to land at Williams AFB, Antarctica. *Navy Photograph Center, Washington DC*

C-130BLC

A standard C-130B, 58-0712 (c/n 3507), which had been modified as the C-130BLC (Boundary Layer Control) test bed and reconverted as an NC-130B, had been employed by NASA at the Johnson Space Center in Texas from July 1968 onward. In September 1969 this aircraft was purchased and received a new registration, N707NA, being re-registered as N929NA in October 1973. Extensively modified, she was named *Earth Survey*, which reflected her role, and served until 1982, when she resumed the N707NA registration. Fitted with type 15 engines, in October 1996 she was flown from NASA Dryden before going into non-flyable storage in October 1999. She is currently in stored for NCAR without engines at Tucson.

C-130BZ

Former USAF machines ex-AMRC, via Pemco, these were modified C-130Bs that Marshalls of Cambridge refurbished with an avionics upgrade to suit the South African Air Force's requirements. This is known was 'Project Ebb' [21st Century Upgrade], under which existing SAAF Boeing 707 airborne refuelling/electronics aircraft operated by 60 SAAF Squadron would be replaced by the upgraded Hercules to conduct the existing Maritime Patrol/Security Aircraft role up to 2016. The two ex-USAF aircraft had already been modified by the fitting of H-model outer wings and a centre wing section.

In December 1996 Marshall Aerospace of Cambridge and Denel Aviation of Kempton Park, Gauteng, South Africa, were contracted to upgrade these aircraft by fitting, inter alia, digital avionics to replace their obsolete electromechanical equivalents. The project ran three years over completion date of June 2002 and was not completed until 2009. Even then ill-fortune dogged the programme; the brakes of one aircraft (402) caught fire while landing at the then Johannesburg International Airport on its final test flight in 2005, resulting in a bitter dispute between the two contractors. Another aircraft undergoing post-upgrading tests was also damaged when its fuel tanks were over-pressurised.

The aircraft were ex-58-0731 (c/n 3526), now SAAF serial 408 and named *40 Years of SAAF Herks*; ex-58-0734 (c/n 3530), now SAAF serial 409; and the 1963-build SAAF 407 (c/n 3769). It has been postulated that ideally (national finances permitting) the remaining SAAF Hercules would be replaced by five C-130Js after 2015 in a phased-in programme of replacement.

C-130C-LM

This designation was assigned to a proposed US Army-operated STOL aircraft, the prototype for which was the NC-130B-LM, serial 58-0712 (c/n 3507), but the concept was never proceeded with.

C-130D-LM

Twelve aircraft, fitted with skis:

Serial	c/n	Type
57-0484	3191	182-1A
57-0485	3192	182-1A
57-0486	3193	182-1A
57-0487	3194	182-1A
57-0488	3195	182-1A
57-0489	3196	182-1A
57-0490	3197	182-1A
57-0491	3198	182-1A
57-0492	3199	182-1A
57-0493	3200	182-1A
57-0494	3201	182-1A
57-0495	3202	182-1A

C-130D-6

Modified from C-130Ds by the removal of ski fittings:

Serial	c/n	Type
57-0484	3191	182-1A
57-0485	3192	182-1A
57-0486	3193	182-1A
57-0487	3194	182-1A
57-0488	3195	182-1A
57-0489	3196	182-1A

C-130E-LM

384 aircraft for USAF Tactical Air Command and Military Airlift Command from 15 August 1961 to March 1974:

Serial	c/n	Type	Serial	c/n	Type	Serial	c/n	Type
61-2358	3609	382-4B	62-1804	3758	382-4B	62-1840	3803	328-4B
61-2359	3651	382-4B	62-1805	3759	382-4B	62-1841	3804	382-8B
61-2360	3659	382-4B	62-1806	3760	382-4B	62-1842	3805	382-8B
61-2361	3662	382-4B	62-1807	3761	382-4B	62-1843	3806	382-8B
61-2362	3663	382-4B	62-1808	3762	382-4B	62-1844	3807	382-8B
61-2363	3681	382-4B	62-1809	3770	382-4B	62-1845	3808	382-8B
61-2364	3687	382-4B	62-1810	3771	382-4B	62-1846	3809	328-8B
61-2365	3688	382-4B	62-1811	3772	382-4B	62-1847	3810	328-4B
61-2366	3706	382-4B	62-1812	3774	382-4B	62-1848	3811	328-4B
61-2367	3712	382-4B	62-1813	3775	382-4B	62-1849	3812	328-4B
61-2368	3713	382-4B	62-1814	3776	382-4B	63-7764	3813	328-4B
61-2369	3714	382-4B	62-1815	3777	382-4B	62-1850	3814	328-4B
61-2370	3715	382-4B	62-1816	3778	382-8B	62-1851	3815	328-4B
61-2371	3716	382-4B	62-1817	3779	382-8B	62-1852	3816	382-8B
61-2372	3717	382-4B	62-1818	3780	382-8B	62-1853	3817	382-8B
61-2373	3720	382-4B	62-1819	3782	382-4B	62-1854	3818	382-8B
62-1784	3729	382-4B	62-1820	3783	382-8B	62-1855	3819	382-8B
62-1785	3730	382-4B	62-1821	3784	382-4B	62-1856	3820	382-8B
62-1786	3731	382-4B	62-1822	3785	382-4B	62-1857	3821	382-8B
62-1787	3732	382-4B	62-1823	3786	382-8B	62-1858	3822	382-8B
62-1788	3735	382-4B	62-1824	3787	382-8B	62-1859	3823	382-8B
62-1789	3736	382-4B	62-1825	3788	382-8B	62-1860	3824	382-8B
62-1790	3737	382-4B	62-1826	3789	328-8B	62-1861	3825	382-8B
62-1791	3738	382-4B	62-1827	3790	382-4B	62-1862	3826	382-8B
62-1792	3739	382-4B	62-1828	3791	382-4B	62-1863	3827	382-8B
62-1793	3743	382-4B	62-1829	3792	382-4B	62-1864	3828	382-8B
62-1794	3744	382-4B	62-1830	3793	328-4B	62-1865	3829	382-8B
62-1795	3746	382-4B	62-1831	3794	382-8B	62-1866	3830	382-8B
62-1796	3747	382-4B	62-1832	3795	382-8B	63-7765	3831	382-8B
62-1797	3748	382-4B	62-1833	3796	382-8B	63-7766	3832	382-8B
62-1798	3752	382-4B	62-1834	3797	382-8B	63-7767	3833	382-8B
62-1799	3753	382-4B	62-1835	3798	382-8B	63-7768	3834	382-8B
62-1800	3754	382-4B	62-1836	3799	328-8B	63-7769	3835	382-8B
62-1801	3755	382-4B	62-1837	3800	328-4B	63-7770	3836	382-8B
62-1802	3756	382-4B	62-1838	3801	328-4B	63-7771	3837	382-8B
62-1803	3757	382-4B	62-1839	3802	328-4B	63-7772	3838	382-8B

Serial	c/n	Type	Serial	c/n	Type	Serial	c/n	Type
63-7773	3839	382-8B	63-7816	3894	382-4B	63-7875	3945	382-4B
63-7774	3840	382-8B	63-7817	3895	382-4B	63-7876	3947	382-8B
63-7775	3841	382-8B	63-7828	3896	382-4B	63-7877	3948	328-8B
63-7776	3842	382-8B	63-7829	3897	382-4B	63-7878	3949	328-8B
63-7777	3843	382-8B	63-7830	3898	382-4B	63-7879	3950	328-8B
63-7778	3844	382-8B	63-7831	3899	382-4B	63-7880	3951	328-8B
63-7779	3845	382-8B	63-7832	3900	382-4B	63-7881	3952	382-8B
63-7780	3846	382-8B	63-7833	3901	382-4B	63-7882	3953	382-4B
63-7781	3847	382-8B	63-7834	3902	382-4B	63-7883	3954	382-4B
63-7782	3848	382-4B	63-7826	3903	382-8B	63-7884	3955	382-8B
63-7783	3850	382-4B	63-7827	3904	382-8B	63-7885	3956	382-8B
63-7784	3851	382-4B	63-7835	3905	382-8B	63-7886	3957	382-8B
63-7785	3852	382-4B	63-7836	3906	382-4B	63-7887	3958	382-8B
63-7786	3853	382-4B	63-8737	3907	382-4B	63-7888	3959	382-4B
63-7787	3854	382-4B	63-7838	3908	382-8B	63-7889	3960	382-4B
63-7788	3855	382-4B	63-7839	3909	382-8B	63-7890	3961	382-4B
63-7789	3856	382-4B	63-7840	3910	382-8B	63-7891	3962	382-4B
63-7790	3857	382-4B	63-7841	3911	382-8B	63-7892	3963	382-4B
63-7791	3859	382-4B	63-7842	3912	382-8B	63-7893	3964	382-4B
63-7792	3860	382-4B	63-7843	3913	382-4B	63-7894	3965	382-4B
63-7795	3861	382-8B	63-7844	3914	382-4B	63-7895	3966	382-8B
63-7796	3862	382-8B	63-7845	3915	382-4B	63-7896	3967	382-8B
63-7797	3863	382-8B	63-7846	3916	382-4B	63-7897	3968	382-8B
63-7798	3864	382-8B	63-7847	3917	328-4B	63-7898	3969	382-8B
63-7799	3865	382-8B	63-7848	3918	382-4B	63-7899	3970	382-8B
63-7800	3866	382-8B	63-7849	3919	382-4B	63-9810	3971	382-8B
63-7801	3867	382-8B	63-7850	3920	382-4B	63-9811	3972	382-8B
63-7802	3868	382-8B	63-7851	3921	328-4B	63-9812	3973	382-8B
63-7803	3869	382-8B	63-7852	3922	382-4B	63-9813	3974	382-4B
63-7804	3870	382-8B	63-7853	3923	382-4B	63-9814	3975	382-4B
63-7793	3872	382-4B	63-7854	3924	382-4B	63-9815	3976	382-4B
63-7794	3873	382-4B	63-7855	3925	328-4B	63-9816	3977	382-8B
63-7805	3874	382-4B	63-7856	3926	382-4B	63-9817	3978	382-8B
63-7806	3875	382-4B	63-7857	3927	382-8B	64-0495	3979	382-8B
63-7807	3876	382-4B	63-7858	3928	382-8B	64-0496	3980	382-8B
63-7808	3877	382-4B	63-7859	3929	382-8B	64-0497	3981	382-8B
63-7809	3879	382-4B	63-7860	3930	382-8B	64-0498	3982	382-8B
63-7810	3880	382-4B	63-7861	3931	382-8B	64-0499	3983	382-8B
63-7811	3881	382-4B	63-7862	3932	382-4B	64-0500	3984	382-8B
63-7812	3882	382-4B	63-7863	3933	382-8B	64-0501	3985	382-4B
63-7813	3883	382-4B	63-7864	3934	382-8B	64-0502	3986	382-4B
63-7818	3884	382-8B	63-7865	3935	382-8B	64-0503	3987	382-4B
63-7819	3885	382-8B	63-7866	3936	382-8B	64-0504	3988	382-8B
63-7820	3886	382-8B	63-7867	3937	382-8B	64-0505	3989	382-8B
63-7821	3887	382-8B	63-7868	3938	382-8B	64-0506	3990*	382-8B
63-7814	3888	382-4B	63-7869	3939	328-4B	64-0507	3991*	382-8B
63-7815	3889	382-4B	63-7870	3940	328-4B	64-0508	3992	382-8B
63-7822	3890	382-8B	63-7871	3941	328-4B	64-0509	3993	382-8B
63-7823	3891	382-8B	63-7872	3942	328-4B	64-0510	3994	382-8B
63-7824	3892	382-8B	63-7873	3943	328-4B	64-0511	3995	382-8B
63-7825	3893	382-8B	63-7874	3944	328-4B	64-0512	3996	382-8B

Serial	c/n	Type	Serial	c/n	Type	Serial	c/n	Type
64-0513	3997	382-8B	64-0556	4057	382-8B	69-6571	4345	382C-15D
64-0514	3998	382-8B	64-0557	4058	382-8B	69-6572	4346	382C-15D
64-0515	3999	382-8B	64-0558	4059	382-8B	69-6573	4347	382C-15D
64-0516	4000	382-8B	64-0559	4062	382-8B	69-6574	4348	382C-15D
64-0517	4001	382-8B	64-0560	4063	382-8B	69-6575	4349	382C-15D
64-0518	4002	382-8B	64-17680	4064	382-8B	69-6576	4351	382C-15D
64-0519	4003	382-8B	64-0561	4065	382-8B	69-6577	4352	382C-15D
64-0520	4004	382-8B	64-0562	4068	382-8B	69-6578	4353	382C-15D
64-0521	4005	382-8B	64-17681	4069	382-8B	69-6579	4354	382C-15D
64-0522	4006	382-8B	64-0563	4071	382-8B	69-6580	4356	382C-15D
64-0523	4007	382-8B	64-0564	4074	328-8B	69-6581	4357	382C-15D
64-0524	4008	382-8B	64-0565	4077	328-4B	69-6582	4359	382C-15D
64-0525	4009	382-8B	64-0569	4079	382-4B	69-6583	4360	382C-15D
64-0526	4010	382-8B	64-0566	4080	382-8B	70-1259	4404	382C-15D
64-0527	4013	382-8B	64-0567	4083	382-8B	70-1260	4410	382C-15D
64-0528	4014	382-8B	64-0570	4085	382-4B	70-1261	4413	382C-15D
64-0529	4017	382-8B	64-0568	4086	382-8B	70-1262	4414	382C-15D
64-0530	4018	382-8B	64-0571	4087	382-4b	70-1263	4415	382C-15D
64-0531	4019	382-8B	64-0572	4090	382-4B	70-1264	4417	382C-15D
64-0532	4021	382-8B	64-18240	4105	382-8B	70-1265	4418	382C-15D
64-0533	4022	382-8B	68-10934	4314	382C-13D	70-1266	4419	382C-15D
64-0534	4023	382-8B	68-10935	4315	382C-15D	70-1267	4420	382C-15D
64-0535	4024	382-4B	68-10936	4316	382C-15D	70-1268	4421	382C-15D
64-0536	4025	382-4B	68-10937	4317	382C-15D	70-1269	4423	382C-15D
64-0537	4027	382-8B	68-10938	4318	382C-15D	70-1270	4424	382C-15D
64-0538	4028	382-8B	68-10939	4319	382C-15D	70-1271	4425	382C-15D
64-0539	4029	382-8B	68-10940	4320	382C-15D	70-1272	4426	382C-15D
64-0540	4030	382-8B	68-10941	4321	382C-15D	70-1273	4428	382C-15D
64-0541	4031	382-8B	68-10942	4322	382C-15D	70-1274	4429	382C-15D
64-0542	4032	382-8B	68-10943	4323	382C-15D	70-1275	4434	382C-15D
64-0543	4033	382-8B	68-10944	4324	382C-15D	70-1276	4435	382C-15D
64-0544	4034	382-4B	68-10945	4325	382C-15D	72-1288	4499	382C-15D
64-0545	4035	382-4B	68-10946	4326	382C-15D	72-1289	4500	382C-15D
64-0546	4039	382-8B	68-10947	4327	382C-15D	72-1290	4502	382C-15D
64-0547	4040	382-8B	68-10948	4328	382C-15D	72-1291	4504	382C-15D
64-0548	4043	382-8B	68-10949	4329	382C-15D	72-1292	4505	382C-15D
64-0549	4044	382-8B	68-10950	4330	382C-15D	72-1293	4506	382C-15D
64-0550	4045	382-8B	68-10951	4331	382C-15D	72-1294	4509	382C-15D
64-0551	4046	382-8B	69-6566	4340	382C-15D	72-1295	4510	382C-15D
64-0552	4047	383-4B	69-6567	4341	382C-15D	72-1296	4517	382C-15D
64-0553	4048	382-4B	69-6568	4342	382C-15D	72-1297	4519	382C-15D
64-0554	4049	382-4B	69-6659	4343	382C-15D	72-1298	4521	382C-15D
64-0555	4056	382-8B	69-6570	4344	382C-15D	72-1299	4527	382C-15D

There were also four built for the US Navy, four for the US Coast Guard, and 109 more for Australia, Brazil, Canada, Iran, Saudi Arabia, Sweden and Turkey (see the appropriate sections).

C/n 3990 marked * in the above table was the former 62-1843 (3806), which crashed at Tuy Hoa in 1965 and subsequently had her aircraft number transferred to c/n 3990. C/n 3991, also thus marked, was the former 63-7785 (3852), which exploded in mid-air over Cam Ranh Bay in 1966 and had her aircraft number transferred to c/n 3991. These two new aircraft, the former USAF 64-0506 and 64-0507, were transferred from the USAF to a 'Special User' in 1964, which oversaw their conversion by Lockheed Aircraft Service Company at Ontario, California, to flying test beds for

Project 'Thin Slice', the development of low-level covert penetration transports for Special Forces operations in SE Asia. Finished in an overall black 'sanitised' paint scheme, they operated into Laos.

Another pair were 1964-build C-130Es from a batch of fourteen that, in December 1965, had been diverted from the USAF to Marietta to convert them to SOG requirements. This pair were taken out of that group in August 1966 and alternatively modified to carry out Operation 'Heavy Chain', a series of covert and still partly classified missions conducted from Norton AFB, California, until it was finally wound up on 31 December 1973. These aircraft were given the code name 'Rivet Yard', and were USAF C-130Es 64-0564 (c/n 4074) and 64-0565 (c/n 4077); subsequently they were modified to 'Rivet Yank', minus the Fulton Gear at the request of the 'Special User' in 1974, and got the improved Alison T56-15 engines in place of their old -7s, which gave them an improved climb rate.[1]

The four 'Rivet Yanks' replaced existing 'Rivet Clamps' by the Pacific area user ('Combat Spear') and conducted operations in that theatre under the generic name 'Combat Sam'. Meanwhile the four displaced 'Clamp' aircraft moved to Hurlburt AFB, thereby temporarily reinforcing the existing four based there. In the event, two of these aircraft were further retained as Student Flight Trainers for the Central & South America and Africa operative ('Combat Knife'). The remaining pair of the displaced quartet, 64-0571 (c/n 4087) and 64-0572 (c/n 4090), had their ECM suite and other SOG apparatus removed at AFLC/AZ and were loaned out, the former being used as a special test machine at Kirtland AFB and the latter employed by ASD at Wright-Patterson; the pair were classified as 'Rivet Swap' aircraft and later became NC-130Es. When later a 'Combat Spear' aircraft, 64-0564 (c/n 4074), was lost in the South China Sea in 1981, she was replaced by a loaned 'Combat Knife' machine working from Clark AB in the Philippines. To fully compensate, 64-0572 (c/n 4090) was quickly reconverted to 'Rivet Clamp' mode and went to Hurlburt, while 64-0571 (c/n 4087) was retrieved from Kirtland into a 'Rivet Yank' before going out to Clark as the permanent replacement.

ASD C-130E Hercules 64-0571 (c/n 4087), seen in June 1970. *Bruce Stewart, via Nick Williams, AAHS*

The European-based quartet ('Combat Arrow') later had specially adapted ECM configurations more suitable to European operating conditions. As late as 1989-93 'Easy' (later 'Echo') Flight, 21 Tactical Control Squadron (TCS), was operating from the main Rhein Main AFB near Frankfurt, Germany, overtly as a civilian outfit carrying aircraft spares.

[1] See Colonel Jerry L. Thigpen's heavily edited book, *The Praetorian STARship: The untold story of the Combat Talon* (Air University Press, 2001) and also Michael E. Haas, *Apollo's Warriors: US Air Force Special Operations during the Cold War* (University of the Pacific, 2002).

To revert, the following conversions took place:

Serial	c/n	Type
64-0523	4007	382-8B
64-0547	4040	382-8B
64-0551	4046	382-8B
64-0555	4056	382-8B
64-0558	4059	382-8B
64-0559	4062	382-8B
64-0561	4065	382-8B
64-0562	4068	382-8B
64-0563	4071	382-8B
64-0566	4080	382-8B
64-0567	4083	382-8B
64-0568	4086	382-8B

These twelve aircraft had been flown into Donaldson AFB at Greenville, South Carolina, where they were repainted with Dupont low-radar reflective paint by Ling-Temco-Vought Electrosystems, the resultant 'Velvet Black and Green' paint job leading them to be dubbed as 'Blackbirds', a name that survived until the 1980s. This extra 'shielding' (a forerunner of today's Radar Absorbent Material [RAM]) increased each aircraft's weight by some 370lb. At Marietta, Georgia, Fulton Air Recovery System (ARS) equipment, later known as the Fulton Surface-to-Air-Recovery System (STARS)[2], was fitted together with the Texas Instruments (TI) AN/APQ-115 navigational radar and the 'Rivet Clamp' electronics and countermeasures Infra-Red (IR) suites, in four monthly batches of three; the first quartet was completed in March 1966, these aircraft initially being dubbed simply as 'Clamps' (C-130E-(CT)) together with the two 'Rivet Swap' C-130E-(S) until, in 1967, the official title of 'Combat Talon' was adopted. The following year two further machines, 64-0571 (c/n 4087) and 64-0572 (c/n 4090), were both converted, but *sans* Fulton gear, to replace the combat losses of 64-0563 (destroyed by mortar fire at Nha Trang AB, South Vietnam, in November 1967) and 64-0547 (which crashed during a combat mission near Dien Bien Phu in December 1967).

Between 1971 and 1973 all sixteen aircraft in service had MOD-70 comprehensive radar upgrades installed, combining the AN/APQ-122-based Adverse Weather Aerial Delivery System (AWADS) with Litton LN-15J inertial Navigation System (INS) incorporating Terrain-Following/Terrain-Avoidance TF/TA technology, and this remained in place for the next decade.

In 1980, during preparations for the failed Iranian rescue mission ('Eagle Claw'), four 'Combat Talons' began to experiment with a palletised fuelling system comprising two 1,800-gallon Benson tanks carried on rails in the cargo hold, and linked to the existing pressurised fuel dump pumps. With these embarked, three 'Combat Talons' were earmarked to become Forward Area Refuelling Points (FARP) for helicopters to extend their range into hostile territory, but in the event only one was ready in time. A proposed second rescue mission, Operation 'Credible Sport' (which never finally materialised), involved planning for the use of a 'Super STOL' mission. Three C-130Hs were acquired in August 1980, one of which was initially designated as XFC-130H to be used as the experimental machine, leaving two for modification for the actual mission as YMC-130Hs. Only the first received modification, but that was lost on 29 October 1980 during trials.

[2] In 1982 there was a terminal incident with this equipment, which led to an intense three-year programme in an effort to make a safer version, codenamed Project 46, but the results were never implemented and, by 1998, all STARS equipment was discontinued and removed.

Camouflaged Hercules C-130E 63-7822 (c/n 3890) is seen at RAF Lakenheath, England, on 28 May 1966. *Nick Williams, AAHS*

USAF C-130E Herk 62-1804 (c/n 3758) of 4442 Combat Crew Training Group, with wavy pattern camouflage, is seen in May 1967 at Hickam, Hawaii. *Nick Williams, AAHS*

A nice view of Military Airlift Command (MAC) C-130E 63-7816 (c/n 3894), of 1611 TAW from McGuire AFB but seen here at Lakehurst NAS in July 1967. *Nick Williams, AAHS*

Wheels down as C-130E 63-7829 (c/n 3897) of 438 MAW, MAC, makes her final approach to Hickam AFB in 1967. *Nick Williams, AAHS*

C-130E 63-7880 (c/n 3951), of 516 TCW, is seen at Sioux City, Iowa, in 1967. *Clyde Gerdes, via Nick Williams, AAHS*

USAF C-130E 62-1804 (c/n 3758), of 37 TAS, with wavy pattern camouflage, is seen in June 1968 leaving Hickam AFB, Hawaii. *Nick Williams, AAHS*

Engines roar at Hickam AFB on 31 January 1968 as C-130E 62-1792 (c/n 3739), of 516 TAW, prepares to leave. *Nick Williams, AAHS*

On 2 June 1968, shimmering in the desert sun, is C-130E 63-7776 (c/n 3842) of 516 TCW. *Nick Williams, AAHS*

At Hickam AFB, Hawaii, in May 1968, Military Airlift Command Hercules C-130E 63-7831 (c/n 3899) of the 438th Military Airlift Wing (MAW) revs up on the main ramp. *Nick Williams, AAHS*

Carrying MAC markings, C-130E 63-9814 (c/n 3975), also of 438 MAW, revs up on the deck at Hickam in 1968. *Nick Williams, AAHS*

C-130E 68-10942 (c/n 4322) of 317 TAW was photographed in March 1969. *Author's collection*

Seen here at Kai Tak Airport, Hong Kong, on 9 October 1971 is C-130E 63-7765 (c/n 3831) of 314 TAW, 776 TAS, at that time based at Ching Chuan Kang Air Force Base, Taiwan. *Mauro Trovato Finard*

C-130E 64-0504 (c/n 3988) of 62 Marine Airlift Wing is seen at McChord MAS on 19 October 1978. One wing was burned off at McChord, and she is seen when rebuilt, conducting tests with a new two-tone grey camouflage scheme. *Nick Williams, AAHS*

THE LOCKHEED MARTIN C-130 HERCULES

The two-tone grey/grey cameo paint job is seen again under test on the same aircraft, of 317 TAW, named *Spirit of Lafayetteville*, pictured here in June 1980 *Nick Williams, AAHS*

With full flaps, MAC C-130E 63-7892 (c/n 3963), of 314 TAW, makes a steady descent over Hickam AFB, Hawaii, in 1979. *Nick Williams, AAHS*

USAF MAC 64-0510 (c/n 3994), of 36 TAS, pictured on 21 February 1980. *Werner Hartman, via Nick Williams, AAHS*

C-130E 63-7807 (c/n 3876), of 317 TAW, on the mat in December 1980. *Werner Hartman, via Nick Williams, AAHS*

Tail-coded PB for Pope AFB, North Carolina, this is C-130E 63-7770 (c/n 3836) on the grass at RAF Lakenheath, England. *Nick Williams, AAHS*

A brace of AFRES C-130E Herks in June 1970; 63-7874 (c/n 3944), with 37 TAS, is closest to the camera. *Nick Williams, AAHS*

THE LOCKHEED MARTIN C-130 HERCULES

C-130E 62-1819 (c/n 3782) carries the LM tail-code of 36 TAS, 316 TAW. *McDonnell Douglas*

C-130E-I

Seventeen 'Combat Talon' aircraft, modified from C-130Es, plus one aircraft (*), modified from an NC-130E:

Serial	c/n	Type	Serial	c/n	Type
62-1843	3806	382-8B	64-0561	4065	382-8B
63-7785	3852	382-4B	64-0562	4068	382-8B
64-0508	3992	382-8B	64-0563	4071	382-8B
64-0523	4007	382-8B	64-0564	4074	382-8B
64-0547	4040	382-8B	64-0565	4077	382-8B
64-0551	4046	382-8B	64-0566	4080	382-8B
64-0555	4056	382-8B	64-0567	4083	382-8B
64-0558	4059	382-8B	64-0568	4086	382-8B
64-0559	4062	382-8B	64-0572*	4090	382-4B

C-130E-II

Ten aircraft, C130E conversions into ABCCC aircraft:

Serial	c/n	Type
62-1791	3738	382-4B
62-1809	3770	382-8B
62-1815	3777	382-4B
62-1818	3780	382-8B
62-1820	3783	382-4B
62-1825	3788	382-8B
62-1832	3795	382-8B
62-1836	3799	382-8B
62-1857	3821	382-8B
62-1863	3827	382-8B

In April 1967 these were re-designated as EC-130s.

C-130F-LM

Seven aircraft, US Navy Transport GV-1Us, redesignated in September 1962:

BuOrd Noc/n		Type
149787	3636	282B-3B
149790	3645	282B-3B
149793	3660	282B-3B
149794	3661	282B-3B
149797	3666	282B-3B
149801	3686	282B-3B
149805	3696	282B-3B

United States Navy C-130F 149787 (c/n 3636), tail-coded RZ, of VR-21, is seen at Naval Air Station Atsugi in 1967. *Nick Williams, AAHS*

Another US Navy RZ-coded C-130F, 149805 (c/n 3696), of the US Navy, at NAS Barbers Point. *Nick Williams, AAHS*

THE LOCKHEED MARTIN C-130 HERCULES

US Navy C-130F 149787 (c/n 3636), of VRC-50 and tail-coded RG for Anderson AFB, Guam, displays her striking prop markings at Yakota Airfield, Japan, in September 1978. *Bob Stewart via Nick Williams, AAHS*

C-130H-LM

306 aircraft, for USAF Tactical Air Command, Air National Guard, Air Force Reserves and Air Combat Command, from June 1974 to December 1996:

Serial	c/n	Type	Serial	c/n	Type	Serial	c/n	Type
73-1580	4542	382C-33D	74-1675	4640	382C-41D	74-2133	4730	382C-41D
73-1581	4543	382C-33D	74-1676	4641	382C-41D	74-2134	4735	382C-41D
73-1582	4544	382C-33D	74-1677	4643	382C-41D	78-0806	4815	382C-80D
73-1583	4545	382C-33D	74-2061	4644	382C-41D	78-0807	4817	382C-80D
73-1584	4546	382C-33D	74-1678	4645	382C-41D	78-0808	4818	382C-80D
73-1585	4547	382C-33D	74-1679	4646	382C-41D	78-0809	4819	382C-80D
73-1586	4548	382C-33D	74-2062	4647	382C-41D	78-0810	4820	382C-80D
73-1587	4549	382C-33D	74-1680	4651	382C-41D	78-0811	4821	382C-80D
73-1588	4550	382C-33D	74-2063	4655	382C-41D	78-0812	4822	382C-80D
73-1590	4554	382C-33D	74-1682	4657	382C-41D	78-0813	4823	382C-80D
73-1592	4557	382C-33D	74-1683	4658	382C-41D	79-0474	4854	382C-88D
73-1594	4563	382C-33D	74-2064	4659	382C-41D	79-0475	4855	382C-88D
73-1595	4564	382C-33D	74-1684	4663	382C-41D	79-0476	4856	382C-80D
73-1597	4571	382C-33D	74-1685	4666	382C-41D	79-0477	4857	382C-80D
73-1598	4573	382C-33D	74-2065	4667	382C-41D	79-0478	4858	382C-88D
74-1658	4579	382C-41D	74-1686	4669	382C-41D	79-0479	4859	382C-88D
74-1659	4585	382C-41D	74-1687	4670	382C-41D	79-0480	4860	382C-88D
74-1660	4592	382C-41D	74-2066	4671	382C-41D	80-0320	4900	382C-5E
74-1661	4596	382C-41D	74-1688	4675	382C-41D	80-0321	4902	382C-5E
74-1662	4597	382C-41D	74-2067	4678	382C-41D	80-0322	4903	382C-5E
74-1663	4598	382C-41D	74-1689	4681	382C-41D	80-0323	4905	382C-5E
74-1664	4603	382C-41D	74-1690	4682	382C-41D	80-0324	4906	382C-5E
74-1665	4604	382C-41D	74-1691	4687	382C-41D	80-0325	4908	382C-5E
74-1666	4611	382C-41D	74-1692	4688	382C-41D	80-0326	4910	382C-5E
74-1667	4613	382C-41D	74-1693	4693	382C-41D	81-0626	4939	382C-18E
74-1668	4616	382C-41D	74-2068	4694	382C-41D	81-0627	4941	382C-18E
74-1669	4617	382C-41D	74-2069	4699	382C-41D	81-0628	4942	382C-18E
74-1670	4620	382C-41D	74-2070	4700	382C-41D	80-0332	4943	382C-18E
74-1671	4621	382C-41D	74-2071	4703	382C-41D	81-0629	4944	382C-18E
74-1672	4623	382C-41D	74-2072	4705	382C-41D	81-0630	4945	382C-18E
74-1673	4627	382C-41D	74-2131	4718	382C-41D	81-0631	4946	382C-18E
74-1674	4631	382C-41D	74-2132	4722	382C-41D	82-0054	4968	382C-35E

Serial	c/n	Type	Serial	c/n	Type	Serial	c/n	Type
82-0055	4970	382C-35E	86-0415	5105	382C-74E	90-1057	5240	382C-14F
82-0056	4971	382C-35E	86-0418	5110	382C-74E	90-1058	5241	382C-14F
82-0057	4973	382C-35E	86-1397	5111	382C-74E	90-1791	5242	382C-14F
82-0058	4975	382C-35E	86-1398	5112	382C-74E	90-1792	5245	382C-14F
82-0059	4977	382C-35E	86-0419	5113	382C-74E	90-1793	5246	382C-14F
82-0060	4979	382C-35E	87-9281	5122	382C-81E	90-1794	5247	382C-14F
82-0061	4982	382C-35E	87-9282	5123	382C-81E	90-1795	5248	382C-14F
83-0486*	5008	382C-46E	87-9283	5124	382C-81E	90-1796	5249	382C-14F
83-0491	5010	382C-47E	87-9284	5125	382C-81E	90-1797	5250	382C-14F
83-0487*	5012	382C-46E	87-9285	5126	382C-81E	90-1798	5251	382C-14F
83-0488*	5014	382C-46E	87-9286	5127	382C-81E	91-1231	5278	382C-22F
83-0489*	5018	382C-46E	87-9287	5128	382C-81E	91-1232	5282	382C-22F
84-0204	5038	382C-60E	87-9288	5129	382C-81E	91-1233	5283	382C-22F
84-0205	5039	382C-60E	88-4401	5154	382C-88E	91-1234	5284	382C-22F
84-0475	5041	382C-59E	88-4402	5155	382C-88E	91-1235	5285	382C-22F
84-0476	5042	382C-59E	88-4403	5156	382C-88E	91-1236	5286	382C-22F
84-0206	5043	382C-60E	88-4404	5157	382C-88E	91-1237	5287	382C-22F
84-0207	5044	382C-60E	88-4405	5158	382C-88E	91-1238	5288	382C-22F
84-0208	5046	382C-60E	88-4406	5159	382C-88E	91-1239	5289	382C-22F
84-0209	5047	382C-60E	88-4407	5160	382C-88E	91-1651	5290	382C-22F
84-0210	5049	382C-60E	88-4408	5161	382C-88E	91-1652	5291	382C-22F
84-0211	5050	382C-60E	88-1301	5162	382C-88E	91-1653	5292	382C-22F
84-0212	5051	382C-60E	88-1302	5163	382C-88E	91-9141	5293	382C-22F
84-0213	5052	382C-60E	88-1303	5164	382C-88E	91-9142	5295	382C-22F
85-1361	5071	382C-71E	88-1304	5165	382C-88E	91-9143	5296	382C-22F
85-1362	5072	382C-71E	88-1305	5166	382C-88E	91-9144	5297	382C-22F
85-0035	5073	382C-71E	88-1306	5167	382C-88E	92-3021	5312	382C-35F
85-0036	5074	382C-71E	88-1307	5168	382C-88E	92-3022	5313	382C-35F
85-1363	5075	382C-71E	88-1308	5169	382C-88E	92-3023	5314	382C-35F
85-1364	5076	382C-71E	89-1181	5188	382C-96E	92-3024	5315	382C-35F
85-0037	5077	382C-71E	89-1182	5190	382C-96E	92-0550	5321	382C-33F
85-1365	5078	382C-71E	89-1183	5192	382C-96E	92-1533	5322	382C-33F
85-0038	5079	382C-71E	89-1184	5193	382C-96E	92-1534	5323	382C-33F
85-0039	5080	382C-71E	89-1185	5194	382C-96E	92-1535	5324	382C-33F
85-1366	5081	382C-71E	89-1186	5195	382C-96E	92-1536	5325	382C-33F
85-1367	5082	382C-71E	89-1187	5196	382C-96E	92-1537	5326	382C-33F
85-0040	5083	382C-71E	89-1188	5197	382C-96E	92-1538	5327	382C-33F
85-1368	5084	382C-71E	89-1051	5198	382C-96E	92-1532	5328	382C-33F
85-0041	5086	382C-71E	89-1052	5199	382C-96E	92-1452	5329	382C-33F
85-0042	5089	382C-71E	89-1053	5201	382C-96E	92-1453	5330	382C-33F
86-1391	5093	382C-74E	89-1054	5203	382C-96E	92-3281	5331	382C-33F
86-0410	5094	382C-74E	89-1055	5204	382C-96E	92-0547	5332	382C-33F
86-1392	5095	382C-74E	89-1056	5205	382C-96E	92-1454	5333	382C-33F
86-1393	5096	382C-74E	89-9101	5216	382C-96E	92-3282	5334	382C-33F
86-0411	5097	382C-74E	89-9102	5217	382C-96E	92-0548	5335	382C-33F
86-0412	5098	382C-74E	89-9103	5218	382C-96E	92-3283	5336	382C-33F
86-1394	5099	382C-74E	89-9104	5220	382C-96E	92-0549	5337	382C-33F
86-0413	5100	382C-74E	89-9105	5221	382C-96E	92-3284	5338	382C-33F
86-1395	5101	382C-74E	89-9106	5223	382C-96E	92-0551	5346	382C-33F
86-0414	5102	382C-74E	90-9107	5238	382C-14F	92-3285	5347	382C-33F
86-1396	5103	382C-74E	90-9108	5239	382C-14F	92-0552	5348	382C-33F

Serial	c/n	Type	Serial	c/n	Type	Serial	c/n	Type
92-3286	5349	382C-33F	93-7311	5374	382C-42F	94-6708	5400	382C-53F
92-0553	5350	382C-33F	93-1040	5375	382C-42F	94-7320	5401	382C-53F
92-3287	5351	382C-33F	93-1041	5376	382C-42F	94-7321	5403	382C-53F
92-0554	5352	382C-33F	93-7312	5377	382C-42F	95-6709	5417	382C-57F
92-3288	5353	382C-33F	94-6701	5378	382C-42F	95-6710	5418	382C-57F
93-1455	5360	382C-42F	93-7313	5379	382C-42F	95-6711	5419	382C-57F
93-1456	5361	382C-42F	93-7314	5380	382C-42F	95-6712	5420	382C-57F
93-1457	5362	382C-42F	94-6702	5382	382C-42F	95-1001	5421	382C-57F
93-1458	5363	382C-42F	94-7315	5389	382C-53F	95-1002	5422	382C-57F
93-1459	5364	382C-42F	94-7316	5390	382C-53F	96-1003	5423	382C-57F
93-1561	5365	382C-42F	94-7317	5391	382C-53F	96-1004	5424	382C-57F
93-1562	5366	382C-42F	94-7318	5392	382C-53F	96-1005	5425	382C-57F
93-1563	5367	382C-42F	94-6703	5393	382C-53F	96-1006	5426	382C-57F
93-1036	5368	382C-42F	94-6704	5394	382C-53F	96-1007	5427	382C-57F
93-1037	5369	382C-42F	94-7319	5395	382C-53F	96-1008	5428	382C-57F
93-2041	5370	382C-42F	94-7310	5396	382C-53F	96-7322	5431	382C-57F
93-2042	5371	382C-42F	94-6705	5397	382C-53F	96-7323	5432	382C-57F
93-1038	5372	382C-42F	94-6706	5398	382C-53F	96-7324	5433	382C-57F
93-1039	5373	382C-42F	94-6707	5399	382C-53F	96-7325	5434	382C-57F

* Fitted with skis

USAF Rescue 65-0985 (c/n 4140) lifts off from Hickam AFB. *Nick Williams, AAHS*

Military Airlift Command's Hercules HC-130H 65-0983 (c/n 4138), with 41 ARRS, seen in September 1968. *Nick Williams, AAHS*

A 19 January 1968 view of a USAF 'Crown Bird' Herk over Hickam AFB, Hawaii. *Nick Williams, AAHS*

Hercules HC-130H 64-14861 (c/n 4088), of 57 ARRS. *Author's collection*

An impressive overhead aerial view of WC-130H 65-0977 (c/n 4127) , of the 920th Weather Reconnaissance Wing (WRW), USAF Reserve, based at Kessler AFB, Missouri, seen in June 1977. *USAF*

In addition, eight USAF Hercules were converted to C-130H standard for the USAF, as follows: one NC-130H, serial 64-14854 (c/n 4038), in April 1986; six WC-130Hs, serials 65-0964 (c/n 4104); 65-0969 (c/n 4111); 65-0972 (c/n 4120); 65-0976 (c/n 4126); 65-0977 (c/n 4127); and 65-0985 (c/n 4140) between July 1990 and March 1992; and one EC-130H, serial 64-14859 (c/n 4082), in June 1993.

The C-130H was the most widely used variant and additionally served with the US Navy, US Coast Guard, and fifty foreign air forces (see the appropriate sections).

C-130H-(CT)

Eleven C-130E-I 'Combat Talon' aircraft:

Serial	c/n	Type
64-0523	4007	382C-8B
64-0551	4046	382C-8B
64-0555	4056	382C-8B
64-0559	4062	382C-8B
64-0561	4065	382C-8B
64-0562	4068	382C-8B
64-0566	4080	382C-8B
64-0567	4083	382C-8B
64-0568	4086	382C-8B
64-0571*	4087	382C-4B
64-0572*	4090	

Nine were subsequently redesignated as MC-130Es and two (*) as MC-130E-Cs.

C-130H-(S)

Four aircraft, C-130Hs 'stretched' by 4.6m to L-100-30 standards for the air forces of Canada and Portugal, and fifty-six new-builds to the same specification for twelve more air forces.

These were subsequently redesignated as C-130H-30s.

C-130H-30

Four aircraft, C-130Hs 'stretched' by 4.6m to L-100-30 standards for the air forces of Canada and Portugal; serials 6801 (c/n 4749); 6802 (c/n 4753); 130343 (c/n 5307), formerly civilian N41030; and 130344 (c/n 5320), formerly civilian N4080M.

Fifty-five aircraft, new-builds to the same specification for twelve more air forces:

Serial	c/n	Type	Serial	c/n	Type	Serial	c/n	Type
A-1317	4864	382T-3E	7T-WHA	4997	382T-56E	60107	5208	382T-17F
A-1318	4865	382T-3E	NAF918	5001	382T-41E	471	5211	382T-27F
A-1319	4868	382T-3E	TL10-01	5003	382T-52E	1622	5212	382T-27F
A-1320	4869	382T-3E	5006	5006	382T-51E	7T-WHB	5224	382T-13F
A-1321	4870	382T-3E	5019	5019	382T-51E	61-PK	5226	382T-20F
7T-VHO	4897	382T-16E	5030	5030	382T-62E	61-PL	5227	382T-20F
7T-VHN	4894	382T-16E	5036	5036	382T-62E	6806	5264	382T-25F
7T-VHM	4919	382T-30E	61-PD	5140	382T-91E	M30-10	5268	382C-05F
7T-VHP	4921	382T-30E	61-PE	5142	382T-91E	G-273	5273	382T-50F
A-1321	4925	382T-21E	61-PF	5144	382T-91E	G-275	5275	382T-50F
A-1324	4927	382T-21E	60105	5146	382T-93E	M30-12	5277	382T-34F
TJX-AE	4933	382T-20E	60106	5148	382T-93E	60111	5280	382T-38F
60104	4959	382T-38E	61-PG	5150	382T-94E	60112	5281	382T-38F
312	4961	382T-39E	61-PH	5151	382T-94E	M30-11	5309	382T-44F
NAF916	4962	382T-40E	61-P1	5152	382T-94E	M30-14	5311	382T-44F
NAF917	4963	382T-40E	61-PJ	5153	382T-94E	M30-15	5316	382T-44F
HZ-MS8	4986	382T-55E	TT-AAH	5184	382T-09F	M30-16	5319	382T-44F
7T-WHD	4987	382T-45E	1293	5187	382T-10F			
7T-WHL	4989	382T-45E	1295	5206	382T-10F			

C-130H (AEH)

Four aircraft, converted from C-130Hs:

Serial	c/n	Type
7T-WHZ-MS019	4837	382C-93D
7T-WHZ-116	4914	382382C-25E
7T-WHZ-MS021	4918	382C-32E
7T-WHZ-MS7	4922	382C-26E

HZ-MS7 (c/n 4922) was operated by Saudia.

Six aircraft, converted from L-100-30s:

Serial	c/n	Type
7T-WHZ-117	4954	382CG-63C
7T-WHZ-MS05	4950	382G-60C
7T-WHZ-MS06	4952	382G-60C
7T-WHZ-MS09	4956	382G-61C
7T-WHZ-MS10	4957	382G-61C
7T-WHZ-MS14	4960	382G-61C

C-130H-MP

Three aircraft – serials FM2451 (c/n 4847), FM2452 (c/n 4849) and FM2453 (c/n 4866) – were produced for the Malaysian Air Force in 1980. They were later modified to aerial tankers and re-registered as M30-7, M30-08 and M30-09 respectively.

One aircraft, *Tentera Nasional Indonesia-Angkatan Udare*, serial AI 1322 (c/n 4898), was built for the Indonesian Air Force in November 1981. This machine was lost on 21 November 1985 when she crashed into Sibyak volcano.

C-130J

Thirty-four aircraft. At the time of writing, thirty-four standard C-130Js are built or building for the British, American (ANG) and Italian air forces, these being serials 94-3026 (c/n 5413), later civilian N130JC; 94-3027 (c/n 5415), later civilian N130JG; 96-8153 (c/n 5454), former civilian N4099R; 96-8154 (c/n 5455); 97-1351 (c/n 5469); 97-1352 (c/n 5470); 97-1353 (c/n 5471); 97-1354 (c/n 5472); ZH880 (c/n 5478), former civilian registration N73238; ZH881 (c/n 5479), former civilian N4249Y; ZH882 (c/n 5480), former civilian N4081M; ZH883 (c/n 5481), former civilian N4242N; ZH884 (c/n 5482), former civilian N4249Y; ZH885 (c/n 5483), former civilian N41030; ZH886 (c/n 5484), former civilian N73235; ZH887 (c/n 5485), former civilian N4187W; 98-1355 (c/n 5491); 98-1356 (c/n 5492); 98-1357 (c/n 5493); 98-1358 (c/n 5494); 46-20 (c/n 5495); ZH888 (c/n 5496), former civilian N4187; 46-21 (c/n 5497); 46-22 (c/n 5498); ZH889 (c/n 5500); 46-46 (c/n 5510); 46-47 (c/n 5511); 46-48 (c/n 5512); 46-49 (c/n 5513); 46-50 (c/n 5514); 46-51 (c/n 5520); 46-53 (c/n 5521); 46-54 (c/n 5523) and 46-55 (c/n 5529, 46-56 (c/n5530), 46-57 (c/n5531), 46-58 (c/n5539), 46-59 (c/n5540).

C-130J-30

Originally there were some ninety-eight aircraft, stretched C-130Js, thirty-seven for the USAF, twenty-five for the RAF, twelve for the RAAF, twenty for the Italian Air Force, and four for the Kuwaiti Air Force. Serials included ZH865 (c/n 5408), former civilian N130JA; ZH866 (c/n 5414), former civilian N130JE; ZH867 (c/n 5416), former civilian N130JJ; A97-440 (c/n 5440), former civilian N130JQ; A97-441 (c/n 5441); A97-442 (c/n 5442), former civilian N130JR; ZH868 (c/n 5443), former civilian N130JN; ZH869 (c/n 5444), former civilian N130JV; ZH870 (c/n 5445), former civilian N73235; ZH871 (c/n 5446), former civilian N73238; A97-447 (c/n 5447), former civilian N73232; A97-448 (c/n 5448), former civilian N73230; A97-449 (c/n 5449), former civilian N73233; A97-450 (c/n 5450), former civilian N4187W; ZH872 (c/n 5456), former civilian N4249Y; ZH873 (c/n 5457), former civilian N4242N; ZH874 (c/n 5458), former civilian N41030; ZH875 (c/n 5459), former civilian N4099R;

382V-37J C-130J-30 02-8155 (c/n 5546) taking off with the Air Force Reserve Command (AFRC). *Courtesy of US Defense Department*

ZH876 (c/n 5460), former civilian N4080M; ZH877 (c/n 5461), former civilian N4081M; ZH878 (c/n 5462), former civilian N73232; ZH879 (c/n 5463); A97-464 (c/n 5464); A97-465 (c/n 5465); A97-466 (c/n 5466); A97-467 (c/n 5467); and A97-468 (c/n 5468).

The 'stretched' version has proved most popular and orders continue to come. The most recent C-130J-30 additions are:

Customer	Serial	c/n	Type	Customer	Serial	c/n	Type
ANG	99-1431	5517	382V-30J	USAF	07-8602	5608	382V-44J
ANG	99-1432	5518	382V-30J	USAF	08-8601	5609	382V-44J
ANG	99-1433	5519	382V-30J	USAF	07-46312	5610	382V-44J
ANG	01-1461	5525	382V-37J	USAF	08-8602	5611	382V-44J
ANG	01-1462	5526	382V-37J	USAF	08-8604	5612	382V-44J
USAF	02-0314	5545	382V-37J	USAF	08-8603	5613	382V-44J
AFRES	02-8155	5546	382V-37J	USAF	08-8606	5614	382V-44J
ANG	02-1434	5547	382V-37J	USAF	08-8605	5615	382V-44J
ANG	02-1463	5551	382V-37J	USAF	08-8607	5616	382V-44J
ANG	02-1464	5552	382V-37J	USAF	06-8611	5619	382V-44J
AFRES	04-3144	5560	382V-44J	USAF	06-8612	5620	382V-44J
USAF	04-3142	5558	382V-44J	USAF	06-8610	5621	382V-44J
USAF	04-3143	5559	382V-44J	USAF	07-8608	5622	382V-44J
USAF	04-3144	5560	382V-44J	USAF	07-8609	5623	382V-44J
AFRES	04-8153	5561	382V-44J	USAF	06-8613	5624	382V-44J
USAF	05-8152	5566	382V-44J	USAF	07-8614	5625	382V-44J
USAF	05-3146	5567	382V-44J	USAF	07-31701	5628	382V-44J
USAF	05-3147	5568	382V-44J	USAF	06-31701	5641	382V-44J
USAF	05-3145	5569	382V-44J	USAF	08-31703	5642	382V-44J
USAF	05-8157	5570	382V-44J	USAF	08-31704	5643	382V-44J
USAF	05-8156	5571	382V-44J	USAF	08-31705	5648	382V-44J
ANG	05-1435	5572	382V-44J	USAF		5670	382V-44J
USAF	05-8158	5573	382V-44J	USAF		5671	382V-44J
ANG	05-1465	5574	382V-44J	USAF		5672	382V-44J
ANG	05-1436	5575	382V-44J	USAF		5673	382V-44J
ANG	05-1466	5576	382V-44J	USAF		5674	382V-44J
USAF	06-8159	5581	382V-44J	USAF		5675	382V-44J
USAF	06-4631	5582	382V-44J	USAF		5678	382V-44J
USAF	06-1438	5584	382V-44J	USAF		5679	382V-44J
USAF	06-1467	5585	382V-44J	USAF		5683	382V-44J
USAF	06-1437	5586	382V-44J	USAF		5684	382V-44J
USAF	06-4632	5587	382V-44J	USAF		5685	382V-44J
USAF	06-4633	5588	382V-44J	USAF		5686	382V-44J
USAF	06-4634	5589	382V-44J	USAF		5691	382V-44J
USAF	07-1468	5594	382V-44J	USAF		5692	382V-44J
USAF	07-4635	5595	382V-44J	USAF		5693	382V-44J
USAF	07-4636	5596	382V-44J	USAF		5694	382V-44J
USAF	07-4637	5597	382V-44J				
USAF	07-4638	5598	382V-44J				
USAF	07-4639	5599	382V-44J				
USAF	07-4640	5600	382V-44J				

In addition, the following C-130J-30s were built for the Canadian Armed Forces:

Serial	c/n	Type	Serial	c/n	Type
130601	5626	382V-44J	130610	5664	382V-47J
130602	5627	382V-44J	130611	5665	382V-47J
130603	5635	382V-47J	130612	5666	382V-72J
130604	5636	382V-47J	130613	5667	382V-72J
130605	5637	382V-47J	130614	5687	382V-47J
130606	5649	382V-47J	130615	5688	382V-47J
130607	5650	382V-47J	130616	5689	382V-47J
130608	5651	382V-47J	130617	5690	382V-47J
130609	5652	382V-47J			

C-130K-LM

Sixty-six aircraft, British equivalents of the C-130H, and known as the Hercules C. Mk 1 in RAF service (all RAF aircraft):

Serial	c/n	Type	Serial	c/n	Type	Serial	c/n	Type
XV176	4169	382C-19B	XV198	4219	382C-19B	XV220	4247	382C-19B
XV177	4182	382C-19B	XV199	4220	382C-19B	XV221	4251	382C-19B
XV178	4188	382C-19B	XV200	4223	382C-19B	XV222	4252	382C-19B
XV179	4195	382C-19B	XV201	4224	382C-19B	XV223	4253	382C-19B
XV180	4196	382C-19B	XV202	4226	382C-19B	XV290	4254	382C-19B
XV181	4198	382C-19B	XV203	4227	382C-19B	XV291	4256	382C-19B
XV182	4199	382C-19B	XV204	4228	382C-19B	XV292	4257	382C-19B
XV183	4200	382C-19B	XV205	4230	382C-19B	XV293	4258	382C-19B
XV184	4201	382C-19B	XV206	4231	382C-19B	XV294	4259	382C-19B
XV185	4203	382C-19B	XV207	4232	382C-19B	XV295	4261	382C-19B
XV186	4204	382C-19B	XV208	4233	382C-19B	XV296	4262	382C-19B
XV187	4205	382C-19B	XV209	4235	382C-19B	XV297	4263	382C-19B
XV188	4206	382C-19B	XV210	4236	382C-19B	XV298	4264	382C-19B
XV189	4207	382C-19B	XV211	4237	382C-19B	XV299	4266	382C-19B
XV190	4210	382C-19B	XV212	4238	382C-19B	XV300	4267	382C-19B
XV191	4211	382C-19B	XV213	4240	382C-19B	XV301	4268	382C-19B
XV192	4212	382C-19B	XV214	4241	382C-19B	XV302	4270	382C-19B
XV193	4213	382C-19B	XV215	4242	382C-19B	XV303	4271	382C-19B
XV194	4214	382C-19B	XV216	4243	382C-19B	XV304	4272	382C-19B
XV195	4216	382C-19B	XV217	4244	382C-19B	XV305	4273	382C-19B
XV196	4217	382C-19B	XV218	4245	382C-19B	XV306	4274	382C-19B
XV197	4218	382C-19B	XV219	4246	382C-19B	XV307	4275	382C-19B

The hand-over ceremony of the first RAF Herk, XV176 (c/n 4169), in August 1967. *Author's collection*

Pristine Hercules XV177 (c/n 4182) is seen on the mat at Marietta prior to delivery to the RAF. The policy at the time was for the aircraft to be delivered in natural metal finish and without some 80% of the standard Lockheed equipment, so that both camouflage and internal fitting could be done in the UK to the required standard. *Lockheed-Georgia, Marietta via Audrey Pearcy*

A hand-over ceremony at Marietta as another RAF aircrew receives a Hercules from Lockheed officials. The badge of RAF Lyneham, with its most appropriate motto 'Support and Save', is also on display in the foreground. *Lockheed-Georgia, Marietta*

Taking her maiden flight at Marietta on 10 October 1966 is RAF Hercules XV177 (c/n 4182), the first C.1. The correct RAF paint job was applied on arrival in the UK by Marshalls of Cambridge. *Lockheed-Georgia, Marietta*

An RAF C-130K line-up at Lyneham, including XV292 (c/n 4257) nearest the camera. *RAF*

RAF C-130K XV193 (c/n 4213) is being towed down the runway at Lyneham. *RAF*

C-130T

Twenty aircraft, C-130Ts, which were C-130H transports fitted with T56A-16 engines and carried refuelling packages for the USMC (all USMC aircraft):

BuOrd No	c/n	Type	BuOrd No	c/n	Type	BuOrd No	c/n	Type
164762	5255	382C-21F	165158	5341	382C-36F	165350	5407	382C-55F
164763	5258	382C-21F	165159	5342	382C-36F	165351	5409	382C-55F
164993	5298	382C-31F	165160	5344	382C-36F	165378	5429	382C-59F
164994	5299	382C-31F	165161	5345	382C-36F	165379	5430	382C-59F
164995	5300	382C-31F	165313	5383	382C-52F			
164996	5301	382C-31F	165314	5384	382C-52F			
164997	5304	382C-31F	165348	5404	382C-55F			
164998	5305	382C-31F	165349	5406	382C-55F			

At Tyndall Air Force Base, Florida, on 28 March 2004 is C-130T 04-0328 N-7559C-01, a specially designed Lockheed C-130 'Fat Albert', carrying forty-five personnel and 25,000lb of equipment. She belongs to the US Navy's flight demonstration team, the 'Blue Angels', and is taxiing near a row of F/A-18C Hornet aircraft just prior to a scheduled air show. The Herk is crewed by US Marines and generally starts each show by demonstrating the aircraft's short take-off distance using Jet Assisted Take-off (JATO) rockets. The 'Blue Angels' perform more than seventy shows at thirty-four different locations throughout the USA each year. *Photographer's Mate 2nd Class Ryan J. Courtade, US Navy official*

CG-130G-LM

Four aircraft, C-130Es with T56-A-16 engines and Navy radio suites, received this US Navy designation (all USN aircraft):

BuOrd No	c/n	Type
151888	3849	382-4B
151889	3858	382-4B
151890	3871	382-4B
151891	3878	382-4B

They were subsequently redesignated as EC-130G (TACAMO) aircraft.

DC-130A-LM

Eight aircraft in total with extended nose radome (except for those indicated *) for drone launching.

Two aircraft, former USAF 182-1A C-130Ds, serials 57-0496 and 57-0497, converted in 1957 and originally designated as GC-130As.

Four more aircraft of the type were also former USAF C-130As: 56-0491; 56-0514; 56-0527; 56-461.

One aircraft, the former C-130D, 55-0021.

One aircraft the former RL-130A, 57-0523.

Serial	c/n	Type
57-0496	3203	182B-1A
57-0497	3204	182B-1A
56-0491	3099*	182-1A
56-0514	3122	182-1A
56-0527	3135	182-1A
56-0461	3168	182-1A
55-0021	3048*	182-1A
57-0523	3230	182A-2A

DC-130A Herk 56-0491 (c/n 3099) cruises past the 12,395-foot-high Mount Fujiyama, in central Japan, on 7 February 1958. She is working with Pacific Air Command from Ashiya Air Force Base. *Lockheed-Georgia, Marietta, via Audrey Pearcy*

DC-130E-LM

Seven drone and APV launchers modified from C-130Es with wing-mounted carry-and-launch pylons and an extended nose radome (all USAF aircraft):

DC-130E 61-2371 (c/n 3716), of the 355th Tactical Fighter Wing, 432 TDG, 22 TDS DM, is seen at Edwards Air Force Base on 12 November 1978. *Nick Williams, AAHS*

THE LOCKHEED MARTIN C-130 HERCULES

DC-130E 61-2362 (c/n 3663), of the 355th Tactical Fighter Wing, 22nd TDS, stands in the static park at an air display on 22 October 1978. *Nick Williams, AAHS*

Serial	c/n	Type
61-2361	3662	382-4B
61-2362	3663	382-4B
61-2363	3681	382-4B
61-2364	3687	382-4B
61-2368	3713	382-4B
61-2369	3714	382-4B
61-2371	3716	382-4B

DC-130H-LM

One aircraft, a former 383-12B HC-130H, serial 65-979 (c/n 4131).

Following conventional service with various ARRS units, this aircraft was in 1976 made-over into a test vehicle, hauling four under-wing 10,000lb simulated loadings; it later became a drone and APV launch aircraft working on the Lockheed 'Senior Prom' stealth missile trails over the Groom Lake test range facility at the former Nellis Auxiliary Field 1 east of the Dry Lake, some 100 miles north of Las Vegas and close to Yucca Flats. This missile had been developed from Lockheed's 'Have Blue' demonstrator, and was powered by a single turbofan in the sharply angled tail. Six examples of this Low Radar Cross Section (LRCS) were built and all were tested successfully near the US Atomic Energy Commission's (AEC) nuclear test facility, where they proved their value by failing to be detected by the site's radar system. After each flight the missile made a parachute-assisted landing onto an inflatable bag, and all were recovered.

The DC-130H made a total of thirteen test flights and launches between October 1978 and the termination of the project in 1981. Subsequently this machine continued with test programme work at Edwards AB and Duke Field, before being loaned to VX-30, then transferred to the US Navy; it later became the test vehicle for high-energy laser experiments with Boeing.

EC-130E

One aircraft, a former EC-130S, was redesignated thus on delivery in 1966, a USCG 382-4B, serial CG1414 (c/n 4158). There were ten further aircraft, former C-130E-IIs (all USAF aircraft):

Serial	c/n	Type
62-1791	3738	382-4B
62-1809	3770	382-8D
62-1815	3777	382-4B
62-1818	3780	382-8D
62-1820	3783	382-4B
62-1835	3788	382-8B
62-1832	3795	382-8B
62-1836	3799	382-8B
62-1857	3821	382-8B
62-1863	3827	382-8B

These aircraft are utilised as Airborne Battlefield Command & Control Centers (ABCCC) and carry upon their internal load/unload railing the 40-foot-long USC-48 ABCCC Capsule (ABCCC III). The contents of the capsule include twenty-three secure radios, telex (teletype) machines and digitally controlled communication systems, with computer-generated colour information display combined with rapid data retrieval (RDR). The system incorporates a Joint Tactical Information Distribution System (JTIDS) enabling instantaneous air-to-air tracking, relay and data-sharing.

In addition to the three top-mounted aerials, these Hercules have under-belly external antennae for the numerous radio systems in the capsule, and also feature HF radio probes on the outer wing tips. These aircraft are fitted with heat exchanger pods, with intakes in front of the engines, to enhance cooling of the electronics, and they also incorporate aerial refuelling.

EC-130E-(CL)

Five aircraft, former C-130Es, were modified by Lockheed to 'Comfy Levi'/'Senior Hunter' aircraft. As part of the 'Coronet Solo II'/'Volant Solo'/'Commando Solo' set-up[3], these aircraft were configured for Senior Scout and/or Senior Hunter Electronic Intelligence-gathering (ELINT) and Signals Intelligence SIGINT gathering (all USAF aircraft).

Serial	c/n	Type
63-7783	3850	382-4B
63-7815	3889	382-4B
63-7816	3894	382-4B
63-7828	3896	382-4B
63-9816	3977	382-8B

EC-130E-(RR)

Three aircraft, former C-130Es, modified to EC-130E-(RR) 'Rivet Rider'/'Volant Scout' electronic surveillance aircraft (all USAF aircraft):

Serial	c/n	Type
63-7773	3839	382-8B
63-7869	3939	382-4B
63-9817	3978	382-8B

[3] 'Coronet Solo' is the Operational Order for EC-130E (RR) 'Rivet Rider' Psychological Warfare operations with WWCTV, C3CM. 'Volant Solo' (ex-'Coronet Solo II') is the MAC Operation Order for EC-130-(VS) Psychological Operations (PSYOP) and C3CM to 'Commando Solo' similar to 'Rivet Rider'. 'Senior Hunter' aircraft are used on 'Senior Scout' reconnaissance and ELINT missions and as support aircraft for EC-130E-(RR)/RC-130CCL 'Commando Solo' missions.

EC-130G

Four aircraft, former CG-130G-*LM*s all USN aircraft):

BuOrd No	c/n	Type
151888	3849	382-4B
151889	3858	382-4B
151890	3871	382-4B
151891	3878	382-4B

They were subsequently redesignated as EC-130G (TACAMO) aircraft.

EC-130H (CCCCM)

Four aircraft, former EC-130Hs (all USAF aircraft):

Serial	c/n	Type
64-14859	4082	382-12B
64-14862	4089	382-12B
65-0962	4102	382-12B
65-0989	4150	382-12B

Plus a further twelve aircraft, former C-130Hs (all USAF aircraft):

Serial	c/n	Type
73-1580	4542	382C-33D
73-1581	4543	382C-33D
73-1583	4545	382C-33D
73-1584	4546	382C-33D
73-1585	4547	382C-33D
73-1586	4548	382C-33D
73-1587	4549	382C-33D
73-1588	4550	382C-33D
73-1590	4554	382C-33D
73-1592	4557	382C-33D
73-1594	4563	382C-33D
73-1595	4564	382C-33D

Modified for Command, Control & Communications Control (CCCC) 'Compass Call' aircraft under this designation.

EC-130H-(CL)

Three aircraft, former C-130Hs, converted to EC-130H-(CL)s for 'Senior Scout' clandestine electronic intelligence gathering and jamming missions – serials 74-2130 (c/n 4711), 74-2134 (c/n 4735) and 89-1185 (c/n 5194).

EC-130J-LM

Three modified C-130Js, with 'Commando Solo II' electronic reconnaissance variants packages on a pallet (*), and two upgrades from C-130J (all ANG aircraft):

Serial	c/n	Type
97-1931*	5477	382U-09J
98-1932*	5490	382U-17J
99-1933*	5502	382U-17J
00-1934	5522	382U-32J
01-1935	5532	382U-32J

EC-130Q-LM

A total of eighteen aircraft, built as US Navy aerial relay stations and featuring dual wing-tip electronics pods. These C-130Hs were improved by the T56-A-16 engine for TACAMO duties (all USN aircraft):

BuOrd No	c/n	Type	BuOrd No	c/n	Type
156170	4239	382-12B	159348	4601	382-12B
156171	4249	382-12B	160608	4781	382-12B
156172	4269	382-12B	161223	4867	382-12B
156173	4277	382-12B	161494	4896	382-12B
156174	4278	382-12B	161495	4901	382-12B
156175	4279	382-12B	161496	4904	382-12B
156176	4280	382-12B	161531	4932	382-12B
156177	4281	382-12B	162312	4984	382-12B
156469	4595	382-12B	162313	4988	382-12B

A line-up of US Navy EC-130Q aircraft, with 156175 (c/n 4279) in the foreground, in November 1975. *R. C. Stewart, via Nick Williams, AAHS*

EC-130V

One aircraft, fitted out for the US Coast Guard as an early-warning aircraft with rotodome and AN/APAS-14S EC-130V, serial CG1721 (c/n 5121).

GC-130A/B/CLM

This designation was allocated to what later became the DC-130A. Later it was applied to all Hercules aircraft that were permanently grounded as instructional airframes. The first to be so designated was serial 54-1621 (c/n 3008) (see also the next entry).

The following additional Hercules served in the ground training role in various capacities and *some*, but by no means all, received this designation at some period (all USAF aircraft):

Serial	c/n	Type	Duty
53-3131	3003	182-1A	Ground trainer
54-1634	3021	182-1A	Fire trainer
54-1637	3024	182-1A	Ground trainer
54-1640	3027	182-1A	Ground trainer
55-0018	3045	182-1A	Loadmaster trainer
55-0019	3046	182-1A	Ground loading trainer
55-0047	3074	182-1A	Paratroop ground trainer
55-0048	3075	182-1A	Evacuation trainer
56-0469	3077	182-1A	Ground and Gun trainer
56-0492	3100	182-1A	Paratroop trainer
56-0498	3106	182-1A	Ground trainer
56-0513	3121	182-1A	Loadmaster trainer
56-0511	3218	182-2A	Instructional airframe
56-0524	3132	182-1A	Instructional airframe
56-0525	3133	182-1A	ECM test bed
56-0539	3147	182-1A	Loadmaster trainer
56-0550	3158	182-1A	Loadmaster trainer
57-0462	3169	182-1A	Fuel-loading trainer
57-0464	3171	182-1A	Loading trainer
57-0469	3176	182-1A	Ground trainer
57-0471	3178	182-1A	Maintenance, electrical and air-conditioning trainer
57-0472	3179	182-1A	Paratroop trainer
57-0477	3184	182-1A	Repair trainer
57-0478	3185	182-1A	Aircraft battle damage trainer
57-0483	3190	182-1A	Ground and loading trainer
57-0486	3193	182-1A	Instructional airframe
57-0489	3196	182-1A	Instructional airframe
57-0490	3197	182-1A	Ground trainer
57-0524	3231	182A-2A	Battle damage repair trainer
57-0528	3504	282-1B	Loadmaster trainer
58-0740	3537	282-1B	Ground and loader trainer
58-6973	3542	282-2B	Loadmaster trainer
61-2081	3638	282-2B	Loadmaster trainer
61-2083	3650	282-2B	Loadmaster trainer
61-2362	3663	382-4B	Maintenance trainer
61-2364	3687	382-4B	Crew Chief trainer
61-2368	3713	382-4B	Loadmaster trainer
61-1794	3744	382-4B	Crew Chief trainer
62-1807	3761	382-4B	Crew Chief trainer
62-1830	3793	382-4B	Non-flying Crew trainer
62-1860	3824	382-8B	Ground trainer
63-7779	3845	382-8B	Engine Maintenance trainer
63-7795	3861	382-8B	Maintenance trainer
63-7801	3867	382-8B	Paratroop trainer
63-7820	3886	382-8B	Loadmaster trainer
64-0500	3984	382-8B	Ground trainer
64-0524	4008	382-8B	Loadmaster trainer
64-0556	4057	382-8B	Maintenance trainer
64-0569	4079	382-8B	Ground trainer
156170	4239	382C-4D*	Loadmaster trainer
69-6579	4354	382-19B*	Ground maintenance trainer
72-1298	4521	382C-15D	Crew Chief trainer
74-1693	4693	382C-43D	Loadmaster trainer

GC-130D/GC-130D-6

Confusingly, both these designation have also been applied to a pair of permanently grounded C-130D-6 airframes (marked * in the table above) down the years.

GVI

Two USAF aircraft, the original US Marine Corps designation applied to the first aerial tanker on loan from the USAF. Both Type 182-1A, they are serials 55-0046 (c/n 3073) and 55-0048 (c/n 3075). See the KC-130F-LM section.

GV-1U

Seven US Navy tanker aircraft (all USN aircraft):

BuOrd	Noc/n	Type
149787	3636	282B-3B
149790	3645	282B-3B
149793	3660	282B-3B
149794	3661	282B-3B
149797	3666	282B-3B
149801	3686	282B-3B
149805	3696	282B-3B

See C-130F section.

HC-130B-LM

Twelve transfers from the USAF for US Coast Guard service (all USCG aircraft):

Serial	Ex-USAF	c/n	Type	Serial	Ex-USAF	c/n	Type
CG 1339	58-5396	3529	282-2B	CG 1346	61-0958	3638	282-2B
CG 1340	58-5397	3533	282-2B	CG 1347	61-2082	3641	282-2B
CG 1341	58-6973	3542	282-2B	CG 1348	61-2083	3650	282-2B
CG 1342	58-6974	3548	282-2B	CG 1349	62-3753	3745	282-2B
CG 1344	60-0311	3594	282-2B	CG 1350	62-3754	3763	282-2B
CG 1345	60-0312	3595	282-2B	CG 1351	62-3755	3773	282-2B

They were variously based at Elizabeth City, Barbers Point, Clearwater and Sacramento during their twenty years of service, and the bulk were finally retired to the MASDC from 1982 onward. Eleven of them still survived in the AMARC Park, as it was redesignated, in 1985, but were due to depart to various CFs that October.

HC-130E-LM

One aircraft, a former Coast Guard EC-130E, built as a Long Range Navigation (Loran) A&C calibration aircraft; serial CG 1414 (c/n 4158).

HC-130G

Twelve former USAF aircraft (all now USCG aircraft):

Serial	Ex-USAF	c/n	Type	Serial	Ex-USAF	c/n	Type
CG 1339	58-5396	3529	282-2B	CG 1346	61-2081	3638	282-2B
CG 1340	58-5397	3533	282-2B	CG 1347	61-2082	3641	282-2B
CG 1341	58-6973	3542	282-2B	CG 1348	61-2083	3650	282-2B
CG 1342	58-6974	3548	282-2B	CG 1349	62-3753	3745	282-2B
CG 1344	60-0311	3594	282-2B	CG 1350	62-3754	3763	282-2B
CG 1345	60-0312	3595	282-2B	CG 1351	62-3755	3773	282-2B

All were redesignated as HC-130B-*LM*s early on (see above).

HC-130H

Forty-three aircraft for ARRS, fitted with AN/ARD-17 Cook aerial tracker, Fulton STAR recovery yoke ('Skyhook'), Hose Recovery Unit (HRU) pods, Inertial Navigation Systems (INS) Omega, Long Range Navigation (Loran), LORAN-C low frequency (LF) terrestrial radio navigation system[4], and Global Positioning Systems (GPS), plus ten launch tubes for flares. The modern HC-130 has a reach of 4,815km (2,600 nautical miles) and a 14-hour endurance. These are all USAF aircraft:

Nosed into Hangar No 9 at Hickam AFB, Hawaii, in May 1969 is HC-130H 65-0981 (c/n 4133), of 76 ARRS. *Nick Williams, AAHS*

An USAF Military Airlift Command HC-130H with 'Rescue' flash, this is 65-0962 (c/n 4102) of 67 ARRS, seen in July 1969. *Nick Williams, AAHS*

[4] In November 2009 the USCG announced that it was terminating transmissions of US LORAN-C signals from February 2010, despite considerable opposition from those who still feel it remains a secure and viable system. Funding cutbacks no doubt contributed to this decision.

Serial	c/n	Type	Serial	c/n	Type	Serial	c/n	Type
64-14852	4036	382-12B	65-0962	4102	382-12B	65-0977	4127	382-12B
64-14853	4037	382-12B	65-0963	4103	382-12B	65-0978	4130	382-12B
64-14854	4038	382-12B	65-0964	4104	382-12B	65-0979	4131	382-12B
64-14855	4055	382-12B	65-0965	4106	382-12B	65-0980	4132	382-12B
64-14856	4072	382-12B	65-0966	4107	382-12B	65-0981	4133	382-12B
64-14857	4073	382-12B	65-0967	4108	382-12B	65-0982	4135	382-12B
64-14858	4081	382-12B	65-0968	4110	382-12B	65-0983	4138	382-12B
64-14859	4082	382-12B	65-0969	4111	382-12B	65-0984	4139	382-12B
64-14860	4084	382-12B	65-0970	4112	382-12B	65-0985	4140	382-12B
64-14861	4088	382-12B	65-0971	4116	382-12B	65-0986	4141	382-12B
64-14862	4089	382-12B	65-0972	4120	382-12B	65-0987	4142	382-12B
64-14863	4094	382-12B	65-0973	4121	382-12B	65-0989	4150	382-12B
64-14864	4097	382-12B	65-0974	4123	382-12B	65-0990	4151	382-12B
64-14865	4098	382-12B	65-0975	4125	382-12B			
64-14866	4099	382-12B	65-0976	4126	382-12B			

Twenty-four aircraft for USGC, twelve from USAF (all USCG aircraft):

Serial	Ex-USAF	c/n	Type	Serial	Ex-USAF	c/n	Type
CG 1452	67-7183	4255	382-12B	CG 1710	5028		382-12B
CG 1453	67-7184	4260	382-12B	CG 1711	5031		382-12B
CG 1454	67-7185	4265	382-12B	CG 1712	5033		382-12B
CG 1500	72-1300	4501	382-12B	CG 1713	5034		382-12B
CG 1501	72-1301	4507	382-12B	CG 1714	5035		382-12B
CG 1502	72-1302	4513	382-12B	CG 1716	5023		382-12B
CG 1503	73-0844	4528	382-12B	CG 1717	5104		382-12B
CG-1504	73-0845	4529	382-12B	CG 1718	5106		382-12B
CG 1603	77-0320	4764	382-12B	CG 1719	5107		382-12B
CG 1602	77-0319	4762	382-12B	CG 1720	5120		382-12B
CG 1601	77-0318	4760	382-12B	CG 1721	5121		382-12B
CG 1600	77-0317	4757	382-12B	CG 1715	5037		382-12B

HC-130H-7

Eleven aircraft for the USGC with SLAR, and FLIR pods (all USCG aircraft):

Serial	c/n	Type	Serial	c/n	Type
CG 1700	4947	382C-37E	CG 1706	4996	382C-50E
CG 1701	4958	382C-37E	CG 1707	4999	382C-50E
CG 1702	4966	382C-37E	CG 1708	5002	382C-50E
CG 1703	4967	382C-37E	CG 1709	5005	382C-50E
CG 1704	4969	382C-37E	CG 1790	4931	382C-22E
CG 1705	4993	382C-50E			

HC-130H-(N)

Six aircraft produced for the Air National Guard, Alaska in the 1990s (all ANG aircraft):

Serial	c/n	Type
88-2101	5202	382C-98E
88-2102	5210	382C-98E
90-2103	5294	382C-24F
93-2104	5381	382C-43F
93-2105	5387	382C-43F
93-2106	5388	382C-43F

HC-130J-LM

Six aircraft, all USCG:

Registration	c/n	Type
CG2001	5524	383U-35J
CG2002	5533	383U-35J
CG2003	5534	383U-35J
CG2004	5535	383U-35J
CG2005	5541	383U-35J
CG2006	5542	383U-35J

The -Js for the USCG incorporate new mission and sensor packages in addition to combat search & rescue and cargo-carrying capacity. The upgraded package includes belly-mounted 360-degree long-range search radar, controlled by two mission system operator stations situated to the rear of the pilot and co-pilot. They are equipped with the multi-mode radar, electro-optical infra-red technology and improved mission communications systems. The US Coast Guard uses its aircraft for search & rescue, illegal drug patrols, monitoring marine environmental problems, International Ice Patrol and illegal immigration problems. They use USCG airfield bases at Barbers Point, Elizabeth City, Sacramento, Clearwater and Kodiak.

Environmental mission: rescued monk seals are flown to safety by a US Coast Guard Hercules. *Courtesy of NOAA*

HC-130N-LM

A total of fifteen aircraft. With Search & Rescue (SAR) command aircraft platform as their principal mission assignment, together with a secondary function of aerial refuelling tanker for helicopters, the HC-130N was also capable of conducting tactical air-drop assignments of specialised amphibious para-rescue teams; also embarked was a basic mission team of three PJ specialists – fully trained to deal with Emergency Trauma Medicine (ETM), Harsh Environment Survival (HES) and Assisted Evasion (AE) skills) – Zodiac inflatable boats and even four-wheel drive, all-terrain (AT) vehicles. Many served with the AFRES. A further fifteen planned were later cancelled and eleven of the existing aircraft were converted to MC-130Ps in 1996. They were all USAF aircraft:

Registration	c/n	Type	Registration	c/n	Type
69-5189	4363	382-20B	69-5827	4376	382-20B
69-5820	4367	382-20B	69-5828	4377	382-20B
69-5821	4368	382-20B	69-5829	4378	382-20B
69-5822	4370	382-20B	69-5830	4379	382-20B
69-5823	4371	382-20B	69-5831	4380	382-20B
69-5824	4372	382-20B	69-5832	4381	382-20B
69-5825	4374	382-20B	69-5826	4375	382-20B
69-5826	4375	382-20B			

HC-130P-LM

Twenty aircraft, upgraded from the HC-130N, the -P series incorporated GPS navigation, missile and radar warning receivers, chaff and flare dispensers, airborne integrated satellite communications radios, and armoured cockpits. Some are being further modified by the provision of Night Vision Goggles (NVG) together with compatible interior and exterior lighting; Cubic Defense V-12 Personnel Locator Systems (PLS) with both voice and text capability, which are fully compatible with such devices as the AN/PRC-112 Survival Radio; and improved digital Low-Power (LP) colour radar and Forward-Looking Infra-Red (FLIR). Low-level missions are currently conducted by 71 Rescue Squadron (RQS) of Air Combat Command (ACC), the 102, 129 and 210 RQS of the Air National Guard (ANG), and 39 and 303 RQS of the Air Force Reserve Command (AFRC). All are USAF aircraft:

A line-up of Herks of all nations at the 1979 Paris Air Show, with USAF HC-130P 66-0223 (c/n 4185) in the foreground of the first picture, with twenty bombing mission makers and RAF XV200 (c/n 4223) beyond her. *All Audrey Pearcy*

Registration	c/n	Type	Registration	c/n	Type
65-0988	4143	382-12B	66-0217	4173	382-12B
65-0991	4152	382-12B	66-0218	4174	382-12B
65-0992	4155	382-12B	66-0219	4175	382-12B
65-0993	4156	382-12B	66-0220	4179	382-12B
65-0994	4157	382-12B	66-0221	4183	382-12B
66-0211	4161	382-12B	66-0222	4184	382-12B
66-0212	4162	382-12B	66-0223	4185	382-12B
66-0213	4163	382-12B	66-0224	4186	382-12B
66-0214	4164	382-12B	66-0225	4187	382-12B
66-0215	4165	382-12B			
66-0216	4166	382-12B			

HC/MC-130J-LM

Lockheed describes this next generation of the Hercules family as a 'tailored common-core special operations variant' specifically designed to replace the whole range of 'Heritage Hercules' types (from a total of eighteen MC-130Es, twenty-four MC-130Hs, twelve MC-130Ws and twenty-eight MC-130Ps that had been built) employed by the Air Force Special Operations Command (AFSOC). There is an official Acquisition Decision Memorandum for sixty-eight aircraft, while the overall 'programme of record' requirement is for a total of 115. It is probable that not all of this ambitious projected replacement programme will survive the 'Obama' cutbacks, however.

The HC/MC-130J incorporates in-flight refuelling receiver capability, is fitted with the 250kt ramp and cargo door and air-to-air refuelling pods of the KC-130J, has an EO/IMR imaging system like the HC-130H, and has an enhanced service life wing (which means in actuality a 920lb increased durability wing box modification) as the MC-130H. There is a special dual-display combat systems operator station. The maiden flight is due in 2010 with deliveries to meet the IOC date of 2012 with a minimum of ten aircraft in service by that date. The Indian Air Force has shown interest in a similar concept but based on the L-100J-30 airframe.

The first aircraft are as follows, ordered for Air Force Special Operations Command (AFSOC):

Serial	c/n	Type
09-	5633	382U-73J
09-	5634	382U-73J
09-	5656	382U-73J
09-	5657	382U-73J
09-	5658	382U-73J
09-	5659	382U-73J

There is also an USAF air tanker variant of the MC-130J for SOC based on the USMC KC-130J being completed, which promises electro-optic/infra-red sensor, higher-capacity generators and enhanced cargo-handling systems in her repertoire.

JC-130A-LM

Sixteen aircraft, modified from C-130As for Missile Tracking Atlantic with removable test equipment. They are all USAF aircraft:

Serial	c/n	Type	Serial	c/n	Type
53-3129	3001	182-1A	54-1627	3014	182-1A
53-3130	3002	182-1A	54-1628	3015	182-1A
53-3131	3003	182-1A	54-1629	3016	182-1A
53-3132	3004	182-1A	54-1630	3017	182-1A
53-3133	3005	182-1A	54-1639	3026	182-1A
53-3134	3006	182-1A	56-0490	3098	182-1A
53-3135	3007	182-1A	56-0493	3101	182-1A
54-1625	3012	182-1A	56-0497	3105	182-1A

JC-130B-LM

Fourteen aircraft, modified from C-130Bs for Satellite Tracking and other temporary functions. They are all USAF aircraft:

Serial	c/n	Type	Serial	c/n	Type
57-0525	3501	282-1B	58-0715	3510	282-1B
57-0526	3502	282-1B	58-0716	3511	282-1B
57-0527	3503	282-1B	58-0717	3512	282-1B
57-0528	3504	282-1B	58-0750	3549	282-1B
57-0529	3505	282-1B	58-0756	3557	282-1B
58-0713	3508	282-1B	61-0962	3647	282-1B
58-0714	3509	282-1B	61-0963	3648	282-1B

JC-130D

A Hercules was used as the test model for the ski-fitted aircraft used in Antarctica, the machine selected being USAF 55-0021 (c/n 3048). As the first ski-equipped C-130, the initial flight took place on 29 January 1957 and the following month extensive testing with this ski-wheel configured aircraft took place at Bernidji Lake, Minnesota, during that year. These tests conclusively proved that the Hercules could perform perfectly satisfactorily in that role. As a result Lockheed was asked by the USAF to modify twelve further C-130As, 57-0484 to 57-0495 (c/ns 3191 to 3202 inclusive) to C-130Ds, and these were delivered between February and April 1959 to the 61st Troop Carrier Squadron at Sewart AFB, Tennessee, and first flew on mission on 23 March 1959.

Meanwhile, following the initial trials 55-0021 was attached to the 3254 ABG at Hanscom Air Force Base and listed as a JC-130D. In 1969 she was modified to a DC-130A and later transferred to the US Navy as its 158228, serving with VC-3. The completion and support of the DEW line of radar stations required fewer ski-equipped Hercules by 1963, and six of the twelve C-130Ds reverted back to their original configuration by having their skis removed, and became C-130D-6s, but they all had their hydraulic systems left in place so that, if required, their skis could be refitted.

JC-130E-LM

One aircraft, serial 61-2358 (c/n 3609). Completed as a trials aircraft in 1964, it was converted to a standard C-130E in 1972.

JC-130H-LM

One aircraft, serial 64-14858 (c/n 4081). An HC-130H with 6593rd Test Squadron, Hickam AFB, Hawaii, it was subsequently redesignated HC-130P.

JHC-130H-LM

Seven aircraft, modified HC-130Hs, all USAF aircraft:

Serial	c/n	Type
64-14852	4036	382-12B
64-14853	4037	382-12B
64-14854	4038	382-12B
64-14855	4055	382-12B
64-14856	4072	382-12B
64-14857	4073	382-12B
64-14858	4081	382-12B

Modified in 1965-66, they were redesignated as HC-130H in 1986-87.

JHC-130P

One aircraft, serial 65-0988 (c/n 4143), which was modified from an HC-130P for the US Aerospace Rescue & Recovery Service (ARRS) for tests.

On 20 February 1972 this aircraft, commanded by Lieutenant Commander Edgar Allison Jr, with a representative of the Federation Internationale Aeronautique (FIN) aboard, flew 8,790 miles (14,146.13km) from Taiwan to Scott AFB, Illinois, at heights of between 37,000 and 39,000 feet (11,277.6 and 11,887.2 metres) and set a new long-distance flight record for a turboprop aircraft. Taking advantage of 70mph (112.3km/h) tail winds, the aircraft landed with 4,500lb (2,041.16kg) of reserve fuel.

KC-130B-LM

The KC series for the US Marine Corps initiated a tactical air tanker and transport aircraft capable of multiple roles and fulfilling missions as various as those undertaken by the Corps itself. As a tanker, a removable 3,600-gallon stainless steel fuel tank can be uploaded into the cargo compartment, and two wing-mounted hose-and-drogue-type refuelling pods can each pump 300 gallons per minute, and refuel two applicants (either pairs of aircraft or pairs of helicopters) simultaneously. Additionally, the Hercules's natural functions of cargo or troop delivery, re-supply to forward temporary landing strips, and emergency Medevac facilities are all readily available.

Six aircraft, C-130Bs modified as tankers for the Indonesian (two) and Singapore (four) Governments.

Customer	Serial	c/n	Type
AURI	A-1309	3615	282-9B
AURI	A-1310	3616	282-9B
Singapore AF	720	3519	282-1B
Singapore AF	721	3557	282-1B
Singapore AF	724	3611	282-1B
Singapore AF	725	3620	282-1B

KC-130F-LM

Two C-130A aircraft on loan from the USAF for the US Navy, serials 55-0046 (c/n 3073) and 55-0048 (c/n 3075), formerly designated as GVIs.

Forty-six aircraft, former C-130Bs:

On the apron at NAS Barbers Point, Hawaii, in June 1969 is KC-130F 150684 (c/n 3727), tail-coded QB. *Nick Williams, AAHS*

United States Marines KC-130F 149816 (c/n 3726), of VMGR-353, tail-coded QB, is seen at Naval Air Station Atsugi. *Nick Williams, AAHS*

California USMC KC-130F 150690 (c/n 3742) touching down in the heat. *McDonnell Douglas, via Audrey Pearcy*

BuNo	c/n	Type	BuNo	c/n	Type	BuNo	c/n	Type
147572	3554	282B-3B	149788	3640	282B-3B	149810	3710	282B-3B
147573	3555	282B-3B	149789	3644	282B-3B	149811	3711	282B-3B
148246	3566	282B-3B	149791	3657	282B-3B	149812	3718	282B-3B
148247	3573	282B-3B	149792	3658	282B-3B	149813	3719	282B-3B
148248	3574	282B-3B	149795	3664	282B-3B	149814	3723	282B-3B
148249	3577	282B-3B	149796	3665	282B-3B	149815	3725	282B-3B
148890	3592	282B-3B	149798	3680	282B-3B	149816	3726	282B-3B
148891	3605	282B-3B	149799	3684	282B-3B	150684	3727	282B-3B
148892	3606	282B-3B	149800	3685	282B-3B	150685	3728	282B-3B
148893	3607	282B-3B	149802	3693	282B-3B	150686	3733	282B-3B
148894	3608	282B-3B	149803	3694	282B-3B	150687	3734	282B-3B
148895	3619	282B-3B	149804	3695	282B-3B	150688	3740	282B-3B
148896	3623	282B-3B	149806	3703	282B-3B	150689	3741	282B-3B
148897	3627	282B-3B	149807	3704	282B-3B	150690	3742	282B-3B
148898	3631	282B-3B	149808	3705	282B-3B			
148899	3632	282B-3B	149809	3709	282B-3B			

KC-130H-LM

Twenty-two aircraft. Tankers, with under-wing refuelling pods. (There are also six converted aircraft).

Customer	Registration	c/n	Type
Israeli AF	75-0522	4660	382C-53D
Israeli AF	75-0545	4664	382C-53D
Argentine AF	TC-69	4814	382C-82D
Argentine AF	TC-70	4816	382C-82D
Saudi AF	N7992S	4503	382C-29D
Saudi AF	457	4511	382C-39D
Saudi AF	458	4532	382C-29D
Saudi AF	459	4539	382C-29D
Saudi AF	1616	4746	382C-61D
Saudi AF	1617	4750	382C-61D
Saudi AF	1620	4872	382C-96D
Saudi AF	1621	4873	382C-96D
Singapore	734	4940	382C-29E
Brazil AF	2461	4625	382C-47D
Brazil AF	2462	4636	382C-47D
Morocco AF	CNA-OR	4907	382C-12E
Morocco AF	CNA-OS	4909	382C-12E
Spanish AF	TK10-5	4642	382C-55D
Spanish AF	TK10-6	4648	382C-55D
Spanish AF	TK10-7	4652	382C-55D
Spanish AF	TK10-11	4871	382C-98D
Spanish AF	TK10-12	4874	382C-98D

KC-130J-LM

A total of forty-six built or on order at the time of writing. With the arrival of the -J series, the USMC took the opportunity to modernise its aging fleet of KC-130Fs. Refuelling speeds have been increased from the previous 100-knot maximum to 270 knots indicated air speed (IAS) with no loss of safety, while the tankers' offload has likewise increased, and at 1,852km (1,000 nautical miles) the offload is 20,412kg (45,000lb). Four are to be modified to USAF Special Operations Command tankers. All are USNC aircraft:

BuOrd No	c/n	Type	BuOrd No	c/n	Type
165735	5488	382U-11J	167110	5579	382U-72J
165736	5489	382U-11J	167111	5580	382U-72J
165737	5499	383U-11J	167112	5602	382U-72J
165738	5506	383U-11J	167923	5590	382U-72J
165739	5507	382U-11J	167924	5591	382U-72J
165809	5508	383U-11J	167925	5592	382U-72J
165810	5509	382U-11J	167926	5593	382U-72J
165957	5515	382U-33J	167927	5618	382U-72J
166380	5516	382U-33J	167981	5617	382U-72J
166381	5527	382U-38J	167982	5603	382U-72J
166382	5528	382U-38J	167983	5604	382U-72J
166472	5543	382U-38J	167984	5605	382U-72J
166473	5544	382U-38J	167985	5606	382U-72J
166511	5553	382U-38J	168074	5631	382U-72J
166512	5554	382U-38J	168075	5632	382U-72J
166513	5555	382U-72J	168065	5644	382U-72J
166514	5556	382U-72J	168066	5645	382U-72J
166762	5562	382U-72J	168067	5646	382U-72J
166763	5563	382U-72J	168068	5647	382U-72J
166764	5564	382U-72J	168069	5660	382U-72J
166765	5565	382U-72J	168070	5661	382U-72J
167108	5577	382U-72J	168071	5676	382U-72J
167109	5578	382U-72J	168072	5677	382U-72J

KC-130R-LM

Fourteen air tanker/transport aircraft, all USMC:

BuOrd No	c/n	Type
160013	4615	382C-43D
160014	4626	382C-43D
160015	4629	382C-43D
160016	4635	382C-43D
160017	4677	382C-43D
160018	4683	382C-43D
160019	4689	382C-43D
160020	4696	382C-43D
160021	4702	382C-58D
160240	4712	382C-58D
160625	4768	382C-68D
160626	4770	382C-68D
160627	4773	382C-68D
16028	4776	382C-68D

KC130R 148895 (c/n 3619) of VMGR-234 from NAS Forth Worth, Texas, coded QH, is seen in October 1976 undergoing engine maintenance at Tucson, Arizona. *Bruce Stewart, via Nick Williams, AAHS*

KC-130T

A total of twenty-six former USAF aircraft, with upgrade as refuelling base for the US Marine Corps and given Navy Bureau of Ordnance (BuOrd) serials. All USMC aircraft:

BuOrd No	c/n	Type	BuOrd No	c/n	Type
162308	4972	382C-34E	164106	5149	382C-83E
162309	4974	382C-34E	164180	5174	382C-95E
162310	4978	382C-34E	164181	5176	382C-95E
162311	4981	382C-34E	164441	5219	382C-11F
162785	5009	382C-48E	164442	5222	382C-11F
162786	5011	382C-48E	164999	5302	382C-32F
163022	5040	382C-58E	165000	5303	382C-32F
163023	5045	382C-58E	165162	5339	382C-39F
163310	5085	382C-70E	165163	5340	382C-39F
163311	5087	382C-70E	165315	5385	382C-51F
163591	5143	382C-83E	165316	5386	382C-51F
163592	5145	382C-83E	165352	5411	382C-56F
164105	5147	382C-83E	165353	5412	382C-56F

KC-130T-30

Two aircraft, 'stretched' versions of the KC-130T for the USMC. Both Type 382-18Fs, the BuOrd Nos are 164597 (c/n 5260) and 164598 (c/n 5263).

LC-130F-LM

Four aircraft, fitted with skis, all for USN:

BuOrd No	c/n	Type
148318	3562	382C-6B
148319	3564	382C-6B
148320	3565	382C-6B
148321	3567	382C-6B

LC-130H

Seven aircraft, ski-equipped LC-130Hs, were thus redesignated for the USAF:

Serial	c/n	Type
83-0490	5007	382C-47E
83-0491	5010	382C-47E
83-0492	5013	382C-47E
83-0493	5016	382C-47E
92-1094	5402	382C-47F
92-1095	5405	382C-47F
93-1096	5410	382C-47F

Serial 83-0490 (c/n 5007) was named *Pride of Clifton Park*; 83-0491 (c/n 5010) *City of Albany*; 83-0492 (c/n 5013) *City of Amsterdam*; 83-0493 (c/n 5016) *Pride of Scotia*; 92-1094 (c/n 5402) *Pride of Glenville*; 92-1095 (c/n 5405) *City of Cohoes*; and 93-1096 (c/n 5410) *City of Christchurch NZ*.

They are currently flown by the 109 Airlift Wing, New York Air National Guard, based at Stratton ANGB in Schenectady County Airport, Scotia, New York.

This unit also has the following four ski-equipped C-130Hs on its strength: 83-0486 (c/n 5008) *Pride of Rotterdam*; 83-0487 (c/n 5012) *City of Troy*; 83-0488 (c/n 5014) *City of Saratoga Springs*; and 83-0489 (c/n 5018) *City of Schenectady*.

LC-130R-LM

Six aircraft, ski-fitted, three later upgraded to LC-130H. Two additional machines of this type were cancelled. All are USN aircraft:

BuOrd No	c/n	Type
155917	4305	382C-9D
159129	4508	382C-26D
159130	4516	382C-26D
159131	4522	382C-26D
160740	4725	382C-65D
160741	4731	382C-65D

Ski-equipped LC-130R 155917 (c/n 4305) of the US Navy's VXE-6, tail-coded JD and from Point Magu, California, is seen at NAS Barbers Point in September 1969. *Nick Williams, AAHS*

MC-130E-C

Ten aircraft, converted for the Special Operations role ('Rivet Clamp'). All are USAF aircraft:

Serial	c/n	Type
64-0523	4007	383-8B
64-0551	4046	383-8B
64-0555	4056	383-8B
64-0559	4062	383-8B
64-0561	4065	383-8B
64-0562	4068	383-8B
64-0566	4080	383-8B
64-0567	4083	383-8B
64-0568	4086	383-8B
64-0572	4090	383-8B

MC-130E-S

One aircraft ('Rivet Swap'), serial 64-0571 (c/n 4087).

MC-130E-Y

Four aircraft ('Rivet Yank'), two of which adopted the serials of crashed Herks and were used in clandestine operations. All are USAF aircraft:

Serial	Ex-USAF	c/n	Type
62-1843	64-0507	3991	382-8B
62-7785	63-7785	3852	382-4B
64-0564		4074	383-8B
64-0565		4077	382-8B

MC-130H-LM ('Combat Talon II')

Total of twenty-four aircraft for 'Combat Talon II' for multi-role and covert operations with SOC. All are USAF aircraft:

Serial	c/n	Type	Serial	c/n	Type	Serial	c/n	Type
83-1212	5004	382C-49E	87-0125	5115	382C-92E	88-0264	5135	382C-87E
86-1699	5026	382C-73E	87-0126	5117	382C-92E	88-1803	5173	382C-89E
84-0475	5041	382C-59E	87-0127	5118	382C-77E	89-0280	5236	382C-01F
86-0476	5042	382C-59E	88-0191	5130	382C-87E	89-0281	5237	382C-01F
85-0011	5053	382C-59E	88-0192	5131	382C-87E	89-0282	5243	382C-01F
85-0012	5054	382C-59E	88-0193	5132	382C-87E	89-0283	5244	382C-01F
87-0023	5091	382C-77E	88-0194	5133	382C-87E	90-0161	5265	382C-05F
87-0024	5092	382C-77E	88-0195	5134	382C-87E	90-0162	5266	382C-05F

MC-130J-LM

All Air Force Special Operations Command (AFSOC):

Customer	Serial	c/n	Type
AFSOC		5680	382U-73J
AFSOC		5681	382U-73J
AFSOC		5682	382U-73J
AFSOC		5695	382U-73J
AFSOC		5696	382U-73J
AFSOC		5697	382U-73J

MC-130P-LM

Twenty-nine aircraft, former HC-130N/Ps, were thus redesignated ('Combat Shadows') from February 1996 when assigned to Air Force Special Operations Command (AFSOC). Their main missions are to fly chiefly nocturnal low-visibility or secret missions into enemy territorial air space and refuel AFSOC helos on clandestine mission deployments against 'sensitive' areas of potential hostile forces. They are also used to fly infiltration units in and out. Upgraded suites include Night Vision Goggles (NVG) and compatible internal lighting; Heads-up Display (HUD); a fully integrated inertial navigation and Global Position System (GPS); Forward-Looking Infra-Red (FLIR) radar; missile and radar warning receivers; chaff and flare dispensing chutes; and satellite and data-burst communications capabilities. All are equipped as a recipient (but not a donor) for in-flight refuelling.

These aircraft serve with three SOS units – 9 (based at Eglin AFB, Florida), 17 (at Kadena AB, Okinawa) and 67 (at RAF Mildenhall, UK). A further unit employing 'Combat Shadow' machines is 130 Rescue Squadron (RS) of the California Air National Guard (ANG) at Moffett Federal Airfield, with four aircraft. All are USAF aircraft:

Serial	c/n	Type	Serial	c/n	Type	Serial	c/n	Type
64-14854	4038	382-12B	66-0215	4165	382-12B	69-5821	4368	382-20B
64-14858	4081	382-12B	66-0216	4166	382-12B	69-5822	4370	382-20B
65-0971	4116	382-12B	66-0217	4173	382-12B	69-5823	4371	382-20B
65-0975	4125	382-12B	69-0218	4174	382-12B	69-5825	4374	382-20B
65-0991	4152	382-12B	66-0219	4175	382-12B	69-5826	4375	382-20B
65-0992	4155	382-12B	66-0220	4179	382-12B	69-5827	4376	382-20B
65-0993	4156	382-12B	66-0223	4185	382-12B	69-5828	4377	382-20B
65-0994	4157	382-12B	66-0225	4187	382-12B	69-5831	4380	382-20B
66-0212	4162	382-12B	69-5819	4363	382-20B	69-5832	4381	382-20B
66-0213	4163	382-12B	69-5820	4367	382-20B			

MC-130W-LM

A crash contingency programme was introduced to supplement and replace cheaply and quickly the existing MC-130 'Combat Talon' and 'Combat Shadow' aircraft lost in accidents by modifying twelve 1987-90-build C-130H-2 airframes serving with Air National Guard and Air Force Reserve units. This gave a reduced cost over new -Js, the conversions working out at $60 million per plane (plus a $14.1 million training programme for the fleet's specialised aircrew). The full programme was scheduled for completion by 2010, whereupon the aircraft were assigned to the 73rd Special Operations Squadron based at Cannon AFB, New Mexico.

Although their initial conversion specification excluded Terrain Following/Terrain Avoidance (TF/TA) installations, they were fitted with the following Special Operations Force (SOF) package: fully-integrated Global Positioning System (GPS) and LN-100R Embedded Inertial Navigation System (INS); Grumman-Northrop AN/APN-24 Low Power Colour (LPC) Weather/Navigation radar; integral Aircraft Health Monitoring System (AHMS); interior/exterior Night Vision Goggles (NVG)-compatible lighting for American Technologies Network Corporation's (ATN) NVG-7; and Advanced Threat Detection and Automated Countermeasures – these incorporated AN/AAQ-24(V) Nemesis Directional Infra-Red Countermeasure (DIRCM) and chaff and flare dispensers, as well as upgraded communications suites and dual satellite communications with data burst transmission to complicate trackback by providing ultra-brief transmission times giving Low Probability of Intercept (LPI) and Low Probability of Recognition (LPR).

In addition, these aircraft had aerial tanker capability via Mk 32B-902E refuelling pods capable of in-flight replenishment of CV-22 Osprey observation aircraft and helicopters.

The first ten of the aircraft (all USAF) thus selected are:

Serial	c/n	Type
87-9286	5127	382C-81E
88-1301	5162	382C-88E
88-1302	5163	382C-88E
88-1303	5164	382C-88E
88-1304	5165	382C-88E
88-1305	5166	382C-88E
88-1306	5167	382C-88E
88-1307	5168	382C-88E
88-1308	5169	382C-88E
88-1051	5198	382C-96E

Two more were pending at the time of writing.

In May 2007 these converted machines, codenamed 'Whiskey' (W), were retitled as 'Combat Spear' in homage to the 'Combat Talon' (although, of course, this allowed their aircrews to immediately dub them as the 'Combat Wombat').

In 2009, following the failure to achieve a replacement for the AC-130 Gunship, proposals were put forward to further convert a select number of MC-130Ws and make them available for this role. This involved simply fitting wing-mounted air-to-ground Hellfire-II 2.75-inch (70mm) rocket missiles, which are linked to Lockheed's DAGR semi-active laser-guidance kit, into existing aircraft. In addition, internal provision was announced of a Roll-on/Roll-off (Ro-Ro) armaments package, which could be quickly installed by the provision of an Adaptive Carriage Environment (ACE) installation when and as required. This package incorporates the Alliant Techsystems (ATK) 'Bushmaster II' Mk 44 30mm chain-fed autocannon, with accompanying sensors, guidance and communications systems, together with the 'Gunslinger' Precision-Guided Munitions (PGM) weapons system, which can precisely deliver ten stand-off Guided Bomb Units (GBU) via Northrop Grumman's GBU-44/B 'Viper Strike' GPS-aided, laser-guidance glide bomb. A supplementary funding package to the 2010 Defense Authorization Bill has initially allowed for two such installed gunship packages to be funded, resulting in the granting of a contract on 17 November 2009.

NC-130

Two aircraft. The original prototypes, YC-130-LOs , serials 53-3396 (c/n 1001) and 53-3397 (c/n 1002), were both redesignated as NC-130s in 1959, having come to the end of their useful test bed lives. They were scrapped at Warner Robins AFB in October 1969 and April 1962 respectively.

NC-130A-LM

Six aircraft, temporarily redesignated C-130As and JC-130As, while being utilised as the Air Force Special Weapons Centre test vehicles at Kirtland AFB, New Mexico. The designation was also applied to those Hercules used in the Airborne Seeker Evaluation Test System (ASSETS). All are USAF aircraft:

Serial	c/n	Type
53-3133	3005	182-1A
54-1622	3009	182-1A
54-1635	3022	182-1A
55-0022	3049	182-1A
55-0023	3050	182-1A
55-0024	3051	182-1A

C-130A 53-3133 (c/n 3005), with 3245 ABW, is seen at Hanscom AFB in July 1968, just before being converted to an NC-130A.
Nick Williams, AAHS

NC-130B-LM

Four aircraft.

One aircraft, serial 58-0712 (c/n 3507), used in STOL experimentation with BLC, and later employed in the NASA Earth Survey Programme and as an Airborne Instrumentation Research Programme machine.

One aircraft, 58-0717 (c/n 3512), used as a special testing machine with the 6593rd Test Squadron; another, 58-0716 (c/n 3511), was used by the 514 Test Squadron, and one former JC-130B, serial 61-0962 (c/n 3647).

NC-130E-LM

Two aircraft, former C-130Es, were used as lead aircraft for the Electronic Special Operations Support (SOS) aircraft. They were serials 64-0571 (c/n 4087), used for Electronic Intelligence-gathering (ELINT), and 64-0572 (4090). In 1979 their designations changed to MC-130E-S and MC-130E respectively.

NC-130F

Two 1961-build aircraft – ex-148893 (c/n 3607) and ex-148897 (c/n 3627) – modified from US Marine Corps KC-130Fs in 2007 and 2009 to become Permanent Test Station Platforms. The various modifications to fit this mission include Range Surveillance and Clearance via the Active Protection System (APS) APS-115 radar outfit; and Aerial Target Carriage, with wing-mounted pylons for drone launch; Target Command and Control Mission capabilities.[5]

NC-130H-LM

Five aircraft, modified HC-130Hs for test usage. All are USAF aircraft:

Serial	c/n	Type	Test Sqn
64-14854	4038	382-12B	1551
64-14857	4073	382-12B	6593
65-0971	4116	382-12B	1551
65-0979	4131	382-12B	514
87-0157	5121	382C-84E	418

The designation was later changed to JHC-130H.

PC-130H (see C-130H-MP)

Four aircraft, built as Maritime Patrol aircraft, three for Malaysia and one for Indonesia.

Customer	Serial	c/n	Type
Malaya	FM2451	4847	382C-97D
Malaya	FM2452	4849	382C-97D
Malaya	FM2453	4866	382C-97D
Indonesia	AI-1322	4898	382C-97E

The designation was changed to C-130H-MP before delivery.

[5] See DOD 4120.15.L – Addendum – MDS Designations allocated after 19 August 1998 (until March 2009).

This Military Airlift Command Hercules RC-130A, 57-0519 (c/n 3226), was photographed on 18 April 1969. *Nick Williams, AAHS*

RC-130A-LM

One aircraft, trial converted to an RC-130A, serial 54-1632 (c/n 3019) (R for Reconnaissance), from a TC-130A. She was subsequently converted back to a standard C-130A.

Fifteen aircraft, new-build RC-130As, specifically built for the Hiran Electronic Surveying, Hiran Controlled Photography and Mapping Photography missions. All are USAF aircraft:

Serial	c/n	Type	Serial	c/n	Type	Serial	c/n	Type
57-0510	3217	182A-2A	57-0515	3222	182A-2A	57-0520	3227	182A-2A
57-0511	3218	182A-2A	57-0516	3223	182A-2A	57-0521	3228	182A-2A
57-0512	3219	182A-2A	57-0517	3224	182A-2A	57-0522	3229	182A-2A
57-0513	3220	182A-2A	57-0518	3225	182A-2A	57-0523	3230	182A-2A
57-0514	3221	182A-2A	57-0519	3226	182A-2A	57-0524	3231	182A-2A

RC-130B-LM

Thirteen new-builds, but modified back to C-130B-IIs. All are USAF aircraft:

Serial	c/n	Type	Serial	c/n	Type	Serial	c/n	Type
58-0711	3506	282-1B	59-1527	3568	282-1B	59-1533	3586	282-1B
58-0723	3518	282-1B	59-1528	3571	282-1B	59-1535	3585	282-1B
59-1524	3560	282-1B	59-1530	3576	282-1B	59-1537	3589	282-1B
59-1525	3561	282-1B	59-1531	3579	282-1B			
59-1526	3563	282-1B	59-1532	3581	282-1B			

All were redesignated as C-130B-IIs ('Sun Valley IIs').

RC-130S

Two aircraft, JC-130As, modified under the 'Shed Light' programme to illuminate the Ho Chi Minh Trail in Vietnam as 'Bias Hunters'. Both Type 182-1A, they were USAF serials 56-0493 (c/n 3101) and 56-0497 (c/n 3105).

However, both were later reconverted back to standard C-30As. Two others were to be so converted, but this was not done.

R8V-1G

Twelve aircraft converted for Search & Rescue missions as either the SC-130B (USAF) or R8V-1G (USN). These designations were changed when they joined the US Coast Guard as HC-130B-LMs, as follows (all USCG aircraft):

Serial	Ex-USAF	c/n	Type
CG 1339	58-5396	3529	282-2B
CG 1340	58-5397	3533	282-2B
CG 1341	58-6973	3542	282-2B
CG 1342	58-6974	3548	282-2B
CG 1344	60-0311	3594	282-2B
CG 1345	60-0312	3595	282-2B
CG 1346	61-2081	3638	282-2B
CG 1347	61-2082	3641	282-2B
CG 1348	61-2083	3650	282-2B
CG 1349	62-3753	3745	282-2B
CG 1350	62-3754	3763	282-2B
CG 1351	62-3755	3773	282-2B

SC-130B-LM

Twelve aircraft, as R8V-1Gs above.

TC-130A-LM

One aircraft, the prototype RC-130A, serial 54-1632 (c/n 3019) (R for Reconnaissance), modified from a TC-130A. She was subsequently converted back to a standard C-130A.

TC-130G

Three aircraft, retired from the TACAMO mission, were allocated this designation as Trainer/Utility aircraft. All Type 382-4Bs, they were USN BuNos 151888 (c/n 3849), 151889 (c/n 3858) and 151891 (c/n 3878).

In the event only the first two received this designation before being struck off charge, while the latter became a support aircraft for the 'Blue Angels' formation team.

TC-130H

A solitary USAF C-130H, 65-0962 (c/n 4102), was modified at LASC, Ontario, California, in 1985 and redesignated as a Trainer. It served with the 41 ECS and the 7 ACCS as *The Lone Wolf*, but without EC equipment. It is currently with 55 Electronic Combat Group, comprising 41 and 43 Electronic Combat Squadrons and 755 Aircraft Maintenance Squadron out of Davis-Monthan AFB, training crews for EC-130H 'Compass Call' duties under the overall command of 44 Wing at Offutt AFB, Nebraska.

TC-130Q

Four aircraft, former US Navy EC-130Qs, thus redesignated for use as trainers and utility transports. All are USN aircraft:

BuNo	c/n	Type
156170	4239	382C-4D
156174	4278	383C-4S
159469	4595	382C-32D
159348	4601	382C-32D

UV-1L

Four aircraft, ski-equipped for the US Navy (ordered by the USAF as the C-130BL on behalf of the Navy). All are USN aircraft:

BuNo	Ex-USAF	c/n	Type
148318	59-5922	3562	282C-6B
148319	59-5923	3564	282C-6B
148320	59-5924	3565	282C-6B
148321	59-5925	3567	282C-6B

On delivery the Navy redesignated them as the UV-1L. In September 1962 they became LC-130F-*LM*s.

VC-130B-LM

One aircraft, serial 58-0715 (c/n 3510), a former JC-130B, modified as a 'Staff Transport' under this designation and used for convert courier missions. It was later remodified to a C-130B.

VC-130H-LM

Seven aircraft, modified C-130Hs as VIP aircraft with larger, squared windows in the main fuselage, 1st Class seating accommodation, deeper soundproofing and a built-in service galley and toilet module. Built for the Government of Egypt (two) and the Government (two) and Royal Family (three) of Saudi Arabia between July 1975 and 1984. They are registrations SU-BAM (c/n 4803) and SU-BAV (c/n 4811); serials 102 (c/n 4605) and 112 (c/n 4737); and registrations HZ-115 (c/n 4845), HZ-114 (c/n 4843) and HZ-116 (c/n 4915).

WC-130A

Three aircraft modified from C-130As for weather experimentation services, including the Operation 'Popeye' rain-inducement trials in December 1970. All Type 182-1As, they were USAF serials 56-0519 (c/n 3127), 56-0522 (c/n 3130) and 56-0537 (c/n 3145).

WC-130B-LM

Five aircraft, all USAF, modified C-130Bs:

Serial	c/n	Type
62-3492	3702	282-1B
62-3493	3707	282-1B
62-3494	3708	282-1B
62-3495	3721	282-1B
62-3496	3722	282-1B

WC-130E-LM

Three aircraft, modified C-130Es.

Three aircraft, former serving C-130Es. All are USAF aircraft:

Serials	c/n	Type
64-0552	4047	382-4B
64-0553	4048	382-4B
64-0554	4049	382-4B
61-2360	3659	382-4B
61-2365	3688	282-1B
61-2366	3706	382-4B

WC-130H-LM

Fifteen aircraft, former HC-130Hs and C-130Hs in 1957. All are USAF aircraft:

Serial	c/n	Type	Serial	c/n	Type	Serial	c/n	Type
64-14861	4088	382-12B	65-0966	4107	382-12B	65-0976	4126	382-12B
64-14866	4099	382-12B	65-0967	4108	382-12B	65-0977	4127	382-12B
65-0963	4103	382-12B	65-0968	4110	382-12B	65-0980	4132	382-12B
65-0964	4104	382-12B	65-0969	4111	382-12B	65-0984	4139	382-12B
65-0965	4106	382-12B	65-0972	4120	382-12B	65-0985	4140	382-12B

One aircraft (65-0965) was lost over the Taiwan Straits on 13 October 1974.

WC-130J-LM

Total of ten aircraft built or on order at time of writing. Modern replacements for the aging WC-130H weather-monitoring fleet, and capable of making continuous meteorological observations and data recording at 30-second intervals.

Customer	Serial	c/n	Type
AFRES	96-5300	5451	382U-04J
AFRES	96-5301	5452	382U-04J
AFRES	96-5302	5453	382U-04J
USAF	97-5303	5473	382U-07J
USAF	97-5304	5474	382U-07J
USAF	97-5305	5475	382U-07J
USAF	97-5306	5476	382U-07J
USAF	98-5307	5486	382U-12J
USAF	98-5308	5487	382U-12J
USAF	99-5309	5501	382U-12J

XFC-130H Super STOL

Three aircraft. In 1980 they were modified to take part in a planned second rescue of US citizens illegally held in Iran, following the failed earlier Operation 'Eagle Claw'. Those to be modified were designated as XFC-130H in readiness for Operation 'Credible Sport'.

They were to be modified C-130Hs with a DC-130 radome, a tail-hook fitted for landing back safely aboard an aircraft carrier in the Indian Ocean, a dorsal fin and two ventral fins fitted to the rear fuselage for additional stability, double-slotted flaps and lengthened ailerons, in-flight refuelling and five sets of ventral-activating retro-rockets totalling thirty in all, arranged with eight facing to the rear to aid take-off, eight angled vertically to aid braking during the planned descent into a football stadium, and eight aimed forward to assist in braking, with a further pair aft designed to keep the tail off the ground due to over-rotation. The 'Combat Talon'-type TF/TA radar was fitted, together with an ECM outfit, Doppler radar and GPS linkage to the Inertial Navigation System (INS).

All Type 382C-41D, they were USAF serials 74-1683 (c/n 4658), 74-2065 (c/n 4667) and 74-1686 (c/n 4669). Of these, 74-1683 (c/n 4658), designated as XFC-130H, was lost in an accident at Wagner Field, an auxiliary to Elgin AFB's Dukes Field, on 29 October 1980, due to premature use of the retros, and in November 1984 one of the two survivors, 74-2065 (c/n 4669), reverted to C-130H status. The other aircraft, 74-2065 (4667), was retained for further experiments in conjunction with Operation 'Credible Sport II' and became the solitary YMC-130H test bed.

YC-130-LO

Two aircraft, the original prototype YC-130-LOs (Model 082-44-01) completed in 1955. They were USAF serials 53-3396 (c/n 1001) and 53-3397 (c/n 1002).

They were redesignated as NC-130s in 1959

YMC-130H-LM

One of the surviving pair of aircraft originally selected for conversions under the aborted 'Credible Sport' mission programme, 74-2065 (c/n 4667) was retained for further experimental work in connection with a planned replacement Operation 'Credible Sport II' (so called because the aircraft hoped to use a football stadium on which to land and rescue American citizens from their Embassy, illegally held by the Revolutionary Iranian Government as hostages).

Rigorous testing was done under Phase I of a test programme, with the aircraft in an XFC-130H-converted state, over a period from 24 August to 11 November 1981, which revealed many defects. Phase II incorporated the recommended amendments and improvements to the original conversion, and further testing was done between June and October 1982.

This resulted in an acceptable design of what was, in effect, the prototype for the 'Combat Talon II', twelve such aircraft being ordered, but funding problems and the transfer of the Special Operations Force (SOF) to Military Airlift Command (MAC) caused the programme to be temporarily put on hold. Fresh requirements for twenty-one 'Combat Talons IIs' in 1983 suffered many delays and the first aircraft – 83-1212 (c/n 5004) – was not delivered until June 1984.

Meanwhile 74-1686, after being on the books of 4950TW for some years, ended her days in the Air Museum at Warner-Robins AFB Museum in 1988.

The EC-130V AEWAC aircraft developed for the US Coast Guard in 1992 by General Dynamics, with rotodome containing the APS-125 radar atop the after fuselage. The USAF later developed her utilising the APS-145 radar system. Recently the same concept has been revived once more, built around an idea using the C-130J-30 equipped for the same AEWAC mission with the AN/APS-145 and the Northrop Grumman (ESID) GroupII+ Mission System. *Authors collection*

Chapter 4

The worldwide operators of Hercules: military

Abu Dhabi & Dubai (United Arab Emirates Air Force – UAEAF)

Two C-130H Type 382C-40Ds, registrations 1211 (c/n 4580) and 1212 (c/n 4584), were purchased for Abu Dhabi & Dubai (the former Trucial States of the Arabian Gulf) in March 1975. They served for seven years and in September 1982 were sold back to Lockheed in part exchange for two replacement aircraft, C-130H Type 382-54Es, registrations N4161T (c/n 4983) and N4249Y (c/n 4985), which took over their registration numbers.

Major Nasser Saadeh (right), the C-130 project manager with the Abu Dhabi Air Force, and Captain Taher Mohid Rawashdeh. *Lockheed-Georgia, Marietta, via Audrey Pearcy*

In 1976, following a state visit two years earlier by President Habib Bourguiba of Tunisia, Sheikh Zayed Bin Sultan Al Nahyan used the Hercules to fulfil his dream of turning his tiny city-state green, by making it an oasis of trees and flowers. The Tunisian leader offered to help by gifting date palm trees of the Tunisian variety, the hardiest known, which were secretly cultivated. One of the most unusual cargoes hauled by the C-130, each Hercules carried approximately 2,000 of the 4-foot-high, 20lb (9.0718kg) date palms on each journey. Under mission commander Major Nasseer Saadeh, each date palm was dug up, the roots carefully packed in wooden boxes, and the delicate fronds sprayed just prior take-off to keep the moisture level satisfactory for the long haul. On arrival in Abu Dhabi the military precision of the operation continued, with twenty trucks shuttling the precious cargo to special nurseries.

Two more C-130H Type 382C-14Es, registrations N4140M (c/n 4879) and N4147M (c/n 4882), were purchased in February 1981, and took the registrations 1213 and 1214 respectively. In 2002 two former Gabon L-100-30s, TR-KKD (c/n 4895) and TR-LBV (c/n 5024), were purchased via Derco, becoming serials 1215 and 1216 respectively; the first was subsequently leased out to Maximus Air Cargo in 2007, and the second was used as a prop for the movie *Batman* at Hong Kong in 2008.

In 2009 the UAEAF announced that it was to order twelve C-130J-30s from Lockheed-Martin, Bethesda, Maryland, together with a substantial Logistics Support and Training Support package. Whether this deal survives the recent financial problems encountered by Dubai remains to be seen, especially as it was being procured through a Direct Commercial Sale.

Angola Air Force (*Força Aéra Nacional* – FAN)

A 1991 Type 382G-70C L-100-30, N4161T (c/n 5225), original owned by Frameair, was refurbished in France in 2005 to become the FAN's T-312. Located at EADS Sogerma, Bordeaux, France, in 2008, she was placed on the sales list by Sikorski subsidiary Derco Aerospace Inc.

Algerian Air Force (*Al Quwwat al Jawwiya al Jaza'eriya*)

The then *Force Aérienne Algérienne* took delivery of two 'Combat Talon' C-130H-30s, registrations 7T-VHN 8112 (c/n 4894) and 7T-VHO 8112 (c/n 4897), in July and August 1981 respectively.

A total of eleven C-130Hs were obtained between April and September 1982: registrations 7T-WHT (c/n 4911); 7T-WHS (c/n 4912); 7T-WHY (c/n 4913); 7T-WHZ (c/n 4914); 7T-VHM (c/n 4919), later re-registered as 7T-WHM; 7T-VHP (c/n 4921), later re-registered as 7T-WHP; 7T-WHR (c/n 4924); 7T-WHQ (c/n 4926); 7T-WHJ (c/n 4928); 7T-WHI (c/n 4930); and 7T-WHF (c/n 4934).

Algerian Air Force C-130H 7T-VHO (c/n 4897) made regular cargo runs through London Stansted Airfield in Essex before it became London's Third Airport. This view was taken on 10 July 1987. *George W. Pennick*

THE LOCKHEED MARTIN C-130 HERCULES

Algerian Air Force C-130H L-382 7T-WHE (c/n 4935) at RAIT Fairford, Gloucestershire. *Courtesy of Alastair T. Gardiner*

They were supplemented by four further C-130H-30 'Combat Talons' – registrations 7T-WHE (c/n 4935); 7T-WHD (c/n 4987); 7T-WHL (c/n 4989); and 7T-WHA (c/n 4997) – which arrived between September 1982 and June 1984. Finally, a fifth aircraft of this type, registration 7T-WHB (c/n 5224), was not delivered until November 1990.

One of their first missions was a search for the son of British Prime Minister Margaret Thatcher, who lost himself in the Sahara near the border with Mali during a car rally. One of the Herks, with a joint Algerian trainee crew/Lockheed instructional crew, found him at noon on 14 January 1982. After pinpointing Mark Thatcher's position using the Herks' Inertial Navigation System (INS), they called up a ground rescue team before refuelling at Tamanrasset. Later that same day they flew the lost rally driver's father, and the British Ambassador, Benjamin Strachan, and vectored a Land Rover rescue team to his location.

The surviving aircraft are operated by the *Escadrilles* 31, 32, 33 and 35.

Argentine Air Force (*Fuerza Aérea Argentina*)

Three former USAF C-130Bs were delivered to Argentina: ex-58-0720 (c/n 3515) in January 1994, which became TC-56; ex-58-0741 (c/n 3538) in November 1992, which became TC-58; and ex-59-1526 (c/n 3563) in November 1994, which became TC-57.

Three C-130Es were delivered in 1968: registrations TC-61 (c/n 4308), modified in 1977 to a C-130H; TC-62 (c/n 4309), which was destroyed in a bomb explosion at Tucuman airfield on 28 August 1975; and TC-63 (c/n 4310), which was destroyed in combat by a Sea Harrier during the Falklands War on 1 June 1982.

Five C-130Hs arrived fresh from the Lockheed factory between December 1971 and March 1976: TC-64 (c/n 4436); TC-66 (c/n 4437); TC-66 (c/n 4464); TC-67 (c/n 4576); and TC-68 (c/n 4578), the latter made over into a makeshift bomber during the Falklands War of 1982.

A solitary KC-130H was delivered in April 1974; this was TC-69 (c/n 4814). Most of these aircraft were flown by the 1 *Esquadron de Transporte, Grupo 1 de Transporte Aero,* and based at El Plomar. In 1979 TC-69 was joined by a second, which became TC-70 (c/n 4816).

Argentine Air Force C-130E TC-62 (c/n 4309). *Lockheed-Georgia, Marietta, via Audrey Pearcy*

Finally, a single Lockheed L-100-30 demonstration aircraft, N4248M (c/n 4891), was purchased by *Fuerza Aérea Argentina* in December 1982. Re-registered as LV-APW in February 1982, she was operated by the LADE company.

Austrian Air Force *(Osterreichische Luftstreitkräfte)*

In March 2003 the *Osterreichische Luftstreitkräfte*, as the flying arm of Austria's *Bundesheer*, purchased three ex-RAF Hercules C-130Ks – 8T-CA (c/n 4198), 8T-CB (c/n 4256) and 8T-CC (c/n 4257) – to equip *Fliegerregiment 3, 4 Transportstaffel*, at Linz/Horshing. These were renovated and joined from February 2008 onward.

Bangladeshi Air Force *(Bangladesh Biman Bahini)*

The Bangladeshi Government took delivery of four former USAF C-130Bs in the late 1990s: ex-58-0754 (c/n 3553); ex-59-1537 (c/n 3589); ex-61-0962 (c/n 3647); and ex-61-2640 (c/n 3676). After refurbishment at the Donaldson Center at Greenville in South Carolina between 2002 and 2004 they became S3-AGA, S3-AGB, S3-AGC and S3AGD with 101 Squadron based at Kurmitola Air Force Base.

Belgian Air Force *(Force Aérienne Belge)*

Twelve C-130Hs were delivered to Belgium between June 1972 and 1973, and formed 20 *Amaldeel, Groupement de Transporte*, with 15 Wing, based at Melsbroek Airfield near Brussels. Operated by Force *Aérienne Belge*, they have been widely utilised in humanitarian and relief roles for the United Nations.

They are CH-01 (c/n 4455); CH-02 (c/n 4460); CH-03 (c/n 4461); CH-04 (c/n 4467); CH-05 (c/n 4470); CH-06 (c/n 4473); CH-07 (c/n 4476); CH-08 (c/n 4478); CH-09 (c/n 4479); CH-10 (c/n 4481); CH-11 (c/n 4482); and CH-12 (c/n 4483).

In April 2007 a former USAF C-130E, 64-0552 (c/n 4047), which had been lying in storage after service with the Evergreen Aviation Educational Institute at McMinnville, Oregon, was sold to Sabena Technics for refurbishment for the FAB, becoming its CH-14 the following year.

The first Belgian Air Force C-130H, CH-01 (c/n 4455), in 1972. *Lockheed-Georgia, Marietta, via Audrey Pearcy*

A line-up of Belgian Air Force C-130Hs. *Jean-Charles Boreux, via Nick Williams, AAHS*

Bolivian Air Force *(Fuerza Aérea Boliviana)*

The following aircraft were on the strength of the *Fuerza Aérea Boliviana* at various times, but mainly operated by the peacetime civilian arm, the *Transporte Aéro Bolivano* (TAB – see the appropriate section), and painted in airline colours performing commercial as well as civic airlift missions, and operated from the world's highest commercial airport, La Paz International, at 14,100 feet (4,297.68m) high. This made Bolivia the eighth South American nation to fly the C-130.

Seven former USAF C-130As were registrations TAM64 (c/n 3023); TAM65 (c/n 3034); TAM66 (c/n 3144), which became CP-2187 in 1996; TAM61 (c/n 3181); TAM62 (c/n 3187); TAM63 (c/n 3188); and TAM69 (c/n 3228), which became CP-2184.

Five former USAF C-130Bs were registrations FAB-61 (c/n 3549); TAM60 (c/n 3559); TAM66 (c/n 3560); TAM67 (c/n 3581); and TAM68 (c/n 3655). TAM67 was lost at Trinidad Airport, Bolivia, on 31 December 1994, and TAM60 crashed on take-off from Chimorre Airfield, Bolivia, on 14 January 2000, while the rest were ultimately placed in storage.

Two C-130Hs, registrations TAM90 (c/n 4744) and TAM91 (c/n 4759), were directly purchased in 1977.

Finally, the Bolivian Government purchased a single L-100-30 from Lockheed in October 1979, the former N4083M (c/n 4833), for the *Fuerza Aérea Boliviana*, which became its TAM92 and was leased and operated for it by TAB as CP-1564.

Hercules are operated by *Escuadrón de Transporte 710, by Fuerza de Tarea Diablos Negros,* and by *Transporte Aéreos Bolivianos*

The Republic of Bolivia took delivery of its first C-130H Hercules on 22 July 1977. *Lockheed-Georgia, Marietta, via Audrey Pearcy*

Landing at Yokota AB, Japan, is C-130B 59-1532 (c/n 3581). She would later become the Bolivian Air Force's TAM67. *Nick Williams, AAHS*

Botswana Air Force

Three former USAF C-130 and B-IIs were made available to the Botswana Government: ex-58-0711 (c/n 3506) in November 1996; ex-58-0742 (c/n 3539) in October 1999; and ex-58-0746 (c/n 3544) in February 1997. They were re-registered as OM-1, OM-3 and OM-2 respectively.

A Brazilian Air Force C-130H collects ground-handling equipment and parts at Marietta on 13 February 1967. *Lockheed-Georgia, Marietta, via Audrey Pearcy*

Brazilian Air Force *(Forca Aérea Brasileria)*

The *Forca Aérea Brasileria* took delivery of eight brand-new C-130Es: registrations 2450 (c/n 4091), delivered in November 1965; 2451 (c/n 4092); 2452 (c/n 4093), which crash-landed on 26 October 1966; 2453 (c/n 4113), delivered in December 1965 and which served for the United Nations in Angola in 1999; 2454 (c/n 4114); 2455 (c/n 4202), delivered in March 1967; 2456 (c/n 4287), delivered in July 1968; and 2457 (c/n 4290), delivered in August 1968, which crashed in fog near Santa Maria air base on 24 June 1985.

Three further C-130Es, but featuring three-windowed paratroop doors, were also received, these being registrations 2458 (c/n 4291), delivered in November 1968; 2459 (c/n 4292); and 2460 (c/n 4293), which was burnt out at Formosa Airfield, Brazil, on 14 October 1994.

Four C-130Hs arrived between March and November 1975, these being registrations 2463 (c/n 4570); 2464 (c/n 4602); 2465 (c/n 4630); and 2462 (c/n 4636). They were joined by a solitary KC-130H, registration 2461 (c/n 4625), in October 1975.

They were joined by three later C-130H acquisitions from the Lockheed pool, registrations 2466 (c/n 4990), in February 1984; 2467 (c/n 4991), in October 1988; and 2468 (c/n 4998) in January 1987, which crashed into the sea off Fernando de Noronha on 14 December 1987.

They all mainly served with *1º Esquadrao of 1 Gruppo*, based at Galeão near Rio de Janeiro, as paratroop carriers, but some were fitted with skis and had a stint with the *2º Esquadrao* running down to Antarctica before reverting back again. Like most South American nations, the Herks were widely used in Governmental commercial projects, like aiding the construction of the Trans-Amazon Highway.

Brazilian Air Force C-130H FAB-2473 (c/n 4451) at Recife-Guararapes, Brazil. *Courtesy of Rafael Nunes*

Ten former Italian C-130Hs were procured from 2001, these being MM61988 (c/n 4441), which became FAB 2470; MM61989 (c/n 4443), FAB 2478; MMS61990 (c/n 4446), FAB 2471; MM61992 (c/n 4449) FAB 2479; MM61993 (c/n 4451), FAB 2473; MM61994 (c/n 4452), FAB 2472; MM61995 (c/n 4491), FAB 2475; MM61997 (c/n 4493), FAB 2476; MM61998 (c/n 4494), FAB 2472; and MM61999 (c/n 4495), which became FAB2477.

Two units currently use the Herk, *1.Grupo de Transporte* at Galeão and *1 Gruppo de Transporte de Tropas* at Campo dos Afonsos.

Cameroon Air Force *(l'Armée de l'Air due Cameroon)*

A pair of C-130Hs were obtained in August and September 1977, which operated services from Douala to other Cameroon cities with Cameroon Airlines. One, TJX-AC (c/n 4747), crashed at Marseilles airport in December 1989, and was subsequently rebuilt at Bordeaux. The other was TJX-AD (c/n 4752). These two were joined by a single C-130H, registration TJX-AE (c/n 4933), in June 1982, which was later registered as TJX-CE.

Although carrying civilian registrations and being used as President Omar Bongo's official aircraft, the Herks were frequently used in the passenger/freight role. Their routine was to pick up transferred imported air cargo from Douala and haul it to Yaounde, Garouda, Marou and Ngounder in the Cameroon, Libreville in Gabon, Bangui in the Central African Republic, and Malabo in Equatorial Guinea. They also made twelve flights to transport 1,104 pilgrims, ninety-two at time, from Douala to Mecca, Saudi Arabia, and football teams to Nairobi, Kenya, Accra, Ghana and Lagos, Nigeria. These Herks also performed in the counter-insurgency war role as necessary, working out of Batouri, Garoua and Yaounde airfields.

Central African Republic
(L'Armée de l'Air of the Forcesarmée Centralaficines – FAC)

A former USAF C-130A, 55-0025 (c/n 3052), was purchased by the President and Head of Armed Forces, François Bozize, in June 2008 from Wurst David Trustee, Medford, Oregon (as civilian N226LS) and transferred to the Central African Republic, becoming its TL-KNK. It is currently based at the capital's airport at Bangui.

Chad Air Force *(Force Aérienne Tchadienne)*

Seven Hercules have served with the *Force Aérienne Tchadienne* since 1963, these being four former USAF C-130As: the ex-54-1633 (c/n 3020) in August 1984, registered as TT-PAB, but subsequently crashing on take-off on 7 March 1986; ex-55-0010 (c/n 3037), re-registered as TT-PAE, but impounded by the Portuguese Government in 1990, which subsequently sold her for spare parts; ex-56-0551 (c/n 3159), re-registered as TT-PAC, but crash-landed on 16 November 1987; and ex-57-0473 (c/n 3180), re-registered as TT-PAD but also impounded, then sold off by the Portuguese Government.

One further C-130A was obtained in November 1983 by the French *Securité Civile* for the Chad Government, being the former Australian 57-0501/A97-208 (c/n 3208), which became TT-PAA.

More recently two brand-new Herks were obtained, these being a C-130H, registration N73238 (c/n 5141), from Gelac in 1988 and re-registered as TT-PAF, and a C-130H-30 (c/n 5184) in 1989, which became TT-AAH.

Chilean Air Force *(Fuerza Aérea de Chile)*

Two C-130Hs were purchased in 1972, these being 995 (c/n 4453) and 996 (c/n 4496). This pair has been supplemented in the *10 Grupo de Aviacon* by four old former USAF C-130Bs, obtained in 1992: ex-58-0752 (c/n 3551), which became 997; ex-60-0310 (c/n 3622), becoming 994; ex-61-0957 (c/n 3637), becoming 993; and ex-61-2647 (c/n 3690), re-registered as 998. They are all based at Merino Benitz air base near Santiago.

Colombian Air Force *(Fuerza Aérea Colombiana)*

To operate with the Air Force's *Escuadron de Transporte* from Eldorado Airfield, near Bogata, the *Fuerza Aérea Colombiana* initially obtained three former RCAF C-130Bs, purchased from Lockheed in 1968: ex-RCAF 10301/Lockheed N4652 (c/n 3572), which became FAC 1003 in 1969, and which ran out of fuel due to navigation error and was lost in the sea off Cape May, New Jersey, on 16 October 1982; ex-RCAF 10302/Lockheed N4653 (c/n 3575), which became FAC 1001 in 1968; and ex-RCAF 10303/Lockheed N4654 (c/n 3587), which became FAC 1002, but crash-landed and burned at Bogata on 26 August 1969.

Eight further surplus USAF C-130Bs were acquired on loan to the Colombia Government from 1990 onward, to help with anti-drug-running operations: ex-USAF 58-0717 (c/n 3512), which became FAC 1006; ex-USAF 58-0726 (c/n 3521); ex-58-0735 (c/n 3531), which was subsequently lost in a crash-landing in July 1995; ex-USAF 58-0757 (c/n 3558); ex-59-1535 (c/n 3585), which became FAC1011; ex-61-0956 (c/n 3635), which became FAC 1012; ex-61-2639 (c/n 3675) which became FAC1008; and ex-62-3487 (c/n 3697), which became the FAC1009.

The Colombian Air Force's first Herk, FAC 1001 (c/n 3575), at Merino Benitez Airfield near Santiago in 1972. *Lockheed-Georgia, Marietta, via Audrey Pearcy*

Columbian Air Force C-130B FAC 1010 (c/n 3521) at Santa Fe de Bogota – El Dorado. *Courtesy of Pablo Andrés Ortega Chávez*

Two brand-new C-130Hs were obtained in 1983, FAC1004 (c/n 4964) and FAC 1005 (c/n 4965). In 1992 four former USAF C-130Bs were added: 61-0956 (c/n 3635), becoming FAC1012; 61-2638 (c/n 3674), becoming FAC 1014; 61-2639 (c/n 3675), becoming FAC1008; and 62-3486 (c/n 3697), becoming FAC1009. Also, in 2008, a solitary ex-Italian C-130H, ex-MM 62001 (c/n 4498), was delivered as FAC1015.

Dubai Air Force (UAE)

Two L-100-30s, registrations 311 (c/n 4834), the former Lockheed stock N4085M, in January 1981, and the new-build 312 (c/n 4961) in April 1984, were purchased by Dubai and work as part of the United Emirates Air Forces.

Ecuador Air Force *(Fuerza Aérea Ecuatoriana)*

A quartet of former USAF C-130Bs were utilised by the Government of Ecuador: registrations 57-0525 (c/n 3501), which was purchased in 1992 and became 894; 57-0529 (c/n 3505), purchased in 1993, becoming 895; 58-0733 (c/n 3528), 1992, becoming 896; and 61-2645 (c/n 3683), becoming 897.

The *Fuerza Aérea Ecuatoriana* also purchased new three C-130Hs in 1977/79: registrations HC-BEF (c/n 4743), lost in a crash in 1982; 748 (c/n 4748), which also crashed on the Pinchincha Mountains a year later; and HC-BGO (c/n 4812), as 892.

Seen in June 1982 is this *Fuerza Aérea Ecuatoriana* C-130H of 11 Squadron, FAE 743 (c/n 4743), with its special camouflage, undergoing maintenance. She later crashed into a mountain near Marisal Sucre Airport, Quito, on 29 April 1982. *Nick Williams, AAHS*

A solitary L-100-30, N4175M (c/n 4893), was purchased from Lockheed and became FAE893. She was damaged in an accident at Guayaquil in June 1992.

Egyptian Air Force *(Al Quwwat Ali Jawwiya Ilmisriya)*

Six C-130Hs were allocated to Egypt from the 1976 USAF schedule, and delivered between December 1976 and April 1977. These were registrations SU-BAA (c/n 4707), later re-registered as 1270, and which was burnt at Larnaca, Cyprus, during an anti-terrorist operation; SU-BAB (c/n 4709), re-registered as 1271; SU-BAC (c/n 4714), re-registered as 1272; SU-BAD (c/n 4719), re-registered as 1273; SU-BAE (c/n 4721), re-registered as 1274; and SU-BAF (c/n 4728), re-registered as 1275.

Egypt's first Hercules, SU-BAA/1270 (c/n 4707), is pictured over the Great Pyramid near Cairo on 21 March 1977. *Lockheed-Georgia, Marietta, via Audrey Pearcy*

Egyptian Air Force C-130H SU-BAS/1286 (c/n 4808) departs from runway 23 at Getafe, Spain. *Courtesy of Diego Ruiz de Vargas*

They were followed into service by a further four C-130Hs delivered in October/November 1978: registrations SU-BAH (c/n 4792), later re-registered as 1276, which crashed on take-off from Cairo West Airport on 29 May 1981; SU-BAI (c/n 4794), re-registered as 1277; SU-BAJ (c/n 4795), re-registered as 1278; and SU-BAK (c/n 4797), which became 1279.

Between January and March 1979 ten further brand-new C-130Hs were delivered: registrations SU-BAL (c/n 4802), which became 1280; SU-BAM (c/n 4803), later 1281; SU-BAN (c/n 4804), later 1282; SU-BAP (c/n 4805), later 1283; SU-BAQ (c/n 4806), later 1284; SU-BAR (c/n 4807), later 1285; SU-BAS (c/n 4808), later 1286; and SU-BAT (c/n 4809), later 1287. They were based at Cairo East Airfield, near Heliopolis.

A tenth C-130H, registration SU-BAV (c/n 4811), was also delivered in March 1979, but was modified to a VC-130H for VIP use. She was later re-registered as 1289.

Yet a third batch of three new C-130Hs arrived in September/October 1982: registrations SU-BEW (c/n 4936), later re-registered as 1290; SU-BEX (c/n 4937), later 1291; and SU-BEX (c/n 4938), later 1292. The latter two have been converted to conduct ECM/ELINT duties, while the remainder are utilised as conventional transports.

A second 'stretched' C-130H arrived in June 1990, also for use as a VIP aircraft; this was SU-BKS (c/n 5187), which took the number 1293. A third of the same type, SU-BKT (c/n 5191), later 1294, arrived in August of the same year, but was lost in an accident near Dover, Delaware, in May 1999. The fourth and final C-130H, registration SU-BKU (c/n 5206), was delivered in August 1990 and took the number 1295.

In 2004 a trio of former Royal Danish Air C-130Hs were obtained: ex-B-678 (c/n 4572), which became SU-BKV; ex-B-679 (c/n 4587), becoming SU-BKW; and ex-B680 (c/n 4599), becoming SU-BKX.

Ethiopian Air Force (EAF)

Two former USAF C-130Bs were operated by the Ethiopian Air Force for a decade from 1998, after purchase from store; they were 61-2635 (c/n 3671), which became 1562, and 61-2636 (c/n 3672), which became 1563.

Two L-100-3s, formerly with Ethiopian Airlines, were taken into Government control in 2007, these being the former ET-AJK (c/n 5022) and ET-AKG (c/n 5306).

French Air Force (*l'Armée de l'Air*)

Despite a strong nationalistic policy of only using home-built aircraft, the versatile Hercules proved irresistible and finally featured in the *l'Armée de l'Air* inventory with the arrival of two confiscated Zaire Air Force C-130Hs, which were impounded at Malpensa Airfield, Milan, in February 1982, and were later used to equip the *Escadron de Transport 2/61*, based at Bricy Airfield near Orleans.

They were the former 9T-TCF (c/n 4588) and 9T-TCC (c/n 4589), which were initially given the French registrations 61-PM and 61-PN, and later became F-RAPM and F-RAPN respectively.

Three more brand-new C-130Hs joined them in December 1987: registrations F-RAPA (c/n 5114), later 61-PA; F-RAPB (c/n 5116), later 61-PB; and F-RAPC (c/n 5119), later 61-PC.

To further increase the unit's capability, three 'stretched' C-130H-30s were purchased in August/September 1988: registrations F-RAPD (c/n 5140), later 61-PD; F-RAPE (c/n 5142), later 61-PE; and F-RAPF (c/n 5144), later 61-PF.

A further batch of four L-130H-30s was purchased in March 1989: the former Lockheed N4242N (c/n 5150), which became F-RAPG, later 61-PG; F-RAPH (c/n 5151), later 61-PH; F-RAPI (c/n 5152), later 61-PI; and the former Lockheed N73235 (c/n 5153), which became F-RAP, later 61-PJ.

Finally, another brace of C-130H-30s arrived in March 1991, these being registrations F-RAPK (c/n 5226), later 61-PK, and F-RAPL (c/n 5227), later 61-PL. RET 02.621 *Franche-Comté*, based at Orléans Bricy AB, is the main operator.

French *Securité Civile*

Two C-130As, the former USAF 54-1631 (c/n 3018) and the former USAF 56-0478 (c/n 3086), which had both been modified as water tankers and were flying with T&G Aviation as N117TG and N116TG, were used by the French Government's *Securité Civile* in that role in Corsica in 1992/95; there are claims that this organisation is the French equivalent of the CIA[1] and also conducted convert operations with the aircraft in Chad for two years. At one time they carried the names *Iron Butterfly* and *City of Phoenix* respectively, and later reverted to T&G once more.

Two more C-130As, the former USAF 56-0530 (c/n 3138) and 56-0540 (c/n 3148), similarly converted to water bombers and registered with Aero Fire Fighting Service as N131FF and N135FF respectively, were sub-leased to the French Government from Hemet in 1993, taking the numbers 81 and 82, before reverting once more.

The *Securité Civile* also acted as a broker for the Chad Government in 1983 by obtaining two further C-130As, the former USAF 57-0501 (c/n 3208) and 57-0512 (c/n 3219), modified as water bombers and registered with Ford & Vlahos as N4445V, and with T&G as N118TG respectively, the latter for spares.

Gabon Air Force *(Force Aérienne Gabonaise)*

The West African state of Gabon operated two L-100s commercially, and in 1977 ordered a further single C-130H, registration TR-KKC (c/n 4765), which was delivered in February 1978 and was still flying in 1998.

One of Gabon's two L-100 Hercules taking off on 18 July 1977. *Lockheed-Georgia, Marietta, via Audrey Pearcy*

[1] See John Titus, 'Who's Who in the C-130 Scandal (an Update)', article in *Portland Free Press*, March/April 1997.

An L-100-20, registration TR-KKB (c/n 4710), was purchased from Lockheed in December 1976, and, despite a ground accident and being placed on sale, was still flying as late as 1997.

The Gabonese Government utilised its Hercules as flying trucks to support country-building projects like the construction of the Trans-Gabon Railway and the airlifting of people and products into and out of interior communities not served by a good surface transportation system. She also flew them on cargo-hauling to and from Europe. The aircraft were also flown as passenger aircraft, with the quick-change pallet system being employed to roll on seating for ninety-one passengers, with a double toilet and a hot and cold galley. They also had a decorative ceiling and extra soundproofing, with an overhead stereo system. One strange cargo – strange even by the Herk's catholic standards – was the transference of a whole supermarket complex from Libreville to a provincial town.

Two L-100-30s were purchased from Lockheed – TR-KKA (c/n 4582) in April 1975 and TR-KKD (c/n 4895) in September 1981 – the latter, named N'tem, for use as the Presidential aircraft. They served with the *Escadrille de Transport* from Leon M'Ba Airport near Libreville until 1989 and July 1988 respectively, when the former was sold to Pegasus Aviation and the latter was leased to Schreiner Airways.

Hellenic Air Force (HAF) *(Polemiki Aéroporia)*
– formerly Royal Hellenic Air Force *(Ellinki Aéroporia)*

Under Mutual Aid Programmes, the United States allocated four former USAF C-130Hs to the *Ellinki Aéroporia* in 1992, and they joined the Air Material Command's 356 *Mira* and 112 *Pterix*. This quartet was serials 741 (c/n 4622); 742 (c/n 4632); 743 (c/n 4665); and 744 (c/n 4672). They were later modernised, mounting ECM antennae.

No new aircraft arrived to reinforce this initial quartet until September 1975, due to Greece's withdrawal from NATO over the Cyprus question. But from that date through to May 1977, the United States Government allocated eight C-130Hs, diverted from USAF allocations. These eight aircraft were serials 745 (c/n 4716); 746 (c/n 4720); 747 (c/n 4723); 748 (c/n 4724), which crashed on Mount Billiuras on 5 February 1991; 749 (c/n 4727); 750 (c/n 4729), which crashed into a mountain near Tanagra on 20 December 1997; 751 (c/n 4732); and 752 (c/n 4734). Some have been re-equipped with MAFFS packages for fire-fighting, others for ELS duties.

In 1992 five former USAF C-130Bs were allocated to build up the force: ex-58-0723 (c/n 3518), which became serial 723; ex-60-0296 (c/n 3597), which became 296; ex-60-0300 (c/n 3604), which became 0300; ex-60-0303 (c/n 3613), which became 303; and ex-61-0948 (c/n 3624), which became 948. These veterans were still in service in 1998 with 112 *Pterix* 356 *Mira* at Elefsis.

Honduras Air Force *(Fuerza Aéra Hondurena)*

Four C-130As were obtained between 1986 and 1989 and operated by the *Escadrilla de Transporte* from Tocontin Airport, at Tegucigalpa. for many years; they were the former USAF serials 54-1635 (c/n 3022), which became FAH560; 55-0003 (c/n 3030), which became FAH557; 55-0015 (c/n 3042), which became FAH558; and 57-0476 (c/n 3183), which became FAH559.

A solitary C-130D, the former USAF 57-0487 (c/n 3194), was purchased in 1986 and became FAH556, but she crashed at Wampusirpi on 14 August 1986.

Indian Air Force (IAF) – *(Bhartiya V yu Sen)*

India announced the placement of orders with Lockheed-Martin in 2008 for eight of the 'stretched' C-130J-30s modified for Special Operations, together with the option for a further six. Deliveries of the first batch were to commence by 2011. These 382V-50Js are K-3801 (c/n 5638); K3802 (c/n 5639); K3804 (c/n 5640); K3803 (c/n 5653); K3005 (c/n 5654); and K3806 (c/n 5655).

A Honduras Air Force C-130A 182-1A (c/n 3042) at Tegucigalpa-Tocantins International, Honduras. *Courtesy of Juan K. Benitez*

Indonesian Air Force *(Angkatan Udara Republik Indonesia)*

As with so many Third World nations, there was much blurring of the edges with regard to the use of Hercules as military or civilian aircraft; often aircraft switched roles frequently, which has led to much confusion. Also, the official naming of the air force was changed almost as often!

With regard to the *Angkatan Udara Republik* Indonesia proper, three new C-130Bs were delivered between January and November 1960: serials T-1301 (c/n 3546), which later carried the civilian registration PK-VHD in 1978 as part of Pelita Air Services fleet, before reverting in 1982 as A-1301; T-1302 (c/n 3578) in October 1960, later renumbered as A-1302; and the former Lockheed demonstrator, N9298R (c/n 3580), which became T-1303 and was later re-serialed as A-1303. All three served with 31 Squadron at Halim Airfield, near Djarkarta, on the island of Java.

Four more C-130Bs were purchased in 1960: registrations T-1304 (c/n 3582); T-1305 (c/n 3583); T-1306 (c/n 3598); and T-1307 (c/n 3599). During the confrontation with Britain in defence of Malaysia in 1964/65 the latter two were lost. The former two were later re-registered as A-1304 and A-1305 respectively.

One brand-new C-130B, serial T-1308 (c/n 3601), arrived in March 1961, was subsequently leased to Pelita Air Services in 1969 as PK-VHA, then returned and was re-registered as A-1308.

A C-130B, former USAF serial 60-0305 (c/n 3614), was received in 1975 and was given the serial T-1311, being later re-registered as A-1311.

Two new C-130Bs, serials T-1309 (c/n 3615) and T-1310 (c/n 3616), were modified to KC-130Bs and re-registered as A-1309 and A-1310 respectively.

Two further former USAF C-130Bs, serials 60-0306 (c/n 3617) and 60-0309 (c/n 3621), were also received in 1975, and took the serials T-1312 and T-1313, being later renumbered as A-1312 and A-1313 respectively.

Sequence of Indonesian C-13MP Maritime Patrol aircraft being handed over and demonstrating.
All Lockheed via Audrey Pearcy

The 1600th Hercules, TNI-AU/A-1321 (c/n 4870) of the Indonesian Air Force, at Marietta on 15 December 1980. *Lockheed-Georgia, Marietta, via Audrey Pearcy*

Two Indonesian Air Force Herks, T-1302 (c/n 3578) and T-1030 (c/n 3580), in close formation. *Lockheed-Georgia, Marietta, via Audrey Pearcy*

In 1979 three L-100-30s were to be purchased at a cost in excess of $40 million, including spares, training and technical support, and all three were to be delivered in July, August and September. The planned use was by Pelita Air Services to airlift families from Java to Sumatra. A Lockheed demonstrator had carried out a series of thirteen twice-daily demonstration flights in mid-1978, which proved the feasibility of such an internal migration, in which 1,300 people were transported the 600 miles (965.606 km) from Djakarta to Padang and Jambi, Sumatra.

An L-100-30, registration A-1314 (c/n 4800), was purchased from Lockheed in December 1978. Another, A-1315 (c/n 4838), was purchased in December 1979, and another, registration A-1316 (c/n 4840), in January 1980. (Two further L-100-30s, registrations PK-PLU (c/n 4824) and PK-PLKW (c/n 4828), were not *Angkatan Udara Republik Indonesia* aircraft as such but were leased from Mitsui Corporation at various times between 1979 and 1991 – (but see also the Pelita Air Services section.)

The first ever 'stretched' C-130H-30, registration A-1317 (c/n 4864), was soon joined by six more: registrations A-1318 (c/n 4865); A-1319 (c/n 4868); A-1320 (c/n 4869); A-1321 (c/n 4870); A-1322 (c/n 4898); and A-1323 (c/n 4899). (Similarly, three other C-130H-30s, registrations PK-PLS (c/n 4917), PK-PLR (c/n 4889) and PK-PLT (c/n 4923), were not *Angkatan Udara Republik Indonesia* aircraft at all, but were purchased by the Indonesian Government and leased to Pelita between 1982 and 1992 – see the appropriate section.)

Two more C-130H-30 aircraft that did belong to the *Tentera Nasional Indonesia – Angkatan Udara* – were serials A-1324 (c/n 4925) and A-1325 (c/n 4927), but the latter crashed at Halim-Perdanakasuma, near Djakarta, on 5 October 1991.

Iraqi Air Force *(Al Quwna al Jawniya Al Iraqiya – IQAF)*

Following the total elimination of the IQAF during the Second Gulf War, a start was made under the newly elected democratic government to rebuild some of its defensive capabilities so that it was no long reliant on Allied forces. Three former USAF C-130Es were purchased in 2006, becoming IQAF's YI-301 (c/n 3802), YI-302 (c/n 3789) and YI-303 (c/n 3903). They are currently based at Baghdad International.

In 2008 the US Defense Department announced that the Iraq Government planned to purchased six C-130J-30s for the IQAF, the final order being placed in August 2009. They will equip 23 Squadron at the new Al Muthana Air Base. At the time of writing no c/ns have been identified for these six machines.

Islamic Republic of Iran Air Force (IRIAF) – formerly Imperial Iranian Air Force *(Nirou Haval Shahanshahiye Iran)*

While the pro-western Shah was still in power in Iran, he took the greatest pride in building up the *Nirou Haval Shahanshahiye Iran*, together with Iran's other armed forces, with the latest technology, and large orders were placed; these included orders for the Hercules, and Iran's Herk force was at one time one of the strongest outside the USA, only ranking below that of the RAF.

The first order, in June 1962, was for a quartet of new C-130Bs, obtained through the US Government's Military Assistance Programme, and these aircraft were initially assigned USAF serials: 62-3488 (c/n 3698), which became Iran's 5-101; 62-3489 (c/n 3699), which became 5-102; 62-3490 (c/n 3700), which became 5-103; and 62-3491 (c/n 3701), which became 5-104. In use with 5 Air Transport Squadron based at Mehrabad International Airport, near Teheran, these were all soon sold off to Pakistan (see the appropriate section).

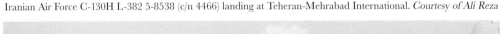

Iranian Air Force C-130H L-382 5-8538 (c/n 4466) landing at Teheran-Mehrabad International. *Courtesy of Ali Reza*

An Iranian Herk. *Lockheed-Georgia, Marietta, via Audrey Pearcy*

Four brand-new C-130Es followed, from December 1965 to January 1966: serials 5-105 (c/n 4115), subsequently re-numbered 5-101, then 5-850; 5-106 (c/n 4117), later 5-102 and sold to Pakistan as 10687; 5-107 (c/n 4118), which was struck by lighting and burnt out on 18 April 1967; and 5-108 (c/n 4119), later 5-103, then sold to Pakistan as 10689.

A second batch of four more C-130Es followed in June/July 1966: serials 5-109 (c/n 4148), later 5-104, then sold to Pakistan as its 64310; 5-110 (c/n 4149), later 5-105, then 5-8502; 5-111 (c/n 4153), later 5-106 and sold to Pakistan as its 64312; and 5-112 (c/n 4154), later 5-112, which crashed at Shiraz during engine trials on 7 April 1969.

Nine more C-130Hs formed the third order, between May and October 1968: serials 5-113 (c/n 4276), later 5-107, then 5-8503; 5-114 (c/n 4282), later 5-108, and sold to Pakistan as their 14727; 5-115 (c/n 4283), later 5-109, then 5-8504; 5-116 (c/n 4284), later 5-110, then 5-8505; 5-117 (c/n 4294), later 5-111, then 5-8506, and sold to Pakistan as its 97706; 5-118 (c/n 4295), later 5-112, then 5-8507; 5-119 (c/n 4296), later 5-113, then 5-8508; 5-120 (c/n 4297), later 5-114, then 5-8509; and 5-121 (c/n 4298), later 5-115, then 5-8510.

A fourth and final order for eleven more C-130Es followed between January 1970 and January 1971: serials 5-122 (c/n 4365), later becoming 5-116, then 5-8511; 5-123 (c/n 4386), later 5-117, then 5-8512; 5-124 (c/n 4387), later 5-118, then 5-8513; 5-125 (c/n 4389), later 5-119, then 5-8514; the former Lockheed demonstrator N7927S (c/n 4390), which became 5-126, then 5-120 and later 5-8515; 5-127 (c/n 4392), September 1970, later 5-121; 5-128 (c/n 4393), September 1970, later 5-122, which crashed near Mehrabad on 28 February 1974; 5-129 (c/n 4394), October 1970, later 5-123, then 5-8517; 5-130 (c/n 4398), November 1970, later 5-124, then 5-8518; 5-131 (c/n 4399), December 1970, later 5-125, then 5-8519; and 5-132 (c/n 4402), January 1971, later 5-126, then 5-8520, which crashed at Shiraz on 19 June 1979.

With the arrival of the C-130H, even larger orders were placed by the *Nirou Haval Shahanshahiye Iran*, the first batch of thirty such aircraft being delivered between November 1971 and April 1973:

Serial	c/n	Later serials	Serial	c/n	Later serials
5-133	4432	5-127, 5-8521*	5-148	4463	5-142, 5-8536
5-134	4433	5-128, 5-8522	5-149	4465	5-143, 5-8537
5-135	4438	5-129, 5-8523	5-150	4466	5-144, 5-8538
5-136	4439	5-130, 5-8524	5-151	4468	5-145, 5-8539
5-137	4440	5-131, 5-8525	5-152	4469	5-146, 5-8540
5-138	4442	5-132, 5-8526	5-153	4471	5-147, 5-8541
5-139	4444	5-133, 5-8527	5-154	4474	5-148, 5-8542
5-140	4445	5-134, 5-8528	5-155	4480	5-149, 5-8543
5-141	4448	5-135, 5-8529	5-156	4484	5-150, 5-8544
5-142	4454	5-136, 5-8530	5-157	4485	5-151, 5-8545
5-143	4456	5-137, 5-8531	5-158	4486	5-152, 5-8546
5-144	4457	5-138, 5-8532	5-159	4487	5-153, 5-8547
5-145	4458	5-139, 5-8533	5-160	4488	5-154, 5-8548
5-146	4459	5-140, 5-8534	5-161	4489	5-155, 5-8549
5-147	4462	5-141, 5-8535	5-162	4490	5-156, 5-8550

* destroyed by Armenian guerrillas at Stepanakert, Nagorno-Karabach, on 17 March 1994.

Two final C-130Hs reached Iran in May 1975, ordered before the overthrow of the Government and the violently anti-western Ayatollahs took over; these were serials 5-157 (c/n 4591), later 5-8551, and 5-158 (c/n 4594), later 5-8552; the latter crashed at Kahrisak on 29 September 1981 with the Defence Minister aboard.

Most of these aircraft initially served with transport units based at Shirah, but four have been converted to perform the ELINT intelligence-gathering role. Since the overthrow of the Shah seven have been lost in accidents, while many of the remainder, some of which served through the Iran/Iraq conflict, have been grounded through lack of maintenance and spares, and only a few remain operational. It is currently estimated that around fourteen Hercules of various types are still capable of limited flight operations through the cannibalisation of written-off aircraft parts.

Israeli Air Force *(Heyl Ha'Avir)*

Twelve former USAF Tactical Air Wing C-130Es were obtained by the *Heyl Ha'Avir* in the period 1971-72, but to fool international observers who did not look too hard, they were given both civilian and military serials. These were the former USAF serials 62-1796 (c/n 3747), which became the civilian 4X-FBE, but was the military number 304; 63-7774 (c/n 3840), becoming the dual 4X-FBF/301; 63-7810 (c/n 3880), 4X-FBG/310; 63-7843 (c/n 3913), 4X-FBH/305; 63-7844 (c/n 3914), 4X-FBI/314; 63-7855 (c/n 3925), 4X-FBK/318; 63-7862 (c/n 3932), 4X-FBL/313; 63-7870 (c/n 3940), 4X-FBM/316; 63-7873 (c/n 3943), 4X-FBN/307; 64-0509 (c/n 3993), 4X-FBO/203; 64-0516 (c/n 4000), 4X-FBP/208; and 64-0528 (c/n 4014), 4X-FBQ/311, which was re-registered as 4X-FBD.

Twelve additional brand-new C-130Hs were delivered in 1976-77 to serve with the 131 Squadron based at Lod airfield, Tel Aviv, and their registrations/serials were treated in the same way, the dual serials being 4X-JUA/102 (c/n 4430), later re-registered as 4X-FBA; 4X-JUB/106 (c/n 4431), later 4X-FBB, then 4X-EBB; 4X-FBC/109 (c/n 4530); 4X-FBD/011 (c/n 4533), which crashed on Gebel Halai on 25 November 1975; 4X-FBQ/420 (c/n 4653), which was converted into a KC-130H in November 1989; 4X-FBY/522 (c/n 4660); 4X-FBS/427 (c/n 4662); 4X-FBZ/545 (c/n 4664); 4X-FBT/435 (c/n 4668); 4X-FBU/448 (c/n 4680); 4X-FBW/436 (c/n 4686), which was converted into a KC-130H; and 4X-FBX/428 (c/n 4692).

Apart from those aircraft currently in storage in Israel, those operational are with 103 ('Elephant') Squadron and 131 ('Yellow Bird') Squadron, both based at Nevatim.

The Israeli Government placed orders for four C-130Js, at a cost of $130 million apiece, with options for a further five. With the President of Iran threatening to erase Israel from the map and enriching uranium, it is not surprising that Israeli defence contracts are shrouded in the greatest secrecy, but it has been reported that the first deliveries are due in 2012 and that these aircraft will incorporate Israeli-build weapons systems including an in-flight refuelling receptacle that would allow them to receive fuel from Israel's Boeing 707 air-tankers. There is a requirement for long-range missions and total-precision air-dropping to forward combat units, often with yards of the enemy. To achieve this, trials are in hand with GPS-guided parachutes, allowing such drops to be made accurately from an altitude of 7,620m (25,000 feet), with the use of a radiosonde that would measure wind speeds at the target zone and transmit them back to the dropping Hercules. Aircrewing is likely to be increased by the addition of a third pilot, and an additional flight engineer or navigator. At the time of going to press no c/n numbers have been released and the IDFAF has recently changed its aircraft registration system.

Italian Air Force *(Aeronautica Militaire Italiana)*

Seven C-130Hs were delivered to the *Aeronautica Militaire Italiana* between March 1972 and May 1972: serials MM61988 (c/n 4441); MM61989 (c/n 4443); MM61990 (c/n 4446); MM61991 (c/n 4447); MM61992 (c/n 4449), which was later adapted as a fire bomber; MM61993 (c/n 4451); and MM61994 (c/n 4452).

They were followed by a second batch of seven more of the same type, delivered between April and June 1973: MM61995 (c/n 4491), scrapped in 1976 but rebuilt and later used for Antarctic supply work in 1989; MM61996 (c/n 4492), which crashed on Monte Serra, near Pisa on 3 March 1977; MM61997 (c/n 4493), which was converted to a fire bomber and later used in Antarctica; MM61998 (c/n 4494); MM61999 (c/n 4495); MM6200 (c/n 4497), converted to a fire bomber, but scrapped after a ground accident on 23 January 1979; and MM62001 (c/n 4498).

These fourteen aircraft served with the *50º Gruppo, 46ª Aerobrigata,* based at San Giusto Airfield near Pisa. They were replaced from March 2000 onward by a batch of twelve C-130Js: serials 46-20 (c/n 5495); 46-21 (c/n 5497); 46-22 (c/n 5498); 46-23 (c/n 5503); 46-44 (c/n 5504); 46-45 (c/n 5505); 46-46 (c/n 5510); 46-47 (c/n 5511); 46-48 (c/n 5512); 46-49 (c/n 5513); 46-50 (c/n 5514); and 46-51 (c/n 5520). These being MM62175 to MM62186 respectively.

In addition there are ten of the 'stretched' C-130J-30s: serials 46-53 (c/n 5521); 46-54 (c/n 5523); 46-55 (c/n 5529); 46-56 (c/n 5530); 46-57 (c/n 5531); 46-58 (c/n 5539); 46-59 (c/n 5540); 46-60 (c/n 5548); 46-61 (c/n 5549); and 46-62 (c/n 5550). These being MM62187 to MM62196 resspectively. These were all delivered between 2002 and 2005.

The main operators are *46 Brigata Aerea, 2 Gruppo,* and *46 Brigata Aerea, 50 Gruppo,* both based at Pisa San Giusto Airfield.

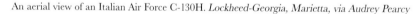

An aerial view of an Italian Air Force C-130H. *Lockheed-Georgia, Marietta, via Audrey Pearcy*

Dropping down to land is Italian Air Force MM62001 (for Matricola Militare) (c/n 4498), code 46-15, which was originally delivered in May 1973. *F. Ballista*

This Italian Hercules, MM61992 (c/n 4449), coded 46-06, took part in the Italian Everest expedition of 1973 and the ECM trials in 1978, and served with MAFFS. *J. Ballista*

The same aircraft is seen again at Istrana Airport in 1999, carrying the new low-visibility code. *F. Ballista*

MM61992 is seen again on 11 September 1976. *Balldur Sveinsson, via Nick Williams, AAHS*

At rest on a rain-sodden runway on 3 March 1977 is Italian Hercules MM61996 (c/n 4492), coded 46-10. *F. Ballista*

Seen at Treviso Airport in 1980 is MM61997, coded 46-11. She is a C-130H (c/n 4493) and carries the name *Portobello*. Her tail marking shows that she belongs to MAFFS (Modular Airborne Fire Fighting System); she was one of two such examples used by 46ª *Aerobrigata* for firefighting duties from June 1978 onward. *F. Ballista*

Dropping down at the UK Air Tattoo of 1983 is Italian Hercules MM61995 (c/n 4491), coded 46-06. She also carried the MAFFS firefighting system in 1978-79. *F. Ballista*

Pictured at Istrana Airport in 1983 is Italian Hercules MM61991 (c/n 4447), coded 46-05. She had originally been delivered on 14 April 1972. *F. Ballista*

At rest at Treviso Airport in 1986 is MM 61990 (c/n 4446), coded 46-04, which had originally been delivered on 30 March 1972. *F. Ballista*

Revving up all four engines at Villafranca Airfield in 1991 is MM 61991 (c/n 4447). She is wearing the new livery that was introduced from 8 February 1985. The red titles behind the cockpit read 'Best Maint. Best Pre-Flight earned at Airlift Rodeo in 1982 and 1984'. *F. Ballista*

Japanese Air Self-Defence Force *(Koku Jietai)*

The Japanese Self-Defence Force Air Section, the *Koku Jietai*, received a total of fifteen C-130Hs in a number of batches with which it equipped its *401st Hikotai,* which belonged to *1 Kokutai*, at Komaki Air Base, near Nagoya. The first pair of these Japanese Herks were serials 82-0051 (c/n 4976) and 82-0052 (c/n 4980), which arrived in December 1983. They were followed by a second pair, serials 45-1073 (c/n 5015) and 45-1074 (c/n 5017), which arrived in October and November 1984 respectively. A further duo, serials 75-1075 (c/n 5088) and 75-1076 (c/n 5090), reached them in November and December 1986, and yet two more, serials 75-1077 (c/n 5108) and 75-1078 (c/n 5109), in July 1987. Another two, serials 85-1079 (c/n 5136) and 85-1080 (c/n 5138), reached them in June and July 1988, while three more were purchased from Gelac in 1989, arriving the following year, these being serials 95-1081 (c/n 5170), 95-1082 (c/n 5171) and 95-1083 (c/n 5172). Another pair, serials 05-1084 (c/n 5213) and 05-1085 (c/n 5214), arrived in September 1990, and the fifteenth and last C-130H to enter Japanese service, serial 85-1086 (c/n 5435), was a former Lockheed aircraft that was not delivered until March 1998.

Japan's C-130H 05-1084 (c/n 5213), with her distinctive tail art, drops down on 13 November 1999. *Nick Williams, AAHS*

A port bow aerial view of three Japanese C-130Hs – 75-1076 (c/n 5090), 75-1077 (c/n 5108) and 75-1082 (c/n 5171) – of 401 Squadron JASDF, stacked up in close formation over their home base of Komaki AB prior to deployment to Thimol. *Hayakawa, JASDF*

The JASDF has modified some of these aircraft locally for the aerial minelaying role, while serials 85-1079 and 95-1083 have been used for United Nations relief work.

The *401st Hikotai* provided the following data on its Hercules fleet in 2000:

Type	c/n	JASDF serial	Delivery date	Serial no
382C-27E	4976	35-1071	12-12-1983	82-0051
328C-27E	4980	35-1072	12-12-83	82-0052
382C-44E	5015	45-1073	12-1984	83-0001
382C-44E	5017	45-1074	12-1984	83-0002
382C-68E	5088	75-1075	1987	85-0025
382C-68E	5090	75-1076	1987	85-0026
382C-75E	5108	75-1077	1987	86-0372
382C-75E	5109	75-1078	1987	86-0373
382C-82E	5136	85-1079	1988	87-0137
382C-82E	5138	85-1080	1988	87-0138
382C-90E	5170	95-1081	1989	88-1800
382C-90E	5171	95-1082	1989	88-1801
382C-90E	5172	95-1083	1989	88-1802
382C-02F	5213	05-1084	1990	88-0118
382C-02F	5214	05-1085	1990	89-0119
382C-60F	5435	85-1086	3-1998	75-1086

A splendid aerial view of C-130H 95-1082 (c/n 5171), of 401 Squadron JASDF, over the central mountains in 1999. *Hayakawa, JASDF*

Kuwait Air Force *(al-Quwwat al-Jawwija al-Kuwaitiya)*

The air force flew two L-100-20s from 1970, the former N7954S, which became its 317 (c/n 4350), and 318 (c/n 4412). The first aircraft served for a decade before crashing near Montelimar on 5 September 1980 after being hit by lightning. The second survived her to be sold back to Lockheed in May 1982, becoming the HTTB (see the appropriate section).

The Kuwait Government acquired four L-100-30s from Lockheed in 1983: ex-N4107F, which became its number KAF322 (c/n 4949); ex-N4349Y, which became KAF323 (c/n 4951); ex-N4242N, which became KAF324 (c/n 4953); and ex-N4232B, which became KAF325 (c/n 4955). In the Iraq invasion the first aircraft was damaged at Kuwait City Airport and taken over by the Iraqis, who flew her back to Baghdad as loot. She was again damaged by a bomb there and, although subsequently returned to Kuwait, was only fit for scrap. The other three were hastily flown to safety in Saudi Arabia and survived. They now fly with N.41 Squadron based at Kuwait International Airport itself.

Liberia

The former RAAF/Bob Geldof C-130A, registration N22FV (c/n 3207), was briefly registered in Liberia as EL-AJM in April 1986 during her varied and frequent changes of ownership, carrying the name *Wizard of Oz*. The Liberian Air Force had comprehensively dissolved itself over the years of internal feuding, but was officially declared null and void in 2005.

Libyan Arab Republic Air Force (ARFL) – *(al Quwwat al Jawwiya al-Libiyya)*

Prior to September 1969 this moderate and pro-western nation purchased many Hercules aircraft, but following the installation of a revolutionary dictatorship, clandestine means have been used to keep them operational. The nation's civilian operators, Jamahiriya Air Transport and Libyan Air Cargo, both based at Tripoli Airport, utilised many of these former Air Force Hercules.

Eight brand-new C-130Hs were lawfully delivered in 1970/71 before relations with the west were severed: registrations LAAF 111 (c/n 4366); LAAF 112 (c/n 4369); LAAF113 (c/n 4373); LAAF114 (c/n 4395); LAAF 115 (c/n 4400); LAAF 116 (c/n 4401), all in 1970; and LAAF 117 (c/n 4403) and LAAF 118 (c/n 4405) in 1971.

A Libyan Air Force C-130H (c/n 4401). *Lockheed-Georgia, Marietta, via Audrey Pearcy*

Following severing of relations, the following new C-130Hs on order and completed in 1973/74 were refused an export licence and were not delivered, and are still stored under embargo at Gelac: registrations LAAF 119 (c/n 4515); LAAF 120 (c/n 4518); LAAF121 (c/n 4523); LAAF 122 (c/n 4525); LAAF 123 (c/n 4536); LAAF 124, (c/n 4538); LAAF 125 (c/n 4540); and LAAF 126 (c/n 4541).

Two L-100-30 'stretched' Hercules, N4248M (c/n 4992), which became 5A-DOM, and N4269M (c/n 5000), delivered in May 1985, were obtained by Armoflex from the West German company POP; it was said that they were to be used for 'oil exploration in Benin, Nigeria'. In fact, they were both destined for Libya and, with Libyan aircrews aboard, they duly successfully evaded the US ban on sales to that country. They were operated by Jamahiriya Air Transport from 1985 onward.

In 2004 Libya was thought to have acquired the former Tripoli-based United Aviation's L-100-20 5A-DJR (c/n 4302), now the Libyan Air Force 112, and the former United Aviation L-100-30 5A-DJQ (c/n 4798), which is flying as the Libyan Air Force 116.

Mexican Air Force *(Fuerza Aérea Mexicana)*

In July 1987 the *Fuerza Aérea Mexicana* took delivery of two of the oldest former USAF Hercules, these being the ex-53-3132 (c/n 3004) and ex-53-3135 (c/n 3007), and although these ladies had been round the block more than a few times, they became FAM 10601 and FAM 10602 respectively. They were operated by *302 Escuadron Aereo Transporte Pesada*, based at Santa Lucia Airfield.

They were joined in 1988 by a further seven elderly aircraft of the same type and vintage: ex-54-1638 (c/n 3025), which became FAM 10603; ex-55-0027 (c/n 3054), which was delivered as a source of spare parts for the rest; ex-55-0028 (c/n 3055), which became FAM 10604; ex-55-0031 (c/n 3058), which became FAM 10605; ex-55-0035 (c/n 3062), which was also delivered as a source of spare parts for the rest; ex-56-0479 (c/n 3087), after being fully refurbished by Warner Robins at the Air Logistics Centre for Presidential Flight duties – her FAM serial 10606 was changed to TP-300 and she also received the civilian registration XC-UTP for these duties; and ex-56-0508 (c/n 3116), which became FAM 10607.

Finally, a single RC-130A, the former USAF 57-0510 (c/n 3217), was acquired the same year for use with the Presidential Flight as support aircraft. She received the FAM serial 10610, but crashed north-east of Mexico City on 17 September 1999.

The *Fuerza Aérea Mexicana* also took over the former Pemex L-100-30 in April 1993 as its 10611 (c/n 4851)

In 2003 the FAM secured a quartet of former RAF C-130Ks: XV191, (c/n 4211), which became 3614; XV215 (c/n 4242), which became 3615; XV222 (c/n 4252), which became 3616; and XV223 (c/n 4253), which became 3617.

In 2004 the FAM obtained two former USAF C-130Es from Israel: ex-C-130E 63-7855 (c/n 3925), which became 3612, and 63-7870 (c/n 3940), which became 3613.

Niger Air Force *(Force Aérienne Niger)*

Two brand-new C-130Hs were obtained by the *Force Aérienne Niger* in September and October 1979 respectively: registrations 5U-MBD (c/n 4829) and 5U-MBH (c/n 4831). Both served with the *Escadrille Nationale du Niger* based at Niamey, and were used for governmental heavy-lifting cargo duties as well as Presidential transport for President Seyni Kountche from time to time. One, 5U-MBD, was placed in storage at Oberpfaffenhoven, Germany, in 1986. She crashed at Sorei, near Niamey, on 16 April 1997, after two engines caught fire. 5U-MBH was similarly placed in storage, at Brussels Airport, in 1996 before returning to Niamey two years later.

Nigerian Air Force *(Federal Nigerian Air Force)*

The Nigerian Air Force purchased six brand-new C-130Hs, commencing with serial NAF910 (c/n 4619), in September 1975, which was later renumbered AT619, and serial NAF911 (c/n 4624), in October 1975, which was renumbered as AT624 and which crashed at Lagos Airport on 26 September 1992 after three engines failed due to contaminated fuel.

Four more quickly joined the first pair between December 1975 and February 1976: serials NAF912 (c/n 4638), which became AT744, then AT638 and later NAF912 again; NAF913 (c/n

Lift-off for Nigerian Herk NAF910 (c/n 4619) on 23 September 1975. *Lockheed-Georgia, Marietta, via Audrey Pearcy*

4639), which became AT639, then NAF913 again; NAF914 (c/n 4649), which became AT649, then reverted to NAF914 again; and NAF915 (c/n 4650), which became AT450, then AT650 before reverting to NAF915 again.

These Herks worked out of Murtala Muhammed Airfield, near Lagos, with the 88 MAG.

In 1984 the Federal Nigerian Air Force acquired two former Lockheed C-130H-30s: N4081M (c/n 4962), which became NAF916, and N4099R (c/n 4963), which became NAF917. This pair was joined by a third of the same type, the new NAF918 (c/n 5001), in June 1986.

Pakistan Air Force (PSAF) – *(Pakistan Fiza'ya)*

The first Herks on the force's books were four new C-130Bs delivered between January and March 1963: serials PAF 24140 (c/n 3751); PAF 24141 (c/n 3766); PAF 24142 (c/n 3768); and PAF 24143 (c/n 3781). They were operated by No 6 Squadron from Chaklala Airport, near Rawalpindi, West Pakistan. One, serial 24142, was shot down while conducting a bombing run during the Indo-Pakistan war in July 1966, while another, with civilian registration AS-HFO, was destroyed in a ground collision with serial 23491 (c/n 3701) at Chaklala on 10 September 1998.

A Pakistan Air Force C-130E (c/n 4180) at Dubai International. *Courtesy of Richard Vandervord*

In 1964 the *Pakistan Fiza'ya* acquired five former USAF C-130Bs to supplement these aircraft and equip No 6 Tactical Support Squadron, 35 (Composite) Transport Wing, based at Chaklala air base. These were former USAF serials ex-58-0739 (c/n 3536), which became PAF 58739; ex-61-2646 (c/n 3689), which became PAF 12646, later receiving civilian registration AK-MOB; ex-61-2648 (c/n 3691), in December 1964, which became PAF 12648, and which crash-landed on 18 August 1965; ex-62-3492 (c/n 3702), which became PAF 23492; and ex-62-3494 (c/n 3708), which became PAF 23494, and which crashed near Bahawalpur with President Zia-ul-Haq and his retinue aboard, the result of suspected sabotage, on 17 August 1988.

There were also four former *Nirou Haval Shahanshahiye* Iran C-130Bs serving in the same unit: former Iranian serials ex-5-101 (c/n 3698), which became PAF 23488 and was involved in a ground accident in March 1979 and scrapped; ex-5-102 (c/n 3699), which became PAF 23489 and was scrapped in March 1970; ex-5-103 (c/n 3700), which became PAF 23490 and was burnt out at Islamabad on 8 July 1969; and ex-5-104 (c/n 3701), which became PAF 23491 and was burnt in collision with PAF 10687 at Rawalpindi on 10 September 1998.

In 1975 more modern replacements arrived in the shape of five former *Nirou Haval Shahanshahiye Iran* C-130Es: former Iranian serials ex-5-102 (c/n 4117), which became PAF 10687 and subsequently collided with PAF 23488 in March 1979 and was scrapped; ex-5-103 (c/n 4119), which became PAF 10689; ex-5-104 (c/n 4148), which became PAF 64310; ex-5-106 (c/n 4153), which became PAF 64312; and ex-5-108 (c/n 4282), which became PAF 1427.

In addition, there were two L-100s bought in October 1966 by the Pakistani Government for PIA but, confusingly, operated by the *Pakistan Fiza'ya*. These were AP-AUT (c/n 4144), which operated as PAF 64144, and AP-AUU (c/n 4145), which operated as PAF 64145, and which crashed near Chaklala on 30 April 1968.

In 2007 the PAF acquired former RAAF C-130Es A97-159 (c/n 4159); A97-171 (c/n 4171); A97-177 (c/n 4177); A97-178 (c/n 4178); A97-180 (c/n 4180); A97-181 (c/n 4181); and A97-189 (c/n 4189).

In 2005 it had also obtained the wing from the former Argentine C-130H TC-67 (c/n 4576) as spares. Currently C-130s are serving with No 6 (Antelope) Squadron or 35 Composite Air Transport Wing at Chaklala PSAF Base.

Peruvian Air Force *(Fuerza Aéra Perunana)*

Five (originally six) former USAF C-130As were obtained in 1988 and operated by *841 Escuadron, 8 Grupo Aereo de Transporte*, based at Jorge Chavez Airport, Lima: former USAF serials ex-55-0025 (c/n 3052), which became FAP381 and was later disposed of to Lester Sumrail Evangelistic Association and received the civilian registration N226LS in November 1990, carrying the names *Mercy Ship Zoe* and *Feed the Hungry* (see the appropriate section); ex-55-0030 (c/n 3057), which became FAP394 and in 1996 was converted to an aerial tanker aircraft; ex-56-0483 (c/n 3091); ex-57-0455 (c/n 3162), which became FAP393 and was also converted to an aerial tanker in October 1995; and ex-57-0470 (c/n 3177), which became FAP395.

The sixth C-130A, ex-56-0522 (c/n 3130), was part of the original sale in 1988 but the deal failed through lack of payment for this aircraft; instead she went to the AMARC in Arizona before being utilised as a static loading trainer at Kelly Air Force Base.

The *Fuerza Aéra Perunana* also obtained two former USAF C-130Ds in 1986: ex-57-0484 (c/n 3191), which became FAP383, and ex-57-0491 (c/n 3198), which became FAP399. Both aircraft were scrapped in August 1993. Similarly the former USAF C-130A 57-0455 (c/n 3162) was sold to Peru in 1987, becoming its FAP393, and modified as a tanker aircraft eight years later; it has been stored without wing since 2001.

Eight L-100-20s were flown by the Peruvian Air Force's *41 Grupo Aereo de Transporte*.

Two former Lockheed demonstrators were purchased in October 1970. Registration N7985S (c/n 4358) became FAP394. She crash-landed at Lima on 24 November 1992, and went to the *Comercial Proveedorn del Oriente SA* as OB-1376 in 1994, before reverting to the *Fuerza Aéra Perunana* under her old serial once more. Registration N7986S (c/n 4364) became FAP395. She was leased to SATCO as OB-R-1004 before reverting to the *Fuerza Aéra Perunana*, but crashed at Tarapoto on 19 February 1978.

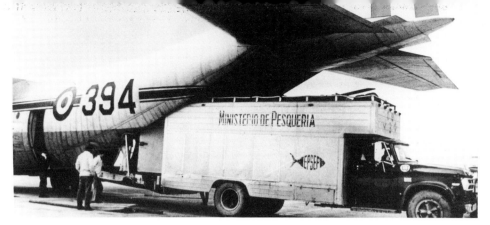

Peruvian Herk FAP394 (c/n 3057) loading a cargo of frozen fish. *Lockheed-Georgia, Marietta, via Audrey Pearcy*

A third L-100-20 was purchased new in April 1972. This was FAP396 (c/n 4450), which was also leased to SATCO as OB-R-956 and returned in 1976. She survived take-off damage from Iquitas in June 1973, but was lost on 24 October 1981 in an emergency night landing due to lack of fuel close to San Juan.

The *Fuerza Aéra Perunana* also operated three further L-100-20s: serials FAP382 (c/n 4706), civilian registration OB-1377; FAP383 (c/n 4708), which crashed at Puerto Maldonado on 9 June 1983; and FAP384 (c/n 4715), civilian OB-1378.

Finally there were two further former Lockheed demonstrators, registrations N4115M (c/n 4850), which became FAP397, civilian OB-1377, OB-1355, OB-1375, etc, and N4119M (c/n 4853), which became FAP398, civilian registration OB-1376.

Cargoes varied enormously. One L-100-20 flew eight bulls from Mexico City to Lima for a bullfight. Others transported twenty-six steel barges to Pacullpa, which were to be used as transports between there and Iquitos on the River Amazon. Much of the work of the Peruvian Herks was in trans-Andes flights to develop oilfields in the Amazonian headwaters, as well as the transport of livestock cattle and bulk cargoes of frozen fish from Lima to Aycucho in the interior across the Andes barrier. The early completion of the Carra Terra Marginal national highway was credited by President Belaunde as due 'almost entirely to this aircraft'. But persistent reports also claim that clandestine missions were conducted to Colombia.

FAP 394 is seen again helping with a Peruvian oil pipeline on 8 March 1976. *Lockheed-Georgia, Marietta, via Audrey Pearcy*

Mention should also be made of a single C-130A, which was to be purchased as a VIP aircraft for the Peruvian Navy. This was the former USAF serial 55-0008 (c/n 3035), which in February 1987 was flown to Aero Corporation at Lake City, Florida, to be modernised. As payment was never received for this, she was subsequently sold in 1993 to Snow Aviation and became the civilian N130SA.

Philippines Air Force *(Hukbong Himpapawid ng Pilipinas)*

In 1991 the Philippines Air Force obtained eight former USAF C-130Bs, and equipped its 222 Heavy Airlift Squadron with them, based at Mactan Airfield. These veteran Herks were serials ex-58-0725 (c/n 3520), which became 0725; ex-58-0738 (c/n 3535), which became 0738; ex-58-0747 (c/n 3545), which became 3545; ex-58-0749 (c/n 3547), which became 0749; ex-58-0753(c/n 3552), which became 3552; ex-60-0294 (c/n 3593), which became 0294 and was grounded in 1996; and ex-61-0961 (c/n 3646), which became 0961 and was grounded in 1996.

A ninth machine, a C-130A-50-LM obtained by the Philippines Government, was the former USAF/RAAF serial 57-0504/A97-211 (c/n 3211), which was registered to Aboitiz at Manila in May 1988 as NRP-R3211 and which in March 1991 was re-registered as RP-C3211 and finally bought from storage at Manila in 1998 by Total Aerospace of Miami, for spare parts.

In August 1973 the Philippines Government also purchased two L-100-20s from Saturn: registrations N30FW (c/n 4302), which became Pl99, and NF40FW (c/n 4303), which became Pl98. They were leased respectively to the Philippines Air Force as 4302 and to Phil Aero Transport as RP-C98. Both were disposed of, the former to UAA in 1982 and the latter to James Bay Energy Corporation in 1973.

Two additional L-100-20s were obtained in October 1973 and May 1975 respectively: the former Lockheed N7967S (c/n 4512) and the new RP-C101 (c/n 4593). They were both leased to Philippine Aero Transport, the former in 1973, before being sold to Philippines Aerospace Development Corporation (PADC); she became Philippines Air Force serial 4512 in 1983, and retired from service in 1991 for use as spares. The latter became Philippines Air Force serial 4593 in July 1983.

Three new C-130Hs joined 222 Squadron in November 1976 and August 1977 respectively, these being Philippines Air Force serials 4704 (c/n 4704), 4726 (c/n 4726) and 4761 (c/n 4761).

Former USAF C-130B 61-0954 (c/n 3633) became 0954 on 2001; ex-61-0961 (c/n 3646) became 0961; and a solitary L-100 Lockheed demonstrator, N1130E (c/n 3946), modified to an L-100-20, was acquired from PADC in 1983.

Hercules currently serve with 222 Airlift Squadron, part of 220 Airlift Wing based on Mactan Island, Cebu, at Benito Ebuen Air Base.

Polish Air Force *(Sily Powietrzne Rzeczypospolitej Polskiej)*

The Polish Government purchased five ex-USAF C-130Es, which had to have their centre wing sections replaced at AMARG together with other modifications and updates. These aircraft became the SPRP's 1501, the former 70-1273 (c/n 4428), with a centre wing section from the former 59-1525 (c/n 3561); 1502, formerly 70-1272 (c/n 4426), with centre wing section from former 59-5957 (c/n 3584); 1503, formerly 70-1262 (c/n 4414), with centre wing section from former 58-0714 (c/n 3509); 1504, formerly 70-1276 (c/n 4435), with centre wing section from former 59-1529 (3569); and 1505, formerly 70-1263 (c/n 4415), with centre wing section from former 61-0958 (c/n 3639).

The first two were handed over at Powidz Air Base for *14 Eskadra Lotnictwa Transportowego*, with the remaining trio due during 2010.

Portuguese Air Force *(Forca Aérea Portuguesa)*

The Portuguese Government became the 41st to take delivery of the Hercules, when the first of five C-130Hs, acquired by the *Forca Aérea Portuguesa* between August 1977 and June 1978, arrived in October 1977. One of a batch of five of that variant, she was received in a ceremony at Lisbon by the Director of Materiel Services of the Air Force, while the commander of *501 Esquadra de Transporte*, at Montijo. Lieutenant Colonel Manuel Alvarenga and his crews completed their training at Marietta. These four aircraft worked out of the Montijo Air Base on both NATO duties and on patrols to maintain the 200-mile economic zone, and on supply runs to the Azores.

The original five were serials 6801 (c/n 4749), stretched to a C-130H-30 in 1992, and used for United Nations work in Angola; 6802 (c/n 4753), stretched to a C-130H-30 in 1995; 6803 (c/n 4772); 6804 (c/n 4777); and 6805 (c/n 4778).

In addition, a third factory-fresh C-130H-30 was obtained from Gelac in October 1991, this being serial 6806 (c/n 5264).

Qatar *(Qatari Eimri Air Force)*

Qatar announced the purchase contract for four C-130J-30 Super Hercules in October 2008. A whole package worth US$393.6 million was announced at Marietta, which included training of aircrew and maintenance technicians, spares, ground support and test equipment (carts, forklifts, loaders, pallets), together with a team of specialists. The four 382V-51Js are serials 1107 (c/n 5662); 1106 (c/n 5561); 1108 (c/n 5668); and 1109 (c/n 5669).

Romanian Air Force *(Fortele Aderiene Romaniei)*

The Lockheed-Martin Aeronautical Systems Support Company, at Marietta, Georgia, was awarded a $6,358,170 firm fixed-price contract to provide Contractor Logistic Support for four C-130Bs, with completion by September 1968. The company provided the necessary replenishment spares, component overhaul, technical service representatives and simulator training as well as technical publications and a scheduled Maintenance Program Continuous Airworthiness Inspection Program. Twenty-nine firms were solicited in May 1996, and three proposals received. The contracting activity was Warner Robins Air Logistic Centre at Robins Air Force Base, Georgia. The Aircraft & Logistics Centres, based at Greenville, South Carolina, and the company promised to engage local Romanian companies in support of the programme, with a certain amount of locally produced parts, saving the long air journey back to the States for overhauls.

The four former USAF C-130Bs were subsequently delivered from Ogden Air Logistics Centre to the *Fortele Aderiene Romaniei* as follows: ex-USAF 59-1527 (c/n 3568) in October 1996, which became serial 5927; ex-59-1530 (c/n 3576) in November 1996, which became 5930; ex-61-0950 (c/n 3626) in October 1996, which became 6150; and ex-61-0966 (c/n 3653) in December 1996, which became 6166. They equipped 90 Airlift based at Otopeni near Bucharest.

In 2004 the former Italian Air Force C-130H, MM 61991 (c/n 4447), was obtained and became serial 6191.

Royal Air Force (RAF)

The British version of the C-130H, originally ordered in 1965, featured the T56-A-15 engine, which developed 4,508eshp, as well as special electronics and other equipment manufactured in the United Kingdom to RAF specifications, and this variant was known as the C-130K. They were all allocated US serial numbers for bureaucratic reasons and were known as the Hercules C Mk 1 under the archaic RAF system. The lead aircraft, US serial 65-13021 (c/n 4169), received the RAF serial XV176 and made her maiden flight at Marietta on 19 October 1966, joining No 27 Operational Conversion Unit based at Thorney Island the following April.

She was the precursor of a fleet of a further sixty-five machines of basically the same configuration, delivered in several batches, as follows:

Ex-US serials	c/n	RAF serials	Notes
65-13022	4182	XV177	c
65-13023	4188	XV178	a
65-13024	4195	XV179	a
65-13025	4196	XV180	crashed at Fairford on 24 March 1969
65-13026	4198	XV181	a
65-13027	4199	XV182	a
65-130028	4200	XV183	c, named *Hector*

RAF Support Command took delivery of its first C-130K, XV176 (c/n 4169), in August 1967, with No 36 Squadron. The aircraft is seen landing. *Author's collection*

Touch-down of first RAF Herk. *Author's collection*

A ceremonial welcome to No 36 of the first RAF Herk, XV176. *Author's collection*

THE LOCKHEED MARTIN C-130 HERCULES

Ex-US serials	c/n	RAF serials	Notes
65-13029	4201	XV184	c
65-13030	4203	XV185	a
65-13031	4204	XV186	a
65-13032	4205	XV187	a
65-13033	4206	XV188	c
65-13034	4207	XV189	c
65-13935	4210	XV190	c
65-13036	4211	XV191	a
65-13037	4212	XV192	b
65-13038	4213	XV193	c; named *Horatius*, and crashed at 3,000 feet in a 'very inaccessible' mountain area near Beinn A'Ghlo, north-east of Blair Atholl, Perthshire, Scotland, on 27 May 1993, killing the nine-man crew
65-13037	4214	XV194	lost in a ground accident at Tromsö, Norway, on 12 September 1972
65-13040	4216	XV195	a
65-13041	4217	XV196	a
65-13042	4218	XV197	c
65-13043	4219	XV198	crashed at Colerne on 10 September 1973
65-13044	4220	XV199	c
66-8559	4223	XV200	a
65-8551	4224	XV201	b
66-8552	4226	XV202	c
66-8553	4227	XV203	b
66-8554	4228	XV204	b
66-8555	4230	XV205	
66-8556	4231	XV206	a
66-8557	4232	XV207	c
66-8558	4233	XV208	
66-8559	4235	XV209	c
66-8560	4236	XV210	a
66-8561	4237	XV211	a
66-8562	4238	XV212	c
66-8563	4240	XV213	b
66-8564	4241	XV214	c
66-8565	4242	XV215	a
66-8566	4243	XV216	crashed off Melovia, Italy, on 9 November 1971
66-8567	4244	XV217	c
66-8568	4245	XV218	a
66-8569	4246	XV219	c
66-8570	4247	XV220	c
66-8571	4251	XV221	c
66-8572	4252	XV222	c
66-8573	4253	XV223	c
66-13533	4254	XV290	c

Royal Air Force C-130K XV293 (c/n 4258) being refuelled. *Nick Williams, AAHS*.

A fine aerial view of an RAF Hercules. *Marshall of Cambridge Aerospace Ltd, via Martin Bowman*

Ex-US serials	c/n	RAF serials	Notes
66-13534	4256	XV291	a
65-13534	4257	XV292	a
65-13536	4258	XV293	a
65-13537	4259	XV294	c
65-13538	4261	XV295	a, named *Hephaestos*
65-13539	4262	XV296	b
65-13540	4263	XV297	a
65-13541	4264	XV298	a
65-13542	4266	XV299	c
65-13543	4267	XV300	a, named *Homer*
65-13544	4268	XV301	c
65-13545	4270	XV302	c
65-13546	4271	XV303	c
65-13547	4272	XV304	c
65-13548	4273	XV305	c
65-13549	4274	XV306	a, named *Hyperion*
65-13550	4275	XV307	c

Notes

a Subsequently fitted with in-flight refuelling probes and equipment in the light of the Falklands campaign, by Marshalls Engineering of Cambridge, becoming C Mk 1Ps. This followed the fitting of an ex-Vulcan probe above the flight deck on one RAF Hercules in 1982. Thus modified, she was able to make a contribution to Operation 'Corporate', and even set the world endurance record for a Hercules of 28hr 4min flight time.

b Modified with air-refuelling coupled with palleted drum/hose equipment to become C Mk 1Ks.

c Stretched by 15 feet (4.57m). The prototype, XV223 (c/n 4253), stretched by Lockheed, first flew thus on 3 December 1979, and twenty-nine others were modified by Marshalls. They could thus accommodate ninety-two paratroops against sixty-four, and 129 infantry as opposed to only ninety-two. These became the C Mk 3 Hercules, and were subsequently converted to C Mk 3Ps. The following year AN/ALQ 157 infra-red jammers and chaff and flare ECM dispensing gear was fitted to both C Mk 1Ps and Ks. Some were also equipped with the Racal Orange Blossom wing-tip ECM pods.

The RAF pilots copied the US Marine Corps, who had nicknamed their tanker aircraft 'Fat Albert' after the American comic-book character, and the name has stuck with British aircrews ever since. The RAF C-130Ks were as fully extended as their American counterparts, flying missions all over the globe, with relief and rapid reinforcement operations in Aden, Anguilla, Belize, Cambodia, Cyprus, Egypt, Ethiopia, Lebanon, northern Iraq (supplying the Kurds), India and Pakistan, as well as supporting Commonwealth peacekeeping operations in Rhodesia (Zimbabwe).

Perhaps one of the most bizarre cargoes ever carried by an RAF Hercules, XV297 (c/n 4264), was the delivery to Bavaria of the body of Rudolf Hess, the former Deputy Leader of the Nazi Party under Hitler, who died in suspicious circumstances at Spandau Jail in Berlin on 17 August 1987. The coffin was transferred from the British Military Hospital to RAF Gatow, flown to the USAF base at Grafenwohr, the nearest airfield to the Hess family home at Wunsiedel, and unloaded amid strict security for burial in the family plot.[2]

---

[2] See John England, 'Security veils Hess's last journey to small Bavarian town', article in *The Times*, 21 August 1987.

A comprehensive display of flare defences by an RAF Herk. *MOD*

THE LOCKHEED MARTIN C-130 HERCULES

C.Mk 1P Royal Air Force XV305

The Royal Air Force's Hercules wing has diversified its force capabilities since the
Falklands war of 1982. Many aircraft were fitted with inflight-refuelling gear, while
several were used as tankers, notably on the Falklands supply route. Additionally, 32
aircraft were 'stretched' to increase airlift capacity in the existing force.

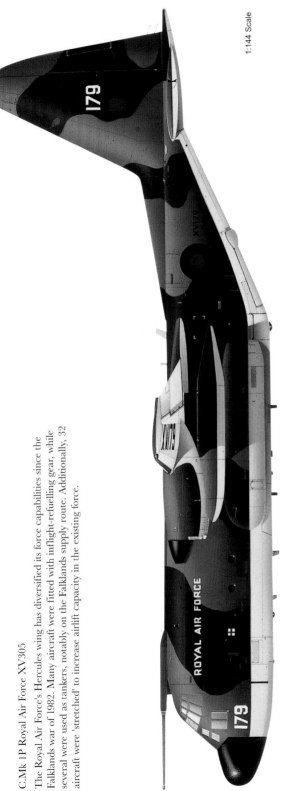

EC-130E 'Volant Solo II' United States Air National Guard

The giant dorsal fillet and underwing 'axe-head' antennae identify the EC-130E
'Volant Solo II' aircraft. Used for electronic reconnaissance, this 'Volant Solo' aircraft
served with the 193rd SOS, Pennsylvania Air National Guard.

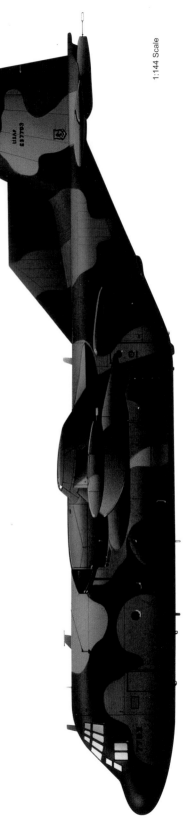

1:144 Scale

1:144 Scale

I

Various low-visibility camouflage schemes were used by MC-130E special operation gunships over the years, including this one. Those in Germany later adopted the 'European One' pattern, but were virtually anonymous.

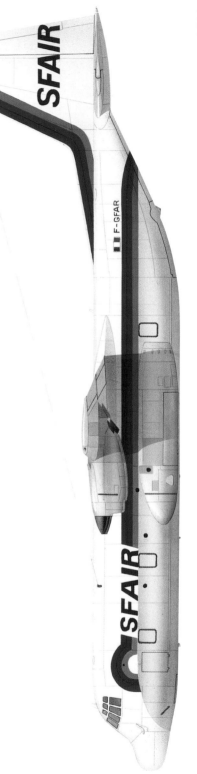

SFAIR was the first European civil operator of the L-382, taking delivery of its first example in 1981 with a second following shortly afterwards. Among the early operations carried out by the Nantes-based carrier were flights on behalf of the French postal service.

Wearing one of the most colourful Hercules schemes, Cameroon's three C-130s came in the 'H' and 'H-30' versions. One has since been written off (in 1989). They were occasionally used as civilian transports.

1:160 Scale

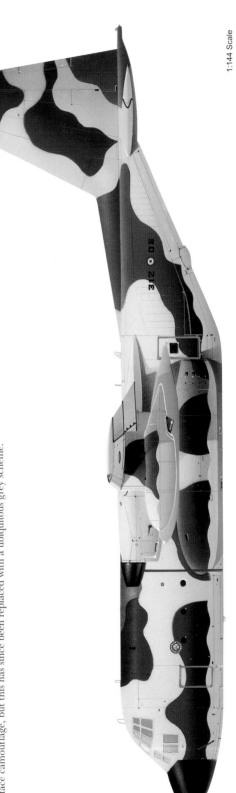

Ejercito del Aire Air Transport Command is responsible for the operations of the two Hercules units. The aircraft used to wear a two-tone brown and dark green upper surface camouflage, but this has since been replaced with a ubiquitous grey scheme.

1:144 Scale

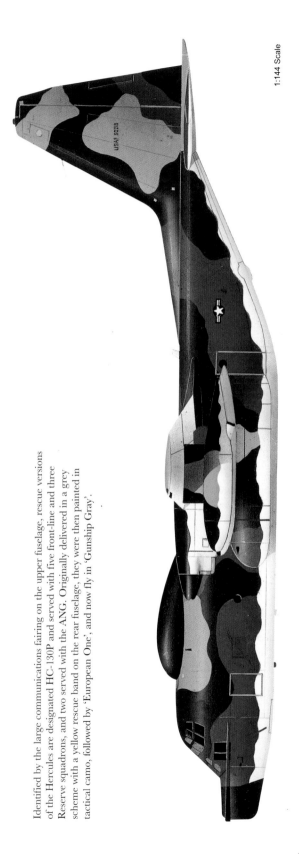

Identified by the large communications fairing on the upper fuselage, rescue versions of the Hercules are designated HC-130P and served with five front-line and three Reserve squadrons, and two served with the ANG. Originally delivered in a grey scheme with a yellow rescue band on the rear fuselage, they were then painted in tactical camo, followed by 'European One', and now fly in 'Gunship Gray'.

This C-130B is one of two that were supplied to the Royal Jordanian air force from USAF stocks. Subsequently a total of five C-130H models was acquired. These aircraft are operated together with CASA Aviocars from King Abdullah Air Base outside Amman. The flush fin VOR aerial is white fibreglass in this case.

This KC-130F (originally styled GV-1) was the Marine Corps support aircraft for the US Navy's Blue Angels aerobatic team, being responsible for a considerable amount of special transport every time the team makes a public appearance.

There are over 500 C-130s of various marks in USAF service, and there is no doubt that this highly important transport will see further front-line service for a very long time. This aircraft is a United States Air Force Lockheed C-130H in a 1980s 'lizard' tactical camouflage.

Argentine Air Force (Fuerza Aérea Argentina)

The FAA currently operates 10 aircraft as part of I Brigada Aérea. Both national and international transport duties are assigned, while the KC-130Hs (like this 1 Escuadrón de Transporte example) provide tanking facilities for the FAA interceptor force. The FAA also operates the C-130B (2), C-130H (5), KC-130H (2) and a solitary L-100-30.

1:144 Scale

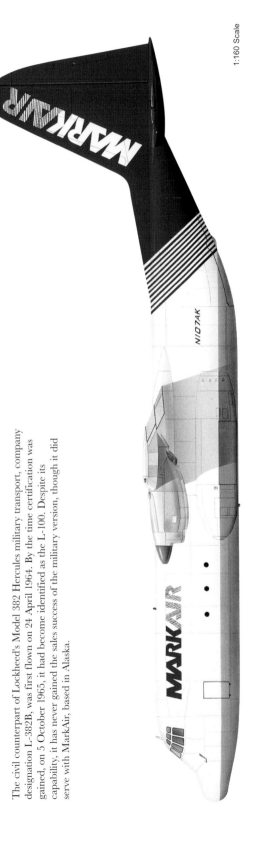

The civil counterpart of Lockheed's Model 382 Hercules military transport, company designation L-382B, was first flown on 24 April 1964. By the time certification was gained, on 5 October 1965, it had become identified as the L-100. Despite its capability, it has never gained the sales success of the military version, though it did serve with MarkAir, based in Alaska.

1:160 Scale

The Al Quwwat al Jawwiya il Misriya's (Egyptian Air Force and Air Defence Command) move away from Soviet aircraft types to Western designs was first evidenced by the supply of six C-130Hs. The current C-130H force, based at Cairo West, numbers 22 machines.

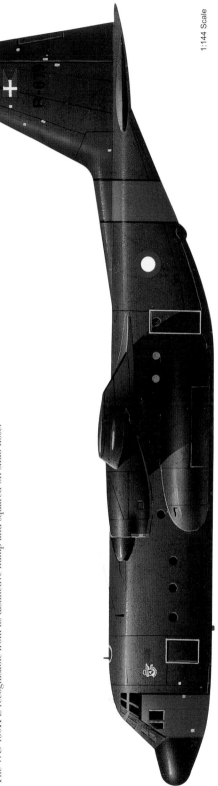

The 54th Weather Reconnaissance Squadron, then part of the Air Weather Service of Military Airlift Command, used this WC-130H when based at Andersen AFB, Guam. The WC-130H is recognisable from its distinctive hump and squared-off snub nose.

1:144 Scale

1:144 Scale

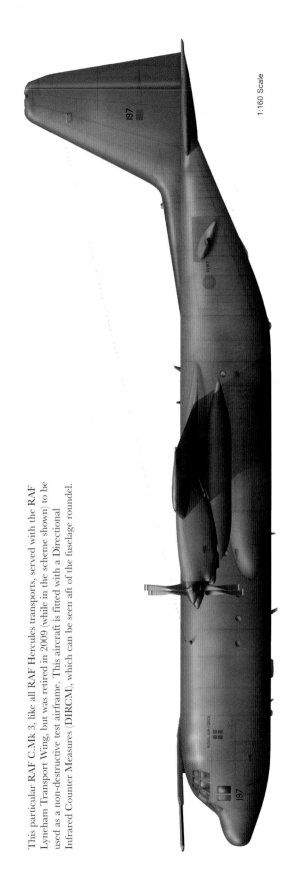

This particular RAF C.Mk 3, like all RAF Hercules transports, served with the RAF Lyneham Transport Wing, but was retired in 2009 (while in the scheme shown) to be used as a non-destructive test airframe. This aircraft is fitted with a Directional Infrared Counter Measures (DIRCM), which can be seen aft of the fuselage roundel.

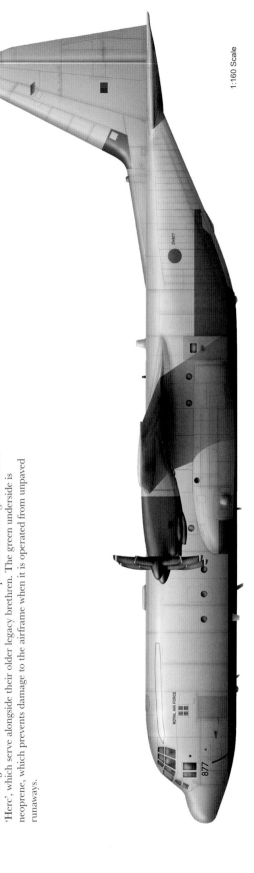

The C-130J is known as C.Mk 4 in RAF service and represents the new generation of 'Herc', which serve alongside their older legacy brethren. The green underside is neoprene, which prevents damage to the airframe when it is operated from unpaved runaways.

Concentrated at RAF Lyneham, near Chippenham, Wiltshire, the RAF Hercules force was part of No 2 Group within RAF Strike Command, and comprised Nos 24, 30, 47, 70 (LXX) and 57 (Reserve) Squadrons, all equipped with the C1/C3, with a solitary C1 of 1312 Flight, based in the Falkland Islands. All units operate in the Air Transport profile, carrying freight and passengers around the world, but Nos 47 and 70 Squadrons specialise in the Tactical Support role, dropping paratroops and supplies, while No 57 (Reserve) Squadron was the Hercules Operational Conversion Unit and provided conversion and refresher training for aircrew. Here also is the UK Mobile Air Movement Squadron (UKMAMS) – which processes all freight and passengers while also deploying mobile teams at various bases around the world to load/unload Hercules – and No 47 (Air Despatch) Squadron, Royal Logistics Corps, which is responsible for the preparation, loading and despatch of all air-dropped stores. The Hercules Engineering Development & Investigation Team (H-EDIT) is also based at Lyneham and undertakes engineering development and investigations resulting from any changes in tactics, role or application.

The Plotting and Communications room at RAF Lyneham. *RAF*

In the aftermath of the Gulf War, when retreating Iraqi troops had set fire to all the Kuwaiti oil-wells in a wanton fit of obnoxious vandalism, there was great concern about the worldwide spread of pollution from the enormous blazes and columns of black smoke. The result was that acid rain, black snow and similar fallout began to pollute the skies over Iran, southern Turkey and even as far afield as Afghanistan. In March *Snoopy* was flown into the area from RAE Farnborough and criss-crossed the zone during 55 hours of daylight sorties, made at altitudes of up to 25,000 feet. Measurements were taken up to 62 miles from the fires, which revealed that the maximum concentrations of smoke particles were layered at 6,000 feet. Concentrations were found of 30,000 smoke particles per cubic centimetre, which fell to about 3,000-5,000 particles per cubic centimetre some 125 miles downwind.

A Flight Deck Simulator at RAF Lyneham. *RAF*

The Main Instrument Training Panel at RAF Lyneham. *RAF*

An RAF C-130K line-up at Lyneham, with XV222 (c/n 4252) nearest the camera. *RAF*

An RAF Hercules banks over Port Stanley in the Falkland Islands. One Herk is permanently stationed there since the Falklands War. *RAF*

In the late 1990s a replacement programme of extended-length C-130J-30s was initiated, following successful trials with the Lockheed prototypes, these being registrations N130JA (c/n 5408), which became ZH865, and the two follow-up aircraft, N130JE (c/n 5414), which became ZH866, and N130JJ (c/n 5416), which became ZH867. This trio was followed by a further thirteen of the same type: RAF serials ZH868 (c/n 5443); ZH869 (c/n 5444); ZH870 (c/n 5445); ZH871 (c/n 5446); ZH872 (c/n 5456); ZH873 (c/n 5457); ZH874 (c/n 5458); ZH875 (c/n 5459); ZH876 (c/n 5460); ZH877 (c/n 5461); ZH878 (c/n 5462); ZH879 (c/n 5463); and ZH889 (c/n 5500).

They were followed by a programme of standard C-130Js: RAF serials ZH880 (c/n 5478); ZH881 (c/n 5479); ZH882 (c/n 5480); ZH883 (c/n 5481); ZH884 (c/n 5482); ZH885 (c/n 5483); ZH886 (c/n 5484); ZH887 (c/n 5485); ZH888 (c/n 5496); and ZH889 (c/n 5500). The Kuwaiti Air Force currently has four more of the same type on order.

The British Ministry of Defence (MoD) took delivery of the first aircraft, ZH 865 (c/n 5408), when it was handed over to the Defence Evaluation & Research Agency (DERA) at Boscombe Down on 26 August 1998, later joined by ZH 871 (c/n 5446) on 30 November and ZH 880 (c/n 5478) on 22 April 1999. The first of the C-130Js, ZH 875 (c/n 5459), was officially received by the RAF's Transport Wing at RAF Lyneham, Wiltshire, on 23 November 1999, by Air Vice Marshal Philip Sturley, AOC 38 Group, Strike Command, more than two years behind schedule. According to some press reports, so many late penalty points had been racked up by this delay that Lockheed was forced to present the RAF with a 'free' aircraft![3] The first squadrons to re-equip with the new Hercules were No 57(R) followed by No 24.

[3] See Peter Almond, 'RAF's new Hercules arrives 2 years late', article in the *Daily Telegraph*, 25 November 1999.

The first C-130-J, N130JA (c/n 5408), which became ZH865, rolls out at Lockheed-Martin, pipers and all, on 18 October 1995. The aircraft is a C-130-J-30 for the Royal Air Force. *Lockheed-Martin Aeronautical Systems Company*

Rolling along the runway is an RAF C-130-30J, showing her fine lines. *Martin Bowman*

A purpose-built training facility for conversion of aircrew and groundcrew to the new aircraft (known as The School House) was built at Lyneham, with eight classrooms and eight computer terminals linked to a central server, and a cockpit simulator with a digital moving map linked to the radar. No 57(R) Squadron was designated as the Hercules Operational Conversion Unit, with nine aircrew courses per year, and three crews per course.[4]

Another record fell on 7 December 1999 when an RAF Hercules, ZH 866 (c/n 5414), made the 4,127.73-mile journey from Marietta to the UK in 9hr 58min 14sec, averaging 414.054mph, the fastest flown by an aircraft of this class without refuelling. Although there is great enthusiasm for the C-130J throughout the RAF, what has not yet been revealed by the MoD is whether stories of weaker jacking points and resultant damage to the new aircraft are rumour or fact. Users are Nos 24, 30, 47 and 70 Squadrons together with 2 Group Hercules Operational Evaluation Unit. 1312 Flight at Mount Pleasant in the Falkland Islands operated C1s spasmodically.

Currently a question mark hangs over the RAF C-130J programme. This results from the planned closure of RAF Lyneham and the move of the remaining Hercules to RAF Brize Norton; the suing of the MoD for the loss by small-arms fire of C-130K XV179 (c/n 4195) at an altitude of just 500 feet on 30 January 2005 between Basrah and Balad, alleged by some to be partly due to lack of Explosive Suppressant Foam (ESF) and others to suspected metal fatigue in a fairly old aircraft[5]; the self-destruction of two RAF Intelligence-gathering Herks after they had made forced landings in Iraq and Afghanistan; and yet another defence review planned for 2010.

[4] See Bob Archer, 'Hercules joins the RAF', article in *The Royal Air Force Yearbook, 2000* (PRM Aviation, Bristol).
[5] The Ministry of Defence took the unusual step of calling in the Air Accidents Investigation Branch (AAIB) to pin down the cause of the loss of the 1965-built XV179, but a spokesman said that they 'had reached no conclusions'. At the same time the USAF grounded thirty of its C-130Es and placed sixty others on Restricted Flight Status (RFS), and had been monitoring the wing box structure since 2001. An AMC spokesman stated at Robins Air Force Base that the cracks found 'were greater in number and severity than originally expected'. See 'Hercules Crash in Baghdad Points to Metal Fatigue in C130's Wing Center – "Whirl-Mode" Phenomenon May Also be at Play', article in *Air Safety Week*, 21 February 2005.

Aircrew members load an M777 A2 Howitzer onto a C-130J Hercules on 14 March 2009 at Bagram Airfield, Afghanistan. The C-130J is part of the 772nd Expeditionary Airlift Squadron (EAAS) at Kandahar Airfield, established to assist with the increase of US troops in the region – the 'Obama Surge'. *Staff Sergeant James L. Harper, Jr, USAF official*

Against that, the RAF's Herks have been performing sterling work in both combat zones, and withdrew more than 4,000 troops and their kit to the UK in 2009 as well as ferrying a host of VIPs to and from Basrah. Safety concerns have been and are continuing to be addressed via the Royal Air Force's C-130 Structural Programmes, conducted at the Hercules IPT, at RAF Wyton, Huntingdon, under Squadron Leader David Saunders BEng CEng MIMechE RAF, concerning themselves with structural test and evaluation on both the C-130K – with Operational Loads Measurement (OLM) analysis, outer wing Fatigue Tests and Fuselage Fatigue Tests between 1999 and 2002, utilising the wingless and tailless hull of XV302 (c/n 4270) – and the C-130J (OLM, Tip-to-Tip Wing Fatigue Tests, and Fuselage Fatigue).

Royal Australian Air Force (RAAF)

The first overseas customer to purchase the Hercules was the RAAF, for which, on 8 November 1958, the Menzies Government commissioned twelve C-130A-50-LMs to take over the duties of the existing DC-3 Dakotas of No 36 Squadron, based at Richmond, NSW. The aircraft were delivered between December 1958 and March 1959: former USAF serials 57-0498 (c/n 3205), which became A97-205 and later civilian registration N205FA with Fowler Aeronautical Services; 57-0499 (c/n 3206), which became A97-206 and later civilian registration RP-C3206 with Aboitiz Air Transport; 57-0500 (c/n 3207), which became A97-207, and later civilian N22FV with Ford & Vlahos; the former 57-0501 (c/n 3208), which became A97-208 and later civilian registration N12FV with Ford & Vlahos; the former 57-0501 (c/n 3208), which became A97-208, and later civilian registration N4445V with Ford & Vlahos; 57-0503 (c/n 3210), which became A97-210, and later civilian registration N12FV with Ford & Vlahos; 57-0504 (c/n 3211), which became A97-211 and later civilian registration N5394L with Ford & Vlahos; 57-0505 (c/n 3212), which became A97-212 and later civilian registration N13FV with Ford & Vlahos; 57-0506 (c/n 3213), which became A97-213 and later RP-R3213 with Aboitiz; 57-0507 (c/n 3214), which became A97-214 and ended up in the RAAF Museum, Point Cook; 57-0508 (c/n 3215), which became A97-215 and later civilian N4469P with Ford & Vlahos; and 57-0509 (c/n 3216), which became A97-216 and later civilian HK-3017X for Aviaco. All served with No 36 and No 27 Squadrons, RAAF, based at Richmond Airfield, New South Wales.

Opposite: A low-level pass by an RAAF C-130H. *Lockheed-Georgia, Marietta, via Audrey Pearcy*

Below: Royal Australian Air Force C-130E A97-167 (c/n 4167) catches the sun as she climbs from Hickam AFB, Hawaii, in June 1968. *Nick Williams, AAHS*

RAAF C-130A A97-205 (c/n 3205) over Sydney Harbour. *Lockheed-Georgia, Marietta, via Audrey Pearcy*

No 36 Squadron, RAAF, notched up 100,000 accident-free hours of flying time with its C-130As in 1972, and they were not finally retired until the late 1970s. They were given civilian registrations as they were sold or leased out, and many had very varied subsequent careers (see the appropriate sections). One, A97-209, minus wings and engines, was retained at Richmond as a ground trainer for cargo-loading techniques. The other eleven had more eventful and turbulent careers.

Parmax-Global Jet, an American company, made an offer to buy all eleven aircraft and appointed Mr Peter Hocking as its contact. However, not a single aircraft was pre-sold by Parmax-Global Jet and in April 1980 the Department of Administrative Services called for tenders for the sale of the eleven. An Australian consortium under Jack Ellis tendered for the disposal, but failed, even though they apparently had buyers lined up for them all, eight for the Mexican Government and three for the World Health Organisation (WHO). Instead the tender was awarded to Ford & Vlahos, a firm of San Francisco attorneys, with John J. Ford at its head, which appointed Peter Hocking and Kenneth Oliver as its contacts. Between the award of the tender on 13 May 1981 and September 1985 not one of the aircraft was sold, but the Department of Administration granted Ford & Vlahos eleven extensions.

In September 1985 the French Government bought A97-208 for $3 million, of which just $1 million went to the Australian Government, and she received the civilian registration N445V. She was used to assist the armed struggle in Chad, a former French colony threatened by Libyan-back insurgents. Next two more aircraft, A97-0121 and A97-0217, were sold to Aviaco Ltd for $4.5 million; the Australian Government gave its approval, but without consulting the US State Department, even though all eleven aircraft were theoretically under the latter's control. The proviso was that the two machines (which took civilian registrations HK 3016X and HK-3017X respectively) were be used strictly for non-military, humanitarian duties. Both machines therefore flew out to the States in October 1983, but the US refused to sanction the deal and duly informed the Australian Department of Foreign Affairs of the fact. The two aircraft were left stranded, one at the Lockheed facility at Dotham, Alabama, the other in Oakland, California. The $985,000 deposit paid by Aviaco to Ford & Vlahos was apparently unaccounted for. A third machine, A97-0215, was also purchased by Ford & Vlahos, receiving the civilian registration N4469. She was leased to the US Nuclear Defense Agency for atomic testing on avionics tests, but was returned to Ford & Vlahos and stored in Alabama. In June 1985 she was flown to England, and, after some maintenance work, was used for relief work in the Sudan for the British Government.

In January 1986, after two years, John J. Ford's exclusive right of sale was terminated and the disposal contract passed to another company, Defence Equipment, whose directors were Peter Hocking and Kenneth Oliver. Next the World Freedom from Hunger campaign, headed by pop singer Bob Geldof, approached the Australian Government for permission to use the unwanted stripped and parked Hercules. The Hawke Government was now in power and the Australian Development Bureau contracted another company, International Air Aid (directors Peter Hocking, Kenneth Oliver and Peter Commins) to handle the $1.7 million refurbishment programme for them. The first aircraft, A97-0207, was moved to RAAF Richmond in January 1986 for the refurbishment to commence, and International Air Aid received $1.5 million for the job. With the civilian registration N22FV, this aircraft flew to Sogerma at Bordeaux, France, for heavy structural checks to be carried out and was subsequently handed over to the International Red Cross (IRC). The Red Cross, in turn, contracted a company to manage the operational side, appointing Integral Air Aid, Cyprus, whose directors were Peter Hocking, Kenneth Oliver and Peter Commins. The contract between Integral Air Aid and IRC was later cancelled after the aircraft had flow for only four months, and the whole exercise cost the Australian taxpayer $1.5 million.[6]

Between August 1966 and January 1967 a second batch of twelve aircraft was purchased; these were C-130Es and joined No 37 Squadron in the 86th Wing (Airlift Group), also based at Richmond. These aircraft were serials A97-159 (c/n 4159); A97-160 (c/n 4160); A97-167 (c/n 4167); A97-168 (c/n 4168); A97-171 (c/n 4171); A92-172 (c/n 4172); A97-177 (c/n 4177); A97-178 (c/n 4178); A97-180 (c/n 4180); A97-181 (c/n 4181); A97-189 (c/n 4189); and A97-190 (c/n 4190).

[6] See the 'Hangared' article, 'C130 "A" Hercules', by Mark Farrar, in *Flightpath* magazine, 1988.

A ceremonial fly-past by No 37 Squadron RAAF over Sydney on 12 September 1977; the leading aircraft is A97-4172 (c/n 4172). *Lockheed-Georgia, Marietta, via Audrey Pearcy*

A No 37 Squadron C-130J Hercules and a visiting Royal Danish Air Force C-130J fly over the RAAF base at Richmond. One the ground are C-130H Hercules during Exercise 'Combined Strength 09'. *RAAF*

A group photo of Royal Danish Air Force, Royal Air Force and Royal Australian Air Force members involved in Exercise 'Combined Strength 09' at the RAAF base at Richmond. The three nations' Herk crews practiced search and rescue, air drop and tactical airlift. *RAAF*

All two dozen Australian Herks were employed during that country's involvement in the Vietnam War transporting troops, military equipment and supplies and evacuating wounded. Some of them were subsequently used in Antarctic survey work. In September 1977 one of the Australian C-130Es, flown by Flight Lieutenant John Smith RAAF, matched the C-130A's achievement of 100,000 hours of accident-free flying time, covering 31 million statute miles (49,889,664km), the equivalent of fifty-eight round trips to the moon, or 1,200 earth orbits. In achieving this impressive total No 37's Herks had made the first landing by the light of kerosene flares at night on a devastated Darwin Airport after Cyclone 'Tracey' had wrecked it; had made mercy flights to Fiji, Noumea and Christmas islands; had resupplied Australian forces acting as United Nations peacekeepers in Egypt and Pakistan; had flown cargoes as diverse as priceless archaeological exhibits and livestock to China and back; and had ferried wounded troops from Butterworth, Malaysia, to Richmond, NSW, during the Vietnam War.

Between July and October 1978 the C-130As were replaced with twelve new C-130Hs: serials A97-001 (c/n 4780); A97-002 (c/n 4782); A97-003 (c/n 4783); A97-004 (c/n 4784); A97-005 (c/n 4785); A97-006 (c/n 4786); A97-007 (c/n 4787); A97-008 (c/n 4788); A97-009 (c/n 4789); A97-010 (c/n 4790); A97-011 (c/n 4791); and A97-012 (c/n 4793). Some of these have been used for Antarctic supply work.

In 1999 it became the turn of No 37 Squadron to have its aircraft replaced by twelve C-130J-30s, between August 1999 and March 2000: the former Lockheed N130JQ (c/n 5440), which became A97-440 and later carried the civilian registration N4080M for a time; A97-441 (c/n 5441); ex-Lockheed N130JR (c/n 5442), which became A97-442; ex-Lockheed N73232 (c/n 5447), which became A97-447; ex-Lockheed N73230 (c/n 5448), which became A97-448; ex-Lockheed N72322 (c/n 5449), which became A97-49; ex-Lockheed N4187W (c/n 5450), which became A97-450; serial A97-464 (c/n 5464); serial A97-465 (c/n 5465); serial A97-466 (c/n 5466); serial A97-467 (c/n 5467); and serial A97-468 (c/n 5468). These are flown by 37 Squadron based at Richmond Air Force Base, NSW.

Royal Canadian Air Force (RCAF)
– now known as Canadian Armed Forces (CAF)

The first Hercules to serve with the Royal Canadian Air Force (later the amalgamated Canadian Armed Forces) were four C-130Bs purchased from Lockheed stock, which arrived between October and November 1960: RCAF serials 10301 (c/n 3572), which was sold back to Lockheed, becoming its N4652; 10302 (c/n 3575), also sold back to Lockheed and becoming its N4653; 10303 (c/n 3587), sold back to Lockheed to become its N4654; and 10304 (c/n 3590), which was lost in an accident in Saskatchewan in April 1966. During their RCAF period they all served with No 435 Squadron. The three survivors were returned to Lockheed in July 1967, which sold them on to Colombia.

A Royal Canadian Air Force C-130E Hercules, 130313 (c/n 4066), carrying Military Airlift Command markings, flies straight and steady from Hickam Air Force Base, Hawaii, on 31 January 1968. *Nick Williams, AAHS*

RCAF C-130B T-1302 (c/n 3578) over the Rockies. *Lockheed-Georgia, Marietta, via Audrey Pearcy*

Two dozen C-130Es were purchased between December 1964 and August 1968: RCAF serials 10305 (c/n 4020), later 130305; 10306 (c/n 4026), later 130306 (these two were later modified to carry pallet-mounted training consoles for use as a navigation trainers and redesignated as C-130(NT)s, then to Search & Rescue aircraft and finally as Early Warning aircraft; 10307 (c/n 4041), later 130307, modified to C-130(NT) and later as SAR; 10308 (c/n 4042), later 130308, modified to C-130(NT) and later as Early Warning aircraft; 10309 (c/n 4050), later 130309, and lost in an accident at Trenton on 27 April 1967; 10310 (c/n 4051), later 130310, modified to C-130(NT) then as SAR; 10311 (c/n 4060), later 130311; 10312 (c/n 4061), later 130312, lost in an accident near Chapais, Quebec, on 15 October 1980; 10313 (c/n 4066), later 130313; 10314 (c/n 4067), later 130314, modified to Early Warning role; 10315 (c/n 4070), later 130315, modified to Early Warning; 10316 (c/n 4075), later 130316, modified to Early Warning; 10319 (c/n 4095), later 130319, modified to Early Warning; 10320 (c/n 4096), later 130320; 10317 (c/n 4122), later 130317, modified to Early Warning; 10318 (c/n 4124), later 130318, crashed at Wainwright Army Airfield, Arkansas, due to severe icing on 29 January 1989; 10321 (c/n 4191), later 130321, crashed at Wainwright field on 22 July 1993; 10322 (c/n 4192), later 130322, crashed at Alert, Ellesmere Island, North-West Territories, on 30 November 1991; 10323 (c/n 4193), later 130323, modified to Early Warning; 10324 (c/n 4194), later 130324, modified to Early Warning; 10325 (c/n 4285), later 130325; serial 10326 (c/n 4286), later 130326, modified to Early Warning; 10327 (c/n 4288), later 130327; and 10328 (c/n 4289), later 130328.

Fourteen C-130Hs were diverted to the RCAF from USAF Tactical Air Force allocations between October 1974 and February 1991: RCAF serials 130329 (c/n 4553), which crashed at Namao on 16 November 1982; 130330 (c/n 4555), lost in a mid-air collision over Namao with 130331 on 29 March 1985; 130331 (c/n 4559), lost in a mid-air collision with 103330 on 29 March 1985[7]; 130332 (c/n 4568), modified as an Early Warning aircraft; 130333 (c/n 4574), modified to Early Warning; the former Lockheed N4246M and CAF G-52-18 (c/n 4580), which became 130336; the former Lockheed N4247M and CAF G52-17 (c/n 4584), which became 130337 and was later modified as an Early Warning aircraft; 130334 (c/n 4994), modified to Early Warning; 130335 (c/n 4995), modified to Early Warning; an unregistered former Lockheed stock aircraft that became 130338 (c/n 5175); 130339 (c/n 5177), modified to Early Warning, then modified again for aircrew training aircraft; a former unregistered Lockheed stock aircraft that became 130340 (c/n 5189), modified to the aerial tanker role, then later remodified as an Early Warning aircraft; another former unregistered Lockheed stock aircraft that became 130341 (c/n 5200), also modified to an aerial tanker then remodified to Early Warning; and 130342 (c/n 5207), again modified to an aerial tanker then to Early Warning.

Two late-build L-100-30s, CAF registration 130343 (c/n 5307) and RCAF 130344 (c/n 5320), were purchased by the Canadian Armed Forces in March 1996 and modified to C-130H-30s by CAE, Trenton, and given the designation of CC-130.

On 20 December 2007 the Canadian Government placed an order for seventeen C-130-30s for the CAF's Airlift Capability Project Tactical Plan at a total cost of $1.44 billion. Delivery of these was due to be completed by December 2010. Actual confirmed details of these 382V-47Js confirm

[7] The following description of the crash is given in *Propos de*, Vol 2, 1985, and *Alberta Report*, 8 April 1985. The squadron was tasked to carry out a fly-past in commemoration of the 61st anniversary of the RCAF in conjunction with other base aircraft. At the conclusion of the fly-past the three CC130 crews planned to recover on RWY 29 utilising a low-level 'battle' break manoeuvre. They positioned themselves in echelon right with wing-span spacing. The briefed procedure was to pull up 10° and turn left with 60° of bank maintaining 2g, climbing to 1,000 feet above ground level (AGL) to position themselves downwind. Nos 2 and 3 would follow, each with a 3-second spacing. After approximately 50° of turn at 900 feet AGL, No 2 collided with the underside of the lead aircraft, forward of the port-side main gear, punching a 5-foot-square hole in the aircraft floor structure. The No 2 aircraft had its forward fuselage section separate from the aircraft and free-fall into a field. The Nos 3 and 4 propellers separated and landed some distance from the main wreckage. The tail section of the lead aircraft also separated prior to ground impact. Control of either aircraft after the collision was impossible. The four occupants of the lead aircraft and the six occupants of No 2 all sustained fatal injuries. Both aircraft exploded in mid-air and crashed inverted over an area the size of four city blocks. A 300 feet by 50 feet storage building (from which 150 military personnel had left just a quarter of an hour earlier) and several vehicles were destroyed in a very intense fire.

the number as seventeen, as follows: 130601 (c/n 5626); 130602 (c/n 5627); 130603 (c/n 5635); 130604 (c/n 5636); 130605 (c/n 5637); 130606 (c/n 5649); 130607 (c/n 5650); 130608 (c/n 5651); 130609 (c/n 5652); 130610 (c/n 5664); 130611 (c/n 5665); 130612 (c/n 5666); 130613 (c/n 5667); 130614 (c/n 5687); 130615 (c/n 5688); 130617 (c/n 5690); and 130616 (c/n 5689). The first pair were scheduled for delivery in May and June 2010 respectively.

Canadian Forces Air Command has the following C-130 users: 8 Wing, comprising 424, 426 and 436 Squadrons at Trenton, Ontario; 14 Wing with 413 Squadron at Greenwood, Nova Scotia; and 17 Wing with 435 Squadron at Winnipeg, Manitoba.

Royal Danish Air Force (*Kongelige Danske Flyvevaabnet*)

Becoming the 30th nation to operate the Hercules, three C-130Hs carrying USAF serials were acquired under the Mutual Air Aid Programme between April and July 1975, and equipped the *Kongelige Danske Flyvevaabnet's* Tactical Air Command unit, flying with *721 Eskadrille, Flyvertaktisk Kommando*, from its base at Vaerose. These three Herks were ex-73-1678 (c/n 4572), which became B-678; ex-73-1679 (c/n 4587), which became B-679; and ex-73-1680 (c/n 4599), which became B-680. All three were modernised and carry ECM/ESM pods mounted on their wing tips. They equip the *721 Eskadrille* based at Aalborg.

Royal Danish Air Force C-130H B-678 (c/n 4572) of 721 *Eskadrille* is on display to the public at an air base at Reykjavik, Iceland, on 1 May 1977. *Balldur Sveinsson, via Nick Williams, AAHS*

This Danish C-130H Hercules, B-680 (c/n 4599), of 721 *Eskadrille*, is seen in dark olive green paintwork with orange highlighting and carrying a further festooning of patches on 7 July 1977. *Balldur Sveinsson, via Nick Williams, AAHS*

A Royal Danish Air Force midnight mail drop in Greenland on 16 May 1976. *Lockheed-Georgia, Marietta, via Audrey Pearcy*

More recently, between 2003 and 2007, the KDF took delivery of a trio of new C-130J-30s to replace the older aircraft, and they are based at Aalborg. These 382V-36Js are B-536 (c/n 5536), B-537 (c/n 5537) and B-538 (c/n 5538). A fourth C-130J-30, a 382V-44J, serial number B-583 (c/n 5583), the former N51004 at Marshalls of Cambridge, was acquired in January 2009.

Royal Jordanian Air Force *(Al Quwwat Almalakiya)*

A quartet of former USAF C-130Bs was obtained by the *Al Quwwat Almalakiya* in 1973 and equipped its No 3 Squadron, which operated from Ling Abdullah Airport, Amman. These aircraft were: ex-60-0301 (c/n 3610), which became serial 141, and was later renumbered 341; ex-60-0302 (c/n 3611), which became serial 142, and was sold to Singapore in 1976; ex-60-0304 (c/n 3612), which became serial 140 and was later renumbered as 340; and ex-60-0308 (c/n 3620), which became serial 143 and was also sold to Singapore in 1976.

These veterans were supplemented by a pair of brand-new C-130Hs – serials 144 (c/n 4779), later renumbered as 744 then 344, and 345 (c/n 4813) – which were received in June 1978 and April 1979 respectively.

In May and July 1982 a second pair of the same type arrived at Amman, serials 346 (c/n 4920) and 347 (c/n 4929).

Finally, a solitary HC-130H (c/n 4073), the former USAF serial 64-14857, was acquired in February 1992, receiving the serial 348. The operational C-130H aircraft are with 3 Squadron based at Al Matar Air Base close to Amman.

Royal Malaysian Air Force *(Tentera Udara Diraja Malaysia)*

Six new C-130Hs were obtained by the Malaysian Government between March and October 1976, and accepted at a ceremony by Prime Minister Datuk Hussein Onn, being sprinkled with holy water. They equipped No 14 (Transport) Squadron based at Subang Airfield, near Kuala Lumpur. They were serials FM2401 (c/n 4656), which was later re-registered as M30-01; FM2402 (c/n 4661), later re-registered as M30-02; FM2403 (c/n 4674), later M30-03, which crash-landed at Sibu, Sarawak, on 25 August 1990; FM2404 (c/n 4685), later M30-04; FM2405 (c/n 4690), later M30-05; and FM2406 (c/n 4697), later M30-06.

A trio of new C-130H-MPs arrived between April and December 1980: FM2451 (c/n 4847), later re-registered as M30-07; the former Lockheed demonstrator N4123M (c/n 4849), which became FM2452, and later M30-08; and FM2453 (c/n 4866), later M30-09. All three were modified to aerial tankers.

The Royal Malaysian Air Force was yet another customer for the C-130, and six of the C-130H models were delivered to Kuala Lumpur. The top photo shows Lieutenant Colonel Kake Kok Lye (right) and Lieutenant Colonel Kong Kok Wah (centre) of the Royal Malaysian Air Force with Lockheed officials after inspecting one of the new aircraft, FM2401 (c/n 4656). The facing picture shows that the capacity of the Herk, with her 40.4-foot-long, 10-foot-wide and 9-foot-high cargo/troop compartment, was a great attraction, as was the truck bed height of only 3.5 feet for ease of loading and unloading of cargo at primitive airstrips with minimum capacity. Malaysia proved to be the 37th sovereign nation to take delivery of the C-130. *Lockheed-Georgia, Marietta, via Audrey Pearcy*

On 17 July 1976 the Royal Malaysian Air Force took formal delivery of its first two Lockheed C-130H transports, FM2401 (c/n 4656), in ceremonies held at Kuala Lumpur Airport. Here the commander of the RMAF's 14 Squadron, Lieutenant Colonel Mustapha Bakri (right), is seen with the aircraft just prior to departure from the Marietta plant airfield. On the left is Lieutenant Colonel Kong Kok Wah and Lockheed instructor pilot Les Hewitt. Five more C-130s were delivered to Malaysia that same year. They operated on troop lifts and cargo flights, and on scheduled runs between West and East Malaysia across the South China Sea, a journey that took a week by sea, but which was cut by the Herk to 2 hours with a 25-ton payload. *Lockheed-Georgia, Marietta, via Audrey Pearcy*

Another view of Royal Malaysian Air Force C-130H FM2401 (c/n 4656). *Lockheed-Georgia, Marietta, via Audrey Pearcy*

RMAF C-130H-30 M30-04 (c/n 4685) at Subang/Sultan Abdul Aziz Shah. *Courtesy of Kian Hong*

Finally six C-130H-30 long-stretch Herks were obtained between December 1991 and April 1993: M30-10 (c/n 5268); M30-12 (c/n 5277); M30-11 (c/n 5309); M30-14 (c/n 5311); M30-15 (c/n 5316); and M30-16 (c/n 5319). They are serving with 14 Squadron at Labuana and 20 Squadron at Subang.

Royal Maroc Air Force *(Al Quwwat Ali Jawwiya Almalakiya Marakishiya)*

Commencing in 1976, the *Force Aérienne Royal Morocaine* took delivery of no fewer than seventeen C-130H aircraft in three deliveries, all of which were given civilian registrations. Their primary duties were military logistic support, but they were also invaluable for up-country industrial development haulage and support flights. They also featured in a purely mercantile role, making regular produce export runs to Paris with fresh fruit, vegetables, frozen fish and other local products, for which there was high demand in France. On the return runs imports of machinery and products were taken back home. One machine, serial CNA-OM (c/n 4875), was fitted with MAFFS equipment to spray locusts as part of a pest-control programme.

The first six aircraft were serials CNA-OA (c/n 4535), CNA-OB (c/n 4537), CNA-OC (c/n 4551), CNA-OD (c/n 4575), CNA-OE (c/n 4581) and CNA-OF (c/n 4583), with another four – serials CNA-OG (c/n 4713), CNA-OH (c/n 4717), CNA-OI (c/n 4733) and CNA-OJ (c/n 4738) –

delivered from May 1974 onward. The second delivery comprised a further five – serials CNA-OK (c/n 4739), CNA-OL (c/n 4742), CNA-OM (c/n 4875), CNA-ON (c/n 4876) and CNA-OO (c/n 4877) – commencing in August 1981. The last pair, serials CNA-OP (c/n 4888) (N4162M) and CNA-OQ (c/n 4892), arrived in mid-1982. Both the latter were equipped with Side-Looking Airborne Radar (SLAR) fitted to the port main undercarriage fairing. In addition, two KC-130Hs were taken on strength in November and December 1981, serials CAN-OR (c/n 4907) (N4216M) and CAN-OS (c/n 4909) (N4221M) respectively.

A more warlike mission also came the way of the Hercules here, as elsewhere, with operations against the Pollisario guerrilla forces, which were actively backed by peaceful Morocco's more extreme Arab neighbours and entered the country via the Western Sahara. Based at Kenitra, the C-130Hs used in this counter-insurgency role had chaff dispensers and flare dispenser pods fitted. Two of the Hercules became casualties of this conflict, CAN-OB being shot down and destroyed on 4 December 1976 and CAN-OH likewise destroyed at Guelta Zemmour on 12 October 1981. Currently the surviving C-130Hs are with the *Escadrille de Transporte* at Rabat Air Base.

Royal Netherlands Air Force (*Koninklijke Luchtmacht*)

It was not until 1994 that the Dutch *Koninklijke Luchtmacht* rather belatedly joined the 'Herk Club', with the purchase of two former Lockheed C-130H-30s for No 334 Squadron, from its base at Eindhoven. This pair were the ex-N4080M (c/n 5273), which became serial G273 and was allocated the name *Ben Swagerman*, and ex-N4080M (c/n 5275), which became G275 and was named *Joop Mulder*.

Two engineless former US Navy EC-130Qs were acquired from Derco in 2005, ex-160608 (c/n 4781) and ex-162313 (c/n 4988), becoming 4780 and 4781 respectively. They were converted to C-130H standard by Marshalls of Cambridge. They currently fly with 336 Squadron from Eindhoven.

Royal New Zealand Air Force

The RNZAF purchased the very first three C-130Hs in March/April 1965 to replace the elderly Hastings transport aircraft in No 40 Squadron in June 1963. The original order was actually for three C-130Es and five more of the anti-submarine warfare versions, but the latter were dropped on economic grounds and P-38 Orions ordered instead. What were actually delivered were not C-130Es but the superior C-130Hs, the first being serial NZ7001 (c/n 4052), which arrived in April 1965. She was operated by No 40 Squadron based at Whenuapai Airfield, near Auckland, and was quickly joined by NZ7002 (c/n 4053) and NZ7003 (c/n 4054). In July 1965, with New Zealand's

RNZAF and a US Navy Hercules C-130Fs wingtip-to-wingtip over Williams AFB, Antarctica, on 20 October 1970. *Navy Photograph Center, Washington DC*

Five C-130Hs of the Royal New Zealand Air Force on 28 October 1969. *Lockheed-Georgia, Marietta, via Audrey Pearcy*

RNZAF C-130H 7001 (c/n 4052) of No 40 Squadron RNZAF on patrol in October 1986. *RNZAF*

THE LOCKHEED MARTIN C-130 HERCULES

involvement in the Vietnam War, this trio was kept busy, first airlifting then supporting Army artillery, support vehicles and personnel to Bien Hoa Airfield. These three aircraft also flew missions to China and the Soviet Union (the first to either country by a RNZAF aircraft), and flew in relief operations in Bangladesh, Cambodia and Pakistan. In the period 1972-73 all three aircraft returned to the Lockheed plant to have wing centre section modifications made, which almost doubled their operational life.

This work was continued on a regular basis and, to support the workload, another pair of C-130Hs was acquired in December 1968, these being NZ7004 (c/n 4312) and NZ7005 (c/n 4313). They entered service in January 1969. Their duties included the evacuation of New Zealand nationals and officials to the safety of Singapore in the humiliating days of 1975. During 1981 all five aircraft again returned to Lockheed for refurbishment of the outer wing panels at a cost of NZ$4.8 million, the last aircraft returning to Whenuapai in October of that year. Since then their work has included regularly supply runs down to the McMurdo Sound Air Base in Antarctica.

Royal Norwegian Air Force (*Konelige Norske Lufforsvaret*)

In June/July 1969 the *Konelige Norske Lufforsvaret* took delivery of a batch of six C-130Hs for operations with its 335 *Skvadron*, based at Gardemoen Air Station, Ullensaker. They received both military and civilian serials, as well as names from Norse mythology. These Herks were military serials 68-10952 (c/n 4334), also BW-A and named *Odin*; 68-10953 (c/n 4335), BW-B and named *Tor*; 68-10954 (c/n 4336), BW-C and named *Balder*; 68-10955 (c/n 4337), BW-D and named *Froy*; 68-10956 (c/n 4338), BW-E and named *Ty*; and 68-10957 (c/n 4339), BW-F and named *Brage*.

An overhead aerial view of Royal Norwegian Air Force C-130H C-BW (c/n 4336), named *Balder. Lockheed-Georgia, Marietta, via Audrey Pearcy*

Very active with NATO and domestic military duties, the Norwegian Hercules have also played a wide humanitarian role down the years. One famous episode on 31 May 1970 saw them flying a whole surgical unit to Lima, Peru, while the same year saw them flying helicopters from Panama, Vietnam and elsewhere to operate from the US Navy carrier *Guam* anchored off Chimbote, to fly relief missions into the interior.

The Royal Norwegian Air Force took delivery of the first of four C-130J-30s for No 335 Squadron in November 2008, another in 2009, and two more are due in 2010 under the US Foreign Military Sales Program. These 382V-46Js are *Frigg* 5601 (c/n 5601); *Idunn* 5607 (c/n 5607); 5629 (c/n 5629); and 5630 (c/n 5630).

Royal Saudi Air Force *(Al Quwwat Ali Jawwiya Assa'udiya)*

The Saudi Government purchased Hercules in several batches down the years. Initially in 1965 they purchased two C-130Es, serials 451, the former N9258R (c/n 4076) and 452 (c/n 4078). The following year they obtained another pair, serials 453 (c/n 4128) and 454 (c/n 4136). In 1967 another was purchased, serial 455 (c/n 4215), and the following year four more, serials 1606 (c/n 4304); 1607 (c/n 4306); 1608 (c/n 4307); and 1609 (c/n 4311).

In 1970 a pair of C-130Hs was purchased, serials 1610 (c/n 4396) and 1611 (c/n 4397), with another pair in 1973, serials 456 (c/n 4503) and 457 (c/n 4511). These were followed by another six of the same type purchased in 1974, serials 458 (c/n 4532), 459 (c/n 4539), 460 (c/n 4566), 461 (c/n 4567), 1612 (c/n 4552) and 1614 (c/n 4560).

A single VC-130H, serial 102 (c/n 4605), was bought in 1977 for use as a VIP aircraft, with square windows; she was re-registered as 111 in 1977.

In 1975 a large order for nine C-130Hs was placed: serials 463 (c/n 4607); 464 (c/n 4608); 465 (c/n 4609); 1601 (c/n 4612); 1602 (c/n 4614); 1603 (c/n 4618); 1604 (c/n 4633); 1605 (c/n 4634); and 1628 (c/n 4637).

A further order for ten more Hercules of this type followed in 1977: serials 112 (c/n 4737); 466 (c/n 4740); 467 (c/n 4741); 468 (c/n 4751); 469 (c/n 4754); 483 (c/n 4756); 1615 (c/n 4745); 1616 (c/n 4746); 1618 (c/n 4755); and 1619 (c/n 4758).

In 1991/92 a fresh order for C-130Hs was delivered: the former N4099R (c/n 5234), which became serial 472, and serials 473 (c/n 5235); 474 (c/n 5252); 475 (c/n 5253); 1623 (c/n 5254); 1624 (c/n 5267); 1625 (c/n 5269); and 1626 (c/n 5270).

Royal Saudi Air Force 451 (c/n 4076) in 1976. *Royal Saudi Air Force*

Two VC-130Hs were delivered in 1980 after being converted to VIP aircraft, for the Saudi Royal Flight; these were the former N4099M (c/n 4843), which became HZ-HM5, and the former N4101M (c/n 4845), which became HZ-HM6. Both were re-registered in 1980 as HZ-114 and HZ-115 respectively.

Three KC-130Hs were also obtained: serial 1617 (c/n 4750) in 1977, followed by serials 1620 (c/n 4872) and 1621 (c/n 4873) in 1980.

Two of the stretched C-130H-30s were purchased in 1992, serials 471 (c/n 5211) and 1622 (c/n 5212).

Many other Saudi Government Hercules are operated by Saudia and these include the following. Seven specially converted C-100-30s were operated as Airborne Emergency Hospital (Medical Services) aircraft, these C-130H(AEH)s being ex-N4253M (c/n 4950), which became HZ-MS05 and later HZ-128; ex-N4254M (c/n 4952), which became HZ-MS06; HZ-117 (c/n 4954); ex-N4255M (c/n 4956), which became HZ-MS09; ex-N4261M (c/n 4957), which became HZ-MS10, and later HZ-129; ex-N4266M (c/n 4960), which became HZ-MS14; and ex-N4243M (c/n 4986), which became HZ-MS8.

There are also four specially converted C-130Hs: ex-N4098M (c/n 4837), which became HZ-MS019; ex-N4185M (c/n 4915), which became HZ-116; ex-N4240M (c/n 4918), which became HZ-MS021 and later MS2; and ex-N4190M (c/n 4922), which became HZ-MS7.

There were also two VC-130Hs, the former N4098M (c/n 4837), which became HZ-MS019, and the former N4099M (c/n 4843), which became HZ-HM5, then HZ-114. (See the Saudia section for more details.)

Current operators of C-130s are Nos 1, 16 and 32 Squadrons flying from Prince Sultan AB, and 4 Squadron working from Jeddah Airfield.

Royal Swedish Air Force *(Svenska Flygvapnet)*

The *Svenska Flygvapnet* has always been at the forefront of aeronautical developments and, for the nation's size and neutrality, has always been one of the best equipped air forces in Europe. It was no surprise therefore that the Swedes were among the first to see the Herk's great potential, nor that Sweden became the very first air force in Europe to operate the type, even before the RAF had taken her on its complement.

This first aircraft, the former USAF C-130E serial 64-0546 (c/n 4039), which had been sold back to Lockheed prior to delivery, was leased by the *Svenska Flygvapnet* as early as February 1965, and was purchased outright that same September, taking the serial 84001. She was assigned to the *7 Flygflottilj Transportglygdivisionen*, which operated from Satenas Airfield, which flew her exhaustively in an intensive test programme. Later, in 1968, she was herself leased to the Red Cross for relief flights into Biafra and carried the temporary civilian registration SE-XBT. In August 1987 she was upgraded to C-130H standard.

Performing at Karlsborg on 19 August 1984 is Swedish Air Force C-130E 382C-8E 846 (c/n 4885), marked out in test colours. She was later fitted out for Electronic Countermeasures (ECM) work. *Sven-Ake Karlson*

Work being carried out on Swedish Air Force Herk 847 (c/n 4887) at Cambridge Airfield in 1967. *Marshall of Cambridge Aerospace Ltd*

Lined up at Karlsborg are several of the Swedish Air Force C-130Es with ECM under-wing pods. They are painted in dark cameo and have black serial numbers. The closest to the camera, with crew disembarking, is serial 847 (c/n 4887), delivered in May 1985. *Sven-Ake Karlson*

Swedish Air Force C-130H 841 (c/n 4039) was modified from a C-130E in 1987. She carries the new (1999) colour scheme of light grey with black markings and carries the national flag on the tail, together with the proud boast 'First C-130 in Europe', underlined in the national colours of blue and yellow. *Sven-Ake Karlson*

A close-up of the tail markings of 841. *Sven-Ake Karlson*

C-130H 841 takes part in a fly-past.
Sven-Ake Karlson

This first Herk was joined by a second C-130E, serial 84002 (c/n 4332), purchased in May 1969, and similarly brought up to C-130H standard with the installation of the -15LFE engines in February 1982. The Swedish Herks were widely used in the humanitarian role, working with the International Red Cross in Bangladesh and Africa, and with the United Nations peacekeeping forces in the Middle East as well as the prime logistical transport for the air force.

Sweden purchased six new C-130Hs between October 1975 and 1982, and designated them as the TP 84. These aircraft were serials 84003 (c/n 4628); 84004 (c/n 4881), which was later ECM-equipped; 84005 (c/n 4884); 84006 (c/n 4885); 84007 (c/n 4887); and 84008 (c/n 4890). The last trio were purchased at a cost of $US 34 million and were delivered in the first half of 1981.

In 1981 aircraft 841 was in Biafra, which was, according to Lars Olausson, 'a rather hairy operation with many aeroplanes in the night searching for the same dimly lit strip.'[8] During Operation 'Bushel' in Ethiopia 842 and 843 both sustained a great deal of damage from landing on strips bestrewn with loose stones. By 20 August 1987 the following aircraft had accumulated these flying hours:

[8] Lars Olausson to Arthur Pearcy, dated 26 August 1987, courtesy of Audrey Pearcy.

A Swedish TP84 firing off ECM flares. *Peter Liander, Swedish Defence Forces*

Serial	Flying hours
84001	9,831
84002	8,324
84003	5,447
84004	2,664
84005	2,469
84006	2,718
84007	2,645
84008	2,827

This represents an average yearly average of 375 hours. Currently Herks fly with *F 7 Skaraborgs flygflottilj, 3 Transportflygenher*, at Såtenäs.

Wing Commander Udomsuk Mahavasu of the Royal Thai Air Force and Lockheed pilot instructor Bob Hill on the flight deck on 30 September 1980. *Lockheed-Georgia, Marietta, via Audrey Pearcy*

Royal Thai Air Force (RTAF)

Three brand-new C-130Hs were acquired by the Royal Thai Air Force under the US Military Assistance Programme (MAP) and Foreign Military Sales (FMS) scheme via the USAF Aeronautical Systems Division in August 1980; they were serials 60101 (c/n 4861), 60102 (c/n 4862) and 60103 (c/n 4863). The Thais thus became the 46th nation to operate the Herky Bird, which replaced the old piston-engined C-123s, and they were flown by No 601 Squadron, 6 Wing, from Don Muang Air Base near Bangkok.

A single C-130H-30 was added in April, 1983, this being serial 60104 (c/n 4959).

In December 1988 two more C-130Hs were purchased, becoming serials 60105 (c/n 5146) and 60106 (c/n 5148), and these were followed in November 1990 by a second C-130H-30 purchased from Lockheed, serial 60107 (c/n 5208), and yet another C-130H, serial 60108 (c/n 5209).

Another pair of C-130Hs followed in November and December 1992, these being serials 60109 (c/n 5272) and 60110 (c/n 5274).

Finally another pair of the stretched C-130H-30s was obtained in April 1992, becoming 60111 (c/n 5280), which was refurbished as a Governmental VIP aircraft, and 60112 (c/n 5281).

Singapore Air Force (Republic of Singapore Air Force)

When the island of Singapore broke away from the Malaysia confederation, it set up its own military air arm, the Republic of Singapore Air Force, and in 1977 obtained its first Hercules transport, a former USAF C-130B, ex-USAF 58-0725 (c/n 3519). She became serial 720 and served with No 122 Squadron; she was converted into a KC-130B aerial tanker in 1988. She was joined in No 122 Squadron by a second of the same type, ex-USAF 58-0756 (c/n 3557), which became serial 721 and was later similarly converted to a KC-130B.

Two further C-130Bs were acquired from the Royal Jordanian Air Force, also in 1977; these were ex-60-0302 (c/n 3611), Jordanian serial 142, which became RSAF serial 724, and ex-60-0308 (c/n 3620), Jordanian serial 143, which became RSAF serial 725. Again, both these were later modified to KC-130Bs. Based at Paya Lebar Airfield with No 122 Squadron, these four aircraft soldiered on until, between January and May 1980, the Squadron was reinforced with four new C-130Hs, RSAF serials 730 (c/n 4842), 731 (c/n 4844), 732 (c/n 4846) and 733 (c/n 4848).

A modern tanker was acquired in October 1982, this being the former Lockheed KC-130H, registration N4237M (c/n 4940), which became serial 734. The final addition to date was the acquisition of a fifth C-130H in October 1986, the former Lockheed N73233 (c/n 5070), which received the serial 735.

South African Air Force

South Africa, once the most prosperous nation in Africa as well as one of the largest, was quick to equip her well-maintained armed forces with the best equipment, and the South African Air Force ordered seven brand-new C-130Bs between November 1962 and 1963: serials 401 (c/n 3724); 402 (c/n 3749); 403 (c/n 3750); 404 (c/n 3764); 405 (c/n 3765); 406 (c/n 3767); and 407 (c/n 3769). These were operated by No 28 Squadron of the Air Transport Command, which has its base at Waterkloof, Transvaal.

More would have joined them but for an arms embargo imposed by the United Nations, so the nineteen much-traded civilian L-100-30s of the ubiquitous Safmarine/Safair Company (see the appropriate section) were earmarked as strategic reserve aircraft to fill the gap, had they been required. Meanwhile, by high-quality care and maintenance, the seven SAAF Herks continued to operate right up to the present day, despite getting rather long in the tooth! Between 1975 and 1976 they supported clandestine operations in Angola, despite the fact that during the rainy season the landing 'fields' turned to 'sheets of water or large expanses of deep, glutinous mud'. They were also used in the humanitarian role of helping evacuate the flood of innocent refugees from the fighting area, and at one point 1,604 people were taken from Angola to AFB Waterkloof, near Pretoria. They also operated round-the-clock search and rescue missions; for example, in November 1965 two of

South African Air Force C-130B 281-1B 401 (c/n 3724) on display at Ysterplaat painted with 75th Anniversary markings. *Courtesy of Cornelius Saayman*

them conducted a search for the crew of an SAAF Buccaneer that had crashed into the sea near Ascension Island on its way south from the UK. They repeated this mission in October 1969, for the crew of another Buccaneer down in the drink north of Durban, as well as hunting for the yacht *Girasol*, lost in the Indian Ocean south of Madagascar in 1975, and the coaster *Induna* lost in the same area four years later.[9] No 28 Squadron also ran a regular shuttle service between Pretoria and Cape Town with up to ninety passengers on webbing seats crammed between pallets of baggage.

When the embargo was finally lifted, two old C-130Bs were obtained from surplus USAF stock in 1997/98, these being the former USAF serial 58-0731 (c/n 3526), which became SAAF serial 408, and the former 58-0734 (c/n 3530), which became SAAF serial 409. Both were re-equipped for the ECM role in 1998.

In addition to this elderly pair, three equally vintage, former US Navy C-130Fs were purchased around the same time: ex-149787 (c/n 3636); ex-149793 (c/n 3660); and ex-149804 (c/n 3695). All were similarly due to be refurbished but were not, and were used for spare parts.

Although as Colonel Steyn Venter, the South African Air Attaché in London, stated, 'We would love to have the J,' he added that 'with our financial constraints we have to have the upgrade. It will allow us to fly these aircraft for the next 20 years.'[10] Certainly the cost of modernisation by Marshall Aerospace at Cambridge, at £9 million, is only a quarter of that of a new J, but gives the thirty-year-old Bs some 65% of the new aircraft's performance, quite a good deal for the SAAF. They are working with 28 Squadron at Waterkloof AFB, Pretoria.

South Korean Air Force (ROKAF)

Four Lockheed test C-130H-30s were purchased, two in July 1987 and two in November/December of the same year. They were the former Lockheed Low Altitude Parachute Eject System (LAPES) test, stretched Herk, N4080M (c/n 5006), which became ROK serial 5006; the former N73232 (c/n 5019), which became ROK serial 5019; the former Lockheed N4249Y (c/n 5030), which became ROK serial 5030; and the former Lockheed N4141T (c/n 5036), which became ROK serial 5036.

Six new C-130Hs were purchased from Lockheed between October 1989 and February 1990: ROK serials 5178 (c/n 5178); 5179 (c/n 5179); 5180 (c/n 5180); 5181 (c/n 5181); 5182 (c/n 5182); and 5183 (c/n 5183). All these Herks were operated by the ROK's Air Transport Wing, based at Kimpo Airfield near Seoul.

Two further C-130Hs were purchased from Lockheed to joined the first six in March 1990, these being ROK serials 5185 (c/n 5185) and 5186 (c/n 5186).

Spanish Air Force (*Ejército del Aire Espanol*)

A quartet of brand-new C-130Hs was acquired between December 1973 and April 1974: EAE serials T10-1 (c/n 4520), later changed to 301-01 and later 311-01, which crashed on Gran Canaria island in the Canary Islands on 28 May 1980; T10-2 (c/n 4526), changed to 301-02 and later 31-02; T10-3 (c/n 4531), changed to 301-03, then later 311-03 and 31-03; and T10-4 (c/n 4534), changed to 301-04, then 311-04 and 31-04. They were initially operated by *Escuadron 301, Manado Aviacon Tactical*, with its base at Zaragoza, Valenzuela, but later by *Escuadron 311, Ala de Transporte 31* (hence the serial changes), but from the same airfield, and also by *Escuadron 312*.

A solitary new C-130H was purchased in January 1976, this being TK10-5 (c/n 4642), later 301-05, then 312-10 and finally 31-50.

A pair of new-build KC-130Hs followed in February and March 1976, these being serials TK10-6 (c/n 4648), later 301-06, 312-02 and 31-51, and TK10-7 (c/n 4652), later 301-07 and 31-52.

Three more new C-130Hs arrived between November 1979 and January 1980 at a price exceeding US$18 million, these being serials T10-8 (c/n 4835), later 311-05 and 31-05; T10-9 (c/n 4836), later 311-6 and 31-06; and T10-10 (c/n 4841), later 312-04 and 31-07. They operated out of Zaragoza with No 301 Squadron on logistic, tactical and humanitarian missions. On NATO exercises the air force utilised its Herks on paratroop drops as well as Container Delivery System

[9] See 'The Lockheed C-130B Hercules – Aircraft for all Seasons', anonymous article in *SAAF News* magazine, 1980.
[10] See Peter Almond, 'RAF's new Hercules arrives 2 years late', article in the *Daily Telegraph*, 25 November 1999.

(CDS) cargo drops. In 1975 it worked with the International Red Cross in Central Africa hauling food and medicines to drought victims, and the following year assisted the Saharan evacuation by airlifting more than 2,200 people and 4.4 million pounds (2 million kilos) of cargo during 341 sorties. The aircraft also worked as pollution-control sprayers when the tanker *Tequila* sank in the Puerto de la Coruna, airlifting in 613,780lb (278,409kg) of detergent.

Two further KC-130Hs were purchased in November and December 1980, these being serials TK10-11 (c/n 4871), which later crashed at Riyadh, Saudi Arabia, on 24 February 1982, and TK10-12 (c/n 4874); both were operated by *Escuadron 32*.

Finally the former Lockheed C-130H-30 serial N7323D (c/n 5003) was acquired in January 1987, and became serial TL10-01; later, with *Escuadron 311*, this changed to 311-01, then 31-01.

Sri Lanka Air Force (SLAF)

In January and February 2000 Sri Lanka joined the long line of Herk users when it purchased two former RAF C-130Ks, ex-XV203 (c/n 4227), which became serial CR-800, and ex-XV213 (c/n 4240), which became CR-881. Both were due to be modified to C.1P standard. New SLAF serials comprising three characters and four digits were adopted in 2009, but neither aircraft appears to be currently operational with 2 Heavy Transport Squadron at Ratmalana Air Base.

Sudanese Air Force (*Silakh al Jawwiya*)

The 43rd nation to operate the Hercules was Sudan. A batch of six C-130Hs was purchased for the Sudaniya for more than $US51 million between January and May 1978: serials 1100 (c/n 4766); 1101 (c/n 4767); 1102 (c/n 4769), which was the 1,500th Hercules delivery; 1103 (c/n 4771); 1104 (c/n 4774); and 1105 (c/n 4775). The plan was for the Sudanese Government to operate them on both economic development and military logistics missions working out of Khartoum Airport.

A Mikoyan MI-9 helicopter being loaded into a Sudanese C-130H for a flight to Yugoslavia on 13 November 1979. *Lockheed-Georgia, Marietta, via Audrey Pearcy*

Lockheed developed a new self-contained and protected high-frequency (H/F) radio antenna, which utilised 2sq ft (0.185m²) of metal and a fibreglass vehicle roof, to create a more durable and reliable mobile communications system for the Sudanese operations; it replaced the more vulnerable whip-type antenna. The antenna incorporated all three C-130 communications systems and a Very High Frequency (VHF) radio system into a four-wheel-drive CJ-7 jeep, and this Mobile Communications Unit (MCU) could be installed in a wide variety of vehicles, and even palletised. The MCU contained radio systems for high, ultra high, and very high frequency AM and FM bands.

One C-130H of the Sudanese air force, serial 1100 (c/n 4766), has been operated exclusively by the civilian arm, Sudan Airways (see the appropriate section for details). The country being in near anarchy, details are hard to obtain on the current status of the surviving aircraft, but most appear to be in storage around Khartoum.

Where's the antenna? Seen on 28 June 1979, Lockheed-Georgia engineers developed an entirely self-contained and protected high-frequency antenna that utilised approximately 2 square feet of metal and a fibreglass vehicle roof to create a more durable mobile communications system. The system was installed in a CJ-7 Jeep for the Sudanese Air Force. The aircraft in the background is the brand-new C-130H 78-0807 (c/n 4817), awaiting delivery to 185 TAS. *Lockheed-Georgia Newsbureau*

Sultanate of Oman – Royal Air Force of Oman (RAFO)

The Sultanate purchased three C-130Hs, the former Lockheed demonstrator N4138M (c/n 4878) in February 1981, which became serial 501, and two brand-new aircraft, serials 502 (c/n 4916) in February 1982 and 503 (c/n 4948) in January 1983. They all served with Nos 4 or 16 Squadrons at Seeb.

In June 2009 Lockheed-Martin announced that an order had been placed by the RAFO for one C-130J for delivery in mid-2012.

Taiwanese Air Force (Republic of China Air Force)

Between July and October 1986 the Republic of China, on the island of Taiwan, received no fewer than a block of twelve new C-130Hs: Republic serials 1301 (c/n 5058); 1302 (c/n 5059); 1303 (c/n 5060); 1304 (c/n 5061); 1305 (c/n 5062); 1306 (c/n 5063); 1307 (c/n 5064); 1308 (c/n 5065); 1309 (c/n 5066); 1310 (c/n 5067); 1311 (c/n 5068); and 1312 (c/n 5069). They joined No 10 Squadron and worked out of Pingtung Air Base. Serial 1310 crashed at SungShan Airfield, near Taipei, on 10 October 1997.

Another C-130H was purchased from Lockheed in December 1991, and became serial 1351 (c/n 5215); she was extensively modified for electronic countermeasures operations and also operated out of Pingtung.

In November 1994 another pair of C-130Hs was purchased from Lockheed and became 1313 (c/n 5271) and 1314 (c/n 5276).

In November/December 1994 two additional new C-130Hs were acquired, serials 1315 (c/n 5308) and 1316 (c/n 5316), and in August a third, serial 1317 (c/n 5318), joined them.

Finally another trio of C-130Hs was obtained between August and December 1997, these being serials 1318 (c/n 5354), 1319 (c/n 5355) and 1320 (c/n 5358), and are all still operational with the 439th Combined Wing.

Tunisian Air Force (*Al Quwwat Al-Jawniya, al-Jamahiriyah, At' Tunisa*)

The Tunisian *Escadrille de Transport et Communication*, based at Bizerta Airfield, operated two brand-new C-130Hs, which the Government purchased from Lockheed's stock fleet in March 1985; these were the former N4249Y (c/n 5020), which although operated by the air force was given the civilian type registration TS-MTA, but later became serial Z21011, and the former N41030 (c/n 5021), which received civilian registration TS-MTB but later became serial Z21012.

To supplement this pair, seven former USAF C-130Bs were acquired between December 1995 and February 1998: ex-58-0728 (c/n 3523), which became serial Z21116; ex-58-0751 (c/n 3550), which became serial Z21115; ex-59-1528 (c/n 3571), which became serial Z21117; ex-59-1533 (c/n 3586), which became Z21114; ex-60-0299 (c/n 3603), which became Z21118, but sometimes carries the civilian registration TS-MTH; ex-61-0949 (c/n 3625), which became serial Z21113; and ex-62-3495 (c/n 3721), which became serial Z21119.

A single former USAF C-130E was added to the Herk fleet in October 1999, this being ex-63-7803 (c/n 3869), which became Z21120.

Finally in March 2002 a former USAF C-130B, 58-0715 (c/n 3510), which had been acquired from the AMARC, became the Tunisian Air Force TS-MTJ.

Turkish Air Force (*Turk Hava Kuvvetleri*)

Five new C-130Es were supplied to the *Turk Hava Kuvvetleri* under the Mutual Assistance Programme and joined *222 Filo*, working out of Kayseri Air Base, in December 1964: USAF serials ex-63-13186 (c/n 4011), which became ETI-186; ex-63-13187 (c/n 4012), which became ETI-187; ex-63-13188 (c/n 4015), which became ETI-188; ex-63-13189 (c/n 4016), which became ETI-189; and ETI-494 (c/n 4100), which joined *131 Filo*, but which crashed near Izmir Airfield on 19 October 1968.

A further batch of new C-130Es was added under the MAP: serials ETI-947 (c/n 4427) in September 1971; ETI-468 (c/n 4514) in November 1973; and ETI-991 (c/n 4524) in February 1974, which served with *222 Filo*.

Most of these aircraft took part in the Turkish paratroop drop that occupied northern Cyprus in 1974, when the island was partitioned, and this led to a United Nations embargo on the supply of further MAP Hercules to this NATO country.

Between December 1991 and August 1992, however, a further seven former USAF C-130Bs were received by the *Turk Hava Kuvvetleri*, and these were to be upgraded with ELINT/SIGINT. They were ex-57-0527 (c/n 3503), which became serial 70527; ex-58-0736 (c/n 3532), which became serial 80736; ex-59-1527 (c/n 3568), which became 59527 but which was returned to the AMARC in 1992 and later sold to the Romanian Air Force (see the appropriate section); ex-61-0969 (c/n 3643), which became serial 10960; ex-61-0963 (c/n 3648), which became serial 10963; ex-61-2634 (c/n 3670), which became serial 12634; and ex-62-3496 (c/n 3722), which became serial 23496. They mainly fly with *222 Filo* out of Erkilet/Kayseri.

Uruguay Air Force *(Fuerza Aérea Uruguaya)*

In August 1982 a former USAF C-130B, ex-60-0295 (c/n 3596), was obtained, and received the serial FAU592; after normal service she was used for supply missions to Antarctica from December 1993 onward. She later took the civilian registration CX-BOX.

A second former USAF C-130B, ex-61-0971 (c/n 3668), was obtained in May 1992 and given the serial FAU591, later becoming the civilian-registered CX-BOW. Both these aircraft were operated by *1 Regimento Tactico* from its base at Carrasco, near Montevideo, and more recently by *3 Escuadrón Aéreo*.

In April 1994 the Uruguay Government acquired a third former USAF C-130B, ex-58-0744 (c/n 3541), from the AMARC park in Arizona, and she became serial FAU593. There is no record that she was ever flown in service by the *Fuerza Aérea Uruguay* and she was finally struck off charge in July 1997.

Venezuelan Air Force *(Fuerza Aérea Venezolana)*

The *Fuerza Aérea Venezolana* placed orders with Lockheed for six new C-130Hs in 1969, and the first quartet were delivered in March 1971 for service with *1 Escuadron, 6 Grupo de Transporte*, working from La Carlota Air Base, near Caracas. The four aircraft were serials FAV3556 (c/n 4406), which subsequently crashed at Caracas on 4 November 1980; FAV4951 (c/n 4407); FAV7772 (c/n 4408), which was also lost in a crash at Lajes, in the Azores, on 27 August 1976; and serial FAV9508 (c/n 4409).

The remaining pair, FAV4224 (c/n 4556) and FAV5320 (c/n 4577), arrived in February and April 1975 respectively.

To replace the two lost Herks, others of the same type were ordered, and these became serial FAV3134 (c/n 4801) in December 1978, and FAV2716 (c/n 5137) in July 1988.

Vietnamese Air Force (Viet Nam Air Force (VNAF) – *(Không Quân Việt)*

Although the C-130 had featured largely in the Vietnam conflict from the earliest days of American aid to the beleaguered southern forces, it was not until the final two years of that tragic war that the Republic of Vietnam Air Force (RVAF) received allocations of C-130A Hercules from the USA. Eventually two squadrons, the 435th and 437th, were both formed in January 1972 with sixteen aircraft each, and initially their main duties were the transporting of personnel and equipment from their base at Tan Son Nhut to the main fighting zones.

The following thirty-two elderly, former USAF C-130As were transferred in November 1972 under Project 'Enhance Plus' to replace the C-123K and mainly to work with these two squadrons:

USAF serials	c/n	Notes
54-1631	3018	returned to USAF
54-1634	3021	returned to USAF
54-1640	3027	returned to USAF
55-001	3028	taken over by North Vietnam in non-operational condition
55-002	3029	burned out in ground accident at Bien Hoa, 6 April 1972
55-0005	3032	taken over by North Vietnam in non-operational condition
55-0006	3033	written off in April 1975
55-0008	3035	returned to USAF
55-0012	3039	returned to USAF
55-0013	3040	taken over by North Vietnam in non-operational condition
55-0016	3043	destroyed by enemy action at Song Be, 25 December 1974

USAF serials	c/n	Notes
55-0017	3044	written off in April 1975
55-0027	3054	returned to USAF
55-0034	3061	returned to USAF
55-0045	3072	written off in April 1975
56-0476	3084	taken over by North Vietnam in non-operational condition
56-0479	3087	written off in April 1975
56-0481	3089	returned to USAF
56-0482	3090	taken over by North Vietnam in non-operational condition
56-0483	3091	returned to USAF
56-0489	3097	written off in April 1975
56-0495	3103	returned to USAF
56-0500	3108	returned to USAF
56-0505	3113	unknown
56-0518	3126	returned to USAF
56-0524	3132	returned to USAF
56-0532	3140	taken over by North Vietnam in non-operational condition
56-0542	3150	written off in April 1975
56-0543	3151	returned to USAF
57-0460	3167	crashed at Phu Bai, near Hue, 2 March 1968
57-0465	3172	written off in April 1975
57-0472	3179	returned to USAF

Three further C-130As were transferred in August 1973 to replace losses, these being the former USAF serials 56-0519 (c/n 3127), taken over by North Vietnam in a non-operational condition; 56-0521 (c/n 3129), destroyed by enemy action at Song Be on 18 December 1974; and 56-0545 (c/n 3153), returned to the USAF.

These Hercules formed the main backbone of the RVAF transport fleet, they were efficiently crewed and operated, and had the lowest accident rate of that force, although, due to their age, it was always a struggle to keep them serviced and maintained; the average serviceability was fourteen aircraft fully operational at any one time. When the North Vietnamese regular army increased the use of its Soviet-supplied AAA and SA-7 ground-to-air missiles, the lumbering Herks became more and more vulnerable during supply drops to isolated garrisons, and were forced higher and higher, losing valuable accuracy. The RVAF worked out its own solution to this, after combat tests in which blocks of ice were substituted for equipment. The new method utilised a drop height of between 9,000 and 10,000 feet (2,743 and 3,048 metres) with a delayed-opening parachute that deployed when falling to 2,000 feet (610m). This reduced wind influence and ensured that most of the drop arrived in the target zone and not among surrounding North Vietnamese forces. These supply drops were radar-controlled, which overcame the frequent heavy cloud cover as well as the enemy missiles and guns. Nonetheless the C-130As were still vulnerable to Surface-to-Air missiles (SAM) at the drop height, and flares were carried that were dropped as heat decoys on the occasions when sufficient warning was available.

When the Americans pulled out and left them to it, lack of heavy bombers was felt, and some C-130As were used as makeshift bombers in the summer of 1974. Under Operation 'Banish Beach', some C-130As were radar-directed at high altitudes over enemy troop concentrations, and parachute-retarded pallets of 55-gallon oil drums filled with napalm, waste oil or petrol were dropped. These fire bombs ignited on impact and were quite effective against Communist troops caught out in the open or in their trenches. The resulting firestorm could incinerate enemy forces in an area some 1,300 feet (396m) long by 700 feet (213m) wide. One Hercules was converted to carry an even more lethal bomb load, this being the 15,000lb (6,804kg) GP 'Daisy Cutter', formerly used by the B-36s. These massive weapons, of which only fifteen were available, were simply rolled out of the tail gate. The effects were demoralising to the enemy, the 150-metre-diameter circular blast area '…levelling trees like toothpicks, and leaving nothing but bare ground.' The Communists claimed that the B-35s had returned, a story taken up by the compliant Western media, but it was just one lone Hercules delivering the goods. Other bomb loads dropped at this period included 250lb (113kg) bombs, which were carried in batches of sixteen to twenty-four at a time and were similarly rolled out of the rear door on multiple passes over enemy positions.

Causalities were few (see the list above) and mainly in the final days, when all surviving Herks were employed in rescuing refugees from the Communist advance, taking 350 of these civilians at a time (the normal capacity was a maximum of 150). Many C-130s were reclaimed by the USAF, after escaping the fall of Saigon, as indicated above, and returned to flying subsidiary duties.

When Tan Son Nhut itself fell to the enemy advance on 20 April 1975, there remained only ten operational C-130As. Seven of these managed to escape to Thailand, while an eighth flew to Singapore, when her crew defected earlier. Of those that are known to have fallen into Communist hands, many were in poor or damaged condition, and only two or three of them were briefly employed by the invaders, until lack of maintenance finally grounded them for good.

Yemeni Air Force *(Yemen Arab Republic Air Force)*

Saudi Arabia presented two of its C-130Hs to the Yemen Arab Republic Air Force in August 1979, these being YARAF serials 1150 (c/n 4825), which later received the civilian registration 7O-ADE, and 1160 (c/n 4827), which later received the civilian registration 7O-ADD, when both were operated by Yemeni Airways.

Zaire Air Force *(Force Aérien Zairoise)*

Between March and July 1971 the *Force Aérien Zairoise* received three new C-130Hs for service with *191º Escadrille, 19 Wing, d'Appui Logistique*, based at N'Djili Airport, near Kinshasa. These were 9T-TCA (c/n 4411); 9T-TCB (c/n 4416), which was impounded at Malpensa Airport, Milan, in October 1994; and 9T-TCD (c/n 4422), which crashed at Kisangani on 18 August 1974. Some of these were used by President Mobuto Sese Sko on official flights.

Commercial flights with the 'stretched' Hercules were also operated by the Bemba Group for in-country and European air cargo haulage operations, with cargoes as diverse as 20-ton loads of coffee and produce to Belgium and France, returning with farm implements, 35,000lb (15,875.73kg) D6 bulldozers, water pumps, electric motors and generators, water tanks, ditch-diggers, Land-Rovers, dump trucks, marine engines, medical equipment, frozen meat and dried fish.

Four further C-130Hs were purchased. These were serials 9T-TCE (c/n 4569) in September 1975, which crashed at Kindu on 14 September 1980 and 9T-TCF (c/n 4588) in May 1975, which was also seized at Malpensa in February 1982. After receiving the French civilian registration F-ZJEP, she joined the *Armée de l'Air* as F-RAPM, then carried the serial 4588 and 61-PN. The other two were serials 9T-TCG (c/n 4589) in April 1975, which was re-registered as 9T-TCC and transferred to the *Armée de l'Air* as serial 4589 and later 61-PN; and serial 9T-TCG (c/n 4736), which arrived in May 1977 but which crashed near Kinshasa on 19 April 1990, leaving 9T-TCA as the sole survivor.

Zambian Air Force

The Government of the Republic of Zambia (GRZ) leased two L-100s, the former Lockheed fleet N9260R (c/n 4101), receiving civilian registration 9J-RCV, and the GRZ N9261R (c/n 4109); both were leased to Zambian Air Cargoes in August 1966, the latter receiving the civilian registration 9J-RCY and being lost in a ground accident at N'dola Airport on 11 April 1968.

A third L-100, the GRZ-owned 9J-REZ (c/n 4209), was similarly leased to Zambian Air Cargoes in April 1967 and later sold to National Aircraft Leasing (see the appropriate section).

Chapter 5

The worldwide operators of Hercules: civilian

Aboitiz Air Transport

This Manila Airport-based company in the Philippines obtained four ex-Australian C-130A Hercules that had never been flown by their RAAF owners: serials 57-0499 (c/n 3206), the former N22669, which was registered as A97-206 in 1988 and after five years of service was grounded for spares in 1993; 57-0503 (c/n 3210), the former N2267W, which was registered as A97-210 in 1988; 57-0504 (c/n 3211), the former N2267W, which was registered as A97-211 in 1988; and 57-0506 (c/n 3213), the former N2268G, which was registered as A97-213. All were finally sold off to Total Aerospace in Miami in 1998 for spare parts.

Advanced Leasing Corporation

A single L-100-30, registration N82178 (c/n 5048), was delivered to the company. She was subsequently registered to the Transadvaree Corporation, Dallas, Texas. She still flies under the Ardmore Leasing banner.

Aerea-Aerovias Ecuatoriansas

A solitary L-100, N9267R (c/n 4146), built in 1966 and purchased by the Bank of America, was leased to this company in April 1968, but was destroyed in a ground accident at Macuma, Ecuador, on 16 May.

Aero Firefighting Services

This company, based in Anaheim, Orange County, California, utilised a quartet of C-130As for wildfire control. One C-130A N45R (c/n 3104), owned by Roy D. Reagan, was leased in December 1990. Another, serial N132FF (c/n 3119), was registered in January 1997, but was later leased to International Air Response (the former T&G Aviation) in November 1998. A third, N131FF (c/n 3138), was registered in July 1990 and was leased to Hemet Valley in June 1991; that company sold her to Michael Zincka Leasing, which in turn sub-leased her to the French *Securité Civile* in August 1993, then, in November 1998, to International Air Response. A fourth, N135FF (c/n 3148), was registered in July 1990 and leased to Hemet Valley; that company again sold her to Michael Zincka Leasing, which sub-leased her to *Securité Civile* in August 1983, then to International Air Response.

In addition, a single RC-130A (c/n 3227) was bought from Pacific Gateway Investments Inc, also of Orange County, in April 1997 and again leased to International Air Response in November 1998.

Aero International

A single L-100-30 Hercules, N8183J (c/n 4796), registered to Rapid Air Transport, Washington DC, in February 1982, was operated by this company in that year, before being leased to Tepper Aviation.

Aero Postal de Mexico

Two former USAF C-130As, serials 56-0487 (c/n 3095) and 56-0537 (c/n 3145), were leased from Pacific Harbor Capital during 1992, carrying the registrations XA-RYZ and XA-RSG respectively. They were replaced by two former USAF RC-130s, 57-0517 (c/n 3224) and 57-0518 (c/n 3225), leased this time from T&G Aviation in 1993/94 and carrying the registrations XA-RSH and XA-RYZ. Painted an overall white colour scheme, they worked out of Mexico City for this Mexican Government-sponsored organisation until about 1996.

AFI International

Two L-100-30 'stretched' Hercules, N4248M (c/n 4992) and N4269M (c/n 5000), were obtained by this company delivered in May 1985, the former from the West German company POP, which was to be used for oil exploration in Benin, Nigeria. In fact, they were both destined for Libya and, with Libyan aircrews aboard, duly successfully evaded the US ban on sales to that country. They were used to support Libyan forces infiltrating and fighting in Chad.

African Air

This L-100-30 was originally delivered to Safair in October 1976. She was briefly transferred from Air Inter (c/n 4695) to become African Air's 9Q-CPF in May 1994, but a month later Safair resumed control and leased her to Lutheran World Food (LWF), operating out of Nairobi.

African AirCargo

This company, registered in Miami, Florida, operated a single C-130A Hercules, N4469P (c/n 3215), which it purchased from the ITT Commercial Finance Corporation in January 1989[1], but it was later impounded by the US Customs Office at Naples, Florida, and kept at Fort Lauderdale until it was sold to F. A. Conner, of Miami. She was registered to the Zotti Group Aviation company of that city until finally sold for scrap in December 1997.

Africargo

Based in the Congo, two Safair Hercules, c/n 4600 and c/n 4606, were utilised by this company in 1987.

AFTI (Advanced Fighter Technology Integration)

Two pairs of Hercules were operated by this Mojave, California, organisation AVTEL, – c/n 3122 and c/n 3168, and c/n 3203 and c/n 3204 – which became AVTEK Flight Test incorporated, working for the US Navy at Point Magu in 1990.

Air Algerie

Two L-100s, N22ST (c/n 4250) and N9232R (c/n 4299), were leased from Saturn in 1981 pending delivery of two (later three) stretched Herks.

Quick-change artist! An Air Algerie L-100-30 undergoes a rapid conversion from cargo aircraft to a passenger airliner. In the top photograph a pallet containing three rows of seats is rolled from a truck into the 55-foot-long cargo compartment of the Super Hercules transport. In the right-hand photograph – hey presto! – the aircraft, which was a cargo hauler earlier that day, has become a wide-body airliner. One pallet, containing a galley and lavatory, is inserted in the centre of the aircraft. Air Algerie operated three of the Lockheed L-100-30 aircraft at this date, 26 October 1981. *Lockheed-Georgia Newsbureau*

[1] In the January 1988 issue of *Trade-A-Plane* (Crossville, Tennessee), page 127, this aircraft was advertised for sale at a knock-down price of $US1.6 million ('Normal retail price $US3 million'). She was credited in the advertisement with 'Approved Part 91 for Corporate use fully Certified for Enclosed Cargo and Packages. Colour all over White Blue Stripe with Polished Leading Edges.'

N4160M (c/n 4886) was the first of three Lockheed Super Hercules 382G-51C L-100-30 passenger/cargo Combi transports acquired by *Air Algerie,* and she is shown here during a test flight on 4 June 1981. The three aircraft featured palletised airliner-type seating and other accommodation for ninety-one passengers, together with a special airliner interior. They were capable of being converted back from passenger to cargo duty in less than an hour, with the removal of the seat pallets. *Lockheed-Martin, Marietta, via Audrey Pearcy*

Three L-100-30s – registrations 7T-VGH (c/n 4880), with doors fitted to the after fuselage; 7T-VHK (c/n 4883); and 7T-VHL (c/n 4886) – were purchased from Lockheed in 1981. These were specially modified versions designed for quick conversion from cargo-hauler to passenger aircraft and back again. Lockheed designed a convertible feature by using seven pallets that contained seating for ninety-one passengers, plus a complete gallery and lavatory, which were loaded via the commercial locking system and locked to the floor in less than an hour.

Of these aircraft, 7T-VHK crashed on landing at Tamanrasset in August 1989, and was a total loss.

Air America

This company operated N7951S (c/n 4301) for Southern Air Transport. It also operated Air Force Hercules, including USAF 56-0510 (c/n 3118) before she crashed in Laos on 10 April 1970, on behalf of the CIA in clandestine operations from Laos during the Vietnam War. There have been many revelations and even more speculation about these so-termed 'shell' companies and even a Hollywood movie, but they have still not given up all their secrets.

A fine study of Southern Air Transport's livery on Air America's N7951S (c/n 4301). *Arthur Pearcy*

Air Atlantique

Working from Orly Airport, Paris, for SNEAS in March 1995, this company leased a single L-100-30 ZS-RSI (c/n 4600) from Safair for a short period.

Air Botswana Cargo (ABC)

This company was formed in 1979 for *ad hoc* charter work worldwide. However, most of its operations were in fact relief missions, and these took it to, among other places, Cambodia, Chad, Cyprus, Ethiopia, Mozambique, Sudan, Tanzania and Uganda. During one particular operation one ABC aircraft was required to move 10,000 tons of supplies in just over three months. Servicing was carried out between schedules and curfew hours to maximise the aircraft's usage, and the task was completed on time.[2]

A single L-100-20, ZS-GSK (c/n 4385), was leased from Safair in November 1984 as ABC's registration A2-AEG for two years.

An L-100-30, ZS-JIY (c/n 4691), fitted with fuselage windows for the passenger-carrying module, was also leased from Safair in October 1979 and re-registered as A2-ABZ, being returned to Safair in August 1983.

A second L-100-30, ZS-JVM (c/n 4701), was similarly leased from Safair in October 1979 and registered as A2-ACA, being returned in February 1987.

At various times these aircraft carried the colours of the Lutheran World Federation and the red cross of the IRC of Geneva for work to Asmara together with a pair of Trans-America Hercules; they also worked in conjunction with Royal Air Force, Belgian Air Force and Swedish Air Force Herks.

Air China

Two L-100-30s, B-3002 (c/n 5025) and B-3004 (c/n 5027), were leased from China Eastern Airlines in 1993.

Air Contractors

In October 1998 this company, based at Swords, Co Dublin, Ireland, leased two L-100-30s, registrations ZS-JIV (c/n 4673), reregistered as EI-JIV, and ZS-JVL (c/n 4676), from Safair, returning the latter in May 1999, which has now become Lynden Air Cargo N406L.

Air Finance

This outfit bought a single L-100-20 N9259R (c/n 4176) from Delta Airlines in September 1983. She was leased to Alaska International Airlines the following month, but was sold to CTA in September 1977.

Air Freight, Ivory Coast

A former Safair L-100-30, TU-TNV (c/n 4698), was briefly registered with this company in September 1991, but re-registered back with Safair the following January.

Air Gabon

The Gabon Air Force used this L-100-20 under the civilian registration of TR-KKB (c/n 4710) until she was badly damaged in an accident in May 1983. In December 1986 the company bought an L-100-30, the former LAC N4274M (c/n 5024), and registered her as TR-LBV.

Air Inter

Another Safair L-100-30 that yo-yoed around for many years, this aircraft, with civilian registration 9Q-CPX (c/n 4695), was transferred to this name in March 1994 before becoming African Air's 9Q-CPF two months later, and was back under Safair's auspices shortly afterward.

---

[2] See B. W. A. Hartridge (ABC Chief Flight Engineer), 'Botswana airline's part in famine relief', article for *Airborne Lifesavers* in *World Airnews* magazine, June 1987 edition.

Airlift International Inc (AII)

Between May and September 1969 an L-100-20 (c/n 3946) was leased from PSL.

L-100s N9248R (c/n 4221) and N9254R (c/n 4222) were also reported to have been utilised. Two L-100s were purchased, N759AL (c/n 4225) and N760AL (c/n 4229).

Air Kenya

Yet another Safair leasing, the tenure of Air Kenya's L-100-30, registration ZS-JIV (c/n 4673), was of brief duration in 1992/93 before Transafrik took her over.

Airplane Sales International

In June and October 1996 this company, based in Santa Monica, California, bought up eleven non-operational former US Navy Hercules that had been dismantled, scrapped or relegated as spare parts at the Aerospace Maintenance & Regeneration Centre (AMARC) in Arizona.

With tail-code TC, this is US Navy EC-130Q 156172 (c/n 4269) of VQ-3, viewed at Barbers Point, Hawaii, in June 1989. She was later sold to Airplane Sales International in June 1996. *Nick Williams, AAHS*

There were two ex-US Navy TC-130Gs, serials 151888 (c/n 3849) and 156170 (c/n 4239), which were registered to the organisation as N93849 and N15674 in June 1996, and nine ex-Navy EC-130Qs: serials 156171 (c/n 4249), reregistered as N34249; 156172 (c/n 4269), as N42699; 156173 (c/n 4277), as N34277; 156174 (c/n 4278), as N14278; 156175 (c/n 4279), as N14279; 156177 (c/n 4281), as N54281; 159469 (c/n 4595), as N54595; 160608 (c/n 4781), as N14781; and 162313 (c/n 4988), reregistered as N9239G.

Alaska Airlines (ASA)

One L-100, N1130E (c/n 3946), a former Lockheed demonstrator, was leased in March 1965. Another, N920NA (c/n 4101), was leased from NAL in April 1969, and a third, N9263R (c/n 4134), was purchased from Lockheed in April 1966.

An L-100, N9267R (c/n 4146), named *City of Anchorage*, was leased from the Bank of America in June 1966. Another, registered N9277R (c/n 4208), and named *City of Juneau*, was purchased in April 1967, while a third, registered N9248R (c/n 4221), was leased from Lockheed in 1968 and modified to an L-100-20 before being sold to Saturn in October 1970.

Alaska International Air (AIA)

This company provided heavy airlift capacity for the Trans-Alaska Oil Pipeline, hauling more than 1 million pounds (453,592 kilos) of air cargo a day during the height of its construction. They pioneered airlifting such equipment into the North Slope. An L-100-20, registration N109AK (c/n 4134), was leased in December 1969. A second L-100-20, registration N105AK (c/n 4176), was leased from Air Finance in October 1973.

One L-100, N9227R (c/n 4208), was purchased from National Aircraft Leasing in November 1972 and sold to Saturn the following March, while another, N921NA (c/n 4209), was leased from National Aircraft Leasing in July 1972, but following an accident in February 1973 it was sold by an insurance company and finally totally destroyed in an explosion at Galbraigh Lake on 30 August 1984. Another L-100, N102AK (c/n 4234), was leased from National Aircraft Leasing in July 1972, and finally written off in a crash in Alaska in October 1974. A third, N101AK (c/n 4248), was similarly purchased after being leased from National Air Leasing (NAL).

An L-100-20, registration N103AK (c/n 4222), was leased and then purchased from Saturn in January 1973, while another, registration N22ST (c/n 4250), was leased from National Aircraft Leasing in October 1975. A third, N104AK (c/n 4300), was leased from Lockheed then purchased in November 1975 and subsequently converted to an L-100-30.

A nice study of Alaska International Air L-100 N105AK (c/n 4176) on 14 June 1976. *Nick Williams, AAHS*

Arctic airlift: the AIA aircraft is N105AK (c/n 4176). *US National Archives, Washington DC*

Herks at work in the arctic wastes. *Lockheed via Audrey Pearcy*

THE LOCKHEED MARTIN C-130 HERCULES

An L-100-30, registration N101AK (c/n 4248), was similarly leased from National Aircraft Leasing then purchased outright in December 1977 and subsequently transferred to Markair in 1984. A second, registration N9232R (c/n 4299), was leased from Saturn in November 1975. Two more L-100-30s, N10ST (c/n 4383) and N11ST (c/n 4384), were leased from Saturn in 1972-76, while another pair, N107AK (c/n 4472) and N106AK (c/n 4477), were leased from Safair in November 1974.

Two L-100-30s, N108AK (c/n 4763) and N501AK (c/n 4798), were purchased in November 1977. In 1982 the former was leased to Cargomaster before going to Markair in February 1984, while the latter was sold to United Trade International.

Alaska World Trade Corporation

A former Pegasus Aviation L-100-30, registration N2189M (c/n 4582), was registered to this company for a few months early in 1990 before being taken over by Flight Cargo Leasing of Dover, Delaware, in April of that year.

American Airlines

L-100-20 (c/n 4299), originally built in 1968 and stretched to a -30 in 1975, had many changes of ownership, but was at one time leased by Southern Air Transport (SAT) to American Airlines in November 1981 under her original N9232R civilian registration. SAT itself, alleged by some sources to be a subsidiary front for the CIA's Pacific Corporation, ran twenty-three Herks at one time, but by 1982 only N9232R remained (66R).[3]

Angolan Air Charter (TAAG)

This Luandan-based company also operated as Angolan Airlines and has operated Hercules for many years now. Among their diverse roles, one was converted with internal fuel tanks carrying 1,800 US gallons (6,813.74 litres) to haul jet fuel to Menongue, Huambo and Luena.

In January 1999 TAAG obtained a single ex-US Navy DC-130A, the former 56-0491/158229 (c/n 3099), from CZX at Wilmington, Delaware, with the civilian registration N9724V. She suffered a couple of crashes while operating for the Angolan Government with Unitrans, the second of which, at the 4 de Fevereiro Airport, Luanda, on 10 June 1991, was terminal. Control was lost following an engine failure and the aircraft, carrying military supplies for the Angolan Ministry of Defence, crashed and caught fire, killing all four crew members and three passengers on board.

In September 1978, Angola Cargo obtained an L-100-20 from CTA, D2-FAF (c/n 4176). She became part of TAAG-Angola Airlines the following April but was scrapped after crash-landing at Sao Tomé Airport on 15 May. Another L-100-20, registration D2-FAG (c/n 4222), was similarly purchased from CTA in November 1977, and used by TAAG-Angolan Airlines from the following April, then Angolan Air Charter. She was twice hit during UNITA (*União Nacional Para a Independência Total de Angola*) actions, once while taking off from Luanda in 1982, then on 5 January 1990, when a missile hit her while she was taking off from Menonque. She crash-landed and was written off.

An L-100-30, N901SJ (c/n 4299), owned by Commercial Air Leasing, was briefly flown for TAAG in 1994 before being leased to Foyle Air, UK. A second L-100-30, registration ZS-RSC (c/n 4475), operated by Safair but leased out to various companies, also flew in Angola for a brief period in 1987. In October 1992 another Safair L-100-30, ZS-RSI (c/n 4600), was leased for a few months by Angolan Air Charter. A third L-100-30, ZS-JIV (c/n 4673), was leased from Safair for a short spell in 1993, and a fourth, ZS-JVL (c/n 4676), similarly leased from that company in 1996/97. A fifth, ZS-JIX (c/n 4684), was also leased from Safair in 1992 and damaged at Ondjiwa in June of that year. Three more L-100-30s, registrations D2-THS (c/n 4691), with fuselage windows, D2-TAD (c/n 4695) and D2-TAB (c/n 4698), were also leased for short periods in 1993/94.

Three further L-100-30s were sub-leased from Mitsui Corporation for a short period during the same period, these being PK-PLU (c/n 4824), PK-PLV (c/n 4826) and PK-PLW (c/n 4828). Finally, another trio of this type – PK-PLR (c/n 4889), which was sub-leased from Heavylift in 1990/91; TR-LBV (c/n 5024), leased from Air Gabon in 1988; and PJ-TAC (c/n 5225), which was leased to TAAG in 1991 as Angola Air Charter – were still operational, despite battle damage, up to the end of 1999.

[3] See Terry Reed and John Cummins, *Compromised: Clinton, Bush and the CIA* (Penmarin Press Inc, 1995) and Victor Marchetti and John D. Marks, *The CIA and the Cult of Intelligence* (Dell Publishing, New York, NY, 1974)

Angolan Airlines purchased two new-build L-100-20s from Lockheed in November 1979, at a price in excess of $US25 million. These became D2-EAS (c/n 4830) and D2-THA (c/n 4832). The former was destroyed by UNITA anti-aircraft fire at Menongue, Angola, on 16 May 1981; the latter made a belly-landing at Dondo, Angola, on 8 June 1986.

AviSto

A Swiss company, Sogerma, purchased the single ex-Ugandan L-100-30 Hercules, 5X-UCF (c/n 4610), which had been impounded and held at Cairo Airport in April 1998, for use with Medecair in central Africa, and she was assigned the company's reserved registration of PH-AID.

Bank of America

A solitary L-100, N9267R (c/n 4146), built in 1966, was purchased by the Bank of America. She was leased as the *City of Anchorage* in June 1966, and again leased, this time to *Aerea-Aerovias Ecuatoriansas,* in April 1968.

Bradley Air Services

In June 1998 this organisation registered ex-NWT L-100-30 as C-GHPW (c/n 4799), and that same October leased it to Schreiner (First Air).

Bush Field Aircraft Company

This organisation inherited the original 1957-built ex-USAF 56-0537 (c/n 3145), a weary and much-travelled C130A with the civilian registration N537UN, from Heavylift International. Her props and engines were sold off and finally, after standing at the Pinal Air Park near Marana, Arizona, Bush sold the remaining carcass to Aero Corporation in January 1999.

Butler Air Cargo

Cal Butler, a pioneer of the early techniques of using aircraft for fighting forest fires, founded this company, which is based at Redmond, east of Seattle, Oregon, close to the Microsoft headquarters. About 70% of the company was at one time owned by TBM Inc. This company purchased a single, flyable former USAF Hercules C-130A, number 56-0531 (c/n 3139), in March 1991, and registered her as N531BA. She is currently a stripped-out hulk without electronics or running gear.

Canadian Airlines International

Formed in March 1987, but tracing its routes back through five predecessor airlines – Canadian Pacific Air Lines (CP Air), Eastern Provincial Airways (EPA), Nordair, Pacific Western Airlines (PWA), and Wardair Canada Ltd – this Vancouver-based company has operated leased L-100-30s from time to time.

Cargolux

An L-100-20, registration CF-PWR (c/n 4355), was bought from PWA in December 1980 and received the registration LX-GCV; it was leased to United African Airlines the following month. Also, an L-100-30, registration N9232R (c/n 4299), was leased from Saturn in July 1981 for a number of months.

Cargomasters (Australia)

Cargomasters leased a pair of L-100-30s, registrations N106AK (c/n 4477) and N108AK (c/n 4763), from Alaska International Air in the summer of 1982, returning them the following year.

Certified Aircraft Parts

This outfit purchased a single former US Coast Guard aircraft, registration HC-130E (c/n 4158), ex CG1414, from WIA in September 1988 for breaking up, selling the cockpit section to Reflections and, finally, the remainder to Asia-Pacific Trading & Simulation PTE in November 1995.

Chani Enterprises

Based in Zambia, this company worked a single former USAF Hercules C-130A, number 9J-BTM (c/n 3095), from the British company May Ventures in March 1997.

Cherry Air Aviation Services

Earl Cherry purchased 1958 ex-RAAF C-130A 57-0505 (c/n 3212) with civil registration N130PS from Alexandria IAP after she had knocked around quite a bit, including stints with QANTAS among others. Flying from Lecompte, LA, with new registration N131EC, she was the only remaining C-130A flying with the three-bladed propeller. She 'starred' in the 2007 Ridley Scott movie *American Gangster* with Denzel Washington and Russell Crowe (about using a C-130A for drug smuggling!), and was later used as a commercial para-drop aircraft, sporting the legend 'Charlie 130 Corp'.

China Air Cargo (CAC)

Two L-100-30s, registrations B-3002 (c/n 5025) and B-3004 (c/n 5027), were purchased from Lockheed in 1987 by this Shanxi-based company, mainly for fish cargo charter Tianjin-Japan. Both these aircraft were subsequently transferred to China Eastern Airlines in 1991.

China Eastern Airlines (CEA)

Two L-100-30s, B-3002 (c/n 5025) and B-3004 (c/n 5027), were transferred from China Air Cargo in 1991 and leased to Air China in 1993 and China Air Cargo before being sold to Safair in 1999.

Comercial Proveedorn del Oriente SA (COPROSA)

This Peruvian organisation, which started and ended its life in 1999, obtained a single, damaged, former *Fuerza Aéra Perunana* L-100-20 Hercules, built in 1970, with civilian registration FAP394 (c/n 4358), formerly with FAP's *41 Gruppo de Transporte* in October 1994, and registered her as OB-1376. She later reverted to her former FAP number and was stored *sans* engines at Lima.

Commercial Air Leasing Inc

In June 1985 this organisation obtained a former Saturn L-100-20, N22ST (c/n 4250), and leased her to IAS/Diamang from 1986 onward. On 2 September 1991 this aircraft was destroyed by mines at Wau, Sudan, while working for the International Red Cross. An L-100-30, registration N520SJ (c/n 4299), was similarly obtained from Saturn on the same date for subsequent leasing, being reregistered as N901SJ in April 1988 and sold to Transafrik in August 1988, which sold her on to the First Security Bank the following month. A second former Saturn L-100-30, N519SJ (c/n 4562), was likewise obtained in May 1988 and reregistered as N904SJ. She ended up at the Hamilton Aviation Air Park at Tucson, Arizona, where she was bought by Derco in August 1997.

Continental Air Services (CAS)

N9260R (c/n 4101) was the very first L-100 to be delivered to any civilian customer, being leased from Lockheed on 30 September 1963. She was sold to GRZ in August 1966. A second, N9261R (c/n 4109), was leased in November 1965 and was also later sold to GRZ at the same time.

CZX Productions Inc (DE)

A single machine, a former USAF/US Navy DC130A, 56-0491/158229 (c/n 3099), was obtained by this Wilmington, Delaware, company in August 1988 from Bob's Air Park at Tucson, Arizona, and sold on to TAAG, Angola, in January 1991.

Delta Air Lines

Based at Atlanta, Georgia, this well-known company operated a fleet of Hercules for many years on scheduled daily all-freight operations, and increased its freight volume by 92% over six years of C-130 working. Three L-100s were purchased – registration N9268R (c/n 4147) in August 1966 and N9258R (c/n 4170) and N9529R (c/n 4176) in October 1966 – and both were later modified to L-100-20s in 1972.

An L-100, registration N7999S (c/n 4234), was leased to Delta by National Aircraft Leasing in January 1970.

Dropping into Los Angeles International Airport is L-100-20 N9268R (c/n 4147) of Delta Airlines. *Nick Williams, AAHS*

Cargo gulper! The same aircraft loads a palleted cargo. *Lockheed-Georgia, Marietta, via Audrey Pearcy*

Delta Airlines L-100-20 N9258R (c/n 4170) arrives at Los Angeles International in 1991. *Nick Williams, AAHS.*

THE LOCKHEED MARTIN C-130 HERCULES

Derco Aerospace

Not strictly an operator, Derco Aerospace, founded in 1979, is a fully owned subsidiary of the Sikorsky Aircraft Corporation with sites at Corpus Christi, Texas, and Milwaukee, Wisconsin. Sikorsky in turn is a subsidiary of United Technologies Corporation (UTX) of Hartford, Connecticut. Part of the company's Derco remit is the purchase and supply of aircraft parts and spares, and in this connection quite a few redundant Hercules aircraft have transited through its hands.

In August 1997 Derco purchased from Globe Air a former 1974-built Safair L-100-30 (c/n 4562), with the civilian registration ZS-RSF. This aircraft was sold on to Transafrik, becoming S9-CAI two months later. The same date saw a sister ship, 1974-built former Safair L-100-30 c/n 4565, registered as ZS-RSG, purchased and also sold to Transafrik, becoming S9-CAJ.

In May 1998 two ex-US Navy EC-130Qs were obtained, these being the engineless 1975-build former 159469 (c/n 4595), registered as N54595, and the 1978-build 160608 (c/n 4781), registered as N14781. The latter was sold on to the Royal Netherlands Air Force two months later, becoming its G-781, while the former had her outer wings sold in February 2009 for fitting to an RAF C-130K.

The 1981-built former Gabon L-100-30, then registered as TR-KKD (c/n 4895), was obtained in August 2000 in a disassembled condition and shipped to the European Aeronautic Defence & Space Company (EADS) of Leiden, Netherlands, whose aircraft maintenance subsidiary, EADS-Sogerma, received her in September 2001. She became the UAE's 1216.

In July 2005 yet a third ex-US Navy C-130Q, 162313 (c/n 4988), originally constructed in 1984, was obtained as an engineless hulk from DMI bearing civilian registration N9239G. In October 2005 she was sold on to the Royal Netherlands Air Force to become G-988 at the same time as c/n 4781.

Another L-100-30, the 1985-build former Tunisian Air Force TS-MTA (c/n 5020), was acquired in December 2007 in a damaged condition. Derco sent her to the Malaysian Aircraft Inspection, Repair & Overhaul Depot (AIROD) at Sultan Abdul Aziz Shah (SAAS) Airport, Subang, for rebuilding, which was done by incorporating the front fuselage section of c/n 4281, and in December 2008 she was offered up for sale.

In August 2000 Derco received a 1985-build former Gabon L-100-30 TR-LBV (c/n 5024). She became the Abu Dhabi 1215 and in November 2007 was to go on to 'star' in the Christopher Nolan film *The Dark Knight* in June 2008, with Michael Caine, Gary Oldman and Heath Ledger.

January 2008 saw a 1991-build ex-Frameair L-100-30 (c/n 5225) carrying the Angolan Air Force coding T-312 for sale by Derco, having been in the hands of EADS-Sogerma for a considerable period.

More recently, in February 2009, the forward section fuselage of the former US Navy EC-130Q 156177 (c/n 4281), built in 1968, was transferred by Derco to AIROD at Subang, to be used in the reconstruction of c/n 5020.

EARL

Based in Tampa, Florida, EARL was briefly and intermittently involved with three 1975/76-build former Safair L-100-30s, these being the former ZS-RSI (c/n 4600), ZS-JVL (c/n 4676) and ZS-JIX (c/n 4684).

EAS (Europe Air Service) Air Cargo

Based at Perpignan, this company operated a leased L-100-30 for a short period.

Echo Bay Mines

A well-travelled L-100-20, CF-DSX (c/n 4303), was obtained from the James Bay Energy Corporation in July 1980, and received the name *Smokey Heel*. She worked with Worldways Canada and her name was changed to *Bob Burton* before she was registered to the Florida Corporation, American Aircraft, at Hialeah in July 1988.[4]

---

[4] This aircraft was advertised for sale in the February 1988 issue of *Trade-A-Plane*, under registration N39ST, by Transamerica Airlines Inc of Oakland, 'Fully Equipped for International Operation Including Dual Litton INS'. The advertisement carried the proviso, 'The aircraft is subject to prior sale, commitment or withdrawal from market without prior notice' and no price was mentioned.

ENDIAMA

ENDIAMA is the Angolan State Diamond Mining Organisation with mines at Luzamba, Catoca and the Cuanago Valley, the latter under continual threat from UNITA rebels. Based in Angola, the company purchased a single Hercules, D2-EHD (c/n 4839), which had already been twice damaged by UNITA action in that country. The aircraft was flown by a Transafrik crew and later reregistered as T-650; it was again damaged by UNITA action at Luena in February 1992 and repaired in Portugal. Returning to Luanda, she continued her dangerous work until UNITA finally got her at the fourth attempt, shooting her down at Huambo on 2 January 1999.

Ethiopian Airlines (RRC Air Services)

In July 1988 two Hercules L-100-30s – ET-AJK (c/n 5022) and ET-AJL (c/n 5029) – were leased from Relief & Rehabilitation Commission (RRC Air Services) after being in storage since 1984/85. ET-AJL was lost in a crash south of Djibouti on 17 September 1991. A third, ET-AKG (c/n 5306), was purchased in November 1996.

European Air Transport

This company, located at Zaventem, Brussels, Belgium, is a subsidiary of DHL Parcels, specialising in dangerous cargoes and livestock. The company leased a Safair L-100-30, ZS-JIX (c/n 4684), between September and October 1998.

Evergreen International Aviation Inc

Evergreen Holdings, which included Evergreen International Aviation and Evergreen Helicopters, was originally established at McMinnville, Oregon. Following the Senator Frank Church hearings, in 1975 the CIA was pressured to sell off its lucrative business-front companies, and this included Marana field, which was taken over by Evergreen. The manager of the CIA's proprietary airlines, George Dole, worked for Evergreen, as did former CIA pilots Gary Eitel and Dean Moss, the latter dying in mysterious circumstances.[5]

The company grew rapidly with government contracts and currently has seven subsidiary companies, one of which specialises in air cargo. In February/May 1999 it bought two former USAF WC-130E Hercules, 61-2365 (c/n 3688) and 64-0552 (c/n 4047), from Wright-Paterson Airfield, Ohio, after both had been retired from service; they were both ex-stock from Western Intentional Aviation salvage yard at Tucson, Arizona.

Due to heavy debts and financial problems, in December 1997 the company announced that an 'unnamed' financial institution would help buy back $US125 million of bonds, but a sell-off of some aircraft assets seemed inevitable. Both Hercules were offered up for resale in January 2000, and are located at the Pinal Air Park, Marana, Arizona, pending their disposal. Their attributes are listed as upgraded wing modifications completed in 1986 and 1988, low flight times (19,485 and 20,357 hours respectively), and the fact that both aircraft were well maintained by the US Air Force (any rumoured covert CIA backing and usage is not authenticated!).

Fédération Européenne des Sociétés (EFIS)

A French company, with headquarters at Chateauroux, EFIS employed a single Hercules, L-100-30 F-GNM (c/n 4695), which it leased from Safair between February 1996 and May 1997.

First Air Canada

Formerly Bradley Air Services, this company, owned by the Makivik Corporation of Kuujjuaq, currently operates two L-100-30s – the former Safair ZS-RSI (c/n 4600) and the previous PWA C-GHPW (c/n 4799) – out of Yellowknife on air freight and cargo hauls up through the Arctic Circle. It is the only civilian Hercules operator in Canada.

---

[5] See John Titus, 'Evergreen Pilot murdered on Weapons Flight', article in *Portland Free Press*, March/April 1994, and 'Air Force Investigates Evergreen', article in *Portland Free Press*, May/June 1996 issue.

First Air Canada's C-GHPW (c/n 4799) makes a night rendezvous at Cambridge Bay Airport. *Courtesy of Alan Sim*

First National Bank of Chicago

A single L-100-20, N92656R (c/n 4300), was purchased by the bank on behalf of Interior Airways, which leased it at various periods from 1968 until it was sold to AIA in October 1975. AIA had her modified to an L-100-30.

Flight Cargo Leasing Inc

Based at Dover, Delaware, this organisation registered a former Alaska World Trade L-100-20, N2189M (c/n 4582), in April 1990 and leased her to Tepper Aviation and Rapid Air Transport for Eastern European operations.

Flight Systems Inc (AVTEL Flight Tests Inc)

Three ex-USAF DC-130As – numbers 56-0514 (c/n 3122), 57-0496 (c/n 3203) and 57-0497 (c/n 3204) – were operated by Flight Systems for the US Navy between April 1986 and October 1990, and by AVTEL Flight Tests Inc at Mojave, California, and Donaldson Center, Greenville, South Carolina. The first aircraft was finally scrapped for parts at the end of 1993, while the other two went to Point Mugo.

Flying W Airways (FWA)

This company flew a former Lockheed L-100-20 demonstrator as N50FW (c/n 3946) under lease to PSL in 1969 before she was leased to Airlift International. It also leased two other L-100-20s, registrations N30FW (c/n 4302) and N50FW (c/n 4303), from the Giraud Trust in April 1964, before they went to the subsidiary RDA that same December. Finally two further L-100-20s, N60FW (c/n 4358) and N70FW (c/n 4364), were purchased from Lockheed in July 1970, but later went to back to Lockheed as N785S and N7986S respectively and were resold to the *Fuerza Aérea del Peru* instead.

Ford & Vlahos

This company was headed by John J. Ford, assistant secretary of T&G Aviation and head of a firm of attorneys in San Francisco, which acted for Pacific Harbor Capital. On its behalf Southern Cross, owned by Multitrade, duly acquired seven unused RAAF C-130As – registrations 57-0500/N2267B (c/n 3207); 57-0501/N2267N (c/n 3208); 57-0503/N2267U (c/n 3210); 57-0504/N2267W (c/n 3211); 57-0505/N2268A (c/n 3212); 57-0508/N2268V (c/n 3215); and 57-0509/N2268W (c/n 3216) – out of storage from Laverton RAAF base (N2267W from the School of Technical Training, Wagga) and reregistered them as N22FV (November 1985), N4445V (September 1986), N12FV (March 1986), N5394L (July 1984), N13FV (October 1983), N15FV (September 1986) and N15FV (February 1985) respectively.

The first was used for the BandAid relief flights in Ethiopia and operated by International Air Aid for the International Red Cross until April 1986. Three others (the second, fifth and sixth) were originally to be sold to the Government of Colombia, but this was blocked by the USA Government and instead they were registered to Ford & Vlahos in August 1983. The second was finally sold to *Securité Civile* for the Chad Government in October 1979, and the fifth was embargoed at Oakland, California, until returned to the RAAF in November 1986. The third and fourth were also returned to the RAAF in 1986, then leased to Hayes Industries, Alabama, the following month. The sixth was eventually sub-leased to the US Nuclear Defense Agency, then stored at Chico, California, and later operated by International Air in the Sudan in 1985 before being registered to ITT Commercial Finance Corporation in August 1986.

Fowler Aeronautical Services

This company, based at Van Nuys Airfield, California, obtained four former unused RAAF C-130As – registrations N205FA (c/n 3205), N207GM (c/n 3207), N213DW (c/n 3212) and N216CR (c/n 3216) – which had been originally registered to Ford & Vlahos (see above) but were returned to the RAAF. They were registered by Fowler in 1989 for resale. The first was returned to the RAAF in 1990 and was demolished for parts and training in 1990-91; the second and fourth were eventually registered to IEP, IEPO, at Chatsworth, California, in September 1992, and the third was sold to Peter Suarez at Van Nuys in July 1994.

Foyle Air UK

Based at Luton Airport, this company utilised three Hercules aircraft over a four-year period. An L-100-30, registration N901SJ (c/n 4299), was leased from Commercial Air Leasing in January 1994 for use as an oil-spill spraying aircraft, as was a second of the same type, N908SJ (c/n 4300), the following year, and a third, N923SJ (c/n 4301), in 1997.

Frameair (TAC Holdings)

A single L-100-30, PJ-TAC (c/n 5225), was purchased by this Netherlands Antilles company in August 1991 and subsequently leased to TAAG as Angola Air Charter in April 1993. A second (c/n 5307), was ordered in February 1992, but cancelled in January 1996. She was subsequently sold to the Canadian Armed Forces in March 1996.

Four further L-100-30s – registrations S9-NAD (c/n 4475), ZS-JVL (c/n 4676), D2-TAD (c/n 4695), and D2-TAB (c/n 4698) – were leased from Safair to TAC Holdings (Frameair) at various times for work for the Angolan Government.

GIA International

This aircraft charter, dealer and brokerage company, based at Medford, Oregon, bought the 1957-build ex-USAF C-130A 55-0025 (c/n 3052) in May 2002, and reconstructed her at Chandler, reregistering her as N130HGL in June 2003, when she began to be operated by Heavylift International. From December 2004, as N226LS, she was operated by Wurst David Trustees, of Medford, Oregon. Her registration was cancelled by the FAA on 26 July 2006.

Globe Air Inc

This holding company had four of the ubiquitous and much-touted former Safair L-100-30s registered to it for a while, most of which were operated by Saturn before going into storage and being resold. They were N517SJ (c/n 4558), which was registered in April 1987 but crashed on an initial training flight at Travis Air Force Base on the 8th of that month; N904SJ (c/n 4562), which was assigned from Saturn in July 1995, but which was in storage at Tucson until sold by Hamilton Aviation to Derco in August 1978; N250SJ (c/n 4565), which was registered in April 1987 and later reregistered as N515SJ, operated by Saturn and stored at Tucson, being returned to Globe Air and finally also sold to Derco in August 1997; and N516SJ (c/n 4590), registered in April 1987, reregistered as N516SJ in July, being operated by Saturn, and also stored at Tucson in 1993-95, returning to Globe in March 1996 before being sold to Lynden Air Cargo in July 1997.

Hawkins & Powers

This Wyoming-based concern had two C-130As, the former USAF 56-0496 (c/n 3104) and USAF 56-0507 (c/n 3115), registered as N8053R and N8055R in May 1989. They leased one of the Hercules to British Aerospace Corporation and the other to Multitrade International, a company linked to a previous C-130 sale. Both eventually went to Roy D. Reagan in August 1998.

A trio of Herk firefighters who flew for Hawkins & Powers in the 1990s: pilot Mike Lynn (left), flight engineer Wage Bargslein (centre) and co-pilot John Lancaster (right). *Chuck Stewart*

Three more C-130As, the former USAF 56-0534 (c/n 3142), 56-0535 (c/n 3143) and 56-0538 (c/n 3146), which had later served with the US Forest Service, were obtained from Hemet in 1988/89 and registered as N131HP, N132HP and N130HP respectively.

Finally the company acquired another quartet of C-130As: ex-USAF 57-0459 (c/n 3166), obtained in February 1990 and registered as N135HP; 57-0482 (c/n 3189), in March 1989, registered as N133HP; 57-0511 (c/n 3218), in October 1990, registered as N134HP; and 57-0513 (c/n 3220), which was obtained for spare parts in August 1998 and registered as N8230H.

Hayes Industries

Based in Birmingham, Alabama, this company leased a former RAAF C-130A, 57-0508/A97-215 (c/n 3215) from Ford & Vlahos in November 1983, and sub-leased her to the US Nuclear Defense Agency in 1984. She was stored at Chico, California, for a while before being utilised by Sudan International Aid the following year, and was finally taken over by the ITT Commercial Finance Corporation in August 1986. The company became Pernco Aerospace Incorporated in 1989.

Heavylift

This Stansted-based company has leased six L-100-30s from various owners down the years: serials N15ST (c/n 4391); ZS-JIX (c/n 4684); PK-PLU (c/n 4824); PK-PLV (c/n 4826); PK-PLW (c/n 4828); and PK-PLR (c/n 4889).

Heavylift International

This corporation, based at Sparks, Nevada, purchased two former USAF C-130As, N487UN (c/n 3095) and N537UN (c/n 3145), from Pacific Harbor in March 1995 and resold the former to May Ventures GB and the latter to Bush Field Aircraft Corporation, which sold her on to Aero Corporation in January 1999.

Hemet Valley Flying Services Incorporated

This Californian fire-fighting company purchased or leased several much-travelled ex-Forestry Service C-130As as water bombers and re-registered them. Among them was N137FF (c/n 3092), which remained at Tucson until sold to Mace Aviation in August 1998; N134FF (c/n 3104); N132FF (c/n 3119), which was leased to FAASA before going to Aero Firefighting Services Company in 1997; and N131FF (c/n 3138) in 1988, before she went to Michael Zicka Leasing in September 1989 and was again leased back, this time from Aero Firefighting in June 1991, and sub-leased to *Securité Civile* in France in 1993. Hemet also acquired six further C-130As – N132FF (c/n 3142); N133FF (c/n 3143); N134FF (c/n 3146); N135FF (c/n 3148); N136FF (c/n 3149); and N138FF (c/n 3227) – most of which were also sub-leased and finally sold to Aero.

Herc Airlift Corporation

A single former RAAF C-130A, 57-0508/A97-215 (c/n 3215), registered as N4469P, was leased by this organisation from the ITT Commercial Finance Corporation for a while in 1987, when she was named *Lennie Marie*.

HSL Company

Based in Dallas, Texas, this company obtained a single L-100-30 (c/n 5055) direct from Lockheed, which was registered N8213G.

Hunting Air Cargo

This company leased three former Safair L-100-30s, N920SJ (c/n 4561) in March 1994, ZS-RSI (c/n 4600) in March 1996, and ZS-JIY (c/n 4691) in February 1997.

InterAgency Ecological Program (IEP) – IEPO

Based at Chatsworth, California, in 1992, this organisation registered two former RAAF C-130A Hercules, 57-0500/A97-207 (c/n 3207) and 57-0509/A97-216 (c/n 3216), as N207GM and N216CR respectively.

IAAFA (Inter-American Air Forces Academy)

Based at Homestead Air Force Base, three former USAF Hercules were employed as ground training aircraft: C-130A 56-0517 (c/n 3125) and a C-130B (c/n 3537), both of which were destroyed in a Hurricane on 24 August 1992, and C-130B-II 59-1531 (c/n 3579).

Intercargo Service (ICS)

This French-based company operated a single L-100-30, F-GFZE (c/n 4698), on behalf of Zimex in 1990; it was reregistered to Zimex as HB-ILG before being reregistered back to her original owners, Safair, the same year.

Interior Airways

Based at Fairbanks, Alaska, this company made two L-100-20 registrations, N9265R (c/n 4248) and N9265R (c/n 4300), which they operated for the First National Bank of Chicago from 1968 before being first leased and then sold to Alaska International Airlines in 1975.

Five L-100s were leased from National Aircraft Leasing: serials N921NA (c/n 4209), from 1969 to 1972; N760AL (c/n 4229), in 1967, which crashed at Prudhoe Bay, Alaska, on 24 December 1968; N7999S (c/n 4234), in April 1969; N9262R (c/n 4248), in November 1969; and N9266R (c/n 4250), in December 1968.

They hauled scientific equipment and other supplies to scientists on the ice island in the Arctic, some 300 miles (482.8km) north of Point Barrow, Alaska, having to land on an ice strip only 3,400 feet (1,036.32m) long and 6 feet (1.8288m) thick. They also moved oil-drilling equipment into the North Slope.

All these aircraft were subsequently transferred to Alaska International Airlines.

International Aerodyne (IA)

One L-100, registration N9262R (c/n 4248), was purchased in 1968 and passed to National Aircraft Leasing.

International Air Response (IAR)

The former T&G Aviation, IAR's predecessor, located at Chandler, Arizona (see below), had entered into an exchange agreement with the Forest Service under the terms of which T&G took delivery of three USAF surplus C-130As, 57-0512 (c/n 3219), 57-0517 (c/n 3224) and 57-0520 (c/n 3227), which had been modified for the air tanker role as RC130As, then converted back. With their new owners, N118TG, N3226B (ex-Valley National Park of Arizona) and N119TG (ex-Aero Firefighting) were either already modified or scheduled to be modified to be water bombers, the former at Chandler MAP. In exchange, IAR (in common with five other companies) delivered three specified historic aircraft to museums designated by the Forest Service.

However, on 28 November 1998 the Forest Service stated that it had lacked the authority to enter into the exchange agreement with IAR, as it had by then become, that the agreement was void *ab initio,* and that the three aircraft were to be returned. Complex legal proceedings followed with the US Government's involvement. In the end, after bankruptcy seizures, cannibalisation for spares and various other woes, in June 2002 c/n 3219 was registered to International Air Response Inc but was used for various Department of Defense tests and trials to November 2003, even making a 50th Anniversary of the Hercules Commemoration Flight in October 2004 before being transferred to Coolidge. C/n 3224 was in storage at Marana Air Park until October 1990 when it was leased to Trans Latin Air as HP1162LN before returning to T&G as N3226B in 1992, then *Aero Postal de Mexico* as XA-RSH in 1992. Finally c/n 3227 went into storage at Chandler, was bought by IAR in 2006 and registered as N119TG, and also stored at Chandler.

International Aviation Services (IAS)

Headquartered at Shannon, Ireland, and with a subsidiary on Guernsey, Channel Islands, this company leased several L-100-30s, including N3847Z (c/n 4839), in December 1984. They later merged with Transmeridian Air Cargo at Luton Airport and became British Cargo Airlines.

International Aviation Services (IAS), Cargo Airlines (UK)

One L-100-30 was briefly operated for *Air Algerie* by this UK-registered company in 1989, 7T-VHK (c/n 4883), but she was written off in a crash at Tamanrasset on 1 August of that year. The company later became part of Dan Air London.

International Aviation Services (IAS), Guernsey

Several Hercules leased from SAT/TAMAG including N521SJ (c/n 4250) in 1986 and TAM69 (c/n 4759) in 1989, while ND-ACWF (c/n 4839) was purchased from Wirtschafsflug of Frankfurt in December 1984, reregistered as D2-EHD and operated for Diamang before being damaged by a UNITA missile in 1986 and subsequently sold to ENDIAMA.

International Telephone & Telegraph (ITT) Commercial Finance Corporation

In August 1986 this corporation registered the former RAAF C-130A 57-0508/A97-215 (c/n 3215), from Ford & Vlahos, and leased her to the Herc Airlift Corporation and others before finally selling her to African Air Transport of Miami in June 1988.

Investment Capital Xchange

Based at Helena, Montana, this organisation registered a solitary former Lockheed L-100-30 Hercules, N898QR (c/n 5032), in December 1997.

Jamahiriya Air Transport

This Tripoli-based company operated two L-100-30 'stretched' Hercules – N4248M (c/n 4992), which became 5A-DOM, and N4269M (c/n 5000) which became 5A-DOD – delivered in May 1985. The former was obtained from the West German company POP, and was to be used for oil exploration in Benin, Nigeria. In fact, they were both destined for Libya and, with Libyan aircrews aboard, they duly successfully evaded the US ban on sales to that country.

5A-DOM was successfully hijacked by its defecting aircrew and flown to Egypt in March 1987, but the aircraft was subsequently returned to Libya despite its illegal origins.

James Bay Energy Corporation

This hydro-electrical supply company was based in northern Quebec and bought a single L-100-20, registration RP-C98 (c/n 4303), from the Government of the Philippines in September 1973 and leased her to Quebecair for operations. There were two Quebecair aircrew each working twelve-hour shifts per day to give round-the-clock operating from Schefferville to the outlying camps on the complex of reservoirs, dykes, dams and powerhouses with foodstuffs, fuel and other essential supplies for the construction workers, including thousands of gallons of beer. The aircraft was finally sold to Echo Bay Mines in July 1980.

L-100 Leasing

Yet more of the much-circulated former Safair aircraft briefly found their way to this organisation; they were two L-100-30s, registrations ZS-RSJ (c/n 4606), operated in Angola by SFAir in 1987 and returned to Safair the following year, and ZS-JJA (c/n 4698), returned to Safair in 1987.

Larkins, Gary R. CA

This Auburn, California, company registered a former Time Aviation C-130A, N9539G (c/n 3224), in July 1982. Another ex-Time Aviation aircraft, DC-130A N3149B (c/n 3230), was similarly registered with the company but only used for spare parts before both went to Humberto Montano in Arizona.

LESEA – Lester E. Sumrail Evangelistic

A single C-130A, the former USAF 55-0025 (c/n 3052), was registered as N226LS from the *Fuerza Aéra Perunana* in 1990 and christened *Mercy Ship Zoe* for use in relief work. She later carried the name *Feed the Hungry* before being grounded at Stansted, then South Bend, Indiana, where she was offered for sale.

Lineas Aéreas del Estade (LADE)

A single Lockheed L-100-30 demonstration aircraft, N4170M (c/n 4891), was purchased by *Fuerza Aérea Argentina* in December 1982. Reregistered as LV-APW in February 1982, she was operated by the LADE company.

Lockheed-Georgia Company (GELAC)

Although the Lockheed company registered many completed Hercules on its books, as the Lockheed Aircraft Service Company, prior to their sale, it only actually retained five Hercules for its own use, mainly as demonstrators; these included an L-100, N1130E (c/n 3946), which was leased out and later converted to an L-100-20.

An L-100-20, N4174M (c/n 4412), originally sold to Kuwait in April 1971, was repurchased in May 1982 and became the famous High Technology Test Bed (HTTB) aircraft (see the appropriate section for further details).

An L-100-30, N4110M (c/n 4839), was built in March 1980 and retained as a demonstrator until sold to Wirtschafsflug in October 1981, but she returned to Lockheed in November 1983 and was sold to IAS, Guernsey, Channel Islands, in December 1984.

A second L-100-30 demonstrator, N4170M (c/n 4891), was an all-white aircraft with a red stripe for LADE, but was sold to the Argentine Air Force in December 1982.

A KC-130H, N4237M (c/n 4940), was retained as a Tanker Demonstrator until sold to the Singapore Air Force in July 1987.

Lynden Air Cargo

This Alaska-based company obtained five former Safair/Saturn L-100-30 Hercules: NJ903SJ (c/n 4590), purchased in July 1997 and reregistered as N403LC in 1997; S9-NAJ (c/n 4606), reregistered as N401LC in 1999; D2-TAB (c/n 4698), purchased in February 1997 and reregistered as N402LC; and N909SJ (c/n 4763), purchased in May 1999 and reregistered as N404LC. The fifth was another former Safair aircraft, ZS-OLG (c/n 5025), which was leased in July 1999.

A Lynden Air Cargo L-100-30 9L-382G at Ted Stevens International, Anchorage, Alaska, in July 2009. *Courtesy of Mark T. Smith*

Maple Leaf Leasing

Two L-100-20s were registered to this company: the former Zambian Air Cargo's 9J-RBW (c/n 4129), which was purchased in 1969 and leased to Pacific Western, being rebuilt as an L-100-20 after crash damage and finally sold to Pacific Western in 1977, and former Lockheed and National Aircraft Leasing N7960S (c/n 4355), which was leased then sold to Pacific Western in 1977.

Markair

Markair utilised several L-100-30s, including the former Alaska International Air machines N101AK (c/n 4248), leased then sold to Transamerica International Airlines in 1984; N104AK (c/n 4300), also leased to Transamerica and sold to Saturn in 1987; N107AK (c/n 4472), sold to Saturn in 1992; N106AK (c/n 4477) in 1984, which it leased to Zantop International, then sold to Saturn; and N108AK (c/n 4763), which was sold to Saturn in 1991.

Marshall Aerospace

This company, based in Cambridge, UK, has for decades specialised in refitting military aircraft. In 1975 1967-built former RAF C-130K XV208 (c/n 4233) was modified as the sole Hercules W.2 Meteorological Research aircraft. She was run by the A&AEE and operated by the RAE, Farnborough, until July 2002. In 2005 she was reacquired by Marshalls from QinetiQ to be utilised as the flying test bed for Risk Reduction flight trials to test the Europrop International TP400-D6 turboprop engine for the Airbus A400M Military Transporters. The engine is mounted on the inner port wing location and is fitted with an eight-bladed Ratier-Figeac propeller 5.33m (17.5 feet) in diameter. Ground tests commenced in 2008 and flight testing the following year.

More typical of Marshall's work is the recovery of two ex-US Navy EC-130Qs, originally retired to the Aerospace Maintenance & Regeneration Center at Davis-Monthan AFB, Arizona, in 1991, and which were sold in 1997 and moved next door to the Dross Metals Inc/ARM yard at Tucson. They have to undergo massive restoration before joining the Royal Netherlands Air Force. The contract for these two veterans, the former 160608, N14781 (c/n 4781) and 162313, N9239G (c/n 4988), was signed on 22 November 2005. The deal included a third machine, the former 159469, N54595 (c/n 4595), which will be cannibalised for spare parts. The Dutch had hoped to acquire two further such aircraft from Great Britain, but this failed due to procrastination by the Ministry of Defence.

Working in conjunction with Derco Aerospace, the logistics behind such moves were impressive. The first of the two aircraft was disassembled by Derco, then trucked in convoy to the port of Houston, Texas, and shipped to London, arriving at Tilbury Docks on 28 March 2008. The aircraft parts were then trucked up the M11 motorway to Cambridge, arriving in the early hours of a Sunday morning. The second aircraft followed the same route, reaching Marshalls on 23 April.

The work to bring these machines up to modern requirements was extensive and involved an integrated modification package (the full 'glass cockpit' make-over treatment), which included a Communications Navigation Surveillance/Air Traffic Management (CNS/ATM) compliant solution centred on the Ville St Laurant, Quebec, company CMC's Flight Management System, featuring LCD display, TacView portable mission displays, Integri-Flight CMA Global Positioning System (GPS) with system sensors with the Federal Aviation Authority's (FAA) Wide-Area Augmentation System (WAAS) capability. These are integrated with a Inertial Navigation System (INS), VHF Omnidirectional Range navigation system (VOR), the Defence Measuring Equipment (DME) transponder-based navigation system, Active Dynamic Filtering (ADF) and Global Position System (GPS). In addition there is a Rockwell Collins communications package incorporating Very High Frequency (VHF), Ultra High Frequency (UHF), High Frequency (HF), Satellite Communications (Satco), Aircraft Communications Addressing & Reporting System (ACARS), and an intercom system. Further upgrading includes Weather Radar, Engine Instrumentation, Lighting Sensors, Traffic Collision Avoiding System (TCAS), Enhanced Ground Proximity Warning System (EGPWS) and Emergency Locator Transmitters (ELT). The pilots are provided with the Exton, Pennsylvania-based Innovative Solutions & Systems (IS&S) display including moving maps. All these improvements are incorporated, together with specialist requirements for the Dutch Air Force. The aircraft are assigned to 334 Squadron based at Eindhoven to back up existing C-130H-30s, which are also due to be updated.

Maximus Air Cargo

Advertising itself as the largest all-cargo and outsize cargo carrier in the UAE, this Abu Dhabi airlift company was established in 2005. Although its main fleet comprises Russian-built Anatovs, it leases three ex-Air Gabon L-100-30s through Derco, these being A6-MAC (c/n 5024), since July 2008, and the former 1215 (c/n 4895), A6-MAX, and D2-THS (c/n 4691), later UAE1217.

Maximus Air Cargo L-100-30 L-382E A6-MAX (c/n 4895), with a 'Care by Air' sticker for humanitarian relief flights, is seen at Dubai International, UAE. *Courtesy of Konstantin von Wedelstaedt*

Maxturbine

The former RAAF C-130A 57-0505 (c/n 3212) was carrying the company logo on her fuselage between November 1999 and November 2001, while at Falcon Field, Mesa, together with the registration N131EC, before being sold on to Fowler Aeronautical Services.

May Ventures, UK

This British company purchased a single, much-travelled C-130A, N487UN (c/n 3095), in 1995 and registered her as 9J-AFV with the name *Tanganyika*. She was operated by Shabair in Zambia, then went into storage at Johannesburg until being sold to Chani Enterprises in 1998.

Megatrade

A single former Lockheed L-100-30 was registered as N8218J (c/n 5056) in 1993 by this company, but five years later she was registered under the same number to the Ruftberg Company, of Dallas, Texas.

Merpati Nusantara Airlines

This Indonesian airline based at Djakarta Airport operated two Hercules L-100-30s, PK-PLS (c/n 4917) and PK-PLT (c/n 4923), which were purchased by the Indonesian Government in 1982 and leased to Pelita before going to Merpati in 1990 and 1986 as that company's PK-MLS and PK-MLT respectively. Both were placed in storage in the early 1990s and subsequently sold to Tentera Nasional Indonesia-Angkatan Udare (TNI-AU).

Micronesia Aviation Corporation

In 1993 a former RAAF C-130A, 57-0506/A97-213 (c/n 3213), was leased by this company from the Philippines Air Force, which had her in storage at Manila Airfield for many years. Registered as RP-C3213, she carried the name *Equator Traders*, but was eventually obtained by Total Aerospace for spare parts.

Military Aircraft Restoration Corporation

In August 1986 a former USAF C-130A, 57-0518 (c/n 3225), was registered by this Anaheim, California, corporation and finally sold to *Aero Postal de Mexico* in 1993. Likewise, a second former USAF C-130A, 56-0500 (c/n 3108), was registered to this corporation as N223MA in February 1992, but utilised by the United Nations in central Africa between 1994 and 1995, before being offered up for sale as spare parts.

Mitsui Corporation

Three L-100-30s, PK-PLU (c/n 4824), PK-PLV (c/n 4826) and PK-PLW (c/n 4828), were purchased by this company in July 1979 and leased to Pelita (see Pelita below for further details).

Montano, Huberto

This Arizona-based company acquired via Gary R. Larkins two former Time Aviation Hercules, C-130A N9539G (c/n 3224) in July 1982 and DC-130A N3149B (c/n 3230). Both ended up as scrap at the Western International Aviation yard at Tucson.

Multitrade Aircraft Leasing

Based in Las Vegas, Nevada, this company acquired a single former USAAF C-130A, 56-0500 (c/n 3108), from the Air Force in July 1990 and registered her as N223MA, naming her *The Phoenix*. She was used in central African operations and registered to Military Aircraft Restoration in 1992. Multitrade leased another from Hawkins & Powers. The company's subsidiary, Southern Cross, flew a number of RAAF C-130s,

National Aeronautics & Space Administration (NASA)

A standard C-130B, 58-0712 (c/n 3507), which had been modified as the C-130BLC (Boundary Layer Control) test bed and reconverted as an NC-130B, was employed by NASA at the Johnson Space Center in Texas from July 1968. In September 1969 the aircraft was purchased and received a new registration, N707NA, being re-registered as N929NA in October 1973. Extensively modified, she was named *Earth Survey*, which reflected her role, and served until 1982, when she resumed the N707NA registration. Fitted with type 15 engines, in October 1996 she was flown from NASA Dryden before going into non-flyable storage in October 1999.

A standard US Navy EC-130Q, registration 161494 (c/n 4896), originally delivered in September 1981 and serving with VQ-3 and VQ-4, was used by NASA at Wallops Island in December 1991 as a remote sensing research aircraft for a period before being grounded and broken up for spare parts.

A second EC-130Q, registration 161495 (c/n 4901), and a third, 161496 (c/n 4904), both with similar historics, were registered to NASA in October and November 1992, the former taking the registration N427NA, after their special equipment had been removed.

National Aircraft Leasing

Together with Pepsico Air Lease, this company owned Hercules aircraft for lease to various operators. L-100 N920NA (c/n 4101) was purchased from GRZ in March 1969, and leased to ASA, then Saturn, before being modified to an L-100-30 in November 1972.

A second L-100, registration N9227R (c/n 4208), was purchased from ASA in 1967 and sold in turn to AIA in November 1972.

Her sister, N921NA (c/n 4209), was purchased from GRZ in 1969 and leased to various companies before being damaged in February 1972. The insurance company sold on the aircraft to AIA.

Two L-100s, N7999S (c/n 4234) and N9266R (c/n 4250), were purchased in 1969 and 1968 respectively and were both leased to Interior Airways (see above). A third, N9262R (c/n 4248), was obtained from International Aerodyne in 1968 and leased to Interior Airways.

A single L-100-20 (c/n 4355), registered as N7960S by Lockheed, was purchased by this company and Maple Leaf Leasing in November 1969 and leased to Pacific Western Airlines, which later purchased the aircraft in January 1977.

National Oceanic & Atmospheric Administration (NOAA)

Formerly the Research Flight Facility (RFF), the aeronautical arm of the Environmental Research Laboratories, the US Commerce Department's NOAA operated two WC-130B Hercules in the 1970s, conducting atmospheric research that included participation in such international ventures as the International Field Year for the Great Lakes (IFYGL) in 1971 and the Global Atmospheric Research Program's Atlantic Tropical Experiment (GATE) in 1974.

In August 1970 the NOAA took over a WC-130B, 58-0731 (c/n 3526), which received the registration N6541C under the Department of Commerce in March 1972. This machine was operated out of Miami with the name *NOAA's Ark* and was reregistered as N8037 before reconverting to a standard C-130B again in 1981 and resuming USAF duties.

The Research Flight Facility, US Department of Commerce, was part of the National Oceanic & Atmospheric Administration's Environmental Research Laboratories. It later became NOAA's Office of Aircraft Operations at Miami, Florida. In 1975 it was operating a single specially equipped WC-130B Hercules, 58-0731 (c/n 3526), which also carries civilian registration N6541C. *US Department of Commerce, Rockville, MD*

A US Navy EC-130Q, registration 161531 (c/n 4932), was allocated to NOAA in May 1992 and was later assigned to the National Centre for Atmospheric Research at Denver, Colorado, in January 1997. She was struck off for salvage in 1997.

An L-100-30, N4281M (c/n 5032), which had been stored at Lockheed between 1985 and 1988 and registered to Worldwide Trading at Delroy Beach, Florida, in January 1989, was reregistered as N898QR in April 1989 and flew in a overall white paint scheme with NOAA decals until October 1993, when she was struck off.

These aircraft carried additional equipment in order to measure weather elements and position, a wide variety of cloud physics instrumentation for sampling the interiors of clouds, including an infra-red (IR) temperature radiometer, ice-nuclei counter, aerosol detector, liquid water content sensors, and a hydrometer foil sampler. In 1974 the WC-130B was modified to carry the Airborne Weather Reconnaissance System (AWRS), a minicomputer-centred airborne meteorological data system developed by Kaman Aerospace Corporation. She could also carry the Omega dropsonde, which sensed temperature, humidity, pressure and position (or winds); the position-sensing capability used an Omega-updated inertial navigation system. She also had side nose radar and vertical cameras providing time-lapse photographic coverage. Thus fitted out, she took part in NASA's Skylab earth-sensor experiments, and was extensively used in the development of new remote-sensing techniques developed for use aboard satellites. She was also heavily involved in weather modification experiments, carrying four seeding racks on each side of her fuselage containing a total of 416 silver iodide flares. A push-button firing mechanism located at the visiting scientist station built onto the flight deck, and connected to an electrical sequencer, was used to ignite and launch the flares during cloud penetration flight.

A typical annual period of service for '41-Charlie', as the Herk was christened, was the logging of a flight time of 478hr 45min in 1972, which included Project StormFury (63 hours); hurricane research (63hr 50min); Naval Research Laboratory projects (142hr 30min); laser profilometer research (20hr 20min); fisheries research (19hr 15min); National Center for Atmospheric Research projects (2hr 15min); NASA projects (27hr 5min); and hail project support (71hr 55min), together with essential calibration and proficiency (66hr 35min).

National Science Foundation (NSAF)

C-130Rs operated by the US Navy for the NSAF included 160740 (c/n 4725) and 160471 (c/n 4731). Former EC-13Qs of the US Navy allocated to the NSAF were 161496 (c/n 4904), 161531 (c/n 4932) and 162312 (c/n 4984). The latter was fitted with an extended sampling boom to the starboard forward fuselage in November 1998, and used for atmospheric research, based at Boulder, Colorado, and taking the civilian registration N130AR from October 1993.

A single LC-130H, 93-1096 (c/n 5410), built in December 1995, flew for the Foundation until recently.

Northcap LLC

This limited liability company is located on the 10th Floor of the Brandywine Building, at 1000 West Street, Wilmington, Delaware. It has been associated by various sources with Tepper Aviation, Rapid Air Services, VPC Planes and Phoenix Air. The sole aircraft is an ex-China Air 283G-44K-30 L-100-30 (c/n 5027). It has been registered since April 2008 with the FAA as N3796B (and was formerly registered in March 2007 as N4557C), and is listed as an 'Experimental' and 'Research and Development' aircraft.

Persistent claims from several published and internet sources[6] link this, and similar, aircraft with the CIA and covert 'Rendition' flights transporting Islamic terrorist suspects for interrogation, transiting via Shannon Airport, but no proven links have been presented to substantiate the claim. She is certainly a most controversial and well-travelled Herk.

---

[6] Grey, Stephen, *Ghost Plane* (St Martins Press, New York, 2006); Gup, Ted, *The Book of Honor* (Anchor, 2001); Shannon Watch; Indymedia Ireland; and others.

Northwest Territorial Airways

This Yellowknife, Canada, company operated six Hercules aircraft.

A single L-100, registration C-FPWK (c/n 4170), was leased from Pacific West Airlines in April 1981, and while being used as a fuel tanker was burned out on the 11th.

Of several L-100-30s that served, registrations C-FNWF (c/n 4562) and C-FNWY (c/n 4600) were leased from Safair during the years 1979/82, while ZS-JIV (c/n 4673) was leased from Safair in 1996/97.

Finally yet another L-100-30, C-GHPW (c/n 4799), was leased in 1983 and purchased outright in 1987 from Pacific West Airlines and utilised by the Red Cross in Angola in the following years, carrying the name *Captain Harry Sorenson*, before being sold to Bradley Air Services.

Oil Spill Response Limited (OSRL)

Established in 1985 and jointly owned by a combination of twenty-nine oil companies, with its headquarters at Southampton, UK, OSRL's mission statement included a 24/7/365 state of readiness to deal with oil slicks or spillages, with at one period at least two specially adapted Hercules aircraft on standby at constant readiness.

The aircraft used included four former Safair 1974/76-build L-100-30s; Safair leased these to Air Contractors Limited, which in turn sub-leased them to OSL for periods. Between 1999 and 2003 it was the former Safair ZS-JVL (c/n 4676) that was so employed; ZS-JIY (c/n 4691) was utilised in that role from 2002 to 2005. ZS-RSG (c/n 4565) was operated under her civilian registration ZS-RSG from 2004 until 2008, and finally ex-Safair ZS-JIV (c/n 4673), with civilian registration EI-EIV, was similarly sub-leased over the same period.

These machines are ready-loaded for specialist equipment deployment with pre-packaged containers, all pre-documented for instant deployment to remote locations such as Central Asia, West Africa and Russia. The Herks themselves are equipped with Aerial Dispersant Spraying (ADS) apparatus. The company had two outstation bases, one located in Bahrain with Air-Mobile Response Equipment, and the other at Aberdeen, Scotland.

Pacific Gateway Investments

A single former firefighting C-130A, N138FF (c/n 3227), from Hemet Valley Flying Services, was registered to this Orange County, California, company in January 1990, which leased her back to Hemet Valley for several years until she finally became an Aero Firefighting machine in 1997.

Pacific Harbor Capital Inc

Based at Portland, Oregon, this company is a subsidiary of PacifiCorp, which, according to some claims, has CIA links.[7] The company registered a former T&G Aviation C-130A, N120TG (c/n 3095), in 1993 and leased her to Aero Postal Mexico at Mexico City in 1993/94, then sold her to Heavylift International in 1995. A second C-130A, registration N130RR (c/n 3145), was obtained from Roy D. Reagan in 1990 as a fire bomber, but she then became a normal transport plane with T&G Aviation and was also leased to Aero Postal Mexico, returning to Pacific Harbor in 1993 as N537UN and, after a spell at the Marana (Pinal Air Park), was also sold to Heavylift International in 1995.

Pacific Rim Airlines (PRA)

The former First National Bank of Chicago 1968-built L-100-30 N9265R (c/n 4300) served for a short period between October 1996 and March 1997 under lease to the moribund Pacific Rim Airlines, which ceased trading in 2003.

---

[7] See *Seattle Post Intelligencer*, 25 October 1975 issue. In the 1975 Senate hearings Senator Frank Church stated that the holding company for all of the then CIA airlines was 'The Pacific Corporation'. See John Titus, 'Who's Who in the C-130 Scandal (an Update)', article in *Portland Free Press*, March/April 1997 issue.

Pacific Western Airlines (PWA)

Pacific` Western Airlines, based in Vancouver, British Columbia, leased a single L-100, registration N92623R (c/n 4134), from Lockheed; it then went to ASA in 1963 before being sold to the latter in 1966. A second, CF-PWO (c/n 4197), the former Lockheed registered N9269R, became number 382 in May 1967 and was leased to TMA in 1967.

Pictured at the old Tokyo International Airfield is L-100-20 CF-PWO (c/n 4197) of Pacific Western Airlines. *Nick Williams, AAHS*

Another view of the same aircraft. *Lockheed-Georgia, Marietta, via Audrey Pearcy*

With its Lockheed registration N926R, the aircraft is being towed at arrival at headquarters. *Lockheed-Georgia, Marietta, via Audrey Pearcy*

The range of cargo hauled by the company's C-130s include breeding cattle from Canada to Japan, with textiles coming back in return, and oil rigs all over the world, from the Canadian Arctic to the Middle East, Africa and South America. At one period in 1971 a PWA Herk was based at Resolute Bay in the Canadian Arctic for more than a month, lacking a hangar or indeed any kind of shelter in temperatures that plummeted as low as -70°C, but was able to operate.

A third L-100, registration N109AK (c/n 4129), was leased from Maple Leaf Leasing in March 1969 as number 383, and, after being damaged in an accident at Eureka, North West Territories, in August 1968, was rebuilt as an L-100-20 and leased to Alaska International Airlines.

An LC-100-20, registration CF-PWX (c/n 4361), was purchased in December 1969 and became number 384. She was finally lost in an accident in Zaire on 21 November 1976. Another, registration CF-PWR (c/n 4355), was leased from Maple Leaf Leasing in November 1969 and became number 385. She was sold to PWA in January 1977, which sold her on to Cargolux in December 1980. A third, registration CF-PWK (c/n 4170), was purchased from Delta Airlines and became number 386. She was leased to NWT in April 1981 and was lost in that company's service.

A solitary LC-100-30, registration C-GHPW (c/n 4799), was purchased in December 1978, becoming number 387. She was leased and finally sold to NWT in 1983.

PWA operated mainly between November and May servicing both the Distant Early Warning (DEW) Line radar chain and later Panarctic Oil's oil-drilling sites in the Arctic regions of Alaska and Canada, flying to within a few hundred miles of the North Pole. The cargo was mainly drill rigs, bulk fuel, equipment, personnel and supplies, and in one case an entire oil-rig community, houses, rigs, fuel and food. They landed anywhere that had an ice depth of at least 54 inches (137cm), which was capable of supporting the L-100, conditions that limited their period of operation. In order to operate in such sub-zero conditions PWA's engineers invented a pre-heating system for the propellers to engine start, utilising bleed from the APU. Outside this operational period PWA shifted its supply missions to Cornwallis, Ellesmere and Melville islands, where they landed on gravel airstrips and sandbars.

Pacific Western Hercules also operated 'air charter' work for oil-rigs to Ethiopia, and diamond mine support in Angola, according to Harry Zelinski (although these mission might not have been what they seemed), together with airlifting two F-104 StarFighter aircraft at a time from Europe to Canada for overhauls.

Pakistan International Airlines (PIA)

Two L-100s, registrations AP-AUT (c/n 4144) and AP-AUU (c/n 4145), were purchased directly by the Government of Pakistan in October 1966 for the national airline, PIA, becoming its 64144 and 64145 respectively.

Pegasus Aviation Incorporated

A former *Force Aérienne Gabonaise* L-100-30, registration TR-KAA (c/n 4582), was purchased by the company in 1989 and reregistered as N2189M; she was reregistered to the Alaska World Trade Corporation in March 1990. A second L-100-30, this time one of the former Safair fleet, 9Q-CBJ (c/n 4796), was taken out of storage at Brussels Airport in 1989 and registered as N123GA. She passed into the hands of Rapid Air Transport the same year.

Pelita Air Services

This Indonesian Government-sponsored company, headquartered at Djakarta, operated six L-100-30s, three of which were officially accepted at Marietta on 18 December 1981 by the Ambassador, Mr Danoedirdjo Ashari. Others were leased from Mitsui Corporation in July 1979. They were registrations PK-PLU (c/n 4824), named *Bina* (later *Toili*); PK-PLW (c/n 4828), named *Sentiaki* (later *Nimbo Krang*); PK-PLR (c/n 4889), named *Sitiung*; PK-PLS (c/n 4917), with doors and named *Rimbo Bujang*; PK-PLT (c/n 4923), named *Pasir Pangarian*; and PK-PLV (c/n 4826), named *Hanonan*.

The laden Hercules N7988S (c/n 4388) taking off. The great advantages of the Herk were, of course, her bulk carrying capacity in this role and the fact that her short take-off and landing ability enabled her to deliver the families close to their new homes. *Lockheed-Georgia, Marietta, via Audrey Pearcy*

Their initial role was as part of the Indonesian transmigration airlift programme, under Operations 'Relita I', 'II' and 'III', when 500,000 families (2,500,000 people) were transported by air, 128 people per trip, from overpopulated areas of the country to less settled regions. In a six-month period from January to June 1981 alone, 100,000 passengers and 14 million pounds (6,330,293.18kg) of cargo were shifted. After a decade of service, many were sub-leased to a wide variety of companies (see the appropriate sections), PK-PLV being lost in a crash at Kai Tak Airport, Hong Kong, on 24 September 1994. Others went to *Tentera Nasional Indonesia-Angkatan Udare* in April 1994 (see the appropriate sections).

Opposite: Pakistan International Airways AP-AUT (c/n 4144). *Lockheed-Georgia, Marietta, via Audrey Pearcy*

Seen aloft on 25 September 1979 is Lockheed Super Hercules PK-PLV (c/n 4826) taking part in the same 'transmigration' programme. *Lockheed-Georgia, Marietta, via Audrey Pearcy*

Pemex *(Petroleole Mexicanos)*

A single L-100-30, registration XC-EXP (c/n 4851), was purchased from Lockheed Aircraft Corporation in April 1980, and used until the early 1990s before she went to the *Fuerza Aérea Mexicana* as its number 10611.

Philippine Aerotransport (PADC)

The Government of the Philippines took delivery of its first Hercules in April 1973, with two more in July and August. These were used by the Philippines Government to airlift agricultural produce such as corn, rice, tomatoes and bananas across the many islands of the republic. The aircraft also transported millions of fingerlings, seedlings and plants to support the nation's Green revolution. Other hauls included thousands of school books to the southern islands from Manila to spread education, and of course oil construction, road and bridge-building supplies have also been hauled by the Herky Bird all over the 7,000-island archipelago.

A former Lockheed L-100 demonstration aircraft, converted to an L-100-20, N50FW (c/n 3946), was obtained by the Philippines Government in 1973 as its RP-97, but was sold to PADC five years later. After being placed in storage, the Philippines Air Force took her over again in 1995.

An ex-Saturn L-100-20, N30FW (c/n 4302), was purchased by the Philippines Government in August 1973 and became this company's RP-C99 in 1978. She was resold to UAA in 1982.

A third L-100-20, N40FW (c/n 4303), was obtained by the Philippines Government in 1973 and leased as RP-C98 before being sold to the James Bay Energy Corporation.

Two more L-100-20s were direct sales from Lockheed to the Philippines Government, in 1973 and 1975. The first, N7967S (c/n 4512), was sold to the company in 1983 and flown for eight years before being broken up for spares, while the second, RP-C101 (c/n 4593), was leased then stored at Manila before being used by the Philippines Air Force in the 1990s.

Prescott Aviation

Bearing the old paint scheme of the notorious Southern Air Transport, itself a descendant of Air America, it is inevitable that this little-known outfit has aroused more claims of being a CIA 'shell' company. Whether true or not, Atlanta Air Services Leasing, a limited liability company of Missoula, Montana, leased a former Lockheed Aircraft Corporation L-100-30, ex-N4281 (c/n 5032), as N3755P to Prescott in 2007, and she operates carrying only the numerals '41901' as identification. She also has lower cockpit windows, and when she arrived at Liverpool Airport on 12 January 2009 from Stephenville she was cordoned off and isolated before departing for Athens with eleven people aboard.

A second L-100-30, the former N8213G (c/n 5055), registered to the HSL Company of Dallas, Texas, has also been operated by Prescott since 2001.[8]

Protex SA De CV

In September 1994 this company, located in Mexico City and advertised there as a machinery, equipment and computer company, purchased 1980-build former L-100-30 N4116M (c/n 4851), built for Pemex and subsequently operated by the *Fuerza Aérea Mexicana* (FAM) as XC-EXP. Within a few years she was carrying FAM's registration 10611 and currently carries the registration 3611.

PSCI

A single C-130A, the former refurbished Snow Aviation's N130SA (c/n 3035), was registered to this Fayetteville, Arizona, organisation in 1997.

PSL Air Lease Corporation

The PSL Air Leasing Corporation operated a single L-100-20, the former Lockheed demonstrator N50FW (c/n 3946), in 1969, which was operated by the Flying W organisation.

Q20 LLC

This was another limited liability company operating on the 10th floor of a building on West Street in Wilmington, Delaware, and suspected by some of being yet another 'shell' company front for CIA operations. The company's L-100-30 (c/n 4796), originally built in 1978 and first registered to Safair in that year, subsequently passed through the hands of SCIBE, Pegasus Aviation, Rapid Air Transport, Aero International and Tepper Aviation. In October 2006 she was briefly registered as N8183J with Q20, before being reregistered as N2679C, before returning to Tepper once more.

Quebecair

In September 1973 another much-travelled L-100-20, which frequently changed ownership and registration, and which ultimately met a sticky end in Angola, was leased to Quebecair, a short-lived airline based in St Laurent, Montreal. Build in 1968, and first registered to the Girard Trust as N9237R (c/n 4303), she was leased to Flying W Airways the following April. By 1973 she had passed through several more ownerships and was operating as the James Bay Energy Corporation's CF-DSX when she was leased to Quebecair, which sold her on to Echo Bay Mines soon after.

Questline

Registered in Florida with one Hercules, the former USAF C-130A 56-0491 (c/n 3099), this organisation flew her in Angola on behalf of the Government, but she crashed and burned out at Luanda on 10 June 1991.

---

[8] To discover more about the alleged participation in 'Extraordinary Rendition' flights by these, and other, aircraft around the globe, see the European Parliament 2004-09 working document No 8, compiled by Giovananit Claudio Fava, 'Temporary Committee on alleged use of European countries by CIA for transport and illegal detention of prisoners', dated 16 November 2006 (DT/64133EN). The Malta newspaper *Independent of Sunday*, 20 November 2005 issue, cited stop-overs by Prescott-logoed N8213G in March and August 2004 at Malta.

Rapid Air Transport

This company, located at Suite 300, 10606 Baltimore Avenue, Beltsville, Maryland, is a Washington DC-based company operating two former Pegasus L-100-30 Hercules, N2189M (c/n 4582) and N8183J (c/n 4796), from 1989. It has leased them out to a variety of users, mainly Tepper Aviation Inc, since that time. Rapid also owned a third L-100-30, originally LAC's N4278M (c/n 5027) built in 1985 and once registered to Safair, but now registered to Northcap at Wilmington. Amnesty International has made allegations[9] linking the company to 'Extraordinary Rendition' flights (conveying both Islamic terrorists and terrorist suspects for interrogation in various countries), but whether true or not some mystery surrounds the movements of these aircraft.

Roy D. Reagan

A former USAF man based in Oregon, Roy Reagan established a network of contacts and became a successful broker of former US military aircraft on the open market. He and Fred Fuch, a former director of the Forest Service programme, are said to have held talks with the Department of Defense and General Services Administration officials in Washington DC and convinced them that any C-130s transferred would remain strictly under Forest Service control for forest and range-land firefighting duties. In 1987 Reagan and Hemet Valley Flying Services came up with the idea of doing a deal whereby surplus aircraft from the Davis-Monthan Park would be exchanged for outdated firefighting aircraft and the latter given to air museums around the country. A trio of Air Force Generals involved in the later discussions later testified that they didn't understand that the titles of the C-130s would leave Government control, or else they would not have approved of these exchanges.

Gary Eitel's contention is that the Hercules would be used to fight fires during the fire season, but used for clandestine operations during the off-season. Both the CIA and the Forestry Service deny such collusion, however, but a University of Georgia History Professor, William Leary, has claimed that from the 1950s the two agencies colluded in such covert activity in South East Asia and that they together set up Intermountain Aviation, which worked from the Pinal Air Park in Marana, until it was taken over by Evergreen in 1975.[10]

Republican Congressman Curt Weldon, of Pennsylvania, investigated the crash of one of these aircraft in Angola in which Robert Weldon, his nephew, was killed, and claimed that it was on a CIA mission at the time and that Reagan had sold the aircraft to Detrich Reinhardt (who had owned St Lucia Airlines) and Peter Turkelson in 1986, both of whom, so the Congressman claimed, had CIA connections.[11]

True or not, Mr Reagan certainly handled some much-travelled and brand-changing C-130A Hercules: ex-USAF 56-0487 (c/n 3095), ex-MASDC, Tucson, and registered as N6585H in January 1991, which went to T&G Aviation in January 1991; 56-0491 (c/n 3099) in October 1986, which went to World Wide Aeronautical Industries in 1986; 56-0496 (c/n 3104) and 56-507 (c/n 3115), both from Hawkins & Powers Aviation in May 1989, the first of which went to Aero Firefighting Services in December 1990, the second back to Hawkins & Powers; and 56-0537 (c/n 3145) as N537TM in August 1989, which went to Pacific Harbor Capital Inc in December 1990.

Red Dodge Aviation (RDA)

A subsidiary of Flying W, Red Dodge Aviation (after Captain 'Red' Dodge, a famous flyer) acquired two brand-new L-100-20s from their parent company in 1969. These were N7952S (c/n 4302) and N9237R (c/n 4303), both originally owned by the Girard Trust and leased to Flying W on

[9] See for example 'Below the radar: Secret flights to torture and "disappearance"', http://web.amnesty.org/library/Index/ENGAMR51052006?open&of=ENG-313.

[10] See William Leary, *Perilous Missions* (University of Alabama Press, 1984).

[11] See John Titus, 'Who's Who in the C-130 Scandal (an Update)', article in *Portland Free Press*, March/April 1997. Both Reagan and Fuch were convicted of conspiracy in April 1998, concerning twenty-two C-130s, and sentenced to terms of imprisonment by Judge William Browning. See David E. Hendrix, 'Whistleblower case takes aim at reputation of Forest Service', article in *The Press-Enterprise* (Riverside, California), 5 April 1998, and Tim Steller, 'Aircraft in scam may have flown for CIA', article in *The Arizona Daily Star*, 1 April 1998, and subsequent story in 2 April 1998 issue.

completion, where they became N30FW and N40FW respectively. The first was sold to Southern Air Transport in February 1973 and the latter to the Philippines Government.

Ruftberg

This Dallas, Texas, company obtained a single L-100-30, N8218J (c/n 5056), from Mega Trade in 1998.

Safair Freighters (Pty)

Formed in 1969 and based at Jan Smuts Airport, Johannesburg, Republic of South Africa, this company, a subsidiary of Safmarine and Rennies Holdings Ltd, has been the major Hercules user, with no fewer than twenty-one aircraft on lease, charter and haulage to a huge variety of companies. Its Hercules fleet has traditionally also been available as a military reserve unit should the need arise.

A solitary L-100-20 (c/n 4385) was leased from Safmarine (see below).

A fleet of seventeen L-100-30s was widely utilised with the following aircraft in service with the company at various dates from December 1972 onward. Many were leased out to other companies before being finally sold on. These 'stretched' civilian Herks were registrations ZS-RSB (c/n 4472); ZS-RSC (c/n 4475); ZS-RSD (c/n 4477); ZS-RSE (c/n 4558); ZS-RSF (c/n 4562); ZS-RSG (c/n 4565); ZS-RSH (c/n 4590); ZS-RSI (c/n 4600); ZS-RSJ (c/n 4606); ZS-JIV (c/n 4673); ZS-JVL (c/n 4676); ZS-JIW (c/n 4679); ZS-JIX (c/n 4684); ZS-JIY (c/n 4691); ZS-JIZ (c/n 4695); ZS-JJA (c/n 4698); and ZS-JVM (c/n 4701). One, ZS-RSI (c/n 4600), was leased to DHL at Luton in 1995 and worked to Boulogne.

Another L-100-30 was purchased in November 1978 and leased to SCIBE in Zaire as its 9Q-CBJ (c/n 4796).

Finally, two further L-100-30s were purchased from China Eastern Airlines in May 1999, ZS-OLG (c/n 5025) and ZS-JAG (c/n 5027), the former being leased to Lynden Air Cargo.

First registered in June 2008 was L-100-30 Oil Spill Response ZS-ORA (c/n 4208).

Safair, the South African-based company, operated a fleet of twenty-four Hercules air freighters. The one shown here in the company's service (formerly with Safmarine) is ZS-GSK (c/n 4385), named *Boland*, an early L-100-20. These were later superseded by the L-100-30 type. *Arthur Pearcy*

Of some interest are the almost identical company paint schemes on these L100-30s of Safair... *Safair via Audrey Pearcy*

... and Northwest Territorial. The latter is C-FXNF (c/n 4562), operating in the northern wastes of Canada at the same period. *Northwest Territorial via Audrey Pearcy*

Safair later repainted its Hercules fleet with a slightly different scheme, as seen here. *Safair via Audrey Pearcy*

A splendid in-flight view of a Safair L-100.
Safair via Audrey Pearcy

Maximum capacity load as a container is
eased into a Safair L-100's capacious hold.
Safair via Audrey Pearcy

Various types of cargo ingested by Safair's L-100 fleet down the years. *Safair via Audrey Pearcy*

Safair L-100-30 Oil Spill Response ZS-ORA (c/n 4208) at Sepang. *Courtesy of W. T. Liew*

Safair Freighter (USA)

This New Jersey-based subsidiary operated three Hercules L-100-30s purchased in late 1974/early 1975: registrations ZS-RSE (c/n 4558), which became N46965 and went to Globe Air in April 1987, crashing at Travis Air Force Base on the 8th of that month; ZS-RSG (c/n 4565), which became N250SF, was subsequently leased and re-leased, registered to Globe Air and sold and resold; and ZS-RSH (c/n 4590), which became N251SF, and was subsequently leased and operated by Saturn while registered to Globe Air before being sold and resold.

Safmarine

A single L-100-20 (c/n 4385) was delivered to this company in August 1970 and registered as ZS-GSK with the name *Boland*. She was immediately leased to Safair and was purchased by that company in February 1980.

St Lucia Airways

Owned by Detrich Reinhardt, in May 1984 this company purchased a single L-100-20 aircraft, J6-SLO (c/n 4129), which was named *Juicy Lucy* and was allegedly used on covert CIA missions to smuggle missiles into Iran by Oliver North during the embargo and also to supply ammunition and supplies to UNITA in Angola[12], before being sold to Tepper Aviation.

SATCO

This Peruvian based organisation operated two L-100-20s. The former *Fuerza Aéra Perunana* FAP 395 (c/n 4364) was leased by the company as its OB-R-1004 and FAP 396 (c/n 4450) as OB-R-956 in 1976, but both were lost in accidents, the former crashing at Tarapoto on 19 February 1978, the latter crash-landing at San Juan on 24 April 1981.

Saturn Airways (Trans-International)

Before becoming part of Trans-International (TIA), this company operated a large fleet of nineteen Hercules of varying types. Many of its early operations were LOGAIR daily freight-hauling runs to various air force bases in the CONTUS (Continental USA) area. One of the company's Hercules hauled out the earth station to Beijing, China, for use during the ground-breaking first visit of President Richard Nixon. Another was chartered by the Disney Corporation to fly camera crew and equipment to worldwide locations for Disneyworld movie sets.

[12] See John Titus, 'Who's Who in the C-130 Scandal (an Update)', article in *Portland Free Press*, March/April 1997.

Among the many diverse cargoes airlifted by the Herk was a complete oil-rig. The Chevron company rig was disassembled into 37,000lb units, then loaded into leased Transamerica Airlines L-100-30 Super Hercules N10ST (c/n 4383) *Rudolph*. One such unit is shown being loaded into the aircraft at Port Sudan on 8 October 1981, for shipment to the oil drill site deep in the Sudanese interior. *Lockheed-Georgia, Marietta, via Audrey Pearcy*

A Trans-International Airlines Super Hercules air freighter offloads a Rolls Royce RB.211 fanjet engine at the Lockheed-California company's Palmdale plant on 29 April 1977, following a flight from England. The Super Herk, stretched 15 feet longer than the regular L-100 Hercules, was able to haul three of the Jumbo jet engines at a time. Trans-International merged with Saturn Airways in late 1976 and operated twelve Lockheed Super Hercules air freighters, which was the largest fleet of L-100-30s in the USA at that time. A TIA Hercules became the first to top 30,000 flight hours. *Lockheed-Georgia Newsbureau via Audrey Pearcy*

N12ST takes off with three Rolls Royce RB.211 engines for the 6,000-mile flight to Georgia. *Lockheed-Georgia, Marietta, via Audrey Pearcy*

Saturn Airways L-100-30 N12ST (c/n 4388) loading a jet engine at night. *Lockheed-Georgia, Marietta, via Audrey Pearcy*

A Rolls Royce RB.211 jet engine being loaded into the same aircraft. *Lockheed-Georgia, Marietta, via Audrey Pearcy*

THE LOCKHEED MARTIN C-130 HERCULES

One L-100-20, registration N24ST (c/n 4101), was leased from NAL in June 1972 and was later modified to an L-100-30.

An L-100 (c/n 4134), registered as N16ST, was purchased from ASA in July 1971 and modified to an L-100-30 in April 1972.

An L-100-20, registration N19ST (c/n 4147), was purchased from Delta in September 1973, and was subsequently modified to an L-100-30 in March 1974. This aircraft, which had undergone two 'stretch' modifications since being first delivered to Delta in 1966 – to -20, then, with Saturn, to -30 – later achieved fame with TIA as the first of that type to achieve 30,000 hours' flying time. This milestone was reached during a LOGAIR/QUICKTRANS military charter supply route flight from Tinker AFB, Oklahoma, and Hill AFB, Denver, Colorado, with Captain Bill Thomas at the helm.

As the Transamerica Company, based in Oakland, California, it airfreighted oil-rig parts into the Guatemalan jungle for Texaco. In 1981 it undertook a similar operation when two Transamerica L-100-30s were leased to the Chevron Overseas Petroleum Company, to airlift an oil-rig in sections from Port Sudan to primitive airstrips at Adar, El Muglad and Malaka, in the Sudan, together with 200,000 US gallons (757,082.35 litres) of diesel and aviation fuel and rig support equipment, in less than thirty days flying around the clock. Five rotating aircrew were used, with each crew resting for 14 hours after each duty day at Khartoum.

A second L-100, registration N18ST (c/n 4208), was purchased from Alaska International Airlines in January 1973 and was modified to an L-100-30 in February 1972.

An L-100-20, registration N9248R (c/n 4221), was purchased from ASA in October 1970, but almost at once crashed at McGuire Air Force Base. Her sister, N13ST (c/n 4222), purchased at the same time, was later leased then sold to Alaska International Airlines.

A third, registration N14ST (c/n 4225), named *Bozo*, was later converted to an L-100-30.

An L-100-30, registration N37ST (c/n 4248), was leased from Transamerica in July 1987, then purchased outright in October. An L-100-20, registration N22ST (c/n 4250), was leased several times from National Aircraft Leasing, then finally purchased in September 1991; she was then leased out to various parties until she was mined and destroyed in the Sudan in September 1991 while working for the International Red Cross.

Four more L-100-20s were acquired by Saturn. One, N38ST (c/n 4300), was first leased from Markair, then purchased in October 1987. A second, N7951S (c/n 4301), was leased from Air America in November 1968 and sold outright in July 1970. She was returned, modified to an L-100-30, in September 1971 and sold outright to Saturn in January 1974, being registered as N23ST. The third, N7952S (c/n 4302), was purchased from the Girard Trust subsidiary Red Dodge Aviation (RDA) in February 1973. The fourth (c/n 4333) was leased from Lockheed in May 1970 and subsequently purchased outright in October 1972 as N17ST (*Wimpy*) and was subsequently modified to an L-100-30.

Two L100-20s (c/ns 4383 and 4384) were purchased in June 1970 and were registered as N10ST (*Rudolph*) and N11ST (*W. C. Fields*) respectively. Both were subsequently modified to L-100-30s in February 1971 and leased to Alaska International Airlines. They were followed by two L100-30s (c/ns 4388 and 4391) in December 1970 and June 1971, which received the civilian registrations N12ST (*Schnozz*) and N15ST (*Barney G.*). The latter was leased to Southern Air Transport and crashed at Kelly Air Force Base on 4 October 1986.

A further pair of L-100-30s, N20ST (c/n 4561) and N21ST (c/n 4586), were purchased in November and April 1974 respectively. They subsequently went to TIA in December 1976.

Saturn achieved early fame by carrying the largest ever shipment for the service-contracted LOGAIR system, a mean 50,058lb. It regularly shipped podded and crated Rolls-Royce RB.211-22B engines for the Lockheed L-1011 TriStar jet transport from Short Brothers & Harland's plant in Belfast, Northern Ireland, to Marietta.

Lockheed officials examine a cut-away model of the Saudi Arabian L-100-30HS Hospital Ship, which contained an operating theatre, medical supplies and equipment, patient monitoring equipment, beds and medical personnel facilities. *Lockheed-Georgia, Marietta, via Audrey Pearcy.*

Saudia

Fourteen Hercules aircraft have been operated by this company for the Saudi Government. Seven specially converted L-100-30s were purchased from Lockheed Aircraft Corporation in 1983: ex-N4253N, which became HZ-MS05 (c/n 4950) and was modified as a Hospital aircraft prior to delivery; ex-N425M, which became HZ-MS06 (c/n 4952) and was modified as a Dental Hospital aircraft prior to delivery; HZ-MS11 (c/n 4954), delivered as the personal VIP aircraft of Sheikh Ibrahim; ex-N4255M, which became HZ-MS09 (c/n 4956); N4261M, which became HZ-MS10 (c/n 4957); N4266M, which became HZ-MS14 (c/n 4960); and ex-N4243M, which became HZ-MS08 (c/n 4986); the latter five had also been converted to Hospital aircraft prior to delivery.

Another L-100-30, registration N15ST (c/n 4391), was leased from Saturn in March 1978.

Four C-130Hs were the former N4098M (c/n 4837), which was modified to a Surgical Hospital prior to delivery and became HZ-MS019; ex-N4185M (c/n 4915), purchased in September 1982, converted to a VC-130-H in 1995, and operated by the company as part of the Saudi Royal Flight; and the former N4240M (c/n 4918) and N4190M (c/n 4922), purchased in March and May 1982 respectively and converted to Hospital aircraft prior to delivery, becoming HZ-MS021 and HZ-MS07.

Two VC-130Hs were the former N4098M (c/n 4837), purchased from Lockheed in January 1980, which was modified as a Surgical Hospital aircraft prior to delivery and became HZ-MS019, and the former N4099M (c/n 4843), purchased from Lockheed Aircraft Corporation in July 1980, operated by the company as a VIP aircraft of the Saudi Royal Flight as HZ-HM05, then reregistered as HZ-114 in February 1981.

Of these special aircraft, HZ-MS05 and HZ-MS10 were later stripped of their medical equipment and converted back to orthodox L-100-30s.

Schreiner Airways

Based at Schipol, Netherlands, Schreiner of Leiden has operated six different leased Hercules L-100-30s: registrations PH-SHE (c/n 4895), leased from Gabon in 1989/90; N909SJ (c/n 4763), leased from Saturn in 1992/93; ZS-JVL (c/n 4676), leased from Safair in 1997; ZS-JIV (c/n 4673), leased from Safair in 1998; ZS-JIY (c/n 4691), also leased from Safair in 1998; and C-GHPW (c/n 4799), leased from Bradley Air Services in 1998.

SCIBE – *Society Commerciale*, Zaire

A single L-100-30, 9Q-CBJ (c/n 4796), was leased by this organisation from Safair in November 1978. Its itinerary included three flights to Bunia, Zaire, transporting 132,000lb (59,874.12kg) of equipment to construct a slaughterhouse. A flight to Gbadolite took 20 tons of cargo, including cars, spare parts and household appliances, returning with 16 tons of fresh produce.

SFAir

This French regional air carrier, based at Bordeaux, flew cargo missions throughout Europe and Africa beginning in April 1981. After the French civil aviation authority, *Direction Générale de l'Aviation Civile* (DGAC), issued a provisional certificate for the Hercules, an L-100-20, registration N4174M (c/n 4412), was leased from Lockheed between July 1983 and February 1984.

An L-100-30, ZS-RSI (c/n 4600), was leased from Safair in April 1981 and registered as F-WDAQ; a second, F-GFAS (c/n 4606), from L-100 Leasing, was operated for Africargo in the

Congo in 1987; and a third, ZS-JJA (c/n 4698), was also leased from Safair from May 1984. These aircraft were transferred to Jet Fret in 1988 before returning to their owners.

Shabair

This Zambian company operated a single C-130A Hercules, the *May Venturers* number 9J-AFV (c/n 3095), during the period 1995/96.

Snow Aviation International Inc

Based in Ohio, the company bought a single C-130A, N130SA (c/n 3035), from Aero Corp at Lake City, Florida, in 1995, which had allegedly been destined for modernisation for the Peruvian Navy, but which was never paid for. Under Snow Aviation's auspices this modernisation was carried out in 1995, and she was registered to PSCI Inc in 1997.

South African Airways (SAA)

Two further former Safair L-100-30s were leased to South African Airways from 1974, these being ZS-RSB (c/n 4472) and ZS-RSC (c/n 4475).

Southern Air Transport (SAT)

This company, based in Miami, Florida, operating between 1947 and 1998, became a high user with twenty-three Hercules passing through its hands down the decades. Their haulage record included electronics equipment, textile equipment, construction helicopters and jet engines; the company even used one Herky Bird to transport meat from Argentina to Chile, and airlifted oil-drilling equipment to Ecuador.

In March 1983 one L-100-30, N916SJ (c/n 4134), was leased from Saturn to commemorate the company's fiftieth anniversary, carrying the name *Southern Air Transport 50 Years 1947-1997* before being sold to Transafrik. Another, N9232R (c/n 4299), was converted to an L-100-30 in January 1974 after an early accident in February 1972.

An L-100-20, registration N7984S (c/n 4362), was purchased by Saturn in December 1969 and became N522SJ in November 1985.

L-100-20 382-E-18C Hercules N7984S (c/n 4362) was leased from Southern Air, based at Miami, Florida, for airborne relief. It is seen here ready to depart from Long Beach, California, on 4 July 1972, for airlift work in Bangladesh with a disassembled Lake Buccaneer (N5056L) and a Bell 47 (N66AR) embarked. *Nick Williams, AAHS*

Somalis unloading Southern Air Transport's Lockheed L-100-30. *Robert E. Dorr, via Nick Williams, AAHS*

An L-100-30, registration N106AK (c/n 4477), was purchased by Saturn in February 1992 and re-registered as N906SJ for leasing.

Purchased by Safair and registered as ZS-RSE (c/n 4558), this L-100-30 was later registered to Safair Freighters in the United States.

There were also several former Saturn/Safair-operated aircraft, including N19ST (c/n 4147), a former Saturn, TIA and Transamerica L-100 leased from July 1986 to 1992, which became N919ST; a former AIA, Saturn and Transamerica L-100-30 (c/n 4208) leased then bought in 1986/87, which became N918SJ; another former AIA, TIA and Transamerica L-100-30, operated by SAT as N37ST, then N907SJ (c/n 4248); an ex-Interior and Saturn L-100-20 leased by SAT in 1972 and 1977 as N22ST (c/n 4250); a trio of L-100-30s, all former Transamerica or Girard Trust aircraft leased by SAT from 1986, these being N908J (c/n 4300), N23ST (c/n 4301) and N30FW (c/n 4302); the former Transamerica N910SJ, re-registered as N910SJ from 1986 (c/n 4383); the ex-AIA, TIA and Transamerica N912J (c/n 4388); the ex-Transamerica and Heavylift L-100-30 N15ST (c/n 4391), which was lost during a night take-off from Kelly AFB in 1985; another L-100-30, the ex-Markair N905SJ (c/n 4472); N911SJ (c/n 4384); and the former Transamerica N920SJK (c/n 4561), N519SJ (c/n 4562), N250SF (c/n 4565), N921SJ (c/n 4586), N251SF (c/n 4590), and N108AK (c/n 4763) (see also the appropriate sections).

Despite the CIA being ordered to divest itself of its airline interests in 1976, covert operations into El Salvador, Nicaragua, Angola, Rwanda and other countries continued, including the famous Oliver North/Contra affair, blown wide open when, on 3 October 1986, a Southern Air Transport Fairchild C-123K Provider was shot down over Nicaragua.[13] On 10 March the remaining assets of SAT were taken over by Southern Air Inc. which began operating the following month.

Southern Cross Airways

Owned by Multitrade, this aircraft operator brought in a number of former RAAF Hercules for use by private firms. One of these aircraft, it was claimed, was involved in the Mena, Arkansas, CIA operation. Another (c/n 3215, allegedly tail-coded N69-P) was stated to have operated on Roy Reagan's certificate on contract for the US Nuclear Defense Agency and was allegedly busted by the DEA in Miami, Florida, on a cocaine-smuggling mission! This aircraft was sold to a US customs agent and flown to T&G Aviation to be refitted, then went on to work in Africa.

The California company certainly briefly operated a former RAAF C-130A, serial 57-0508/A97-215 (c/n 3215), in 1986 for Herc Airlift, which leased her from ITT Commercial Finance Corporation. She was later sold to African Air Transport, a Miami-registered company, in June 1988, which subsequently sold her to African Cargo, Miami, in January 1989. She was impounded at Naples, Florida, by US Customs and stored at Fort Lauderdale before being sold to F a Conno, Miami, in March 1995, and registered to Zotti Group Aviation, Miami, in May of that year.

Suarez, Peter

Another former RAAF C-130A, 57-0505/A97-212 (c/n 3212), was purchased by this Van Nuys, California, outfit from Fowler Aeronautical Services in July 1994 and re-registered as N130PS, ending up for sale by Kreuger Aviation Inc, California, from October 1996.

Sudan Airways

One C-130H of the Sudanese Air Force, 1100 (c/n 4766), was operated by the civilian arm, Sudan Airways, between 1983 and 1991 and registered initially as ST-AHR, then ST-AIF.

TAB *(Transporte Aereo Boliviano)*

A former RC-130A, reconverted to a standard C-130A, 57-0521 (c/n 3228), was purchased by the *Fuerza Aérea Boliviana* in October 1988 and became its TAM69. Painted white overall, she was operated by the company as CP-2184 until going into storage at La Paz in 1997.

Two C-130Hs, registrations TAM90 (c/n 4744) and TAM91 (c/n 4759), were purchased by the *Fuerza Aérea Boliviana* in July and October 1977 respectively and operated by TAB on its behalf. The former was lost in a night crash into the sea off Tacumen, Panama, on 28 September 1979; the other was leased to IAS/Transafrik for United Nations operations in Sudan and Angola, and was twice damaged in this risky work. She was finally returned to Bolivia in January 2000.

The Bolivian Government purchased a single L-100-30 from Lockheed in October 1979, the former N4083M (c/n 4833), for the *Fuerza Aérea Boliviana*, which became its TAM92 and was leased and operated for it by TAB as CP-1564. In 1988 this aircraft was sub-leased to Transafrik and was destroyed on 16 March 1991 by enemy action close to Malanje, Angola.

T&G Aviation (International Air Response)

With the late Jack Chisum as a Vice President, this 1968-established organisation was based in Chandler, Arizona, and obtained six former USAF C-130A Hercules for modification into firefighting water bombers: 54-1631 (c/n 3018) in October 1989, registered as N117TG; 56-0478 (c/n 3086) in October 1989, re-registered as N116TG; 56-0487 (c/n 3095), via Roy D. Reagan in January 1991 and re-registered as N120TG; 56-0537 (c/n 3145) via Pacific Harbor Capital in December 1990; 57-0512 (c/n 3219) in October 1989, re-registered as N118TG; and 57-0517 (c/n 3224) via Valley National Bank of Arizona in October 1990, already registered as N9539G before the company became International Air Response (IAR) in 1998.

[13] See Victor Marchetti and John D. Marks, *The CIA and the Cult of Intelligence* (Dell Publishing Company Inc, New York, NY, 1974) and Joanne Omang and George C. Wilson, 'Questions about Plane's Origins Grow', article in *The Washington Post*, Washington DC, 9 October 1986 issue, ppA-1 and A-32.

Woody Grantham purchased two of these C-130s from Roy Reagan for $US688,000 and had US State Department approval for their work. The other three C-130s were exchanged for two helicopters and two obsolete aircraft. Some T&G Forest Service Hercules were contracted for the Bechtel Corporation via MARTECH to haul oilfield equipment to the Gulf in the aftermath of the war,[14] but the aircraft were ordered to return to Marana, Arizona, according to some sources. Jack Chisum himself was subsequently knocked down and killed by a car in Arizona.

International Air Response, with Woody Grantham as its President, originally worked out of Chandler Memorial Airport 14 miles south-east of Phoenix. That field had been leased from the Gila River Indian Community, and was a Second World War auxilliary airfield with a 9,000-foot (2,743.2m) asphalt runway, but IAR more recently moved its operations to Coolidge. At least three of the original six C-130s – N116TG (c/n 3086), which crashed on 6 September 2000, N117TG (c/n 3018) and N118TG (3219) – were initially based at Coolidge during the winter months, moving out to locally sited airstrips according to the Wildfire threat pattern and in conjunction with the US Forest Service. In 2009, in addition to the IAR aircraft the following C-130 Air Tankers were identified as operational: TBMs N473TM (c/n 3081), N531BA (c/n 3139) and N466TM (c/n 3173), and Hawkins & Powers N131HP (c/n 3142) and N133HP (3189). However, in 2010 there were none listed on the Federal Contract Airtankers List.

TBM Inc

This company, founded in 1957 by Henry Moore, Doug Gandy, Harvey Miller, Bob Nunch, Milt Watts, Bob Phillips, Wayland Fink, Jim French and Elmer Johnson, originally based at Redmond, Oregon, and at Tulare, California, was named after the US Navy's Avenger torpedo bomber, in particular the variant built by General Motors during the war (the TBM), which was the company's first aircraft when purchased at a military surplus sale. TBM has been in the airtanker business since 1959 and has provided continuous state and federal airtanker services since that time as aerial firefighters. They cover the areas of Fresno and Ramona in California, Fort Smith and Fort Huachuca in Arkansas, Silver City in New Mexico, Minden in Nevada, West Yellowstone in Montana, and Pocatello in Idaho.

The company obtained four old former USAF C-130A Hercules: 54-1639 (c/n 3026) in 1990, which was unregistered and used for spare parts; 56-0473 (c/n 3081) in 1989, re-registered as N473TM; 57-0466 (c/n 3173) in 1989, re-registered as N466TM; and 57-0479 (c/n 3186) via US Forestry Service in 1991, re-registered as N479TM. Two Hercules are still currently flying.

Tepper Aviation

Based at Bob Sikes Airport, Crestview, Florida, this company had one L-100-20, used for operations in Angola, allegedly supplying arms to UNITA. This was the former St Lucia Airways J6-SLO (c/n 4129), which was purchased in 1988 and re-registered as N9205T, receiving the name *Grey Ghost*; it crashed at Jamba on 27 November 1989. Two L-100-30s were also leased for operations in Eastern Europe and for the US Government; they were registrations N2189 (c/n 4582), from Flight Cargo Leasing in 1990, which went to Rapid Air in 1995 and recently to JJS&D LLD; and N8183J (c/n 4796), from Rapid Air in 1989, and currently with Q2P LLD as N2679C.

Tepper C-130s were first linked to the CIA operations when they were claimed to be flying in arms to support UNITA against the Marxist Angolan Government during the 1980s, working from Kamina, Uganda, after St Lucia Airways dropped out of the scene. The head of Tepper during this period was one Pharies 'Bud' Petty, and he categorically denied that any Tepper aircraft went to Angola or Uganda, a denial that rather lost its sheen when Petty himself died when piloting the *Grey Ghost* N9205T (c/n 4129) laden with arms, guerrilla fighters and several European 'advisers' into Jamaba Airfield, Angola, on 29 November 1989.[15] Pharies's widow, Gracie T. Petty, was secretary and treasurer of Tepper, according to Ted Gup.

[14] See NewsHawk ® Inc, via David Hoffman, Haight Ashbury Free Press, 'C-130s Said Diverted From US Forest Service Duty by CIA', 31 October 1999.

[15] See 'Angolan CIA Hercules air crash kills Tepper Aviation chief', article in *Flight International*, 13 December 1989 issue, and Richard K Kolb, *Into the Heart of Darkness: Cold War Africa, Part Two: Angola*, http:web.archive.org/web/20000119063105/www.vfw.org/magazine/may99/38.shmtl.

In more recent times Tepper aircraft have been seen operating as far apart as Riga, Latvia, Barbados, Mojave Spaceport, Puerto Rica, Guam and the Philippines, as well as at the CIA training Camp Peary, near Galveston, Texas, and the Department of Energy's allegedly disused Desert Rock Airport, Nevada. These flights have been linked by some to the 'Extraordinary Rendition' traffic, although this strong speculation has not been demonstratively proven.

Time Aviation

Based in Sun Valley, California, this company had two ex-USAF aircraft, C-130A ex-57-0517 (c/n 3224) in 1981, registered as N9539G, and DC-130A 57-0523 (c/n 3230), registered as N9539Q. Both went to Gary R. Larkins the following year.

Transafrik

Working out of São Tomé and Principe, this African company has used twenty-five Hercules, both purchased and leased, over the years.

A single C-130H, registration TAM69 (c/n 4759), was leased from *Fuerza Aérea Boliviana* in 1987 for UN operations in Sudan and Angola, and was damaged by UNITA action and later by an accident at Mongu Airport, before being returned to the FAB in January 2000.

Seven L-100-20s have been used, including registrations S9-CAW (c/n 4300), operated by Transafrik for TWL Ltd, Mauritius, from 1998; S9-CAV (c/n 4301), bought from Saturn in 1998; S9-NAI (c/n 4303), bought from American Aircraft Corporation, Florida, in 1988, but finally brought down by UNITA action at Luanda Airport on 9 April 1989 and written off; and S9-NAL (c/n 4385), bought from Safair in 1989, and used by the United Nations in Africa.

Two more, registrations N522SJ (c/n 4362) and N910SJ (c/n 4383), were bought from Saturn in 1999, while registration N901SJ (c/n 4299) was also bought in 1999 from Commercial Air Leasing, but immediately resold to First Security Bank.

No fewer than fifteen L-100-30s have been employed, including registrations N916SJ (c/n 4134), S9-CAX (c/n 4248), S9-BOQ (c/n 4388), N905SJ (c/n 4472), S9-BOP (c/n 4477), and S9-CAO (c/n 4561), all bought from Saturn in 1998/99. Two of these have been lost to date, S9-CAO (c/n 4561), destroyed by UNITA action on 26 December 1998, and S9-BOP (c/n 4477), written off in an accident at Luzamba, Angola, on 27 December 1999.

Three others were purchased, registrations S9-CAI (c/n 4562), bought from Derco in 1998; S9-CAJ (c/n 4565), bought from Globe Air in 1999; and N921SJ (c/n 4586), bought from Hamilton Aviation, Tucson, in 1999.

Seven more L-100-30s have been leased down the years: CP-1564 (c/n 4833), leased from *Fuerza Aérea Boliviana* in 1988, but shot down by UNITA forces at Malanje on 16 March 1991; D2-EHD (c/n 4839), owned by ENDUAMA but flown by Transafrik, damaged by UNITA action several times before finally being shot down by a SAM missile while in cruise at FL170, 32km from Malanje, on 16 March 1991, with the loss of all three crew members and six passengers; S9-CAY (c/n 4208), operated by Transafrik for TWL, Mauritius, from 1998; S9-NAD (c/n 4475), leased from Safair for United Nations work in Cambodia in 1992, and returned in 1993; S9-NAJ (c/n 4606), leased from Safair in 1989 and damaged in a mid-air collision on 30 January 1990, but continuing to work for the United Nations worldwide and returned to Safair in 1992; ZS-JIV (c/n 4673), leased from Safair in 1993; and S9-NAT (c/n 4695), leased from Safair in 1991/93.

Trans-Latin Air (TLA)

Based in Panama, it used one former USAF C-130A, 57-0517 (c/n 3224), from Valley National Bank of Arizona and the Marana Air Park; she was reregistered as HP1162TLN in 1990, but went to T&G in 1992.

Trans-Mediterranean Airways (TMA)

A solitary L-100, the ex-Lockheed N9269R (c/n 4197), was leased in 1967 but crashed at Cayaya, Peru, on 16 July 1969.

T3D&H LLC

This limited liability company operates from Suite 1000 at 824 Market Street, Wilmington, Delaware, and owns an alleged CIA 'Spook' aircraft operated by Tepper Aviation and working out of Bob Sikes Airport (KCEW) and Montgomery regional airports, including parachute drops over Blackstone AFB. This aircraft, N3867X (c/n 4684), is an L-100-30 built in 1976 for Safair, and has been run by a whole variety of operators including Angola Air Charter, Heavylift, European Air Transport and Earl.

Uganda Airlines

This Kampala-based company registered a single L-100-30, N108AK (c/n 4610), purchased from Page Airways in August 1975 and becoming UA's 5X-UCF. She worked for Uganda Air Cargo, carried the name *The Silver Lady*, and had a host of misadventures, including fire damage and being impounded twice, before finally being sold to AviSto of Switzerland for Medecair.

United African Airlines

This Libyan company used several Hercules aircraft. An ex-Philippines Government L-100-20, registration PI-99 (c/n 4302), was purchased in 1982 and re-registered as 5A-DJR, and a former Cargolux L-100-20, LX-GCV (c/n 4355), was leased in 1981 and re-registered as 5A-DHJ (later 5A-DHI0).

A Lockheed L-100-30, registration N501AK (c/n 4798), which had been originally purchased from Alaska International Air by United Trade International in 1979 but was impounded at Tripoli in October of that year, was leased in January 1980. Also the two L-100-30s, registrations 5A-DOM (c/n 4992) and TY-BBU (c/n 5000), which beat the blockade, were claimed to be registered with the company before they were transferred to Jamahiriya Air.

United Trade International (UTI)

A former Alaska International Air L-100-30, registration N501AK (c/n 4798), was purchased in 1979 but impounded at Tripoli that October and later went to United Arab Airlines (see the appropriate section).

Unitrans

Dieter Reinhardt briefly utilised a TAAG C-130A, N9724V (c/n 3099).

Vansco Air Freight

In September 1991 Vansco Air Freight, registered in Côte d'Ivorie (Ivory Coast) as a 'Freight & Forwarding' company, obtained a former Safair L-100-30 built in 1976 and originally registered as ZS-JJA (c/n 4698); she was re-registered as TU-TNV. Vansco became implicated in UN sanctions-busting flights to aid the rebel UNITA forces in Angola. Arms, equipment, fuel and commodities were allegedly flown in from Eastern European suppliers via air bases in various Africa nations despite the international arms embargo. It was claimed in a UN Report that John Marques Kakumba, a UNITA spokesman, was the sole owner of Vansco at one time[16], while the leader of UNITA, Jonas Savimbi, was himself alleged to be the owner, or a major shareholder, in several airline companies, of which Vansco was allegedly one. Southern Air Transport aircraft leased from a Texas company and operated by St Lucia Airways were also rumoured to have been involved, according to the same UN Report.

However, whether involved or not in such trafficking, which was widespread at the time[17], by 1992 c/n 4698 was registered once more with Safair.

---

[16] See Robert R. Fowler, Chairman, Security Council, 'Report of the Panel of Experts established by the Security Council pursuant to Resolution 1237, on violations of Security Council Sanctions against UNITA' ('The Fowler Report'), S/2000/203, paragraph 143 (Vansco Air Freight), dated 10 March 2000.

[17] See John Peleman, *The Logistics of Sanction Busting: The Airborne Component*.

VOAR Linhas

This Angolan freight line briefly leased two, and maybe three, 1972/76-build former Safair L-100-30s in 1996 – the former ZS-RSC (c/n 4475), ZS-JIX (c/n 4684) and ZS-JJA (c/n 4698) – although the latter is not confirmed.

Von Hoff

In 1993 this company briefly leased one, and possibly two, 1976-build former Safair L-100-30s in Angola, these being the former ZS-JIY (c/n 4691) and possibly the former ZS-JIX (c/n 4684).

Wirtschaftsflug

This company, based in Frankfurt, Germany, purchased a former L-100-30 demonstrator from Lockheed in October 1981, registered her as D-ACWF (c/n 4839), and used her on charter flights throughout Europe, the Middle East and Africa. She returned to Lockheed in November 1983.

Worldways

The Echo Bay Mines L-100-20, CF-DSX (c/n 4303), was utilised by this Canadian company in 1983, when she was named *Bob Beaton*.

World Wide Aeronautical Industries

This company, based at Ashland, Oregon, was among the many that handled the former USAF/USN C-130A, 56-0491/158229 (c/n 3099), obtaining her from Roy D. Reagan in December 1986 and transferring her to Bob's Air Park at Tucson the following year.

Worldwide Trading

Based at Delroy Beach, Florida, this company had a single ex-Lockheed L-100-30, N4281M (c/n 5032), which was reregistered as N898QR in April 1989 and went to Investment Capital Xchange in 1997.

Yemenia

Yemen Airways, based at Sanaa, has operated two C-130H Hercules, given to it by Saudi Arabia in 1979, these being 7O-ADE (c/n 4825) and 7O-ADD (c/n 4827).

Zaire Air Services

This company leased two Hercules from the all-embracing Safair in 1988, these being an L-100-30, 9Q-CZA (c/n 4606) in 1982, which was damaged in a ground collision, and an L-100-20, ZS-GSK (c/n 4385), re-registered as 9Q-CHZ in 1988.

Zaire Cargo

Leased by this company from Safair in 1985 were three L-100-30s: registrations ZS-RSC (c/n 4475) in 1985, re-registered as 9Q-CZS; ZS-RSJ (c/n 4606) in 1982, re-registered as 9Q-CZA; and ZS-JIY (c/n 4691) in 1983/84, re-registered as 9Q-CZS.

Zambian Air Cargoes

Purchased in April 1996 was an L-100-20, registration 9J-RBW (c/n 4129) and named *Alexander*, which was sold to Maple Leaf Leasing in 1969. A single L-100, which was also purchased in April 1966, 9J-RBX (c/n 4137), was named *Ajax*, but was lost in a ground collision at N'dola on 11 April 1968.

This company also used three more L-100s – registrations 9J-RCV (c/n 4101), 9J-RCY (c/n 4109) and 9J-REZ (c/n 4209) – which it leased from the Government of Zambia (GRZ) in August 1966 and April 1967 (see the appropriate section).

An aerial view of Zambian Air Cargo L-100-20 9J-RCY (c/n 4109). *Lockheed-Georgia, Marietta, via Audrey Pearcy*

Zantop International

This organisation leased a solitary former Alaska International Airlines L-100-30, registration N106AK (c/n 4477), from Markair in April 1986 to March 1991.

Zimex Aviation

Two more much-traded former Safair L-100-30s saw brief service with this company, based in Zurich, Switzerland, which mainly operates as aerial support for oil and engineering concerns, but also operates aircraft on behalf of the Red Cross when required. The two machines were HB-ILG (c/n 4698) in 1988 and HB-ILF (c/n 4701) in Angola in 1987, the latter being shot down by UNITA while taking off from Cuito Airport on 14 October 1987.

Michael Zincka Leasing

Michael Zincka Leasing had two firefighting C-130As on its books in 1989, the former Hemet Valley Aviation N131NF (c/n 3138) and N136FF (c/n 3148). They were later registered to Aero Firefighting Services, which leased them back to Hemet; Hemet sub-leased them to the French Government agency, *Securité Civile,* for two years.

Zotti Group Aviation

After being purchased from the US Customs pound at Fort Lauderdale, Florida, by F. A. Conner of Miami, the much-travelled C-130A, N4469P (c/n 3215), was registered to this organisation in May 1995, and broken up there over the next two years.

Appendix 1

Model summary

Model	First delivered	Delivery ceased
C-130A	1956	1959
C-130B	1959	1963
C-130E	1962	1974
C-130H	1964	1998
C-130H2	1978	1992
C-130H3	1992	1997
C-130J	1996	-
L-100	1964	1968
L-100-20	1968	1981
L-100-30	1970	1998
C-130H-30	1980	1997

Appendix 2

Model list

Model	Applied to	From c/n	Initial customer
82	YC-130	1001	US Air Force
182-1A	C-130A, C-130D	3001	US Air Force
182-2A	RC-130A	3217	US Air Force
282-11B	C-130B	3724	South African Air Force
282-1B	C-130B, HC-130B	3501	US Air Force
282-2B	HC-130B	3594	US Coast Guard
282-3B	KC-130F	3554	US Marine Corps
282B-3B	C-130, KC-130F	3554	US Marine Corps
282-4B	C-130E	3651	US Air Force

An aerial head-on view of USAF C-130E Model 282-4B 61-2359 (c/n 3651), a 'Weatherbird', on 26 November 1962. *Lockheed-Georgia, Marietta via Audrey Pearcy*

Model	Applied to	From c/n	Initial customer
282-7B	C-130B	3546	Indonesian Air Force
282C-6B	LC-130F	3562	US Navy
382-12B	HC-130H, HC130P	4036	US Air Force
382-13B	C-130E	4011	Turkish Air Force
382-14B	C-130H	4052	Royal New Zealand Air Force
382-15B	C-130E	4020	Royal Canadian Air Force
382-16B	C-130E	4091	Brazilian Air Force
382-17B	L-100	3946	Lockheed Aircraft Corporation
382-19B	C-130K	4169	Royal Air Force
382-20B	HC-130N	4363	US Air Force
382-4B	C-130E	3609	US Air Force
382-4B	EC-130E	4158	US Coast Guard
382-5E	C-130H	4900	US Air National Guard
382-8B	C-130E	3779	US Air Force
382B-10C	L-100	4221	Aircraft International Incorporated
382B-14C	L-100	4234	Lockheed Aircraft Corporation
382B-1C	L-100	4101	Continental Air Services
382B-2C	L-100	4129	Zambian Air Cargoes
382B-3C	L-100	4134	Lockheed Aircraft Corporation
382B-4C	L-100	4144	Pakistan International Airlines
382B-5C	L-100	4146	International Aerodyne
382B-6C	L-100	4147	Delta Airlines
382B-7C	L-100	4208	Alaska Airlines
382B-8C	L-100	4197	Lockheed Aircraft Corporation
382B-9C	L-100	4209	Zambian Government
382C-01F	MC-130H	5236	US Air Force
382C-02F	C-130H	5213	Japanese Air Force
382C-03F	C-130H	5137	Venezuelan Air Force
382C-04F	C-130H	5141	Chad Government
382C-05F	MC-130H	5265	US Air Force
382C-06F	C-130H	5179	Republic of Korea
382C-07F	C-130H	5215	Taiwan
382C-10D	C-130E	4294	Imperial Iranian Air Force
382C-11D	C-130E	4304	Royal Saudi Air Force
382C-11E	C-130H	4875	Royal Moroccan Air Force
382C-11F	KC-130T	5219	US Marine Corps
382C-12D	C-130E	4308	Argentine Air Force
382C-12E	KC-130H	4907	Royal Moroccan Air Force
382C-13D	C-130H	4312	Royal New Zealand Air Force
382C-13E	C-130H	4878	Sultanate of Oman
382C-13F	C-130H-30	5224	Algerian Air Force
382C-14D	C-130H	4334	Royal Norwegian Air Force
382C-14E	C-30H	4879	Abu Dhabi
382C-14F	C-130H	5238	US Air Force Reserve
382C-15D	C-130E	4314	US Air Force
382C-15D	C-130E	4404	US Air Force
382C-15E	C-130H	4890	Indonesian Air Force
382C-15F	C-130H	5209	Royal Thai Air Force

Model	Applied to	From c/n	Initial customer
382C-17D	C-130E	4365	Imperial Iranian Air Force
382C-17D	C-130E, C-130H	4386	Greek Air Force
382C-17F	C-130H-30	5208	Royal Thai Air Force
382C-18D	C-130H	4366	Libyan Republic Air Force
382C-18E	C-130H	4939	US Air Force Reserve
382C-18F	KC-130T-30	5260	US Marine Corps
382C-19D	C-130H	4396	Royal Saudi Air Force
382C-19E	C-130H	4916	Sultanate of Oman
382C-19F	AC-130U	5256	US Air Force
382C-1D	C-130	4115	Imperial Iranian Air Force
382C-1E	C-130H	4861	Royal Thai Air Force
382C-20D	C-130H	4406	Venezuelan Air Force
382C-21D	C-130H	4411	Government of Zaire
382C-21F	C-130T	5255	US Naval Reserve
382C-22D	C-130H	4441	Italian Air Force
382C-22E	HC-130H-7	4931	US Coast Guard
382C-22F	C-130H	5278	US Air National Guard

A dedication ceremony at the main hangar base of the Kentucky Air National Guard, celebrating the first flight of C-130H Model 382C-22F 91-1231 (c/n 5278) for the ANG, and marking the fact that she was the 2,000th production aircraft. She was also the first to mount the SATIN missile detector with chaff and flare dispersal inbuilt. *Robert F. Dorr, via Nick Williams, AAHS*

382C-23D	C-130H	4436	Argentine Air Force
382C-24D	C-130H	4430	Israeli Defence Forces
382C-24E	C-130H	4936	Egyptian Air Force
382C-24F	HC-130H(N)	5294	US Air National Guard
382C-25D	C-130H	4456	Imperial Iranian Air Force

Model	Applied to	From c/n	Initial customer
382C-25E	C-130H	4911	Algerian Air Force
382C-26E	C-130H	4915	Saudi Arabian Government
382C-26F	C-130H	5175	Canadian Armed Forces
382C-27C	L-100-20	4450	Portuguese Air Force
382C-27D	HC-130H	4507	US Coast Guard
382C-27D	HC-130H	4528	US Coast Guard
382C-27E	C-130H	4976	Japanese Air Force
382C-27F	C-130H-30	5211	Saudi Arabian Government
382C-28D	LC-130R	4508	US Navy
382C-28E	C-130H	4920	Royal Jordanian Air Force
382C-28P	C-130H	4458	Safair
382C-29D	KC-130H	4503	Lockheed Aircraft Corporation
382C-29E	KC-130H	4940	Singapore Air Force
382C-29F	C-130H	5234	Saudi Arabian Government
382C-2D	C-130E	4159	Royal Australian Air Force
382C-2E	C-130H	4842	Singapore Air Force
382C-30D	C-130H	4515	Lockheed Aircraft Corporation
382C-30F	C-130H	5253	Saudi Arabian Government
382C-31D	C-130E	4519	US Air Force
382C-31F	C-130T	5298	US Naval Reserve
382C-31F	C-130T	5304	US Naval Reserve
382C-32D	EC-130Q	4595	US Navy
382C-32E	C-130H	4918	Saudi Arabian Government
382C-32F	KC-130T	5302	US Marine Corps
382C-33D	C-130H	4542	US Air Force
382C-33E	C-130H	4948	Sultanate of Oman
382C-33F	C-130H	5310	US Air National Guard
382C-33F	C-130H	5321	US Air Force
382C-34C	L-100-30	4610	Government of Uganda
382C-34D	C-130H	4530	Israeli Defence Forces
382C-34E	KC-130T	4974	US Marine Corps
382C-35D	C-130H	4535	Royal Moroccan Air Force
382C-35E	C-130H	4968	US Air National Guard
382C-35F	C-130H	5312	US Air Force Reserve
382C-36D	C-130H	4588	Government of Zaire
382C-36F	C-130T	5341	US Naval Reserve
382C-37C	L-100-20	4706	Peruvian Air Force
382C-37D	C-130H	4591	Imperial Iranian Air Force
382C-37E	HC-130H-7	4947	US Coast Guard
382C-37F	C-130H	5272	Royal Thai Air Force
382C-38D	C-130H	4572	Royal Danish Air Force
382C-39D	C-130H	4552	Royal Saudi Air Force
382C-39F	KC-130T	5339	US Marine Corps
382C-3D	C-130	4128	Royal Saudi Air Force
382C-40D	C-130H	4580	Abu Dhabi Air Force
382C-40F	AC-130U	5279	US Air Force
382C-41D	C-130H	4579	US Air Force
382C-42D	C-130H	4556	Venezuelan Air Force
382C-42E	C-130H	4964	Colombian Air Force

Model	Applied to	From c/n	Initial customer
382C-42F	C-130H	5360	US Air National Guard
382C-43D	KC-130R	4615	US Marine Corps
382C-43F	C-130H	5380	US Air Force Reserve
382C-44E	C-130H	5015	Japanese Air Force
382C-45D	C-130H	4570	Brazilian Air Force
382C-46D	C-130H	4605	Royal Saudi Air Force
382C-46E	C-130H	5008	US Air National Guard
382C-47D	KC-130H	4625	Brazilian Air Force
382C-47E	LC-130H	5007	US Air National Guard
382C-47F	LC-130H	5402	US Air National Guard
382C-48D	C-130H	4576	Argentine Air Force
382C-48E	KC-130T	5009	US Marine Corps
382C-49D	C-130H	4619	Nigerian Air Force
382C-49E	MC-130H	5004	US Air Force
382C-4D	EC-130Q	4239	US Navy
382C-4E	VC-130H	4843	Royal Saudi Air Force
382C-50E	HC-130H-7	4993	US Coast Guard
382C-50E	C-130H	5058	Taiwan
382C-51D	C-130H	4553	Canadian Armed Forces
382C-51F	KC-130T	5385	US Marine Corps
382C-52D	C-130H	4653	Israeli Defence Forces
382C-52F	C-130T	5383	US Naval Reserve
382C-53D	KC-130H	4660	Israeli Defence Forces
382C-53F	C-130H	5389	US Air Force Reserve
382C-54D	C-130H	4622	Greek Air Force
382C-54E	C-130H	4983	Abu Dhabi Air Force
382C-54F	C-130H	5271	Taiwan
382C-55D	KC-130H	4642	Spanish Air Force
382C-55E	C-130H-30	4986	Saudia Arabian Government
382C-55F	C-130T	5404	US Naval Reserve
382C-56D	C-130H	4628	Royal Swedish Air Force
382C-56F	KC-130T	5411	US Marine Corps
382C-57D	C-130H	4656	Malaysian Government
382C-57E	HC-130H-7	5028	US Coast Guard
382C-57F	C-130H	5417	US Air National Guard
382C-58D	KC-130R	4702	US Marine Corps
382C-58E	KC-130T	5040	US Marine Corps
382C-59D	C-130H	4716	Greek Air Force
382C-59E	MC-130H	5041	US Air Force
382C-59F	C-130T	5429	US Naval Reserve
382C-5D	C-130E	4202	Brazilian Air Force
382C-60D	C-130H	4737	Royal Saudi Air Force
382C-60E	C-130H	5038	US Air Force Reserve
382C-60F	C-130H	5435	Japanese Air Force
382C-61D	KC-130H	4750	Royal Saudi Air Force
382C-61E	HC-130H-7	5031	US Coast Guard
382C-61F	C-130H	5318	Taiwan
382C-62F	C-130H	5358	Taiwan
382C-63D	C-130H	4704	Philippines Air Force

Model	Applied to	From c/n	Initial customer
382C-63E	C-130H	4994	Canadian Armed Forces
382C-64D	C-130H	4707	Egyptian Air Force
382C-65D	LC-130R	4725	National Science Foundation
382C-65E	C-130H	5020	Tunisian Air Force
382C-66D	C-130H	4736	Government of Zaire
382C-66E	C-130H	5070	Singapore Air Force
382C-67D	C-130H	4713	Royal Moroccan Air Force
382C-68D	KC-130R	4768	US Marine Corps
382C-68E	C-130H	5088	Japanese Air Force
382C-6D	C-130E	4276	Imperial Iranian Air Force
382C-69D	C-130H	4747	Cameroon Air Force
382C-70D	HC-130H	4757	US Coast Guard
382C-70E	KC-130T	5085	US Marine Corps
382C-71D	C-130H	4780	Royal Australian Air Force
382C-71E	C-130H	5071	US Air National Guard
382C-72D	C-130H	4744	Bolivian Air Force
382C-73D	C-130H	4749	Portuguese Air Force
382C-73E	MC-130H	5026	US Air Force
382C-74D	C-130H	4743	Ecuador Air Force
382C-74E	C-130H	5093	US Air National Guard
382C-75D	EC-130Q	4781	US Navy
382C-75E	C-130H	5108	Japanese Air Force
382C-76D	C-130H	4768	Sudanese Government
382C-76E	HC-130H-7	5023	US Coast Guard
382C-77D	C-130H	4761	Philippines Air Force
382C-77E	MC-130H	5091	US Air Force
382C-78D	C-130H	4772	Portuguese Air Force
382C-79D	C-130H	4765	Government of Gabon
382C-79E	HC-130H-7	5106	US Coast Guard
382C-7D	C-130E	4285	Canadian Armed Forces
382C-80D	C-130H	4815	US Air National Guard
382C-80E	C-130H	4990	Brazilian Air Force
382C-81D	C-130H	4792	Ecuador Air Force
382C-81E	C-130H	5122	US Air Force Reserve
382C-82D	KC-130H	4814	Argentine Air Force
382C-82E	C-130H	5138	Japanese Air Force
382C-83D	C-130H	4779	Royal Jordanian Air Force
382C-83E	KC-130T	5143	US Marine Corps
382C-84D	C-130H	4801	Venezuelan Air Force
382C-84E	HC-130H-7	5121	US Coast Guard
382C-85D	EC-130Q	4867	US Navy
382C-85E	C-130H	4998	Brazilian Air Force
382C-86D	C-130H	4825	Northern Yemeni Government
382C-86E	AC-130U	5139	US Air Force
382C-87D	C-130H	4812	Ecuador Air Force
382C-87E	MC-130H	5130	US Air Force
382C-88D	C-130H	4852	US Air National Guard
382C-88E	C-130H	5151	US Air Force Reserve
382C-89D	C-130H	4813	Royal Jordanian Air Force

Model	Applied to	From c/n	Initial customer
382C-89E	MC-130H	5173	US Air Force
382C-8D	C-130E	4287	Brazilian Air Force
382C-8E	C-130H	4881	Royal Swedish Air Force
382C-90D	C-130H	4829	Government of Niger
382C-90E	C-130H	5170	Japanese Air Force
382C-92D	C-130H	4835	Spanish Air Force
382C-93D	C-130H	4837	Saudi Arabia
382C-92E	C-130H	5114	French Air Force
382C-93E	C-130H-30	5146	Royal Thai Air Force
382C-94D	C-130H	4838	Indonesian Air Force
382C-95D	C-130H	4841	Spanish Air Force
382C-95E	KC-130T	5174	US Marine Corps
382C-96D	KC-130H	4872	Royal Saudi Air Force
382C-96E	C-130H	5188	US Air National Guard
382C-97D	C-130H-MP	4847	Malaysian Government
382C-97E	AC-130U	5228	US Air Force
382C-98D	KC-130H	4871	Spanish Air Force
382C-98E	HC-130(N)	5202	US Air National Guard
382C-9D	LC-130R	4305	US Navy
382C-9E	C-130-MP	4898	Indonesian Air Force
382E-11C	L-100-20	4299	Lockheed Aircraft Corporation
382E-13C	L-100-20	4300	First National Bank of Chicago
382E-15C	L-100-20	4302	Flying W Airways
382E-16C	L-100-20	4412	Government of Kuwait
382E-18C	L-100-20	4350	Lockheed Aircraft Corporation
382E-20C	L-100-20	4362	Lockheed Aircraft Corporation
382E-19C	L-100-20	4355	Lockheed Aircraft Corporation
382E-21C	L-100-20	4333	Lockheed Aircraft Corporation
382E-22C	L-100-20	4383	Saturn Airways
382E-25C	L-100-20	4385	Safair
382E-26C	L-100-20	4358	Lockheed Aircraft Corporation
382E-29C	L-100-20	4512	Lockheed Aircraft Corporation
382E-33C	L-100-20	4593	Philippines Government
382E-44C	L-100-20	4830	Government of Angola
382E-47C	L-100-20	4850	Government of Peru
382G-23C	L-100-30	4388	Lockheed Aircraft Corporation
382G-28C	L-100-30	4472	Safair
382G-30C	L-100-30	4582	Government of Gabon
382G-31C	L-100-30	4558	Safair
382G-32C	L-100-30	4561	Saturn Airways
382G-35C	L-100-30	4673	Safair
382G-38C	L-100-30	4763	Alaska International Airways
382G-39C	L-100-30	4796	SCIBE Zaire
382G-40C	L-100-30	4798	Alaska International Airways
382G-41C	L-100-30	4800	Indonesian Air Force
382G-42C	L-100-30	4799	Pacific Western Airlines
382G-43C	L-100-30	4824	Pelita Air Services
382G-45C	L-100-30	4833	Bolivian Air Force
382G-46C	L-100-30	4839	Lockheed Aircraft Corporation

Model	Applied to	From c/n	Initial customer
382G-48C	L-100-20	4851	Petroleole Mexicanos
382G-50C	L-100-30	4834	Government of Dubai
382G-51C	L-100-30	4880	Air Algerie
382G-52C	L-100-30	4889	Pelita Air Services
382G-53C	L-100-30	4891	Argentine Air Force
382G-54C	L-100-30	4893	Ecuador Air Force
382G-57C	L-100-30	4917	Pelita Air Services
382G-58C	L-100-30	4895	Government of Gabon
382G-59C	L-100-30	4949	Government of Kuwait
382G-60C	L-100-30	4950	Saudi Arabian Government
382G-61C	L-100-30	4956	Saudi Arabian Government
382G-62C	L-100-30	4992	Alliance Funding International
382G-63C	L-100-30	4954	Saudi Arabian Government
382G-64C	L-100-30	5000	Alliance Funding International
382G-65C	L-100-30	5024	Government of Gabon
382G-67C	L-100-30	5022	Ethiopian Airlines
382G-68C	L-100-30	5048	Advanced Leasing Corporation
382G-69C	L-100-30	5025	China Air Cargo
382G-70C	L-100-30	5225	Frameair
382G-71C	L-100-30	5307	Frameair
382G-71C	L-100-30	5320	Canadian Armed Forces
382G-72C	L-100-30	5306	Ethiopian Airlines
382T-09F	C-130H-30	5184	Government of Chad
382T-10F	C-130H-30	5187	Egyptian Government
382T-16E	C-130H-30	4894	Algerian Air Force
382T-20E	C-130H-30	4933	Cameroon Air Force
382T-20F	C-130H-30	5226	French Air Force
382T-21E	C-130H-30	4925	Indonesian Air Force
382T-25F	C-130H-30	5264	Portuguese Air Force
382T-28F	C-130H-30	5268	Government of Malaysia
382T-30E	C-130H-30	4919	Algerian Air Force
382T-34F	C130H-30	5277	Government of Malaysia
382T-38E	C-130H-30	4959	Royal Thai Air Force
382T-38F	C-130H-30	5280	Royal Thai Air Force
382T-39E	C-130H-30	4961	Government of Dubai
382T-3E	C-130H	4864	Indonesian Air Force
382T-40E	C-130H-30	4962	Nigerian Air Force
382T-41E	C-130H-30	5001	Nigerian Air Force
382T-44F	C-130H-30	5309	Government of Malaysia
382T-45E	C-130H-30	4987	Algerian Air Force
382T-50F	C-130H-30	5273	Royal Netherlands Air Force
382T-51E	C-130H-30	5006	Republic of Korea
382T-52E	C-130H-30	5003	Spanish Air Force
382T-56E	C-130H-30	4997	Algerian Air Force
382T-62E	C-130H-30	5030	Republic of Korea
382T-91E	C-130H-30	5140	French Air Force
382T-94E	C-130H-30	5150	French Air Force
382U	C-130J-30	5523	Lockheed Aircraft Corporation
382U-04J	WC-130J	5451	US Air Force Reserve

Model	Applied to	From c/n	Initial customer
382U-06J	C-130J-30	5478	Royal Air Force
382U-07J	WC-130J	5473	US Air Force Reserve
382U-08J	C-130J-30	5469	US Air National Guard
382U-09J	EC-130J	5477	US Air National Guard
382U-11J	KC-130J	5488	US Marine Corps
382U-12J	WC-130J	5486	US Air Force Reserve
382U-13J	C-130J-30	5495	Italian Air Force
382U-16J	C-130J-30	5491	US Air National Guard
382U-17J	EC-130J	5490	US Air National Guard
382U-31J	C-130J-30	5520	Italian Air Force
382U-32J	EC-130J	5522	US Air National Guard
382U-33J	KC-130J	5515	US Marine Corps
382U-35J	HC-130J	5524	US Coast Guard
382U-38J	JC130J	527	US Marine Corps
382U-48F	C-130J-30	5413	US Air Force Reserve
382U-72J	KC130J	5644	US Marine Corps
382U-73J	HC/MC-130J	5633	Air Force Special Operations Command (AFSOC)
382V-01J	C-130J-30	5443	Royal Air Force
382V-03J	C-130-J	5440	Royal Australian Air Force
382V-05J	C130J-30	5446	Royal Air Force
382V-30J	C-130J-30	5517	US Air National Guard
382V-31J	C-130J-30	5510	Italian Air Force
382V-34J	C-130J-30	5521	Italian Air Force
382V-36J	C-130J-30	5536	Royal Danish Air Force
382V-37J	C-130J-30	5525	US Air National Guard
382V-44J	C-130J-30	5557	US Air Force/AFRES
382V-46J	C-130J-30	5601	Norway
382V-47J	C-130J-30	5635	Canadian Armed Forces
382V-49F	C-130J-30	5408	Royal Air Force
382V-50J	C-130J-30	5638	India
382V-51J	C-130J-30	5662	Qatar
382V-52J (?)	C-130J-30(?)	?	UAE (twelve-aircraft order 2009)
382V-73J	HC/MC-130J	5634	AFSOC

Appendix 3

C-130: major sub-contractors

C-130A-H

Allison Division, General Motors, Indianapolis	Engines
Alcoa, Pittsburgh, Pennsylvania	Aluminium forgings, etc
Avco, Nashville, Tennessee	Empennage
Collins Radio, Cedar Rapids, Iowa	General avionics
Garrett Corporation, Los Angeles and Phoenix	Environmental controls
General Electric, Binghamton, New York	Electrical generators
Goodyear Aerospace, Rockmart, Georgia	Fuel cells
Goodyear Company, Akron, Ohio	Brakes
Hamilton Standard, Windsor Locks, Connecticut	Propellers
Honeywell Corporation, Minneapolis	Fuel quantity gauges
Kaiser Aluminium, Oakland, California	Aluminium forgings, etc
Martin-Marietta, Torrance, California	Aluminium castings, etc
Menasco, Burbank, California	Landing gear
Rohr, Chula Vista, California	Nacelles
Ronson Hydraulics, Charlotte, North Carolina	Flight controls
Scottish Aviation, Prestwick	Fuselage side panels
Sperry-Vickers, Jackson, Michigan	Hydraulic pumps
Stainless Steel Products, Burbank, California	Ducting
Texas Instruments, Dallas, Texas	Radar System (APQ 122)

C-130J

Aero-Maoz	Lighting systems
Aerostructures Corporation	Wings, wing components and empennages
Aerotech World Trade Ltd	Databus test analysis and simulation systems
AiResearch	APUs
Airtechnology Group	Fans, fan heaters, motors, generators, switches and sensors
Alliant Defense	Missile-warning system
Ametek Aerospace Gulton-Statham Products	Aviation sensors and instrumentation
Ametek Rotron Technical Motor Division	Brushless motors, fans and blowers
ATC Power Systems Inc	AC/DC and DC/DC power supplies
Aviation Spares International Ltd	Military aircraft spares
Avionic Display Corporation	High-resolution, active matrix, flat-panel, liquid-crystal displays (LCD)
BCF Designs Ltd	Databus and EMC test solutions
B. F. Goodrich Lighting Systems	Lighting systems
Dowty Aerospace, Staverton, Gloucestershire	Composite propellers
DRS Headland Ltd	Airborne video systems for flight test and mission data
Filtronic Components Ltd	Microwave subsystems and airborne surveillance and targeting
Flight Dynamics (Collins-Kaiser)	Holographic Head-Up Display (HUD)
GFM GmbH	Ultrasonic cutting and high-speed routing machines
Hella Aerospace GmbH	Aircraft lighting systems
Honeywell	Dual embedded INS/GPS and digital mapping systems
Judd Wire	Insulation systems for electrical wire and cable
Lockheed-Martin	Infra-red countermeasures system

Lucas Aerospace	Full-authority, digital engine-control system
Mercury Computer Systems	High-performance real-time multicomputers
Metronor ASA	High-precision portable coordinate measuring machines
MPC Products Corporation	Electromechanical components and systems
Northrop Grumman	Colour weather and navigation radar
PTC	Integrated software solutions for aircraft development
Radom Aviation Systems Ltd	Aircraft upgrades and modifications
Rolls-Royce	Turboprop engines
ROTRAN Simulator Logistics Ltd	Flight simulator relocation
Saft	Aircraft batteries
SBS Technologies Inc	MIL-STD-1553, ARINC 429 & Telemetry Products
Senior Aerospace	Metallic and non-metallic products and systems
SKY Computers Inc	High-performance real-time multicomputers
Timken Aerospace & Super Precision	Speciality bearings
Torotel Products Inc	Magnetic components
Tracor	Countermeasures systems
Westinghouse	Weather/navigation radars

Appendix 4

Verifiable losses of C-130s

Note: Several known casualties have no positive confirmations, or are subject to varying degrees of speculation, notably aircraft lost to the Revolutionary Government of Iran, with its obsessive secrecy, and Somalia, with its chaotic system. Any such aircraft are not included in the main body of this list, nor are any aircraft of any nationalities that crashed but were subsequently restored.

1958

2 September (c/n 3136): C-130A-II 56-0528, 7406th CCS, destroyed by Soviet MiG-17 Fresco interceptors north-west of Yerevan, Armenia, while conducting a 'Sun Valley' covert SIGINT sortie.

19 September (c/n 3134): C-130A 56-0526, mid-air collision with a French *Armée de l'Air* Super Mystère jet over France.

1959

20 May (c/n 3175): C-130A 57-0468, crashed at Ashiya, Japan, due to single-engine failure.

1961

27 May (c/n 3570): C-130B 59-1534, left runway due to single-engine failure landing at Ramstein Air Base, Germany.

October (c/n 3543): C130A 58-0745, damaged by fire at Évreux-Fauville Air Base, France, and scrapped. Front part salvaged and used to repair C-130A c/n 3530 in October 1969.

1962

8 March (c/n 3047): C-130A 55-0020, crashed in bad weather conditions 11km from North Alencon, France.

17 May (c/n 3154): C-130A 56-0546, crashed on mountain near Nairobi, Kenya, in bad weather.

26 November (c/n 3096): C-130A 56-0488, crashed with power loss on two engines at Sewart Air Force Base, Tennessee, while conducting go-round during a training flight.

1963

27 August (c/n 3082): C-130A 56-0474, refuelling accident, burned out at Naha Air Base, Okinawa.

1964

2 May (c/n 3100): C-130A 56-0492, struck edge of runway and crashed while landing at Ie Shima Island, Japan.

3 September (c/n 3599): C-130B *Angkatan Udara Republik Indonesia*, crashed into Malacca Straits, trying to outmanoeuvre RAF Javelin interception from RAF Tengah.

1965

11 January (c/n 3514): C-130B 58-0719, jumped from wheel chocks while running up engines at Forbes Air Force Base, Kansas, and careered into 58-0730 (c/n 3525). Resultant fire consumed both machines.

25 March (c/n 3863): C-130E 63-7797, struck high-tension line near Alençon, France.

24 April (c/n 3182): C-130A 57-0475, lost two engines and crashed while conducting a go-around in bad weather conditions at Korat Air Force Base, Thailand.

1 July (c/n 3066): C-130A 55-0039, destroyed by satchel charges at Da Nang Air Base, South Vietnam.

1 July (c/n 3069): C-130A 55-0042, destroyed by satchel charges at Da Nang Air Base, South Vietnam.

18 August (c/n 3691): C-130B Pakistani Air Force 12648, left runway while landing and irreparably damaged.

24 August (c/n 3693): KC-130F USMC BuNo 149802, swerved off runway, hit wall and went into harbour while taking off from Kai-Tak Airport, Hong Kong.

16 September (c/n 3598): AC-130B *Angkatan Udara Republik Indonesia* T-1306, hit by friendly fire and crashed at Bawang.

18 September (c/n 3065): C-130A 55-0038, hit water and crashed while trying a VFR landing approach to Qui Nhon, South Vietnam, in very poor weather conditions.

8 December (c/n 3110): C-130A 56-0502, crashed in bad weather, suspected engine difficulties, while taking off from Chu Lai, South Vietnam.

12 December (c/n 3123): C-130A 56-0515, crashed while lifting off from Bitburg Airfield, Germany.

20 December (c/n 3805): C-130E 62-1842, crashed into hill while making landing approach in murky weather to Tuy Hoa, South Vietnam, due to suspected, but not confirmed, enemy ground fire. In 1973 this aircraft's serial number was covertly reassigned to C-130E 64-0506 (c/n 3990), which subsequently flew Air America clandestine missions.

1966

6 January (c/n 3669): C-130B 61-0972, shot down by enemy fire west of Pleiku, South Vietnam.

9 January (c/n 3667): C-130B 61-0970, left runway and crashed while landing at An Khe, South Vietnam.

1 February (c/n 3709): KC-130F USMC BuNo 149809, damaged by enemy action and crashed in sea 65km east of Dong Hoi.

19 March (c/n 3677): C-130B 61-2641, crashed into Svanfjellet, Senja Island, while making approach to Bardufoss Air Station, Norway.

26 March (c/n 3114): C-130A 56-0506, damaged when swerved to avoid truck while landing at Tuy Hoa, South Vietnam, with propeller reversal failure. Subsequently written off and fuselage utilised for a makeshift Officers Club.

29 March (c/n 3630): C-130B 61-0953, hit ground short of runway during night approach at Pleiku, South Vietnam, and irreparably damaged.

15 April (c/n 3590): CC-130B RCAF 10304, suffered decompression when forward cargo accidentally opened and forced to make wheels-up landing in field; subsequently written off.

31 May (c/n 3995): C-130E 64-0511, destroyed by enemy AAA while attempting to destroy the Thanh Hoa Bridge with 5,000lb bomb during Operation 'Carolina Moon'.

17 June (c/n 3852): C-130E 63-7785 working with US Navy's VR-7, exploded in mid-air over sea near Phu Hiep, north of Nha Trang, after leaving Cam Ranh Bay, Vietnam, suspected enemy sabotage. This aircraft's original USAF serial number was covertly transferred to C-130E 64-0507 (c/n 3991) in 1972, which machine subsequently flew Air America missions as part of CIA clandestine operations mission.

15 July (c/n 3768): C-130B Pakistani Air Force 24142, destroyed when flew into mountain in Pakistan.

6 September (c/n 3949): C-130E 63-7878, flew into mountain from Ching Chuan Kang, Taiwan, allegedly due to a navigation error.

2 October (c/n 3803): C-130E 62-1840, destroyed by enemy fire 30km south of Cam Ranh Bay, South Vietnam.

12 October (c/n 3957): C-130E 63-7886, flew into ground 30km north-north-west of Aspermont, Texas, while conducting night training.

25 October (c/n 3634): C-130B 61-0955, encountered air turbulence from next ahead while landing at Fort Campbell, Kentucky, veered off runway and was irreparably damaged.

26 October (c/n 4093): C-130E Forca Aérea Brasileira FAB 2452, crashed when landing at Galeao, Rio de Janeiro.

1967

17 February (c/n 3618): C-130B 60-0307, suffered split flap failure and crashed into paddy field shortly after leaving Tay Ninh, South Vietnam. Scrapped in situ.

12 March (c/n 3838): C-130E 63-7772, air turbulence from helicopter allegedly caused terminal crash when lifting off at An Khe, South Vietnam.

16 April (c/n 3517): C-130B 58-0722, crashed while undertaking go-around at Bao Loc Airfield, South Vietnam, and cargo of ammunition detonated on impact.

18 April (c/n 4118): C-130E Iranian Air Force IIAF, struck by lightning and burned out.

27 April (c/n 4050): CC-130E RCAF 10309, crashed after take-off from Trenton, suspected elevator trim failure.

9 June (c/n 3534): C-130B 58-0737, crashed 20km east of Tan Son Nhut, South Vietnam, suspected enemy AAA.

17 June (c/n 3591): C-130B 60-0293, crashed and irreparably damaged after aborted take-off from An Khe, South Vietnam.

22 June (c/n 3867): C-130E 63-7801, wing detached while landing at Pope Air Force Base, North Carolina. Fuselage used for paratrooper and subsequently loadmaster training before finally being scrapped in 1999.

15 July (c/n 3036): C-130A 55-0009, destroyed in enemy mortar attack on Da Nang Air Base, South Vietnam.

15 July (c/n 3777): EC-130E 62-1815, destroyed in enemy mortar attack on Da Nang Air Base, South Vietnam.

8 October (c/n 3692): C-130B 61-2649, crashed into mountain 25km south-east of Phu Bai, Hue, South Vietnam.

Hercules 58-0722 (c/n 3517) impresses the crowds and assembled photographers as she unburdens herself of various items of military hardware at Hill AFB, Utah. She was later destroyed at Bao Loc Airfield, South Vietnam, on 16 April 1967 when her load of ammunition blew up on the ground – sabotage was suspected. *Robert F. Dorr, via Nick Williams, AAHS*

12 October (c/n 3174): C-130A 57-0467, crashed into bulldozer while taking off from Dak To, South Vietnam. Managed to land at Cam Ranh Bay but irreparably damaged.

15 October (c/n 4043): C-130E 64-0548, crashed short of runway at Khe Sanh, South Vietnam.

15 November (c/n 3829): C-130E 62-1865, hit and burned out during enemy rocket attack on Dak To, South Vietnam.

15 November (c/n 3904): C-130E 63-7826, hit and burned out during enemy rocket attack on Dak To, South Vietnam.

25 November (c/n 4071): C-130E(I) 'Combat Talon' 64-0563, hit and burned out during enemy rocket attack on Nha Trang, South Vietnam.

29 December (c/n 4040): C-130E(I) 'Combat Talon' 64-0547, flew into mountain 65km north-east of Dien Bien Phu while on leaflet drop sortie.

1968

10 February (c/n 3719): KC-130F USMC BuNo 149813, hit by enemy AAA causing fire in fuel storage and forcing crash-landing on runway at Khe Sanh, South Vietnam.

18 February (c/n 3540): C-130B 58-0743, took direct hit internally and burned out by enemy mortar attack on Tan Son Nhut Air Base, South Vietnam.

28 or 29 February (c/n 4006): C-130E 64-0522, hit by enemy ground fire while taking off at Song Ba, South Vietnam, made crash-landing but burned out (exact date is a matter of dispute).

2 March (c/n 3157): C-130A 56-0549, crashed while attempting night landing at Phu Bai, Hue, South Vietnam.

3 March (c/n 3776): C-130E 62-1814, suffered electrical fire and crashed at Cam Ranh Bay, South Vietnam; electrical fire in aft cockpit.

11 April (c/n 4137): L-100 Zambian Air Cargoes, lost as result of brake failure at Ndola Airport, resulting in ground collision with same company's 9J-RCY (c/n 4109); both machines written off.

11 April (c/n 4109): L-100 Zambian Air Cargoes 9J-RCY, destroyed in ground collision with c/n 4137 at Ndola Airport due to brake failure.

13 April (c/n 3654): C-130B 61-0967, suffered engine failure during touch-down at Khe Sanh, left runway and burned out.

16 April (c/n 3088): C-130A 56-0480, crash-landed at Special Forces Camp Bunard, 80km north of Bien Hoa, South Vietnam, and subsequently destroyed.

26 April (c/n 3602): C-130B 60-0298, heavily damaged by enemy AAA over A Loui, South Vietnam, crash-landed and irreparably damaged.

30 April 30 (c/n 4145): L-100 Pakistan Air Force-operated 64145, suffered broken wing due to weather near Chaklala, Rawalpindi, Pakistan, and crashed.

12 May (c/n 3156): C-130A 56-0548, damaged by enemy small arms fire at Kham Duc, South Vietnam, with feathered propellers and brakes shot away; crash-landed and subsequently abandoned.

12 May (c/n 3600): C-130B 60-0297, hit by enemy ground fire while taking off from Kham Duc, South Vietnam, and crashed.

15 May (c/n 3945): C-130E 63-7875, port wing broke away while landing at Quang Tri, South Vietnam, and scrapped.

16 May (c/n 4146): L-100 (delivered June 1966) *Aerea-Aerovias Ecuatoriansas* N9726R, propeller struck ground while taxiing at Macuma, Ecuador, and burned out.

22 May (c/n 3085): C-130A 56-0477, shot down over Laos while engaged in carrying out 'Blind Bat' flare-dropping sortie.

25 June (c/n 3825): C-130E 62-1861, hit in port outer engine by enemy AAA fire over Katum, South Vietnam, and subsequent fire spread along wing. Forced to make crash-landing at Tay Ninh, using only nose and starboard landing gear; left runway and exploded.

29 July (c/n 4164): HC-130P 66-0214, destroyed by satchel charges at Tuy Hoa, South Vietnam.

29 July (c/n 4174): HC-130P 66-0218, destroyed by satchel charges at Tuy Hoa, South Vietnam.

6 September (c/n 3730): C-130E 62-1785, shot down by enemy AAA fire at Tan Phat, near Bao Loc, South Vietnam.

19 October (c/n 4100): C-130E *Türk Hava Kuvvetleri* ETI-949, flew into mountain on approach to Akhisar AB, Manisa, Turkey.

28 November (c/n 3682): C-130B 61-2644, overshot runway at Tonie Cham, South Vietnam.

24 December (c/n 4229): L-100 United States Department of the Interior, given go-around in snowstorm at Prudhoe Bay, Alaska, but crashed and destroyed.

1969

1 January (c/n 4136): C-130E Royal Saudi Air Force 454, destroyed in crash at Le Bourget Airport, Paris, France.

27 January (c/n 3846): C-130E 63-7780, destroyed in enemy mortar attack on Tonie Cham, South Vietnam.

4 February (c/n 4151): HC-130H 65-0990, developed faults and forced to make water landing on SAR mission off Taiwan.

8 March (c/n 4035): C-130E 64-0545, crashed while on bad-weather landing approach to Ching Chuan Kang Air Base, Taiwan.

24 March (c/n 4196): C-130K RAF XV180, stalled on take-off for training flight from RAF Fairford, Gloucestershire, and crashed into field beyond runway.

7 April (c/n 4154): C-130E Imperial Iranian Air Force 5-112, crashed at Shiraz, Iran, while running on just two engines in training.

29 April (c/n 3673): C-130B 61-2637, struck by enemy AAA in wheel-well and crash-landed at Loc Ninh, South Vietnam; burned out.

18 May (c/n 3723): KC-130F USMC BuNo 149814, involved in a head-on collision with one of two F-4B fighters while engaged in refuelling them over Phu Bai, Vietnam.

23 May (c/n 3856): C-130E, 63-7789, stolen from RAF airfield by apparently distressed USAF Crew Chief from RAF Mildenhall, who reputedly wanted to return home and wanted to fly her to Langley Air Force Base, Virginia, but who instead flew along the English Channel. Eventually aircraft crashed into sea off Alderney, Channel Islands. Persistent stories that aircraft was shot down by USAF fighter planes continue to this day and examination of official USA records that have been made available to date found them to be rather ambiguous, somewhat vague and little help in clearing up that point.

24 May (c/n 3016): AC-130A 54-1629, SOE gunship hit by enemy fire while operating over Laos, and forced to crash land at Ubon Royal Thai Air Force Base, Thailand, where she burned out.

27 May (c/n 3080): C-130A 56-0472, damaged by enemy ground fire on landing approach to Katum, South Vietnam; managed to get down but lost starboard wing in subsequent fire.

USAF C-130E 63-7789 (c/n 3856) drops into base. She was hijacked from RAF Mildenhall, England, on 23 May 1969 and crashed into the sea off Alderney. *Author's collection*

30 May (c/n 3794): C-130E 62-1831, suffered ground accident at Fairchild Maintenance Facility, St Petersburg, Florida, and later scrapped.

23 June (c/n 3652): C-130B 773rd Tactical Airlift Squadron 61-0965, shot down on approach to Katum, South Vietnam.

8 July (c/n 3700): C-130B Pakistani Air Force 62-3490, serial 23490, caught fire and burned while being refuelled at Islamabad.

16 July (c/n 4197): L-100 Trans-Mediterranean N9269R, crashed when one wing touched ground in thick fog when given go-around at Cayaya, Peru.

26 August (c/n 3587): C-130B *Fuerza Aérea Colombiana* 1002, crashed while attempting to land at Bogotá and burned out.

6 October (c/n 3513): C-130B 58-0718, exploded in mid-air close to Chu Lai, South Vietnam; sabotage suspected.

24 November (c/n 3141): C-130A 56-0533, destroyed by enemy AAA over Ban Salou, Laos, while undertaking 'Blind Bat' flare-dropping mission.

13 December (c/n 3107): C-130A 56-0499, crashed and destroyed while endeavouring to take off from Bu Dop, South Vietnam.

15 December (c/n 3754): C-130E 62-1800, propeller reversed during flight and crashed in Taiwan.

1970

10 April (c/n 3118): C130-A Air America 56-0510, flew into mountain while on approach to Long Tieng, Laos.

10 April (c/n 3124): C-130A 56-0516, two engines cut out apparently due to bleed air faults; forced to ditch in sea off Okinawa.

22 April (c/n 3012): AC-130A 54-1625, shot down near Ban Tanag Lou.

30 July (c/n 3728): KC-130F USMC BuNo 150685, crashed at Marine Corps Air Station, El Toro, Lake Forest, California; attempted a 'maximum effort' landing that resulted in broken wings, upturned fuselage and burn-out.

31 July (c/n 3756): C-130E 62-1802, crashed close to Piggott, Arkansas, during training flight.

2 October (c/n 4025): C-130E 64-0536, encountered problems during take-off and subsequently crashed at Cha Tien Shan Mountain, Taipei, Taiwan.

11 October (c/n 4221): L-100 Saturn Airways N9248R, went in at Fort Dix while attempting bad-weather landing approach to McGuire Air Force Base, New Jersey.

1971

15 February (c/n 3562): LC-130F USN BuNo 148318, taxied into snow wall at McMurdo, Antarctica, one wing touched ground and broke then burned.

21 February (c/n 3678): C-130B 61-2642, damaged by enemy rockets at Da Nang Air Base, South Vietnam, and subsequently scrapped, with tail used to repair a damaged AC-130A.

9 November (c/n 4243): C-130K RAF XV216, took off from Melovia but crashed into sea off Pisa, Italy.

12 November (c/n 4353): C-130E 69-6578, apparently suffered fin stall during take-off from Little Rock Air Force Base, Arkansas, and crashed.

1972

15 January (c/n 3710): KC-130F USMC BuNo 149810, caught fire while filled with oxygen at Lake City, Florida; fuselage fully burnt with only tail section salvageable.

15 January 15, (c/n 3871): EC-130G USN TACAMO III BuNo 151890, fire in No 1 fuel tank while at Naval Air Station Patuxent River, which subsequently spread to rest of aircraft, leaving her irreparable.

19 February (c/n 3775): C-130E 62-1813, collided in mid-air with Cessna T-37 6km north-east of Little Rock, Arkansas.

28 March (c/n 3071): AC-130A 55-0044, shot down by North Vietnamese SA-2 Guideline surface-to-air missile south-east of Sepone, Laos.

30 March (c/n 4345): AC-130E Special Air Squadron 69-6571, shot down over Ho Chi Minh Trail, Laos.

18 April (c/n 3841): C-130E 63-7775, hit by enemy fire and crash-landed near Lan Khe, South Vietnam; subsequently written off.

25 April (c/n 3992): C-130E 64-0508, shot down near An Lôc, South Vietnam.

3 May (c/n 3748): C-130E 62-1797, shot down near An Lôc, South Vietnam.

17 May (c/n 3864): C-130E 63-7798, shot down, possible enemy rocket strike while taking off from Kontum, South Vietnam.

22/23 May (c/n 3818): C-130E 62-1854, hit by enemy rocket and burned out at Kontum, South Vietnam.

5 June (c/n 3202): C-130D 57-0495, suffered rudder stall and crashed during over-shoot at Dye III, 320km east of Söndreström Air Base, Greenland; scrapped.

5 June (c/n 3759): C-130E 62-1805, crashed in sea off Makung, Pescadores Islands, after explosion in aircraft landing gear set off chain reaction in hydraulic fuel pipes.

18 June (c/n 3070): AC-130A Special Operations Squadron 55-0043, shot down by enemy SA-7 surface-to-air over A Shau Valley, south-west of Hue, South Vietnam.

12 August (c/n 3817): C-130E 62-1853, shot down while taking off from Soc Trang, South Vietnam.

12 September (c/n 4214): C-130 RAF XV194, left irreparably damaged when left runway and tipped into ditch while landing at Tromsø/Langnes Airport (TOS), Norway.

5 December (c/n 4059): C-130E(I) Special Operations Squadron 'Combat Talon' 64-0558, in night collision with ANG aircraft north-east of Myrtle Beach Air Force Base, South Carolina.

9 December (c/n 3989): C-130E 64-0505, crashed and burned while attempting to land at Naval Air Station Agana, Brewer Field, Guam.

21 December (c/n 3098): AC-130A Special Air Squadron 56-0490, shot down 40km north-east of Pakse, Laos.

1973

28 January (c/n 4305): LC-130R USN BuNo 155917, crashed as result of late go-around call while in white-out weather conditions at South Pole Station, Antarctica.

10 September (c/n 4219): C-130K RAF XV198, crashed and destroyed at RAF Colerne, Wiltshire. While conducting co-pilot training she overshot runway while simulating engine failure, but second engine on same side also failed at non-recoverable height of only 400 feet.

15 October (c/n 3808): C-130E USAF 62-1845, flew into the north face of Sugarloaf Mountain, 45km south of Fort Smith, Arkansas; exploded on impact and totally destroyed.

1974

28 February (c/n 4393): C-130E Imperial Iranian Air Force 5-122, crashed on mountain near Mehrabad, Iran.

20 April (c/n 3804): C-130E USAF 62-1841, crashed into ocean and sank while attempting take-off from Andersen Air Force Base, Guam.

23 May (c/n 4225): L-100 Saturn Airways N14ST, lost when wing snapped off due to turbulence at Springfield, Illinois.

The main emergency access steps on US Navy LC-130R 155917 (c/n 4305) are duly adorned with symbols of her allies (note the Kiwi 5s and RAAF roundel), as well as the New Zealand symbol with 'Ao-Te'a-Roa', seen in September 1969. On 28 January 1973 she later crashed at the Amundsen-Scott South Pole Station. *Nick Williams, AAHS*

4 July (c/n 4295): C-130E Imperial Iranian Air Force 5-8507, reported crashed at Shiraz, Iran., but date is disputed.

18 December (c/n 3107): C-130A VNAF 56-0521, destroyed on ground at Song Be, South Vietnam.

25 December (c/n 3043): C-130A VNAF 55-0016, shot down while landing at Song Be, South Vietnam.

18 August (c/n 4422): C-130H Zaire Air Force 9T-TCD, crashed at Kisangani, Zaire.

30 August (c/n 4209): L-100 Alaska International Air, totally gutted by cargo explosion while on ground at Galbraith Lake, Alaska, 200km south of Prudhoe Bay.

30 September (c/n 3868): C-130E 63-7802, crashed during landing attempt at Kadena Air Base, Japan.

13 October (c/n 4106): WC-130H 65-0965, vanished without trace, assumed caught in Typhoon 'Bess' over Taiwan Strait.

27 October (c/n 4234): L-100 Alaska International Air N102AK, suffered wing fracture during landing approach to Old Man's Camp, Alaska.

18 December (c/n 3129): C-130A VNAF 56-0521, destroyed on ground at Song Be, South Vietnam.

25 December (c/n 3043): C130-A South Vietnamese Air Force 55-0016, shot down while landing at Song Be, South Vietnam.

1975

1 February (c/n 3516): C-130B 58-0721, crashed due to engine failure when attempting take-off from Naval Air Station, New Orleans, Louisiana.

6 April (c/n 3029): C-130A South Vietnamese Air Force 55-0002, left runway at Bien Hoa, South Vietnam, damaged and burned.

28 April (c/n 4519): C-130E 72-1297, hit and burned out by NVA rocket attack on Tan Son Nhut Air Base, South Vietnam.

26 July (c/n 3161): C-130A 57-0454, blade from starboard inner engine detached and struck outer engine; aircraft crashed north of Imlay City, Michigan.

28 August (c/n 4309): C-130E *Fuerza Aérea Argentina* TC-62, destroyed by bomb explosion on runway ahead of her while taking off from Tucuman, Argentina.

25 November (c/n 4533): C-130H Israeli Air Force 203/4X-FBO, destroyed when flew into side of Jebel Halal, 55km south-south-east of El Arish, Israel.

1976

3 September (c/n 4408): C-130 *Fuerza Aérea Venezolana* FAV-7772, destroyed with heavy loss of life while making repeated efforts to land at Lajes Air Base Terceira Island, in the Azores. Aircraft finally crashed after three go-around attempts in atrocious weather conditions.

21 November (c/n 4361): L-100-20 Pacific Western Airlines N7982S, crashed into jungle near Eastville, Kisangani, Zaire. Arrived very low on fuel and attempted emergency night landing in fog; airfield landing lights were off and aircraft came down in jungle.

4 December (c/n 4537): C-130H Royal Moroccan Air Force CN-AOB, shot down over Sahara by Polisario rebels.

21 December (c/n 4463): C-130H Imperial Iranian Air Force, delivered as 5-148, crashed while making bad-weather approach into Shiraz Airfield, Iran.

1977

3 March (c/n 4492): C-130H Italian Air Force MM61996, flew into Monte Serra, 15km east of Pisa, Italy.

21 June (c/n 4280): EC-130Q US Navy TACAMO III BuNo 156176, crashed into sea soon after nocturnal take-off from Wake Island airstrip.

1978

19 February (c/n 4707): C-130H Egyptian Air Force 1270, suffered electrical fire that destroyed nose of aircraft while on ground at Larnaca Airport, Cyprus, and scrapped.

19 February (c/n 4364): L-100-20 SATCO OB-R-1004, suffered engine shut down and crashed while attempting take-off from Tarapoto, Peru.

15 April (c/n 3854): C-130E 63-7787, suffered fin stall and crashed at Barstow, California.

28 April (c/n 3832): C-130E 63-7766, came down some distance from runway during approach to Sparrevohn Air Force Station, Alaska; irreparably damaged and scrapped.

12 July (c/n 4748): C-130H *Fuerza Aérea Ecuatoriana* 748, crashed in Pinincha Mountains, Ecuador.

8 September (c/n 4021): C-130E 64-0532, flew into mountain in Arkansas during bad weather.

19 September (c/n 4457): C-130H Imperial Iranian Air Force 5-8532, crashed in go-around after one engine failed over Doshan Tappah Air Base, Iran.

30 November (c/n 4316): C-130E 68-10936, came down after lightning strike, 55km west of Charleston, South Carolina.

10 December (c/n 4331): C-130E 68-10951, crashed during approach to Fort Campbell Army Air Field, Kentucky, due to faulty engine control wire.

1979

23 January (c/n 4497): C-130H Italian Air Force MM62000, jumped chocks while making engine run-up on ground and careered into tree; irreparably damaged and scrapped. Parts were used in repair of MM61995 (c/n 4491) after damage at Pisa in January 1999.

1 February (c/n 3698): C-130B Pakistani Air Force A5-HFP, also jumped chocks during night engine test, colliding with 10687 (c/n 4117); both written off as total losses.

1 February (c/n 4117): C-130E Pakistani Air Force 10687, struck heavily by 23488 (c/n 3698) in accident on ground; both aircraft subsequently scrapped.

7 April (c/n 4401): C-130H LAAF 116, shot down by RPG-7 while taking off from Entebbe, Uganda.

15 May (c/n 4176): L-100 TAAG Angola Airlines, overshot runway while attempting to land at São Tomé and subsequently scrapped.

19 June (c/n 4402): C-130E Imperial Iranian Air Force 5-8520, reported as crashed at Shiraz, Iran; date disputed.

28 September (c/n 4744): C-130H *Transporte Aéreo Boliviano* CP-1375, came down in sea after attempting night take-off from Panama-Tocumen.

1980

14 March (c/n 4659): C-130H 74-2064, suffered internal explosion and crashed 15km west of Incirlik, Turkey.

24 April (c/n 3770): EC-130E 62-1809, struck in wing root by USN RH-53D Sea Stallion helicopter in nil visibility conditions during Operation 'Eagle Claw' in Great Salt Desert of Eastern Iran, near Tabas, and abandoned.

28 May (c/n 4520): C-130H Spanish Air Force 311-01, crashed into mountain near Rocqu Noblio, central Gran Canaria, Canary Islands.

5 September (c/n 4350): L-100-20 Kuwait Air Force 317, struck by lightning and crashed close to Montelimar, France.

14 September (c/n 4128): C-130E Royal Saudi Air Force 453, suffered catastrophic engine fire while taking off from Medina Airfield, Saudi Arabia, and crashed with heavy loss of life.

14 September (c/n 4569): C-130H Zaire Air Force 9T-TCE, crashed and burned while attempting to take off from Kindu, Zaire, with only three functioning engines while fully laden.

2 October (c/n 3112): C-130A 56-0504, crashed near McMinnville, Tennessee, after section of leading edge of port wing fell away.

15 October (c/n 4061): CC-130E Canadian Forces 130312, crashed after low-level stall during SAR sortie near Chapais, Quebec.

29 October (c/n 4658): YMC-130H 74-1683, crashed at Eglin AFB Auxiliary Field 3 at Duke Field, Florida, while making landing during demonstration flight concerning the proposed Operation 'Credible Sport' rescue mission in Iran. Arrester rockets either failed to fire or fired out of sequence, resulting in crash-landing and fire when starboard wing came off; wreck deemed unsalvageable.

4 November (c/n 4406): C-130H *Fuerza Aérea Venezolana* FAV-3556, suffered catastrophic engine failure and crashed near Caracas, Venezuela.

1981

14 January (c/n 4357): C-130E 69-6581, suffered fin stall and crashed while attempting to take off at Ramstein Air Base, Germany.

26 February (c/n 4074): MC-130E-Y Special Operations Squadron 64-0564, went into ocean off Tabone Island, Philippines, while attempting low-level turn.

24 April (c/n 4450): L-100-20 *Fuerza Aérea del Peru* FAP-396, written off while attempting emergency night landing after running out of fuel at San Juan, Peru.

16 May (c/n 4830): L-100-20 Angola Air Charter D2-EAS, shot down by infra-red missile near Menongue, Angola.

29 May (c/n 4792): C-130H Egyptian Air Force 1276, crashed shortly after taking off at Cairo West Airport, Egypt.

21 September (c/n 4623): C-130H 74-1672, came down well short while attempting night landing on desert air strip close to Springs Air Base, Nevada, and suffered irreparable damage.

29 September (either c/n 4594 or c/n 4495 – sources differ): C-130H Islamic Republic of Iran Air Force either S-158 or S-8552, confirmed as crashing close to Kahrisak, south of Tehran, killing the then Minister of Defence and a number of senior officers.

12 October (c/n 4717): C-130H Royal Moroccan Air Force 17, shot down by Polisario rebels over West Sahara.

1982

11 April (c/n 4170): L-100 Northwest Territorial Airways, accidentally caught fire and burned out on ground 69°N 124°W near Paulatuk, Northwest Territory, during discharge of cargo including gasoline.

13 April (c/n 4645): C-130H 74-1678, suffered catastrophic engine failure in both starboard engines, severing whole wing, and crashed near Sivas, Turkey.

13 May (c/n 4033): C-130E 64-0543, wing broke away while on training flight and aircraft crashed close to Judsonia, Arkansas.

29 April (c/n 4743): C-130H *Fuerza Aérea Ecuatoriana* 743, flew into mountain while attempting go-around from Marisal Sucre Airport near Quito, Ecuador.

1 June (c/n 4310): C-130H *Fuerza Aérea Argentina* TC-63, shot down by Royal Navy FRS.1 Sea Harrier XZ451 from aircraft-carrier HMS *Invincible* using AIM-9L Sidewinder missile and guns during the Argentine invasion and illegal occupation of the Falkland Islands.

30 July (c/n 4757): HC-130H USCG CG1600, crashed and burned while attempting bad-weather landing approach at Attu, Aleutian Islands.

16 October (c/n 3572): C-130B *Fuerza Aérea Colombiana* 1003, suffered loss of all navigation systems, and as a result flew around until ran out of fuel and was forced to make water landing some 330km east of Cape May, New Jersey. Most remarkably the hull remained afloat in the Atlantic swells for 56 hours.

16 November (c/n 4553): CC-130H Canadian Forces 130329, cargo hung up while conducting Low Altitude Parachute Extraction System (LAPES) operation; aircraft went out of control and crashed near Namao, Edmonton, Canada.

1983

13 February (c/n 4693): C-130H 74-1693, badly damaged by ground fire at Pope Air Force Base, North Carolina, and subsequently written off; fuselage later utilised for loadmaster training.

9 June (c/n 4708): L-100-20 *Fuerza Aérea del Peru* 383, crashed at Puerto Maldonado, southern Peru.

28 June (c/n 4694): C-130H 74-2068, stalled at low altitude while taking part in 'Red Flag' exercise and crashed some 100 miles north of Nellis Air Force Base, Nevada.

27 August (c/n 4333): L-100-20 Transamerica N17ST, flew into mountain south of Dundo, Angola, in dense fog.

1984

28 February (c/n 4324): C-130E 68-10944, flew into mountain 55km north-west of Zaragoza, Spain.

2 November (c/n 4326): C-130E 68-10946, written off following crash-landing at Giebelstadt Army Air Field, Germany; nose section later used to repair damaged 64-0539 (c/n 4029).

1985

22 January (c/n 3109): C-130A USAF 56-0501, crashed in sea during approach to Trujillo Airport, Honduras.

24 February (c/n 4872): KC-130H Royal Saudi Air Force 1620, overshot runway, turned at low level, stalled and crashed at Riyadh, Saudi Arabia.

12 March (c/n 4044): C-130E 64-0549, stalled and crashed while conducting supply drop training exercise at Fort Hood, Texas.

29 March (c/ns 4555 and 4559): CC-130H Canadian Forces 130330 and 130331, 435 Squadron, collided in mid-air above CFB Namao, Edmonton, Alberta; both destroyed.

24 June (c/n 4290): C-130E *Força Aérea Brasileira* FAB 2457, crashed while making landing approach in fog at Santa Maria Air Base, Brazil.

21 November (c/n 4898): C-130H-MP Indonesian Air Force TNI-AU, lost when crashed into volcano at Sibyak, Indonesia, and irreparably damaged.

1986

7 March (c/n 3020): C-130A *Force Aérienne Tchadienne* TT-PAB, stalled and crashed while attempting take-off, location unconfirmed.

2 April (c/n 4161): HC-130P 66-0211, encountered severe turbulence at low altitude, causing starboard wing to break away; crashed north of Magdalena, New Mexico.

8 June (c/n 4832): L-100-20 Angola Air Charter D2-THA, made belly-landing at Dondo, Angola, and damaged beyond repair.

14 August (c/n 3194): C-130D-6 Honduras Air Force 556, crashed at Wampusirpi, Honduras.

9 September (c/n 3076): C-130A 56-0468, suffered broken throttle cable and crashed at end of runway, Fort Campbell, Kentucky; written off.

4 October (c/n 4391): L-100-30 Southern Air Transport N15ST, tried to take off at night from Kelly Air Force Base, Texas, with cockpit control lock still in place; crashed into hangar and written off.

1987

8 April (c/n 4558): L-100-30 Global Air (SAT) N517SJ, all power on both port engines failed during transport training operations at Fairfield-Travis Air Force Base, California, and port wing struck ground ahead of runway; crashed and burned.

1 July (c/n 4325): C-130E 68-10945, while conducting LAPES display in front of guests at Fort Bragg Special Warfare School, North Carolina, which featured a low-level parachute-assisted air-drop of an M551 tank, involving the 'touch-and-go' technique, aircraft did not gain sufficient altitude after drop and struck trees, burning out.

14 October (c/n 4701): L-100-30 Zimex Aviation HB-ILF, shot down after taking off at Cuito, Angola.

16 November (c/n 3159): C-130A *Force Aérienne Tchadienne* TT-PAC, crashed during landing in Chad, location unconfirmed.

9 December (c/n 4522): LC-130R USN BuNo 159131, crash-landed at Site D59, Antarctica, and written off as unsalvageable.

12 December (c/n 4998): C-130H *Força Aérea Brasileira* 2468, went into sea while making landing approach at Fernando de Noronha island, Brazil; no survivors.

1988

8 June (c/n 3720): C-130E 61-2373, went into ground some 5km short of runway while making landing approach at Greenville, Mississippi.

17 August (c/n 3708): C-130B Pakistan Air Force 23494, eyewitness reports stated that this aircraft exploded in mid-air soon after it took off from Bahawalpur; later claims were made of bombs hidden in crates loaded aboard without proper security checks, but all these were discounted by Pakistani and American authorities, although they have themselves have not yet released official findings of subsequent investigations. The crash killed everyone aboard at the time, which included the President of Pakistan, Muhammad Zia-ul-Haq, the United States Ambassador to Pakistan, a US General and seventeen top brass of the Pakistan Army. What little remained of the aircraft was quickly removed.

1989

29 January (c/n 4124): CC-130E Canadian Forces 130318, hit ground some 600 feet sort of runway while making night approach to Fort Wainwright, Alaska, in temperatures of -46°C, and was destroyed.

27 March (c/n 4752): C-130H Royal Saudi Air Force 470, heavily damaged while attempting to take off from Jeddah, Saudi Arabia; deemed irreparable and written off.

9 April (c/n 4303): L-100-20 IAS/Transafrik S9-NAI, suffered fires in two engines forcing crash-landing at Luena, Moxico Province, Angola; scrapped.

1 August (c/n 4883): L-100-30 *Air Algérie* 7T-VHK, left runway during attempted landing at Tuareq (Tamanrasset), Algeria; badly damaged and subsequently written off.

9 August (c/n 4654): C-130H 74-1681, crashed when load hung-up but parachute deployed, during LAPES demonstration at Special Operations base, Fort Bragg, North Carolina.

This Herk is C-130H 74-1681 (c/n 4654) of 463 TAW, seen here in June 1980. On 9 August 1989 she crashed at Fort Bragg during exercise drops, when a Sheridan tank became hung up in her hold but the parachute deployed. *Nick Williams, AAHS*.

27 November (c/n 4129): L-100 Tepper Aviation N9205T, made emergency crash-landing at Jamba, Huíla, Angola; written off.

21 December (c/n 3187): C-130A Bolivian Air Force TAM62, crashed at Guayaramerin, Bolivia, while attempting three-engine take-off.

1990

5 January (c/n 4222): L-100 Angola Air Charter D2-TH, hit and damaged by missile at Menonque, Angola, crash-landed and written off.

19 April (c/n 4736): C-130H Zaire Air Force 9T-TCG, suffered broken propeller blade and crashed close to Kinshasa, Zaire.

12 August (c/n 4384): L-100-20 Southern Air Transport N911SJ, one engined failed shortly after taking off from Juba, Sudan, and while attempting to land back safely aircraft overshot runway and burned; subsequently written off.

25 August (c/n 4674): C-130H Malayan Air Force M30-03, crash-landed at Sibu, Sarawak and written off as beyond repair.

1991

31 January (c/n 4341): AC-130H Special Operations Squadron 69-6567, shot down by Iraqi SA-7 missile at dawn during Battle of Khafji, about 110km south-south-east of Kuwait City, Kuwait.

5 February (c/n 4724): C-130H Hellenic Air Force 748, flew into Mount Othrys while making landing approach to Nea Anchialos with heavy loss of life.

27 February (c/n 4949): L-100-30 Kuwait Air Force KAF322, after being damaged by ground fire at Kuwait City Airport on 2 August 1990, flown to Iraq and badly damaged by bomb. Hull was subsequently returned to Kuwait by road transport in March 1995 and scrapped. Cannibalised to help repair of Zaire Air Force C-130H 9T-TCA (c/n 4411).

16 March (c/n 4833): L-100-30 Transafrik TAM-92, shot down by UNITA FIM-92 Stinger missile near Malanje, Angola.

21 March (c/n 4754): C-130H Royal Saudi Air Force 469, crashed and irreparably damaged while making approach in poor visibility to Ras Al-Mishab Airport, Saudi Arabia.

10 June (c/n 3099): DC-130A Angolan Government/Questline 9J-SLQ, insecurely stored cargo shifted during attempted take-off from Launda, causing aircraft to crash and burn out.

2 September (c/n 4250): L-100 IAS/Diamang N521SJ, blown up by mine while preparing to take off at Wau, Sudan.

17 September (c/n 5029): L-100-30 ET-AJL, crashed into Mount Arey, south of Djibouti, Ethiopia.

5 October (c/n 4927): C-130H-30 *Tentera Nasional Indonesia-Angkatan Udara* A-1324, suffered catastrophic engine failure and crashed after taking off from Halim-Perdanakasuma, Jakarta, Indonesia.

30 October (c/n 4192): CC-130 CAF 130322, crashed some 18 miles from airstrip while making visual sight landing final approach to Canadian Forces Station (CFS) Alert on Ellesmere Island.

1992

6 February (c/n 3527): AC-130B 58-0732, stalled and crashed on US 41 Highway while attempting take-off from Evansville Regional Airport, Evansville, Indiana, killing all five crew and nine motorists.

28 April (c/n 3985): AWADS equipped C-130E 64-0501, fell into Blewett Falls Lake, North Carolina.

24 August (c/ns 3125 and 3537): C-130A Inter-American Air Forces Academy 56-0517 and C-130B 58-0740 reduced to ground trainers, both destroyed at Homestead Air Force Base, Miami, Florida, by Hurricane 'Andrew'.

27 August (c/n 3661): C-130F USN BuNo 149794, suffered severe damage on ground at Guam during Typhoon 'Omar', written off and finally scrapped circa August 1994.

26 September (c/n 4624): C-130H Nigerian Air Force 911, port inner engined failed while attempting heavily laden take-off from Lagos Airport, Nigeria, and 3 minutes after take-off she crashed and was destroyed.

7 October (c/n 3952): C-130E 63-7881, during low-level mission one wing clipped power lines at Berkeley Springs, West Virginia, spun in and destroyed.

1993

3 February (c/n 4412): L-100-20 N130X, Lockheed HTTB (High Technology Test Bed) used to evaluate fly-by-wire rudder actuator and ground minimum control speed (VMCG) at Dobbins Air Reserve Base, Marietta, Georgia. While undergoing final high-speed ground test run, she somehow got out of control, careered to port and lifted off. The aircraft managed to climb approximately 250 feet before crashing close to Naval Clinic, killing her seven-man test crew.

27 May (c/n 4213): C-130K 65-13038 RAF C Mk. 1 XV193, stalled and crashed at Glen Tilt, Blair Atholl, Perthshire, Scotland, while making practice cargo drop, killing all aboard.

22 July (c/n 4191): CC-130E Canadian Forces 130321, crashed when struck barn while conducting practice LAPES low-level air-drop at CFB Wainwright, Alberta, and broke into three pieces on hitting ground.

16 December (c/n 4761): C-130H Philippines Air Force 4761, flew into Mount Manase during landing approach to Naga Airport, some 250km south-east of Manila.

1994

14 March (c/n 4351): AC-130H Special Operations Squadron 69-6576, live Howitzer round exploded in gun barrel after taking off from Mombasa Airport, Kenya, with military cargo, triggering fire in port engines; crashed in sea 7km south of Malindi..

17 March (c/n 4432): C-130H IRIAF 5-8521, shot down by Armenian insurgents north of Stepanakert in Nagorno-Karabakh while on flight from Moscow to Tehran, with heavy loss of life.

7 April (c/n 4679): L-100-30 TAAG Angola Airlines D2-THC, brakes overheated during landing at Malenge, Angola; resultant fire left aircraft irreparably damaged and written off.

13 August (c/n 3148): C-130A Hemet Valley Flying Services Tanker 82, crashed in hills above Pearblossom, California, and totally destroyed along with crew.

24 September (c/n 4826): L-100-30 Heavylift PK-PLV, overspeed fault in starboard outer propeller while taking off from Kai Tak Airport, Hong Kong, caused crash into harbour; total loss.

14 October (c/n 4293): C-130E *Força Aérea Brasileira* 2460, cargo of ammunition ignited in mid-air and crashed at Formosa, north-east of Brasília, Brazil.

31 December (c/n 3581): C-130B Bolivian Air Force TAM67, crashed at Trinidad, Bolivia, while attempting three-engine take-off.

1995

13 May (c/n 3801): C-130E 62-1838, port inner engine caught fire soon after departure from Boise, Idaho, while at altitude of 26,000 feet. Initially fire was extinguished but reignited. While attempting to divert to Mountain Home AFB, Idaho, engine came off its mounting, damaging both fuselage and port wing, which also finally fell off. Aircraft crashed with loss of entire crew.

1996

15 May 15 (c/n 4576): C-130H *Fuerza Aérea Argentina* TC-67, severely damaged on impact when attempting bad-weather landing at Tandil, Argentina, and written off.

15 July (c/n 4473): C-130H Belgian Air Force CH-06, victim of bird-strike that knocked out three engines while making go-around over Eindhoven AB, Eindhoven, Netherlands. On striking runway, caught fire and burned out with very heavy loss of life among passengers and crew.

17 August (c/n 4597): C-130H 74-1662, took off from Jackson Hole, Wyoming, but flew into Sleeping Indian Mountains and was total write-off.

22 November (c/n 4072): HC-130P 64-14856, suffered total fuel starvation while over Pacific, causing every engine to seize up whereupon she went into sea some 113km west of Eureka, California.

1997

1 April (c/n 5161): C-130H 88-4408, overshot runway at Toncontín International Airport, Honduras, and was total write-off.

16 April (c/n 4829): C-130H *Force Aérienne Niger* 5U-MBD, flew into ground close to Sorei while making approach to Niamey, Niger.

10 October (c/n 5067): C-130H Taiwan Air Force 1310, crashed into ground at Tapei-SungShan, Taiwan, while endeavouring to make go-around in heavy rain.

20 December (c/n 4729): C-130H Hellenic Air Force 750, crashed at Pastra, Greece, while making landing approach to Tanagra Air Base.

1998

10 September (c/n 3701): C-130B Pakistani Transport Conversion School AQ-ACV, crashed into by c/n 3781 while on ground at Rawalpindi, caught fire, burned and was subsequently scrapped.

26 December (c/n 4561): L-100-30 Transafrik S9-CAO, shot down by UNITA rebels while taking off from Huambo, Angola, on United Nations mission.

1999

2 January (c/n 4839): L-100-30 Transafrik T-650, shot down by UNITA just after taking off from Huambo, Angola.

11 June (c/n 4264): C-130K RAF XV298, cargo shifted while attempting to take off from Kukës, Albania; crash-landed, caught fire and was subsequently written off.

17 September (c/n 3217): C-130A *Fuerza Aérea Mexicana* 3610, crashed in mountains 80km north-east of Mexico City, Mexico.

10 December (c/n 3924): C-130E 63-7854, badly damaged after wheels-up landing at Kuwait International Airport. Hulk was subsequently shipped to AMARC Davis-Monthan Air Force Base, Arizona, to await disposal.

27 December (c/n 4477): L-100-30 Transafrik S9-BOP, control lost while making wet landing at Luzamba, Angola, and aircraft ended up in 40-foot-deep ravine, irreparably damage and scrapped.

2000

14 January (c/n 3559): C-130B Bolivian Air Force TAM60, crashed while attempting to take off from Chimorre Airport, Bolivia; ran off runway into culvert, then ploughed into nearby forest with total loss of crew and passengers.

26 July (c/n 4073): HC-130H Royal Jordanian Air Force 348, crashed after taking off from al-Mafraq Air Base, north of Amman, Jordan.

6 September (c/n 3086): C-130A *Sécurité Civile* N116TG, converted water-bomber used for firefighting, crashed into hill near Burzet, France, while making second water delivery run over forest fire.

Minimal national insignia feature on C-130E Hercules 63-7854 (c/n 3924) of the Military Air Command at Atsugi Air Base, Japan, on 21 February 1980. On 10 December 1999 she was badly damaged after a wheels-up landing at Kuwait International Airport. *Werner Hartman, via Nick Williams, AAHS*

2001

27 September (c/n 4202): C-130E *Força Aérea Brasileira* FAB 2455, flew into mountain soon after taking off from Rio de Janeiro Airport, with no survivors.

20 December (c/n 4824): L-100-30 *Tentera Nasional Indonesia-Angkatan Udara* TNA-AU, left runway while attempting to land at Malikul Saleh, Lhokseumawe, and suffered irreparable damage; written off.

2002

9 January (c/n 4702): KC-130R USMC BuNo 160021, flew into mountain while making approach to land at Shamsi, Pakistan, with no survivors.

12 February (c/n 3619): KC-130F USMC BuNo 148895, suffered catastrophic engine failure and crashed during touch-and-go landings exercises at Twenty-Nine Palms, California.

13 February (c/n 4163): MC-130P Special Operations Squadron 'Combat Shadow' 66-0213, lost over eastern Afghanistan while involved in nocturnal refuelling sortie. Made emergency climb in poor visibility to avoid ridge but crash-landed, wheels up, in deep snow.

12 June (c/n 5041): MC-130H Special Operations Squadron 'Combat Talon' II 84-0475, crashed at Bande Sardeh Dam near Gardez, Afghanistan, during night exfiltration mission to lift out two SF soldiers. Pilot apparently ignored two failed acceleration time checks and continued take-off, crashing less than 3 miles from strip.

17 June (c/n 3146): C-130P Hawkins & Powers Aviation N130HP, became second converted water bomber loss when centre wing box failed while pulling up after making firefighting run near Walker, California. Both wings folded up and detached, and aircraft went into ground inverted with loss of entire crew. This accident was filmed, and such a series of alarming losses prompted Interior Department to cancel its contract for all heavy firefighting aircraft. It also led to rigorous and ongoing investigations into stability of all C-130 centre wing sections, and considerable work for the AMARG.

7 August (c/n 5265): MC-130H Special Operations Squadron 'Combat Talon II' 90-0161, crashed into Monte Perucho, south of Caguas, after taking off from Naval Station Roosevelt Roads, Puerto Rico, on training mission.

2003

30 June (c/n 4926): C-130H Algerian Air Force 7T-WHQ, suffered engine fire after departure from Boufarik Air Force Base and crashed on Beni Mered, Blida, with heavy loss of life.

19 September (c/n 3025): C-130A *Fuerza Aérea Mexicana* 10603, suffered in-flight fire and came down close to La Quemada, Mexico.

2004

28 September (c/n 5050): C-130H ANG 84-0211, suffered heavy ground damage from tornado at New Castle County Airport, Delaware, and was written off as not worth repairing.

29 December (c/n 5054): MC-130H Special Operations Squadron 'Combat Talon II' 85-0012, made unscheduled night landing at Q-West airstrip, Mosul, an Iraqi airfield that was under repair, resulting in terminal damage and write-off.

2005

30 January (c/n 4195): C-130K RAF C.1 XV179, damaged by enemy light arms fire during take-off from Baghdad Airport; resultant fire caused starboard wing fuel tank to explode and aircraft crashed at Al Taji, Iraq.

31 March (c/n 5118): MC-130H Special Operations Squadron 'Combat Talon II' 87-0127, stalled when climbing to gain height, hit mountain ridge, crashed and burned with loss of entire complement aboard.

6 December (c/n 4399): C-130E IRIAF 5-8519, flew into Air Force Apartment Block in Tehran, Iran, while transporting party of eighty-four journalists and observers to witness military manoeuvres, plus aircrew of ten; very heavy loss of life. This was one of many similar (five or six) Revolutionary Iran Air Force C-130 losses, but one of the few that can actually be verified.

2006

5 May (c/n 4460): C-130H Belgian Air Component CH-02, totally destroyed in hangar fire at Zaventam, Brussels Airport, Belgium.

24 May (c/n 4231): C.1P RAF Special Forces XV206, struck anti-tank mine while landing at Lashkar Gar, Helmand Province, Afghanistan; explosion ruptured port external fuel tank, setting port inner engine alight. All crew and passengers, which included the British Ambassador, SAS troops and civilians, managed to evacuate, but aircraft was total write-off.

11 June (c/n 5141): C-130H *Force Aérienne Tchadienne* TT-PAF, overran runway while attempting to land in sandstorm at Abéché, Chad; irreparably damaged and written off.

28 July (c/n 5028): HC-130H USCG CG1710, crash-landed at Saint Paul Island, Alaska, and written off.

13 August (c/n 4880): L-100-30 Air Algérie 7T-VHG, made 'high-rate descent' from 24,000 feet and crashed at Piacenza, Milan, Italy.

2007

12 February (c/n 5460): C-130J-30 RAF C.4 ZH876, damaged by bomb on unspecified runway in Maysan Province, Iraq, close to Iranian border, carrying secure communications equipment to monitor passage of arms and ammunition into Iraq from Iran. Decision was made to have it blown up to prevent equipment falling into hostile hands, as it was deemed too dangerous to attempt salvage. Details of precise cause of damage are sparse.

23 August (c/n 4230): C.1P RAF Special Force Flight XV205, made heavy landing on unspecified southern Afghanistan airstrip in area dominated by Taliban, and badly damaged. Equipped with FLIR turret and night cameras, it was deemed too dangerous to recover it, so was blown up by British Army engineers to prevent secret equipment falling into enemy hands.

2008

27 June (c/n 5098): C-130H Air Force Reserve Command 86-0412, written off as total loss after suffering catastrophic engine failure on all engines and being forced to make emergency field landing north-east of Baghdad, Iraq. Following salvage operations, hulk was dismantled and recovered by American Civil Engineer Squadron.

4 August (c/n 4985): C-130H United Arab Emirates (Abu Dhabi) 1212, overran end of runway and burned while attempting to land at Bagram Air Base, Kabul.

25 August (c/n 4593) L-100-20 *Hukbong Himpapawid ng Pilipinas* 4593, crashed into sea at 20.55 soon after taking off from Davao City, Mindanao, Philippines, after communications with tower suddenly ceased; cause still unknown.

2009

24 February (c/n 4714): C-130H Egyptian Air Force 1272, hit ground hard and crashed while making nocturnal touch-and-go landings at unspecified airfield.

20 May (c/n 4917): L-100-30 TNI-AU A-1325, crashed into paddy fields close to Magetan, east of Yogyakarta, Java, while carrying more than 100 passengers, including many soldiers and their families, from Djakarta to Papua via Magetan; very heavy loss of life.

30 October (c/n 4993): HC-130 USCG CG1705, destroyed in collision with USMC AH-1W Cobra helicopter off San Clemente Island, San Diego, California; no survivors from either aircraft.

24 November (c/n 5497): KC130J Italian Air Force MM62176, made sharp turn to port shortly after touch-and-go landing at Galileo Galilei Airport, Pisa, and suddenly lost altitude, snagged power cables on way down and crashed on main railway line with no survivors.

Appendix 5

Museum Hercules

Quite a number of retired C-130s found their way into various Air Museums in the USA and elsewhere, although it should be noted that not all of them are on public display. (Some others were preserved as Gate Guards or Static Displays, but with the cutting back of the US Defense budgets these are gradually being dismantled.)

1   USAF serial 53-3129 (c/n 3001) *First Lady*, USAF Armament Museum, Eglin AFB, Florida
2   USAF serial 54-1626 (c/n 3013) *Vulcan Express*, USAF Museum, Wright-Patterson AFB, Ohio
3   USAF serial 54-1630 (c/n 3017) *Azrael*, USAF Museum, Wright-Patterson AFB, Ohio
4   USAF serial 55-0014 (c/n 3041)*Jaws of Death*, Robbins AFB Museum, Houston County, Texas
5   USAF serial 55-0023 (c/n 3050) *City of Ardmore*, Linear Air Park, Dyess AFB, Abilene, Texas
6   USAF serial 55-0037 (c/n 3064) *Sayonara*, Octave Aerospace Museum, Rantoul Aviation Complex, Chanute, Illinois
7   USAF serial 56-0509 (c/n 3117) *Raids Kill Um Dead*, Hurlburt Field Memorial Air Park, Okaloosa County, Florida
8   USAF serial 57-0453 (c/n 3160) *Nite Train to Memphis*, National Vigilance Park, Fort George G. Meade, Maryland. Dedicated to the C-130 aircrew lost over Armenia in 1958.
9   USAF serial 57-0457 (c/n 3164), Pima Air Museum, Tucson, Arizona
10 USAF serial 57-0478 (c/n 3185), Museum of Aviation, Wright-Patterson AFB, Ohio
11 USAF serial 57-0485 (c/n 3192) *Snowshoe*, Minnesota Air National Guard Historical Museum, St Paul, Minnesota
12 USAF serial 57-0490 (c/n 3197), Empire State Air Museum, Schenectady County Airport, New York
13 RAAF serial A97-214 (c/n 3214), RAAF Museum, Point Cook, Melbourne, Australia
14 USAF serial 57-0514 (c/n 3221) *Miasis Dragon*, Selfridge Military Air Museum, Mount Clements, Michigan

Seen at Da Nang in standard camouflage scheme in August 1968 is C-130A 55-0037 (c/n 3064) of 35 TAS, based at Naha, Okinawa. She carried the name *Sayonara*, and is now preserved at the Octave Aerospace Museum, Chanute, Illinois. *Nick Williams, AAHS*

THE LOCKHEED MARTIN C-130 HERCULES

15 USAF serial 57-0526 (c/n 3502), Hill AFB Museum, Salt Lake City, Utah

16 USAF serial 62-1787 (c/n 3732), USAF Museum, Wright-Patterson AFB, Ohio

17 US Navy serial 159348 (c/n 4601), TACAMO facilities Static Park at Tinker AFB, Oklahoma City

18 USAF serial 56-0518 (c/n 3126), Gate Guard at Little Rock AFB Visitor Center, Little Rock, Arkansas

19 USAF serial 57-0453 (c/n 3160), National Vigilance Park, National Security Agency, Fort George Meade, Maryland

20 US Marine Corps BuNo 149798 (c/n 3680), National Museum of Naval Aviation, NAS Pensacola, Florida

21 US Marine Corps BuNo 151891 (c/n 3878), National Museum of Naval Aviation, NAS Pensacola, Florida

US Navy C-130G 151891 (c/n 3878) is pictured at NAS Atsugi, Japan, in November 1968, and can be seen at the National Museum of Naval Aviation, NAS Pensacola, Florida. *Nick Williams, AAHS*

22 RAAF serial A97-160 (c/n 4160), RAAF Museum, Point Cook, Melbourne, Australia

23 USAF serial 69-6580 (c/n 4356), Air Mobility Command Museum, Dover AFB, Delaware

24 USAF serial 70-1269 (c/n 4423), Pope Air Park, Pope AFB, Fayetville, North Carolina

25 USAF serial 68-10953, ex-RNAF 953 (c/n 4335), Norwegian Armed Forces Museum, Oslo Gardemoen Airport, Oslo, Norway

26 Royal Saudi Air Force serial 460 (c/n 4566), Riyadh Air Base Museum

27 USN BuNo 159348 (c/n 4601), Tinker AFB

28 USAF serial 74-1686 (c/n 4669), Robbins AFB Museum, Georgia

29 Royal Canadian Air Force serial 13-0315 (c/n 4070), 426 Transport Training Squadron Air Base, Trenton, Ontario, Canada

Appendix 6

Chase the Herk: strange happenings!

In the murky world of convert actions, allegations of misuse of C-130s obtained from the Arizona boneyards for all manner of CIA operations, including arms smuggling and drug importation, and, more recently, 'Extraordinary Rendition' flights, continue to abound. However, whether or not every one of Gary R. Eitel's claims and those of other organisations' researchers are true, the complications are so labyrinthine that tracking down the many ramifications seems almost beyond human powers. To give just one example from many, in 1990 the US Forest Service is alleged to have transferred two aircraft to TBM Inc. TBM transferred them to Roy Reagan, who sold them to T&G Aviation. Woody Grantham of T&G in turn is alleged to have sold them to Pacific Harbor Capital, which then sold them back to T&G. In 1993 the same two aircraft were transferred by T&G back to Pacific Harbor Capital, as repossession (according to the two companies) or as a sale (according to a Federal Aviation Administration document – what John Titus regards as part of 'sheep-dip' cleansing operations).

Although during investigations US Attorney Claire Lefkowitz stated that no evidence of CIA involvement with Forestry Service and ex-service C-130s was found[1], the rumours persist. The exchange of twenty-eight C-130 and P-3 aircraft for ageing Second World War firefighting aircraft belonging to such companies as Hemet Valley Flying Services; Hawkins & Powers Aviation, Greybull, Wyoming; TBM Inc/Butler Aircraft; Aero Union Corporation, Chico, California; T&G Aviation; Heavylift International; and Pacificorp, Portland, Oregon, remains shrouded in some confusion, although current operations have been declared legitimate enough.[2] The General Services Administration stated in September 1995 that these exchanges were illegal and instructed the Forest Service to recover all the aircraft.

Whatever happened with the Contras in Nicaragua and the drug deals, the denial by a Herk operator of covert landings in Angola that was followed by the death of that same denier in a Herk crash in that very country soon afterwards, together with all the other allegations of misuse, one thing is clear – the full story has still not yet been told. The highly mysterious deaths of many of the people who may have known some aspects of the story are a warning that not everything is as it seems about this peculiar aspect of the C-130's otherwise unblemished and splendid history.[3]

---

[1] See Tim Steller, 'Aircraft in scam may have flown for CIA', article in *The Arizona Daily Star*, 1 April 1998, and subsequent story in 2 April 1998 issue.

[2] See Jay Reynolds, 'Major Deception on Contrails Unmasked (Part 3)', article in *Veritas News Service*, 26 April 1999.

[3] See Gary Null, 'The Strange Death of Colonel Satow' (www.garynull.com/Documents/satow/htm) where, among others, computer specialist Tom Wade, Marine Colonel Jerry Agenbroad and Marine Colonel James E. Satow all died sudden and violent deaths in the same manner as Jack Chisum of T&G. See also Alexander Cockburn and Jeffrey St Clair, *Whiteout: the CIA, Drugs and the Press* (Verso Books, 1999); Peter Dale Scott and Jonathan Marshall, *Cocaine Politics: Drugs, Armies and the CIA in Central America* (University of California Press, 1998); and Gary Webb, *Dark Alliance: The CIA, the Contras and the Crack Cocaine Explosion* (Seven Stones Press, 1998).

Appendix 7

Latest USAF C-130 Serial Numbers

Equipment ID	Serial Number	Equipment ID	Serial Number
A4151	9400008151	A6437	600001437
A4152	9400008152	A6438	600001438
A7351	9700001351	A6467	600001467
A7352	9700001352	A6631	600004631
A7353	9700001353	A6632	600004632
A7354	9700001354	A6633	600004633
A8355	9800001355	A6634	600004634
A8356	9800001356	A6159	600008159
A8357	9800001357	A6610	600008610
A8358	9800001358	A6611	600008611
A9431	9900001431	A6612	600008612
A9432	9900001432	A7468	700001468
A9433	9900001433	A7170	700003170
A1461	100001461	A7635	700004635
A1462	100001462	A7636	700004636
A2314	200000314	A7637	700004637
A2434	200001434	A7638	700004638
A2463	200001463	A7639	700004639
A2464	200001464	A7608	700008608
A2155	200008155	A7609	700008609
A3154	300008154	A7613	700008613
A4142	400003142	A7614	700008614
A4143	400003143	A7310	700046310
A4144	400003144	A7311	700046311
A4153	400008153	A7312	700046312
A5435	500001435	A8601	800008601
A5436	500001436	A8602	800008602
A5465	500001465	A8603	800008603
A5466	500001466	A8604	800008604
A5145	500003145	A8605	800008605
A5146	500003146	A8606	800008606
A5147	500003147	A8607	800008607
A5152	500008152		
A5156	500008156		
A5157	500008157		
A5158	500008158		

Select bibliography

Archer, Bob, Dorr, Robert F. and Hewson, Robert 'Lockheed C-130 Hercules' in *World Air Power Journal*, Vol 18 (Aerospace Publishing Ltd, 1992), pp50-109

Archer, Bob and Keep, Mike *Lockheed C-130 Hercules* (Aviation News/Sky Books Press, 1979)

Badrocke, Mike and Gunston, Bill *Lockheed Aircraft Cutaways: The History of Lockheed Martin* (Osprey, 1998)

Ballard, Jack S. *Development and Employment of Fixed-Wing Gunships 1962-1972* (Office of the Air Force History, 1982)

Bowers, Ray L. *Tactical Airlift: The United States Air Force in Southeast Asia* (Office of Air Force History, 1983)

Chinnery, Philip D. *Any Time, Any Place: Fifty Years of the USAF Air Commando and Special Operations Forces 1944-1994* (United States Naval Institute, Annapolis, 1994)

Bowman, Martin W. *Lockheed C-130 Hercules* (Crowood Publishing, 1999)

Brown, Albert *C-130 and the Blue Angels* (privately published via A4 Sky Jt, 1981)

Bunrin-Do *Famous Airplanes of the World – No 79: Lockheed C-130 Hercules* (Tokyo, 1976)

Caidin, Martin *The Long Arm of America* (E. P. Dutton & Co, 1963)

Caidin, Martin *The Mighty Hercules* (E. P. Dutton & Co, 1964)

Campbell, R. L. *Tasks of Hercules* (Lockheed-Georgia, 1975)

Cockburn, Alexander and St Clair, Jeffrey *Whiteout: the CIA, Drugs and the Press* (Verso Books, 1999)

Dabney, Joseph Earl *Herk, Hero of the Skies* (Cobblehouse Books, 1986)

Davis, Larry *Gunships: A Pictorial History of Spooky* (Squadron/Signal Publications, 1981)

Drendel, Lou *C-130 Hercules in Action*, Aircraft No 47 (Squadron/Signal Publications, 1981)

Francillon, Rene J. 'C-130 Hercules Variant Briefing, Parts 1, 2 & 3' in *World Air Power Journal*, Vols 6-8 (Aerospace Publishing Ltd, 1991-92)

Gaines, Mike and Goulding, James *Hercules* (Jane's Aircraft Spectacular, 1985)

Grey, Stephen *Ghost Plane* (St Martins Press, New York, NY, 2006)

Haas, Michael E. *Apollo's Warriors: US Air Force Special Operations during the Cold War* (University of the Pacific, 2002)

Hinebaugh *Flying Upside Down* (United States Naval Institution, Annapolis, 1999)

Jolly, Randy *Air Commandos* (Aero Graphics, 1994)

Laming, Tim *Hercules: The C-130 in Service* (Motorbooks International, 1992)

Kyle, James H. *The Guts to Try* (Primer Publications, 1994)

Leader, Ray *Colours and Markings of the C-130 Hercules* (Colours and Markings, Vol 7, 1987)

Leary *Perilous Missions* (University of Alabama Press, 1984)

Lee, Robert Mason *Death and Deliverance* (Macfarlane Walter & Ross, 1992)

McGowan, Sam *The C-130 Hercules: Tactical Airlift Missions, 1956-1975* (Tab Books Inc, 1988)

Mackintosh, Ian *C-130 Pictorial* (Airline Publications, 1979)

Marchetti, Victor and Marks, John D. *The CIA and the Cult of Intelligence* (Dell Publishing Company Inc, New York, NY, 1974)

Mason, Francis K. *Lockheed Hercules* (Patrick Stephens Ltd, 1984)

Maxell, H. G. 'History of the Hercules ...with pilot's report' (*Air Classics* magazine, June 1974)

Middleton, Peter 'Antarctic Shuttle' (*Flight International* magazine, January 1985)

Mikesh, Robert C. *Flying Dragons: The South Vietnamese Air Force* (Osprey, 1988)

Morris, M. E. *C-130: The Hercules* (Airpower No 1009, Presidio Press, 1989)

Morse, Stan (ed) *Gulf Air War Debrief* (Aerospace Publishing, 1991)

Nye, Frederick F. *Blind Bat: C-130 Forward Air Controller: Ho Chi Minh Trail* (Eakin Publications, 2000)

Olausson, Lars *Lockheed Hercules Production List, 1954-2012* (privately published, 2010)

Orr, Kelly *From a Dark Sky: The Story of US Air Force Special Operations* (Presidio Press, 1996)

Peacock, Lindsay *The Mighty Hercules: The First Four Decades* (RAF Benevolent Fund, 1994)

Pearcy, Arthur *A History of US Coast Guard Aviation* (Airlife, 1989)

Pereira, Wilf *RAF Lyneham: Hercules Super Station in Action* (privately published, 1990)

Pierce, K. J. 'The Lockheed Hercules', series of articles in *South-East Air Review WLAG*, November 1966-March 1967 editions

Reed, Arthur *Modern Combat Aircraft 17: C-130 Hercules* (Motorbooks, 1984)

Reed, Chris *Lockheed C-130 Hercules and its Variants* (Schiffer Publishing Ltd, 1999)

Reed, Terry and Cummins, John *Compromised: Clinton, Bush and the CIA* (Penmarin Press Inc, 1995)

Robbins, Christopher *Air America: The Story of the CIA's Secret Airlines* (Putnams, 1979)

Selby, Earl and Miriam *Hercules: Work-Horse of the Air* (Readers Digest, 1983)

Scott, Peter Dale and Marshall, Jonathan *Cocaine Politics: Drugs, Armies and the CIA in Central America* (University of California Press, 1998)

Tart, Larry and Keefe, Robert *The Price of Vigilance* (Ballantyne Pocket Books, 2002)

Thigpen, Colonel Jerry L. *The Praetorian STARship: the untold story of the Combat Talon* (Air University Press, 2001)

Turner, Paul St John *Lockheed Hercules* (Profile No 223, Profile Publications, Windsor, 1971)

Vaughan, David Kirk *Runway Visions: An American C-130 Pilot's Memoirs of Combat Airlift Operations in Southeast Asia 1967-1978* (Verlinden Productions Inc, 1986)

Webb, Gary *Dark Alliance: The CIA, the Contras and the Crack Cocaine Explosion* (Seven Stones Press, 1998)

White, Molly O'Loughlin *The Foodbirds: Flying for Famine Relief* (Bookmarque Publishing, 1994)

Wilson, Stewart *Dakota, Hercules and Caribou in Australian Service* (Australian Airpower Collection, 1991)

Index

A&AEE (Aeroplane & Armament
    Experimental Establishment) 58, 160, 343

ABCCC (Airborne Battlefield Command
    & Control Center) 112, 114, 205, 222

Aboitiz Transport...282, 294, 324

Abu Dhabi & Dubai (*United Arab Emirates*
    Air Force)....................249-250, 335, 344, 375, 377-378, 399

ACARS (Aircraft Communications
    Addressing & Reporting System) 344

ACE (Adaptive Carriage Techsystems) 242

ACMA (Advanced Civil/Military Aircraft) 69

ACWAR (Advisory Caution & Warning System) 49

ADF (Active Dynamic Filtering)..344

ADM (Acquisition Decision Memorandum) 232

ADS (Aerial Delivery System).........................54, 60, 74, 76, 197

Advanced Leasing Corporation 324, 381

Aerea Aervias Ecuatoriansas...................................324, 332, 388

Aerial Tankers 213, 304

Aeropostal de Mexico...324, 341, 345

Aero Firefighting Services 122, 324, 339, 341, 348, 354, 372

Aero International...324, 353

AE (Assisted Evasion) 230

AEC (Atomic Energy Commission) 221

Aerial Dispersant Spraying (ADS) 54, 348

AEW&C (Airborne Early-Warning & Control) 120, 126

AFB (Air Force Base) 9, 18, 19, 24-25, 28-29, 32-34, 51,
    78, 82, 87, 92, 94-97, 101, 111, 114, 116-119, 123, 125, 127,
    129-130, 133, 138 150, 152, 160-166, 168, 171, 177 180, 182,
    191, 196-200, 203-204, 207, 209-211, 227,233-234, 241-242,
    245, 247-248, 294, 307, 316-317, 343, 363, 366, 370, 387,
    393, 397, 400-401

AFCS (Air Force Communications Service)............................29

AFI International 325

AFRES (Air Force Reserve Command) 9, 28, 56, 112,
    127, 165-166, 204, 214, 230, 247, 382

AFSOC (Air Force Special Operations
    Command)..............................54, 56, 232-233, 240-241, 382

AFTI (Advanced Fighter Technology Integration)...............325

African Air 325, 327, 332, 341, 367

African AirCargo 325

Africargo 325, 364

Agenbroad, Colonel Jerry...402

AHMS (Aircraft Health Monitoring System) 241

Air Algerie 325-326, 341, 381, 395, 399

Air America 326, 353, 363, 386, 389, 404

Air Atlantique...327

Air Botswana Cargo (ABC)..327

Airbus A400M 46, 59, 343

Air China 333

Air Contractors 327, 348

Air Finance 327, 329

Airfreight, Ivory Coast 327, 370

Air Gabon...327, 331, 344

Air Inter 325, 327

Airlift International...328, 337

Air Mobility Command (AMC)................50, 121, 160, 293, 401

AIROD (Aircraft Inspection Repair & Overhaul Depot)......335

AIRP (Airborne Instrumentation Research Programme) 111

Airplane Sales International 166, 168, 328

Air Kenya...328

Air Research Development Command (ARDC) 93

Alaska Airlines...328, 375

Alaska International Air................327, 329, 332, 340, 343, 350,
    363, 370, 372, 380, 391

Alaska Worldwide Corporation 337

Alexander, Julius 126

Algerian Air Force (*Al Quwwat al Jawwiya*
    al Jaza'eriya) 250-251

Allison, Jr., Lieutenant Commander Edgar............................234

Allison Turboprops.........................18, 21-22, 24, 26, 30, 37, 49,
    52, 61, 63, 66, 69-70, 108, 128, 312, 375, 377, 381, 383, 398

ALLTV (All Light-Level Television) 125

Almond, Peter 291, 317

Al Nahyan, Sheikh Zayed Bin Sultan.....................................250

Alvarenga, Lieutenant-Colonel Edgar.....................................282

ALG (Assault Landing Gear) 158

Alvin, Major Dave 46

American Airlines..331

AMARC (Aerospace Maintenance &
    Regeneration Center) 88, 165-166, 168, 180, 226,
    280, 320-321,328, 397

American Gangster, motion picture 333

AMU (Avionics Management Unit)..46

ANG (Air National Guard)...................54, 56, 92, 115, 121, 147,
    157, 165, 213-214, 223, 228, 230, 241, 376, 390, 398

Angolan Air Charter 331, 338, 370, 393-395

Angola Air Force (*Força Aéra Nacional (FAN)*......................250

Antonov An-70T...39

APR (Airborne Profile Recorder) 78

APS (Active Protection System)........26, 120, 128, 159, 180, 243

APU (Auxilliary Power Unit)......22-23, 26-27, 30-31, 37-38, 50,
    52-53, 61, 63, 65-67, 350

APV (Automatically Piloted Vehicle) 220-221

ARS (Aerial Recovery Systems).....................................133, 197

Argentine Air Force (*Fuerza Aérea Argentina*) 251-252,
    342, 375-376, 378-379, 381

Aerial Search & Rescue (ASR) 79, 180, 298, 316

ARRS (Aerospace Rescue & Recovery Service)..........34, 80-83,
    85-86, 89, 91, 131-132, 160, 166, 210-221,227, 234

ART (Aerial Retrieval & Transport) System...................74, 180

ASSETS (Airborne Seeker Evaluation Test System) 242

AT (All-Terrain)..230

ATCS (Automatic Thrust Control System) 46

ATD &AC (Advanced Threat Detection and
    Automated Countermeasures) System..............................241

ATK (Alliant Techsystems)......................................49, 242, 383

Austrian Air Force *(Osterrecihische Luftstreitkräfte)* 252

AviSto 332, 370

AVTEL (Flight Tests Inc.) 97, 337

AWADS (Adverse Weather Aerial
    Delivery System) 46, 197, 396

AWR (Airborne Weather Reconnaissance) 165

BAC Buccaneer..317, 365

Bangladeshi Air Force. *(Bangladesh Biman Bahini)* 252

'Banish Beach', Operation 322

Bank of America 324, 328, 332

Belgium Air Force *(Force Aérienne Belge)* 252

Beltz, Stanley 18

'Bevel Edge', Operation 136

'Big Blue' fuel-air blast bombs 117

'Bird Feeding' inflight refuelling methods 100

'Black Crow' Target Ignition Sensor (TIS) 123-125

Blackwell, Micky 40

Bloodworth, Steve 51

'Blue Angels", USMC display team.........142-143, 166-167, 173,
    176, 178, 219, 245, 403

Boeing B-25 18

Boeing TC-14 143

Bolivian Air Force *(Fuerza Aérea Boliviana)* 253-254, 367,
    379-380, 395-397

Bongo, President Omar 256

Botswana Air Force 254

Boundary Layer Control (BLC) 101, 111, 142, 153-159, 192, 345

Bourguiba, President Habib 250

Boyd, Brigadier-General Albert 18

Bradley Air Services 332, 336, 348, 364

Bragg, James 51

Brazilian Air Force *(Forca Aérea Brasileria)*............36, 255-256,
    375, 378-380

Brennan, Anthony..18

Brown, Al 18

BTR (Beacon Tracking Radar) 123

Budge, Paul 51

BuOrd (U S Navy Bureau of Ordnance)................................238

Burns, Chuck 12

Bush Field Aircraft Company.......................................332, 339

'Bushel', Operation 313

Butler Aircraft Company 332, 402

Butler, Carl..332

C-54 *Skymaster* 11, 69

C-110 *Flying Boxcar* 11

C-124 *Globemaster* 11

C-130 Variants

    AC-130E 123-124, 182-183, 390

    AC-130H 110, 124, 182-183, 395-396

    AC-130U 125, 183, 376-377, 379-380

    C-130A.............13-14, 18, 21, 24-25, 26, 57, 77, 93, 95, 100,
        111, 122-123, 134-135, 137, 145, 147, 160, 163, 181,
        184-188, 235, 242, 244-245, 256-257, 263, 277, 280,
        282, 294, 296, 321,324-325, 332-333, 338-342,
        344-345, 348, 353-354, 365, 367-374, 383,
        385-389, 391-392, 394-398, 400

C-130A-II 157, 159, 162, 165-166, 168, 171, 175, 179-180,
    182-183, 197, 207, 209-213, 215, 218, 221, 223-224,
    227-228, 232-234, 236, 239-241,243, 245-262, 267-270,
    272, 274-280, 282-283, 294, 298-299, 301-311, 313,
    315-323, 343, 344, 347, 364, 367, 369, 371, 373,
    375-381, 388, 391-392, 394-399

C-130 ZZZ 26, 28-29, 57, 75, 80, 100-101, 111-112,
    127, 131-132, 134, 142, 160, 165,

C-130B 173, 188, 190, 192, 246, 254,258, 263, 282,
    300, 315-316, 320-321, 340,
    345-346, 373-375, 385-394, 396-397

C-130B-II 111-112, 190-191, 345

C-130BL 148, 158, 191-192, 246, 345

C-130C 101, 108, 192, 222

C-130D 146-148, 157, 192-193, 219, 226, 233-234,
    262, 280, 374, 390, 394

C-130D-6 ....147, 193, 226, 234, 394

C-130E 32-35, 46, 49, 51, 57, 60, 88, 93, 95, 100, 110,
    112-114, 116-117, 119-120, 123-124, 138-139, 141-142,
    146, 158-159, 165, 179, 182-183, 193, 196-205, 211,
    219-222, 226,232, 234, 240, 243, 246, 251-252,
    255, 267-279,
    278-280, 282, 293-294, 297, 299, 301, 307, 310-313,
    320, 332, 336, 373-380, 385-399, 404

C-130E-II 112, 146, 205, 222

C-130F 97-99, 100-101, 143-145, 148-158, 169-171,
    173, 178, 180,191, 206-207, 226, 235, 237-238, 243, 246,
    307, 317, 374-375, 385-390,396, 398

C-130H....................29-30, 49, 57, 66, 71, 75, 81-89, 93, 96,
    99-101, 110, 117-121, 124-125, 127-129, 134-135, 147

C-130H (CT) 81, 87-88, 117-119,159, 196-197, 205, 211,
    240-242, 247-248, 250-251, 387, 390, 398-399, 404

C-130H (S) 212

C-130H-30..............30, 66, 159, 212, 250-151, 257, 261, 267,
    279, 283, 301, 306-307, 311, 315, 317-318, 344, 373,
    375-378, 380-381, 396

C-130H (AEH) 212

C-130H-MP 128, 159, 213, 243, 304, 380, 394

C-130J...............24, 39-43, 46-47, 50-52, 54-57, 100-101,116,
    125, 127, 158-160, 166, 179, 192, 213-215, 223, 229,
    232-233, 237, 240, 247, 250, 262, 267, 269-270, 283,
    291, 293-294, 298, 299, 303, 310, 320,
    373, 381-383, 399

C-130J-30 ....46, 51-52, 54, 56, 213-215, 250, 262, 267,
    270, 283, 291, 299, 303, 310, 381-382, 399

C-130K 46, 57-58, 215, 218, 252, 278, 283-284,
    286-287, 291, 293-294, 318, 335, 343, 375,
    388, 390, 396-397, 399

C-130(S) 197

C-130T 171, 178-179, 218-219, 238, 375-380

CG-130G 219, 223

DC-130A 78, 93-97, 219-220, 224, 234, 331, 337, 342,
    345, 369, 296

DC-130E 93, 95, 220-221

DC-130H 87, 96, 221

EC-130E 87, 112, 114, 116, 159, 179, 222, 375,
    386, 392

EC-130E (CL) 114, 222

EC-130E (RR) 114, 222
EC-130G 166-167, 219, 223, 390
EC-130H (CCCCM) 223
EC-130H (CL) 118, 223
EC-130J 52, 54, 116, 223, 382
EC-130Q 166, 168, 224, 245, 307, 328, 335, 343,
345-347, 377-379, 392
EC-130V 120, 159, 180, 224
EC-130V AEW&C 159
GC-130A 95, 219, 224
GC-130D 226
GC-130D-6 226
GVI...226, 235
GVI-U 226
HC-130B 79, 145, 180, 226, 245, 374
HC-130E 112, 179, 226, 332
HC-130G 79, 226
HC-130H 81-89, 96, 120, 127, 134, 159, 162, 165-166,
179-180, 209-210, 221, 227, 232, 234, 243, 247,
304, 375, 377, 379, 388, 393, 397, 399
HC-130H-7 ....88, 180, 228, 376, 378-379
HC-130H (N) 92-93, 228, 376, 380
HC-130N 91, 230, 241, 375
HC-130P 88-89, 91-92, 160, 180, 230, 234, 241, 375,
388, 394, 397
JC-130A 24, 78, 95, 123, 130, 223, 242, 244,
JC-130B 130-131, 133, 160, 233, 243
JC-130E 234
JC-130H 87, 234
JHC-130H 87, 234, 243
JHC-130P 160, 234
KC-130B 234, 263, 315-316
KC-130F 97-99, 100-101, 143-144, 173-178, 226, 235,
237, 243, 374, 385-390, 398
KC-130H 100-101, 236, 251, 255, 269, 307, 311,
316-318, 342, 375, 377-380, 394
KC-130J 55, 100-101, 179, 232-233, 237, 382
KC-130R 100-101, 175, 179, 237, 378-379
KC-130T 178-179, 238, 375, 377-380
KC-130T-30 ....238, 376
LC-130F 143-145, 148-158, 169, 191, 238, 246, 375, 389
LC130H.............................147, 157, 239, 347, 378
LC-130R 157, 239, 377, 379-380, 390-391, 394
MC-130E-C 211, 240
MC-130E-S 119-120, 240, 243
MC-130E-Y 120, 240, 393
MC-130H 117-118, 197, 232-233, 240, 247-248, 375,
378-380, 393, 398-399
MC-130P 91-93, 96, 125, 230, 232, 241,398
NC-130.............18, 88, 96, 101, 108, 119-120, 159, 180, 192,
196, 205, 211, 242-243, 347, 345
NC-130A 242
NC-130B 101, 108, 192, 243, 345
NC-130E 88, 119, 196, 205, 243
NC-130H 96, 120, 159, 180, 211, 243
PC-130H 127-128, 135, 243

RC-130A 77-79, 160, 187, 244-245, 278, 367, 374
RC-130B 111, 244
RC-130S 78, 244
R8V-1G 79, 180, 245
SC-130B 79, 190, 245
TC-130A 77, 160, 244-245
TC-130G 166, 145, 328
TC-130Q 245
UV-1L 148, 191, 246
VC-130B 160, 246
VC-130H 246, 260, 310-311, 364, 378
WC-130A 246
WC-130B 163-165, 190, 246, 346-347
WC-130E 246, 336
WC-130H 211, 247, 391
WC-130J 56, 127, 166, 247, 381-382
YC-130-LO 18, 242, 247
YMC-130H...................118, 197, 247-248, 393
Caine, Michael...335
Cameroons Air Force
(l'Armee de l'Air due Cameroons)................71, 256, 379, 381
CAML (Cargo Aircraft Minelayer System) 128-129
Canadian Airlines International 332
Canadian Armed Force (CAF) 215, 299, 301, 338,
377-379, 381-382
Cargolux 332, 350
Cargomaster (Australia) 331-332
CBR (California Bearing Ratio)..........................163
CDS (Container Delivery System) 54, 77, 318
Central African Republic
(L'Armee de l' Air of the Forcesarmee)....................256, 345
Certified Aircraft Parts.............................112, 332
GCAAS (Ground Avoidance System)..........................49
Chad Air Force (Force Aérienne Tchadienne)......................256
Chani Enterprises 333, 344
Cherry Air Aviation Services..............................333
Chilean Air Force (Fuerza Aérea de Chile)............................257
China Air Cargo (CAC) 333, 381
China Eastern Airlines 327, 333, 355
Chisum, Jack...............................367-368, 402
Church, Senator John 336, 348
CIA (Central Intelligence Agency).......................326, 331, 336,
347-348, 353-354, 359, 365, 367-370, 386, 402-404
CNS/ATM (Communications Navigation
Surveillance/Air Traffic Management) 343
Cockburn, Alexander 402-403
'Cold Cowl', Operation...................................165
'Cold Crystal', Operation 165
Colombian Air Force (Fuerza Aérea Colombiana) 257, 377
Colquhoun, Flight Lieutenant M 46
Combat Arrow 196
Combat Knife..196
Combat Shadow..241, 398
Combat Talon.......................81, 88, 117, 119, 196-197, 205, 211,
241-242, 247, 250, 387, 390, 404

Combat Talon II................117-118, 240, 248, 398-399
'Combat Wombat' *(sic)*...242
Comfy Levi/Senior Hunter.....................................222
Commando Solo.............................54, 115, 222-223
Commercial Air Leasing.................331, 333, 338, 369
Comercial Proveedorn del Oriente SA (COPROSA)...........333
Commins, Peter..297
COMINT (Communications Intelligence).....................111, 188
Compass Call.................................118, 223, 245
Conner, F. S..325, 372
Continental Air Services...............................333, 375
CONTUS (Continental United States)...............359
Coronet Solo..115, 222
CPI (Crash Position Indicator)...............................26
'Credible Sport', Operation..............197, 247-248, 393
Crowe, Russell..333
CZX Productions Incorporated (DE)............331, 333
DAGR (Defense Advanced GPS Receiver) System...............242
Dan Air London..341
DCA (Defense Communiations Agency).......................29
DEA (Drug Enforcement Administration)...........367
'Decisive Edge', Operation..119
'Deep Freeze', Operation............................149, 155
'Deliberate Force', Operation..................................119
Delta Air Lines...............327, 333-334, 350, 375
'Deny Flight', Operation...119
DERA (Defence Evaluation & Research Agency)........51, 160, 291
Derco Aerospace.............250, 269, 307, 333, 335, 338, 343-344
'Desert Sabre', Operation..110
'Desert Shield', Operation.....................110, 119, 124, 136
'Desert Storm', Operation..............110, 114, 119, 124, 136
DEW Line (Distant Early Warning) Radar Chain......145, 234, 350
Deylius, Eric P...9, 28
DFCC (Digital Fire Control Computer)............................124
D/F (Direction-Finding)...111
DIRCM (Directional Infra-Red Countermeasures) System......241
DME (Defence Measuring Equipment)..........................344
DMZ (Demilitarized Zone).......................................111
Dodge, Captain 'Red'.................................354, 363
Dole, George..336
Douglas C-47 *Skytrain*.............................11, 122
Dowty Aerospace...................9, 46, 49-50, 52, 383
DSO (Defense Sciences Offices or
    Dropsonde System Operator)...........................127
Dubai Air Force..258
'Eagle Claw', Operation..............99, 197, 247, 392
EARL...333, 335, 370
'Easy' Flight..196
Earth Survey' programmes..............111, 192, 243, 345
EAS (Europe Air Service) Air Cargo 335
Echo Bay Mines...............335, 342, 353, 371
'Echo' Flight...196
ECS (Electronic Countermeasures) System 114, 119, 165, 245
Ecuador Air Force (*Fuerza Aérea Ecuatoriana*).....258, 379, 381

ECM (Electronic Countermeasures) System 92, 96,
    111, 118, 120, 123-124, 196, 225, 247, 260,
    262, 271, 287, 302, 311-312, 314, 317
Edwards, Jerry..51
EGPWS (Enhanced Ground Proximity Warning System) 344
Egyptian Air Force
    (*Al Quwwat Ali Jawwiya Ilmisriya*).................259-260, 376,
    379, 392-393, 399
Eitel, Gary R..336
ELINT (Electronic Intelligence)......111, 119, 222, 243, 260, 269, 321
Ellis, Jack...296
ELT (Emergency Locator Transmitter)................................344
EMP (Electro-Magnetic Pulse)...................................168
ENDIAMA...336, 341
'Enduring Freedom', Operation..................................119
'Enhance Plus', Project...321
EO/IMR (Electro-Objects Imaging Radar).........................232
ERTS (Electric Re-Entry Tracking System).........................180
ESM (Electronic Surveillance Measures).....................168, 302
E-TCAS (EnhancedTraffic Avoidance System).......................49
Ethiopian Air Force..260
Ethiopian Airline (R.R.C. Air Services)................260, 336, 381
European Air Transport.............................336, 370
Evans, Ralph...34
Evergreen International Aviation.........................252, 336, 354
"Extraordinary Rendition" Flights.................353-354, 369, 402
F-104 *Starfighter*...350
Fairchild C-123J *Provider*.......................................367
Fairchild-Republic A-10 *Thunderbolt-II*..............................114
FAA (Federal Aviation Authority) 51, 60, 62, 338, 344, 347
FADEC (Full-Authority Digital-Control) System....................49
FARP (Forward Area Refuelling Points)..............................197
'Fat Albert'...............................166, 172, 219, 287
Fava, Giovananit Claudio..353
FCC (Fixed Convergent Cameras)......................................77
FCS (Future Combat Systems)...71
Fédération Européenne des Sociétés (EFIS).......................336
Fink, Wayland...368
First Air Canada..332, 336-337
First National Bank of Chicago................337, 340, 348, 380
FLA (Future Large Aircraft)...39-40
Flatley, Rear-Admiral James H....................................99
Flight Cargo Leasing Inc.....................331, 337, 368
Flight Systems Inc...337
FLIR (Forward Looking Infra-Red) System 88, 124-125,
    180, 228, 230, 241, 399
Flock, Art..12
Flying W Airways...........................337, 353-354, 380
FOL (Forward Operating Location)........................110
Ford & Vlahos.........................261, 294, 296, 297, 337-339, 341
Ford, John J..296, 337
FMS (Foreign Military Sales)......................................315
Forest Fire Control...120-122
Forrestal, USA Aircraft-carrier (CVA59)..................97-98, 173
FOV (Field of Vision)..46

Fowler Aeronautical Services...........................294, 338, 344, 367
Fowler, Robert R..370
Foyle Air UK..331, 338
Frameair..250, 335, 338, 381
Frank, E C...12
French Air Force (*l'Armée de l'Air*)..........................260, 380-381
French, Jim..368
French *Sécurité Civile*.....257, 261, 324, 337, 339, 364, 372, 397
Frisbee, Lloyd..24
FROG (Free Rocket Over Ground)...........................110, 124
Frost, Eugene...12
Gabon Air Force (*Force Aérienne Gabonaise*)...............261, 327
Gandy, Doug..368
Garrett, Joe..34
GATE (Global Atmospheric Research Program)..................346
GBU (Guided Bomb Unit)...242
Geldof, Bob..277, 297
Gemini Space Vehicle Recovery..180
General Dynamics F-16 *Fighting Falcon*.............................50
GEN-X (Generic Expendable) decoys....................................49
GIA International...338
Giles, Ira...34
Gilley, Jack..18
Girasol, yacht...317
Globe Air Inc......................................335, 338, 359, 369
GMS (Ground Maintenance System)....................................51
GM TBM *Avenger*..368
GPES (Ground Proximity Extraction System)................75-76
GPS System.......................49, 92, 125, 227, 230, 241-242, 247,
                                                                270, 344, 383
Grant, Jim...70
Grantham, Woody..368, 402
Griffin, Marvin..18
Grumman E-2C *Hawkeye* System.........................120, 159
GTC (Gas Turbine Compressor)..146
'Gunboat', Operation..122
Gup, Ted..347, 368
Hansen, Art...24
Hartridge, B. W. A..327
Have Blue, demonstrator...221
Hawker *Sea Harrier*...251, 393
Hawkins & Powers.................338-339, 345, 354, 368, 398, 402
Hawkins, Willis..12
HES (Harsh Environment Survival).....................................230
Hayes Industries...337, 339
HDD (Head-Down Display)..46
H-EDIT (Hercules Engineering Development
    & Investigation Team)..289
'Heavy Chain', Operation...196
Heavylift...331, 339, 366, 370, 396
Heavylift International.....................332, 338-339, 348, 402
Helicopter In-Flight Refuelling (HIFR)............................89, 92
Hellenic Air Force ((*Polemiki Aeroporia*)...............262, 395, 397
Hemet Valley Flying Services Incorporated.........122, 324, 339,
                                                        348, 354, 372, 396, 402

Hendrik, David E...354
Herc Airlift Corporation...............................340-341, 367
'Heritage Hercules'..232
Hess, Rudolf...287
HF (High Frequency)......................78, 115-116, 127, 222, 344
HH-53 Helicopters..80, 91
Hill, Bob...34, 315
Hine, Air Chief Marshal Sir Patrick....................................40
Hitler, Adolf...287
Hocking, Peter...296-297
Hoffman, David...368
Honduras Air Force
    (*Fuerza Aérea Hondurena*)........................262-263, 394, 397
Hospitals and Dental Clinics, Saudi airborne.................99-100
HOW (Hercules on Water)..160
HRS (Human Retrieval System).........................82, 88, 112
HRU (Hose Recovery Unit)............87, 91-92, 100, 179, 227
HS.681...39
HSL Company...340, 353
HTTB (High Technology Test Bed)...................125-126, 142,
                                                        160, 277, 342, 396
HUD (Heads-up Display).............46, 50-51, 124-125, 241, 383
Hughes, Carl..96
Hunting Air Cargo...340
'Hurricane Hunters'..126
Hurricane 'Katrina'..116
Hurricane 'Rita'..116
IAAFA (Inter-American Air Force Academy).......................340
IAS (Indicated Air Speed)........76, 237, 333, 341-342, 367, 395-396
'Ice', Operation..136
Ice Patrols...80, 180, 229
IDA (Integrated Diagnostic System)....................................51
IFYGL (International Field Year for the Great Lakes)..........346
ILS (Instrument Landing System)..49
Imperial Iran Force
    (*Nirou Haval Shahanshahiye Iran*).........267, 269, 388, 390,392
INS (Inertial Navigation System)...............49, 92, 118-119, 125,
                                197, 227, 241, 247, 251, 335, 344, 383
Indonesian Air Force
    (*Angkatan Udara Republik Indonesia*)........36, 72, 139, 190,
                        213, 234, 263-267, 345, 351, 375, 380-381, 394
International Air Response (IAR)....................340-341, 368
International Aviation Services (IAS)......333, 341, 367, 395-396
International Aviation Services – IAS (Guernsey)..........341-342
International Aviation Services -IAS Cargo Airlines (UK)....341
Intercargo Services (ICS)...340
Interior Airways...62, 337, 340, 346
Intermountain Aviation...354
International Aerodyne..............................340, 346, 375
International Telephone & Telegraph (ITT)
    Commercial Finance Corporation....125, 325, 338-341, 367
Investment Capital Xchange.....................................341, 371
Iraqi Air Force (*Al Quwna al Jawniya Al Iraqiya (IQAF)*.........267
'Iraqi Freedom', Operation...116, 119
IRC (International Red Cross)...................................297, 327

IRCN (Infra-Red Counter Measures) 114, 118-119, 125, 197, 241, 383

Islamic Republic of Iran Air Force (IRIAF)..................267, 393

Israeli Air Force (*Heyl Ha'Avir*)..............236, 269, 376-378, 391

Italian Air Force (*Aeronautica Militaire Italiana*) 213, 256, 258, 270-273, 283, 376, 382, 392, 399

Inter-Agency Ecological Program (IEP) IEPO..............338, 340

Jamahiriya Air Transport..................277-278, 341, 370

James Bay Energy Corporation 282, 335, 342, 352-353

Japanese Air Self-Defence Force (*Koku Jietai*)...............274-275, 375, 377-380

JATO (Jet-Assisted Take-Off).....................141-143, 145-147, 219

Johnson, Elmer 368

Johnson, Kelly...18

'Joint Endeavour', Operation..................................136

'Jolly Green Giant' 80, 91

JFTL (Joint Future Theatre Lift).............................71

JTIDS (Joint Tactical Information Distribution System).......114, 222

'Junction City', Operation 109

'Just Cause', Operation 115

Kakumba, John Marques 370

Kelly, Merrill...12

Kountche, President Seyni..278

Kross, General Walt..50

Kuwait Air Force (*al-Quwwat al-Jawwija al-Kuwaitiya*)..............125-126, 277, 342, 380-381, 392, 395

L-100 Leasing 342, 364

LAPES (Low Altitude Parachute Extraction System) 76-77, 317, 393-396

Larkins, Gary R..342, 345, 369

LASC (Lockheed Aircraft Service Company)...........97, 99, 245

Leary, William 354, 403

Lebold, Jack 12

Lechner, Al 12

Ledger, Heath 335

L/F (Low Frequency) 115

Leary, Professor William...................................354, 403

Lefkowitz, Claire 402

LESEA (Lester E. Sumrail Evangelistic)................342

Liberian Air Force...227

Libyan Arab Republic Air Force (*Adwas Alibyan Ujnna*) 277

Lineas Aéreas del Estade (LADE)................252, 342

Ling-Temco-Vought-Electrosystems 197

LCD (Liquid Crystal Display) 46, 343, 383

Littlejohn, Chuck 18

Lockheed-Georgia Company (GELAC)......257, 274, 278, 283, 342

Lockheed DP-2E Neptune..95

Lockheed P-3V Orion...111

LOGAIR System 65, 359, 363

LFL (Long Focal Length) 111

LLLTV (Low Light-Level Television) 123-124

LORAN (Long-Range Navigation)................112, 159, 226-227

LPI (Low Probability of Intercept) System............241

LPC (Low Power Colour) System 241

LPR (Low Probability of Recognition) System 241

LOX (Liquid Oxygen)...21

LRCS (Low Radar Cross Section) 221

LWF (Lutheran World Food).................................325

Lynden Cargo 327, 338, 342-343, 355

MAC (Military Airlift Command) 9, 30, 32, 34, 198-199, 201, 203, 222, 248

McDonnell Douglas F15 *Eagle*..............................50

MAFFS (Modular Airborne Fire Fighting System)...............121, 262, 271-273, 306

MAP (Military Assistance Programme)..................315, 320, 341

MARDEZ (Maritime Defense Zone)....................180

Maple Leaf Leasing 343, 346, 350, 371

Marchetti, Victor 331, 367, 403

Markair..331, 343, 363, 366, 372

Marks, John D 331, 367, 403

Marshalls Aerospace 57-59, 160, 192, 217, 287, 303, 307, 343

Marshall, Jonathan.............57, 192, 286, 312, 317, 343, 402, 404

MASDC (Military Aircraft Storage & Disposition) 96, 112, 179, 226, 354

Martin, Bud 18

Maximus Air Cargo 250, 344

Maxturbine 344

May Ventures UK...344

MCC (Mission Crew Commander).......................118

McDonnell Douglas F-4 *Phantom* 123, 144

McDonnell Douglas YC-15...................................158

Megatrade 345

Merpati Nusantara Airlines 345

Mexican Air Force (*Fuerza Aérea Mexicana*).......................278

Micronesia Aviation Corporation..........................345

Microwave Command Guidance System (MCGS) 93

Military Airlift Command (MAC)........................9, 30, 32, 34, 198-199, 201, 203, 222, 248

MIL-STD-1553 bus 51, 384

Middlewood, Robert W 12

Military Aircraft Restoration Corporation............345

Miller, Harvey..368

Minelaying, Aerial...128-129, 275

Mitsui Corporation 266, 331, 345, 351

Mobuto, President Sese Seko..................................323

Montano, Huberto.........................342, 345, 375

Moore, Henry 368

Moss, Dean 336

MP (Maritime Patrol).......................128, 213, 243, 380, 394

MTBF (Mean Time Between Failure) 46

MTI (Moving Target Indicator)........................123-124

Multitrade Aircraft Leasing......................337-338, 345, 367

Multitrade International...338

National Aeronautics Association (NAA)................52

National Aeronautics and Space Administration (NASA)......................86, 111, 192, 243, 345-347

National Aircraft Leasing.....................323, 329, 331, 333, 340, 343, 346, 363

National Oceanic and Atmospheric Administration (NOAA) 127, 165, 229, 346-347

NATO (North Atlantic Treaty Organisation) 81, 262, 282, 310, 317, 320

NASA (National Aeronautics & Space Administration) 86, 111, 192, 243, 345-347

National Science Foundation (NSAF) 347

NCAR (National Center for Atmospheric Research) 192

NDA (Nuclear Defense Agency) 297, 338-339, 367

NHC (National Hurricane Center) 127

Niger Air Force (Force Aérienne Niger) 278

Nigerian Air Force (Federal Nigerian Air Force) 278-279, 378, 381, 396

NVG (Night Vision Goggles) System..88, 92, 118, 180, 230, 241

Nixon, President Richard M 359

NOAA (National Oceanic & Atmospheric Administration) 127, 165, 229, 346-347

Northcap L.L.C. 347, 354

North, Lieutenant-Colonel Oliver L 359, 367

Northwest Territorial Airways 348, 356, 393

NSWC (Naval Surface Weapons Center) 129

Null, Gary 402

Nunch, Bob 368

NVIS (Night Vision Imaging System) 46

Oil Spill Response Limited 348, 355, 358

Olausson, Lars 9, 314, 404

Oldman, Gary 335

Oliver, Kenneth 296-297

OMC (Office of Munitions Control) 120

Onn, Prime Minister Datuk Hussein 304

'Opbat', Operation 180

Ormsby, Robert B 70

OSC (On-Scene Commander) 80

OZP (Offshore Zone Patrol) 127

Pacific Gateway Investments 324, 348

Pacific Harbor Capital Inc.....324, 337, 339, 348, 354, 367, 402

Pacific Rim (PRA) 348

Pacific Western Airlines (PWA) 332, 336, 349-350

Pakistan Air Force (Pakistan Fiza'ya) 279, 388, 394

Pakistan International Airlines (PIA) 280, 350

PAPI (Precision Automatic Photogrammetric Intervalometer) 77

Pave Aegis 124

Pave Low 117

Pave Pronto 122

Pave Pronto Plus 122-123

Pave Spectre 123-124, 182

PCMCIA (Personal Computer Memory Card) 51

Pegasus Aviation International...........70, 262, 331, 351, 353-354

Pelita Air Services 263, 266, 351, 380-381

Pemex (Petroleole Mexicanos) 278, 352-353

'Penguin Airline' 155, 169

Peruvian Air Force (Fuerza Aérea Perunana) 280, 377

Peterman, E. A 12, 18

Petty, Gracie T 368

Petty, Pharies 'Bud' 9, 368

PGM (Precision-Guided Munitions) System 242

Philippines Aerotransport (PADC) 282, 352

Philippines Air Force (Hukbong Himpapawid ng Pilipinas) 282, 345, 352, 378-379, 396

PLADS (Parachute Low-Altitude Delivery System) 76

PLS (Personnel Locator System) 230, 267, 345, 351

POET (Primed Oscillator Expendable Transponder) 49

Polish Air Force (Sily Powietrzne Rzeczypospolitej Polskiej) 282

'Popeye', Operation 246

Portuguese Air Force (Forca Aérea Portuguesa) 282, 377, 379, 381

Prescott Aviation 353

Price, Bob 46, 51

Prime Vertical Cameras (PVC) 77, 347

'Project Ebb' (21st-Century Upgrade) 192

Protex, Mexico 353

'Proven Force', Operation 119, 124

'Provide Comfort', Operation 119, 136

'Provide Hope', Operation 136

'Provide Promise', Operation 136

'Provide 'Relief', Operation 136

PSCI 353, 365

PSL Air Lease Corp 353

PSYOP (Psychological Operations) 115, 222

Qatar Air Force 283, 382

QinetiQ Bedford 58, 343

Quebecair 342, 353

Questline 353, 396

QUICKTRANS System 65, 363

RAM (Radar Absorbent Material) 95, 197

Rapid Air Transport 324, 337, 347, 351, 353-354, 368

RATOG (Rocket-Assisted Take-Off Gear) 158

RDR (Rapid Data Retrieval) 222

Reagan, Roy D 324, 338, 348, 354, 367-368, 371, 402

Real, Jack 18

Red Dodge Aviation (RDA) 354, 363

Reinhardt, Dietrich 354, 359, 370

'Relita', Operations 351

Rens, Arlen 52

'Restore Relief', Operation 136

Reynolds, J 402

Rivet Clamp 119, 196-197, 240

Rivet Fire Operating System (RFOS) 118

Rivet Rider/Volant Scout 114, 222

Rivet Swap 120, 196-197, 240

Rivet Yank 120, 196, 240

Rivet Yard 196

Robbins, Lieutenant Commander Clyde 145, 400-401, 404

Robinson, Flight Lieutenant Mark 51

ROF (Route of Flight) 46

Rohr Industries Incorporated 383

Romanian Air Force (Fortele Aderiene Romaniei) 283, 321

Royal Air Force 46, 161, 283, 286, 292-293, 327, 375, 382

Royal Australian Air Force (RAAF) 51, 57, 109, 139-141, 187, 213, 277, 280, 282, 294, 296-299, 324, 333, 337-341, 344-345, 367, 391, 400-401

Royal Canadian Air Force (RCAF) 257, 299-301, 386

Royal Danish Air Force (*Kongelige Danske Flyvevaabnet*).........260, 298, 302, 377, 382

Royal Jordanian Air Force (*Al Quwwat Almalakiya*) 303, 316, 377, 379, 397

Royal Malaysian Air Force (*Tentar Udara Diraja Malaysia*).......213, 304-306

Royal Moroc Air Force
(*Al Quwwat Ali Jawwiya Almalakiya Marakishiya*) 306

Royal Netherlands Air Force (*Koninklijke Luchtmacht*).......307, 335, 343, 381

Royal New Zealand Air Force (RNZAF) 36, 109, 307-309

Royal Norwegian Air Force
(*Konelige Norske Lufforsvaret*) 309-310, 375

Royal Saudi Air Force
(*Al Quwwat Ali Jawwiya Assa'udiya*)........310, 375-378, 380, 388, 392, 394-396, 401

Royal Swedish Air Force (*Svenska Flygvapnet*) 138, 311-313, 327, 378, 380

Royal Thai Air Force (RTAF) 123, 160, 315, 375-377, 380-381, 388

Roy D. Reagan 324, 338, 348, 354, 367, 371

RPV (Remotely Piloted Vehicles)...................................96

R.R.C. Air Services 336

Ruftberg 345, 355

Safair Freighters 9, 355, 366

SAFD (Semi-Automatic Flare Dispenser) 123, 307

Safmarine 316, 355, 359

Saville, Lieutenant-General Gordon.................................11

SAM (Surface-to-Air) Missiles Systems........................322, 369

SAR (Search and Rescue) 79, 114, 128, 180, 230, 301, 388, 392

SATCO (Satellite Communications) 280-281, 344, 359, 392

Satow, Colonel James E..402

Saturn Airways (Trans-International -TIA)............65, 282, 325, 328-329, 331-333, 338, 342-343, 346, 352,359-361, 362-366, 369, 380, 389-390

Saudia 99, 212, 311, 364, 378

Savimbi, Jonas..370

Schaefer, Lyle 51-52

Scottish Aviation 57, 383

Scott, Peter Dale 402, 404

Scott, Ridley 333

Schreiner Airways..262, 332, 364

SCIBE-Society Commerciale, Zaire.........................353, 364, 380

Senior Hunter..114, 222

Senior Prom, Stealth Missile Testing..................................221

Senior Scout..115, 118, 222-223

SEALS (Sea – Air- Land Squadron)......................................117

SFAir 342, 364

Shabair 344, 365

Shaw, David 51

'Shed Light' Programme..244

Singapore Air Force (*Republic of Singapore Air Force*).............315, 342, 377, 379

SIGINT (Signals Intelligence)..222

SKE (Station Keeping Equipment)...49

Ski-fitted C-130's 70, 84, 110, 143-152,154-157, 160, 169, 191, 193, 233-234, 239, 246

'Skyhook' recovery system 227

SLAR (Side-Looking Airborne Radar)............88, 180, 228, 307

Smith, Flight Lieutenant John...299

South African Airways (SAA) 365

Snow Aviation International Inc 282, 365

SOF (Special Operations Force).....................................241, 248

SOFI (Special Operations Force Improvement)....................125

SOG (Special Operations Group)..196

SOS (Special Operations Support) Systems 93, 116-119, 125, 241, 243

South African Air Force...............................9,192, 316-317, 374

'Southern Watch', Operation 119

South Korean Air Force (*ROKAF*) 317

Southern Air Transport (SAT)...............331, 341, 365-367, 394

Southern Cross Airways 337, 345, 367

Spanish Air Force (*Ejército del Aire Espanol*)................317, 378, 380-381, 392

Spectre...125, 183

Sri Lanka Air Force 318

'Stabilise', Operation 136, 139

Stanton, Dick 18

STARS (Surface-to-Air Recovery System) 197

St. Clair, Jeffrey 402

St. Lucia Airways 359, 368, 370

Steller, Tim 354, 402

Stites, Joe D 128

STOL (Short Take-off & Landings) Systems 18, 52, 70-71, 101, 108, 125, 141-142, 158-159, 162, 192, 197, 243

'Storm Fury', Project...347

Strachan, Benjamin...251

SRW (Strategic Reconnaissance Wing) 95

'Storm Trackers'..127

Suarez, Peter 338, 367

Sudanese Air Force (*Silakh al Jawwiya*)...................318-319, 367

Sudan Airways...319, 367

Sultanate of Oman – Royal Air Force of Oman (RAFO)........320, 375-377

Sullivan, Leo...18, 24

Sun Valley II..111, 191, 244, 369, 385

Super Chicken/Surprise Package...123

'Super Hercules' – GL-207..68

TAB (*Transporte Aereo Boliviano*) 253, 367

TACAMO ('Take Charge and Move Out') System.............166, 168, 219, 223-225, 390, 392, 401

TAC Holdings..338

T&G Aviation (International Air Response)..........261, 324, 337, 340-341, 348, 354, 367-369, 402

Tactical Drone Group (TDG)..95, 220

'Talking Bird' System..29

TBM Inc 122, 332, 368, 402

TCAS (Traffic Collision Avoiding System) 49, 344

TCS (Tactical Control Squadron) 147, 196

TCW (Troop Carrier Wing) 25, 135, 199-200

Taiwanese Air Force – Republic of China Air Force (Zh nghuá Mingu K ngj n) 320
Teledyne Ryan BQM-34 *Firebee*....................................93
Tepper Aviation 324, 337, 347, 353-354, 359, 368, 370, 395
Test, H. H. 11
TEWS (Tactical Early Warning System) 114
TF/TA (Terrain Following/Terrain Avoidance) Systems 118, 197, 241, 247
Thatcher, Mark 136
Thatcher, Prime Minister Margaret 251
The Dark Knight, motion picture 335
'Thin Slice', Project 196
Thomas, Captain Bill...363
Thossen, Willard 12
'Thunderball', Operation 136
Time Aviation 342, 345, 369
Titus, John 261, 336, 348, 354, 359, 402
TPAS (Tactical Precision Approach System).................26
TPC (Tropical Prediction Center)................................127
Transafrik................328, 333, 335-336, 365, 367, 369, 395, 397
Trans-Latin Air (TSA)..369
Trans-Mediterranean Airways (TMA).................349, 369
'Trash and Ass Haulers'..109-110
T3D&H L.L.C 320, 335, 370
Tunisian Air Force (Al Quwwat Al-Jawniya, al-Jamahiriyah, At' Tunisia)...............................379
Turkelson, Peter 354
Turkish Air Force (Turk Hava Kuvvetleri) 320, 375
Uganda Airlines 370
UHF (Ultra High Frequency)...........................52, 115, 344
UKMAMS (United Kingdom Mobile Air Movement Squadron) 289
UNITA rebels 331-332, 336, 341, 359, 368-370, 372, 395, 397
United African Airlines 332, 370
United States Coast Guard (USCG) 54, 80, 88, 127, 180, 222, 226-229, 245.393, 399
United States Marine Corps (USMC) 55,97, 101, 109, 142, 173-174, 176-178, 218, 233, 235, 237-238, 385-390, 398-399
United States Navy (USN) 79, 99, 168, 219, 223-224, 226, 238-239, 245-246, 371, 389-390, 392, 394, 396, 401
'United Shield', Operation 125
United Trade International (UTI) 370
Unitrans 331, 370
Unpaved Airfield Operations...........................12, 141, 162-163
'Uphold Democracy', Operation 116, 119
'Urgent Fury', Operation 125, 136
Uruguay Air Force (Fuerza Aérea Uruguaya) 321
UTX (United Technologies Corporation) 335
U/V (Ultra-Violet)...123
Vansco Air Freight 370
Venezuelan Air Force (Fuerza Aérea Venezolana) 321, 375-377, 379
Venter, Colonel Steyn..317
VHF (Very High Frequency) 52, 115, 155, 319, 344

Vietnamese Air Force (Viet Nam Air Force (VNAF) – Không Quân Việt)...........109, 117, 123-124, 134, 321-322, 390-391, 403
'Vigilant Warrior', Operation.....................................119
VLAGES (Very Low Altitude Gravity Extraction System)......77
VLS (Volume-Loadability-Speed).................................70
VNAF (Vietnamese Air Force)......................109, 321, 391
VOAR Linhas 371
Volant Solo II 115, 222
Von Hoff..371
VOR (VHF Omnidirectional Range) System.................344
WAAS (Wide-Area Augmentation System) 344
Wade, Tom...402
Washington, Denzel..333
Watts, Milt 368
Wawrzynski, Lieutenant Chester................................145
'Weatherbirds'...163
Webb, Gary 402, 404
Weldon, Curt 354
Weldon, Robert 354
Wellington, The Duke of, General................................11
West, Brigadier-General Randall L 52
WHO (World Health Organisation)..............................296
Wilkniss, Dr Peter 145, 157
Williams, Squadron-Leader Robyn 46, 51
Wimmer, Roy 18
Wirtschafsflug...241
Woodward, L R 32
Worldways 335, 371
World Wide Aeronautical Industries.....................354, 371
World Wide Trading..347, 371
Wurst David Trustees 256, 338
Yemeni Air Force (Yemen Arab Republic Air Force) 323
Yemenia...371
Zaire Air Force (Force Aérien Zairoise).................260, 323, 371, 391-392, 395
Zaire Air Services 371
Zaire Cargo 371
Zambian Air Cargoes....................323, 343, 371-372, 375, 387
Zambian Air Force..323
Zantop International 322, 343
Zelinski, Harry...350
Zia-ul-Haq, President 394
Zicka, Michael, Leasing....................................324, 339, 372
Zimex Aviation..340, 372, 394
Zotti Group Aviation...325, 367, 372

The Junkers Ju 87 Stuka

Peter C Smith

Utilising this slow and relatively lightly-armed WWII warplane the German Luftwaffe spearheaded the Blitzkrieg assaults from Poland in 1939, through to North Africa and beyond. From the very first day of the Second World War to the very last, the Ju 87 operated on the front line.

Famed for its precision bombing the Stuka's accuracy paid handsome dividends against such pin-point targets as rail and road bridges, artillery, communications, fortresses and enemy armour.

Its added ability to linger over the combat zone providing continuous close air support to troops in the field and proven capability in the field proved a major asset to the Luftwaffe throughout WWII.

For a land-based aircraft, the Stuka earned a formidable reputation as an anti-shipping weapon. Off the coast of Norway, Dunkirk, in the Mediterranean and Arctic, the English Channel and Black Sea, the Ju 87 chalked up a fearsome list of destroyed ships. Later in the war she achieved legendary fame as a specialist anti-tank and night attack aircraft.

Peter C Smith, a leading authority on the history of dive-bombers and dive-bombing, relates the history of the Stuka and all its variants in great detail. Complemented by over 250 photographs, comprehensive appendices, equipment and instrument layouts and colour profiles *The Junkers Ju87 Stuka* provides essential reading for researchers, historians and modellers alike.

ISBN: 9 780859 791564, hardback

256pp Price £29.95

The Fw 200 Condor

Jerry Scutts

Born of an idea suggested by the Japanese Navy to arm Germany's elegant Fw 200 Condor airliner for a maritime reconnaissance role, the Luftwaffe's long range Condor proved its worth in the first years of World War II.

A practical anti-shipping raider, the Condor fought a virtually private war against surface vessels in line with the policy of imposing a blockade to strangle Britain's seaborne lifeline. Rapidly neutralised by allied escort carriers and merchant ships the Condor's role switched to staving off the Sixth Army's defeat at Stalingrad. Condor crews hauled supplies in appalling winter conditions – sub-zero temperatures and low visibility and routinely serviced and refuelled aircraft under the guns of the Red Air Force.

For the Germans, maritime patrol duty grew ever more costly in terms of men and machines and new 'stand-off' weapons were introduced to beat the defences. By 1944 the Fw 200 had been all but eclipsed in a combat role and the survivors reverted to the transport role for which they were originally designed.

The Fw 200 Condor describes the development of the aircraft and its varied roles, missions and personnel including the fate of all aircraft built. Colour profiles and a wealth of photographs provide comprehensive information on this elegant aircraft.

ISBN: 9 780859 791311, hardback

264pp Price £29.95

To order or for more details on all our books visit www.crecy.co.uk or telephone +44 (0)161 499 0024

The Hawker Hunter

Tim Mclelland

Tim McLelland's *Hawker Hunter* is both a comprehensive work of reference and an authoritative history. It covers the origins of the aircraft from both the P1040 and P1052 swept-wing versions and moves through design and development of the twin-seat dual-control Hunter T7 to the 'ultimate' FGA.Mk.9. The Hunters varied operational successes are noted with particular emphasis on major foreign users in Switzerland and India, and, amongst others, exports to Oman and Chile.

Extracts from the Hunter's original Aircrew Manual and appendices covering service histories, serial numbers and the fate of each Hunter constructed, combine to provide full details of this Cold War Interceptor and ground attack platform.

Colour profiles by Richard Caruana coupled with storied and anecdotes from former Hunter air and ground crew ensure the complete history of the aircraft is presented in a single volume and provide essential reading for the aviation enthusiast, modeller or historian.

ISBN: 9 780859 791236, hardback

384pp Price £29.95

The Avro Vulcan

Tim Mclelland

The story of the Avro Vulcan is as dramatic as the presence of the aircraft itself. Designed by a team led by Roy Chadwick, the man responsible for the legendary Lancaster, the Vulcan was one of the three bombers designed to carry Britain's nuclear deterrent in the 1950s and 1960's. But it was Avro's delta-winged colossus that became the backbone of the V-force, remaining poised to strike at the heart of the Soviet Union until the very end of the 1960's when the deterrent role passed from the RAF's manned bomber to the Navy's Polaris submarine fleet.

The Vulcan remained in RAF service as a tactical low-level bomber armed with conventional and nuclear weapons, and was only retired following the introduction of the Panavia Tornado. It was nonetheless able to write a spectacular epilogue to its operational career when in 1982 the aircraft was selected to undertake the longest bombing raid flown in British military history – to the Falklands.

This is Sheffield based Tim McLelland's brand new third book on the *Avro Vulcan* and is both a comprehensive work of reference and an authoritative history. It covers the origins of the Vulcan and delta-winged flight, details of every major production variant and also, using newly released information describes the aircraft's use as a test-bed for a variety of missile, engine and equipment technologies. The book reproduces extracts from the Vulcan's original Aircrew Manual together with appendices on both squadron disposal and the fate of every Vulcan built. Also included is a wealth of information and anecdotes from former Vulcan air and ground crews, describing from first-hand experience what it was like to live with the mighty Vulcan.

This comprehensive coverage is completed with over 250 photographs, new scale drawings and colour profiles making the *Avro Vulcan* a vital read for historians, modellers and aviation enthusiasts alike.

ISBN: 9 780859 791274, hardback

368pp Price £29.95

To order or for more details on all our books visit www.crecy.co.uk or telephone +44 (0)161 499 0024